W9-CJW-737

FOURTH EDITION

THE
ADMINISTRATION
AND
MANAGEMENT
OF
CRIMINAL JUSTICE
ORGANIZATIONS

A Book of Readings

Stan Stojkovic
University of Wisconsin–Milwaukee

John Klofas
Rochester Institute of Technology

David Kalinich
Florida Atlantic University

WAVELAND
PRESS, INC.
Long Grove, Illinois

Property of WLU
Social Work Library

DISCARD

Property of the Library
Wilfrid Laurier University

For information about this book, contact:
Waveland Press, Inc.
4180 IL Route 83, Suite 101
Long Grove, IL 60047-9580
(847) 634-0081
info@waveland.com
www.waveland.com

Copyright © 2004 by Waveland Press, Inc.

ISBN 1-57766-310-1

All rights reserved. No part of this book may be reproduced, stored in a retrieval system, or transmitted in any form or by any means without permission in writing from the publisher.

Printed in the United States of America

7 6 5 4 3 2 1

Contents

Section 4
Processes in Criminal Justice Organizations 381

Section 5
Change in Criminal Justice Organizations 473

Introduction

The fourth edition of *The Administration and Management of Criminal Justice Organizations* represents a compilation of new articles and research on the operations of criminal justice organizations. As with the three earlier editions of the book, this edition focuses on new ways of viewing criminal justice administration and management. These new ideas on criminal justice administration and management must be understood in the context of an ever-changing world and expectations for the criminal justice system. Since the third edition of this book, we have seen terrorist actions leveled against the United States, a war in Iraq, dwindling federal and state funding for social service agencies, and a number of difficult problems facing states, including record budget deficits and shrinking local tax revenues. In addition, the country has responded to terrorist actions and threats by creating the Department of Homeland Security, representing an integration of over twenty federal agencies, tens of thousands of employees, and a budget in the billions. This department has been given broad authority to address the threat of terrorism and will require the direct involvement and assistance of criminal justice agencies.

It is within this context that contemporary criminal justice administrators, managers, and employees have been asked to address crime and the nascent threat of terrorism. Many controversial ideas have been generated and proposed to improve the functioning of criminal justice organizations, and many prescriptions have specifically targeted practices and ways of doing business among criminal justice administrators. The fourth edition includes a representative sample of articles that question the traditional methods and practices of criminal justice administrators. Whether discussing the politics of criminal justice agencies, the changing nature of policing within the context of metropolitan development, or the interfacing between criminal justice organizations and other social service agencies, criminal justice entities will be asked to improve their delivery of services to diverse and competing communities and constituent groups.

The twelve new articles added to this edition of the book all address central concerns in how criminal justice organizations will function during very difficult times. These new additions to the book examine very important issues and concerns that will define criminal justice responses to crime for many years to come. As organizational and political entities, criminal justice organizations often times respond to crime based on perceived threats of dangerousness from a class of people. Gangs, for example, represent a serious threat to community safety on a number of dimensions. How serious is the gang threat? McCorkle and Miethe (chapter 2) attempt to address this issue by examining the organizational and political responses to gangs in Nevada. Their analysis raises questions regarding the very nature of the criminal justice response to perceived threats of safety to the community. Similarly, Klofas (chapter 4) explores how police organization is directly tied to the changing nature of community organization. Urban sprawl and the development of metropolitan communities will continue unabated across the country. Policing these areas changes the relationship between police and their communities and has direct implications for how cities within large metropolitan areas are policed. Police organizations will have to respond to the changing nature of community organization in order to fulfill their missions.

The changing nature of police is not the only criminal justice system component that is being affected by changing communities. Research is demonstrating that singular portrayals of criminal justice organizations as functioning outside the influence of other criminal justice components or social service agencies are misleading. Wenzel et al. (chapter 5) demonstrate that some crimes, such as drug offending, require innovative approaches and inter-organizational bridges to other noncriminal justice agencies to be effectively addressed. In chapter 5, the authors underscore the importance of facilitating a linkage between criminal justice organizations and other agencies to address drug usage among criminal offenders. Criminal justice administration is moving from traditional hierarchies to more flexible organizational structures that foster both formal and informal connections with other public and private agencies in managing crime. Changing organizational structures to respond more effectively to crime must be understood within budgetary constraints. Worrall (chapter 6) addresses the importance of budgetary considerations by examining how some law enforcement agencies respond to crime in an era of dwindling budgets. Some police organizations have used civil forfeiture laws created in the 1990's to expand their budgets and to rely on confiscated dollars and assets during tight fiscal times. Such laws, suggest critics, open the door for many types of abuses by police agencies, yet at one level, these agencies are responding to what is seen to be continued shrinking federal, state, and local budgets in an innovative way. Whether one supports civil forfeiture laws or not, the long term implications of these laws clearly question the nature and appropriateness of the laws and how they are used by law enforcement organizations.

Another way to view police organizations is to explore police supervision. Engel (chapter 10) examines a very critical aspect of police work: how rank and file officers are supervised. Many have argued for years that being a front-line supervisor is the toughest job in any organization. Within police organizations we have very little research to guide our understanding of police. Engel (chapter 10) examines the differing styles of supervision found among police supervisors and suggests that differing styles of supervision lead toward discernable behaviors among rank and file police officers. It is the activity of police officers that generates much debate among citizens, scholars, and police administrators. On indicator of police activity is the number of citizen complaints levied against individual police officers. Terrill and McCluskey (chapter 13) address this question and suggest that having more citizen complaints against an officer may actually indicate high police performance and not necessarily problematical behavior. Under such a view, citizen complaints must be viewed as a product of an aggressive police strategy to detect criminals, and more importantly, officers with a high number of citizen complaints are the same officers who apprehend and arrest more criminals as well. For police administrators and managers, the discussion must be focused on what it is they are trying to achieve with their officers and what is acceptable and appropriate behavior on the part of officers given the tasks, objectives, and goals of police organizations.

What is appropriate behavior and inappropriate behavior among correctional employees? Marquart et al. (chapter 14) examine the prevalence and incidence of boundary violations in a southern prison during the late 1990's. The authors provide an interesting description of how these boundary violations occur within the context of an organizational dynamic found within prisons, and that while these boundary violations are pervasive, caution has to be exercised when discussing the specific nature of the violations and their seriousness. In short, not all violations are alike. Not all correctional organizations are alike as well regarding boundary violations. The role of administration and management in addressing these violations and setting an organizational "tone" such that they will not be tolerated is important. These types of violations occur in all human service organizations. Addressing them in an effective way is a difficult matter for criminal justice administrators, since there is no one easy strategy that can be employed that addresses the violations. One way to manage unacceptable behavior within criminal justice organizations is to explore what the appropriate relationship should be between supervisors and subordinates. Souryal and Diamond (chapter 16) examine the issue of personal loyalty to superiors in criminal justice agencies. They highlight the difficulties that devout loyalty brings to criminal justice agencies. They question, as we do, what is the proper role of loyalty in criminal justice organizations, and what duty does the criminal justice employee have to the organization and fellow employees, both similarly situated employees and superiors. For criminal justice administrators, the question becomes: What loyalty do you expect from subordinates and toward what aims? Additionally, how do you distinguish appropriate forms of loyalty from inappropriate forms of loyalty?

Answers to these questions may assist criminal justice administrators and managers to define the focus and direction of their organizations. There has been much written on new directions and foci for criminal justice organizations. Dalton (chapter 19) offers a bold set of prescriptions on the changing nature of police work and how police, along with others, can impact one of the most intractable problems facing urban areas today—homicides. Dalton suggests that criminal justice agencies can make a difference in reducing homicides by taking an innovative approach to the problem by examining the work of the Strategic Approaches to Community Safety Initiatives (SACSI) program. These initiatives are geared toward the integration of efforts by many criminal justice agencies and non-criminal justice organizations to reduce homicides. Similar approaches have been suggested for tackling the drug problem in this country.

Smith et al. (chapter 20) explore the impact of multijurisdictional drug tasks forces. Their analysis indicates that these task forces may offer the perception that multijurisdictional drug task forces improve drug enforcement efforts, but that actual improvement in drug enforcement outputs may not exist. It is the disjuncture between what we believe will have an impact on illegal drug offender behavior and the reality of law enforcement efforts to reduce illicit and illegal drug usage among offenders that is important. How criminal justice administrators and managers address this disjuncture is of critical importance to the allocation of sparse police resources to a problem that is enormously complex. These multijurisdictional drug task forces are just one example of the changing nature and structure of police organization that might produce some increased effectiveness and efficiencies among police organizations. It is the topic of change within criminal justice organizations that the final two additions to this volume explore.

Allen (chapter 25) examines the impediments to organizational change when implementing community policing ideas into a traditionally structured police organization. Allen found that individual attitudes and pressure to change are critical variables when implementing a change from a more traditional police structure to a community policing structure. What will work in the change process is dependent upon many variables, and criminal justice administrators and managers have to be sensitive to what is most critical in their organizations to facilitate effective change. One way to know what is most critical to an organization going through a planned change process is to review what the literature says about what works with specific issues and groups in organizations. Ferguson (chapter 29) shows how applying the knowledge generated from research on effective correctional interventions with offenders can be used by correctional administrators to change their organizations and make them more effective in accomplishing their organizational missions. Research is used not only for efficiency and effectiveness reasons, but in addition, allows the organization to develop a further understanding on how to learn and develop so that future implementation and organizational issues can be more appropriately addressed.

Trying to address the many needs of both employees and offenders becomes one of the most central challenges faced by criminal justice administrators. Oftentimes, criminal justice administrators, politicians, and citizens believe certain efforts will yield specific results, only to be thwarted by uncertainties, poor planning, and a host of unanticipated consequences (see Doleschal, chapter 24). Nevertheless, the criminal justice system continues to respond to crime, and criminal justice administrators are constantly reacting to the vagaries of their environments. As a police chief once told an editor of this volume, "The crime business is always going to be difficult and frustrating, but it is never boring." It is the ways in which these administrators respond to crime that this book was intended to address. As with the first, second, and third editions of the book, the collection of articles in this edition do reflect specific characteristics. Some of these characteristics are unique to criminal justice organizations, while others are common to all organizations. What follows is a brief examination of these characteristics. The reader is asked to consider these characteristics when reading the articles presented in this edition. They will serve as the foundation for understanding the complexity of criminal justice administration and management.

Criminal justice organizations serve people. Whether it is a police officer diffusing a domestic violence situation, a parole agent supervising a sex offender, or a prosecutor presenting information to a grand jury, criminal justice administrators and employees work with people.

Some of these people are offenders, while others may be concerned citizens or crime victims. The primary consideration for criminal justice administrators is how people are served by their organizations. Since an overwhelming majority of criminal justice agencies are public, they are held to standards of accountability by the citizenry they serve. Moreover, communities hold differing expectations of how criminal justice services will be delivered. A significant issue for criminal justice administrators is how they are perceived by their constituents, and fundamentally, this is predicated on both the quantity and quality of service citizens are provided. The social critic Jimmy Breslin is quoted as saying that many current "quality of life" programs initiated by police departments, for example, have slipped into direct forms of brutality. To paraphrase him, "I want the quality of life to be improved by the police, yet what kind of quality-of-life effort includes torturing and brutalizing citizens?" Altering a negative perception of how people are treated by the criminal justice system is a constant effort for many criminal justice administrators.

A second characteristic of criminal justice organizations is a concern for efficiency and productivity. Efforts to reinvent government are a good example of a movement to increase the productivity of public agencies. Criminal justice organizations have not been lost in this effort. The most visible component of the criminal justice system stressing more efficiency and productivity in its operations is corrections. Prisons are the most direct example. Private companies have entered the correctional domain and, in all likelihood, will be a major player in corrections into the next century. Yet, correctional administrators are not the only ones being challenged by the private sector: Increased usage of private security forces in the police field, the computerization and modernization of court systems, and the growth in mediation centers to handle disputes that were formally addressed by the criminal justice system are good examples of where private agencies are competing for tax dollars with traditional criminal justice agencies. Concerns over fiscal integrity, productivity, and efficiency are shaping the contours of the criminal justice system in ways that were unheard of a decade ago.

Criminal justice organizations are also expected to accomplish conflicting and multiple goals. Examples of this are plentiful in criminal justice organizations: Prisons are expected to rehabilitate while they are primarily structured to be secure facilities, police are expected to control crime while having to be sensitive to the rights of suspects, and courts are to guarantee due process rights to defendants while being cognizant of efficiency and case processing issues in the dispensing of justice. For criminal justice administrators, meeting these multiple and conflicting goals is a challenging and daunting task. In fact, how criminal justice officials confront these challenges is what ultimately defines their character. It has been said that necessity is the mother of invention. This aphorism is true for criminal justice administrators who must come up with innovative ideas and approaches when addressing the many conflicting and multiple goals placed upon them by their communities.

Criminal justice goals are defined by external constituencies. This is the fourth characteristic common to criminal justice organizations. Citizen groups demanding that something be done with a sexual predator in their community, politicians legislating that parole boards not release certain types of offenders, or business interests wanting more police protection during specific times and days are all examples of how external constituents define goals for criminal justice organizations. For criminal justice administrators, many of the requests are not unreasonable; in fact, many of the requests make sense, but they must be understood within the context of finite resources chasing infinite demands. They cannot respond to all requests for services; instead, they respond to those that are either the most "rational" from their perspective, or try to pass resources around to as many constituent groups as possible, thereby presenting an image that at least something is being done to meet the demands of the community. The result is that some groups win and get what they want from the criminal justice system while others do not. Most, however, get something. Moreover, all constituent groups are not the same. Some have more influence than others, and criminal justice administrators tend to respond accordingly. Gauging the degree to which external constituencies have political influence is a central activity of criminal justice administrators.

Finally, criminal justice organizations are composed of competing and conflicting internal constituencies. The level of conflict among the rank-and-file within criminal justice agencies has escalated over the past ten years. The conflict is multidimensional. Take, for example, police organizations. The conflict may be split on the following dimensions: age, race, gender, educational level, years of service, and rank, to mention a few. For the police administrator of the twenty-first century, the "troops" will be more diverse. This will make police administration more problematical and difficult. Similar concerns exist for correctional administrators and court personnel. Managing diverse organizations will become one of the most challenging tasks facing criminal justice administration into the next century.

The articles in this volume will reiterate these themes and characteristics. The reader is asked to place the articles within the context of these characteristics. Doing so will broaden the understanding of the reader and allow an appreciation for the complexity of criminal justice administration. Section one examines the nature of criminal justice organizations, placing them in the context of their structures and purposes. Section two explores the individual in criminal justice organizations, stressing the importance of individual adaptation to organizational structure and demands. Section three expands the examination of criminal justice administration and management by looking at group behavior, with a particular emphasis on the interface between formal and informal elements within criminal justice organizations. Section four highlights the importance of criminal justice processes to an understanding of criminal justice administration, and the final section of the book, section five examines change within criminal justice organizations, noting that many reforms engender unintended consequences for both criminal justice administrators and society.

Acknowledgments

We thank the authors of the fine works in this collection. In addition, we are grateful to both colleagues and students who provided input in the selection of these articles. Finally, we would like to dedicate this volume to our families: Ilija Stojkovic, Milan Stojkovic, Mary Beth Klofas, and Carolyn Kalinich.

Section 1

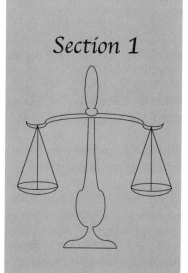

The Nature of Criminal Justice Organizations

Responses to crime have dramatically changed during the last decade of the twentieth century and into the twenty-first century. Criminal justice administrators have had to manage a much different criminal justice system. While there are still many functionally similar entities and purposes associated with the criminal justice system, there have been many changes occurring in how the system is structured and responds to crime concerns of citizens and communities. Section one explores the nature of criminal justice organizations by examining ideas, goals, and structures. The central purpose of this section of the book is to explore both the "core" of criminal justice organizations and some other ideas on what defines their nature.

Malcolm Feeley's article is a classic presentation of two competing models to understanding criminal justice organizations. His comparisons and contrasts between the "goal model" and the "functional systems model" offer some fascinating insights and implications for criminal justice administrators. Depending upon which model you examine, each offers a look at criminal justice administration from various points of view. Feeley notes how criminal justice organizations must be understood as multidimensional entities. Changing or reforming them will depend upon the way you understand their nature and the way they function.

McCorkle and Miethe offer an insightful analysis of how a "moral panic" created a criminal justice response to gangs that was both political and pragmatic at the same time. The criminal justice system responded to the threat of gangs in a way that defined the problem such that additional police and prosecution resources were generated, but generated toward what end? This analysis of a response to a gang problem highlights how criminal justice administrators are, to some degree, sensitive to community and political realities even though the presence of a crime "problem" is not supported by the evidence.

Wright, in the third piece in this volume, moves the discussion about the nature of criminal justice by applying a systemic examination of why goal conflict, while ubiquitous in criminal justice organizations, is actually a good thing. He examines how, out of a primary concern for democracy and freedom, the criminal justice system should not be more rational and efficient. By introducing the principle of "reflective diversity," Wright encourages the reader to come to grips with the fact that there is no monolithic and unifying set of values in our society, nor should there be. He sees goal conflict within criminal justice organizations as both endemic and liberating at the same time. It represents a check on the powers of criminal justice administrators and an opportunity for a diversity of ideas to be expressed within the criminal justice system.

It is the diversity of communities that Klofas explores in his piece on metropolitan development and police organization. Communities across the country are experiencing unprecedented urban sprawl and growth. Police organizations have not kept up with the changes found among these metropolitan communities. Klofas asks a central question regarding how police are to respond to changes in community organization. More importantly, he paints a disturbing picture on the differences found among police agencies in the "outer ring" of metropolitan communities and those in the inner circle or inner city. His analysis raises questions not only about the purposes of police organizations, but in addition, what their role is in the continued growth of metropolitan communities across the country.

In the fifth piece in this section, Wenzel, Longshore, Turner, and Ridgely redirect the discussion of the nature of criminal justice organizations by discussing the importance of interorganizational linkages to increasing the effectiveness of criminal justice responses to crime. In their article, they discuss the importance of bridging to other agencies in the community to address drug crimes. In their discussion, they point out the difficulties courts face when attempting to address drug crime and they suggest that health service agencies should be considered part of the criminal justice response to drug offenders. Their analysis posits that the criminal justice system has evolved from being singularly focused organizations (i.e., police, prosecution, courts, and corrections) to networks of organizations that assist in crime reduction and management efforts. This view has profound implications for how criminal justice agencies are understood and managed by criminal justice officials.

In the concluding piece of this section, Worrall examines an unsettling but continuing practice found among law enforcement agencies to supplement, and in some cases augment, their budgets. Faced with dwindling resources, some law enforcement agencies have used the civil forfeiture laws created in the 1990s to meet their budgetary shortfalls. In this engaging piece, Worrall discusses the problems with using civil forfeiture laws to supplement and augment police budgets. The analysis provided underscores a more serious question concerning the usage of market-generated assets in public organizations. For decades, we have viewed criminal justice agencies as "nonmarket" entities; civil forfeiture laws changed that focus and now enable police administrators to structure financial incentives into their calculations on how police services will be provided and the direction of police efforts. Should this be the case? The answer to this question cuts to the core issue of what exactly is the nature of criminal justice organizations and how they are administered and managed.

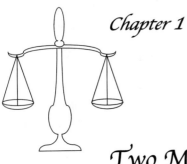

Chapter 1

Two Models of the Criminal Justice System
An Organizational Perspective

Malcolm M. Feeley

Despite the scholarly and popular interest in the administration of criminal justice, there are few *theoretical* discussions of the process. Consequently, this article is an attempt to develop an explicit theoretical framework by which the practices in the administration can be depicted and explained. In it I characterize the criminal justice system in terms of the theory of large-scale organizations, and then examine some of the tasks of administration in terms of established concepts and criteria supplied by this perspective. Following Etzioni, by organization I mean "social units devoted primarily to the attainment of specific goals" (1961). In this case the formal task of the criminal justice system is to process arrests, determine guilt or innocence, and in the case of guilt to specify an appropriate sanction. The major actors in the organization include the defendant, prosecutor, defense counsel, judge, arresting officer, court clerk, and to varying degrees, other persons such as witnesses, additional policemen, clerks, parole officers, court psychiatrists and social workers, and the defendants' families and friends. A system of the administration of justice, whether it is adversarial or inquisitorial, entails the key elements of organization: institutionalized interaction of a large number of actors whose roles are highly defined, who are required to follow highly

Malcolm M. Feeley, "Two Models of the Criminal Justice System," An Organizational Perspective," *Law and Society Review*, Vol. 7 No. 3, 1973, pp. 407–425. Reprinted by permission of the Law and Society Review.

defined rules and who share a responsibility in a common goal—that of processing arrests.[1]

In this discussion, I will outline two models of, or approaches to, organizational analysis and then use them to characterize and evaluate much of the recent systematic research on the administration of criminal justice. Finally, some of the concerns raised by the theories of large-scale organizations generally, but which have been overlooked by students of the administration of justice, will be examined.

Two Models of Organization and a Modification

At the risk of oversimplification, let me suggest that a good portion of the systematic studies of the administration of justice in the United States can be classified into two general models of organization—models which I have adapted from Etzioni's discussion of organizational analysis. They are the *goal model* and the *functional-systems model* (1960). The former, he argues, is an approach which is concerned primarily with "organizational effectiveness," in which the criteria for the assessment of effectiveness is derived from organizational goals (Etzioni, 1960:257). Thus the announced public goals of an organization are usually regarded as the "source for standards by which actors assess the success of their organization" (Etzioni, 1960:257). This approach, its adherents claim, facilitates an "objective" analysis because it does not insert the observer's own values, but takes the "values," i.e., the goals, of the organization as the fixed criteria of judgment. On the other hand, Etzioni (1960:259) identifies what he has termed the functional-systems model of organizational analysis. It is sharply distinguished from the goal model in that:

> The starting point for this approach is not the goal itself, but a working model of a social unit which is capable of achieving a goal. Unlike a goal, or a set of goal activities, it is a model of a multi-functional unit. It is assumed *a priori* that some means have to be devoted to such non-goal functions as service and custodial activities, including means employed for the maintenance of the unit itself. From the viewpoint of the system model, such activities are functional and increase the organizational effectiveness.

The key difference between the models, Etzioni argues, is that the latter approach is more open-ended in its analysis of the function and "needs" of an organization than is the former, and the researcher is likely to be more attentive to a wide range of influencing factors and as a result apt to show a less biased point of view.

In applying this very general typology to a analysis of approaches to the study of the administration of criminal justice, I have made certain adjustments. In particular it seems appropriate to join the *goal model* with Weber's *rational-legal* model of organization, and produce what I call a *rational-goal model* of the criminal justice system. Etzioni has identified the key distinction between these two models. The rational model "differs from the goal model by the types of functions that are included as against those that are neglected. The rational model is concerned almost solely with *means* activities, while the goal model focuses attention on *goal* activities" (Etzioni, 1960: fn. 16, 263). In the administration of criminal justice, however, it is possible to join these two models, because means and goals merge. While on a highly abstract level, the goal—as opposed to the means—of the criminal justice system might be stated in terms of achieving justice, this goal has no clear empirical referent or context by itself. In the dominant tradition of the West at least, the goal, justice, usually acquires meaning in a normative, legal, and empirical context, only when operationalized in terms of procedure, i.e., means.[2] Thus, particularly in the administration of justice, the means become the end, at least in terms of viewing "organizational effectiveness" and "formal goal activities."[3]

The Rational-Goal Model

There is a large body of research focusing primarily upon means or formal goals of the administration of criminal justice. Although there is no consensus or common methodology among the writers adopting this rational-goal approach, their common theme is a primary concern with formal rules. One approach in this style of research is the logical analysis of the interrelationship of the rules of criminal procedure in order to identify and overcome problems of ambiguity, fairness, and discretion. These studies are analogous to the analysis and continuous refinement of formal organizational schema. Another form of research this model uses is the empirical description of practices in the administration of justice, which is then contrasted to the formal rules and goals of the system in an attempt to identify and measure discrepancies between reality and ideal.

This preoccupation with formal goals and rules has as its most eloquent theoretical spokesman Max Weber, who regarded the organization of the administration of justice in the West as the prime example of rational organization. According to Weber, the drift of history in the West has been an ever-increasing reliance upon rational modes of thinking, organization, and authority (1954). In terms of organization this has resulted in a system of depersonalized, rulebound, and hierarchically structured relationships, which produce highly predictable, rationalized, and efficient results. The system of the administration of justice, he argued, is an excellent example of this phenomenon (Weber, 1954:350):

> Above all, bureaucratization offers the optimal possibility for the realization of the principle of division of labor in administration according to purely technical considerations, allocating individual tasks to functionaries who are trained as specialists and who continuously add to

their experience by constant practice. "Professional" execution in this case means primarily execution "without regard to person" in accordance with calculable rules. The consistent carrying through of bureaucratic authority produces a leveling of differences in social "honor" or status, and, consequently, unless the principle of freedom in the market is simultaneously restricted, the universal sway of economic "class position." The fact that this result of bureaucratic authority has not always appeared concurrently with bureaucratization is based on the diversity of the possible principles by which political communities have fulfilled their tasks. But for modern bureaucracy, the element of "calculability of its rules" has really been of decisive significance. . . . Bureaucracy provides the administration of justice with a foundation for the realization of a conceptually systematized rational body of law on the basis of "laws" as it was achieved for the first time to a high degree of technical perfection in the late Roman Empire.

On the formal level, and from a broad perspective, most legal scholars would tend to concur with this characterization of the administration of justice in the West.[4] However, on a more specific level, does this rational goal model characterize the actual organization of criminal justice? Weber has characterized the major components of all organizations as: (1) a continuous organization of official functions bound by rules; (2) a specific sphere of competence, i.e., a sphere of obligations, in the division of labor to be performed by a person who is provided with the necessary means and authority to carry out his tasks; (3) the organization of offices following the principle of hierarchy; and (4) a set of technical rules and norms regulating the conduct of the offices (Etzioni, 1964:43).

These conditions applied to the organization of the administration of criminal justice imply an elaborate apparatus which processes arrests according to highly defined rules and procedures undertaken by "experts" who perform the functions ascribed to them by highly defined formal roles, under a rigorous division of labor, and who are subject to scrutiny in a systematic and hierarchical pattern. This model seems to be the dominant view or ideal of the criminal justice process held by appellate judges and lawyers, and many of the academic students of the courts. Much of their discussion and research, therefore, has centered on the problems with the formal rules of operation, i.e., increasing the "rationality" by minimizing discretion and arbitrary administration, through specifying with increasing precision the roles of the actors. Lawyers under the auspices of the American Bar Association go to great lengths to articulate and refine the precise role of the advocate in criminal justice; many appellate court decisions are attempts at further defining and refining the rules and roles for the various actors in the organization; law journals and appellate court opinions are filled with discussions of the proposals for rules to minimize discretion and more completely define the rules of procedure; and social scientists continue to point out that no one is following the formal rules.

One form of planning by utilizers of the rational-goal model is to examine and explicate the operative rules to determine whether or not they are internally consistent. Abraham Goldstein's discussion of the rules of criminal procedure is an excellent example of this type of analysis (1960). He attempts to show by logical analysis and example that certain alterations of the rules of criminal procedure have the effect of undercutting other, more generalized and basic rules and norms of "equality" among the parties. Since the system is conceived of as a meticulous application of highly defined and prescribed rules, Goldstein can convincingly argue this point, that certain alterations in procedure undercut the power of the defense and thereby weaken or destroy the more fundamental rule of "balanced advantage" between the adversaries. An analogy is that the equilibrium or balance of power in a game of chess is disturbed if a new rule permits White additional moves that are not granted to Black.

The rational-goal approach has not, however, concerned itself entirely with speculative and logical analysis of the rules and norms of the system; it has an empirical component as well. As Etzioni has noted, one of the major objects of the empirical studies adopting a goal model approach is to measure organizational "effectiveness" by contrasting observed, actual behavior with the stated, formal goals of the organization, and a good deal of social science research has followed this pattern.

Lefstein, Stapleton, and Teitelbaum's study of juvenile court judges' compliance to the *Gault* decisions is one example of this research (1969). Their basic format was to outline the requirements and implications of the *Gault* and related decisions, and then identify the extent to which the actual practices of judges in various jurisdictions and types of cases conformed to them. While they have demonstrated quite convincingly that the *Gault* decision had a major impact on the administration of juvenile justice, their optimism regarding the eventual full compliance to the standards of that decision seems somewhat unwarranted when one considers the practices of the actors in the administration of justice generally. What is not found in this study is an examination of the variety of factors, goals, and incentives operative (and likely to remain so) for the various individual actors in the system. A skeptical social scientist might well ask of a lower court judge, "So the Supreme Court handed down a decision, why should it affect you?" A full analysis of the dynamics of compliance and a theory of organization effectiveness would have to address itself to this question which assumes that the Supreme Court decision is just one of a number of factors affecting the system.

Likewise some of the studies reporting the impact of the *Miranda* decision on police behavior follow a similar format (Wald, et al., 1966–67, and Medalie, et al., 1968). The requirements specified in the decision are regarded as the formal goals and then actual behavior is observed and contrasted with them. The studies report different levels of compliance and acceptance on the part of the police, but generally note a low level of effectiveness. Various factors are raised and suggested as possible bases for this less than complete compliance. The "newness" of the decision is one such mentioned factor. Another is the generally hostile attitude of the police toward the new requirements. These factors, however, are not examined systematically, nor are they—and others—incorporated into a dynamic model of organization which considers the multiplicity of goals and incentives operating simultaneously within the system.

My criticism of these types of empirical studies echoes Etzioni's criticism of the goal model approach in general. The preoccupation with a set of formal goals and the observation of behavior primarily in terms of how it squares with these goals (or how the rules have altered previous patterns of behavior) is not conducive to theory building and the explanation of the observed patterns of behavior. It tends to produce a *unidimensional* picture of the process by placing undue emphasis on one set of goals and rules without adequately considering other factors which are, perhaps, equally as important in shaping the behavior of the actors in the system. The shortcomings of this approach will become more evident as the functional-systems model is explicated and examples of it are discussed.

Functional Systems Approaches

Turning to the second model, the functional-systems model, a substantially different conception of organization is employed. A different set of practices tends to be focused on, and there is a far greater and explicit concern for "explaining" the behavior of the actors (as opposed to simply "contrasting" it). Etzioni has lumped together a wide variety of studies under the rubric of systems models, and here too, there is a wide variation in the approaches to the analysis of criminal justice which I have placed in this category. There are, however, a number of common and distinguishing characteristics and assumptions which are shared by most of them. They all tend to view the organization of the administration of criminal justice as a system of action based primarily upon *cooperation*, *exchange*, and *adaptation*, and emphasize these considerations over adherence to formal rules and defined "roles" in searching for and developing explanations of behavior and discussing organizational effectiveness. Rather than being the primary focus of attention, formal "rules" and "disinterested professionalism" are viewed as only one set of the many factors shaping and controlling individuals' decisions, and perhaps not the most important ones. The efficacious "rules" followed by the actors are not necessarily the ideal, professional rules; and the goals they pursue are not necessarily the formal "organizational" goals posited by the researcher or even the "public" goals posited by the leaders of the organization.

Rather the "rules" the organization members are likely to follow are the "folkways" or informal "rules of the game" within the organization;

the goals they pursue are likely to be personal or sub-group goals; and the roles they assume are likely to be defined by the functional adaptation of these two factors. These three features of the organization then are the objects to be accounted for, and the functional-systems approach is likely to begin to identify and examine the adaptation of the actors to the environment, the workload and the interests of the persons placed within the system, i.e., other goals of the actors within the organization.

The idealized perspective of the *rational organization* pursuing its single set of goals is replaced by a perspective of the set of *rational individuals* who comprise the system, in this case the prosecutor, defense counsel, police, defendant, clerks, etc. pursuing their various individual goals. Unlike the rational-goal model, this model explicitly recognizes the "normality" of, and emphasizes the reality of, conflict between formal organizational goals, and the goals of the individual actors within the organization. According to this model, the "authority" of legal rules and "professionalism" is not automatically assumed to be efficacious. A more complete system of incentives is required.

In order to account for the actual behavior and practices of the organization, the scholars who to varying degrees utilize this functional-systems model of organization, describe the actual process and then begin to identify and examine the causes and conditions of the patterns of behavior of the various actors. In doing this they focus on the working conditions, the system of controls, incentives, and sanctions at the disposal of the various actors, and the larger environmental effects on the system. However, beyond these very general sets of concerns, there is little in common among the scholars who use this functional systems approach of criminal justice administration.

As with the rational-goal model, analysts utilizing a functional-systems model also tend to be motivated by normative concerns, but they are more likely to move beyond the contrasting of ideal goals with actual practices, to search for and identify the factors contributing to the observed practices. While perhaps personally accepting one set of goals for the system and giving expression to their own values, the functional systems approach is at least open enough to allow for and acknowledge the existence of other goals and not accept as "normal" the perfect coincidence of formal organizational goals with the goals of the individual actors within the system. Thus the perspective not only lends itself to accurate description of actual behavior but also begins to attempt to identify and account for the causes and conditions leading to this behavior.

Herbert Packer's . . . book, *The Limits of the Criminal Sanction* (1968), dramatically illustrates one of the major points of the functional-systems analysts. There can be many "goals" operating simultaneously—and at odds with each other—within any single system of organization, so that even to speak of "the formal goals" of an organization is likely to be misleading. He convincingly argues that there are at least two major sets of distinctly antagonistic values (the "due process" model and the "crime control" model) held by different actors responsible for administering criminal justice. One set emphasizes "due process," strict adherence to legal rules, and a full-fledged adversary relationship; the other emphasizes effective "crime control" for the community, and tends to minimize the concern for formality and individual rights. One's assessment of the "effectiveness" in achieving the "system's goals" would obviously depend upon which of the two sets of goals or models of values he subscribes to. Clearly any analysis of organizational behavior must be open-ended enough to identify and deal with the multiplicity of goals, values, and incentives of the various actors comprising the system. To do otherwise is likely to lead into the trap of reification and away from social theory.

Another body of research using a type of functional-systems approach tends to rely on an exchange model, adapted in varying degrees from Peter Blau's theoretical perspective (1964). The works of Jerome Skolnick (1966), Herbert Packer (1968), Abraham Blumberg (1967), and George Cole (1970) all tend to utilize this framework. The most widely-read work by any of these scholars is Skolnick's *Justice Without Trial*. While it is primarily an analysis of the functioning of the police in the realm of law enforcement, it does touch on police-prosecutor-court relationships, and characterizes them as participating in an elaborate exchange and bargaining system. However, in a related study, he focuses directly on the administration of criminal justice, and in particular on the roles, behavior, and relationships of the public defender and the prosecuting attorney (1967). For purposes of analysis he has suggested that all institutions are based either on norms of cooperation or norms of conflict, and that a major task of the social analyst is to identify and analyze means for countering these norms. That is, in an organization such as the family or corporation, a major concern is maintenance of cooperation and procedures for cooperation, and in other organizations, such as the sporting event or the adversary system, a major concern is maintenance of the institutionalized conflict and procedures for conflict. In both sets of institutions, Skolnick argues, the social analyst is interested in identifying the "deviation" from these norms of cooperation or conflict and the conditions and principles accounting for such deviation (Skolnick, 1967:53). Thus his analysis focuses on the institutionalized and structural pressures to reduce the conflict between prosecutor and defense attorney, on the resulting functional adjustments, and also on the normative justifications that support these new practices which seem to violate the *formal* norms of conflict.

Skolnick (1967:53) identifies the main pressures for "deviant" cooperation in this system as *administrative concerns* of each of the sets of actors (e.g., the defense attorney wants to get the best deal for his client and also handle it in the most expeditious manner; the district attorney has many publics to satisfy, an enormous amount of work, and opportunity for a great amount of discretion in selecting cases and charges to develop). As a result, a strong tendency toward cooperation develops in the relationship that is theoretically portrayed as a zerosum game. Strong informal norms to enhance the smooth functioning of the system itself replace the norms of conflict and adversarial relationship (Skolnick, 1967:55). Thus, the main cause for the "deviation" from the conflict norms Skolnick identifies as administrative *convenience*, brought about through an elaborate exchange system of mutually advantageous benefits. Additionally, he notes that the prosecuting and defense attorneys (almost always young, inexperienced and idealistic lawyers) are usually "successfully" socialized into this through an elaborate system of informal controls, or are transferred out.

The main device in which all parties share an interest of administrative convenience is in settlement by a plea of guilty. This serves the administrative purposes of saving time, effort, and—the actors all usually emphasize—in "getting a better deal" for the accused. It also has the effect of replacing the adversary system's norm of "presumption of innocence" with a norm of "presumption of guilt." Skolnick, however, argues in regard to this point that cooperation does "not demonstrably impede the quality of representation," a phrase which is unfortunately quite vague.[5] The operating norms—which rationalize this "deviant" behavior—at least from the public's or layman's perspective—are those of "administrative efficiency" and the "interests" of the accused in securing a reduced sentence.

Similar themes are taken up by other writers, who supply additional evidence to support a functional-systems model of the administration of criminal justice. Cole, in an analysis of the defense counsel/prosecutor relationships in Seattle, describes a similar system of mutually advantageous exchanges which function to displace conflict with cooperation, and produce a smooth-running system which seeks to maximize the administrative and personal goals of the individual actors rather than the formal organizational goals of due process. Stefan Kapsch (1971), in an interesting analysis which characterizes the plea bargaining by prosecution and defense as a mixed-strategy game—rather than the zero-sum game of adversary theory—emphasizes the administrative goals (the reduction of decision-making costs) being served by this substitution of cooperation for conflict, and also goes one to develop an explicit justification for the practice.[6]

Another well-known study of the administration of justice—and virtually the only recent full-length sociological analysis of the operations of a criminal court—is Blumberg's book on the New York City criminal justice system (1967). Despite his strong adherence to the principles enunciated in the "formal organizational goals" and particularly full-fledged adversary proceedings, Blumberg undertakes a functional analysis attempting to identify *causes and conditions* leading to the actual practices. He does this by conceptualizing the organization (the court, as he terms it) as an elaborate system of exchanges by persons who can mutually benefit by cooperating.

In a highly decentralized and complex organization, his model assumes that each of the actors will pursue more immediate goals and interests, and hence either the personal interests of the individual actor or the goals of and pressures for "production" and "efficiency" from his immediate supervisors and peer group will determine his actions. Thus, for example, the prosecutor's office wants high "batting averages," the defense counsel wants to handle cases as quickly as possible either for financial reasons or, in the case of the public defender, for administrative efficiency, and judges are constantly pressed to clear their calendars.

Blumberg identifies two main factors leading to the "displacement" of the formal, organizational goals by this system of mutual adjustment and exchange (1967).

> Intolerably large case loads of defendants which must be disposed of in an organizational context of limited resources and personnel. . . . As a consequence an almost irreconcilable conflict is posed in terms of intense pressures to process large numbers of cases on the one hand, and the stringent ideological and legal requirements of "due process" of law on the other hand. A rather tenuous resolution of the dilemma has emerged in the shape of a large variety of bureaucratically ordained and controlled "work crimes" short cuts, deviations and outright rule violations adopted as court practices in order to meet production norms. (Blumberg, 1967a:22)

Thus he has identified the press of large case loads and the strains on the actors as perhaps the chief reason for the systematic violations and/or tendencies to deviate from the prevailing ideological rules and norms of the adversary system. This makes it literally impossible for the actors to perform their prescribed roles, even if they wanted to. While it is no doubt accurate to identify a crushing case load as one of the factors necessitating functional adjustments and violations of the due process norms, the implication of Blumberg's argument seems to be that, in the absence of heavy case loads, the actors would "naturally" tend to perform their "proper" adversarial roles as defined by the full-fledged fight theory of the adversary system, and as outlined in some of the rational-goal models of the process.

This position is in at least partial conflict with Skolnick's and Cole's analyses of the conditions for cooperation (as opposed to institutionalized adversarial conflict), which emphasize the structural factors of long-term interaction, acquaintanceships, and a variety of personal and administrative factors (including handling of heavy case loads) as the primary factors contributing to a system of cooperation and exchange. Also, there is some evidence to indicate that rapid processing of defendants (and presumably "corner-cutting" by the actors in the system) occurs in situations where the work-load of the court is not pressing (Mileski, 1971). Thus I suspect that Blumberg has somewhat overstated the importance of heavy case loads, and perhaps as well, over-inflated the efficacy of "professional norms" of lawyers, norms which he feels most criminal lawyers have been "forced" to abandon for the purposes of court-dictated expediency.

Blumberg is also interested in the defense counsel, whom he argues is ideally supposed to assume a highly defined "professional" role as advocate and champion of his client, but in fact is usually found—like the prosecutor, judge and other court personnel—to respond to more direct and immediate incentives than those of "professional duty" (Blumberg, 1967a:28).

> The strong incentive of possible fee motivates the lawyer to promote litigation which would otherwise never have developed. However, the criminal lawyer develops a vested interest of an entirely different nature in his client's case: to limit its scope and duration rather than to battle. Only in this way can a case be profitable. . . . In effect, in his role as double agent, the criminal lawyer performs an extremely vital and delicate mission for the court organization and the accused. Both principals are anxious to terminate the litigation with a minimum of expense and damage to each other.

This argument appears reasonable, and Skolnick's reports tend to corroborate it to some extent. However, one still wishes here that Blumberg had been more careful and systematic in collecting and evaluating his data and presenting his arguments on the incentives of defense counsel. His discussions of the two factors which undercut the full-fledged adversary role of the defense counsel, the heavy case load and the financial incentive to quick disposition of cases, tend to contradict each other. On one hand, he argues, the court, in an attempt to cope with the heavy case load, has "co-opted" the defense counsel and "forced" him into acting the part of a "confidence agent" in convincing his client to plead guilty. On the other hand, the discussion of the financial incentives indicates that regardless of the judge's and prosecutor's interests, it is still in the self-interest of the defense counsel to seek a quick termination of the case through a plea of guilty since he is usually paid a flat fee for representation. Consequently, the less time a case takes, the higher the volume of his income. If the financial incentive is an important one, then one would expect the defense counsel to willingly press for pleas of guilty regardless of case load before the court. Furthermore, it is not unreasonable to expect that up to a point, as case load diminishes, the defense counsel's desires for quick and cursory disposition of cases would tend to increase. If business is slackening, then one must hustle even more to maintain volume. Systematically gathered and presented evidence would go a long way toward resolving these rival plausible hypotheses and unsupported assertions. Still, on the whole, one is given the distinct impression from the works of Blumberg, Skolnick, and Cole that the defense counsel is not so much an unwittingly co-opted agent used by the self-serving court bureaucracy, as he is one of the key figures in an elaborate system in which everyone, including himself, has certain commodities to exchange in the pursuit of his own interests.

There is still another set of factors which has been identified and examined by many of the scholars adopting the functional-systems approach. This is the enormous amount of discretion possessed by most of the actors in the criminal justice system, and in particular, the police and prosecutor. Most analysts subscribing to the rational-goal model of the system make little mention of this, tending to emphasize the rational administration according to specified rules and assume that it is an "attainable goal." Likewise many "reformers" and advocates of increased "professionalism" (i.e., rule-following) avoid dealing squarely with the problem posed by discretion. Among those scholars who have focused on this problem, Joseph Goldstein (1969), Packer (1968), and Skolnick (1967) are the most prominent. What they have all noted is that the administrators of justice have tremendous leeway in defining a situation, a vast array of competing rules in their arsenal, and are placed in a situation where it is frequently physically impractical (if not literally impossible) to enforce or administer all, or perhaps even most, of the rules all of the time.

This problem of discretion has two main components: first is the problem of the sheer magnitude of substantive laws and procedural rules; second is the inherent ambiguity of rules. A moment's reflection tells us that it is physically impossible and undesirable in anything approaching a democratic society to attempt to enforce all rules — both substantive criminal law and due process norms in the administration of justice — all the time. There are simply too many rules, and it would require a police state, a totalitarian bureaucracy, and a highly costly apparatus to begin even to approach total enforcement. Therefore, given the virtual impossibility of faithful adherence to and enforcement of all the rules, there is considerable room for discretion in the enforcement and administration of the rules. Discretion in such circumstances is inevitable, and because of the low visibility of most of the criminal activities and administration, it falls primarily on the hands of the police and prosecutors, and is not subject to much public attention and continuous supervision.

The second component of discretion — the ambiguity of rules and the subsequent leeway in defining an action — is more complex and perhaps more philosophically intriguing. For instance, if a person is arrested for burglary, he could also be charged with intent to commit burglary, illegal possession of burglary tools, illegal entry, possession of stolen property, and numerous other criminal violations. In short, a single action can be defined and interpreted in a number of ways. The ambiguity of "facts," of course, further complicates the picture and enhances discretionary practices. The process of selecting which "facts" to consider and which "rule" to apply to define the activity is in itself a discretionary matter of considerable importance. The variety of available "legal" alternatives allows the actor a wide latitude for discretion, and of course a very valuable commodity to bargain with in the system of exchange. In this view the interpretation and use of the rules themselves are viewed as instruments of rationalization, not application. That is, the rules are selected and used as weapons or supports at the whim of, and in the particular interests of, the various actors in the system. Thus ambiguity and discretion are inherent to the very nature of all elaborate systems of rules, and "force" enforcement and administrative officials—the so-called rule "appliers"—into a position of making "lawless" decisions. This poses a major problem in the administration of justice, as Herbert Packer (1968:290) has noted:

> The basic trouble with discretion is simply that it is lawless, in the literal sense of that term. If police or prosecutors find themselves free (or compelled) to pick and choose among known or knowable instances of criminal conduct, they are making a judgment which in a society based on law should be made only by those to whom the making of law is entrusted.

To the extent that this in fact is the case—for the reasons just outlined—a faithful adherence to rational-goal model of the criminal justice system is *impossible* in practice and in principle.

Considerations for Reform

While analysts using the rational-goal model have tended to emphasize the set of formal goals, ideals, and rules which they suggest should be operating in the administration of justice, and have examined the consequences of non-performance of these goals in terms of the normative ideals and consequences to individual rights, they have frequently ignored the factors and conditions contributing to the displacement, violation, and non-performance of these goals, ideals and rules.[7] On the other hand, the functional-systems approach has gone a long way toward identifying the causes and conditions accounting for the observed behavior, and toward demonstrating that there is no particular reason to expect individuals' behavior to coincide with the behavior prescribed by the formal goals of the system. Formal rules and norms obviously affect and guide the behavior of the actors, but they are only one set of considerations among several.

It is therefore unreasonable to expect a perfectly "effective" system for administering criminal justice. This, of course, does not preclude the adoption of policies and practices which incrementally increase the system's "effectiveness." Additional rules of clarification and procedure, reducing the reliance on the criminal sanction, more and better trained personnel, more space, and improved calendars, are all frequently mentioned as measures of reform, and there is little question that their adoption would result in improvement. However, running through such proposals is the assumption that if these steps were taken, the actors in the system would somehow *naturally* begin to assume stronger commitments to the formal goals and rules of the system and act accordingly. This tends to underestimate, I think, the very real and strong individual and sub-group incentives, goals, and values, and underestimates as well the saliency of the "crime control model" as the operative normative ideal among many persons involved in the system. Clearly it is more than a problem of overcoming work-load so that good men can do good work. There exist strong competing norms and incentives which act at cross-purposes to the system's formal goals and norms. The task of institution-alized reform rests squarely on the generation of mechanisms which strengthen the position of the organizational goals and norms vis-à-vis the competing subgroup and individual goals.

At this point it is particularly useful to return to the concerns of the theorists of large-scale organizations, and begin to consider some of the structural features of the system, particularly the compliance-inducing mechanisms. What emerges from the analysis of the operations of the criminal justice system is a clear picture of an organization which has highly specified rules and goals, but has virtually no instruments by which to enforce them. Rather than the highly rationalized rulebound and bureaucratically structured system that Weber depicted the process to be, one finds a highly decentralized and decidedly non-hierarchial sys-tem of exchange, in which there are virtually no instruments to supervise practices and secure compliance to the formal goals of the organization. In the absence of such efficacious compliance securing mechanisms, insti-tutionalized long-term reform is unlikely.

Only two mechanisms are institutionalized to induce actors to comply with the formal rules and goals of the criminal justice system—normative inducements accruing from *professionalism* and the *appellate procedure*—and neither is very effective in relation to the countervailing incentives.

Appeal to the normative considerations of professionalism is a key source of control in many organizations composed of highly trained and skilled personnel, and in many instances is a highly successful instru-ment. Certainly the guild-like pride and clannishness of the legal profes-sional generally and bar associations in particular act as a powerful influence on lawyers. Legal training is marked with a continuing empha-sis on the professional responsibilities of the lawyer and one might expect all these factors to act as a substantial "professionalizing" influence on the actors in the criminal justice system. However, a great many students of professional organizations have noted that the importance of professional norms—in the absence of direct supervision and other formal means of control—are not as powerful as they are popularly believed to be.

This downward revised assessment would particularly seem to be the case in the administration of criminal justice. There is little disagree-ment among knowledgeable observers that the criminal lawyer—includ-ing the office of prosecutor, defense lawyer, and not infrequently the criminal court judge as well—holds the status of anchor-man within the legal profession. This certainly acts to reduce the importance of the norm of "professionalism" as a compliance-inducing mechanism. Likewise, the low visibility of the administration of criminal justice and the generally "low" status of its clients tends to further erode the "professional" environment and leads to a lack of concern on the part of the more prestigious legal professional organizations and the public generally, further undercutting one of the major sources of inducement to professionalism.

The other mechanism — the only formal one — institutionalized to induce compliance to formal organizational norms on the part of the actors within it, is the appellate process, and the continuing opportunity for appeal. This, however, is a highly ineffectual instrument in that it is relatively passive, extremely expensive, can be instituted only at the insistence of a convicted defendant, and usually only if it is pressed by his defense counsel. At best it is a passive instrument, which might function to curb some of the most flagrant violations of administration, but is hardly a powerful and systematic instrument of control in most instances.

In short, what one finds in the system of criminal justice is a highly formalized and defined set of rules, norms, and goals, but also an organization which possesses no corresponding set of incentives and sanctions which act to systematically enforce them. Any far-reaching discussion of reform and proposals for change in the administration within the American system of criminal justice would have to deal with this problem of the nature and distribution of compliance-including mechanisms.[8] Ironically, it seems to lead to a solution requiring more bureaucracy, not less.

Endnotes

[1] I have been criticized on this point by some persons who argue that the American adversary system cannot be considered an "organization," and in fact is designed explicitly to avoid "organizational" and "bureaucratic" processing of cases on a routine basis. The argument is that the adversary system protects individual rights by institutionalizing the lack of an organization to "process" cases, in contrast to (to varying degrees) many of the countries relying on inquisitorial methods. While there are certainly differences between European and American practices in the administration of criminal justice, I think that these differences are easily contained within an organizational framework. One system may be more centralized and hierarchically organized than another, but in all cases there is a group of institutionalized interacting roles which in principle are expected to work together (whether through conflict or cooperation) toward a common set of goals.

[2] Herbert Packer (1968) makes a similar point in his discussion of the two models of criminal justice, the "due process" model and the "crime control" model. He suggests that among academic lawyers, the former tends to be regarded as the "goals" of the system. Likewise John Rawls has made a similar point (1958).

[3] No doubt one of the major reasons for concentrating almost exclusively on "means" — aside from their connection with the concept of justice — in analyzing the activities of the criminal justice system is that there is no way of measuring effectiveness in terms of deciding guilt or innocence, another activity which might reasonably be identified as the "goal" of the organization. That is, if one posed this as the goal of the organization, there would be no reliable measure which would allow him to contrast the "ideal" with the actual in that there is no way of always knowing *factual* guilt or innocence.

4 This position, on a general level, reflects Maine's (1963) celebrated observation that the "movement of the progressive societies has hitherto been a movement from Status to Contract." Likewise similar division of labor and specialization of the administration of justice has been demonstrated systematically in the work of Schwartz and Miller (1964) and Schwartz (1954). On the other hand, many scholars question the extent to which all this has in fact taken place. The legal realists have rather successfully demonstrated the ambiguity of legal rules and the flexibility of rule-application (Llewellyn, 1964). Likewise the judicial behaviorists have rather convincingly demonstrated a relationship between judicial backgrounds and judicial behavior (see Schubert, 1965, and Nagel, 1970). Also, Friedman (1966) has challenged and at least modified Weber's arguments regarding the nature of "rational" legal reasoning, and along with Joseph Goldstein (1969) and others has shown the increasing utilization of discretionary, non-rule specified powers within the "modern" law. Kadi-like justice seems not to have disappeared either in theory or in fact.

5 At any rate, this argument should have been dwelt on in more depth. He offers no real evidence for it, nor does he attempt to operationalize "quality of representation," and it remains an undemonstrated assertion. It is, I think, an example of the conservative bias, i.e., the acceptance of the *status quo* once one "understands" it, which if not inherent in the logic of functional analysis generally is certainly reflected in a good deal of functionalist literature.

6 I think that his is a tortured reading of the traditional theory of the adversary system and the administration of justice, but nevertheless it is one of the few thoughtful discussions of the practices—one that moves away from implicit normative support of the practices, and begins to offer an explicit justification of them.

7 This language assumes that if there is widespread consensus that these are, in fact, the actual goals of the organization, and that they once were—or could have been—achieved. Packer's persuasive analysis of the two models of criminal justice points up the existence of a multiplicity of goals within the organization, and shows that they frequently lead to cross purposes.

8 For an elaboration of the problem of individual incentives and compliance inducing mechanisms, see my discussion of law as a "public good," and the subsequent problem for an explanation of individual incentives and compliance (Feeley, 1970). For a general exposition of the problem of incentives and compliance to organizational goals by "rational actors," see Downs (1967).

References

Blau, P. (1964). *Exchange and power in social life*. New York: John Wiley.

Blumberg, A. (1967). *Criminal justice*. Chicago: Quadrangle Books. (1967a). The practice of law as a confidence game. *Law and Society Review, 1*, 15–29.

Cole, G. (1970). The decision to prosecute. *Law and Society Review, 4*, 331–345.

Downs, A. (1967). *Inside bureaucracy*. Boston: Little Brown.

Etzioni, A. (1960). Two approaches to organizational analysis: A critique and a suggestion. *Administrative Science Quarterly, 5*, 257–278.

Etzioni, A. (1961). *A comparative analysis of complex organizations*. New York: Free Press.

Etzioni, A. (1964). *Modern organization*. Englewood Cliffs: Prentice-Hall.

Feeley, M. (1970). Coercion and compliance. *Law and Society Review, 4*, 505–519.

Friedman, L. (1966). On legalistic reasoning—a footnote to Weber. *1966 Wisconsin Law Review*, 148–171.

Goldstein, A. S. (1960). The state and the accused: Balance of advantage in criminal procedure. *Yale Law Journal, 69*, 1149–1199.

Goldstein, J. (1969). Police discretion not to invoke the criminal process: Low visibility decisions in the administration of justice. *Yale Law Journal, 69*, 543–594.

Kapsch, S. (1971). *The adversary system and the assistance of counsel.* Unpublished Ph.D. Thesis, Department of Political Science, University of Minnesota.

Klonoski, J., & Mendelsohn, R. (Eds.). (1970). *The politics of legal justice.* Boston: Little Brown.

Lefstein, N., Stapleton, V., & Teitelbaum, L. (1969). In search of juvenile justice. *Law and Society Review, 5,* 491–563.

Llewellyn, K. (1960). *The common law tradition.* Boston: Little Brown.

Maine, H. (1963). *Ancient law.* Boston: Beacon Press.

Medalie, R. J., et al. (1968). Custodial police interrogation in our nation's capital: The attempt to implement *Miranda. Michigan Law Review, 66,* 1347–1422.

Mileski, M. (1971). Courtroom encounters. *Law and Society Review, 5,* 473–538.

Nagel, S. (1970). *The judicial process from a behavioral perspective.* Chicago: Dorsey.

Packer, H. (1968). *The limits of the criminal sanction.* Stanford: Stanford University Press.

Rawls, J. (1958). Justice as fairness. *Philosophical Review, 67,* 164–197.

Schubert, G. (1965). *The judicial mind.* Evanston: Northwestern University Press.

Skolnick, J. (1966). *Justice without trial.* New York: John Wiley.

Skolnick, J. (1967). Social control in the adversary system. *Journal of Conflict Resolution, 11,* 52–67.

Schwartz, R. D. (1954). Social factors in the development of legal control. *Yale Law Journal, 63,* 471–491.

Schwartz, R. D., & Miller, J. (1964). Legal evolution and societal complexity. *American Journal of Sociology, 70,* 159–169.

Wald, M. S., et al. (1966). Interrogations in New Haven: The impact of *Miranda. Yale Law Journal, 76,* 1521–1648.

Weber, M. (1954). Rational and irrational administration of justice. In M. Rheinstein (Ed.), *Max Weber on Law in Economy and Society.* Cambridge: Harvard University Press.

Chapter 2

The Political and Organizational Response to Gangs
An Examination of a "Moral Panic" in Nevada

Richard C. McCorkle
Terance D. Miethe

The past decade has witnessed increasing concern about street gangs and their role in violent crime and drug trafficking. According to a recent national survey, more than 80 percent of prosecutors in large cities now acknowledge that gangs are a problem in their jurisdiction, that their numbers are growing, and that levels of gang-related violence are increasing (Johnson, Webster, and Connors, 1995). A seasoned observer of the gang problem has asserted that contemporary street gangs are now "more numerous, more prevalent, and more violent . . . than anytime in the country's history" (Miller, 1990:263).

The recognition of a gang problem has not been uniform. Initially, many cities remained in what Huff (1990) calls a state of *denial*, officially disavowing the problem because of public relations fears. Many of these cities now acknowledge gang activity on their streets, a concession that frequently followed the commission of one or more high-profile gang-

Richard C. McCorkle and Terance D. Miethe, *"The Political and Organizational Response to Gangs: An Examination of a "Moral Panic" in Nevada," Justice Quarterly*, Vol. 15 No. 1, March 1998, pp.41–64. Reprinted by permission of the Academy of Criminal Justice Sciences.

related crimes (Klein, 1995). After the "discovery" of a gang problem, however, public officials react in a standard fashion: gangs are defined as a law enforcement problem, police and prosecutorial "gang units" are formed, and suppression strategies are promoted vigorously (Huff, 1990).

Gangs recently have emerged as a major social problem, it is argued, because of a significant increase in the objective threat posed by such groups. This explanation for the current crisis—overwhelmingly embraced by those who study, police, or prosecute gangs—is characteristic of objectivism, one of two dominant approaches to social problems in general. According to this model, a condition becomes a social problem when it threatens the quality or length of life of a substantial number of people (Manic, 1974). Objectivism ignores or minimizes the subjective nature of social problems and assumes that empirical measures of a condition accurately reflect the objective threat it poses. The state acts only in response to that threat and does not attempt to shape or influence public opinion to further its own agenda (Beckett, 1994). According to this perspective, the gang problem is real, growing, and deserving of public attention and state resources. Huff's conclusion that public officials typically "overreact" to a gang problem thus should be viewed more as a criticism of the form than of the level of that response; indeed, Huff advocates a massive, "coordinated, comprehensive effort" to address the fundamental social and economic conditions that give rise to gangs (1990:316).

Some observers, however, question the magnitude of the threat posed by contemporary street gangs (Jackson and Rudman, 1993; Zatz, 1987). Despite surveys suggesting an increase in gang activity across the country, many wonder how such findings should be interpreted, given the lack of a consensus about how even to define a "gang" or what constitutes "gang-related crime." The definitions currently employed are the outcome of an extremely subjective process and vary greatly across jurisdictions, agencies, and researchers; thus it is extremely difficult to make statements about the nature and trends in gang activity (Decker and Kempf-Leonard, 1995; Mein and Maxson, 1989). Some observers have gone farther, asserting that the gang crisis, in certain jurisdictions, was manufactured by social control agencies to obtain resources and expand their authority (Zatz, 1987). Public support for state expansion is generated, these critics argue, by creating and promoting images which suggest that the community is under attack from warring tribes of drug-dealing sociopaths.

Those who look askance at the current state and direction of gang policy represent the constructionist approach, the other dominant approach to social problems. According to this model, the objective status of a condition—for example, gang activity—is largely irrelevant in determining what is defined as a social problem. Instead a social problem is understood more accurately as a product derived from the "activities of individuals or groups making assertions of grievances and claims with respect to some putative condition" (Spector and Kitsuse, 1977:75). The important point is not the actual nature of the condition, but what claimsmakers *say* about that condition. Conceivably any number of conditions, even those presenting only minor threats, could exist. Yet because public attention and resources are limited, intense competition exists among claimsmakers in public arenas where social problems are framed and funded (Hiltgartner and Bosk, 1988). Many apparently are called, but few are chosen.

Gangs have become a major social problem, according to constructionists, because law enforcement officials have been successful in these public arenas. This success has been enhanced by their access to the media and to government officials, by their monopoly of crime information, and by our cultural preoccupations with crime and race. Like other claimsmakers, these officials also have found it "necessary to lie or exaggerate a little" so as to distinguish themselves from other groups seeking recognition and funding (Goode and Ben-Yehuda, 1994:120). Unlike the case with most social problems, however, the distortions and exaggerations by law enforcement officials necessarily entail a focus on a particular group of individuals in the community. One possible result is a "moral panic," a situation in which public fears and state interventions greatly exceed the threat posed by the targeted group. Such moral panics purportedly have occurred in response to various groups in American history, as shown by the anti-Catholic movement of the 19th century and the satanic cult scare of the past decade (Hofstadter, 1966; Jenkins and Meier-Katkin, 1992).

Gangs and Moral Panics

The concept of moral panic actually grew out of research on British youth gangs conducted during the 1960s. Cohen (1972) believed that the term most accurately characterized the reactions of the media, agencies of social control, and the public to a brief melee between the "Mods" and the "Rockers" at a seaside resort. He defined a moral panic as follows:

> A condition, episode, person or group of persons emerges to become defined as a threat to societal values and interests; its nature is presented in a stylized and stereotypical fashion by the mass media; the moral barricades are manned by editors, bishops, politicians and other right thinking people; socially accredited experts pronounce their diagnoses and solutions; ways of coping are evolved or . . . resorted to; the condition then disappears, submerges or deteriorates and becomes invisible. Sometimes the subject of the panic is quite novel and at other times it is something which has been in existence long enough, but suddenly appears in the limelight. (Cohen, 1972:9)

A few scattered fistfights and broken windows, according to Cohen, were transformed by the media into "an orgy of destruction," an event characteristic of a wave of hooliganism spreading across the country. Although local law enforcement officials were aware of the embellishment by the media, they played along, seizing the opportunity to increase funds and expand police powers. Even the British Parliament got involved, enacting stiffer sentences against youth offenders and at least entertaining the notion of a return to corporal punishment.

One of the most frequently cited illustrations of a moral panic is taken from events in Britain during the early 1970s (Hall et al., 1978). Britain, at that time, was mired in a deep economic recession, which fomented social unrest and generated challenges to the capitalistic system. To deflect attention from the economic problems, Hall et al. argue, the British ruling class manufactured a moral panic, manipulating the press and the criminal justice system so as to convince the public that street crime had reached epidemic proportions. By exploiting the public's fear of crime, the ruling class shifted the focus from an ailing British economy to street muggings, thereby protecting their own economic interests and legitimating the more strongly authoritarian social control measures employed to quell social unrest.

At least two gang researchers have characterized the reaction to street gangs in the United States as a moral panic. Zatz (1987) accused law enforcement officials in Phoenix during the late 1970s of manufacturing a Chicano youth gang problem as a means of acquiring LEAA funds for a new gang crime unit. Police spokesmen, she contended, exploited the media penchant for violence, sensationalism, and crime "themes" by providing a regular stream of violent, random crimes committed by alleged gang members. Estimates on the number of gangs were ratcheted up by officials regularly and without justification, she reported, and were accompanied by dire warnings of impending social disorder if law enforcement interventions were not beefed up. Analysis of juvenile court records, however, provided little to support law enforcement claims. Chicano youth gang members referred to juvenile court were no more a threat to the community than nongang referrals;. most gang youths had been arrested for fighting, primarily among themselves, and for minor property crimes. From interviews with social service agencies in Phoenix that dealt with Chicano youths, Zatz (1987) also concluded that police wildly exaggerated both the number and the size of gangs in the area.

Zatz's designation of the response to gangs in Phoenix as a moral panic may have been premature, however, given that she examined only the criminal activities of youthful gang members. Although there are disturbing accounts of 8- and 10-year-old gang members, the upper age range actually has "expanded dramatically" (Klein, 1995:105). Because gang violence is primarily a young adult, not a juvenile, problem (Maxson, Gordon, and Mein, 1985; Maxson, Klein, and Cunningham, 1992; Spergel, 1984), Zatz (1987) may have underestimated the nature and level of the threat posed by gangs during that period.

More recently, Jackson and Rudman (1993) suggested that antigang initiatives in California, such as the Street Terrorism Enforcement and

Prevention Act, have been excessive and extreme, shaped by stereotypic portrayals of gangs provided by law enforcement and the media. Yet because the authors had not examined actual levels and trends in gang activity in California, they could only conclude that "on the surface," the gang response was "similar to past inquiries finding support for the idea of a 'moral panic'" (Jackson and Rudman, 1993:271).

Whether the gang problem in fact constitutes a moral panic in certain jurisdictions thus remains unknown. Certainly a great deal of mythology surrounds gangs: The research simply does not support tales of highly organized, entrepreneurial, drug-dealing urban gangs on the move in search of new markets (Klein, 1995). Nonetheless, large numbers of young males grouped in rival factions would pose significant problems for the community. Yet the determination that the response to those groups represents a moral panic requires a more extensive examination of gangs than has been conducted to this point; such an examination must include a detailed analysis of gang activity over a period of years. Moreover, the concept used in previous studies of gang crises has not yet been operationalized adequately. Researchers such as Zatz (1987) and Jackson and Rudman (1989) used the concept in the loosest fashion: They did not properly specify in advance, or subsequently examine, the empirical indicators necessary for demonstrating that a moral panic in fact had occurred.

The concept of moral panics, however, has not been without its critics. For Waddington (1986), the problem is "establishing the comparison between the scale of the problem and the scale of the response to it" (p. 246). At what point, he asks, can we say that a reaction is disproportional to the objective threat, that a "moral panic" has occurred? Furthermore, critics such as Waddington believe that the objective threat of a condition can never be known; consequently, judgments as to whether a reaction was disproportional must remain arbitrary.

In response to such criticisms, Goode and Ben-Yehuda (1994) note that many (if not most) objective threats can be measured, particularly those which are "familiar, ongoing, and based on behavior" (p. 43). They further contend that specific criteria can be used to determine the proportionality of a response to a given problem. Indicators of a disproportional response—a "moral panic"—include the exaggeration or fabrication of figures purporting to measure the severity of the problem and wild fluctuations in the attention given to a condition without corresponding changes in its severity. In this study, we gave careful attention to these criteria to determine whether the response to gangs in Las Vegas could accurately be described as a moral panic.

Methods

In this paper we present the results of a study applying the concept of moral panic to the gang problem in Las Vegas, Nevada. Using a variety of sources, we attempted to understand the process by which gangs, present in the city for more than a decade, came to be defined as a major social problem during the late 1980s. To construct the timetable in which the problem unfolded in Las Vegas, we conducted a search for all gang-related stories published from 1983 to 1994 in the city's two largest newspapers, the *Review Journal* and the *Sun*. We also examined state and local government records including minutes of legislative hearings on gangs, archival data; and law enforcement publications. In reviewing these materials, we identified and subsequently interviewed key actors—police officers, school officials, prosecutors, and politicians active in the definition and response to gangs in Las Vegas. These interviews provided further details about the history of the gang response in Las Vegas.

To assess the appropriateness of that response to gangs, we examined all felony charges filed in Clark County district courts from 1989 through 1994. Previous studies did not use prosecutors' filings as a measure of the objective threat posed by gangs; gang crime typically was measured by self-reports (Esbensen and Huizinga, 1993; Hagedorn, 1988; Thornberry et al., 1994) or by arrest data (Maxson, Klein, and Cunningham, 1992; Tracy, 1987). We believe that prosecutors' filings are at least as valid an indicator of gang crime as self-reports or arrest data, if not more so.

One of the surest paths to overstating gang members' criminal activity is to take the accounts provided by the gang members themselves (Klein, 1995; Spergel, 1995). They are prone to exaggerate their own criminal activity, and possess unreliable and biased information on the scope of the group's crimes. Arrest statistics suffer a different set of problems: Because gangs consist primarily of minorities (Klein, 1995), and because race is not independent of the decision to arrest (Black, 1971; Smith and Visher, 1981; Smith, Visher, and Davidson, 1984), arrest statistics may be a more accurate indicator of enforcement patterns than of criminal activity. Indeed, the higher rejection and dismissal rates for members of minorities strongly suggest that police often use arrests for nonlaw enforcement purposes: for example, to harass or punish troublesome, disrespectful populations (Hepburn, 1978; Petersilia, 1985; Pope, 1978).

On the other hand, there is little or no evidence that race is a factor on a prosecutor's decision to file charges (Albonetti et al., 1989; Miethe, 1987; Miethe and Moore, 1986). That decision is a function primarily of the severity of the offense and the quality of the available evidence. Consequently we believe that prosecutors' filings are a valid measure of the objective threat posed by gangs over the period in question.

One problem with using felony charges, of course, is that the juvenile gang members' delinquent acts would not be included in our assessment of gang activity during the period under study; those acts are under the exclusive jurisdiction of the juvenile court. Thus the measure of objective gang threat used in this study underestimates the threat posed by these groups, but not by much. Research has confirmed that serious gang activity is attributable primarily to older adolescent and young adult males (Spergel, 1995). Furthermore, juveniles age 15 and older in Nevada, when charged with committing serious violent crimes, are automatically certified as adults and prosecuted in the adult court system.

Some might argue that our measure actually overstates the threat posed by gangs. By labeling any crime committed by a known gang member or associate as a "gang-related" incident, we are employing the broader of the two definitions in use (Klein, 1995; Spergel, 1995). As a measure of gang activity, these crimes did not necessarily spring from intergang rivalries, turf conflicts, or efforts to increase gang revenues. A crime was committed, an arrest was made, and the suspect's name showed up in the gang file. The alleged crime may have been independent of gang affiliation: For example, an individual robbed a convenience store not to help the gang but to purchase his next fix or put gas in his car. This "member-based" definition, in fact, is used by law enforcement officials in Las Vegas and is the basis of reports on the incidence of gang crime in the city (C. Owens, June 12, 1995, personal communication). Using a "motive-based" definition, and counting a crime as gang-related only if it was gang-motivated, might have reduced the reported incidence of gang crime in the city by as much as half (Klein, 1995).

Gangs and Moral Panic in Las Vegas

Before the mid-1980s, Las Vegas essentially had no gang problem (M. Hawkins, March 3, 1995, personal communication). Gangs existed, but they were few, were not particularly troublesome, and were confined to public housing projects and minority communities, particularly on the west side of the city (Nerlander and Ferguson, 1990). Nonetheless, in 1985 the Las Vegas Metropolitan Police Department (LVMPD) assigned two officers full-time to an experimental Gang Diversion Unit (GDU). The unit's function was largely intelligence gathering; officers made no arrests, arranged no drug busts, and answered no dispatches. Procedures for identifying and recording gang members and their associates were also developed. These provided the first official "count" of gangs in late 1985: 15 gangs with some 1,000 members ("Special Police Units," 1985). The GDU reports also concluded that Las Vegas gangs were not heavily involved in the illicit drug market.

Early in 1986 the Gang Diversion Unit abruptly announced that there were now 4,000 gang members in 28 distinct gang sects; many were involved heavily in selling illicit drugs ("Group Examines," 1986). More disturbing than the increased number was the apparent movement of gang activity, reported in the media, from the traditionally "troubled" neighborhoods to recreation centers, theaters, and public schools across the city. GDU officers now also reported that area street gangs, in addition to drug trafficking, were involved increasingly in burglary, vandalism, animal abuse, and satanism ("Group Examines," 1986).

Concern about the gang problem increased quickly, as indicated by trends in media coverage during the late 1980s. Figure 1 presents the trend in gang coverage by the two major Las Vegas newspapers over that period. In 1983, only 4 stories on gangs appeared in local papers; at its peak in 1989, the number of gang related stories reached 174. Local papers continued to carry well over 100 stories a year through 1991. The growing apprehension was also reflected in a public survey of Las Vegans in 1989 (Center for Survey Research, 1989): 77% of residents were "very concerned" about gangs in the community, up from 67 percent from 1987. Moreover, 89% of those polled believed that the gang problem was worsening and perhaps was out of control.

The Law Enforcement Response

The official response to gangs began to take shape in early 1988, when the county provided funding for an additional 16 officers for the Gang Diversion Unit. That mobilization of forces was accompanied by a radical shift in strategy, from an emphasis on intelligence gathering and selective enforcement to a harder position on deterrence and punishment. Gang-infested areas were to be targeted; aggressive sweeps were to be conducted, which would "rid Las Vegas of hoodlum gangs" once and for all ("Metro Mobilizes," 1988). Throughout the year, press reports trumpeting the success of the new GDU appeared in local papers. Television news reporters frequently accompanied police on drug sweeps of areas purportedly controlled by gangs, filming raids of crack houses and the

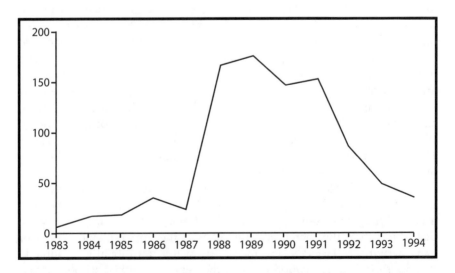

Figure 1 Gang Stories in Clark County (NV) Newspapers, 1983–1994

arrests of "high-level" gang leaders. Because of this sustained assault, law enforcement officials (while not declaring victory), claimed that the tide had turned; gangbangers were retreating in the face of "superior forces" ("Gang Diversion Unit," 1988).

Talk of victory would have been premature, particularly because of the outbreak of gang violence on high school campuses in spring 1989 (J. Lazzarotto, September 29, 1995, personal communication). Law enforcement officials offered an explanation for the disruptions, claiming that gangs were moving from the street to the campus to recruit new members and expand drug distribution networks. In response, the Las Vegas Metropolitan Police Department (LVMPD) stepped up patrols, undercover police officers wandered on and near campuses, and school district police, usually unarmed, were allowed to carry weapons ("Bonanza students," 1989).

Calm eventually returned to high school campuses; only a few, very minor interruptions were reported in the spring semester of 1990. The alarm was sounded once again, however, after the shooting death of a student in a school cafeteria on the first day of the 1990–1991 academic year. The gunman, a 15-year-old Hispanic male, was arrested and charged with murder. Police described his act as a "gang-related slaying," an accusation never substantiated despite repeated challenges from the attorney assigned to represent the youth ("Eldorado Teen," 1990).

The Legislative Response

During the 1989 session, state lawmakers had enacted a number of statutes targeting gang crime, particularly that which occurred on school property (Nerlander and Ferguson, 1991). The cafeteria slaying of 1990 was viewed as part of a larger pattern of gang activity, suggesting that gang members were not deterred by the passage of this legislation. In an impassioned speech delivered on the day after the cafeteria shooting, the governor of Nevada announced what he believed would be the *coup de grace*: a complete ban on gang membership. The statute, he promised, would be written broadly to ensure that "wearing gang colors, hanging around gangs, or even bragging about being in a gang" would be a criminal offense and subject to swift, severe sanctions ("Governor Miller," 1990). The initial draft of this "Gang Abolishment Act" drew sharp criticism from local ACLU officials, who claimed that the bill had disturbing racial overtones because the majority of gang members were members of minorities (C. Kendrick, July 18, 1995, personal communication).

The initial draft consequently underwent major revisions; the LVMPD and the Clark County Prosecutor's Office were placed in charge of producing a workable gang bill. Redactors relied heavily on California's Street Terrorism and Enforcement and Prevention Act, a comprehensive piece of gang legislation that had withstood the scrutiny of California's appellate court (Committee on Judiciary, 1991). In the new version (known as the Gang Enhancement Statute), gang membership in Nevada would not be criminalized. Any person, however, who committed a crime "knowingly for the benefit of, at the direction of, or in association with a criminal gang" would be subject to a term of incarceration in addition to, and consecutive to, the term prescribed by the statute for the crime (Committee on Judiciary, 1991:316). For felonies, prison sentences would be doubled. The bill sailed through the state senate and assembly; it drew only four opponents, the most critical a black senator who characterized the legislation as a "veiled effort to incarcerate more minorities" (J. Neal, August 13, 1995, personal communication). In fall 1991, a specialized gang prosecution unit was developed, which would apply the statute more effectively.

The Abatement of the Panic

By 1992 the Special Enforcement Detail was asserting that it had "control over the gang problem" (Hartung and Roberts, 1993:32). Hundreds of gang members reportedly had been imprisoned; the sentences of many were doubled under the Gang Enhancement Statute as a result of their expert testimony. In the months following the passage of the Gang Enhancement Statute and the creation of a gang prosecution unit, media attention to street gangs in Las Vegas declined sharply (see figure 1). The problem of gangs apparently had been addressed. Even if it had not, the media now were dominated by more dramatic issues: deepening state budget deficits, an unscrupulous battle between a university president and the basketball coach, the federal government's plan to store radioactive waste only 90 miles from the city.

Assessing the Objective Threat Posed by Gangs

Perhaps the declining criterion of a moral panic is the lack of proportionality between the objective threat posed by a condition and the reaction to that threat. To assess the appropriateness of the response to gangs in this jurisdiction, we examined data on all felony charges filed in Clark County District Courts from 1989 through 1994. We obtained a list of all known gang members and associates from the Gang Investigation Section (GIS) of the LVMPD. The list contained the identification numbers (no names) of 4,752 individuals, assigned at their first contact with GIS officers in the field. Individuals also were distinguished by whether they were juveniles or adults. When a gang member or associate had been arrested by LVMPD, a defendant identification number also was recorded. The Clark County District Attorney's Office uses these numbers to monitor the flow of cases through the court system. We excluded the 2,152 juveniles on the list, and then matched the remaining 2,600 adults with the case-monitoring data. By doing so, we could document the level and the trends of officially recorded gang crime during the period of the ostensible moral panic.

Table 1 presents the percentage of UCR index crime and felony drug charges filed against known gang members from 1989 to 1994. For violent offenses in general, the objective threat posed by gangs increased during that period. The proportion of violent index crimes attributable to gangs more than doubled from 1989 to 1993. Despite this disturbing trend, however, the percentage of violent crime linked to gangs was (and remained) quite low. When the gang panic erupted in 1989–1990, known gang members accounted for only about 3 percent of all reported violent crimes

Table 1 Proportion of index crimes and felony drug charges[a] filed against known gang members, 1989–1994[b]

	1989	1990	1991	1992	1993	1994
Violent Index	03	.04	.05	.07	.07	.05
Offenses	(4,032)	(4,771)	(5,017)	(5,904)	(6,349)	(6,195)
Murder	.13	.08	.18	.18	.19	.15
	(266)	(355)	(346)	(493)	(488)	(354)
Rape	.01	.00	.03	.09	.02	.05
	(181)	(135)	(66)	(70)	(126)	(79)
Aggravated	.02	.03	.03	.03	.04	.05
Assault	(2,945)	(3,597)	(3,550)	(4,402)	(4,507)	(4,493)
Robbery	.04	.06	.08	.14	.16	.14
	(640)	(684)	(1,055)	(1,299)	(1,228)	(1,269)
Property Index	.02	.04	.06	.06	.05	.03
Offenses	(3,604)	(3,558)	(3,967)	(4,915)	(5,629)	(7,564)
Burglary	.02	.03	.04	.05	.04	.03
	(1,716)	(1,736)	(2,003)	(2,461)	(2,400)	(2,932)
Larceny/theft	.01	.05	.04	.04	.03	.01
	(1,104)	(1,001)	(1,141)	(1,396)	(2,206)	(3,467)
Motor vehicle	.04	.06	.12	.11	.12	.10
Theft	(774)	(800)	(819)	(1,054)	(1,010)	(1,161)
Arson	.00	.05	.00	.25	.08	.00
	(10)	(21)	(13)	(4)	(13)	(4)
Drug Offenses						
Drug sales	.02	.01	.02	.03	.05	.04
	(1,419)	(1,111)	(700)	(992)	(775)	(929)
Drug	.02	.03	.03	.07	.05	.05
Trafficking	(639)	(787)	(1,054)	(1,415)	(1,349)	(1,479)

[a] Includes attempted crime and conspiracy to commit crime.

[b] Numbers in parentheses represent the total number of charges for the specific offense filed during the year.

committed in the county. Gang members were responsible for even a smaller share of property crimes, although again the data show increased activity. Perhaps most striking are the figures related to drug crimes, which law enforcement officials have linked closely to the gang phenomenon: Official court records give no indication that gangs were particularly active in the illicit drug market during this period.

Having concluded that traditional criminal statutes were inadequate for prosecuting crimes typically committed by gangs, the legislature (as discussed above) enacted several pieces of antigang legislation (Nerlander and Ferguson, 1990). Table 2 shows that some of these laws were useful, but most were rarely, if ever, applied. The most frequent charges based on the antigang statutes were those directed at the random and reckless use of firearms, typical of gang retaliatory crimes. (These figures represent the total number of charges filed; they are not separate criminal events in which the law was invoked.) It was not uncommon for 15 or more charges under this law to be filed against a gunman who (for example) fired a single shot in the air near a crowd. Most of these charges, of course, would be dismissed during plea negotiations.

The number of defendants actually convicted under each of these antigang statutes is shown in parentheses in table 2. Although these statutes, with the exception of the Gang Enhancement Statute, were enacted to deal with "gang crimes," most of those convicted under the antigang laws had not been identified as members of street gangs.

The Gang Enhancement Statute was used only once in the year after it was signed into law. Prosecutors undoubtedly needed some time to research the attendant legal issues, cultivate expert witnesses, and plot trial strategies. In 1993, 84 charges were filed with the statute as an enhancement; in 1994 the number had risen to 117. Ninety percent of the Gang Enhancement charges, however, were dismissed before final disposition. As of 1994, only 18 defendants had been convicted of felonies under the Gang Enhancement Statute.

Understanding the Gang Panic in Nevada

The reaction to gangs in Las Vegas fits the pattern established in previous studies of moral panics. Questions remain, however. Why did the gang hysteria break out in 1988? In the absence of a gang crime wave, why did gangs become the focus of a moral panic? How can we account for the end of the gang crisis? Two complementary perspectives, drawn from the moral panic literature, provide insight into such questions (Ben-Yehuda, 1986).

The first perspective focuses on the *timing* of moral panics and requires us to consider the social, political, and economic motivations behind the creation and cultivation of the gang crisis in Las Vegas. This perspective emphasizes the role of established interest or pressure groups, particularly those with direct access to policy makers and legislators.

Table 2 Number of charges filed and persons or convicted[a] under Anti-Gang Legislation, 1989–1994[b]

	1989	1990	1991	1992	1993	1994
Additional penalty for procurement of solicitation of minor to commit certain violations as agent (effective 7/6/89)	0	0	0	0	0	0
Additional penalty for commission of certain violations at or near school, school bus stop, or recreational facilities for minors (effective 7/6/89)	0	0	0	0	0	0
Additional penalty: Felony committed on school bus (effective 7/6/89)	0	0	0	0	0	0
Possession of dangerous weapon on property or in vehicle of school (effective 10/1/89)	0	0	0	7 (2)	27 (1)	15 (0)
Discharging of firearm out of motor vehicle (effective 6/28/89)	0	3 (1)	2 (2)	12 (6)	47 (5)	89 (3)
Aiming firearm at human being, discharging weapon where person might be endangered	27 (2)	205 (26)	193 (16)	247 (29)	377 (36)	392 (40)
Gang Enhancement Statute: Felony committed to promote activities of criminal gang	—	—	0	1 (1)	84 (9)	117 (8)

[a] Includes attempted crimes and conspiracy to commit crimes.
[b] Numbers in parenthesis represent number of persons convicted.

The second perspective emphasizes issues of *morality* as a means of understanding moral panics. Panics purportedly emerge when society's deeply held moral values are threatened. The reaction to the deviant group constitutes "boundary maintenance" and represents a collective effort to reinforce socially approved behaviors (Ben-Yehuda, 1986; Cohen, 1972; Gusfield, 1963; Trebach, 1982).

The Inspiration for the Gang Panic

The response to gangs in Las Vegas can be understood only in the broader national context of the gang phenomenon during those years. Street gangs were deemed "unnewsworthy" for more than a decade. In the late 1980s, however, the national press began to focus considerable attention on gangs, linking them to the distribution of illicit drugs and to senseless acts of violence. From Hollywood came powerful and frightening dramatizations of urban gangs, such as *Colors, Boyz in the Hood,* and *Warriors.* These films often depicted the "supergang" Crips and Bloods of Los Angeles engaged in urban guerilla warfare, turning communities into war zones over reputations and drug turf, and regularly taking the lives of innocent bystanders. These images were disturbing to the people of Las Vegas, only a four-hour drive away.

The national and local media clearly played a role in the moral panic examined here, similar to that documented in previous studies of moral panics (Cohen, 1972; Goode and Ben-Yehuda, 1994). Yet the moral panic in Las Vegas could not have been inspired by the media; what reporters and filmmakers knew about gangs came from the police. A number of studies have directly implicated the police in moral panics, revealing how law enforcement used its control of crime information to serve its own bureaucratic interests (Ben-Yehuda, 1986; Fishman, 1978; Zatz, 1987).

The possibility that the local Las Vegas police instigated the moral panic is further suggested by the intense and sustained lobbying efforts of police organizations during that period. At county and state hearings, police representatives testified on the growing threat posed by gangs; they fostered the impression that war-weary officers were outgunned and outstaffed in street confrontations with gangbangers; they helped to draft new gang legislation and lobbied vigorously for its passage ("Senate Airs," 1991; "Senate Judiciary," 1991). In short, police representatives were extremely active in politicizing the gang problem.

There is nothing unusual about LVMPD's activity; law enforcement in the United States has always been extremely active politically (Benson, 1990). The unique position of enforcement bureaucracies—easy access to legislative and executive leaders, the potential for creating social disorder, the monopoly of information about crime—grants them a great deal of political power, which they have wielded successfully to protect and advance their own interests (Ben-Yehuda, 1986; Fishman, 1978; Glaser, 1978; Jackson and Rudman, 1993; Roby, 1969; Zatz, 1987). Police activism invariably is accompanied by repeated references to the public safety, and certainly there is much truth to that claim. All bureaucracies, however, are subject to strong pressures to conflate public and organizational interests, particularly during periods of retrenchment or threats to legitimacy (J. Wilson, 1989).

Las Vegas police operated under such pressures throughout the 1980s. A deep and prolonged recession early in the decade forced hiring freezes and reductions in operating budgets in law enforcement, as well as in other government agencies across the state (Nevada Employment Security Department, 1983). Even after economic recovery in 1983, wary public officials continued to exercise tight fiscal policies for fear of being caught unprepared once again. By 1987, because of this situation and a population boom during the decade, the officer-civilian ratio in Las Vegas was only about half the national average ("New Positions," 1987).

In February 1988, in response to these social and economic conditions, top law enforcement officials introduced the "Four-Year Plan," an ambitious long-range budget calling for (among other things) 200 additional police officers. The requisite funding would come from four consecutive years of property tax increases, a measure to be decided by referendum in the November elections ("Metro Seeks," 1988). Over the next several months, police officials campaigned heavily to increase public awareness of the need for more officers ("LV Police," 1988). During this campaign the public was informed of the growing menace posed by criminal street gangs, largely through a steady stream of "gang-related" crimes released to the media. In November 1988, voters approved the property tax increases needed to fund the Four-Year Plan and bolster police resources in the war on gangs.

During the late 1980s, local police also faced a crisis of legitimacy, dogged by persistent allegations of police harassment, brutality, and warrantless searches (known in the LVMPD as "home visits") ("Police Trample," 1990). The number of citizens' complaints filed against LVMPD officers skyrocketed from less than 300 in 1984 to nearly 900 in 1989. Alleged victims of police brutality—transients and tourists, prostitutes and preachers, cab drivers and corporate attorneys—also received increased media coverage (figure 1). Across the valley, police lawlessness was denounced in organized rallies featuring nationally known speakers such as Jesse Jackson, Angela Davis, and Nation of Islam leader Louis Farrakhan ("Farrakhan," 1990). Organizations such as the NAACP and ACLU filed numerous suits seeking redress in federal courts.

Revelations of the gang menace in the late 1980s directed the public attention back to the streets and away from the police department. Local media coverage of police misconduct moved from the front page, to be replaced by stories of drive-bys, turf wars, and drug deals. Suddenly the police were once again the "good guys," arresting gangbangers, busting crack houses, and generally making the world safe again for decent people. In keeping with moral panics, the threat posed by gangs overshadowed other social problems.

Gangs and Morality

The above discussion suggests that the local police department created and sustained a moral panic to obtain needed resources and to repair a badly tarnished image. The District Attorney's Office also supported the panic, in part because of a genuine concern about gang crime, but also because its association with the gang panic brought funding for additional staff attorneys (Lucherino, 1995).

The emotional intensity that defines a moral panic, however, derives not from perceptions of physical danger per se but from more fundamental threats to the "moral-symbolic universe" (Goode and Ben-Yehuda, 1994). Street gang crime constitutes such a threat, much more so than crime in general. Gangs are the most visible manifestation of a subculture typically associated with the underclass found in inner cities across the country (Anderson, 1990; W. Wilson, 1987). The values and lifestyle of the underclass are perceived as antithetical to those of the larger community, and its apparent resistance to state and market-oriented interventions has only intensified public fear and anger (Magnet, 1993). Gangs have become the media icons of the underclass, flaunting the values perceived to be endemic to the underclass culture itself: the glorification of violence, the rejection of the work ethic, irresponsible sexuality, and drug abuse. Gangs' rejection of mainstream culture is accentuated by their street language, their manner of dress, and their music.

Thus it is not surprising that gangs provoke such hostility in the public. More disturbing, however, are perceptions that the gang culture is diffusing into the middle class. White middle-class youths now routinely "play the dozens," the highly stylized, sexually explicit repartee traditionally engaged in primarily by lower-class black males (Majors and Billson, 1991). White youths who talk and dress black have become so common as to constitute a new hybrid of American teenagers, known on the streets as "wiggers" (Bernstein, 1995). Rap or "gangsta" music, inspired by and reflecting the deprivations of the inner city, now finds its largest market among white youths despite their parents' denunciation of its angry, violent, and misogynistic lyrics (Nelson, 1995). Gangster clothes—baggy pants, Pendleton-type wool shirts, and starter jackets—are the rage on junior high school and high school campuses across the country; mainstream retailers now offer a full line of "ghetto wear" for those who seek the pretense of oppression. In effect, today's celebration of the gang culture by middle-class youths is blurring moral boundaries and fostering "in-group" deviance even in the best-ordered communities.

Conclusions and Implications

On the basis of the sources examined here, we believe it is fair to conclude that events in Las Vegas during the late 1980s land early 1990s indeed constituted a moral panic. Street gangs, composed primarily of Hispanic and African-American males, became the focus of intense concern and hostility throughout the community. The crisis came suddenly, then disappeared almost as quickly as it had emerged. Despite its relatively brief duration, the intensity expressed at the height of the gang panic had a significant and enduring impact on the community: an expansion of social control agencies, new legislation, metal detectors on school campuses, more liberal juvenile certification procedures, and a proliferation of public and private antiviolence programs targeting at-risk youths.

The actual threat posed by gangs, however, was less real than imagined. Two specific findings reported here support this claim. First, despite an increase in the proportion of charges attributed to gang members during the period, court data reveal that this figure never exceeded 15 percent for any type of violent crime. Second, and contrary to law enforcement claims, gangs played only a minor role in the Las Vegas drug market: Not even 4 percent of changes filed for drug sales from 1989 to 1994 involved known gang members.

Even so, the figures presented here suggest that gang-related crime increased during the period; thus, perhaps, the response by authorities was proportionate to the objective threat. The proportion of violent crime attributable to gangs more than doubled, increasing from 6 percent in 1988 to 14 percent in 1993. Whether these numbers constitute a "wave" of gang crime is debatable. We believe, however, that such figures greatly exaggerate the actual level of gang members' criminal activity during those years.

Because law enforcement officials in Las Vegas use a "member-based" definition, the levels of "gang-related" crime during the (period are almost certainly overstated. Furthermore, as in most jurisdictions across the country, the method by which offenders are identified as "gang members" in Las Vegas is highly questionable; as a result, marginal gang members or "wannabees" are placed on official lists of known gang members (Huff, 1990). According to GIS officers in Las Vegas, distinctions among minority males — who is a gang member and who is not — can be made accurately on the basis of clothing (e.g., "saggy pants"); monikers (a nickname given by the gang; this is usually written on the inside of a baseball cap, standard headware for gang members); and hand signs ("a manipulation of the hands, arms and fingers to form a cryptic message") (Hartung and Roberts, 1993:26). Though they may have originated in gangs, such dress, sobriquets, and gestures are no longer confined to those groups. The glamorization of the gang culture through music and movies has popularized certain mannerisms and styles of clothing once peculiar to street gangs. Consequently the markers used to identify gang members are no longer valid. In certain neighborhoods, residents may even feel pressured to adopt certain styles or colors for defensive purposes, to avoid being mistaken for rival gang members.

Other identifiers are equally suspect. According to a federal public defender in Las. Vegas, a veteran of several high-profile gang cases, "minorities are often identified and entered into the record as gang members or associates, without being informed, simply because they happen to be in the company of a known gang member, and that member probably got labeled in a similar fashion" (F. Forsman, September 30, 1995, personal communication). In subsequent contact with police, she added, such persons are often genuinely surprised to find that they have been placed in LVMPD's "gang file." The problem of overlabeling gang members is further indicated by the comments of a gang unit officer who asserted, "It is safe to assume that when you run across a young, black drug dealer, he's probably a gang member" ("Police Units," 1986). This mindset makes the problem of "false negatives" (gang crime not labeled as such) seem unlikely. Coupled with organizational pressures to identify and respond to gangs, such stereotypes make it likely that a young minority male would be labeled a gang member.

Our suspicions regarding the official data on gang-related crime were confirmed by sources in the District Attorney's Office. The chief deputy prosecutor admitted that he was not "comfortable" with the way LVMPD labeled gang members, and suggested that we "take whatever numbers they give you and divide them by two" (W. T. Koot, August 30, 1995, personal communication). In view of the problems surrounding the identification and labeling of gang members, a "ripple," not a wave, may be a better characterization of the trend in gang activity during the period examined. The additional resources allocated to police and prosecution agencies during those years, as well as the organizational restructuring within those agencies, thus appear to be vastly disproportionate to the objective threat posed by gangs.

The infrequency with which antigang legislation was used during those years also suggests that the threat from gangs was exaggerated. For example, under the Gang Enhancement Statute, the most forceful of the laws, only 18 defendants were convicted tom 1991 to 1994. Given the alleged magnitude and nature of the threat posed by criminal street gangs, why was the law not used more frequently and more effectively? According to criminal justice officials interviewed for this study, supporters of the statute made assumptions about gangs that simply proved to be false. Lawmakers had been influenced strongly by media stereotypes of gangs as highly organized, routinely violent, and dominating illicit markets in drugs and weapons. The language of the Gang Enhancement Statute targeted this type of criminal organization. In the course of prosecuting gangs, however, prosecutors discovered that the reality of gangs was far from the stereotype. Gangs were not "criminal enterprises" but simply loose, shifting associations without stable leadership, role expectations, or collective goals. In most cases processed, "gang crime" amounted to little more than the impulsive acts of marginal persons attempting to gain immediate, easy, *individual* short-term pleasure. Nor have officials "cracked down" on gang members who commit conventional steet crimes. In Las Vegas, gang defendants actually stand a greater chance than nongang defendants that the charges against them will be dismissed. If prosecuted and convicted, they are less likely to be sentenced to prison (Miethe and McCorkle, 1997).

Law enforcement officials figured prominently in the creation of such a stereotype, and in the moral panic itself. The timing of the panic corresponded to a vigorous public campaign aimed at bolstering police resources, a campaign hindered by perceptions of lawlessness and violence within the police department itself. The "discovery" of a gang problem in the late 1980s diverted public attention from ongoing police scandals, and also provided a justification for increased agency budgets. Officially acknowledging a gang problem might discourage tourists from visiting Las Vegas and injure LVMPD's efforts to obtain additional revenues. That risk however, was probably minimalized; gangs and tourism appeared to coexist in Los Angeles, only a short drive away (Huff, 1990).

In addition, law enforcement officials certainly believed that the politicization of gangs served the public interest; many abhorrent and irrational acts of violence, in fact, were committed by offenders with gang affiliations. Yet the threat posed to the community by such persons was subject to interpretation, and it is generally accepted that the function and interests of any organization necessarily influence the manner in which its members perceive, interpret, and respond to the environment (Edelman, 1988; J. Wilson, 1989). Moreover, in many organizations, and certainly in law enforcement, the development of expertise leads to a sense of dedication that often is erroneously identified with the public interest (Niskanen, 1971). Thus, in short, bureaucrats attempting to protect and advance the organization's interests can "easily persuade themselves of the rationality and morality of their appeals" (Edelman, 1988:22).

Despite the nature of organizational behavior, generalizations from this study to other jurisdictions can only be speculative. Estimates regarding the prevalence and activity of gangs will be affected by the distinctive political and economic environments in which law enforcement agencies operate. Conditions in one jurisdiction may exert pressure to overestimate the problem; in another, circumstances may dictate a "denial" of any gang problem (Huff, 1990).

A necessary, but not sufficient, condition for a moral panic is some level of public fear toward certain minority groups, which Goode and Ben-Yehuda, (1994) call the "raw material" for moral panics. Because of the tremendous growth of minority populations in Nevada during the 1980s, the raw material for the crisis was in ample supply; a scratch probably would have been sufficient to ignite the moral panic examined here. During the decade, the number of unemployed black and Hispanic males age 16 to 24 in Las Vegas nearly doubled (U.S. Bureau of the Census, 1983, 1992). Nonetheless, according to the moral panic concept, public concern about such "threatening" populations would have remained at the level of general unease without the activities of claimsmakers.

In this regard we believe that the concept of moral panic may be useful in refining the "threat hypothesis" (Liska, 1992), an essentially objectivist perspective that posits a link between the growth of minority populations and the expansion of social control agencies. Missing from the threat hypothesis is a comprehensive examination of the "sequence of events by which threatening acts, people, and distributions of people influence social control . . . why specific acts, people, and distributions of people are perceived as threatening" (Liska, 1992:176). The moral panic concept provides this level of analysis by examining how control agencies advance their political and organizational interests by labeling certain groups as "threatening" to the community. By ignoring the social construction of threatening populations, the threat hypothesis remains unembedded in more general theories of social structure and social process.

Although generalizations from this study are limited, we can say that law enforcement agencies, like organizations in general, struggle constantly to maintain legitimacy and to protect and increase the flow of resources (Meyer and Rowan, 1983). In that struggle, the pursuit of organizational interests can easily obscure the public good. The findings of this study clearly show that in addition to responding to crime, law enforcement agencies are involved in the social construction of crime itself. Law enforcement, in some sense, creates the demand for its services; therefore we cannot discount the possibility that gangs are the object of a moral panic in other jurisdictions.

References

Albonetti, C., Hauser, J., Hagan, J., & Nagel, I. (1989). Criminal justice decision-making as a stratification process: The role of race and stratification resources in pretrial release. *Journal of Quantitative Criminology, 5,* 57–82.

Anderson, E. (1990). *Street wise: Race, class, and change in an urban community.* Chicago: University of Chicago Press.

Beckett, K. (1994). Setting the public agenda: "Street crime" and drug use in American politics. *Social Problems, 41,* 425–447.

Benson, B. L. (1990). *The enterprise of law: Justice without the state.* San Francisco: Pacific Research Institute.

Ben-Yehuda 1963, cited p. 22.

Ben-Yehuda, N. (1986). The sociology of moral panics: Toward a new synthesis. *Sociological Quarterly, 27,* 495–513.

Bernstein, N. (1995). Goin' gangsta, choosin' cholita. *Utne Reader, 68,* 87–90.

Black, D. (1971). The social organization of arrest. *Stanford Law Review* 23:63–77.

Center for Survey Research. (1989). Department of Sociology, University of Nevada at Las Vegas.

Cohen, S. (1972). *Folk devils and moral panics: The creation of the mods and rockers.* London: MacGibbon and Kee.

Committee on Judiciary. (1991). Minutes of the joint senate and assembly committee on judiciary. February 13, 1991. Mimeographed copy.

Decker, S., & Kempf-Leonard, K. (1995). Constructing gangs: The social definition of youth activities. In M. Klein, C. Maxon, & J. Miller (Eds.), *The Modern Gang Reader* (pp. 112–137). Los Angeles: Roxbury.

Edelman, M. 1988. *Constructing the spectacle.* Chicago: University of Chicago Press.

Esbensen, F. P., & Huizinga, D. (1993). Gangs, drugs, and delinquency in a study of urban youths. *Criminology, 68*, 262–73.

Fishman, M. (1978). Crime waves as ideology. *Social Problems, 25*, 531–543.

Glaser, D. (1978). *Crime in our changing society.* New York: Holt, Rinehart and Winston.

Goode, E., & Ben-Yehuda, N. (1994). *Moral panics: The social construction of deviance.* Cambridge, MA: Blackwell.

Gusfield, J. R. (1963). *Symbolic Crusade: Status politics and the American temperance movement.* Urbana: University of Illinois Press.

Hagedorn, J. (1988). *People and folks: Gangs, crime, and the underclass in a rust belt city.* Chicago: Lake View Press.

Hall, S., Critcher, C., Jefferson, T., Clark, J., & Roberts, B. (1978). *Policing the crisis: Mugging, the state, and law and order.* London: Macmillan.

Hartung, V., & Roberts, L. (1993). *Identification of Hispanic gangs.* Las Vegas Metropolitan Police Department (Nov/Dec).

Hepburn, J. (1978). Race and the decision to arrest: An analysis of warrants issued. *Journal of Research in Crime and Delinquency, 15*, 54–73.

Hiltgartner, S., & Bosk, C. (1988). The rise and fall of social problems: A public arenas model. *American Journal of Sociology, 94*, 53–78.

Hofstadter, R. (1966). *The paranoid style in American politics and other essays.* New York: Knopf.

Huff, R. (1990). Denial, overreaction and misidentification: A postscript on public policy. In R. Huff (Ed.), *Gangs in America* (pp. 310–317). Beverly Hills: Sage.

Jackson, P., & Rudman, C. (1993). Moral panic and the response to gangs in California. In S. Cummings & D. Monti (Eds.), *Gangs: The origin and impact of contemporary youth gangs in the United States* (pp. 257–275). New York: SUNY Press.

Jenkins, P., & Miler-Katkin, D. (1992). Satanism: Myth and reality in a contemporary moral panic. *Crime, Law and Social Change, 17*, 53–75.

Johnson, C., Webster, B., & Connors, E. (1995). *Prosecuting gangs: A national assessment.* Washington, DC: GPO.

Klein, M. (1995). *The American street gang: Its nature, prevalence, and control.* New York: Oxford University Press.

Klein, M., & Maxson, C. (1989). Street gang violence. In M. Wolfgang & N. Weiner (Eds.), *Violent crime, violent criminals* (pp. 198–234). Beverly Hills: Sage.

Bonanza students fear more violence. (1989, March 14). *Las Vegas Review Journal,* p. B1.

Eldorado teen gunned down: Gunfire erupts in gang-related cafeteria fight. (1990, August 27). *Las Vegas Review Journal,* p. B1.

Farrakhan: Stop killing. (1990, October 22). *Las Vegas Sun,* p. B6.

Gang diversion unit called a success. (1988, May 3). *Las Vegas Sun,* p. B1.

Gov. Miller wants gangs outlawed. (1990, August 28). *Las Vegas Sun,* p. B1.

Group examines gang problem. (1986, March 13). *Las Vegas Sun,* p. B2.

LV police urge voters to approve property tax hike. (1988, August 7). *Las Vegas Review Journal,* p. B3.

Metro mobilizes against LV gangs. (1988, March 24). *Las Vegas Sun,* p. B1.

Metro seeks 79.4 million, 50 new officers. (1988, February 25). *Las Vegas Review Journal,* p. B1.

New positions cut from metro budget. (1987, February 24). *Las Vegas Review Journal,* p. B4.

Police trample rules in searches. (1990, September 18). *Las Vegas Review Journal*, p. B1.

Police units target increasing gang activity. (1986, April 4). *Las Vegas Review Journal*, p. B2.

Senate airs metro-designed bill to target crimes committed by gangs. (1991, February 2). *Las Vegas Review Journal*, p. B1.

Senate judiciary committee considers new anti-gang bill. (1991, March 6). *Las Vegas Sun*, p. B3.

Special police units probe gangs in southern Nevada. (1985, May 9). *Las Vegas Sun*, p. B2.

Liska, A. (1992). Developing theoretical issues. In A. Liska (Ed.), *Social threat and social control* (pp. 165–190). New York: SUNY Press.

Lucherini, R. (1991). *Gang unit proposal.* [Mimeographed document.] Clark County District Attorney Office.

Magnet, M. (1993). *The dream and the nightmare: The sixties' legacy to the underclass.* New York: William Morrow.

Majors, R., & Billson, J. M. (1991). *Pose: The dilemmas of black manhood in America.* New York: Lexington Books.

Manis, J. (1974). The concept of social problems: Vox populi and sociological analysis. *Social Problems, 21,* 305–315.

Maxson, C., Gordon, M., & Klein, M. (1985). Differences between gang and non-gang homicides. *Criminology, 23,* 209–222.

Maxson, C., Klein, M., & Cunningham, L. (1992). *Defining gang crime: Revisited.* Presented at the meetings of the Western Society of Criminology, San Diego, CA.

Meyer, J., & Rowan, B. (1983). Institutionalized organizations: Formal structure as myth and ceremony. In J. Meyer & W. Scott (Eds.), *Organizational environments: Ritual and rationality* (pp. 199–215). Beverly Hills: Sage.

Miethe, T. (1987). Charging and plea bargaining practices under determinate sentencing: An investigation of the hydraulic displacement of discretion. *Journal of Criminal Law and Criminology, 78,* 155–176.

Miethe, T., & McCorkle, R. (1997). Gang membership and criminal processing: A test of the "master status" concept. *Justice Quarterly, 14,* 407–427.

Miller, W. (1990). Why the United States has failed to solve its youth gang problem. In R. Huff (Ed.), *Gangs in America* (pp. 263–287). Beverly Hills: Sage.

Nelson, H. (1995, November). Hip-hop jumps cultural lines. *Billboard,* 34.

Nerlander, D., & Ferguson, J. (1990). Street gangs. [Unpublished manuscript.] Carson City, NV: Research Division of the Legislative Counsel Bureau.

Nevada Employment Security Department. (1983). *Economic update.* [Quarterly Report.] Carson City: Nevada Employment Security Department.

Niskanen, W. A., Jr. (1971). *Bureaucracy and representative government.* Chicago: Aldine.

Petersilia, J. (1985). Racial disparities in the criminal justice system: A summary. *Crime and Delinquency, 31,* 15–34.

Pope, C. E. (1978). Post-arrest release decisions: An empirical examination of social and legal criteria. *Journal of Research in Crime and Delinquency, 15,* 35–53.

Roby, P. (1969). Politics and criminal law: Revision of the New York state penal law on prostitution. *Social Problems, 17,* 83–109.

Smith, D., & Visher, C. (1981). Street-level justice: Situational determinants of police arrest decisions. *Social Problems, 29,* 167–177.

Smith, D., Visher, C., & Davidson, L. (1984). Equity and discretionary justice: The influence of race on police arrest decisions." *Journal of Criminal Law and Criminology, 75,* 234–249.

Spector, M., & Kitsuse, J. (1973). Social problems: A reformulation. *Social Problems, 21,* 145–159.

Spergel, I. A. (1984). Violent gangs in Chicago: In search of social policy. *Social Service Review, 58,* 199–226.

Spergel, I. A. (1995). *The youth gang problem: A community approach.* New York: Oxford University Press.

Thornberry, T., Lizotte, A., Krohn, M., Farnsworth, M., & Joon Jang, S. (1994). Delinquent peers, beliefs, and delinquent behavior: A longitudinal test of interactional theory. *Criminology, 32,* 47–83.

Tracy, P. (1987). Race and class differences in official and self-reported delinquency. In M. Wolfgang, T. Thornberry, & R. Figlio (Eds.), *From boy to man, from delinquency to crime* (pp. 87–121). Chicago: University of Chicago Press.

Trebach, A. S. (1982). *The heroin solution.* New Haven: Yale University Press.

U.S. Bureau of the Census (1983). Census of the population, 1980. Washington, DC: U.S. Government Printing Office.

U.S. Bureau of the Census (1992). Census of the population, 1990. Washington, DC: U.S. Government Printing Office.

Waddington, P. A. J. (1986). Mugging as moral panic: A question of proportion. *British Journal of Sociology, 37,* 245–259.

Wilson, J. Q. (1989). *Bureaucracy: What government agencies do and why they do it.* New York: Basic Books.

Wilson, W. J. (1987). *The truly disadvantaged.* Chicago: University of Chicago Press.

Zatz, M. (1987). Chicago youth gangs and crime: The creation of a moral panic. *Contemporary Crisis, 11,* 129–158.

Chapter 3

The Desirability of Goal Conflict within the Criminal Justice System

Kevin N. Wright

Conflicting Goals in the Non-System

Experts in the field of criminal justice have recently displayed a growing obsession with the idea of creating a monolithic system for the administration of justice. This obsession is reflected in a diversity of writings, yet a common theme can be found throughout the literature: if criminal justice is to fulfill its function of crime control, then a transformation must occur which will create a rational, well-integrated system in which a common set of goals can be pursued through a compatible set of strategies and techniques.

One source of this trend is found in the various theoretical and philosophical treatises which are intended to serve as a framework for revamping the criminal justice system. Duffee (1980:4) has succinctly described the nature of these works:

> Whether the analysis of criminal justice has been done by radicals, liberals or conservatives, most analysts from van den Haag, to Packer, to Quinney have assumed that centralized planning and program devel-

Reprinted from *Journal of Criminal Justice*, Vol. 9. Kevin N. Wright, "The Desirability of Goal Conflict within the Criminal Justice System." pp. 209–218, 1980, with permission of Elsevier.

opment dealing with criminal justice can or could influence significantly the frequency with which crime is committed, the proportion of offenders who are apprehended, and the degree to which punishment for crimes would feedback upon the political, economic and social conditions which give rise to crime and the means with which society responds to it.

Radicals such as Quinney (1969; 1974 and 1977) and Chambliss (1969; 1971; 1972; 1975 and 1979) generally perceive the existing system to be coherent in that the system functions to protect the interests of the powerful, and individuals are punished for the inequities of society. Change of the system is considered in terms of broader social change but is aimed at creating a new form of coherence. Conservatives such as Packer (1968), van den Haag (1975), and Wilson (1975) and liberals such as Clark (1971) and Menninger (1969), on the other hand, generally perceive the existing system as lacking coherence and continuity in that a single set of goals is not pursued. Each indicates, however, that coherence could be built into the system and the problem of crime control resolved.

A second source of advocacy for a monolithic system can be found in the structural analyses of the organizational aspects of the criminal justice system as reflected in the work of Skoler (1977) and Kellogg (1976). These assessments focus on the inability of the "system" to function as a true system, i.e., one which is coherent and well integrated and has a unitary set of goals. Consequently, this group of analysts refer to the criminal justice system as a "non-system." Criminal justice is characterized by conflicting goals, a lack of integration, and overlapping jurisdictions which promote inequities of justice and create inefficiencies which result in higher costs of operation:

> Official decisions affecting the criminal offender are made by a patchwork of separate jurisdictions, in a system of independent prosecutors, judges, prison administrators, and parole and probation officers. Respective policies vary arbitrarily from place to place, or even from time to time within the same place. Sentencing decisions within the same jurisdiction, not to mention among different ones, vary widely with the attitudes of individual judges. Decisions are based upon limited and inconsistent information, generally without adequate explanation to benefit other officials in the decision-making process. (Kellogg, 1976:50)

In fact, the components of criminal justice are characterized as being noncooperative and even hostile toward one another. It has been suggested that the inability of the criminal justice system to function as a true system results in a fragmented output and often an undesirable outcome (Skoler, 1977; Kellogg, 1976; O'Neill, et al., 1976:4–17).

Unlike the theoretical and philosophical treatises which propose frameworks for revamping the system, the structural analysts focus their attention on remedial structural changes. In other words, the structural analysts concentrate on the mechanics of change rather than the content and direction of change within the system. Various proposals (see Skoler [1977] for a comprehensive review) have been made to alleviate the problems of conflict and fragmentation within the criminal justice system. Such suggestions range from integration and cooperation to direct unification of the system. However, more attention has been given to the former than the latter. Statewide and comprehensive planning and fiscal incentives have been advocated as mechanisms for integration. Structural change has also been suggested as a mechanism for integrating the components. Reorganization of state government is quite often cited as a potentially effective method of structural change. Skoler (1977:289) has even suggested that the "fragmented, duplicative, and uncoordinated character of criminal justice services" can best be resolved through the consolidation and unification of the system's components. Services should be combined and centrally administered.

The inherent desirability of creating a monolithic system for the administration of justice, however, deserves further consideration. As suggested above, the lack of integration, coordination, and goal and technique compatibility within the criminal justice system seems to be quite inefficient and ineffective. The system lacks the rationality associated with systemic organization. Additional assessment, however, may not support this conclusion. Proposals for unification seem to ignore the environment in which criminal justice exists. Furthermore, there are at least three reasons why goal conflict within the system is desirable. The purpose of this article is to consider these factors in order to assess the desirability of a monolithic system.

The Sociopolitical Environment

The theoretical and philosophical treatises and the structural analyses which advocate a monolithic criminal justice system seem to have conveniently ignored the sociopolitical environment in which the system exists. Such an oversight may be helpful in gaining public attention to one's ideas but is most unfortunate from a practical and pragmatic standpoint. The essence of a system as complex as criminal justice simply cannot be understood from the perspective which considers it as an isolated system. Nor can any proposal for significant planned change of the system claim any validity without considering the effects and constraints of the environment on that system.

In order to understand fully the implications of this idea, it is necessary to assess what type of a system criminal justice is. Numerous authors (Emery and Trist, 1965; Terryberry, 1968; March and Simon, 1958; Cyert and March, 1963) have argued that there are at least two types of social systems: simple and complex. In a simple system, goals can be specified, tasks to accomplish those goals can be undertaken, and progress can be monitored so that the system is self-regulating. These activities are possible because the internal and external environments of the system are relatively stable. It is this model of the criminal justice system which the theoretical and structural analysts noted above have used. A complex system, on the other hand, does not exist in stable environments but rather finds itself in a complex and rapidly changing, or turbulent, environment which produces unpredictable changes within the system itself. This situation precludes rational, long-range, and macro-planned change. Because the environment is turbulent, and thus drastically and dynamically affecting the system, it is simply impossible to identify and specify a set of goals and to bring about some change to remodel the system (Emery and Trist, 1965, Terryberry, 1968). Duffee (1980:101) has made a very strong case that criminal justice is in fact a complex system:

> There is a wide variety of information available pertaining to the fact that criminal justice is not a monolithic, commonly conceived routine exercise. Criminal justice may well have different meanings in different places, or behave differently under contrasting conditions. Before we attempt to change actual operating agencies so that they might conform to a unitary motive of criminal justice operation, we may wish first to ask why such variations occur, whether these variations are functional equivalents, or whether the contrasting practices provided to the locality in which they are observed contributions to social order that might be lost if all criminal justice agencies behaved appropriately to the expectations of the analyst.

Duffee goes on to argue that criminal justice is, in fact, an institution much like the family or religion, and that its existence and what happens to it are unrelated to goal accomplishment.

Just as Duffee noted that there is a wide variety of information which indicates that criminal justice is not a monolithic system, there is, in particular, considerable information which indicates the political nature of criminal justice. Both conservatives and radicals concur that the basis of criminal justice, criminal law, is generated within an interest structure (see Pound, 1943; Quinney, 1969:20–30.) Society is characterized by an interest structure in which various kinds of interests are distributed throughout that structure. Laws are the product of different interest groups vying for power to see their interests represented or realized. Theorists differ, however, in their perceptions concerning the output of the process as to whether the result is a product of compromise or domination.

Beyond the law, the actual administration and allocation of justice can also be viewed within the political context. Cole (1973:15–16) has provided one of the most concise reviews of this idea:

> Rather, like all legal institutions, the criminal justice system is "political" since it is engaged in the formulation and administration of public policies where choice must be made among such competing values as the rights of defendants, protection of persons and property, justice

and freedom. That various groups in society interpret these values differently is obvious. Decisions result from the influence of the political
power of decision makers and relative strength of competing elites.

Cole (1973:16) continues by noting that there is a wide range of discretion within the administration of justice. Laws are often ambiguous and
full enforcement of them is neither possible nor desirable. Decisions must,
therefore, be made within the context of the community and its interest
structure. Legal personnel, judges and prosecutors, must operate within a
political environment. Their decisions must rest on the selection among
competing dispositions which reflect dominant political interests. The
actions of police executives are similarly influenced by the political nature
of the position. To summarize, "in many ways the administration of criminal justice is a community affair; political influentials and interest groups
work to insure that the law will be applied in ways consistent with their
perception of local values" (Cole, 1973:17). (For an excellent discussion of
the political reality of the administration of justice see chapter 4, "The Making of Criminal Justice Policy" in Levine, Musheno, and Palumbo, 1980.)

Suggestions to create a monolithic, unified system deny the very existence of an interest structure characterized by a specific distribution of
power. Therefore, to analyze the criminal justice system as if it did not exist
within a political environment seems to be particularly naive. There are
actors within the system who have a vested interest in its organization and
operation, as well as influential persons within the community who want to
see their particular interests represented. We know that interests vary from
area to area. What is "justice" in an urban area may not be similarly perceived in a rural area. We know that what is "justice" to a police officer may
not be "justice" to a young offender and his or her liberal public defender.

Radicals, to a degree, seem to understand the political context of the
administration of justice in that their proposals for change are couched in
terms of broader social changes. They realize that massive change in the
system rests on social change. For example, the proponents of prison abolition fairly consistently advocate such change within a proposal for the
creation of a society characterized by pervasive equality. (See Hawkins,
1976; 5–12 for a review of the abolitionist movement.) Radicals, however,
often fail to consider the likelihood of drastic social change.

Liberals, conservatives, and structural analysts virtually ignore the
political environment. They propose massive change in the system without considering the possibility that actors within the system as well as
politically influential persons would resist that change. They fail to see
that criminal justice is as it is for a reason, that there is a certain rationality
in the seemingly structural irrationality of the system. (See Diesing's *Reason in Society* [1962] for a discussion of this conceptualization of rationality.) To create a monolithic, unified system would require a compatible set
of values to serve as its basis; our complex society is not constituted in
such a manner. Individuals working in the various components of the sys-

tem, personnel in various jurisdictions, and influence bearers who have an interest in the administration of justice are extremely unlikely to agree on a single set of values. Levine, Musheno, and Palumbo (1980:38, 150) in their introductory textbook make this fact clear when they conclude:

> In short, the public interest is constantly being defined and redefined. The balance among its various facets is always shifting. As is true in any area of public policy, the choice of ideals in criminal justice is the result of an unpredictable, ever-changing and very intricate political process. . . . This often means that only incremental rather than sweeping changes can be made.

Furthermore, there are at least three reasons why goal conflict and fragmentation are advantageous to the processes and functioning of the system. Conflict makes it possible to represent and protect different societal interest, establishes a system of checks and balances, and promotes a smoothly operating offender-processing system.

Reflective Diversity

Underlying the ideas of unification and the creation of a monolithic system for the administration of justice is an assumption that there is a compatible set of values, or if you please, a single culture, from whence unification can proceed. As suggested above, there is considerable theoretical and empirical evidence that indicates the existence of a diversity of values within the criminal justice environment. The fragmentation and lack of integration within criminal justice would thus seem possibly to allow different interests to be incorporated into the system. As such, different societal interests may be reflected or represented by the different, and often conflicting, goals within criminal justice. This idea has been verified on a number of different levels.

First, the representatives of different interests can be seen among different jurisdictions. Wilson's study of the police (1968) indicated that styles of law enforcement vary from community to community. While the day-to-day routine of police work was not directly affected by political influence, the political culture of the community was found to influence directly the style and policies of the department. Similarly, Levin (1980) found in his study of criminal courts that the handling of defendants varied according to the political culture of the community. The lack of consistency between judicial decisions in Pittsburgh and Minneapolis was explained by their different political systems. If it is assumed that the political culture and public interests vary from area to area, then the seemingly fragmented system of justice may serve to fulfill those diverse interests. This conclusion is reflected in the research of both Wilson and Levin. For example, the influence of both a middle- and lower-class culture in Pittsburgh as opposed to a predominantly middle-class cultural influence in Minneapolis was found to be reflected in judicial practices.

On a second level, different interests can be represented by the fragmentation and inconsistencies within a single component. This situation is evidenced in the corrections' search for an alternative to rehabilitation. Certain interests are advocating community supervision and reintegration, while other groups stress increased incapacitation and retribution. These considerations are further complicated by new demands for lowering state budgets with correspondingly rising cost of incarceration and demands for the protection of the rights of offenders. Trends seem to be toward greater use of community supervision with simultaneous specification of mandatory sentences for particularly "fear-invoking" offenses. We thus see quite different and conflicting interests being considered, incorporated, and implemented within corrections.

A study by Cole (1980) of the Office of the Prosecuting Attorney in King County, Washington also supports the contention that different interests are represented within the seemingly conflicting processes of a single agency. Cole's research indicated that the prosecutor's office could be viewed as an organization within an exchange system that operated in a marketlike fashion. The decision to prosecute or not to prosecute could occur at various times during processing and was often based on the influence of a variety of officials. In this manner, the prosecutor could only exercise discretion within the exchange framework. As Cole (1980:166) points out, "the police, court congestion, organizational strains, and community pressures are among the factors that influence prosecutorial behavior."

In a most informative paper, Ohlin (1974) has outlined the manner in which conflicting interests influence organizational objectives and policy. (While Ohlin focused his analyses on correctional organizations, his ideas seem to be applicable to all criminal justice components.) Ohlin notes that interest groups arise when they feel that particular issues will directly affect them. The group may perceive that existing or possible activities will serve as a means to the achievement of its own objectives, it may be threatened by some existing or proposed activity, or it may view support of some issue as a way to fulfill some other obligation to another group. (See Bauer, 1968:17 for a discussion of obligatory activities which develop between interests groups.) A group's involvement in a particular issue will be determined by the advertency, saliency, and potency of the issue to that group. If the issue or activity is deemed important enough for the interest group's involvement or influence, the group can either try to obtain representation in the decision-making process or to support or penalize the organization for its particular decision. Over time and issues, the influence of various interest groups will change. As Ohlin (1974:149) describes, "the old, routinized ways of doing things gradually create problems. These problematic situations become the focus of new conflicts of interest, out of which new patterns of activity emerge."

The activities of an organization cannot be understood without considering the influence of interest groups. In that policies and activities of the organization reflect the influence of different interest groups, they may appear actually to conflict with one another, yet that conflict may be necessary in mediating among conflicting values within the community. The nature and activities of the organization may vary considerably as control passes from one group to another and as the interest structure shifts. Such dynamics are imperative for organizational survival in a complex environment.

On a final level, it would also seem possible that different interests are represented by the different components of criminal justice. Unfortunately, there is a lack of empirical analysis of this possibility, yet some support for the proposition can be inferred from what we know about the system. As suggested throughout this article, it is certainly reasonable to suggest that various aggregates of society desire different things from the justice system. The American Friends Service Committee seem to have a very different set of values than law-and-order traditionalists such as the International Association of Chiefs of Police. In attempting to see that their respective values are realized, these two groups advocate very different justice policies. However, each group tends to concentrate the exertion of its influence on a different component of the system, corrections and law enforcement respectively. In responding to the interests of these and similar groups, it is quite possible for the components to focus on different and conflicting goals.

It is clear that criminal justice incorporates a number of different goals, including crime prevention, public tranquility, justice, due process, efficiency, and accountability (Levine, Musheno, and Palumbo, 1980:19–35). It is also known that the components differentially incorporate these goals into their operations. For example, it is often noted that the police tend to be more concerned with efficiency than due process, while the courts tend to focus on due process over efficiency. The different orientations of the police and the courts may very well make it possible to represent different interests within the community.

The apparent incoherence of the criminal justice goals does seem to serve a useful function when we view the environment in which the system exists. That environment is characterized by different values and interests. The fragmentation among jurisdictions, the goal conflict within a single component of the system, and the conflict among components allow different interests to be incorporated into the system. As we will see in the following section, the existence of goal conflict allows for continual mediations of interests and adaptability of the system.

Mediations of Interests and System Adaptation

A second advantage of conflicting goals within the criminal justice system is that they promote a process of checks and balances within the system. Fragmentation ensures that no single component of the system can dominate all other components, nor can any unitary interest be over-emphasized. The various components can and do influence the operations of the other elements.

As Coser (1956) has demonstrated, conflict establishes and maintains a balance of power within the structure of the system. To make oneself understood and to achieve at least partial realization of goals, power must be exercised. Specifically, one's interest will not be considered in the negotiating process unless that individual's presence is felt. As Coser (1956:137) has stated, "struggle may be an important way to avoid conditions of disequilibrium by modifying the basis for power relations. . . . Conflict, rather than being disruptive and dissociating may indeed be a means of balancing and hence maintaining a society as a going concern." In an environment which is characterized by a high degree of diversity of interest, conflict may well serve to produce an equilibrium, a balance, rather than a state of disequilibrium. Interest groups are forced continually to negotiate and compromise. Differences are thus mitigated, and the system changes and adapts over time. Given the high diversity of attitudes about justice and its administration, the conflicts and fragmentation within the criminal justice system probably provide the only means of maintaining equilibrium among the various interest groups. Thus, a strong law enforcement orientation can exist in a system which is also committed to a program of diversion. Lack of specificity is thus an effective device that allows various and diverse interests to be presented.

Lack of integration allows the system to adapt to special problems. For example, in reacting to public sentiment a local prosecutor may attempt to see that a particular offender is sentenced to a very long period of incarceration. Other than promoting the goal of retribution, such a sentence may be incongruent with other criminal justice goals. In a fragmented system, corrections may modify the prosecutor's action through some form of early release. The correctional decision as such directly conflicts with the values and goals of the local prosecutor and the public which he or she represents but may be consistent with contemporary trends of corrections and justice.

Blumstein and Cohen (1973) have suggested that levels of punishment are consistent over time within cultures. They contend that as crime increases the boundaries of criminality and the severity of punishment will be modified in order to maintain a consistent level of punishment. Lack of unification within the criminal justice system seems to serve a similar function. Discretion, such as corrections mediating a prosecutor's long sentence, allows for an equalization process to occur. In this manner, the motivation of police is modified by the decision of the courts as to what crimes will be prosecuted. Corrections monitors and modifies court decisions by implementing forms of early release, thus mitigating the overemphasis of incapacitation and retribution. The police and the courts monitor correctional decisions by being particularly attuned to previous offenders. This interactive process within the system makes it possible, at least to some degree, to maintain levels of punishment at consistent levels.

It is important to realize that the influence which components exert on one another is less than total domination. Because of the circular nature of influence, each component has the ability to modify the output of every other component and consequently that influence can be reciprocated. Also, no single component can totally reverse or change the action or activity of another component. Therefore, influence is limited to a specific extent. In this manner, the courts' insistence on police practices which are consistent with due process does not eliminate the law enforcement orientation toward efficiency. Efficiency is simply pursued within the boundaries of the courts' influence. This reality is critically important in that different components may represent different interests. The provision for diversity prevents any single interest from becoming dominant. Unification and the pursuit of a monolithic system would reduce discretion and limit the ability of the system to respond to aberrations and peculiarities. Fragmentation, on the other hand, allows the components to check the behavior of one another and to promote a balanced or equitable system of justice.

Thus, by allowing different interests to be present within an agency or a component, conflict may be played out and resolved among different jurisdictions and among the different components. Negotiation and mitigation may occur. Allowing fragmentation to exist and conflict to surface provides the system with the ability to adapt and evolve over time. Specifically, the system can experiment; it can act and react to the influence of different societal interests. The impetus and implementation of change develops slowly with a unified and monolithic system; a more fragmented system can rely on and use conflict as an impetus for change.

Offender Processing

The final advantage of goal conflict and fragmentation within the criminal justice system is that they may actually promote and support rather than retard and hinder the processing of offenders. This suggestion is contrary to most contemporary claims. For example, Kellogg (1976:50) suggests that "the system functions best when all of its parts most rationally and consistently assess offenders and their offenses, match these with the most appropriate responses, and administer the activities required to maintain the process." To the contrary, the lack of unity may be essential for the smooth operation of offender processing whereby the system is able to move a person through its various stages.

Recent research behind criminal justice consolidation has questioned the assumptions, theory, and evidence and has suggested that polycentricity is actually better than unity and centrality. Skoler (1977:300) has summarized the works of these researchers as follows:

They cite, variously (and persuasively), emerging knowledge on organizational design and behavior, the cost and inefficiency of layered and complex public bureaucracies, new insights on where economies of scale and public service systems are illusory or nonexistent, and a theory of governmental responsiveness and efficiency which suggests greater "payoff" from less orderly, sometimes overlapping, and locally autonomous service units than from large, centralized, policy-uniform hierarchies. New theories of organizational behavior seem to suggest that large centralized organizations are less effective than smaller more autonomous organizations.

Ostrom and Parks (1973), in examining the merits of small versus large police departments, found that the public generally favors small departments, that efficiency is not gained with greater departmental size after a certain point, that fragmentation of agencies within a metropolitan area does not necessarily reduce the service, and that bureaucratization may reduce effectiveness more than increase it (Skoler, 1977:300). There seems to be little evidence that suggests that bigger, more centralized, and more unified systems or organizations are better; most evidence runs to the contrary.

In an attempt to unify a system, it is difficult, if not impossible, to anticipate all idiosyncrasies and probable changes and to formulate rules which will accommodate these future events. A nonunified system can change and make necessary adaptations to events which were not anticipated. Similarly, it is difficult to conjecture how the interest structure will develop and be modified in the future. A formalized and necessarily unified system will have difficulty in adapting to these changes.

Hasenfeld (1974:67–68) noted that the components of the criminal justice system depend on each other for validation of their claimed competence. The police depend on the conviction of apprehended offenders by the courts in order that their action be effective. The criteria that the police use for deciding which suspects to introduce formally into the system are partially defined by the behavior of the courts. Lack of unification within the system provides for the interaction between the various elements of the criminal justice system in this manner and allows the system to make changes in order to maintain a smooth flow of clients. As the use of marijuana became more widespread, the system adapted; courts ceased prosecuting users and the police responded by no longer arresting minor offenders.

Conclusions

Based on the arguments made above, the long-term implications of increased integration and unification cannot be regarded as favorable. Unification would create inequities to the extent that any new structure could not accommodate the diverse interests which currently have an impact on the system. The complex and dynamic process of negotiation which occurs within the decision-making environment of offender processing would accordingly be limited. Any system which exhibits high diversity, even in the form of fragmentation, allows conflicts to be played out and resolved on a continual basis. Any degree of centralization and unification, on the other hand, promotes rigidification and creates bureaucracy which is known to be an inefficient structure for change. A more unified criminal justice system would be more static, less able to respond to various interests. Greater investments of time and energy would be required to change the system.

As Coser has shown, conflict provides system stability rather than reduces it. The dynamic quality of a fragmented criminal justice system promotes a balance of power between antagonistic interests as it encourages adaptation and change. As societal attitudes and values fluctuate, the system can make corresponding changes. Unification would limit the ability of components to adjust their outputs to specific individual cases, to changes that occur over time, and to overreactions and mistakes by the other components. Furthermore, the balance which results from the exertion of influence on components by other components would be limited.

References

Bauer, R. A. (1968). The study of policy formation: An introduction. In R. A. Bauer & K. J. Gregen (Eds.), *The study of policy formation* (pp. 1–26). New York: Free Press

Blumstein, A., & Cohen, J. (1973). A theory of the stability of punishment. *Journal of Criminal Law and Criminology, 64,* 198–207.

Chambliss, W. J. (1969). *Crime and the legal process.* New York: McGraw-Hill.

Chambliss, W. J., & Seidman, R. B. (1971). *Law, order and power.* Reading, MA: Addison-Wesley.

Chambliss, W. J., & Seidman, R. B. (1972). The state, the law and the definition of behavior as criminal or delinquent. In D. Glazer (Ed.), *Handbook of criminology.* Chicago: Rand-McNally.

Clark, R. (1971). *Crime in America.* New York: Irwin and Schuster.

Cole, G. F. (1973). *Politics and the administration of justice.* Beverly Hills: Sage.

Cole, G. F. (1980). The decision to prosecute. In G. F. Cole (Ed.), *Criminal justice: Law and politics* (pp. 155–166). North Scituate, MA: Duxbury.

Coser, L. A. (1956). *The functions of social conflict.* Glencoe, IL: Free Press.

Cyert, R. M., & March, J. G. (1963). *A behavioral theory of the firm.* Englewood Cliffs, NJ: Prentice-Hall.

Diesing, P. (1962). *Reason in society.* Westport, CT: Greenwood Press.

Duffee, D. (1980, reissued 1990). *Explaining criminal justice.* Prospect Heights, IL: Waveland Press, Inc.

Emery, F. E., & Trist, E. L. (1965). The causal texture of organizational environments. *Human Relations, 18,* 21–31.

Hasenfeld, Y. (1974). People processing organizations: An exchange approach. In Y. Hasenfeld & R. A. English (Eds.), *Human service organizations* (pp. 60–71). Ann Arbor: The University of Michigan Press.

Hawkins, G. (1976). *The prison: Policy and practice.* Chicago: The University of Chicago Press.

Kellogg, F. R. (1976). Organizing the criminal justice system: A look at "operative" objectives. *Federal Probation, 40,* 50–56.

Levin, M. A. (1980). Urban politics and policy outcomes: The criminal courts. In G. F. Cole (Ed.), *Criminal justice: Law and politics* (pp. 336–361). North Scituate, MA: Duxbury.

Levine, J. P., Musheno, M. C., & Palumbo, D. J. (1980). *Criminal justice: A public policy approach.* New York: Harcourt Brace Jovanovich.

March, J. G., & Simon, H. A. (1958). *Organizations.* New York: John Wiley.

Menninger, K. (1969). *The crime of punishment.* New York: Viking.

Ohlin, L. E. (1974). Conflicting interests in correctional objectives. In Y. Hasenfeld & R. A. English (Eds.), *Human service organizations* (pp. 135–152). Ann Arbor: The University of Michigan Press.

O'Neill, M. E., Bykowski, R. F., & Blair, R. S. (1976). *Criminal justice planning.* San Jose: Justice Systems Development.

Ostrom, E., & Parks, R. (1973). Suburban police departments: Too many and too small? In Masotti & Hadden (Eds.), *The urbanization of the suburbs: Vol. 7.* Beverly Hills: Sage.

Packer, H. (1968). *The limits of criminal sanction.* Stanford: Stanford University Press.

Pound, R. (1943). A survey of social interests. *Harvard Law Review, 57,* 1–39.

Quinney, R. (1969). *Crime and justice in society.* Boston: Little, Brown.

Quinney, R. (1974). *Critique of legal order: Crime control in capitalist society.* Boston: Little, Brown.

Quinney, R. (1977). *Class, state and crime.* New York: Longman.

Skoler, D. L. (1977). *Organizing the non-system.* Lexington, MA: Lexington Books.

Terryberry, S. (1968). The evolution of organizational environments. *Administration Science Quarterly, 12,* 490–613.

van den Haag, E. (1975). *Punishing criminals: Concerning a very old and painful question.* New York: Basic Books.

Wilson, J. Q. (1968). *Varieties of police behavior.* Cambridge, MA: Harvard University Press.

Wilson, J. Q. (1975). *Think about crime.* New York: Basic Books.

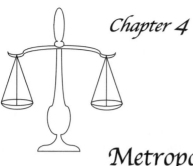

Chapter 4

Metropolitan Development and Policing
The Elephant in the Living Room

John M. Klofas

Introduction

It may seem obvious that the social conditions of American communities have important implications for policing those communities. That theme has been prominent in classical as well as contemporary investigations of police problems including subcultures (Westley, 1970) and the misuse of force (Skolnick and Fyfe, 1993:104): It was also the most pronounced theme in the report of the President's Commission on Law Enforcement and Administration of Justice in 1967.

Ironically, however, although changes in social conditions are widely recognized, these important elements of the context of policing have been largely neglected in the intellectual foundation as well as the practice of many contemporary approaches to policing. Concentrated poverty and racial isolation have become the "elephant in the living room" — obvious and omnipresent but often unacknowledged or ignored. This article will examine recent changes in communities and discuss their possible implications for policing. This will be done by focusing on medium- and small-sized cities in New York State.

John M. Klofas, "Metropolitan Development and Policing: The Elephant in the Living Room," *Criminal Justice Review*, Volume 25 No. 2, Autumn 2000, pp. 234–245. Reprinted by permission of *Criminal Justice Review*.

Policing Then and Now

In 1967 the President's Commission contrasted the "old model," in which policing was regarded as a contest between the officer and the criminal, with a "new model" in which there emerged a role for police in maintaining order in communities. The commission focused on urban policing and identified social conditions in communities as a primary ingredient defining the nature of the police role. Its members wrote, "It is in the cities that the conditions of life are the worst, that social tensions are the most acute, that riots occur, that crime rates are the highest, that the fear of crime and the demand for effective action against it are the strongest" (1967:91).

In its report, the President's Commission elaborated a consistent perspective on the tasks facing criminal justice and the police in particular. It was based on a broad understanding of the causes of crime and included a prominent concern with changing social conditions in America's cities.

Although some have argued that the roots of modern policing can be found in the Commission's report (Walker, 1994:29), its concern with objective, definable conditions of communities does not seem to have the same place in discussions of contemporary policing. Instead, community policing discussions have often invoked idealized visions of self-regulating communities. These discussions, however, have been criticized as ignoring the economic and physical conditions of decline in communities (Buerger, 1994) and even as being circumlocutions designed to conceal the traditional police function (Klockars, 1999).

The literature of community policing pays little attention to the objective condition of communities despite its frequently expressed concern with the quality of life in those communities (Skolnick and Bailey, 1986). The focus of discussion is often internal, on the police and on how to change organizations and implement new strategies (Sparrow, 1999). In the language of management, this might be viewed as tending towards a closed-system perspective (Katz and Kahn, 1978) in which organizational analysis pays little heed to environmental factors.

It is, however, not simply ironic that community policing largely ignores objective community conditions. The theoretical justification for this seems to be the belief in the ability of good policing to overcome the power of other community forces such as poverty, poor housing stock, and racial and economic segregation (Kelling, 1998; Kelling and Coles, 1996). These beliefs are even more pronounced in some other contemporary strategies, most notably those emphasizing quality-of-life arrests.

Thus the contemporary view seems to be that good policing, albeit with strong community support and involvement, can counteract the impact of community conditions. Under this view, the most important condition is the quality of policing. By contrast, the perspective of the President's Commission in 1967 was that problems of crime and order, and ultimately the role of the police, would be shaped by the conditions of communities.

There are at least two possible implications of the contemporary view of the limited relevance of community conditions. First, the assumptions behind the contemporary strategies may be supported or refuted as crime is or is not controlled despite community conditions. That is an empirical question that is beyond the scope of this article.

The second implication may be more relevant to the regular operation of the police. Inattention to community conditions may mean that policing is influenced by forces unseen and that it is shaped in unanticipated and thus unplanned ways. A more open-systems analysis may avoid this outcome. The goal of the rest of this article is to reconsider the perspective of the President's Commission in which contextual variables were seen as relevant and to describe ways in which those variables may influence policing today. The goal is to talk about "the elephant in the living room," as we did in 1967, and to discuss its possible implications for the police in the twenty-first century.

From Urban to Metropolitan Communities

The 1992 presidential election was a milestone in electoral politics. It was the first such election in which a majority of the votes came from suburban communities rather than from cities and rural areas (Schneider, 1992). That was an important landmark in the movement of the population of the nation from a primarily urban to a metropolitan population. It signaled a sea change in American society similar to that when the country moved from a rural and agrarian nation to an urban one a hundred years ago (Jackson, 1985). Just as those early changes had broad implications for communities, so does the metropolitanization of much of American society. There are at least six trends that characterize this shift and that can be illustrated by examining upstate New York cities.

Shrinking Cities — Expanding Suburbs

Many small and medium-sized cities, particularly those in the northeast, have seen dramatic population shifts. For example, peak population levels for upstate New York cities were reached with the 1950 census. An examination of U.S. Census data shows that over the next 40 years the populations of Buffalo, Rochester, Syracuse, Utica, and Albany, declined by between 25% and 43%. The largest loser has been Buffalo. Its population fell from 580,000 to 328,000 during this period. In Rochester the population fell by more than 140,000.

While city populations fell, their suburbs grew, spurred on by highway construction and favorable financing and tax policies (Jackson, 1985). Buffalo's suburbs grew by 100% between the 1950 and 1990 censuses. As the city of Rochester lost nearly one third of its population, its suburbs grew by more than 200%. In 1950 two thirds of all Rochester area residents lived in the city; by 1990 that situation was reversed and two thirds of area residents lived in Rochester's suburbs. As the cities shrank and their suburbs expanded, other changes also occurred.

Increased Racial Segregation

The movement to the suburbs has not been uniform, across demographic groups. Analysis of census data reveals that whites fled many cities in remarkable numbers over the past 40 years. In Buffalo 1 out of every 1.6 whites left the city. It Rochester 1 of every 1.8 whites left. As whites left the cities the nonwhite population grew as a proportion of the total city population and in real numbers,

A nonwhite migration into the cities, by blacks and later by Latinos, has been masked by the overall decline in city populations. As late as 1950 nonwhites composed only 3% of the population of the city of Rochester. That rate was 40% in the 1990 census. From 1950 to 1990, the nonwhite population grew by more than 200% in Buffalo and by more than 350% in Albany. As the proportion of nonwhite residents of the cities grew rapidly, the suburbs remained almost exclusively white. The upstate suburban towns and villages have generally stayed below a level of 5% nonwhite.

Increasing Concentration of Poverty in Cities

As overall city populations fell and their minority populations grew, cities also saw dramatic increases in their rates of poverty (Wilson, 1987). Between, 1970 and 1990 poverty levels increased by 2 to 3 times across the four New York cities. According to the Census Bureau, more than one quarter of Buffalo's population fell below the poverty level in 1990. The other cities all saw poverty levels of around 20%.

In Rochester, half of all census tracts are now classified as "high poverty" tracts where 20% or more of the population live below the federal poverty level. The region's extreme poverty tracts, with poverty levels of 40% or more, are all located in the city of Rochester.

As with the racial gap between cities and suburbs, the poverty gap is also growing. Suburban poverty levels have changed only slightly as urban poverty has grown. Only Utica's suburbs reach as high as 8%. The other metro area suburbs had poverty rates of 4% or 5% for the last census.

Strain on Urban Institutions

A fourth trend associated with the metropolitanization of communities involves the strain that this places on urban institutions. Institutions that functioned for an urban society may not serve their new metropolitan communities as well. The best example may be public education. Many urban school systems appear to be failing as they are overwhelmed by the concentrated poverty of the urban core (G. Orfield, 1997).

The Rochester school system provides an illustration. Although city poverty levels are at the 25% mark, the figure is much higher for children. According to census figures, 38% of Rochester's children fall below the poverty line. That figure is still much higher when the public school system is considered. As late as 1980, 22% of Rochester School District children were from families who met income requirements to participate in the free and reduced-cost lunch program. In 1998 the figure had risen, to 90% (New York State Department of Education, 1999).

Those high poverty levels have also been tied to failing student performance. City schools do not compare well in educational outcomes with their suburban counterparts. Analysis of state education data (New York State Department of Education, 1999) shows that in the Rochester area, out of 100 suburban students entering high school, 85 can be expected to graduate in four years. In the city school district, however, that figure is just 27. And only 5% of city students as compared with 50% of suburban students will earn Regents diplomas—the highest standard in New York and the standard currently being phased in as a general graduation requirement for all students.

The situation in Rochester is not unique. According to Gary Orfield (1997), urban education across the country suffers similar problems. Although there are classrooms and even schools that fair better, no school district as a whole has made significant progress in the face of such high poverty levels.

Spread of Effects to Inner Ring

Movement to the suburbs actually began in the 1930s but escalated dramatically after World War II. The early suburbs that grew on the outskirts of cities were the first of expanding bands of development that now reach many miles out around most cities. And now those early inner-ring suburbs are showing many problems that were once regarded as limited to cities. Increasingly those suburbs are being plagued by decaying infrastructures, faltering local economies, and growing pockets of poverty.

A pattern being repeated around the country shows a decline of many inner-ring suburbs as wealth and resources move ever outward, often clustered in one direction, which has been referred to as a community's "golden crescent" (M. Orfield, 1997). There executive homes, office parks, and upscale retailing thrive while drawing resources from the central city and now the inner suburbs as well. But those inner suburbs lack even the strength of the city's business district or the concentration of social services found in cities, and so they may decline farther and faster than even the urban core (Rusk, 1995).

The trend is illustrated by the condition of Rochester's inner ring of suburbs. The oldest suburbs are seeing population declines and very slow rates of economic growth. The tax base of the city of Rochester has not grown in more than 20 years and is beginning to show significant declines (Metropolitan Forum, 1998). Total assessed value fell by 13% in the most recent year of available data. In fact, the county now provides more funds to the city budget than is raised by property taxes within the city itself.

But problems are also found in the suburbs. In the inner ring of suburbs, tax base growth has averaged 32% over the past 20 years while it has been 132% in the fastest growing "golden crescent" suburbs (Metropolitan Forum, 1998). What were once regarded as differences between cities and their suburbs are now surfacing in the form of disparities across suburbs.

Sprawl to Outer Ring and Rural Areas

The final trend, which can be recognized as part of the metropolitanization of communities, is the continued sprawl of suburban development. In many areas the pace of low-density development of the American landscape around cities has escalated. Since 1970 the population of the greater Rochester metropolitan area, for example, has grown by a mere 30% but the overall urbanized land use has grown by more than 100%. Similar patterns are found for other cities across the country. Recognition of urban sprawl has spawned concern with a wide range of issues including environmental degradation, loss of productive farmland, architectural aesthetics, increased transportation and utility costs, and the impact on rural culture. In recent years many initiatives have begun to try to slow or reverse these trends through preservation of farmland and protection of undeveloped land (American Farmland Trust, 1998).

Implications for Policing

An open-system perspective would suggest that the six trends that characterize metropolitan development have important implications for policing. Furthermore, consideration of contemporary growth patterns suggests that the effects on policing may be related but different in urban, suburban, and rural areas. For urban policing the continued decline of living conditions and problems of maintaining order in poor neighborhoods are likely to be major sources of concern. In suburban communities, police are likely to confront fears about the spread of crime and they may need to address community members' efforts to isolate themselves from their impoverished neighbors. In rural areas the pattern of growth suggests increasing concerns with the spread of crime and criminals to rural areas and with clashes between development interests and agricultural and rural interests. With those broad implications of metropolitan growth in mind, it is possible now to consider several more specific implications.

Increasingly Mobile Crime Problem

One consequence of the metropolitanization of communities is that crime patterns will follow the population. As infrastructure moves outward crime is likely to follow.

In recent years there has been renewed attention to the subject of rural crime (Weisheit, Falcone, and Wells, 1999; Weisheit and Wells, 1996). The subject of crime and justice across metropolitan areas has received less attention. It is clear, however, that gang and drug problems are not limited to urban areas and the crime trends reflect current population shifts (Kleniewski, 1997). The organization of policing, however, continues to follow established patterns of population density. Rural departments are inevitably small, with few officers covering large geographic areas. Many departments also have little or no capacity for conducting investigations. Suburban departments may grow as populations shift but they too may have few resources. Metropolitan development will put additional demands on a fragmented structure of policing and particularly on suburban and rural departments.

Greater Demands for Order in Cities

As the poverty gap widens in metropolitan areas, city police are likely to face increasing problems associated with the concentration of poverty. Among those problems may be growing demands for the maintenance of order in poor neighborhoods. As the physical and social conditions of neighborhoods grow to reflect poverty conditions many neighborhood residents and community leaders may pressure police to do what may be necessary to maintain order. Many police leaders have supported aggressive police tactics (Bratton and Knobler, 1998; Kelling and Coles, 1996). Sweeps, undercover drug enforcement, and specialized units to address street crime have become common in cities. These and other forms of aggressive policing may increase under growing demands for order. In the face of the personal consequences of structural change in communities, some residents may pressure police for even more aggressive efforts. If left unchecked these may strain the bounds of legal authority.

Strain on Police Community Relations

Police in American society have always shared a complex role marked by competing demands and interests (Bitner, 1970). Metropolitan development is likely to provide further complications. Although support for aggressive policing may grow in some areas, that support is not likely to be universal. The tactics, therefore, will also create additional conflicts with some community members who see themselves as the victims of more politically powerful groups. In a democratic society, current patterns of metropolitan growth seem likely to lead to increasing conflicts over police use of force, surveillance, stop and frisk practices, and other similar tactics.

Increasing "Culture Conflicts"

The race- and class-related consequences of changing metropolitan communities also suggest that these characteristics may play an even greater role in future police controversies. The growing segregation by class and race that marks metropolitan communities can spawn conflicts across those social boundaries. Police are likely to find themselves drawn into these culture conflicts. Divisions between "good" and "bad" neighborhoods and between a city and its suburbs will increase demands on police to contain problems of crime and disorder. Suburban police, in particular, are likely to face public support for activities designed to identify and remove people who are not seen as legitimate members of the community. Race and class can play central roles in such "border patrol" activity. If left unmanaged, pressure to engage in such activity may very well strain the boundaries of legitimate policing.

Mission Creep

As urban institutions experience problems associated with increasingly concentrated poverty in cities, police will be under increasing pressure to respond. Demand for new police interventions will come from those community institutions where the consequences of metropolitan development are most obvious. In Rochester, for example, police officers have been assigned to all middle and high schools on a full-time basis. Unlike the "officer friendly" role of the past, however, these officers are expected to perform a role that emphasizes traditional law enforcement powers.

In addition to schools, police in other communities have expanded their roles in public transportation and in the protection of downtown businesses and entertainment sites. In these and similar areas, police can expect increasing demands for their intervention. Those demands may place police officers in roles that take them beyond traditional approaches to policing.

Growing Problems Associated with Budget Constraints

As urban and inner-ring suburban tax bases fail, police will find themselves facing problems associated with increasingly tight budgets. Thus, at the same time that demands for services are increasing, the traditional sources of police support will be failing. Those problems may first mean greater calls for accountability or reorganizational efforts that stretch resources by moving officers to the street from administrative responsibilities.

There may also be other implications. Police may be forced to seek other revenue sources, perhaps through greater use of forfeiture laws. Local police may also increase reliance on funds from other governmental or private sources. And, too, private agencies may bear an increasing share of metropolitan policing responsibilities. Such changes, driven by the changing structure of American communities, can have very significant implications for the nature of local policing.

Impact of Sprawl on Rural Police

Whereas some of the effects discussed above primarily influence urban and suburban policing, rural police may also be significantly affected by metropolitan growth. As development sprawls outward, clashes are likely between long-term rural residents and the increasingly suburban population. Conflicts over early morning farming, spreading manure near residential neighborhoods, and other farm practices have been documented in metropolitan areas around the country.

The Social Meaning of Metropolitanization

In the nineteenth century, as the nation raced from its agrarian roots toward urbanization, the reform of social institutions and the development of new ones was inevitable. Public health housing reform, and improved public education are only a few of the reforms that grew with burgeoning cities. In criminal justice, institutional treatment of offenders and, later, the juvenile court and alternative sanctions such as probation and parole were all tied to the great change in American society (Rothman, 1971, 1980).

In the midst of this tumultuous change, however, not everyone embraced the new urban America. In the late nineteenth century the Populist Party emerged as a reactionary force in American politics. Populists pushed an agenda of economic and social reform that was meant to support threatened agrarian and rural interests. By the turn of the century the Populist Party had all but disappeared, overwhelmed by the forces of industrialization and urbanization.

Today, a clear reform agenda addressing metropolitanization is only beginning to emerge (Rusk, 1999). As yet, no consistent national policy has developed and states and localities are struggling sporadically with initiatives such as Smart Growth, a planning movement intended to address urban sprawl (Bollier, 1998). Like the Populists of the nineteenth century, many city and suburban interests resist such an agenda and pray for a return to an earlier era.

Despite the modern populists, the social implications of this demographic shift are substantial. Left unchecked, many are also quite harmful.

The pattern of development in metropolitan communities has led many people to home ownership, fine schools, and rising property values. Many have gone to the suburbs in search of the American dream. And many, both whites and minorities, have found it there. But, at a time when technology is making the world smaller and bringing cultures together, this pattern of development also threatens to divide us. With the growth of metropolitan areas there has also been a growth in the distance, both physical and social, between our nation's poor and the middle and upper classes. As William Julius Wilson (1987) has pointed out, it is a distance with significant economic and cultural consequences. As it widens, a burgeoning underclass falls farther from the social mainstream.

Social divisions by class and by race can also be exacerbated as opportunities for success, through education for example, close or remain closed to succeeding generations of poor children. Conditions in poor neighborhoods are also likely to grow worse as local municipal budgets are strained.

The decline of the urban core and the spread to older suburbs cannot occur without still wider social consequences. The great question for the near future will be whether we can build communities without building barriers. Fear can strengthen psychological barriers and engender hostility and conflict in older suburbs. It can spawn gated communities in the developing outer ring and it can push aside the bucolic isolation of rural America as we sprawl ever outward.

Conclusion:
Police Management and Metropolitan Growth

People who study the future in earnest caution against peering too deeply into the crystal ball (Cole, 1995). The future is most likely to resemble evidence-grounded, short-term predictions. It may be tempting to view this article as an attempt to peer deep into the future. But that would be an oversimplification. The forces changing American society are clear and well documented. Perhaps their consequences read like prognostications, but in each case there is already evidence of those consequences occurring across communities. The only element of prediction may be in estimating the magnitude of the consequences if metropolitan changes go unmanaged.

Unlike some fanciful predictions of the future, the forces of metropolitan growth and development have been gathering momentum for some time. In 1967 the President's Commission identified questions of race and class as issues that were central to the field of criminal justice. It recognized the relationship between poverty, discrimination, and crime and it noted the impact that these conditions have on police community relations and on the role of the police.

Although many of the conditions cited by the Commission have gown much worse, academic discussion of these matters in criminal justice has been more reserved, sometimes to the point of ignoring them. Outside of the field, however, a growing body of scholarship has been concerned with the social consequences of metropolitan patterns of development. Scholars and policy makers have used this framework to examine and suggest reform in a broad range of areas including education (G. Orfeld, 1997), fiscal policy (M. Orfeld, 1997), employment (Wilson, 1997), politics (Rusk, 1995), land use (Porter, 1997), and environmental justice (Bullard, 1994).

For managers of the police there are advantages to an open-systems view that encourages them to consider what has become the elephant in the living room. An understanding of population demographics and their consequences can contribute needed information for decisions regarding the management of police resources. Metropolitan development can have implications for police recruitment, training, and deployment of officers. This perspective suggests, at a minimum, that police should adopt regional perspectives that encourage cooperation across urban, suburban, and rural departments. It suggests that managers should be proactive in examining the demands that they face and in planning for expansion of their mission. And it suggests the importance of maintaining and enforcing clear professional standards as police negotiate increasingly complex and competing demands.

The importance of understanding the patterns of change that are altering American communities, however, is not limited to managerial concerns. The focus returns us to a question considered by the President's Commission in 1967: "What . . . is America's experience with crime and how has this experience been shaped by the Nation's way of living?" (1967:v). Now, as then, asking such questions seems important to understanding basic ideas of order and justice in a democratic society.

References

American Farmland Trust. (1998). *Call to action: Farmland protection success stories in the Empire State*. Washington, DC: American Farmland Trust.

Bittner, E. (1970). *The functions of police in modern society*. Washington, DC: National Institute of Mental Health.

Bollier, D. (1998). *How smart growth can stop sprawl*. Washington, DC: Essential Books.

Bratton, W., & Knobler, P. (1998). *Turnaround: How America's top cop reversed the crime epidemic*. New York: Random House.

Buerger, M. E. (1994). The limits of community. In D. P. Rosenbaum (Ed.), *The challenge of community policing* (pp. 270–273). Thousand Oaks, CA: Sage.

Bullard, R. D. (1994). *Dumping in Dixie: Race, class and environmental quality*. New York: Westview Press.

Cole, G. (1995). Criminal justice in the twenty-first century: The role of futures research. In J. Klofas & S. Stojkovic (Eds.), *Crime and justice in the year 2010* (pp. 4–17). Belmont CA: Wadsworth Publishing Company.

Jackson, K. T. (1985). *Crabgrass frontier: The suburbanization of the United States*. New York, NY: Oxford University Press.

Katz, D., & Kahn, R. (1978). *The social psychology of organizations*. New York, NY: John Wiley & Sons.

Kelling, G. L. (1998). Crime control, the police and culture wars: Broken windows and cultural pluralism. In National Institute of Justice (Ed.), *Perspectives on crime and justice: 1997-1998 lecture series* (pp. 31–51). Washington, DC: U.S. Department of Justice.

Kelling, G. L., & Coles, C. M. (1996). *Fixing broken windows: Restoring order and reducing crime in our communities.* New York, NY: Touchstone.

Kleniewski, M. (1997). *Cities, change and conflict: The political economy of urban life.* Belmont, CA: Wadsworth Publishing Company.

Klockars, C. B. (1999). The rhetoric of community policing. In S. Stojkovic, J. Klofas, & D. Kalinich (Eds.), *The administration and management of criminal justice organizations* (pp. 19–36). Prospect Heights, IL: Waveland Press.

Metropolitan Forum. (1998). *The health of Monroe's suburbs: Stagnation in the inner ring.* Rochester, NY: Author.

New York State Department of Education. (1999). *The state of learning: Report to the governor and state legislature* (Chap. 655 report). Albany, NY: Author.

Orfield, G. (1997). *Dismantling desegregation: The quiet reversal of* Brown v. Board of Education. New York, NY: New Press.

Orfield, M. (1997). *Metropolitics: A regional agenda for community and stability.* Washington, DC: Brookings.

Porter, D. R. (1997). *Managing growth in America's communities.* Washington, DC: Island Press.

President's Commission on Law Enforcement and Administration of Justice. (1967). *The challenge of crime in a free society: A report.* Washington, DC: U.S. Government Printing Office.

Rothman, D. (1971). *The discovery of the asylum: Social order and disorder in the new republic.* Boston, MA: Little Brown.

Rothman, D. (1980). *Conscience and convenience: The asylum and its alternatives in progressive America.* Boston, MA: Little Brown.

Rusk, D. (1993). *Cities without suburbs.* Washington, DC: Woodrow Wilson Center Press.

Rusk, D. (1999). *Inside game/outside game: Winning strategies for saving urban America.* Washington, DC: Brookings.

Schneider, W. (1992). The suburban century begins. *Atlantic Monthly, 240*(1), 33–44.

Skolnick, J. H., & Bailey, D. H. (1986). *The new blue line: Police innovation in six American cities.* New York: The Free Press.

Skolnick, J. H., & Fyfe, J. (1993). *Above the law: Police and excessive use of force.* New York: The Free Press.

Sparrow, M. (1999). Implementing community policing. In S. Stojkovic, J. Klofas, & D. Kalinich (Eds.), *The administration and management of criminal justice organizations* (pp. 397–408). Prospect Heights, IL: Waveland Press.

Walker, S. (1994). *Sense and nonsense about crime and drugs* (3rd ed.). Belmont, CA: Wadsworth Publishing Company.

Weisheit, R., Falcone, D., & Wells, E. (1999). *Crime and policing in rural and small town America.* Prospect Heights, IL: Waveland Press.

Weisheit, R., & Wells, E. D. (1996). Rural crime and justice: Implications for theory and research. *Crime and Delinquency, 42*(2), 379–397.

Westley, W. (1970). *Violence and the police: A study of law, custom and morality.* Cambridge, MA: M.I.T. Press.

Wilson, W. J. (1987). *The truly disadvantaged: The inner city, the underclass and public policy.* Chicago, IL: University of Chicago Press.

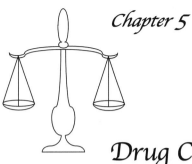

Chapter 5

Drug Courts
A Bridge between Criminal Justice and Health Services

Suzanne L. Wenzel
Douglas Longshore
Susan Turner
M. Susan Ridgely

Introduction

This study investigates the role of drug courts as a bridge between criminal justice and health services in the community for the drug-abusing offender. Drug courts are a burgeoning phenomenon in this nation, but research on drug courts is still in its infancy. On no specific topic is this research deficit more apparent than on drug courts' relationships with community health services for offenders. This article discusses the importance of building bridges and presents a conceptual framework for organizing a comprehensive investigation of them. Using data from a National Institute of Justice (NIJ) sponsored study of 14 drug court programs in the United States and Puerto Rico (Turner, 1998), the study explains linkages between drug courts and health services (including drug treatment providers) in terms of (1) what services are available to drug court clients and (2) the characteristics of the linkage such as information sharing, formality

Reprinted from *Journal of Criminal Justice,* Vol 29, Suzanne L. Wenzel, Douglas Longshore, Susan Turner, and M. Susan Ridgely, Drug Courts: "A Bridge Between Criminal Justice and Health Services," pp. 241–253, 2001, with permission from Elsevier.

of the linkage, reliance on case management, whether Treatment Alternatives to Street Crime (TASC) brokers services, and whether there is a single treatment provider or a network of providers.

Need for a Bridge

The Overlapping Problems of Drug Abuse and Crime

Drug abuse, one of the nation's most intractable public health and safety problems (Lamb, Greenlick, and McCarty, 1998:13), is closely related to criminal activity, and criminal activity is an especially costly correlate of drug abuse. The level of drug abuse among criminal offenders is striking, with as many as three-quarters of males arrested in 24 sites nationwide testing positive for recent illicit drug use (National Institute of Justice (NIJ), 1993; Office of National Drug Control Policy (ONDCP), 1999). Rates for female offenders are thought to be even higher (Cook, 1992:369–371). Studies of entrants to federal and state correctional facilities have shown that the majority of inmates have histories of drug abuse (Leukefeld and Tims, 1992:279). New estimates from the National Household Survey on Drug Abuse reveal that among drug abusers in need of treatment in the US, there are disproportionate numbers who report committing crimes (Woodward et al., 1997:15).

Needs of Drug Abusers

The needs of drug abusers—whether they are offenders or not—extend far beyond treatment for drugs to a broad array of other problems, often including physical and mental health, housing and family assistance, job training and placement assistance, and living skills (Lamb et al., 1998:28; McLellan et al., 1998:1498). Some of these needs may be causes and others consequences of substance abuse (McLellan, Luborsky, Woody, O'Brien, and Kron, 1981), but no matter the temporal or causal ordering of the correlates, substance abusers present significant challenges for service providers.

Due to preoccupation with the acquisition and use of substances, abusers may neglect physical health maintenance and not practice preventive health behaviors. Addiction may result in nutritional deficiencies, below average weight, liver problems, and cerebrovascular disorders (Ericksen and Trocki, 1992; Umbricht-Schneider, Ginn, Pabst, and Bigelow, 1994). Infectious diseases including hepatitis, tuberculosis, sexually transmitted diseases, and HIV/AIDS are related to behaviors involved in acquisition of the drugs, disinhibiting effects of the drugs, and the means of administering the drugs (McBride and Inciardi, 1990:271–72; Piette, Fleishman, Stein, Mor, and Mayer, 1993; Selwyn, 1996:398; Siegal, Wang, Forney, and Carlson, 1994:85–101; Tewksbury,

Vito, and Cummings, 1998:10–11). Co-occurrence of mental health problems with substance problems is more often the rule than the exception (Cuffel, 1996; Regier et al., 1990), and rates of attempted and completed suicide are also greater among substance abusers (Gomberg, 1993). Substance-abusing women face additional problems, including infections and threats to reproductive health, pregnancy complications, and possible harm to the fetus (CSAT, 1994:26–40; Wenzel et al., in press), and they may also be at increased risk of victimization (Wenzel, Gelberg, Koegel, and Leake, 2000).

Need for Multiple Services

Multiple sources of evidence indicate that substance abuse treatment works (Anglin and Hser, 1990; Hubbard, Rachal, Craddock, and Cavanaugh, 1984:42–68; Lipton, 1994:331), even for the most difficult cases (such as chronic heroin and cocaine users with extensive predatory criminal histories) (Lipton, 1994:331). Other sources emphasize that provision of services for the multiple problems of substance abusers (as described above) can only enhance the prospects of successful treatment (Friedman, Alexander, and D'Aunno, 1999; McLellan et al., 1994, 1998:1498; Widman et al., 1997). Provision of multiple services also aids in the treatment and prevention of drug abusers' other problems, such as poor physical health and higher rates of infectious disease (Mathias, 1998).

The Role of the Criminal Justice System

Because the offender population is one that has had minimal access to substance abuse treatment or other health care services, the criminal justice system serves as an important point of service contact (Hammett, Gaiter, and Crawford, 1998:100). Court-ordered treatment has in fact expanded access to treatment for people on probation or parole because the court pays for treatment, although knowledge of the extent and quality of such treatment is lacking (Woodward et al., 1997:16). Efforts to address the interrelated problems of drug abuse and crime through treatment have in fact occurred with some success among those already in jail or prison (Leukefield, Matthews, and Clayton, 1992; Lipton, 1994:334–336; Peters, 1992:53–75), as well as among offenders who are diverted from jail or prison into treatment programs (e.g., TASC, Anglin et al., 1996; and Treatment Drug Courts, Deschenes and Greenwood, 1994:99–115; Drug Courts Program Office, 1997). Screening and services for infectious diseases such as HIV/AIDS and tuberculosis are especially important in jails and prisons because of the possible spread of infection among inmates and staff (see McBride and Inciardi, 1990:268–269, and Tewksbury et al., 1998:1–22 for more details regarding HIV/AIDS in the criminal justice system).

Treatment Alternatives to Street Crime

TASC represents one of the earliest and best linkages or "bridges" between the criminal justice system and community-based substance abuse treatment programs (Anglin et al., 1996:85; Healy, 1999), and is also one of the earliest and largest approaches to case management for providing substance abuse treatment within the context of the criminal justice system. TASC activities have been found to reduce drug use and recidivism and increase use of substance abuse treatment and retention among drug-involved arrestees (Anglin, Longshore, and Turner, 1999; Rhodes and Gross, 1997:41). TASC has a long history and has developed critical elements for the role of case management. TASC critical elements are to identify drug-using offenders qualified for TASC, assess the offenders' basic service needs, refer to appropriate treatment services, monitor treatment progress, use sanctions to ensure compliance with treatment and TASC requirements, and terminate from TASC or provide further referral if necessary. TASC critical elements, in fact, have been recommended as a guide to developing effective drug court programs (Vito and Tewksbury, 1998:50–51). However, TASC, as a "third-party" nonservice organization, cannot ensure that service needs are being met (Anglin et al., 1996:84), and case managers sometimes must manage too many cases with too few resources to provide comprehensive services (Healy, 1999:11–12). Additionally, TASC evaluations have focused on initial assessment activities, and services provided under TASC were often found to be restricted to drug testing (urinalysis).

Even in TASC, attention thus far has been restricted to the criminal justice and substance abuse treatment systems and has not adequately addressed ties with other vital community health services such as physical and mental health care (Anglin et al., 1996:84; Bazelon, 1999; Taxman, 1998). Resource and other constraints make it unlikely that the multiple problems faced by substance abusers can be successfully addressed by any single agency or organization (Lamb et al., 1998:29; Marsden, 1998:6); yet, as previously argued, these needs must be addressed to enhance the prospects of treatment success. Involvement of providers of multiple services through collaborative linkages is therefore necessary and advisable (Anglin et al., 1996:9–10; D'Aunno and Zuckerman, 1987; Marsden, 1998:4; Schlenger, Kroutil, and Roland, 1992:316, 329; Selwyn, 1996:397, 400, 401, 404). Indeed, building such linkages and integrated services has been one of the biggest challenges facing the larger health services system in recent years (National Association of State Alcohol and Drug Abuse Directors [NASADAD]/National Association of State Mental Health Program Directors [NASMHPD], 1998:1).

Drug Courts

Drug courts have roots in programs developed by courts, pretrial, probation, and parole agencies, and they particularly build upon the substantial foundation of TASC (CSAT, 1994; Shannon, 1998). Authorized under Title V of the Violent Crime Control and Law Enforcement Act of 1994, drug courts are one of the newest and fastest growing criminal justice innovations aimed at crime reduction. Between 1995 and 1997, more than 150 communities received roughly 33 million dollars from the Office of Justice Programs (OJP) to plan, implement, or improve drug courts. Over 200 drug courts are operational in 47 states. These courts serve as specialized courts for offenders that include drug treatment, ancillary health and social services, and close judicial monitoring and appropriate provision of rewards and sanctions as key features (Belenko, 1998:1–42, 1999:158; Drug Courts Program Office, 1997:10; Hora, Schma, and Rosenthal, 1999:5–15).

Drug courts represent a promising way of addressing the intersection of drug abuse and crime, as well as the multiple needs of substance abusers, because of the potential bridge they represent between the criminal justice and broader health services systems. As articulated by the Office of Justice Programs (1998), a fundamental premise of the drug court approach is that the cessation of drug abuse requires well-structured treatment services and coordinated and comprehensive programs of other rehabilitation services to address the underlying personal problems of the drug user and to promote his or her reentry into society. A successful drug court and ultimately successful outcomes for offenders depends on collaborative linkages between the court, treatment providers, other social services and community organizations (General Accounting Office [GAO], 1995:15).

According to the 1997 Drug Court Survey Report by American University (Cooper, 1997), which provides information on 97 drug courts in operation as of January 1997 (including seven in the current study), almost all stated that they provide public health services including TB and HIV screening and referral. Many reported that they provide special services to those with mental health disorders in addition to substance abuse, and a number of drug courts use the services of a physician or nurse. Offenders in drug courts typically have multiple needs. For example, 60 percent of all drug court participants have minor children, have been using drugs for 15 years on average, and many are polydrug users. Rates of suicide and other mental health problems are high among drug court offenders (Belenko, 1999:158). Seventy-five percent of the offenders in drug courts surveyed by American University had not been exposed to treatment prior to their drug court experience, but a large majority had already served jail or prison time.

Conceptual Framework for Understanding Drug Court as a Bridge

An in-depth investigation of bridges to health services—and their ultimate importance to offender outcomes—can be guided by the health services research-based quality of care framework described by Donabedian (1980, 1982, 1984, 1988a, 1988b, 1988c), and elaborated upon by McGlynn, Norquist, Wells, Sullivan, and Liberman (1988), for mental health care delivery. In this framework, adapted in figure 1 for the drug court context, there are three interrelated elements: the structure of the service delivery system, the process of care, and client outcomes.

Both structure and process are important to understanding offender outcomes. Structure refers to the organization and resources of each of the relevant institutions delivering services to the target population. Linkages can be conceptualized as another dimension of structure, one that may both directly enhance offenders' access to services and moderate the relationship between program characteristics and access. The structure of care defines the context for the process of care, which refers to the treatments and services that offenders receive (utilize) as a result of their interaction with the system of care. Enhanced access, depicted here as a key process element, should favorably influence offender outcomes. Offender characteristics (case mix) (not depicted in figure 1) are also relevant to client outcomes and are thus typically accounted for in predictive models to understand outcomes.

Linkages imply "working together" (Vigdal, 1995:9) to meet a common goal, and they can occur at differing levels of quantity and quality (Anglin et al., 1996; Baker, 1991; D'Aunno and Zuckerman, 1987; Hammett, Gaiter, and Crawford, 1998:1; Marsden, 1998:4; Mathias, 1998:1; NASA-DAD/NASMHPD, 1998:3; Polivka, Kennedy, and Chaudry, 1997; Ridgely, Lambert, Goodman, Chichester, and Ralph, 1998; SAMHSA, 1997; Selwyn, 1996:397–410; Taxman, 1998): (1) the sharing of information about clients, such as through a management information system; (2) the joint planning of service goals; (3) interagency referrals of clients; (4) documentation of relationships through memoranda of understanding (MOUs), contracts, or other means; (5) joint assessment of clients; (6) the presence and extent of case management and liaisons; (7) favorable (flexible) funding situations and sharing of monetary resources; (8) sensitivity to the concerns of other agencies and organizations providing services to clients; (9) crosstraining of staff; (10) shared philosophies in services provision and administrative structure; (11) regular meetings (e.g., boards) among program leaders. It is reasonable that presence and extent of collaborative linkages across organizations could affect clients' access to needed services.

Method

Overview

RAND received a grant in 1998 from the NIJ (Drug Court Evaluation II: An Assessment of 14 Programs, S. Turner and D. Longshore, PIs)

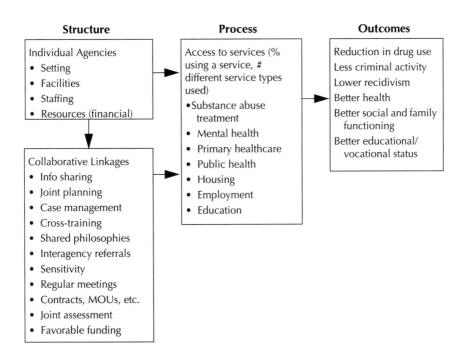

Structure	Process	Outcomes

Figure 1   Conceptual framework for understanding drug court as a bridge.

to investigate fourteen drug court programs that had received implementation funding from the Drug Courts Program Office for 1995–1996. The major objectives of this study are to develop a conceptual description of drug courts, describe implementation of the fourteen drug courts funded by DCPO, determine program evaluability for each, and develop plans for an evaluation of each program's effectiveness. The current study utilizes data collected for the NIJ-sponsored investigation. Data presented here on linkages between drug courts and health services represent the foundation of a more in-depth investigation that has recently begun with sponsorship from the National Institute on Drug Abuse (Wenzel, 1999).

Sample Design and Characteristics

The sample consists of those 14 drug court programs that received implementation funding in 1995–1996 from the Drug Court Program Office. These 14 programs represent jurisdictions in Puerto Rico and nine states (Alabama, California, Florida, Georgia, Illinois, Nebraska, New York, Virginia, Washington) representing the Southern, Northeastern, Western, Northwestern, Plains, and Midwest regions of the United States. Two of the drug court programs in this study are in Alabama, three are in California, and two are in Illinois. One of the California programs, one of the Illinois programs, and the Florida program serve juveniles or young adults; the remainder serve adults. While the sites are not randomly selected, they are diverse and are likely to be representative of other drug courts in the 50 states and Puerto Rico that have met the criteria for federal DCPO funding (one of the major sources of funding). The programs are diverse not only in that they represent different regions of the country but also because they are designed for different offender populations. Additionally, they employ different prosecutorial models and implement supervision strategies of various types and intensities. Persons who have recently committed a violent crime are excluded from the fourteen drug courts, as are individuals with no evidence of a drug problem.

Procedures and Measures

Linkage-relevant descriptive information about the fourteen drug court programs was gathered through a number of different sources, where available: sites' original proposals to DCPO for implementation grant funding, sites' internal process or outcomes evaluations, DCPO site visit reports, sites' progress reports to DCPO, and records of visits to each of the sites. Site visits were conducted in June, July, and August of 1999. At each site, a two-person team made one visit lasting 2–3 days. Information was gathered from judges and other drug court staff through an interview protocol that contained 71 questions for visitors to use as a guide in gathering information on a number of different dimensions including collaborative linkages. In addition to the 71 question protocol, RAND provided site visitors with a guide of individuals to be interviewed (e.g., judge, district attorney, case manager, treatment provider), which individuals were to be asked which sets of questions, and available background materials on sites (e.g., DCPO progress reports and site visit reports). Because the time at each site was limited, visitors had few opportunities to speak with individuals other than drug court staff (e.g., judge, district attorney, public defender, administrator, evaluator) and key substance abuse treatment providers.

Preliminary information on drug courts as a bridge between criminal justice and health services was obtained through five questions in the protocol. The first of the questions — "What is the nature of the collaboration with . . . treatment providers, and other social service or health care providers (e.g., formal, through contracts, or informal)?" — was intended to yield preliminary information on the formality and documentation of any relationships. "How do drug court staff and collaborating agencies know when programmatic changes occur in the drug court (How are agencies apprised)?" and "Are people and agencies involved with serving the client getting the information they need about the client?" were both intended to provide insight on whether and how information about the drug court and about clients in the court is being shared. "Is there an operational management information system that allows for rapid retrieval of exchange of information about clients among existing criminal justice, health, and other service systems?" focuses on a specific and important mechanisms for sharing information about clients. The probe, "Is the system set up in a way that serves all of the agencies well?" was designed to elicit general information about the adequacies or inadequacies of any collaboration.

Given that linkage was but one element investigated as part of the NIJ-sponsored study, site visitors could not devote extensive time to obtaining elaboration on responses to these five questions. Further, these questions were asked only of representative drug court team members and, in most cases, of a single representative substance abuse treatment provider at each site. Additional site materials were examined (as available) to address these questions and to describe the service providers. Even this limited information, however, represents a significant advance on a topic that has not been sufficiently investigated.

Results

Available Services

Table 1 shows the types of health-related services (including drug treatment) that were planned for offenders in each of the fourteen drug court programs, as described in the programs' proposals to DCPO for 1995–1996 implementation grant funding. (We have masked identities of the Drug Courts for confidentiality.) These services included substance abuse treatment, public health (e.g., screening for diseases), mental health, housing, referrals to jobs, and educational services. Judging from this information, sites recognized the importance of providing not only drug treatment but other services for offenders. It was not possible in this study to verify the current availability of all types of health services to offenders, or their frequency or regularity of use by offenders. These characteristics will undergo further investigation under sponsorship by NIDA.

Substance abuse treatment is, of course, a routine health service for the drug court and appears to be the service most available to drug court offenders. It was for this area that site visitors were able to obtain the most detailed information. In table 2, the types of treatment provided to offenders in the fourteen drug courts are described. Inpatient/residential and detox services are not available to all offenders even when the service is listed as available. For example, Site I cannot afford to pay for residential and detox services for its offenders; offenders must have private or public insurance or personal resources to utilize this treatment type. Acupuncture has received increasing attention as a method of drug abuse treatment (Bullock, Kiresuk, Pheley, Culliton, and Lenz, 1999:31–38; McLellan, Grossman, Blaine, and Haverkos, 1993; Shwartz, Saitz, Mulvey, and Bran-

Table 1 Approximate numbers and types of providers for the 14 drug courts.

Site	Key component	Substance abuse	Public health	Mental health	Housing	Jobs	Education	Family
A	Antisubstance Abuse coalition	20	+	+	17	+	+	+
B	Uses TASC services	5	2	+	4	+		
C	Case management	50	+	+	+	+		+
D	Uses TASC-like approach	+				+	+	+
E	Uses TASC case2 managers	2	2	3		1	1	
F		10	3	+		2	2	
G	Has multiagency collaborative in place	1				1	1	
H		+	+	+	+	+	+	+
I	Has local criminal justice planning group	1				+	+	+
J	Uses TASC	5	+	+	+	+	+	+
K	Uses 2 treatment coordinators	+		+	+			+
L	Uses TASC case managers		20	+	+	+	+	+
M								
N		1		1				+

+ = service type mentioned in drug court proposal to DCPO, but number of providers of this type is unclear. Blank for a service category means no information provided.

nigan, 1999) and has been used in the treatment of drug-abusing offenders (Falkin, Prendergast, and Anglin, 1994; Latessa and Moon, 1992:317–33). Acupuncture was provided only at Sites I and K among our fourteen programs, where it was used largely as an adjunct to more traditional treatment approaches and as a means of detoxification and relaxation.

Characteristics of the Bridge

As previously shown in table 1 and verified in other site materials, TASC is a key component of the linkage for five of the fourteen sites. In Site B, individuals are assigned to TASC for urine monitoring, case management, and occasionally treatment prior to their drug court involvement. Once accepted into that drug court program, the judge carefully monitors client progress using information provided by TASC case managers. Drug

Table 2 Types of substance abuse treatment provided by the 14 drug courts.

Site	Outpatient (intensive or other)	Inpatient/ residential	Detox	Methadone	Acupuncture
A	+				
B	+				
C	+	+	+	+	
D	+				
E	+	+	+	+	
F	+	+		+	
G		+	+		
H	+	+	+		
I	+	+	+		+
J	+	+	+		
K	+				+
L	+	+	+		
M	+	+	+		
N	+	+			

court staff reported that the existing TASC infrastructure facilitated a smooth start-up of this drug court. In the opinion of the site visitors, the Site B drug court represents a very organized, institutionalized, and collaborative partnership between TASC and the criminal justice system. Before implementation of the drug court, TASC involvement with the criminal justice system was case specific. Non-TASC case management appears to be key in Site D. At Site L, TASC is described as "the glue between the drug court staff, judge and treatment providers," although the site visitors observed that the local addiction recovery center is more central to decision making about clients in the drug court than TASC.

Preliminary information on drug courts as a bridge was also obtained through five questions in the site visit protocol, as described above. That information is summarized in tables 3–7 below.

Although the information presented in tables 3–7 must also be subjected to further investigation and verification, formal linkages (in terms of contracts, for example) appear to exist primarily with substance abuse treatment providers. Other services are provided on a more informal basis. At one site, offenders may walk a very short distance to a University of California Medical School clinic for emergency MediCal. Drug court sites D and F contract with a regional behavioral health services agency to coordinate all service provision, where the most common service provided is substance abuse treatment.

Table 3 Characteristics of linkages with health service providers: What is the nature of the collaboration?

Site	
A	Drug court operates outpatient treatment center; thus, no treatment linkage. Contacts with other providers are informal.
B	All collaborative partnerships appear informal but are stable.
C	Collaboration with SA treatment providers is by written agreement. Informal collaborations with other agencies but DC is working to formalize them.
D	Formal contract with behavioral health care provider that represents link to all health services.
	Collaborations are informal.
F	Formal contract with treatment coordination agency that represents a link to all health care services.
G	Memoranda of understanding between drug courts and service agencies.
H	All linkages through memoranda of understanding or contract.
I	Treatment services are contracted, but no other formal collaborations with providers.
J	Treatment provided directly by or contracted through PR's Administration for Mental Health and Substance Abuse.
K	Formal MOUs and contracts with treatment providers; informal collaborations with other service providers.
L	Contract with local addiction recovery center for drug abuse treatment. There are no MOUs or formal relationships with other providers.
M	Contract with Agency for Community Treatment Services.
N	Formal collaboration with substance abuse treatment. Informal collaborations with other providers on as needed basis.

Communication, in the sense of getting information about changes in the drug court program process, appears to occur informally. Site visitors typically did not provide yes/no answers to this question, in part because many did not have the opportunity to interview providers other than drug treatment providers. With one known exception, drug court programs may also have been relatively static. Informality, or communication "as needed," appears to characterize the transmission of information. Although meetings provide a somewhat more formal vehicle at some sites, it is not clear whether communication is sufficient from the perspective of the providers.

Answers to this probe may also reflect more heavily the perspectives of drug court team members and perhaps drug treatment staff than other service providers, given that site visitors had fewer opportunities to speak with other providers. Based on the responses summarized above, most providers appear to be receiving sufficient information about offenders, but there may be obstacles including lack of efficiency and regularity. Drug court H, a program reported to have formal collaborations

Table 4   Characteristics of linkages with health service providers: Do collaborating agencies know when changes in drug court occur?

Site	
A	Treatment staff know because they are on site.
B	Monthly meeting of all drug court players where changes are discussed and agreed upon.
C	DC has newsletter for treatment providers.
D	Monthly meeting of all drug court players where changes are discussed and agreed upon.
E	Weekly staff meetings where information is disseminated.
F	Treatment coordinator works closely with drug court and receives necessary information.
G	No formal channels of communication to providers.
H	Drug court coordinator keeps information and shares it "when needed."
I	Informal discussion. Drug court coordinator keeps information and shares it "when needed."
J	TASC and probation case managers communicate information when needed.
K	Changes must be discussed in and approved by oversight committee that includes all key players and agencies.
L	Inconclusive.
M	Weekly meetings are major means of communication.
N	Attendance at drug court sessions, regular meetings, and written communication.

with all of its providers, appears to share information only sparingly in an effort to protect the confidentiality of clients.

In an era where management information systems are critical to effective information sharing, few of the drug courts have sufficient resources in this regard. Some programs have systems that serve on-site needs; some programs have no MIS. There was no evidence of any programs having systems that are networked to other providers and that can provide relevant agencies with immediate access to client information.

This general reflection on the state of collaboration reveals inconsistency across programs, with about half of the agencies reporting that the current drug court system serves their agencies well. Answers to this probe no doubt also reflect that site visitors had fewer opportunities to speak to individuals other than drug court staff and substance abuse treatment providers.

Comment

Drug court programs had proposed to provide a wide variety of services to offenders in their programs, although determination of the availability, depth, and breadth of these services was not possible in the current

Table 5   Characteristics of linkages with health service providers: Are service providers getting needed information about drug court clients?

Site	
A	Apparently, yes.
B	Better communication about client status is needed between drug treatment counselors and TASC case managers.
C	Inconclusive.
D	No problems reported; case manager and DC coordinator are responsible for interagency communication.
E	Apparently, yes.
F	Yes.
G	Yes, although some reports about need for better communication generally between judge and treatment providers.
H	Information not routinely shared; agencies and DC do not feel it would benefit the client to share assessment or progress information among agencies.
I	No formal means of sharing among DC and treatment providers (incl. acupuncturist). SA treatment provider and DC coordinator report getting adequate info; acupuncturist is probably not.
J	Apparently, yes, through case managers.
K	Apparently, yes, but flow could be quicker.
L	Yes.
M	Not clear, lack of MIS said to be a problem.
N	Not clear, but they do not use their MIS and that could pose a problem.

investigation. With few exceptions, the relationships between drug courts and providers of services to offenders in the fourteen drug courts were characterized by informality. Although informality is not necessarily a negative characteristic and in fact may serve small jurisdictions well, it remains to be seen how such an approach can be maintained in an increasingly complicated era of funding and service provision. To the extent that relationships are well documented and formal, they appear to be occurring with substance abuse treatment providers.

Although a key element of a drug court management information system should be effective connection and integration with existing criminal justice, treatment, public health, and other social service agency information systems, sites' management information systems appeared to be insufficient, sometimes even for meeting site-based needs (Drug Courts Program Office, 1998). This has implications for the timeliness of client information sharing and, thus, clients' access to services and outcomes. Apart from having an MIS, there is also the question of its content. Linkages may be more readily made, and referrals more prompt and appropriate, if the drug court's MIS includes data on a full array of client needs and if the assess-

Table 6   Characteristics of linkages with health service providers: Is there an operational MIS that enables efficient information sharing between CJ and provider (treatment and other) agencies?

Site	
A	Paper reports can be distributed and there are ambitious plans to network the DC organization (incl. onsite tx provider).
B	Yes, and treatment counselors can use it. Complaints of delays in processing time and phone line problems, however.
C	Yes, it is sophisticated and exhaustive.
D	DC administrator does not have an MIS.
E	Very limited MIS that can print out reports with detailed information on clients.
F	MIS can generate paper reports to share and are shared with the treatment coordinator.
G	No central MIS—no computerized sharing of information.
H	No MIS system.
I	MIS system but only paper records can be shared.
J	No.
K	There are separate, nonintegrated MIS systems.
L	Yes, but it is not networked across multiple agencies.
M	No MIS.
N	A nonnetworked database that is not used, lack of personnel to input data.

ment tools are suitably rigorous. Peters et al. (2000) recently evaluated brief substance abuse assessment tools such as the Texas Christian University Drug Screen to identify offenders likely to meet drug dependence criteria and for whom more extensive diagnostic assessment might be needed. To be most useful for the purpose of service linkage, an MIS should also include assessments of other health and social problems characteristic of drug-using offenders. The Addiction Severity Index (McLellan et al., 1992:199–213) measures problem severity in medical, psychiatric, and other domains, as well as drug and alcohol use, and its psychometric properties are well established for criminal justice populations (Peters et al., 2000). Similarly, the Offender Profile Index (Inciardi, McBride, and Weinman, 1993:1–15; McBride and Inciardi, 1993:143–160), designed specifically for drug-using criminal offenders, covers service needs in the domains of family, education, work, housing stability, and HIV risk behavior.

Some ideas can be entertained regarding why these linkages appear, at least based on the present information, to be less solid than would be expected for such an intensive criminal justice and health service endeavor as drug court. Lack of resources may be key; some of these programs subsist on a tenuous foundation of funding. Due to stretched

Table 7   Characteristics of linkages with health service providers: Is the current DC system serving the collaborating agencies well?

Site	
A	Inconclusive, all agencies (treatment) being run by the drug court itself.
B	Not serving treatment provider well, in that better communication about client status is needed.
C	Yes, from the court's perspective.
D	No, because of lack of centralized MIS, and because court has difficulty getting ancillary services arranged (treatment pgms do not want to provide these services)
E	Apparently yes.
F	Yes.
G	All communication b/w treatment and court is mediated by probation officer; alternative suggested of having treatment representative attend meetings in chambers.
H	Not clear.
I	No complaints, except for acupuncturists' wish for more communication.
J	Apparently, yes, through case managers.
K	Apparently, yes.
L	Apparently, yes, through TASC case manager.
M	Lack of MIS said to be a problem; also a treatment provider is acting as a case manager, which seems to be causing conflict with other providers.
N	Not clear, but they do not use their MIS and that could pose a problem.

resources, staff are sometimes performing multiple roles (e.g., a supervising probation officer may be the drug court coordinator, administrator, and case manager). Even if a probation officer serving as a case manager does know or suspect that a client has been physically or sexually assaulted and suffers psychological trauma that interferes with program progress, limited staff time and too few resources will limit any intervention. It was not uncommon for sites to speak regretfully about not having sufficient funding for residential treatment, an FTE case manager devoted to client case management, and nursing staff.

Apart from current resource limitations, there is the additional problem of having no assurance of long-term funding and the disincentive such instability may prove to building bridges. The instabilities and shortages of funding not only make purchase of services and formalization of provider relationships difficult for the short term, there may reasonably be less incentive or capacity for the hard work of developing interagency arrangements when the very future of the drug court is in question. Informal, as-needed contacts in the community may be the best that can be expected in some cases.

Site visitors reported that one of the drug courts did not see a clear benefit to sharing client information with other providers. It is possible that limitations in collaborative linkages—and the importance of strong bridges—may not be fully recognized by all drug court staff, depending on who is running the drug court program and that person's exposure to a broader drug court network such as through participation in national drug court conferences. Drug courts operated through probation departments rather than health and human services agencies, for example, may have different orientations to linkages simply because of their different training backgrounds and experiences. Without sufficient staff training, there is no reason why probation staff should be aware that offenders with drug and alcohol problems may also have histories of physical or sexual abuse and mental health difficulties that should be addressed to enhance prospects of treatment success. Site visitors learned that not all drug court judges or team members participate in the annual meetings sponsored by the National Association of Drug Court Professionals, a principal venue for sharing information about the drug courts across the nation. Recognition and awareness are enabled through information. Evaluation studies are a key in demonstrating the importance of linkages and access, yet such studies are rare. Insufficient evidence that bridge building is effective is a reasonable hindrance to developing these ties.

Also noteworthy is that there may be a tension between the supervisory and rehabilitation objectives of drug courts that may interfere with building bridges and access to services. Some of the drug courts visited were under pressures from various sources to process a large number of cases, in some situations exceeding their capacity. In such circumstances, particularly in a climate of limited resources, a rehabilitation focus and, thus, delivery of a fuller range of services may assume a lower level of priority.

The drug court represents a promising bridge between the traditionally separate criminal justice and health services systems. This study provided a preliminary description of the ties between drug courts and health service providers, a critical topic about which far too little is currently known. The present work has highlighted areas for future research on developing linkages between the criminal justice system (drug courts) and health service providers. Such future work ultimately carries implications for the enhancement of service access and opportunities for successful offender outcomes.

References

Anglin, M. D., & Hser, Y. (1990). Treatment of drug abuse. In M. Tonry & J. Q. Wilson (Eds.), *Drugs and crime* (pp. 393–458). Chicago, IL: University of Chicago Press.

Anglin, M. D., Longshore, D., & Turner, S. (1999). Treatment alternatives to street crime: An evaluation of five programs. *Criminal Justice and Behavior, 26,* 168–195.

Anglin, M. D., Longshore, D., Turner, S., McBride, D., Inciardi, J., & Prendergast, M. (1996). *Studies of the functioning and effectiveness of treatment alternatives to street crime (TASC) programs: Final report to the National Institute on Drug Abuse.* Los Angeles, CA: Drug Abuse Research Center.

Baker, F. (1991). *Coordination of alcohol, drug, mental health services.* Rockville, MD: Alcohol, Drug Abuse, Mental Health Services Administration, Office for Treatment Improvement.

Bazelon, D. L. (1999). *Criminalization of people with mental illness.* Washington, DC: Bazelon Center for Mental Health Law.

Belenko, S. (1998). Research on drug courts: A critical review. *National Drug Court Institute Review, 1*(1), 1–42.

Belenko, S. (1999). Research on drug courts: A critical review, 1999 update. *National Drug Court Institute Review, 2*(2), 1–58.

Bullock, M. L., Kiresuk, T. J., Pheley, A. M., Culliton, P. D., & Lenz, S. K. (1999). Auricular acupuncture in the treatment of cocaine abuse: A study of efficacy and dosing. *Journal of Substance Abuse Treatment, 16*(1), 31–38.

Center for Substance Abuse Treatment (CSAT). (1994). *Practical approaches in the treatment of women who abuse alcohol and other drugs.* Rockville, MD: Center for Substance Abuse Treatment, U.S. Department of Health and Human Services.

Cook, F. (1992). TASC case management models. In R. S. Ashery (Ed.), *Progress and issues in case management* (pp. 368–382). Rockville, MD: National Institute on Drug Abuse (NIDA Monograph 127).

Cooper, C. (1997). *Drug court survey report: Executive summary.* Washington, DC: American University.

Cuffel, B. J. (1996). Comorbid substance use disorder: Prevalence, patterns of use, and course. *New Directions for Mental Health Services, 70,* 93–105.

D'Aunno, T., & Zuckerman, H. S. (1987). The emergence of hospital federations: An integration of perspective from organizational theory. *Medical Care Review, 44,* 323–343.

Deschenes, E. P., & Greenwood, P. W. (1994). Maricopa County's drug court: An innovative program for first-time drug offenders on probation. *Justice System Journal, 17*(1), 99–115.

Donabedian, A. (1980). *Explorations in quality assessment and monitoring: The definition of quality and approaches to its assessment* (Vol. 1). Ann Arbor, MI: Health Administration Press.

Donabedian, A. (1982). *Explorations in quality assessment and monitoring: The definition of quality and approaches to its assessment* (Vol. 2). Ann Arbor, MI: Health Administration Press.

Donabedian, A. (1984). *Explorations in quality assessment and monitoring: The definition of quality and approaches to its assessment* (Vol. 3). Ann Arbor, MI: Health Administration Press.

Donabedian, A. (1988a). Monitoring: The eyes and ears of healthcare. *Health Progress, 69,* 38–43.

Donabedian, A. (1988b). Quality assessment and assurance: Unit of purpose, diversity of means. *Inquiry, 25,* 173–192.

Donabedian, A. (1988c). The quality of care: How can it be assessed? *Journal of the American Medical Association, 260,* 1743–1748.

Drug Courts Program Office. (1997). *Defining drug courts: The key components.* Washington, DC: Office of Justice Programs, U.S. Department of Justice.

Drug Courts Program Office. (1998). *Drug court monitoring, evaluation, and management information systems.* Washington, DC: Office of Justice Programs, U.S. Department of Justice.

Ericksen, K. P., & Trocki, K. F. (1992). Behavioral risk factors for sexually transmitted diseases in American households. *Social Science and Medicine, 34*, 843–853.

Falkin, G. P., Prendergast, M., & Anglin, M. D. (1994). Drug treatment in the criminal justice system. *Federal Probation, 58*(3), 31–36.

Friedman, P. D., Alexander, J. A., & D'Aunno, T. A. (1999). Organizational correlates of access to primary care and mental health services in drug abuse treatment units. *Journal of Substance Abuse Treatment, 19*(1), 71–80.

General Accounting Office (GAO). (1995). *Drug courts: Information on a new approach to address drug-related crime.* Washington, DC: U.S. Government Printing Office.

Gomberg, E. S. L. (1993). Gender issues. *Recent Developments in Alcoholism, 11*, 95–107.

Hammett, T. M., Gaiter, J. L., & Crawford, C. (1998). Researching seriously at-risk populations: Health interventions in criminal justice settings. *Health Education and Behavior, 1*, 99–120.

Healy, K. M. (1999). *Case management in the criminal justice system.* National Institute of Justice. Research in Action (online). Available: http://www.ncjrs.org.

Hora, P. F., Schma, W. G., & Rosenthal, J. T. A. (1999). Therapeutic jurisprudence and the drug treatment court movement: Revolutionizing the criminal justice system's response to drug abuse and crime in America. *Notre Dame Law Review, 74*(2), 439–538.

Hubbard, R. L., Rachal, J. V, Craddock, S. G., & Cavanaugh, E. R. (1984). Treatment outcome prospective study (TOPS): Client characteristics and behaviors before, during and after treatment. In F. M. Tims & J. P. Ludford (Eds.), *Drug abuse treatment evaluation: Strategies, progress, and prospects* – 68). Rockville, MD: National Institute on Drug Abuse (NIDA Research Monograph No. 51).

Inciardi, J. A., McBride, D. C., & Weinman, B. A. (1993). *The offender profile index: A user's guide.* Washington, DC: National Association of State Alcohol and Drug Abuse Directors.

Lamb, S., Greenlick, M. R., & McCarty, D. (Eds.). (1998). *Bridging the gap between practice and research: Forging partnerships with community-based drug and alcohol treatment.* Washington, DC: National Academy of Sciences (Institute of Medicine Report).

Latessa, E. J., & Moon, M. M. (1992). The effectiveness of acupuncture in an outpatient drug treatment program. *Journal of Contemporary Criminal Justice, 8*(4), 317–331.

Leukefeld, C. G., & Tims, F. M. (1992). Directions for practice and research. In C. G. Leukefield & F. M. Tims (Eds.), *The challenge of drug abuse treatment in prisons and jails* – 293). Washington, DC: Government Printing Office (NIDA Research Monograph No. 118. DHHS Publication No. ADM 92-1884).

Leukefield, C., Matthews, T., & Clayton, R. (1992). Treating the drug-abusing offender. *Journal of Mental Health Administration, 19*(1), 76–82.

Lipton, D. S. (1994). The correctional opportunity: Pathways to drug treatment for offenders. *Journal of Drug Issues, 24*(2), 331–348.

Marsden, M. E. (1998). *Organizational structure and the environmental context of drug abuse treatment.* Brandeis University, Waltham, MA. http://www.165.112.78.61: Heller School (Issue paper).

Mathias, R. (1998). Linking medical care with drug abuse treatment stems tuberculosis among HIV-infected drug users. *NIDA Notes, 13*(3).

McBride, D. C., & Inciardi, J. A. (1990). AIDS and the IV drug user in the criminal justice system. *Journal of Drug Issues, 20*, 267–280.

McBride, D. C., & Inciardi, J. A. (1993). The focused offender disposition program: Philosophy, procedures, and preliminary findings. *Journal of Drug Issues, 23*(1), 143–160.

McGlynn, E. A., Norquist, G. S., Wells, K. B., Sullivan, G., & Liberman, R. P. (1988). Quality-of-care research in mental health: Responding to the challenge. *Inquiry, 25*, 157–170.

McLellan, A. T., Alterman, A. I., Metzger, D. S., Grissom, G., Woody, G., Luborsky, L., and O'Brien, C. P. (1994). Similarity of outcome predictors across opiate cocaine and alcohol treatments: Role of treatment services. *Journal of Clinical and Consulting Psychology, 62*(6), 1141–1158.

McLellan, A. T., Grossman, D. S., Blaine, J. D., & Haverkos, H. W. (1993). Acupuncture treatment for drug use: A technical review. *Journal of Substance Abuse Treatment, 10*(6), 569–576.

McLellan, A. T., Hagan, T. A., Levine, M., Gould, F., Meyers, K., Bencivengo, M., & Durell, J. (1998). Supplemental social services improve outlook in public addiction treatment. *Addiction, 93*(1), 1489–1499.

McLellan, A. T., Kushner, H., Metzger, D., Peters, R. H., Smith, I., Grissom, G., Pettinati, H., & Argeriou, M. (1992). The fifth edition of the addiction severity index. *Journal of Substance Abuse Treatment, 9*, 199–213.

McLellan, A. T., Luborsky, L., Woody, G. E., O'Brien, C. P., & Kron, R. (1981). Are the "addict-related" problems of substance abusers really related? *Journal of Nervous and Mental Disease, 169*, 232–239.

National Association of State Alcohol and Drug Abuse Directors (NASADAD)/National Association of State Mental Health Program Directors (NASMHPD). *Substance abuse and mental health services links with primary care.* Health Resources and Services Administration, Washington, DC: The Bureau of Primary Health Care.

National Institute of Justice (NIJ). (1993). *DUF 1992 annual report.* Washington, DC: Department of Justice.

Office of Justice Program (OJP). (1998). *Looking at a decade of drug courts.* Washington, DC: American University.

Office of National Drug Control Policy (ONDCP). (1999). *National drug control strategy.* Washington, DC: Office of National Drug Control Policy.

Peters, R. H. (1992). Referral and screening for substance abuse treatment in jails. *Journal of Mental Health Administration, 19*(1), 53–75.

Peters, R. H., Greenbaum, P. E., Steinberg, M. L., Carter, C. R., Ortiz, M. M., Fry, B. C., & Valle, S. K. (2000). Effectiveness of screening instruments in detecting substance use disorders among prisoners. *Journal of Substance Abuse Treatment, 18*, 349–358.

Piette, J. D., Fleishman, J. A., Stein, M. D., Mor, V., & Wilson, D. (1993). Perceived needs and unmet needs for formal services among people with HIV disease. *Journal Community Health, 18*(1), 11–23.

Polivka, B. J., Kennedy, C., & Chaudry, R. (1997). Collaboration between local public health and community mental health agencies. *Research in Nursing and Health, 20*(2), 153–160.

Regier, D. A., Farmer, M. E., Rae, D. S., Locke, B. Z., Keith, S. J., Judd, L. L., & Goodwin, F. K. (1990). Comorbidity of mental disorders with alcohol and other drug abuse. *The Journal of the American Medical Association, 264*, 2511–2518.

Rhodes, W., & Gross, M. (1997). *Case management reduces drug use and criminality among drug-involved arrestees: An experimental study of an HIV prevention inter-*

vention. Washington, DC: U.S. Department of Justice, Office of Justice Programs, National Institute of Justice.

Ridgely, M. S., Lambert, D., Goodman, A., Chichester, K., & Ralph, R. (1998). Maine's dual diagnosis collaborative: A model for interagency collaboration in the treatment and support of people with co-occurring mental and substance abuse disorders. *Psychiatric Services, 49,* 236–238.

Schlenger, W. E., Kroutil, L. A., & Roland, E. J. (1992). Case management as a mechanism for linking drug abuse treatment and primary care: Preliminary evidence from the ADAMHA/HRSA Linkage Demonstration. In R. S. Ashery. (Ed.), *Progress and issues in case management* (pp. 316–330). Rockville, MD: National Institute on Drug Abuse (NIDA Monograph 127).

Selwyn, P. A. (1996). The impact of HIV infection on medical services in drug abuse treatment programs. *Journal of Substance Abuse Treatment, 13*(5), 397–410.

Shannon, M. (1998). Drug courts in California. *California Correctional News, 53,* 14–17.

Shwartz, M., Saitz, R., Mulvey, K., & Brannigan, P. (1999). The value of acupuncture detoxification programs in a substance abuse treatment system. *Journal of Substance Abuse Treatment, 17*(4), 305–312.

Siegal, H. A. J., Wang, M. A., Forney, R. S., & Carlson, R. G. (1994). Incarceration and HIV risk behaviors among injection drug users: A Midwestern case study. *Journal of Crime and Justice, 17,* 85–101.

Substance Abuse and Mental Health Services Administration (SAMHSA). (1997). *National treatment improvement evaluation study.* Rockville, MD: Substance Abuse and Mental Health Services Administration.

Taxman, F. (1998). Reducing recidivism through a seamless system of care: Components of effective treatment, supervision, and transition services in the community. Unpublished report to the Office of National Drug Control Policy, Treatment and Criminal Justice System Conference.

Tewksbury, R. A., Vito, G. F., & Cummings, S. B. (1998). Injection drug users and HIV risk behaviors: The criminal justice professionals' role in identifying and responding to multi-faceted risk behaviors. *Journal of Crime and Justice, 21*(1), 1–23.

Turner, S. (1998). *Drug court evaluation II: An assessment of 14 programs.* [A National Institute of Justice Sponsored Study, Grant #98-DC-VX-K003].

Umbricht-Schneiter, A., Ginn, D. H., Pabst, K. M., & Bigelow, G. E. (1994). Providing medical care to Methadone clinic patients: Referral vs. on-site care. *American Journal of Public Health, 84*(2), 207–210.

Vigdal, G. L. (1995). *Planning for alcohol and other drug abuse treatment for adults in the criminal justice system.* Rockville, MD: U.S. Department of Health and Human Services (CSAT TIP Series 17).

Vito, G. F., & Tewksbury, R. A. (1998). The impact of treatment: The Jefferson County (Kentucky) Drug Court Program. *Federal Probation, 62*(2), 46–51.

Wenzel, S., Gelberg, L., Koegel, P., & Leake, B. (2000). Antecedents of physical and sexual victimization among homeless women: A comparison to homeless men. *American Journal of Community Psychology, 28,* 367–390.

Wenzel, S. L. (1999). *Collaborative linkages: Drug courts and service providers.* Rockville, MD: National Institute on Drug Abuse (R01-DA130997-01).

Wenzel, S. L., Kosofsky, B. E., Harvey, J. A., Iguchi, M. Y, Steinberg, P., Watkins, K. E., et al. (in press). *Prenatal substance exposure: Scientific considerations and pol-*

icy implications. A New York Academy of Sciences/RAND report. New York: New York Academy of Sciences. Available online at http://www. nyas.org.

Widman, M., Platt, J. J., Marlowe, D., Lidz, V., Mathis, D. A., & Metzger, D. S. (1997). Patterns of service use and treatment involvement of Methadone maintenance patients. *Journal of Substance Abuse Treatment, 14*(1), 29–35.

Woodward, A., Epstein, J., Gfroerer, J., Melnick, D., Thoreson, R., & Wilson, D. (1997). The drug abuse treatment gap: Recent estimates. *Health Care Financing Review, 18*(3), 5–17.

Chapter 6

Addicted to the Drug War
The Role of Civil Asset Forfeiture as a Budgetary Necessity in Contemporary Law Enforcement

John L. Worrall

Introduction

Civil asset forfeiture allows for the seizure and forfeiture of property derived from or used to facilitate certain crimes (Kessler, 1993). It is used in a number of criminal contexts, but is largely designed to weaken the economic foundations of the illicit drug trade and assist law enforcement in reducing drug-related crime (Department of Justice, 1994a). There are literally hundreds of state and federal statutes (e.g., President's Commission on Model State Drug Laws, 1993) that authorize the seizure of assets linked to drug offenses (not to mention other types of crime), and courts have consistently ruled that such statutes are constitutional, but civil asset forfeiture continues to be one of the most controversial weapons in the drug war arsenal (Morganthau and Katel, 1990; Pratt and Peterson, 1991; Wisotsky, 1991).

One reason that civil asset forfeiture is controversial is that, depending on the forum in which forfeiture proceedings are pursued (local, state, or federal), law enforcement officials can share in the proceeds derived from forfeitures (Blumenson and Nilsen, 1998:52; Department of

Reprinted from *Journal of Criminal Justice* Vol. 29, John L. Worrall, "Addicted to the Drug War: The Role of Civil Asset Forfeiture as a Budgetary Necessity in Contemporary Law Enforcement, pp. 171–187, 2001, with permission of Elsevier.

Justice, 1994b). This potential for "profit" in law enforcement, otherwise known as "equitable sharing," has contributed to a near decade-old intellectual and legal battle about the disposition and distribution of forfeited assets (e.g., Atkins and Petterson, 1991; Hawkins and Payne, 1999). The law enforcement view is that forfeited assets should be reserved for law enforcement purposes. Alternatively, critics claim that the police should never view their duties as a means of raising revenue for government agencies (McNamara, 1999; Thomas, 1999; Zalman, 1997).

State and federal laws vary in terms of what, if any, proceeds derived from civil asset forfeiture can be returned to the law enforcement agency (or agencies) that initiated the forfeiture proceeding(s) (Blumenson and Nilsen, 1998:54). This has led to fears that state and local agencies are circumventing state requirements, especially state requirements that prohibit law enforcement officials from sharing in the proceeds derived from civil asset forfeiture (e.g., Levy, 1996). Critics have claimed that the state and local agencies that participate with federal officials in civil forfeiture actions inadvertently contribute to an expanded role of the federal government in crime control, a notion antithetical to the ideals of federalism (Blumenson and Nilsen, 1998).

An interesting issue raised by the potential for law enforcement to receive a "kickback" from forfeiture is the role civil asset forfeiture, particularly equitable sharing, plays as a budgetary supplement. There are at least three ways forfeiture proceeds can be viewed with respect to law enforcement agencies' traditional budgets. One view (perhaps the most common) is that forfeiture proceeds can help to assist law enforcement officials by funding continued drug war activities. Another view is that forfeiture can be seen, more generally, as a fortuitous source of income that helps compensate for budgetary shortfalls. A final, perhaps more insidious view is that law enforcement agencies may be coming to depend on forfeiture in light of the revenue that stands to be earned. The latter, dependence-oriented perspective was the focus of the research reported here.

If the amounts of money and property seized from civil forfeiture were scarce and dispersed, there would hardly be a cause for concern. However, because the proceeds from forfeitures run into the hundreds of millions, if not billions, of dollars annually, the potential for "addiction" is not to be taken lightly. For example, in fiscal year 1996 alone, the Justice Department's Asset Forfeiture Program controlled US$338.1 million dollars, not to mention tens of thousands of pieces of real property. That amount was actually down by nearly US$200 million from the year before (Department of Justice, 1991). During the *height* of the drug war the Asset Forfeiture Program routinely oversaw amounts larger than half a billion dollars each year (Hyde, 1995). And with respect to asset forfeiture activities at the state and local level, one researcher recently found that it is not uncommon for single law enforcement agencies in large counties and municipalities to receive tens of millions of dollars from civil forfeiture during relatively short periods of time (Worrall, 1999).

Clearly, civil asset forfeiture can be a useful alternative source of income for law enforcement agencies, but some supporters have gone so far as to claim that forfeiture can, and even should, *supplant* traditional budgets. For example, the Justice Research and Statistics Association has made the following observation:

> Asset seizures play an important role in the operation of [multijurisdictional drug] task forces. One "big bust" can provide a task force with the resources to become financially independent. Once financially independent, a task force can choose to operate without federal or state assistance. (Justice Research and Statistics Association, 1993:9)

Whether or not this is a suggestion that drug task forces should attempt to fund themselves is unclear, but it is not difficult to see what role pecuniary concerns can play when law enforcement officials aggressively target money and property tied to both alleged and actual criminal activity.

The findings from the Justice Research and Statistics Association's report hardly stand alone. Reports from some US Attorneys' offices have shown seizures equal to as much or all of their operating budgets (Hawk, 1993). According to US Attorney Frederick W. Thieman (Hawk, 1993:7), figures from 1993 demonstrated that ". . . $1.9 million in asset forfeitures . . . [paid] for the operation of the entire US Attorney's Office [of the Western District of Pennsylvania]. . . ." Moreover, in reference to a New York Law Journal article, Blumenson and Nilsen (1998:63) reported that "in an eight month period during 1989 . . . the United States Attorney's office in the Eastern District of New York collected $37,000,000 from civil forfeitures," four times its operating budget. Thus, forfeiture laws have permitted governments to become "full financial partners and participants in the drug business" (Kessler, 1993:1.01). And to the extent that law enforcement agencies come to expect revenue from forfeiture, it is possible that other goals (e.g., service and crime control) are compromised.

In light of the hotly contested nature of civil forfeiture, there have been virtually no empirical studies of civil forfeiture (the lone exception appears to be Warchol and Johnson, 1996). Moreover, the fiscal budgeting perspective on civil forfeiture has been ignored entirely. It would seem that additional *empirical* attention to civil asset forfeiture, especially to the pecuniary concerns associated with the seizure of money and property, would be a worthy pursuit. Research in this area may help allay (or reinforce) some of the widespread fears that civil asset forfeiture laws are being abused by law enforcement officials (e.g., Hyde, 1995; Levy, 1996).

In an attempt to fill the gaps left by previous forfeiture research, this article reports on a nationwide survey of 1400 law enforcement executives concerning their experiences with civil asset forfeiture. Specifically, data were gathered on "adoptive" forfeitures, that is, forfeitures where state and local officials participated with federal officials in order to receive a "cut" of the proceeds; amounts of proceeds received from forfeiture; and perceptions of civil asset forfeiture as a tool for managing fiscal constraints. Since there have been no surveys of law enforcement's experiences with civil asset forfeiture, it is hoped that the results of the survey reported here contribute something more than rhetoric to the debate over civil asset forfeiture, as much of the current concern and criticism is linked to "celebrated" cases (e.g., Hyde, 1995).

This article takes a step beyond mere reporting, however. Evidence is offered that, indeed, a substantial proportion of law enforcement agencies *are* dependent on civil asset forfeiture, that forfeiture is coming to be viewed not only as a budgetary supplement, but as a necessary source of income. Potential explanations for "addiction" to civil asset forfeiture are then introduced. These are based on three primary factors: (1) past experiences with civil asset forfeiture; (2) fiscal expenditures; and (3) state regulations concerning the disposition of forfeited assets to law enforcement agencies and other criminal justice entities. Empirical tests of these explanations—including agency size as a control variable—reveal that dependence on civil asset forfeiture is tied to past forfeiture activities and, to a lesser extent, on fiscal expenditures.

Background:
The Controversy Over Civil Asset Forfeiture

Civil asset forfeiture's supporters hail, not surprisingly, from all arenas of local, state, and federal government. Prosecutors, law enforcement officers, Justice Department officials, even US Presidents, as well as others, have supported civil forfeiture with near unanimous consensus. Supporters have argued that civil forfeiture is an essential law enforcement tool, and that the "war on drugs" will never be won so long as criminals profit from their enterprises (e.g., Asset Forfeiture Office, 1994; Department of Justice, 1990, 1994b, 1995; Drug Enforcement Administration, Strategic Intelligence Division, 1993, 1994; Executive Office for Asset Forfeiture, 1994a, 1994b; General Accounting Office, 1990, 1991, 1992; Myers and Brzostowski, 1982). As the President's Commission on Model State Drug Laws (1993:A-29) remarked, forfeiture serves three remedial goals: it "(1) removes financial incentive to engage in illegal activity; (2) restores economic integrity to the marketplace; and (3) compensates society for economic damages suffered due to illegal activity by rededicating forfeited property to socially beneficial uses."[1]

Of course, civil asset forfeiture has just as many, if not more, critics (e.g., NACDL, 1996; Rudnick, 1992). The practice has been attacked by an unlikely coalition of critics, including conservative politicians. Critics have sensationalized the "drug war's hidden economic agenda" (Blumenson and Nilsen, 1997), referring to the means by which forfeiture annihilates due process (Jensen and Gerber, 1996) and encourages egregious law enforcement blunders (Hyde, 1995). Critics have also maintained that civil forfeiture tramples the Bill of Rights, circumvents proper appropriations channels, threatens the freedom of law abiding citizens, and guarantees a conflict of interest between crime control and fiscal management (Levy, 1996).

Both sides have been extremely vocal on the subject of civil forfeiture, but the voices of critics have almost drowned out the competition (e.g., Bauman, 1995; Burnham, 1996; Chapman, 1993; Enders, 1993; Greenburg, 1995; Rosenburg, 1988). In addition to criticisms of equitable sharing, which I address later, the critics have attacked civil forfeiture for its allegedly "perverted procedures" (Hyde, 1995). These procedural matters deserve special consideration.

Procedural Controversies

Civil asset forfeiture should be distinguished from criminal forfeiture. Criminal forfeiture proceedings are in personam, which means they target criminal defendants. Criminal forfeiture proceedings "are implemented in conjunction with the criminal prosecution of a defendant" (Warchol, Payne, and Johnson, 1996:53–54), and criminal forfeiture can only follow a criminal conviction. Moreover, criminal forfeiture is not to be confused with restitution or fines as potential penalties for criminal conduct. Civil forfeiture proceedings, on the contrary, are in rem proceedings, meaning that they target *property*. Civil forfeiture does not require that formal adversarial proceedings be initiated, and the property owner's guilt or innocence is largely irrelevant.

Civil asset forfeiture can be traced to an "archaic and curious legal fiction that personifies property" (Hyde, 1995:17). The personification of property originated in biblical times with deodands, which were things "forfeited, presumably to God for the good of the community, but in reality to the English crown" (Levy, 1996:7). If, for example, an inanimate object was responsible for a person's death, then the object was held in forfeit—as a deodand—in response to the superstition that the victim's soul would not rest until the object was accused and subsequently atoned. The Supreme Court has stated:

> Traditionally, forfeiture actions have proceeded upon the fiction that the inanimate objects themselves can be guilty of wrongdoing. Simply put, the theory has been that if the object is "guilty," it should be held forfeit. In the words of a medieval English writer, "Where a man killeth another with the sword of John at Stile, the sword shall be forfeit as deodand, and yet no default is in the owner." The modern forfeiture

statutes are the direct descendants of this heritage. (*United States v. United States Coin and Currency*, 1971)

The notion that property can be "animate" and somehow responsible for wrongdoing is manifested in administrative and civil judicial proceedings where the government essentially sues property. Consider the names of the parties in two representative cases: *United States v. One Mercedes 560 SEL* (1990) and *United States v. One Parcel of Land at 508 Depot Street* (1992). This is important because the in rem proceeding is what ignites civil asset forfeiture's critics. In rem proceedings are sometimes controversial because they can shift the burden of proof from the state to the property owner (Durking, 1990; Petrou, 1984). Such proceedings can require the property owner to demonstrate, among other things, that the property was not used to facilitate a crime, nor that it was derived from the proceeds of criminal activity.

Asset forfeiture has also been criticized because law enforcement officials often need only demonstrate probable cause that the property is subject to forfeiture, not proof beyond a reasonable doubt as in criminal cases. And as Yoskowitz (1992:575) has pointed out, "as a practical matter, the government usually meets the initial burden of proof of probable cause simply by filing a verified complaint." The courts have allowed the government to use hearsay, circumstantial evidence, tips from anonymous informants (*United States v. All Funds on Deposit or Any Accounts Maintained at Merrill Lynch*, 1992) or information that is obtained *after* the seizure to establish probable cause in hindsight, *even if the initial seizure was illegal* (Yoskowitz, 1992, emphasis added; see also *United States v. One 56-Foot Yacht Named Tahuna*, 1983; *United States v. One 1977 Mercedes-Benz 450 SEL, 1983*).

Civil forfeiture's critics also contend that the law is equivocal about what is subject to forfeiture. Federal civil forfeiture law provides for the forfeiture of property that "facilitated" a drug crime; however, there is not always a clear indication of what constitutes facilitation (e.g., Heilbroner, 1994; *US v. Real Property Located at 6625 Zumirez Drive*, 1994). Moreover, the growing scope of civil forfeiture laws has raised many questions. Federal civil forfeiture laws have evolved from a focus on property to money and, more recently, to all real property.[2] Burnham (1996) has criticized these legislative changes, claiming that law enforcement officials can justify seizures without demonstrating that the property in question is clearly linked to criminal activity.

The legislative progression does not stop with addition of real property, however. Hyde (1995:25) has pointed out that the offenses subject to forfeiture are also growing in number:

> The 1986 Anti-Drug Abuse Act expanded civil forfeiture to include the proceeds of money-laundering activity. Certain 1990 amendments to that act included proceeds traceable to counterfeiting and other offens-

es affecting financial institutions — a bow to the savings and loan scandals. Then in 1992 Congress added more categories of offenses and also covered proceeds traceable to motor vehicle theft.

This broadening progression of federal forfeiture law says nothing about state forfeiture laws. And to the chagrin of the critics, some cases seem to suggest that state laws allow authorities more latitude with forfeiture (e.g., *Bennis v. Michigan*, 1996).

The remedial options for individuals whose property is subject to forfeiture are sometimes problematic as well; all the weight of the justice system can be stacked against property owners (Goldsmith and Linderman, 1989; Kasten, 1991). Sometimes it is "... up to the owner to challenge the seizure in a costly and unpromising hearing" (Blumenson and Nilsen, 1997:47). Thus, in cases where the forfeited property is not very valuable, the owner may have to make a cost/benefit decision, grudgingly conceding that it is best to "let the property go" (Edwards, 1994; Yoskowitz, 1992) because attorney fees can be too costly. As might be expected, the majority of forfeitures go unchallenged (General Accounting Office, 1989).

Forfeiture at the federal level has also been criticized because property owners are allowed less than 2 weeks to file a claim in federal court to challenge a forfeiture, and, until recently, they were required to post a 10 percent cash bond based on the value of the property simply to have their day in court (Hyde, 1995). Furthermore, the government has not always been liable for damage, storage, and maintenance costs while property is in its possession (Hyde, 1995).

Civil forfeiture has also been problematic for innocent owners, again because the owner's guilt or innocence does not matter (see *Bennis v. Michigan*, 1996; Canavan, 1990; O'Brien, 1991; Saltzburg, 1992; Stahl, 1992; Zeldon and Weiner, 1991). If innocent owners can muster the resources to challenge the seizure of their property, they can sometimes raise a successful innocent owner defense. According to 21 U.S.C. § 881(a)(7), property cannot be forfeited if the criminal activity at issue was "committed ... without the knowledge or consent of [the] owner" (e.g., *United States v. Bajakajian*, 1998). However, there is no such protection in the some 200 civil forfeiture statutes at the state level (Levy, 1996), although there are some exceptions. "The federal courts simply have not clearly or uniformly explained the innocent owner defense, and Congress has not intervened to settle the matter" (Levy, 1996:164). In addition, the innocent owner defense is only relevant if the forfeiture is challenged.

Still other questions have been raised concerning the propriety of civil asset forfeiture, including the so-called relation-back doctrine (Jankowski, 1990). The relation-back doctrine is embodied in 21 U.S.C. § 881(h) and provides that "all right, title and interest in property [subject to forfeiture] shall vest in the United States upon commission of the act giving rise to forfeiture" (e.g., *United States v. 92 Buena Vista Ave., Rumson*, 1993). Still other concerns have been raised about the significance of the Fourth Amendment in civil forfeiture activities (Nelson, 1992; Speta, 1990).

One of the most controversial aspects of civil asset forfeiture is, of course, equitable sharing. Many observers have become concerned that the profit motive is winning out over the nobler goal of crime control (Dortch, 1992; Shaw, 1990; Willson, 1990).

The Civil Asset Forfeiture Reform Act of 2000

As this article was under review, the Civil Asset Forfeiture Reform Act of 2000 (CAFRA) was signed into law by the President Clinton. This was a significant victory for civil asset forfeiture's critics. Among other things, the new legislation shifts the burden of proof in federal forfeiture proceedings from the property owner to the state, eliminates the cost bond requirement, provides for reasonable attorney's fees for property owners who prevail in forfeiture proceedings, and creates a uniform innocent owner defense for all federal forfeiture proceedings.

The new legislation certainly minimizes the procedural controversies associated with civil asset forfeiture. Unfortunately, however, CAFRA is binding only on the federal government. States can decide themselves whether or not to follow the procedures outlined in CAFRA or change their own laws. In addition, and more importantly still, CAFRA does nothing to change the law pertaining to equitable sharing. That is, the potential for law enforcement to profit remains unchanged. This controversial feature of civil asset forfeiture is the primary focus of the remainder of this article.

Potential Explanations for "Addiction"

The foregoing has illustrated some of the controversies and problems inherent with civil asset forfeiture. Much of the extant literature seems to suggest that pecuniary concerns can motivate forfeiture activities. This raises at least two questions. First, is law enforcement coming to depend on civil asset forfeiture? Second, to the extent "addiction" is present, what explains this state of affairs? It has already been indicated that the former question will be answered in the affirmative. First, however, potential explanations for the "addiction" are reviewed, as these were incorporated into the multivariate models of "addiction" reported below.

To its critics, civil asset forfeiture is particularly loathsome because the agencies participating in forfeitures can also share in the proceeds. Prior to the Comprehensive Crime Control Act of 1984, the profits from *federal* civil asset forfeitures were deposited in the general fund of the US Treasury. Nowadays, at least at the federal level, the money goes to the Justice Department's Asset Forfeiture Fund and to the Treasury Department's Forfeiture Fund [see 28 U.S.C. § 524(c)(4) (1988 and Supp. IV

1992)]. "The money is then supposed to be used for forfeiture-related expenses and general 'law enforcement purposes,' with no further necessity for congressional appropriations or authorization" (Hyde, 1995:30).

The "equitable sharing" provision of the Comprehensive Crime Control Act of 1984 allows federal agencies to divide the proceeds derived from civil forfeitures with all participating agencies. State laws vary as to whether they return seized assets to participating agencies, but under federal law, participating nonfederal agencies are entitled to a (legal) "kickback" that is currently 80 percent (Executive Office for Asset Forfeiture, 1994a). One of civil forfeiture's most ardent critics has made this observation:

> Nothing revolutionized forfeiture in this country as much as equitable sharing. Its impact has been enormous, because it provides an intense incentive for law enforcement agencies at the state and local levels to search for assets connected with crime and to seize them for forfeiture. The incentive is self-aggrandizement: what the police take they will likely get to keep for their departments under federal law. (Levy, 1996:147)

The potentials for abuse and conflict-of-interest are obvious — equitable sharing not only provides an attractive budgetary supplement, but it encourages the circumvention of state forfeiture laws, thereby expanding the jurisdiction of federal law enforcement officials (Blumenson and Nilsen, 1997). This technique of "federalizing" forfeitures, or giving them up for "adoption" (also known as adoptive forfeitures) has been the target of numerous legislative reform proposals (e.g., Hyde, 1995).

Thus, it is reasonable to assume that increased participation in adoptive forfeitures could be tied to a dependence on civil asset forfeiture. According to Blumenson and Nilsen (1998:51), "at a time when state and local government budgets are shrinking, equitable sharing offers a new source of income, limited only by the energy police and prosecutors are willing to commit to seizing assets." In short, it was predicted that *the incidence of federalized seizures would be positively associated with "addiction."*

Second, in cases where state and local law enforcement officials do not (or cannot) give up forfeiture cases for "adoption," there is still a potential to share in the proceeds derived from forfeiture. As pointed out earlier, state law varies in terms of what percentage of forfeiture proceeds (if any) can go to law enforcement. At least three varieties of state laws are favorable to law enforcement. Each of these are reviewed in detail below (and in appendix A), but for now suffice it to say that state laws governing the distribution of forfeited assets can be expected to related to dependence on forfeiture. For example, some states allow more than 80 percent of the proceeds derived from civil forfeiture to go to law enforcement. Other state legal requirements, found in states that require proceeds to go into the general fund, are less likely to contribute to the growing dependence on civil asset forfeiture. Thus, it was predicted that *state laws authorizing a substantial proportion of civil forfeiture proceeds to go to law enforcement will be associated with "addiction."*

Third, in light of the observations by Hawk (1993) and others that forfeiture can be used to augment, even supplant fiscal budgets in some instances, it is reasonable to expect that past experiences with forfeiture will also be tied to the potential for "addiction." Accordingly, it was predicted that *the proceeds derived from civil asset forfeiture would be positively associated with dependence on civil forfeiture.* Put another way, as agencies come to receive more money and property from civil forfeiture, the more likely it is that they will come to depend on the practice.

Of course, a measure of total proceeds received excludes, a priori, those agencies that are prohibited by state law from sharing in the proceeds obtained from forfeitures. Moreover, just because an agency does not receive forfeiture proceeds does not mean that the potential for "addiction" will be absent. Some law enforcement agencies never receive forfeiture funds but are nonetheless aggressive in seizing money and property. The sheer incidence of attempted forfeitures (i.e., seizures), therefore, can be expected to serve as a useful predictor of "addiction" to civil asset forfeiture. Accordingly, it was predicted that *the incidence of seizures (whether or not money was actually returned to the participating agency) would be positively associated with "addiction."*

Fifth, it was predicted that fiscal expenditures will be inversely related to "addiction." Blumenson and Nilsen (1998:40) have observed that "during the past decade, law enforcement agencies increasingly have turned to asset seizures and drug enforcement grants to compensate for budgetary shortfalls, at the expense of other criminal justice goals." Thus, it is reasonable to expect that agencies with limited or restricted budgets will come to rely on civil forfeiture more than agencies that are better off, at least insofar as Blumenson and Nilsen's (1998) observations are accurate. Either way, the research reported here predicted that *law enforcement agencies with a "fiscal advantage" over other agencies would be less reliant on civil asset forfeiture as a means to compensate for budgetary shortfalls.*

Finally, it is reasonable to expect that *agency size is associated with dependence on civil asset forfeiture,* although there is no theoretical justification for specifying the directionality of such a relationship. It could be that large agencies enjoy large budgets, thereby reducing the need for civil forfeiture. Alternatively, large agencies could be those most in need of supplementary income to finance drug task forces, narcotics squads, and the like. More likely is the latter perspective; large agencies are, on average, confronted with more serious crime problems, and must occasionally be creative and innovative in their endeavors to combat illegal activity. Agency size is thus an important variable that deserves to be included in any model of "addiction" to civil asset forfeiture.

Methods

This article has two interrelated goals. The first goal of this article is to offer evidence that a substantial proportion of law enforcement agencies is dependent on civil asset forfeiture. The second goal is to offer an explanation for this phenomenon. Accordingly, this section describes the sources of data, variables, and statistical techniques used to reach the conclusions that many law enforcement agencies are dependent on civil asset forfeiture and that the dependence is tied to past forfeiture activities and fiscal expenditures.

Sources of Data

Three data sources were used in the analysis reported here. The first data set was obtained from a national survey of law enforcement agencies conducted in 1998. The second source of data was actually several subsources, namely the various civil and criminal codes of the 50 states and the District of Columbia. The third source of data was the Law Enforcement Management and Administrative Statistics (LEMAS) data set for 1993, the most recent year for which data are publicly available. Data from these latter two sources were merged into the 1998 *Policing Issues Survey* data set.

Policing Issues Survey

Under the auspices of the Division of Governmental Studies and Services at Washington State University, a survey was sent to 1400 police executives and county sheriff's nationwide during 1998.[3] The population for the survey was all municipal police departments and county sheriff's executives appearing in the 1998 *National Directory of Law Enforcement Administrators*. Two survey samples were drawn from that source. One was a sample of 700 police agencies employing more than 100 full-time sworn officers/deputies. This first sample attempted to reach *all* agencies with more than 100 officers/deputies, and was patterned after the sample collected in the 1993 LEMAS survey conducted by the Bureau of Justice Statistics. The second sample was of all the municipal police agencies and county sheriff's agencies appearing in the *National Directory* that employed *less than* 100 full-time sworn officers. The second sample was stratified random based on the type of agency (municipal police, county sheriff), size of population served, and number of sworn officers/deputies. Both samples were chosen so that they could be merged with both the LEMAS sample and the *Policing Issues Survey* sample.

The civil asset forfeiture section of the *Policing Issues Survey* asked a series of questions. Municipal police chiefs and county sheriffs were asked several forfeiture-related questions, three of which are pertinent to the research reported here:

1. Of the total number of times in the *previous three years* that your agency seized money or goods through civil forfeiture, on how many separate occasions did federal agencies act in conjunction with your agency?;

2. Please enter the estimated value of money and goods received by your agency during the *previous three years* from civil forfeitures; and

3. Please provide your reaction to the following statement by checking the appropriate response: Civil forfeiture is necessary as a budgetary supplement for my agency.

The responses available for the latter question were "strongly agree," "agree," "neutral," "disagree," and "strongly disagree."[4]

Overall, the survey response rate was 55 percent (770 of 1400 agencies responding). The response rate for large agencies was 60 percent (417 of 700 agencies responding) and the response rate for the small agencies was 50 percent. A probable reason for the low response rate among small agencies was that many small agencies do not have the resources and/or personnel available to complete the survey. Other potential reasons for the overall 55 percent response rate were that the survey took some time to complete and that the questions asked were somewhat sensitive.

After comparing the characteristics of respondents with nonrespondents, it was determined that there was some nonresponse bias. To probe nonresponse bias, particularly regional nonresponse, the author calculated two logistic regression models with response/nonresponse as a dependent variable. The first model included both agency size and population size as independent variables. This first model was unable to predict nonresponse (the model was no improvement over a model with all coefficients equal to zero). The author then calculated a second logistic regression model, this time including the four main census regions (Northeast, Midwest, South, and West). These were coded as three separate dummy variables. This second model was a significant improvement over the model without region as an independent variable, that is, it was able to predict nonresponse. The author coded the Southern Census region as the reference category and found that, relative to Southern agencies, Midwestern and Western agencies were more likely to respond to the *Policing Issues Survey*. This could have been due to the location of the author's university, but this is nothing more than speculation. Accordingly, readers should be aware that there was *some* nonresponse bias in the results reported below.

State Forfeiture Laws

As indicated in the literature, varieties of state laws governing the disposition and distribution of forfeited assets are believed to be of particular relevance to the apparent dependence on civil asset forfeiture.

Accordingly, the author reviewed the relevant statutory provisions for each of the 50 states and the District of Columbia (see appendix A).

It was predicted that the statutory provisions that were most favorable to law enforcement would be the most likely to contribute to dependence on civil asset forfeiture. The author categorized state forfeiture laws in 11 different ways (see appendix A for the categorization and relevant statutory citations). However, the three types of law governing the disposition and distribution of forfeited assets that were expected to contribute to "addiction" were as follows: (1) state laws where 80 percent or more of the proceeds go to law enforcement; (2) state laws that permit agencies to share in forfeiture proceeds based on their contribution; and (3) state laws that specify that forfeiture proceeds go into a crime control fund (e.g., a drug awareness and education fund).

There are various reasons why law enforcement stands to benefit from the three legal arrangements selected for analysis. The first category was chosen because there is arguably less of an incentive to pursue adoptive forfeitures (forfeitures with federal officials), especially if close to 100 percent of the proceeds can be returned to law enforcement. Concerning the second category, state laws that permit agencies to share forfeiture proceeds based on their contribution also have a potential to be rewarding, especially if only one agency initiates forfeiture proceedings. Finally, even though state laws that require forfeiture proceeds to go into a crime control fund do not benefit participating agencies *directly*, such legal arrangement still benefit law enforcement overall (especially when the revenue is used to fund programs such as DARE).

Law Enforcement Management and Administrative Statistics

The third source of data used in the analysis was the LEMAS survey. One variable from the LEMAS data set believed to have a bearing on dependence on civil asset forfeiture concerned total fiscal expenditures. As indicated, the author predicted that total fiscal expenditures will be inversely related to dependence on civil asset forfeiture. Another important LEMAS variable included in the analysis was agency size. The LEMAS data set contains one variable for the average number of sworn officers/deputies that was also used in the analysis, although primarily as a control variable.

It was possible to use the LEMAS data set because the *Policing Issues Survey* sample was patterned after the LEMAS sample. Unfortunately, the most recent publicly archived LEMAS data set is for 1993. The 1997 data are currently being compiled, and, as of this writing, are not available. Nevertheless, it is reasonable to assume that the fiscal expenditures figures reported in 1993 compared to those reported in 1997 are highly correlated. There is no way to know this for sure as of this writing, so the use of 1993 LEMAS data should be acknowledged as a potential limitation of the research reported here.

Variables and Coding

The *Policing Issues Survey* was used to measure the dependent variable (dependence on forfeiture) and two independent variables (incidence of federalized forfeitures and amounts received). Additional variables were measured from the two alternative data sources (state laws and LEMAS), all of which were merged with the *Policing Issues Survey* data set. The analysis of state laws was conducted in order to find state laws most conducive to dependence on civil asset forfeiture. The LEMAS survey was used to measure total fiscal expenditures and agency size.

The dependent variable, dependence on civil asset forfeiture, was coded on a five-point ordinal scale. This corresponds to the five potential responses to the statement: "Civil forfeiture is necessary as a budgetary supplement for my agency." (The ordered responses to this statement appear in table 1 in the Results section.) In terms of the multivariate model of dependence on civil asset forfeiture, a logistic regression model capable of dealing with ordered dependent variable responses was employed. (The results for this model appear in table 4.)

The independent variables were coded in two primary ways. First, the three categories of state laws (80 percent or more of proceeds to law enforcement; proceeds into a crime control fund; and sharing based on contribution) were coded as three separate dummy variables. The presence of one or other of these legal arrangements was coded with a one; zero served as the reference category.

Table 1 Responses to statement: "Civil forfeiture is necessary as a budgetary supplement"

	Large Agencies			Small Agencies		
	Frequencies	Percent	Cumulative	Frequencies	Percent	Cumulative
Strongly disagree[a]	63	16.45	16.45	50	15.97	15.97
Disagree	65	16.97	33.42	71	22.68	38.66
Neutral	79	20.63	54.05	94	30.03	68.69
Agree	77	20.10	74.15	46	14.70	83.39
Strongly agree	99	25.85	100.00	52	16.61	100.00
Total	383[b]	100.00	—	313[b]	100.00	—

[a] Pearson's chi-square = 17.8111; P = .001. Rows and columns are independent at the .001 level of significance.

[b] Total number of responses with complete data (out of 417 large agencies and 353 small agencies).

All of the remaining independent variables were coded as continuous variables. The incidence of total seizures and the incidence of federalized seizures were count outcomes. Both included the incidence of total and federalized seizures for the past 3 years. The total forfeiture proceeds variable was measured by amounts in dollars and included the incidence of federalized seizures for the past 3 years. The total fiscal expenditure was measured in the same way — total amounts in dollars for fiscal year 1993. Finally, department size was a continuous variable representing the average number of sworn personnel in each of the responding agencies.

Results

The results of the analysis were summarized for presentation in three ways. First, evidence is offered that a substantial proportion of law enforcement executives is "addicted" to civil asset forfeiture. Second, the independent variables used to explain the "addiction" were summarized. Finally, a multivariate model of dependence on civil asset forfeiture is reported. This section concludes with a discussion of potential problems posed by multicollinearity in the multivariate analysis.

Addicted to the Drug War

Table 1 reports on law enforcement executives' perceptions of civil forfeiture as a *necessary* budgetary supplement. Fully 176 law enforcement supervisors agreed or strongly agreed that civil forfeiture is necessary as a budgetary supplement, almost 40 percent of all the responding agencies.

Table 1 also suggests that small law enforcement agencies are less likely to depend on civil asset forfeiture. Just over 31 percent of the small agencies agreed or strongly agreed that civil forfeiture is necessary as a budgetary supplement. Even so, whether the focus is on large or small agencies, an "addiction" is still apparent.

In short, a substantial proportion of law enforcement agencies reported that they are coming to *depend* on civil forfeiture. Such a finding gives some support to criticisms that pecuniary concerns may be motivating law enforcement to forfeit money and property tied to criminal activity. To the extent that most of the response were truthful, this represents a potential conflict of interest, seemingly confirming forfeiture critics' worst fears.

Summary Statistics:
State Law, Forfeiture Activities, and Fiscal Expenditures

Table 2 summarizes the three varieties of state laws used in the analysis. The frequencies reported in table 2 are, again, for individual agencies. For example, 68 of the large agencies that responded were from states where forfeiture laws allowed a substantial proportion of forfeiture proceeds to go to law enforcement, a proportion equal to or greater than that which could be obtained by participating with federal officials in civil forfeiture actions. Only 11 agencies in the large agency sample

Table 2   Prevalence of selected state laws governing the distribution of forfeited assets

	Large Agencies		Small Agencies	
	Frequencies	**Percent**	**Frequencies**	**Percent**
Eighty percent or more to law enforcement[a]				
No	345	83.54	272	77.27
Yes	68	16.46	80	22.73
Total[b]	413	100.00	352	100.00
Proceeds into crime control fund[c]				
No	402	97.34	337	95.74
Yes	11	2.66	15	4.26
Total	413	100.00	352	100.00
Distribution based on contribution[d]				
No	360	87.17	312	88.64
Yes	53	12.83	40	11.36
Total	413	100.00	352	100.00

[a] Two-way Pearson's chi-square = 4.7055; $P = .030$. Rows and columns are independent at the .030 level of significance.

[b] Total refers to the number of responses with complete data (out of 417 large agencies and 353 small agencies).

[c] Two-way Pearson's chi-square = 1.4625; $P = .227$. Rows and columns are not significantly independent.

[d] Two-way Pearson's chi-square = 0.3997; $P = .527$. Rows and columns are not significantly independent.

were from states that require that forfeiture proceeds go into a crime control fund. Other agencies were able to receive forfeiture proceeds based on their contribution, but most common among the state laws governing the distribution of forfeited assets was the provision that 80 percent or more of the proceeds go to law enforcement.

A cursory examination of table 2 suggests that there are no *significant* differences in state law by agency size. This is understandable, since the data reported in table 2 are actually state-level data, specifically state laws governing the distribution of forfeited assets. Any number of large and small agencies can be found in each state throughout the union.

Table 3 reports on agency forfeiture activities and fiscal expenditures, specifically the incidence of federalized seizures, total proceeds received, and total fiscal expenditures. These were the other three independent variables believed to influence agencies' dependence on civil asset forfeiture. Because these three variables are continuous, averages are reported instead of frequencies. Additionally, table 3 includes minimums and maximums for each of the three variables.

Table 3   Agency forfeiture activities and fiscal expenditures[a]

Size/Federalized Seizures and Dollar Amount	Obs.[b]	Mean	S.D.	Min.	Max.
Large agencies					
Number of total seizures	413	179	390	0	4500
Number of federalized seizures	349	45	177	0	3000
Total proceeds received (US$)	294	886,838	3,511,927	0	45,000,000
Total expenditures	413	3.06E+07	9.90E+07	129,742	1.70E+09
Small agencies					
Number of total seizures	352	18[c]	30	0	300
Number of federalized seizures	297	2[d]	5	0	60
Total proceeds received (US$)	255	21,697[e]	52,998	0	410,000
Total expenditures	352	2.95E+07[f]	5.33E+08	4800	1.00E+ 10

[a] The figures reported in this table are rounded off to the nearest whole number.

[b] "Obs." refers to observations, the number of cases with complete data for this variable. Observations reported are out of 417 large agencies and 353 small agencies that responded to the *Policing Issues Survey*.

[c] $t = -7.7638$; $P < .0000$. Small agencies participated in fewer total seizures than large agencies.

[d] $t = -4.1299$; $P < .0000$. Small agencies participated in fewer federalized seizures than large agencies.

[e] $t = -3.7512$; $P = .0002$. Small agencies received fewer total proceeds than large agencies.

[f] $t = -0.0435$; $P = .9653$. Small agencies' total fiscal expenditures do not differ significantly from large agencies' total fiscal expenditures.

Not surprisingly, the large agencies were more likely to receive forfeiture proceeds than small agencies. The *t* statistic reported in footnote c of table 3 supports this observation; large agencies received approximately US$887,000 from civil forfeiture, whereas small agencies only received an average of approximately US$22,000. Much the same relationships held for the incidence of federalized seizures and total fiscal expenditures. On average, large agencies were more likely to participate in federalized seizures than small agencies. They also reported greater fiscal expenditures than small agencies.

Though not reported in table 3, the mean size of the large agencies was 526 with a standard deviation of 1673.56. The low-end cutoff for large agencies was, of course, 100 sworn officers/deputies, but the largest of the agencies in the large agency sample was 31,000. The mean size of the small agencies was 22 with a standard deviation of 22.4. The smallest agency included in the small agency sample employed only one sworn officer/deputy. Agency size is an important control variable introduced in the multivariate model that follows.

Explaining the "Addiction": A Multivariate Approach

Table 4 summarizes the logistic regression models of dependence on civil asset forfeiture. The dependent variable was reported dependence on civil asset forfeiture. The independent variables were those variables believed (based on theory and intuition) to be associated with dependence on civil asset forfeiture.

The results reported in table 4 are simultaneously comforting and disheartening. On the comforting side, the incidence of total seizures and the incidence of federalized seizures were not associated with dependence on civil asset forfeiture. This helps quell critics' (e.g., Blumenson and Nilsen, 1998) fears that federal agencies are meddling in the affairs of state and local law enforcement. Table 4 also suggests that state forfeiture laws have no statistically significant relationship to dependence on civil asset forfeiture. Thus, the law enforcement agencies that stand to benefit from state forfeiture laws are neither less nor more dependent on civil asset forfeiture as a tool to manage fiscal constraints. The relationships were in the hypothesized direction, however.

Table 4   Logistic regression models of dependence on civil asset forfeiture

	Large Agencies (n = 363)[a]		Small Agencies (n = 298)[a]	
	Logit	Odds	Logit	Odds
Total seizures[b]	− 0.0000 (0.004)	0.9999 (0.0004)	0.0041 (0.0051)	1.0041 (0.0051)
Federalized seizures	− 0.0007 (0.0022)	0.9992 (0.0022)	− 0.0077 (0.0174)	0.9923 (0.0172)
Total proceeds received[c]	8.44E − 07**	1.0000**	2.01E − 06**	1.0000**
	(2.51E − 07)	(2.51E − 07)	(5.93E − 07)	(5.93E − 07)
Total fiscal expenditures[c]	− 1.04E − 08 *	1.0000 *	8.05E − 10	1.0000
	(5.04E − 09)	(5.04E − 09)	(3.63E − 09)	(3.63E − 09)
Eighty percent or more to law enforcement	0.3412 (0.3023)	1.4066 (0.4252)	− 0.0415 (0.3149)	0.9593 (0.3021)
Crime control fund	0.5792 (0.6891)	1.7845 (1.2297)	0.1578 (0.6826)	1.1710 (0.7993)
Based on contribution	0.5226 (0.3214)	1.6864 (0.5421)	0.0274 (0.4146)	1.0278 (0.4262)
Agency size	− 0.0003 (0.0013)	0.9997 (0.0012)	0.0878 (0.0553)	1.0918 (0.0603)
Constant	− 0.4160	−	− 1.2873	−
Log likelihood	− 237.7430		− 177.9106	
− 2 ln L chi-square	26.74		21.67	
Probability > chi-square	.0008		.0056	
Goodness of fit chi-square	375.79		297.08	
Probability > chi-square	.2039		.3438	

[a] n refers to the number of agencies with complete data on all variables of interest.

[b] Coefficients are close to zero and odds close to one because the units of measurement are small (individual counts of the number of total seizures and federalized seizures).

[c] Coefficients are close to zero and odds close to one because the units of measurement are small (amounts in dollars).

* $P < .05$.

** $P < .01$.

It also appears the agency size is not related to "addiction," but interestingly the logit coefficient suggests an inverse relationship. This would seem to indicate that larger agencies are less likely to rely on civil asset forfeiture, a logical conclusion since large agencies are more likely than small agencies to enjoy larger budgets. However, the presence of more crime in large jurisdictions would suggest an opposite effect.

Somewhat disheartening are the relationships between total proceeds received, total fiscal expenditures, and dependence on civil asset forfeiture. The highly significant relationship between total proceeds received and dependence on civil forfeiture suggests, reasonably enough, that the agencies that not only engaged in comparatively more civil asset forfeitures, but also received generous revenues from such activities, throughout the past 3 years, came to depend on the practice more readily. That is, the more certain law enforcement agencies received in the way of forfeiture proceeds, the more likely they were to depend on such revenues. This was the case for both the large and small agency models.

Similarly, the total fiscal expenditure variable was significant. It was also in the hypothesized direction, but only for the larger agencies. Large agencies (those with 100 or more sworn personnel) with greater fiscal expenditures were *less* likely to depend on civil asset forfeiture. This relationship suggests that law enforcement agencies have stumbled upon a creative solution to the fiscal constraints that continue to plague public agencies. At the least, this poses some conflict of interest problems.

It should be noted that the relationships reported in table 4 are not due to chance. For example, the model chi-square statistics for both the large and small agency models were both significant ($P = .0004$ and $P = .0038$, respectively). The goodness of fit chi-squares reported at the bottom of table 4 also suggest that both models fit the data relatively well (.2178 and .3681, respectively).

A Note Concerning Multicollinearity

Multicollinearity, or too-high intercorrelations among X variables, can cause trouble. Specifically, it leads to unreliable coefficient estimates and large standard errors (Hamilton, 1992). This is important because the incidence of seizures, whether overall or federal, can be expected to correlate with the amount of forfeiture proceeds received by particular law enforcement agencies. Accordingly, steps were taken to ensure that multicollinearity was not a serious problem in the multivariate model reported in the previous section.

There are several methods for diagnosing multicollinearity, two of which were employed in the research reported here. First, a matrix of correlations among X variables was constructed. Table 5 includes the pairwise correlations among the regressors. According to Gujarati (1995:335), ". . . if the pair-wise or zero-order correlation coefficient

Table 5   Correlation matrix of continuous X variables[a]

	Total Seizures	Federalized Seizures	Total Proceeds	Total Fiscal Expenditure	Agency Size
Total seizures	1.000				
Federalized seizures	.6496	1.000			
Total proceeds	.6829	.8512	1.000		
Total fiscal expenditures	.1257	.1461	.1659	1.000	
Agency size	.5728	.7282	.8547	.1793	1.000

[a] Three variables (80 percent to law enforcement, crime control fund, and based on contribution) were excluded from this table because they were coded as dummy variables.

between two regressors is high, say, in excess of .8, then multicollinearity is a serious problem." Two pairwise correlations broke the .8 threshold, thereby indicating relatively high multicollinearity. These were the correlations between total proceeds and federalized seizures and agency size and total proceeds. These high correlations would seem to call the multivariate results into question. However, the correlation matrix method has been deemed fallible for various reasons (Hamilton, 1992, p. 133; Gujarati, 1995, pp. 335–336).

An alternative technique for diagnosing multicollinearity makes use of auxiliary regressions. This involves regressing each X variable on all the other X variables and examining the resulting R^2 values. The resulting R^2 values are then subtracted from one to yield a "tolerance" estimate (Hamilton, 1992). With perfect multicollinearity, tolerance equals zero and regression is not possible. Low tolerance, according to Hamilton (1992), that is, tolerance below .2 or .1, ". . . does not prevent regression but makes the results less stable."

Table 6 reports the tolerance estimates for the continuous independent variables. The tolerance of each variable, also known as the independent variation, is reported in the second column of table 6. Only one of the continuous variables demonstrates low tolerance: federalized seizures. Accordingly, the coefficients on federalized seizures in the multivariate results section should be viewed with some caution. Indeed, *all* coefficients in the multivariate "addiction" model should be viewed in this fashion, especially because many of the "cures" for multicollinearity were not suitable in light of the research design. For example, dropping selected variables, a common remedial measure taken in the presence of multicollinearity, would have left theoretically important variables out of the multivariate model. Similarly, data transformations, attempts to gather new data, polynomial regressions, and other techniques (see Gujarati, 1995 for a review) were not viable alternatives.[5]

Table 6   Tolerances of continuous X variables[a]

Variable	Shared Variation	Independent Variation
Total seizures	.4864	.5136
Federalized seizures	.8544	.1456
Total proceeds	.7339	.2661
Total fiscal expenditures	.0340	.9660
Agency size	.7325	.2675

[a] Three variables (80 percent to law enforcement, crime control fund, and based on contribution) were excluded from this table because they were coded as dummy variables.

Summary, Conclusions, and Implications

This article has offered evidence that a substantial proportion of law enforcement agencies, particularly municipal police departments and county sheriff's agencies, are dependent on the revenue generated from civil asset forfeiture. I then attempted to explain dependence on civil asset forfeiture in terms of three primary factors: (1) fiscal expenditures; (2) past experiences with forfeiture; and (3) state regulations governing the disposition and distribution of forfeited assets. Multivariate tests of these and other explanations for "addiction" suggested that fiscal expenditures were inversely related to dependence on civil asset forfeiture, but only for large agencies. The results also indicated that past forfeiture experiences, namely total proceeds received, were also associated with dependence on civil asset forfeiture, but in the positive direction. The incidence of total seizures, the incidence of federalized seizures, state law, and agency size were not significantly related to "addiction."

The most important finding reported in this article is that many law enforcement agencies are dependent on civil asset forfeiture. Of course, this was not the case for all agencies, or even for the majority, and cross-sectional data cannot reveal trends over time, but nearly 40 percent of the large agency sample reported that forfeiture is *necessary* as a budgetary supplement. The 40 percent figure was for 1998, and could very well be dynamic and changing in either a positive or negative direction, but the results nevertheless seem to confirm forfeiture critics' (e.g., Hyde, 1995; Levy, 1996) worst fears. If law enforcement is "in it for the money," which some agencies clearly are (see Miller and Selva, 1994), then it is difficult to see how the "war on drugs" can ever be won. (Of course, given law enforcement's minimal success in the "war on drugs," it is quite possible the "war" can never be won, even if profit is not a consideration.)

Appendix A   Percentage of proceeds going to law enforcement: State law categories and relevant statutory citations[6]

State	
Alabama	5 [Ala. Code § 20-2-93(e) (1990)]
Alaska	9 [Alas. Stat. § 17.30.122 (1996)]
Arizona	7 [Ariz. Rev. Stat. Ann. § 13-4315 (1997)]
Arkansas	6 [Ark. Stat. Ann. § 5-64-505(k) (1993)]
California	3 [Cal. Health and Safety Code § 11489(a)(2)(A) (1997)]
Colorado	3 [Colo. Rev. Stat. Ann. § 1613-506 (1997)]
Connecticut	3 [Conn. Gen. Stat. Ann. §§ 54-36h(f), 54-36i(c) (1997)]
Delaware	1 (100 percent) [16 Del. Code Ann. § 4784(f)(3) (1995)]
District of Columbia	1 (100 percent) [D.C. Code Ann. § 33-552(d)(4)(B) (1993)]
Florida	11 (depends on agency; not for operating expenditures) [Fla. Stat. Ann. § 932.7055(3)–(6) (1996)]
Georgia	6 [Ga. Code Ann. § 16-13-49(u)(4)(B) (1996)]
Hawaii	4 [Haw. Rev. Stat. § 712A-16(2)(a) (1993)]
Idaho	1 (100 percent) [Ida. Code § 37-2744(e)(2)(C) (1994)]
Illinois	11 (depends on particular statute) [ILCS ch. 720 §§ 550/12(g), 570/505(g) (1997); ILCS ch. 725 § 175/5(g)—(h) (1997)]
Indiana	8 [Ind. Code Ann. § 16-42-20-5(e) (1997)]
Iowa	8 (no discussion of distribution) [Io. Code Ann. §§ 809A.16-809A.17 (1997)]
Kansas	1 (100 percent) [Kan. Stat. Ann. § 60-4117(c)–(d) (1994)]
Kentucky	11 (depends on type of property) [Ky. Rev. Stat. Ann. § 218A.435 (1995)]
Louisiana	3 [La. Rev. Stat. Ann. § 32:1550(k)(1) (1989)]
Maine	10 [Me. Rev. Stat. Ann. § 5821 (Supp. 1996)]
Maryland	1 (100 percent) [Md. Crimes and Punishment Code Ann. §§ 297(f),297(k)(3)(v) (1996)]
Massachusetts	3 [Mass. Ann. Laws ch. 94C, § 47(d) (1995)]
Michigan	1 (100 percent) [Mich. Comp. Laws Ann. § 333.7524 (1997)]
Minnesota	3 [Minn. Stat. Ann. § 609.5315(5) (1997)]
Mississippi	1 (80 percent) [Miss. Code § 41-29-181(2) (Supp. 1997)]
Missouri	9 [Mo. Const., Art. IX, § 7; Mo. Ann. Stat. § 513.623 (Supp. 1997)]
Montana	1 (100 percent) [Mont. Code Ann. § 44-12-206 (1995)]
Nebraska	7 (50 percent only) [Neb. Rev. Stat. §§ 28-431(4), 28-1439.02 (1995)]
Nevada	1 (100 percent, but not for normal operating expenditures) [Nev. Rev. Stat. § 179.1187(2) (1995)]
New Hampshire	4 [N.H. Rev. Stat. Ann. § 318-B:17-b(v)(a)(1) (1995)]
New Jersey	6 [N.J. Stat. Ann. § 2C:64-6(a) (1995)]
New Mexico	0 [N.M. Stat. Ann. § 30-31-35(E), § 22-8-32(A)(1) (1978 and Supp. 1992, 1997)]
New York	11 (40 percent to drug fund; 75 percent of remaining balance to participating agency) [N.Y. Laws 1349(h)(i)]

continued

Appendix A   Percentage of proceeds going to law enforcement: State law
categories and relevant statutory citations[6] (continued)

State	
North Carolina	0 [N.C. Const., Art. IX, § 7; N.C. Gen. Stat. § 90-112(d)(1) (1993)]
North Dakota	2 (100 percent up to US$500,000) [N.Dak. Cent. Code §§ 19-03.1-36(5)(b), 54-12-14 (1997)]
Ohio	1 (100 percent) [O. Rev. Code Ann. §§ 2933.43(D)(1)(c), 2925.43(B)(4)(c), 2925.44(B)(8)(c) (1992)]
Oklahoma	1 (100 percent, but only for enforcing controlled substance laws) [Okla. Stat. Ann. §§ 2503(D)–(F), 2-506(L)(3) (1997)]
Oregon	1 (100 percent, but only for enforcing controlled substance laws) [Ore. Rev. Stat. Notes Preceding ORS 166.05 §§ 10(1)(c)–11(b)(1)(b) (1995)]
Pennsylvania	11 (shared by D.A. and Attorney General) [Pa. Cons. Stat. Ann. § 6801(f)–(h) (1997)
Rhode Island	6 [R.I. Gen. Laws § 2128-5.04(b)(3)(A)(i) (Supp. 1996)]
South Carolina	3 [S.C. Code Ann. § 44-53-530(e) (Supp. 1996)]
South Dakota	7 [S.Dak. Code Laws § 34-20B-89(2) (1994)]
Tennessee	11 (depends on type of property) [Tenn. Code Ann. §§ 53-11-451(d)(4), 5311-452(h)(2)(A) (1991 and Supp. 1996)]
Texas	11 (based on agreement between state and local officials) [Tex. Crim. Pro. Code Ann. § 59.06(a)–(d), (h) (Supp. 1997)]
Utah	1 (100 percent, but only for enforcing controlled substance laws) [Ut. Code Ann. § 5837-13(8)(a) (1997)]
Vermont	9 [18 Vt. Stat. Ann. §§ 4244(d), 4247 (Supp. 1996)]
Virginia	6 [Va. Code § 19.2-386.14(AB) (1995)]
Washington	1 (100 percent, but only for enforcing controlled substance laws) [Wash. Rev. Code Ann. §§ 7.43.100, 43.10.270, 69.50.505(f)(i) (1992 and Supp. 1997)]
West Virginia	10 [W.Va. Code § 60A-4-403a(g) (1992)]
Wisconsin	3 [Wis. Stat. Ann. § 961.55(5)(b) (Supp. 1997)]
Wyoming	9 [Wyo. Stat. § 35-7-1049(e)–(j) (Supp. 1996)]

Key
 0 = none
 1 = 80 percent or more
 2 = 80 percent or more with restrictions
 3 = less than 80 percent, but more than 0
 4 = less than 80 percent, but more than 0 with restrictions
 5 = based on contribution
 6 = based on contribution with restrictions
 7 = paid into state/general law enforcement fund (e.g., antiracketeering fund)
 8 = paid into nonlaw enforcement fund (e.g., school fund) or general fund
 9 = left to discretion of some official with or without restrictions
 10 = law does not specify
 11 = other

Taking this idea one step further, the notion that law enforcement is coming to depend on civil asset forfeiture lends support to perspectives such as Reiman's (1995) Pyrrhic defeat theory, namely that the criminal justice system is designed to fail. It could be that law enforcement has a vested interest in there being a drug problem because of the money and resources that stand to be gained. Of course, there is no way to support this statement, and such an eventuality is as implausible as it is radical, but the "policing for profit" notion is nevertheless intriguing. Nils Christie's (1993) view of crime control as industry also sheds light on the findings reported here. As Christie (p. 14) states, the crime control industry ". . . provides *profit and work* while at the same time producing control of those who otherwise might have disturbed the social process" (emphasis added).

The second most important finding from the research reported here is that past experiences with civil asset forfeiture and fiscal expenditures were associated with "addiction." Of course, these two variables do not fully *explain* dependence on civil asset forfeiture, but it would seem that conflict of interest problems are present in the way civil forfeiture is currently being carried out. Insofar as fiscal expenditures are inversely related to dependence on civil asset forfeiture, it is plausible to conclude that crime control is not the *only* goal among contemporary law enforcement agencies. Organizational survival and fiscal stability are also important considerations.

The finding that past experiences with forfeiture are tied to dependence has important implications. Aside from conflict of interest concerns, this finding helps explain why the CAFRA was tied up in Congress for so long. Numerous forfeiture reform proposals were continually been beaten down by the law enforcement lobby, particularly the International Association of Chiefs of Police, the Fraternal Order of Police, and the Department of Justice. The struggle may have occurred because of law enforcement's apparent dependence on civil asset forfeiture, and because law enforcement officials saw the potential to lose a significant proportion of the revenue generated from civil asset forfeiture.

It is possible that CAFRA's requirement that the burden of proof shift to the state may now improve things, but since the law does not require that forfeiture proceeds be diverted into a general fund, then the revenues generated from civil asset forfeiture will, in all likelihood, remain substantial. Regardless of what legislative changes have occurred, law enforcement agencies (and, to an extent, prosecutors' offices) enjoy a source of revenue that is not available to other public agencies. Any proposed changes to *this* arrangement are likely to confront serious opposition.

Much research remains to be done. Asset forfeiture has been scrutinized on constitutional and procedural grounds, but most research on forfeiture has not been empirical. The handful of empirical studies on civil asset forfeiture (this article included) could be starting points for future research. A host of questions remain, some of which include: What determines forfeitures?; What are the theories and motivations behind forfeiture?; Is forfeiture an effective crime control policy?; and, Are the police, in an attempt to generate money from civil forfeiture, violating people's civil rights? An answer to the latter question could lend additional support to the findings reported here. Other questions include: Is there a time dimension to dependence on civil asset forfeiture?; Is law enforcement really "addicted" to the drug war?; and, Is the "addiction" growing? If so, what can be done to ensure conflict of interest problems do not become more serious?

In closing, the research reported here has substantiated *some* of the concerns raised by civil forfeiture's most ardent critics. Despite noble intentions to strike at the economic foundations of the illicit drug trade, many law enforcement agencies are coming to depend on civil asset forfeiture. Moreover, past experiences and fiscal constraints are intimately tied to that dependence. The most profound consequence of this is that, depending on such variables as leadership philosophy and location, civil asset forfeiture can provide an opportunity for law enforcement officials to behave unethically, circumvent constitutional protections, and act in self-interest rather than in the interest of crime control or public safety.

Despite a number of past and current reform proposals, and despite the heated debate that asset forfeiture inspires, law enforcement's "double-edged sword" (Miller and Selva, 1994) is here to stay. It also appears that equitable sharing will survive well into the future. Given the fact that law enforcement agencies will continue to be able to reap the benefits from civil asset forfeiture, then steps should be taken to ensure that the "addiction" is not irreversible.

Endnotes

[1] Interestingly, the President's Commission failed to notice that most of the proceeds obtained from civil asset forfeiture go to law enforcement, not "society."

[2] The Comprehensive Drug Abuse Prevention and Control Act of 1970 provided, in relevant part, for the forfeiture of ". . . equipment . . . [and] property which is used, or is intended for use . . . in any manner to facilitate the transportation, sale, receipt, possession, or concealment [of controlled substances]" [21 U.S.C. § 881(a) (1988 and Supp. IV 1992)]. The act was amended in 1978, providing for the forfeiture of "[a]ll moneys . . . or other things of value furnished or intended to be furnished by any person in exchange for a controlled substance . . ." [21 U.S.C. § 881(a)(6) (1988)]. In 1984, the act was further amended (or broadened) to provide for the forfeiture of "[a]ll real property . . . which is used, or intended to be used, in any manner or part, to commit, or to facilitate the commission of a violation" [21 U.S.C. § 881(a)(7) (1988)].

[3] Although sheriffs and chiefs were asked to complete the survey, it was clear in some instances that a subordinate completed the survey.

[4] It is possible that some agencies had an incentive to claim that they were dependent on civil forfeiture, perhaps not wishing to lose future revenues.

[5] It has been said that if the goal of regression is prediction, then multicollinearity may not be a serious problem (see Geary, 1963).

[6] Categories 1, 2, 5, 6, and 7 were used in the analysis. The remaining categories were not used in the analysis either because the percentages going to law enforcement are relatively small or because there is no guarantee that *any* proceeds go to law enforcement. Categories 1 and 2 were used to construct the dummy variable specifying that 80 percent or more of proceeds go to law enforcement. Categories 5 and 6 were used to construct the dummy variable specifying that proceeds are based on contribution. Category 7 represents the third dummy variable.

References

Asset Forfeiture Office. (1994). *Asset forfeiture manual: Law and practice*. Washington, DC: United States Department of Justice.

Atkins, D. P., & Patterson, A. V. (1991). Punishment or compensation? New constitutional restrictions on civil forfeiture. *Bridgeport Law Review, 11*, 371–381.

Bauman, R. (1995, February 20). Take it away. *National Review*, 34–38.

Blumenson, E., & Nilsen, E. (1998). Policing for profit: The drug war's hidden economic agenda. *University of Chicago Law Review, 65*, 35–114.

Bumham, D. (1996). *Above the law*. New York: Scribner.

Canavan, P. M. (1990). Civil forfeiture of real property: The government's weapon against drug traffickers injures innocent owners. *Pace Law Review, 10*, 485–517.

Chapman, S. (1993, March 7). Seizing property: Law enforcement's dangerous weapon. *Chicago Tribune*, p. 3, sec. 4.

Christie, N. (1993). *Crime control as industry*. New York: Routledge.

Department of Justice. (1990). *Annual report of the Department of Justice Asset Forfeiture Program*. Washington, DC: Office of the Attorney General.

Department of Justice. (1991). *Points in response to presumed guilty series*. Washington, DC: Office of the Attorney General.

Department of Justice. (1994a). *Annual report of the Attorney General of the United States*. Washington, DC: Office of the Attorney General.

Department of Justice. (1994b). *Guide to equitable sharing of federally forfeited property for state and local law enforcement agencies*. Washington, DC: Executive Office for Asset Forfeiture, Office of the Attorney General.

Department of Justice. (1995). *Audit report: Asset Forfeiture Program*. Washington, DC: Office of the Inspector General.

Dortch, S. (1992, August 19). 356 marijuana plants, hose, weapons seized. *Knoxville News Sentinel*, p. 1.

Drug Enforcement Administration, Strategic Intelligence Division. (1993). *Illegal drug price/purity report – United States: January 1990–March 1993*. Washington, DC: United States Department of Justice.

Drug Enforcement Administration, Strategic Intelligence Division. (1994). *Illegal drug price/purity report – United States: January 1991–June 1994*. Washington, DC: United States Department of Justice.

Durkin, C. (1990). Civil forfeitures under federal narcotics law: The impact of the shifting burden of proof upon the Fifth Amendment privilege against self-incrimination. *Suffolk University Law Review, 24*, 678–709.

Edwards, E. E. (1994). *Review of federal asset forfeiture program (Testimony before the Legislation and National Security Subcommittee of the Committee on Government*

Operations, House of Representatives, June 22, 1993). Washington, DC: U.S. Government Printing Office.

Enders, J. (1993, February 11). Opposition growing to nation's drug forfeiture laws. *Chicago Daily Law Bulletin, 2*.

Executive Office for Asset Forfeiture. (1994a). *Guide to equitable sharing of federally forfeited property for state and local law enforcement agencies*. Washington, DC: United States Department of Justice.

Executive Office for Asset Forfeiture. (1994b). *Annual report of the Department of Justice Asset Forfeiture Program*. Washington, DC: United States Department of Justice.

Geary, R. C. (1963). Some results about relations between stochastic variables: A discussion document. *Review of International Statistical Institute, 31*, 163–181.

General Accounting Office. (1989). *Asset forfeiture: An update*. Washington, DC: General Accounting Office.

General Accounting Office. (1990, June). *Asset forfeiture: Legislation needed to improve cash processing and financial reporting (GAOIGGD-90-94-144FS)*. Washington, DC: U.S. Government Printing Office.

General Accounting Office. (1991, September). *Asset management: Government-wide asset disposition activities (GAOIGGD91-139FS)*. Washington, DC: U.S. Government Printing Office.

General Accounting Office. (1992, September). *Real property dispositions: Flexibility afforded agencies to meet disposition objectives varies (GAOIGGD-92-144FS)*. Washington, DC: U.S. Government Printing Office.

Goldsmith, M., & Linderman, M. J. (1989). Asset forfeiture and third party rights: The need for farther law reform. *Duke Law Journal, 39*, 1253–1301.

Greenburg, J. C. (1995, June 22). Hyde: Easy recovery of seized property. *Chicago Tribune*, p. 14.

Gujarati, D. N. (1995). *Basic econometrics* (3rd ed.). New York: McGraw-Hill.

Hamilton, L. C. (1992). *Regression with graphics: A second course in applied statistics*. Belmont, CA: Duxbury Press.

Hawk, R. (1993, November 8). Western district office pays for itself and more. *Pennsylvania Law Journal, 7*.

Hawkins, C. W., Jr., & Payne, T. E. (1999). Civil forfeiture in law enforcement: An effective tool or cash register justice? In J. D. Sewell (Ed.), *Controversial issues in policing* (pp. 23–34). Boston, MA: Allyn and Bacon.

Heilbroner, D. (1994, December 11). The law goes on a treasure hunt. *New York Times*, p. 70, sec. 6.

Hyde, H. (1995). Forfeiting our property rights: Is your property safe from seizure? Washington, DC: Cato Institute.

Jankowski, M. A. (1990). Tempering the relation-back doctrine: A more reasonable approach to civil forfeiture in drug cases. *Virginia Law Review, 76*, 165–195.

Jensen, E. L., & Gerber, J. (1996). The civil forfeiture of assets and the war on drugs: Expanding criminal sanctions while reducing due process protections. *Crime and Delinquency, 42*, 421–434.

Justice Research and Statistics Association. (1993). *Multijurisdictional drug control task forces: A five-year review 1988–1992*. Washington, DC: Justice Research and Statistics Association.

Kasten, L. (1991). Extending constitutional protection to civil forfeiture that exceeds rough remedial compensation. *George Washington Law Review, 60*, 194–244.

Kessler, S. F. (1993). *Civil and criminal forfeiture: Federal and state practice.* St. Paul, MN: West.

Levy, L. W. (1996). *A license to steal: The forfeiture of property.* Chapel Hill: University of North Carolina Press.

McNamara, J. (1999, June 6). When the police take property, who do you call? *Orange County Register,* 5 [Commentary].

Miller, J. M., & Selva, L. H. (1994). Drug enforcement's double edged sword: An assessment of asset forfeiture programs. *Justice Quarterly, 11,* 313–335.

Morganthau, T., & Katel, P. (1990, April 29). Uncivil liberties? Debating whether drug war tactics are eroding constitutional rights. *Newsweek,* 18–21.

Myers, H. L., & Brzostowski, J. (1982, Summer). Dealers, dollars, and drugs: Drug law enforcement's promising new program. *Drug Enforcement,* 7–10.

National Association of Criminal Defense Lawyers. (1996). *H.R. 1916 ("Civil Asset Forfeiture Reform Act") and the current federal asset seizure and forfeiture program* [Oral testimony presented before the United States House Committee on the Judiciary, July 22, 1996.] Washington, DC: National Association of Criminal Defense Lawyers.

Nelson, W. P. (1992). Should the ranch go free because the constable blundered? Gaining compliance with search and seizure standards in the age of asset forfeiture. *California Law Review, 80,* 1309–1359.

O'Brien, A. M. (1991). Caught in the crossfire: Protecting the innocent owner of real property from civil forfeiture under 21 U.S.C. Section 881(a)(7). *St. John's Law Review, 65,* 521–551.

Petrou, P. (1984, September). Due process implications of shifting the burden of proof in forfeiture proceedings arising out of illegal drug transactions. *Duke Law Journal,* 822–843.

Pratt, G. C., & Petersen, W. B. (1991). Civil forfeiture in the second circuit. *St. John's Law Review, 65,* 653–700.

President's Commission on Model State Drug Laws. (1993). *Volume 1: Economic remedies.* Washington, DC: White House.

Reiman, J. H. (1995). *The rich get richer and the poor get prison: Ideology, class, and criminal justice* (4th ed.). Boston, MA: Allyn and Bacon.

Rosenburg, J. A. (1988). Constitutional rights and civil forfeiture actions. *Columbia Law Review, 88,* 390–406.

Rudnick, A. G. (1992). Cleaning up money laundering prosecutions: Guidelines for prosecution and asset forfeiture. *Criminal Justice, 7,* 2.

Saltzburg, D. G. (1992). Real property forfeitures as a weapon in the government's war on drugs: A failure to protect innocent ownership rights. *Boston University Law Review, 72,* 217–242.

Shaw, B. (1990). Fifth Amendment failures and RICO forfeitures. *American Business Law Journal, 28,* 169–200.

Speta, J. B. (1990). Narrowing the scope of civil drug forfeiture: Section 881. Substantial connection and the Eighth Amendment. *Michigan Law Review, 89,* 165–210.

Stahl, M. (1992). Asset forfeiture, burdens of proof, and the war on drugs. *Journal of Criminal Law and Criminology, 83,* 274–337.

Thomas, C. (1999, May 8). Civil forfeiture laws in desperate need of change. *Arizona Republic,* p. B6.

Warchol, G. L., & Johnson, B. R. (1996). Guilty property: A quantitative analysis of civil asset forfeiture. *American Journal of Criminal Justice, 21,* 61–81.

Warchol, G. L., Payne, D. M., & Johnson, B. R. (1996). Criminal forfeiture: An effective alternative to civil and administrative proceedings. *Police Studies, 19*, 51–66.

Willson, E. (1990, February). Did a drug dealer own your home? (Criminal assets may be seized). *Florida Trend*, 6–9.

Wisotsky, S. (1991). Not thinking like a lawyer: The case of drugs in the courts. *Notre Dame Journal of Legal Ethics and Public Policy, 5*, 651–700.

Worrall, J. L. (1999). *Civil lawsuits, citizen complaints, and policing innovations.* Doctoral dissertation, Washington State University.

Yoskowitz, J. (1992). The war on the poor: Civil forfeiture of public housing. *Columbia Journal of Law and Social Problems, 25*, 567–600.

Zalman, M. (1997, May 9). The insidious side of drug forfeiture laws. *Detroit News*, A11.

Zeldin, M. F., & Weiner, R. G. (1991). Innocent third parties and their rights in forfeiture proceedings. *American Criminal Law Review, 28*, 843–861.

Cases Cited

Bennis v. Michigan, 116 S.Ct. 994 (1996).

United States v. All Funds on Deposit . . . at Merrill Lynch, 801 F. Supp. 984 (E.D. N.Y. 1992).

United States v. Bajakajian, 524 U.S. 321 (1998).

United States v. One Mercedes 560 SEL, 919 F.2d 327 (5th Cir. 1990).

United States v. One 1977 Mercedes-Benz 450 SEL, 708 F.2d 444 (9th Cir. 1983).

United States v. One Parcel of Land at 508 Depot Street, 964 F.2d 814 (8th Cir. 1992).

United States v. One Yacht Named Tahuna, 702 F.2d 1276 (9th Cir. 1983).

United States v. Real Property Located at 6625 Zumirez Drive, 845 F. Supp. 725 (1994).

United States v. United States Coin and Currency, 401 U.S. 715 (1971).

United States v. 92 Buena Vista Ave., Rumson, 507 U.S. 111 (1993).

Section 2

The Individual in Criminal Justice Organizations

Criminal justice organizations influence the individuals who work for them, both on formal and informal levels. How both supervisors and subordinates respond to their environments and work settings is a critical issue facing criminal justice administrators. Issues such as job design, supervisory styles, and organizational structure impact directly how individuals within the criminal justice system view their roles. More importantly, these issues also affect the administration and management of criminal justice organizations. The articles presented in this section of the book examine how individual actors respond to and are influenced by the various structures and environments within and outside the criminal justice system.

Kraska and Cubellis present a fascinating examination of the proliferation of police paramilitary units within police departments across the country at a time when crime rates are falling and police progressives are trying to promote more problem-oriented and community-policing approaches to their departments. Kraska and Cubellis suggest that the development of such units is consistent with the paramilitary history and structure of police departments, yet a movement toward the creation of such units is viewed in stark contrast to other attempts by police organizations to get away from the trappings of a paramilitary structure. The authors suggest that the further development of these units within police departments reflects an interest on the part of the state to further refine the administration of violence through increased bureaucratization consistent with the tenets of "high modernity."

Fyfe, in contrast, argues that what is needed in "good policing" is the adoption of other approaches to police organization and structure. His view is that good policing cannot be defined outside the context of what the police themselves view as the most important principles and practices to provide optimal police service. Fyfe would agree with Kraska and Cubellis that the traditional police structure is the source of many problems, both organizationally and individually, for administrators and officers. He offers a simple and basic remedy to these problems by enlisting the views of regular cops as to how they would organize and deliver police services. In this way, the impossible mandate given to police might become more manageable for both police supervisors and their subordinates the rank-and-file police officer.

The third piece in this section examines an often neglected area in criminal justice research, that being defense attorneys and the court settings in which they work. McIntyre provides a very descriptive profile of the ups and downs of doing criminal defense work. Her analysis shows both the "dos and don'ts" associated with criminal defense work and the various moral dilemmas that defense attorneys face. Yet, the picture painted by McIntyre is revealing of how these dilemmas are addressed within the context of a courtroom work group and, most importantly, how criminal defense work serves the purpose of upholding the law and guaranteeing that the playing field is, at least on the surface, even for all participants in the criminal court process.

Robin Engel examines the supervisory styles exhibited among sergeants and lieutenants within police organizations in the fourth article in this section. This topic has not received much attention in the literature, but it is the individual behaviors of police supervisors that are most critical to the effectiveness of police organizations. The analysis provided stresses the importance of supervisory styles in influencing behaviors among individual police officers and the nexus between supervisory styles and organizational goals. Police supervision, therefore, is critical to how organizational goals are achieved. The implementation of specific styles of supervision will have a profound impact on the behaviors of police officers, the goals attained by police agencies, and the general quality of services provided to the community.

In the next two articles within this section, both Rosecrance and Toch describe the effects of bureaucratization on the organization and individual. Rosecrance brilliantly explores how the increased bureaucratization of a probation department engendered specific patterns of adaptation among probation agents. In the long run, the effect was that many of the old "prima donnas" were weeded out of the organization, but not all. Similar to what was found by Engel regarding the importance of a balance of supervisory styles within police organizations, Rosecrance concludes that a balance of various role types is essential to the effective functioning of probation departments. His analysis requires serious examination by criminal justice reformers and administrators who view greater "rationality" in criminal justice organizations as the panacea to their problems.

Toch also questions such an approach, but his examination is at the individual level and focuses on the effects of bureaucratization on the individual correctional officer. His insightful exploration of the correctional officer role shows that at the core correctional officers are in the human service business and are problem solvers at the micro-level of their organizations. They enforce rules, yet they do more: They exercise discretion in such a way that both keeper and kept can survive the prison experience. Hence, it is the officer who humanizes the work, and he or she requires a structure that recognizes and supports the diversity of correctional work such that prisons can effectively function. Both Rosecrance and Toch present views that have serious implications for criminal justice administration and management.

The final piece of this section explores the definition of what constitutes a problem officer within police organizations. For Terrill and McCluskey, problem officers need to be understood within the context of doing police work. A large part of this work involves direct contact with citizens and a possible outcome of repeated contact with citizens is an increase in citizen complaints. Terrill and McCluskey suggest that officers who are genuinely enforcing the law will naturally receive more citizen complaints; this does not make them "bad" officers. Instead, citizen complaints must be gauged relative to the productivity levels of individual officers. Terrill and McCluskey note the inherent difficulties in viewing citizen complaints in a vacuum without noting the benefits derived from high arrest activities among some officers. The analysis has direct implications for how police administrators and managers supervise rank-and-file officers and how they are viewed by the police organization.

Militarizing Mayberry and Beyond
Making Sense of American Paramilitary Policing

Peter B. Kraska
Louis J. Cubellis

Crime and justice studies have a fundamental interest in society's formal reaction to the breaking of laws (Sutherland, Cressey, and Luckenbill, 1992). Consequently criminologists have examined and debated the changing nature of the criminal justice enterprise. Some penological scholars argue, for instance, that correctional ideology and practice are aligning themselves more closely with the features of a postmodern or high-modern society (Christie, 1994; Feeley and Simon, 1992; Garland, 1990, 1995). Policing scholars, on the other hand, focus predominantly on the "quiet revolution" occurring within the modern police institution, namely community- and problem-oriented policing reforms (Kelling, 1988).

Despite the democratic rhetoric connected with this "revolution," the discourse associated with military activity and war remains a core feature of crime-control ideology (e.g., the war on drugs, crime fighters). Indeed the military model, the armed forces, and a fear of martial control

Peter Kraska and Louis Cubellis, "Militarizing Mayberry and Beyond: Making Sense of American Paramilitary Policing," *Justice Quarterly*, Vol. 14 No. 4, December 1997, pp. 607–629. Reprinted by permission of the Academy of Criminal Justice Sciences.

have all been influential in the development of police (Bailey, 1995; Bittner, 1970; Enloe, 1980; Fogelson, 1977; Manning, 1977). Early police scholarship examined in depth the military model's theoretical and practical importance for civilian law enforcement (Bittner, 1970; Fogelson, 1977; Manning, 1977). Contemporary discussions, however, rarely include the military model as a central influence on the police institution.

An important exception is Skolnick and Fyfe's (1993) recent discussion, similar to Bittner's in 1970, of the continued harmful influence of the military paradigm in contemporary policing. They argue that despite the recent rhetorical turn toward democratic reforms, the military model still lingers as a central feature of police culture and operation. One important manifestation of this paradigm which Skolnick and Fyfe overlooked is the adoption of the military special operations model,[1] embodied in what the international literature calls police paramilitary units (PPUs) (Brewer et al. 1988; Enloe, 1980; Jefferson, 1990; Reiner, 1992). These units are known most commonly in the United States as SWAT or special response teams.

At first glance, the police paramilitary unit imagery exhibited at Waco and Ruby Ridge hardly appear to support the notion that a component of policing is moving toward a military approach. These events were sensational and alarming, but could be regarded as unique events that portended little about trends in law enforcement overall. Kraska and Kappeler (1997), however, in a national study of PPUs in medium-sized to large police departments, found that these units have not only grown in numbers but have become increasingly proactive.

The research presented here stems from a separate national survey of small-locality police agencies. Descriptive and longitudinal data on small-locality PPUs are presented, followed by the implications of these findings. In an effort to begin making theoretical sense of these data, we then situate the small-locality findings with the larger PPU phenomenon. We present additional analyses and discuss how the rise and normalization of PPUs correspond closely to macro-level changes in formal social control.

The Military Model and Paramilitary Units

In this study we shed light on two neglected areas of scholarship in criminology. First, Weisheit (1993:217) charges crime and justice studies with urban ethnocentrism when reviewing the scant literature on rural crime and justice issues. Although the literature includes some case studies of small police departments (Decker, 1979; Gibbons, 1972; Marenin and Copus, 1991), few systematic examinations of these agencies exist (Weisheit, Falcone, and Wells, 1996). The existing literature characterizes small-locality police as oriented toward crime prevention and social service.

Second, until recently no scholarly research on PPUs existed except in the international literature (Jefferson, 1990; Reiner, 1992).[2] Few police scholars have acknowledged that the military and the police have an inherent political connection: both possess a monopoly on and the pre-rogative to exercise the state-legitimized use of force (Bittner, 1970; Enloe, 1980; Kraska, 1994; Turk, 1982). Even internationally, police rarely orga-nize and administer force along any other lines than the military-bureau-cratic model, although the degree of militarization varies widely (Brewer et al., 1988; Chevigny, 1995; Enloe, 1980).

Police academics, however, have criticized the military model as playing a central role in numerous problems that plague policing (Angell, 1971; Bittner, 1970; Fogelson, 1977; Fry and Berkes, 1983; Klockars, 1985; Skolnick and Fyfe, 1993). The military-bureaucratic model, epitomized in the professional model of policing, acts as a barrier to police-community ties by fostering a "we/they" attitude. Military ideology and organiza-tion are also antithetical to more democratic approaches, both internal and external to a police agency. Finally, the military model encourages overemphasis on the crime-fighting function of police work and pro-motes a warlike approach to crime and drug problems.

In the "era" of community- and problem-oriented policing, it may seem inappropriate to examine trends toward rather than away from the military paradigm, particularly in smaller police jurisdictions. Yet today, the military model's influence on the police may be no less significant (Chevigny, 1995; Kraska, 1994; Skolnick and Fyfe, 1993).

Cop-on-the-Beat Police versus Police Paramilitary Units

It is important to distinguish traditional police from policing with PPUs. In the images constructed by the media, PPUs are highly trained and disciplined teams of police officers housed in the largest agencies, which respond to the rare hostage, sniper, barricaded person, or terrorist. Police paramilitary units can be distinguished from what Enloe (1980) calls "cop-on-the beat policing" most simply by their appearance, their heavy weaponry, and their operations.

For a more exact identification, we must clarify the term *paramilitary unit*. We must distinguish between indications that are *necessary* in apply-ing the PPU label and those which would only *contribute* to labeling these units and their activities as paramilitaristic.

First among the necessary factors, the unit must train and function as a military special operations team with a strict military command structure and discipline (or the pretense thereof). Examples include the U.S. Navy Seals teams and foreign police paramilitary squads such as the British Special Patrol Groups. This status as a unique team within a larger organization perpetuates the belief that these units and their members are "elite," a sentiment supported by their administrators (Kraska and Paulsen, 1997).[3]

Second, the unit must have at the forefront of their function to threaten or use force collectively, and not always as an option of last resort (e.g., in conducting a no-knock drug raid).[4] Operationally, PPUs are deployed to deal with situations that require a team of police officers specifically trained to be use-of-force specialists. Historically they have operated as *reactive* units, handling only strictly defined, high-risk situations already in progress.

Finally, the unit must operate under legitimate state authority, and its activities must be sanctioned by the state and coordinated by a government agency. This criterion would exclude common thuggery, militia organizations, and guerilla groups.

Contributing indicators include the hardware they employ and their garb. These teams generally outfit themselves with black or urban camouflage BDUs (battle dress uniforms), lace-up combat boots, full-body armor, Kevlar helmets, and ninji-style hoods. PPUs' weapons and hardware include submachine guns, tactical shotguns, sniper rifles, percussion grenades, CS and OC gas (tear and pepper gas), surveillance equipment, and fortified personnel carriers.

It would seem improbable, given the crime prevention and service orientation attributed to small-locality police agencies, that they would want, need, or be willing to fund these expensive units.[5] Ethnographic research, however, uncovered a flourishing PPU movement in small-town police departments in the north central United States (Kraska, 1996); this work overcame our doubts about using resources and time to conduct a national survey of these agencies.

Methodology

We designed and administered a 40-item (100-variable) survey to collect data on the formation, prevalence, and activities of PPUs in small localities. We developed a sampling frame of all U.S. police agencies (excluding federal agencies), serving jurisdictions between 25,000 and 50,000 citizens.[6] This list yielded a population of 770 law enforcement agencies. In March 1996 we made an initial mailing of the survey to this population of police agencies; the mailing included a letter of introduction and a copy of the survey instrument. Because police agencies are secretive and suspicious (Manning, 1978; Skolnick, 1966; Westley, 1956), and because of the difficulty in researching sensitive topics in policing, the letter was written on a recognized sponsor's letterhead. It was signed by both the principal researcher (the first author) and the director of the professional organization that was sponsoring the research. It also noted the researchers' university affiliation. The language used in the survey encouraged respondents to recognize the study as administratively oriented. It is likely that this orientation, coupled with the authors' familiarity with PPU rhetoric and the promise of confidentiality and anonymity, aided our response rate.

Within five weeks, the first mailing yielded 433 completed surveys, a 56 percent response rate. After approximately six weeks, we mailed a second wave of surveys to the remaining 337 nonrespondents. In the second mailing we emphasized the high level of participation by other police agencies and urged cooperation from departments without a PPU. After six additional weeks, this follow-up mailing yielded an additional 119 surveys for a total response rate of 72 percent (n = 552).

Of the 552 returned surveys, we excluded 79 departments that employed more than 100 sworn officers, and thus obtained a more accurate representation of policing in small localities (N = 473).[7] The resulting sampler of departments contained an average of 62 officers and a median of 60.

Of the 473 agencies, we selected 40 to provide identification and telephone information for semistructured follow-up phone interviews. We sought information on missing data and inquired into some of the more sensitive PPU activities, such as proactive patrol work. Interviews lasted five minutes to one hour; most lasted about 30 minutes.

Analysis and Results

Demographic and Descriptive Characteristics

Over 65 percent (n = 311) of the departments responded that they had a SWAT team. Of the remaining agencies (those without a PPU), 28 percent (n = 46) responded that they planned to develop a team within the next few years. The highest proportion of these agencies (24 percent) used the traditional acronym SWAT. Other departments employed an array of labels for the reorganized or more recently formed PPUs, including SRT (special response team, 21 percent) and ERU (emergency response unit, 15 percent).

Most of the units we surveyed were equipped with the latest "tactical gear." Over 80 percent of the departments had MP5 submachine guns, tactical semiautomatic shotguns, night vision equipment, sniper rifles, flash-bang grenades, tactical shields, battle-dress uniforms, and specialized "dynamic entry tools." Over 50 percent had electronic surveillance equipment, tactical helmets, tactical communication headsets, and a mobile command center (i.e., a SWAT van). Seven percent had armored personnel carriers.

Most of the officers responding to the survey were police supervisors. Thirty-eight percent (n = 119) could be categorized as high-level administrators (chief, sheriff, deputy chief, major, or captain); 50 percent were either sergeants or lieutenants (n = 154); the remainder were patrol officers or deputy sheriffs.

Because the departments were relatively small, it was important to understand how PPUs fit into these agencies' organizational structures. Seven percent (n = 22) of the PPUs were maintained full-time; 93 percent were classified as a part-time arrangement (n = 288). Almost 74 percent (n = 230) of the PPUs served only one department, while 18 percent (n = 58) were multijurisdictional. Follow-up phone interviews revealed that many extremely small departments offset the high costs of forming and operating a paramilitary unit by participating in regional units. Some of these multijurisdictional operations involved 50 to 60 smaller agencies.[8]

There were 17.7 paramilitary officers for every 100 sworn persons. We realize that this finding is due mainly to departmental size. As we discuss later, the proximity of paramilitary police officers to regular patrol officers (in fact, most officers in small-town PPUs function as both) is important in assessing the potential cultural and operational effects of these units on the larger organization.

PPU Activities over Time

Analysis of the longitudinal data revealed important trends in the periods during which PPUs were formed (see figure 1). Only 20 percent (n = 63) of today's PPUs existed at the beginning of 1980. By the end of 1984, the number had risen to 121, a 92 percent increase. This increase foreshadowed the developments in the second half of the 1980s. The number of PPUs formed between 1985 and 1990 increased sharply: 130 new units came into existence during this period, bringing the total to 251 and representing an increase of 107 percent. Between 1985 and 1995, the number of paramilitary units in agencies serving small jurisdictions. increased by 157 percent. This growth is likely to continue. If we consider that 46 of the departments surveyed responded that they would establish a unit within the next few years, three-fourths of departments employing 100 or fewer officers and serving 25,000 to 50,000 persons will have a PPU by the turn of the century.

The formation of numerous but relatively inactive units, however, would lessen the significance of these data. Therefore we collected baseline data on the number of call-outs performed by each department beginning in 1980; we requested longitudinal data from 1980 to the end of 1995. "Call-outs" included any activity requiring deployment of the unit, such as barricaded persons, hostages, terrorists, civil disturbances, and the serving of high-risk search and arrest warrants. These data do not include activities related to proactive patrol work by PPUs.

The number of call-outs from 1980 to 1984 remained relatively stable at an average of 3.6 to 3.8 per year (see table 1). Beginning in 1985, the mean number increased steadily from 4.5 in 1985 to slightly over 12 by the end of 1995. The median rose from 4 in 1985 to 9 in 1995. Between 1980 and 1995 the mean number of call-outs increased by 238 percent.

The total number of call-outs, because of the increase in the number of PPUs in the last 10 years, illustrates more clearly the aggregate rise in police paramilitary activities (see table 1). In 1980 the total was 220. By 1985 the number had more than doubled to 481, by 1988 it had quadrupled to 960, and by the end of 1995 it had reached 3,715, a total increase of 1,589 percent.

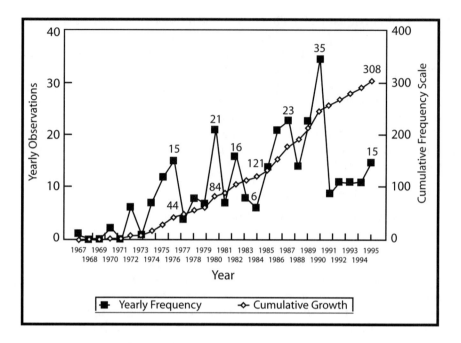

Figure 1 Cumulative growth of PPUs, showing number of new PPUs formed each year

For 1995, traditional reactive functions associated with SWAT units accounted for a surprisingly small proportion of call-outs. Hostage situations ($n = 193$; 5 percent), civil disturbances ($n = 52$; 1 percent), and terrorist incidents ($n = 5$; .1 percent) were quite rare. Barricaded persons accounted for a higher proportion ($n = 874$; 24 percent). By far the most common use of these units was for executing search and arrest warrants: 66 percent ($n = 466$) of the units' call-outs belonged to this category.[9]

Figure 2 displays the number of departments each year that began using their paramilitary units to execute warrants. The total number of departments using PPUs for this purpose has increased steadily over the last 20 years, and increased exponentially (342 percent) between 1985 and 1995. Even though the overall number of units has increased, the percentage of units engaged in warrant work has grown significantly as well. For instance, as shown in table 2, only 40 percent of PPUs were used in this capacity in 1980. This number had risen to 49 percent by 1985, to 81 percent by the end of 1990, and to 94 percent by the end of 1995. These data indicate a dramatic shift in PPUs' activity.

Serving warrants should not be interpreted as a "reactive" deployment of the unit when a felony arrest warrant is served on a high-risk suspect after a thorough investigation. Phone interviews revealed that warrant work consisted almost exclusively of proactive, no-knock "raids"

Table 1 Selected characteristics of call-out data

Year	Mean	Median	Number of Call-Outs	Percentage Increase[a]
1980	3.7	3.0	220	N/A
1981	3.7	3.0	244	10.9
1982	3.6	3.0	274	24.6
1983	3.7	3.0	322	46.4
1984	3.8	3.0	350	59.1
1985	4.5	4.0	481	118.6
1986	5.5	4.0	685	211.4
1987	6.7	4.5	960	336.4
1988	7.1	4.0	1,151	423.2
1989	8.9	5.0	1,633	642.3
1990	10.3	5.0	2,311	950.5
1991	11.1	6.0	2,610	1,086.4
1992	12.1	7.0	3,052	1,287.3
1993	12.0	8.0	3,255	1,379.6
1994	12.2	8.0	3,452	1,469.1
1995	12.5	9.0	3,715	1,588.6

[a] Within the percentage increase column, 1980 is the base year for all calculations.

for the purpose of investigating a residence and collecting evidence such as drugs, guns, and money. About 10 percent of the small-locality departments served 20 to 120 investigatory search warrants a year.

Possibly an even more controversial use of PPUs was their deployment as a patrol force. Seventeen percent of the departments with a paramilitary unit ($n = 55$) used the unit as a proactive patrol force in "high-crime" areas within their jurisdiction. Although a few PPUs performed this function before 1989 ($n = 6$), most of the increase has occurred since then ($n = 49$, a 717 percent increase; see figure 3). Phone interviewees described a variety of approaches used to deploy these units as patrol teams. Some PPUs patrolled in BDUs and carried MP5 submachine guns. These units responded only to the most serious call for service; they spent most of their time conducting "terry-stops."[10] Other departments used similar tactics but dressed less like a military unit (in jeans and jackets identifying their unit) and carried only 9mm. service revolvers and semi-automatic shotguns.

Finally, the PPUs' training deserves mention. Training holds a central place in the police paramilitary subculture (Kraska, 1996; Kraska and Paulsen, 1997). As with military special operations teams such as the Navy

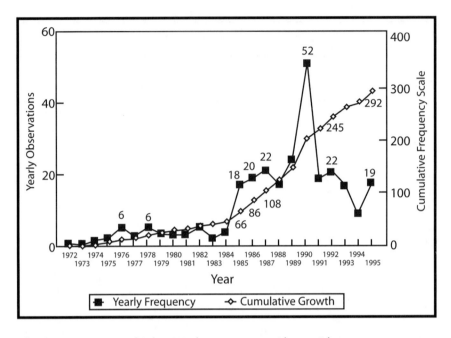

Figure 2   Years in which PPUs began warrant/drug raids

Seals and the Army Rangers, these units' elite status is based in part on their reputation for receiving extensive training in "tactical or special operations."

In medium-sized to large police organizations, each officer in a paramilitary unit receives an average of 225 hours of formal training per year (Kraska and Kappeler, 1997). Most PPU commanders agreed that if a department is moderately active in conducting call-outs (two per month), a tactical officer needs at least 220 hours of training a year. If the unit conducts relatively few call-outs (three a year), it should provide at least an additional 50 hours of formal training per year. The PPUs housed in the small-locality departments studied here conducted a yearly average of

Table 2   Proportion of PPUs conducting warrant work for selected years

	Number of Units in Existence	Number of Units Used for Warrants	Percentage Engaged in Warrant Work
1984	121	48	39.67
1985	135	66	48.89
1990	251	203	80.88
1995	311	292	93.89

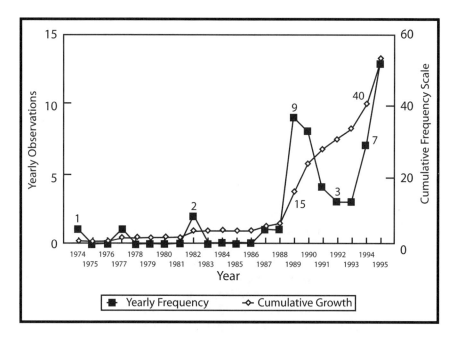

Figure 3   Years in which PPUs began proactive patrol

only 106 hours of formal training per officer. Almost 53 percent of these departments conducted 100 or fewer hours of training per year; 20 percent provided their tactical officers with 50 or fewer hours.

Police paramilitary teams often draw their expertise and training from actual military special operations teams such as the Navy Seals and the Army Rangers (Kraska and Kappeler, 1997). Surprisingly, even in these smaller jurisdictions, 32 percent (n = 101) of the respondents answered "yes" when asked whether they trained with active-duty military experts in special operations. Thirty-one percent (n = 96) responded that they were influenced by "police officers with special operations experience in the military." The two most popular sources of PPU training and/or expertise were the FBI and for-profit, tactical training schools. Forty-one percent (n = 129) of the PPUs worked with the FBI; 63 percent (n = 196) used private tactical schools.

Implications for Small Localities: The Dangers of Militarizing Mayberry

The data demonstrate a significant growth in the number of PPUs and a precipitous rise in PPU activity in small jurisdictions. Because small-locality PPUs engage in proactive patrolling and serve investigatory search warrants, these findings also document the normalization of the PPU approach into small-town police work. Most likely we captured these trends in the midst of their development.[11]

Previous research assessing macro-level shifts in police practices focused mainly on "big-city policy" (Fogelson, 1977). Our research adds a new dimension to the underresearched area of small-locality policing by raising questions about the assumption that these agencies are exclusively service-oriented. Paramilitary units in small towns are even more significant than in big cities because urban police officials and politicians can justify, at least partially, a paramilitary approach to crime and drugs in the media-constructed image of a hostile, crime-ridden, urban environment. How do we reconcile this same type of paramilitary policing imagery and activity in "Mayberry?"

It would be tempting to marginalize this paramilitary phenomenon as an interesting appendage of the multidimensional nature of modern police. Not only do the findings on the normalization of small-locality PPUs into routine police work neutralize this argument, it is also critical to recall that there are almost 18 police paramilitary officers for every 100 regular patrol officers in these small localities. Most of these PPU officers serve in the organization as regular patrol officers during their normal duties. In addition, police administrators view these officers as the "elite" or the "cops' cops" (see note 3). These factors add credence to the possibility that the paramilitary team model today represents a significant cultural and operational influence on small-locality police organizations as a whole (and possibly will do so more strongly in the future).

The small number of training hours in these PPUs raises another important issue: the degree to which these teams approximate the ideal of highly trained, proficient squads of use-of-force specialists. In keeping with the decentralized nature of American policing, departments form these squads in an ad hoc fashion, with no regulatory body or set of standards. Expertise in "tactical operations" often is gained from reading books, watching videotapes, and possibly visiting a 3- to 5-day for-profit, paramilitary training camp.

In view of these conditions, strict military discipline, a rigid command structure, and tight administrative oversight may not be the norm in Mayberry. PPU members in this study claimed autonomy from direct administrative supervision. As one team commander stated, "We're left alone. The brass knows that we know what we're doing more than they do. One of the reasons we're so effective is we have the freedom to handle situations and problems as we see best." Bock (1995) documents how the autonomy enjoyed by these PPUs, even at the federal level, carries high potential for abuse, particularly in serving no-knock search warrants.

Another development that must be tracked closely is departments' tendency to expand paramilitary units' range of applications, especially if we consider their high cost (see note 5) and the extreme concern about officers' safety in the police subculture (Skolnick, 1966; Van Maanen, 1978). PPUs are not only creeping into proactive functions; their existence in small localities also might be contributing to a broader definition of reactive situations requiring a paramilitary response. One small-locality SWAT commander gave the following justification for an inordinately large number of PPU deployments for barricaded suspects in relation to a departmental policy that requires patrol officers to ask "barricades" only once to surrender:

> If the subject refuses once, the SWAT unit is called in, and we almost always either gas 'em or toss in a flash-bang grenade. We're not gonna hang around for hours and beg, and we're sure not going to get killed because we're indecisive.[12]

Beyond Mayberry: Explaining Paramilitary Unit Policing

Theoretical and Causal Analysis

To understand the PPU phenomenon more clearly, we must situate small-locality PPUs within broader changes in the police institution and in formal social control in general. We attempt here to make theoretical sense of the rise and normalization of paramilitary policing.

Trends in small-locality policing lag, by roughly three years, nearly identical shifts in larger departments (see Kraska and Kappeler, 1997). Small-locality paramilitary policing thus follows an even more significant movement in medium-sized to large police agencies. If we combine the data from larger departments with those cited in this study, we see that the paramilitary unit approach is becoming an integral part of contemporary policing in all departments serving localities with 25,000 or more people. In 1995 over 77 percent of police departments had paramilitary units, an increase of almost 48 percent since 1985. The returned surveys alone documented 29,962 paramilitary deployments in 1995, a 939 percent increase over the 2,884 call-outs of 1980. Over 20 percent of all departments with PPUs use the units for proactive patrol work, a 257 percent increase since the beginning of 1989.

Our assertion that these data represent a shift in the police institution should not be interpreted as the announcement of a mutually exclusive shift—that is, the only shift. The police institution has probably shifted as well toward the rhetoric and activities associated with community policing. National-level longitudinal data documenting the degree to which the police institution has structurally transformed and engaged in activities associated with community policing over time, however, have yet to surface (see Maguire forthcoming).[13] As we argue below, it is likely that the two approaches are increasing simultaneously.

As with any macro-social shift, an explanation for the rise of PPUs will likely involve a multitude of intersecting and overlapping factors forming a complex theoretical mix of social, political, economic, and cultural influences. Because of the shortage of relevant longitudinal, national-level data, valid theory testing and model building will be difficult.

Nonetheless we attempted to determine what factors accounted for variance in the dependent variables, paramilitary unit formation and paramilitary unit call-outs ($n = 846$). We collected 73 national-level independent variables that measured economic trends and trends in crime rates, drug use, fear of crime, and criminal justice activity. Using varimax factor analysis and multiple regression, as well as "differencing" to control for the influence of time (Lafree and Drass, 1996), we found that no single variable or construct accounted for a significant amount of variance in our dependent variables.[14]

The inability to account for variance by using these independent variables may be important in itself. We were especially interested in additional testing of the commonsense notion that the rise of PPUs represents a rational reaction by police to changes in crime. Therefore we tested, agency by agency, whether PPU activity corresponds to the occurrence of violent crime. We compared call-out rates from 1980 to 1995, for each jurisdiction, to a UCR violent-crime composite for each of those jurisdictions. We derived the UCR composite by summing the homicide, rape, and robbery rates for each of the responding locations for each year from 1980 through 1995. We excluded aggravated assault rates on the basis of recommendations in the literature (Gove, Hughes and Geerken, 1985; Lafree and Drass, 1996).

Because the data revealed time-based dependence, we differenced the call-out and crime measures at the first level to make them stationary (i.e., to remove the effects of time). A canonical analysis, using the 15 call-out variables and the 15 crime variables for each jurisdiction, revealed that the canonical correlation value of .59 differed significantly from zero at the .000 level. The Stewart-Love index of redundancy, which is directly analogous to the R^2 statistic in multiple regression and is interpreted similarly (Hair et al., 1995), allowed us to determine that only 6.63 percent of the variance in the call-out data was explained by the violent crime composites. Thus we could reasonably exclude changes in violent crime as an important factor explaining the activities of PPUs.

Beyond the Numbers: A Theoretical Exposition

To make sense of this phenomenon beyond the commonsense notion that it reflects a rational response to crime, we must first recognize that the specter of the military model still haunts the real world of contemporary policing, despite the recent rhetoric of democratic reforms. In learning that a component of the police institution is reorganizing itself and conducting operations that could be characterized as militaristic, we find strong support for the thesis that the military model is still a powerful force guiding the ideology and activities of American police. This should not be surprising considering the war/military paradigm remains an authoritative framework for crime-control thinking and action by politicians, bureaucrats, the media, and much of the public (Sherry, 1995).

To understand the revival of militarism in policing, we must point out the close identification between the police paramilitary subculture associated with PPUs and the recent growth of a larger paramilitary culture in the United States during the Reagan-Bush era, and especially since the end of the cold war (Gibson, 1994; Hamm, 1993; Kraska, 1996). Gibson (1994) believes that a ubiquitous culture of paramilitarism has arisen in the last 15 years. Indications include the popularity of paramilitary themes in films, movies, politics, and the news media during the 1980s; the rise of PPUs at the federal and local levels; the popularity of military special operations teams such as the Navy Seals, the Army Rangers, and the Delta Force; the rise of informal militia/paramilitary groups; and the paramilitarism found in some urban gangs (Gibson, 1994).

Within this larger culture, the police paramilitary subculture contains a status hierarchy with military special operations squads such as the Navy Seals at the top, followed by FBI, and BATF police paramilitary teams, large metropolitan paramilitary units, and, finally, PPUs in smaller jurisdictions (Kraska, 1996). In the past decade an enormous police paramilitary community has developed, which includes a 10,000-member professional organization, numerous periodicals, and even its own art work.

A complex of for-profit training, weapons, and equipment suppliers heavily promotes the culture at police shows, in police magazine advertisements, and in police paramilitary training programs sponsored by gun manufacturers such as Heckler and Koch and Smith and Wesson. As evidenced by data in this study, the U.S. armed forces also participate, particularly since the end of the cold war (Kraska, 1996). The allure of police paramilitary subculture stems from the enjoyment, excitement, high status, and male camaraderie that accompany the heavy weaponry, new technologies, dangerous assignments, and heightened anticipation of using force in most PPU work (Kraska, 1996; Kraska and Paulsen, 1997).

Ideologically the government's latest war on drugs, with its rhetoric and actions associated with doing battle (drug war boot camps, drugs as a threat to national security, and the use of the U.S. armed forces), dovetails nicely with Gibson's thesis on the growth of paramilitary culture. The drug war—beginning in the early 1980s, peaking in the late 1980s, and continuing through the 1990s—has profoundly affected all aspects of the criminal justice system (Irwin and Austin, 1997; Miller, 1996). It is no coincidence that the police cracked down on drugs in economically deprived areas concurrently with the great increase in investigatory, no-knock drug raids, conducted mostly by PPUs. Indeed, most of the increases in paramilitary deployments began in 1988, at the apex of drug war activity and hysteria. Nearly all police officials (n = 126) in small and large agencies explained in phone interviews that their agency either formed its PPU or dramatically increased the activities of its PPU to conduct raids on private residences in search of drugs, guns, and "drug money."

The escalation of the drug war and the increase in PPUs coincide as well with reformers' calls for the police to alter their operational focus. Reformers advocate a change from *reacting* to individual calls for service with one or two officers to adopting a *proactive* model, which establishes "teams" of officers that work collectively to "maintain order" or solve "community problems" (Goldstein, 1990; Kelling, 1988; Trojanowicz and Bucqueroux, 1990). As we found in this research, and according to data from larger departments (Kraska and Kappeler, 1997), police paramilitary teams are used as proactive patrol forces to "suppress" highly politicized problems such as guns, drugs, gangs, and community disorder in economically deprived areas. In fact, 63 percent of police agencies serving 25,000 people or more agreed or strongly agreed that PPUs "play an important role in community policing strategies." One PPU commander clarified the rationale behind this belief:

> We conduct a lot of saturation patrol. We do "terry stops" and "aggressive" field interviews. These tactics are successful as long as the pressure stays on relentlessly. The key to our success is that we're an elite crime-fighting team that's not bogged down in the regular bureaucracy. We focus on "*quality of life*" issues like illegal parking, loud music, bums, neighbor troubles. We have the freedom to stay in a hot area and clean it up—particularly gangs. Our tactical enforcement team works nicely with our department's emphasis on community policing (emphasis added).

At first glance one might assume that a trend toward militarization must be in opposition to the community policing "revolution." In the real world of policing, however, some police officials are interpreting the reformers' call to adopt a proactive stance, and to "actively create a climate of order" (Bayley, 1996), as requiring a more aggressive, indeed militaristic approach to enforcing law and order among the "dangerous classes." At least in their minds, PPUs do not supplant a CP or POP approach; they operate in harmony. This reasoning is exemplified most clearly in the recent crackdown on crime and drugs by New York city politicians and police officials.[15]

The rise and the normalization of PPUs, then, correspond to changes in popular culture, drug control operations, and police reform efforts. It should be apparent that a complex combination of factors plays a role in this phenomenon. To explain the final and perhaps most compelling way in which the rise of PPUs corresponds to larger shifts in formal social control, we must revisit the essence of paramilitary unit functioning: PPUs are deployed to deal with situations that police agencies perceive as requiring a team of officers with a strong focus on the threatened or actual use of violence. Street-level policing has always been individually based, discretionary, and unregulated (Bittner, 1970; Skolnick, 1966). Does this shift in policing, away from individual, situational uses of violence and toward the collective use of violence by "well managed" teams of officers, coincide with larger trends in formal social control?

A comparable development in scope, form, and function is occurring in corrections. It cross-validates the notion that paramilitary units may indicate *modernizing* changes in the handling of violence by social control agents in the larger criminal justice apparatus (Christie, 1994; Feeley and Simon, 1992; Garland, 1990). Correctional administrators have adopted the paramilitary unit model in attempting to *rationalize* (in the Weberian sense) correctional officers' use of violence through the establishment of "special operations" or "emergency response" teams. As has occurred in policing, "many departments of corrections created their own emergency response teams modeling them after Police SWAT Teams and military commando units such as the Army Green Beret Special Forces and the Navy Seal Teams" (Bryan, 1995:2). These units, originally designed to react to only the most serious inmate disturbances, have expanded their range of functions in the last few years to include cell searches, lesser inmate disturbances, "extractions" of inmates from cells, and the forced administration of medicines (Beard, 1994; Bryan, 1995).

Why is this paramilitary model so appealing to both corrections and policing? As noted above, part of the answer lies generally in the seductive powers of paramilitary unit subculture as promoted by for-profit industry. The techno-warrior garb, heavy weaponry, sophisticated technology, hypermasculinity, and "real-work" functions are nothing less than intoxicating for paramilitary unit participants and those who aspire to work in such units (Kraska, 1996; Kraska and Paulsen, 1997).

An additional source of allure is the hope that bureaucracies, by creating "violence specialists," can finally control, manage, and make more efficient the state-administered force which is their prerogative. This faith in professionalizing violence by adopting the military model has a long history in both corrections and policing. Thus, to much of the practicing criminal justice community, the recent implementation of the military special operations model represents not a regression in the administration of justice but a step toward further modernizing and refining state violence.

In sum, militarizing state force does not only signal a falling back on a culture of militarism and crude state power in the war on crime and drugs. It also corresponds closely to developments documented by Christie (1994), Cohen (1985), Ericson (1994), Feely and Simon (1992, 1994), Garland, (1990, 1995), Manning (1992, 1993), and of course Foucault (1977). All of these scholars have theorized on what they view as an unpromising, fundamental shift in formal social control: an acceleration of criminal law agencies' uncritical implementation of practices consistent with the tenets of "high-modernity"—accentuated standardization, routinization, technical efficiency, scientificization, risk minimization, technologicalization, actuarial thinking, the "what works" fetish, moral indifference, and a focus on aggregate populations—in a quest to more efficiently manage those who threaten state order. The rise and the normalization of PPUs represents, therefore, an adaptation to conditions of high-modernity in the crime war.

Policy Science and General Schwartzkopf

We cannot assume, however, that this quest for rationality will lead to rational outcomes. Ritzer (1993:121) draws from Weber in asserting that "rational systems inevitably spawn a series of irrationalities that serve to limit, ultimately compromise, and perhaps even undermine, their rationality." The central policy issue related to PPUs is the degree to which this phenomenon constrains police violence, as intended, or escalates it. Except for individual departments, no systematic data have been compiled on the extent to which these units use force. The first author interviewed officials from large and small police departments who claimed that their units had never discharged weapons during a deployment; others stated that they often discharged their weapons on call-outs; some admitted shooting innocent people; and some described casualties to officers caused by "friendly fire."

The paramilitary community is adamant about PPUs' life-saving potential. Few could argue against using well-trained specialists to respond to serious terrorist or hostage situations. Even within these narrow reactive functions, however, we need only recall Waco and Ruby Ridge to appreciate what the adaptation of the paramilitary model implies for civilian law enforcement. Valid system-wide data on PPUs' use of force is needed but will be difficult to obtain.

To determine the rationality of this approach, however, we must consider issues broader than whether these units "save lives" and how often weapons are discharged. Researchers also must track and assess PPUs' "mission creep" into mainstream policing functions. As evidenced by the broad definition of "barricades" in some small-locality agencies, the normalization of the PPU approach carries high potential for expanding the use-of-force options available to the police and the circumstances in which they are utilized in a type of police violence net widening. "Less-lethal technologies," for instance, are becoming extremely popular among PPUs (Kraska, 1996).

These data also demonstrate the expansion of police power in conducting contraband raids. PPUs provide the police institution with a new tool for conducting a crude form of investigation into drug and gun law violations inside private residences. This new approach to drug and gun law enforcement is not necessarily a reaction to a dangerous existing condition (such as a hostage situation). Rather, it is a police-initiated proactive approach, which itself manufactures dangerous situations.

Policy research as it applies to police militarization, however, can provide only limited guidance. The debate on paramilitary policing in the British literature illustrates clearly that normative concerns play a central role in assessing its desirability (Jefferson, 1990; Reiner, 1992). This issue involves heartfelt beliefs, values, and morals. To many people, even among academics, the military model represents constraint, discipline, honor, control, competence, and even a type of patriotism. To others it stands for tyranny, state violence, human rights abuses, war, and an ideology which stresses that problems are best handled by technologized state force. Some will see the rise and normalization of PPUs as a necessary and rational approach to today's crime, gang, and drug problems; others will view it as bureaucracy building and as evidence of a government in crisis moving toward a police state.

Crime and justice academicians nevertheless must be careful not to succumb to what Ericson calls "General Schwartzkopf criminology": an uncritical policy science approach that emphasizes "how military-type bureaucracy, discipline, technology, deployment and coercion fight criminal sources of insecurity" (Ericson and Carriere, 1994:100). The ideological trappings of the General Schwartzkopf approach lie in its close association with military professionalism, scientific rationality, advanced technology, and expedient, value-neutral problem solving through the use or threat of force. Scholars must remain skeptical about applying these tenets of high-modern militarism to the criminal justice apparatus, and must watch closely for the irrationalities it is likely to spawn.

Endnotes

[1] For a more thorough discussion of the war/military paradigm and its connection to paramilitary policing, see Kraska (1996).

[2] *The Iron Fist and the Velvet Glove* (Crime and Social Justice Associates, 1983) was the first work to identify and critique the SWAT phenomenon. Chambliss (1994) conducted field research on the Washington, DC rapid deployment unit (RDU) and discussed its "repressive" tendencies. Stevens and MacKenna (1988) conducted survey research on PPUs in 1986, which yielded only a 40 percent response rate. Their research focussed on administrative issues.

[3] Ninety-six percent ($n = 45$) of the police chiefs responding to this survey agreed or strongly agreed with the statement "Being part of a tactical unit is a prestigious position in the department."

[4] One department of 75 officers sent us professionally made trading cards depicting its 15-man unit. One of the cards was a photograph of the SRT posed around an armored personnel carrier. Members were dressed in full tactical gear; nylon mesh masks covered their faces. The back of the card read, "When citizens need help they call the police. When the police need help they call SRT." The SRT's self-image as the cops' cops illuminates members' self-perception as specialists in the use of force.

[5] In phone interviews with two departments that had just established PPUs, the informants estimated that start-up and first-year costs of a 15-member unit would be $200,000 to $250,000. This figure includes all "tactical gear" and first-year training costs.

[6] The demographic literature makes the break between smaller and larger cities at 50,000 (McGregor-Matlock and Woodhouse, 1987; Shannon and Ross, 1977). In labeling this study "small-locality," as opposed to "small-town," we included 37 county agencies that serve 25,000 to 50,000 people and employ 100 or fewer officers.

[7] Although the N is reduced by truncating the population subset at the 100-officer level, analysis of the larger data set revealed no appreciable differences in our findings.

[8] Some police administrators in small towns and rural counties are developing multijurisdictional PPUs by using existing arrangements designed to assist small communities in natural disasters. A paper agency is formed when departments participating in the disaster relief arrangement also donate one to three officers and associated funds to be a part of a fully operational 40- to 60-member PPU. Several interviewees claimed that their multijurisdictional PPUs gradually developed an independence from political and community oversight; this left them free to collaborate with state police agencies, with little political or community scrutiny.

[9] Three percent (n = 125) of call-outs were categorized as "other."

[10] Interviews revealed that when paramilitary units conducted proactive patrols, they were not required to answer routine calls for service. These units instead were deployed into "high-crime" neighborhoods to conduct street interrogations of "suspicious" pedestrians, occupants of automobiles, and even persons in "drug houses." Three departments said that it was not unusual for their units to conduct "warrantless dynamic entries" into private residences if they saw suspected drug dealers entering a residence to elude police interrogation.

[11] Evidence for this assertion includes the large number of police departments planning to establish a PPU in the future, the recent steep growth in PPUs doing warrant and patrol work, and the fact that much of these data comes from newly formed units.

[12] One of the anonymous reviewers of this paper claimed that similar changes are taking place in hostage/barricade situations:

> Instead of following the tried and true 25-year-old practice of negotiating for a bloodless resolution no matter how long it takes, some departments seem to have adopted the practice of turning scenes over to SWAT after a relatively short time. . . . SWAT then attempts to implement a "tactical resolution" which usually ends in one or more dead bodies. Indeed, members of one SWAT team even told me that their department has given up on negotiating for a bloodless resolution no matter how long it takes. Instead, they have adopted the "LA procedure" which consists of negotiating with hostage takers or barricaded persons for the purpose of putting them in position for a "tactical resolution": an "instantly catastrophic" shot by a sniper to the cerebral cortex.

[13] On the basis of data from 1987–1993, Maguire (forthcoming) finds no significant differences in the extent of structural change between agencies that identify themselves as community policing departments and agencies that do not.

[14] Currently we are collecting data relevant to social threat theory for each of the 846 jurisdictions for 1995. The objective is to determine which (if any) social threat variables account for the variance in paramilitary deployments across jurisdictions.

[15] NYPD officials, with support from the Harvard School of Government, are quite vocal in claiming that their unique brand of proactive, aggressive policing has reduced crime dramatically. In April 1996, NYPD launched a "3,000"-officer offensive to "crush drug trafficking and the drug business," employing the same tactics as discussed in this research (Kraus, 1996:1). NYPD is also aggressively marketing its "success strategy" to other police agencies via national conferences.

References

Angell, J. E. (1971). Toward an alternative to the classic police organizational arrangements: A democratic model. *Criminology, 9,* 195–206.

Bailey, W. G. (1995). *The encyclopedia of police science* (2nd ed.). New York: Garland.

Bayley, D. H. (1994). *Police for the future.* New York: Oxford University Press.

Beard, J. A. (1994, August). Using special management units to control inmate violence. *Corrections Today,* 88–91.

Bittner, E. (1970). *The functions of police in modern society.* Chevy Chase: National Clearinghouse for Mental Health.

Bock, A. W. (1995). *Ambush at Ruby Ridge: How governmental agents set Randy Weaver up and took his family down.* Irvine, CA: Dickens.

Brewer, J. D., Guelke, A., Hume, I., Moxon-Browne, E., & Wolford, R. (1988). *The police, public order and the state.* New York: St. Martin's.

Bryan, D. (1995). Emergency response teams: A prison's first line of defense. *Corrections Compendium, 20*(7), 1–13.

Chambliss, W. J. (1994). Policing the ghetto underclass: The politics of law and law enforcement. *Social Problems, 41,* 177–94.

Chevigny, P. (1995). *Edge of the knife: Police violence in the Americas.* New York: Free Press.

Christie, N. (1994). *Crime control as industry: Toward GULAGS, Western style.* New York: Routledge.

Cohen, S. (1985). *Visions of social control: Crime, punishment and classification.* Cambridge: Polity.

Crime and Social Justice Associates. (1983). *The iron fist and the velvet glove: An analysis of the U.S. police* (3rd ed.). San Francisco: Garret.

Decker, S. (1979). The rural county sheriff. An issue in social control. *Criminal Justice Review, 4,* 97–111.

Enloe, C. (1980). Police, military, and ethnicity: Foundations of state power. New Brunswick, NJ: Transaction.

Ericson, R. (1994). The division of expert knowledge in policing and security. *British Journal of Sociology, 45,* 149–70.

Ericson, R., & Carriers, K. (1994). The fragmentation of criminology. In D. Nelken (Ed.), *The Futures of Criminology* (pp. 89–109). Beverly Hills: Sage.

Feeley, M., & Simon, J. (1992). The new penology. *Criminology, 39,* 449–74.

Feeley, M., & Simon, J. (1994). Actuarial justice: The emerging new criminal law. In D. Nelken (Ed.), *The Futures of Criminology* (pp. 173–201). Beverly Hills: Sage.

Fogelson, R. M. (1977). *Big-city police.* Cambridge, MA: Harvard University Press.

Foucault, M. (1977). *Discipline and punish: The birth of the prison.* New York: Vintage.

Fry, L. W., & Berkes, L. J. (1983). The paramilitary police model: An organizational misfit. *Human Organization, 42,* 225–34.

Garland, D. (1990). *Punishment and modern society: A study in social theory.* Chicago: University of Chicago Press.

Garland, D. (1995). Penal modernism and postmodernism. In T. G. Blomber & S. Cohen (Eds.), *Punishment and social control: Essays in honor of Sheldon L. Messinger* (pp. 181–210). New York: Aldine.

Gibons, D. C. (1972). Crime in the hinterland. *Criminology, 10,* 177–91.

Gibson, J. W. (1994). *Warrior dreams: Manhood in post-Vietnam America.* New York: Hill and Wang.

Goldstein, H. (1990). *Problem-oriented policing*. New York: McGraw-Hill.

Gove, W. R., Hughes, M., & Geerken, M. (1985). Are uniform crime reports a valid indicator of the index crimes? An affirmative answer with minor qualifications. *Criminology, 23,* 111–120.

Hair, J. F., Jr., Anderson, R. E., Tatham, R. L., & Black, W. C. (1995). *Multivariate data analysis with readings* (4th ed.). Upper Saddle River, NJ: Prentice-Hall.

Hamm, M. S. (1993). *American skinheads: The criminology and control of hate crime.* Westport, CT: Praeger.

Irwin, J., & Austin, J. (1997). *It's about time: America's imprisonment binge.* Belmont, CA: Wadsworth.

Jefferson, T. (1990). *The case against paramilitary policing.* Bristol, PA: Open University Press.

Kelling, G. L. (1988). *Police and communities: The quiet revolution.* Washington, DC: National Institute of Justice.

Klockars, C. B. (1985). *The idea of police.* Beverly Hills: Sage.

Kraska, P. B. (1994). The police and the military in the post-cold war era: Streamlining the state's use of force entities in the drug war. *Police Forum, 4,* 1–8.

Kraska, P. B. (1996). Enjoying militarism: Political/personal dilemmas in studying U.S. police paramilitary units. *Justice Quarterly, 13,* 405–429.

Kraska, P. B., & Kappeler, V. E. (1997). Militarizing American police: The rise and normalization of paramilitary units. *Social Problems, 44,* 1–18.

Kraska, P. B., & Paulsen, D. J. (1997). Grounded research into U.S. paramilitary policing: Forging the iron fist inside the velvet glove. *Policing and Society, 7,* 253–270.

Kraus, C. (1996). NYC police to start big drug offensive using new approach. Posted on World Wide Web, April 4. *New York Times* Company.

LaFree, G., & Drass, K. A. (1996). The effects of changes in intraracial income inequality and educational attainment on changes in arrest rates for African Americans and whites, 1957 to 1990. *American Sociological Review, 61,* 614–634.

Maguire, E. R. (Forthcoming). Structural changes in large municipal police organizations during the community policing era. *Justice Quarterly.*

Manning, P. K. (1977). *Police work: The social organization of policing.* Cambridge, MA: MIT Press.

Manning, P. K. (1978). The police: Mandate, strategies and appearances. In P. K. Manning & J. Van Maanen (Eds.), *Policing: A view from the street* (pp. 53–70). Chicago: Goodyear.

Manning, P. K. (1992). Economic rhetoric and policing reform. *Criminal Justice Research Bulletin, 7,* 1–8.

Manning, P. K. (1993). The preventive conceit: The black box in market context. *American Behavioral Scientist, 36,* 639–650.

Marenin, O., & Copus, G. (1991). Policing rural Alaska: The village public safety officer (VPSO) program. *American Journal of Police, 10,* 1–26.

McGregor-Matlock, L., & Woodhouse, L. (1987). *The state of the small city: A survey of the nation's cities and towns under 50,000.* Washington, DC: National League of Cities.

Miller, J. G. (1996). *Search and destroy: African-American males in the criminal justice system.* New York: Cambridge University Press.

Reiner, R. (1992). *The politics of the police.* Toronto: University of Toronto Press.

Ritzer, G. (1993). *The McDonaldization of society: An investigation into the changing character of contemporary social life.* Thousand Oaks, CA: Pine Forge.

Shannon, J., & Ross, J. (1977). Cities: Their increasing dependence on state and federal aid. In J. Herrington (Ed.), *Small cities in transition: The dynamics of growth and decline* (pp. 211–229). Cambridge, MA: Ballinger.

Sherry, M. S. (1996). *In the shadow of war: The United States since the 1930s.* New Haven: Yale University Press.

Skolnick, J. H. (1966). *Justice without trial: Law enforcement in a democratic society.* New York: Wiley.

Skolnick, J. H., & Fyfe, J. J. (1993). *Above the law: Police and the excessive use of force.* New York: Free Press.

Stevens, J. W., & MacKenna, D. W. (1988). Police capabilities for responding to violent criminal activity and terrorism. *Police Studies, 11,* 116–123.

Sutherland, E. H., Cressey, D. R., & Luckenbill, D. F. (1992). *Principles of criminology.* Dix Hills, NY: General Hall Inc.

Trojanowicz, R., & Bucqueroux, B. (1990). *Community policing: A contemporary perspective.* Cincinnati: Anderson.

Turk, A. (1982). *Political criminality: The defiance and defense of authority.* Beverly Hills: Sage.

Van Maanen, J. (1978). Kinsmen in repose: Occupational perspectives of patrolmen. In P. K. Manning & J. Van Maanen (Eds.), *Police and policing: A view from the street* (pp. 28–39). Chicago: Goodyear.

Weisheit, R. A. (1993). Studying drugs in rural areas: Notes from the field. *Journal of Research in Crime and Delinquency, 30,* 213–232.

Weisheit, R. A., Falcone, D. N., & Wells, L. E. (1996). *Crime and policing in rural and small-town America.* Prospect Heights, IL: Waveland Press.

Westley, W. A. (1956). Secrecy and the police. *Social Forces, 34,* 254–257.

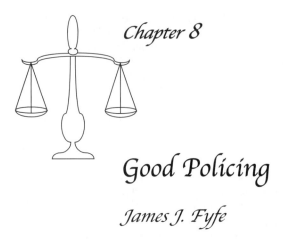

Chapter 8

Good Policing

James J. Fyfe

According to Peter K. Manning (1977), the social mandate of the American police is a hodge-podge of conflicting duties and responsibilities that has developed with little input from the police themselves. He is correct. Firefighting, the uniformed public service frequently compared to policing, has a clear mandate that firefighters have helped to fashion: the fire service exists to prevent fires and to extinguish as quickly and as safely as possible all those it did not prevent. It is virtually impossible to derive a similarly succinct and comprehensive statement of the police role. Instead, it is safe to say only that police perform a variety of services that must be available seven days a week, 24 hours a day, that may require the use or threat of force, and that are not readily available from any other public agency or private institution.[1]

Doing What Nobody Else Does

Police responsibility for these tasks not handled by others has meant that the police sometimes are called upon to do the impossible or to attempt to provide services they have not been adequately prepared to perform. The historic reluctance of police to intervene in domestic disputes,[2] for example, probably has more to do with the difficulty of straightening out other peoples' arguments in the middle of the night than with the purported danger to police of such assignments. A line of research has recently demonstrated that *domestics* are not nearly the police job hazard they were

James F. Fyfe, "Good Policing," in Brian Forst, Ed., *The Socioeconomics of Crime and Justice*. Reprinted by permission of M. E. Sharpe, Inc., Armonk, New York 10504.

assumed to be (see, e.g., Margarita, 1980; Konstantin, 1984; Garner and Clemmer, 1986). The difficulty of resolving these arguments while they are at flashpoint, however, has long been clear, and is a task that might better be handled by social workers provided with protective police escorts. Social workers understandably have not volunteered to play such a role. Consequently, the police have been stuck with it on grounds that they are available and that their duties include order maintenance.

In the past, the ready, round-the-clock availability of the police has caused them to be assigned to many duties that fit under this *order mainte-nance* rubric only by the most liberal definition. In the late nineteenth cen-tury, Philadelphia police provided lodging for more than 100,000 people every year. Early in the twentieth century, New York police stations were the distribution points for food and coal doled out to the poor under "home relief" programs (Monkonnen, 1981:81–106).

In addition, the close ties of the police to the powerful have, in many places, made police departments a major vehicle of job patronage. A major factor in historic analyses of policing is the great extent to which attainment of formally stated police goals has continually been affected by use of police departments as means of politically dispensed upward mobility for newly arrived ethnic groups and recently empowered racial minorities (Fogelson, 1977; Walker, 1977; Wilson, 1964).

The closeness of the police to communities and to politicians has also led to corruption, especially in inner cities where police have been charged with enforcing laws that had been enacted by conservative rural-dominated legislatures, but that found little support in the hurly-burly of urban life. In such places, it became the job of locally controlled police to protect illegal businesses—most notably, gambling and prostitution—from disruptions caused by both other law enforcement agencies and by unruly clientele who might scare off paying customers.[3]

This trend reached a peak during Prohibition, when official corrup-tion became the standard operating procedure of many American police departments (Citizens' Police Committee, 1969). By the time Prohibition ended, however, the United States was deep in the Great Depression, and a constricted job market made policing an attractive career option to well-educated people who in better times would have gone into more tradi-tional white collar and professional work. In many cases, this new breed was repulsed by old school corruption and sought to turn policing into a respectable undertaking.

Police as Crime Fighters

Two icons of these new professionals were J. Edgar Hoover, whose FBI waged a bloody and successful war against the gangsters of the early 1930s, and August Vollmer, who earlier had made the Berkeley Police Department an exemplar of efficiency and technological excellence (Carte and Carte, 1975). These two role models led many local police to attempt to do away with the ambiguity of their mandate by redefining themselves first and foremost as professional crime fighters. These new professionals among police believed that, like FBI agents, local police would win their war by adopting the selective personnel standards and high technology employed with such apparent success by both Hoover and Vollmer. Unfortunately, the police were to find over the long run that the experiences of Hoover and Vollmer were not readily generalizable to other times and places.

J. Edgar Hoover

Hoover's Depression-era successes came not in a broad-fronted war, but in a series of skirmishes against a small number of spectacular outlaws. When local police attempted to apply this same model of *the resolute and professional lawman on the track of bad guys*, however, they eventually became stymied. Police used this strategy over three decades and took great credit for the comparative domestic tranquility that then prevailed. Then, in the 1960s, American crime exploded. Since that watershed decade, the police have learned that the techniques that had been so useful to the FBI in its war against a few colorful characters meant little when a huge baby-boomer generation entered its crime-prone adolescent years, or in inner city crime factories that systematically turn out criminals in overwhelming numbers. Hoover could declare victory when his agents had rounded up or killed the likes of John Dillinger, "Pretty Boy" Floyd, "Babyface" Nelson, and other legendary bandits of the era. But no such easy victory is possible over the rampant and ubiquitous street crime that has literally consumed many inner cities.

August Vollmer

In the same way that police were misled by Hoover's victories, police attempts to emulate Vollmer's example generally have been based on an inexact analogy. Without question, Vollmer turned the Berkeley Police Department into the early twentieth-century American ideal. The Berkeley department was extremely selective, allowing only the very best young men to wear its uniforms. Under Vollmer, the department's apparent success in stifling crime, combined with its great responsiveness to the needs of the *good people* of the community, won it universal admiration at home (Carte and Carte, 1975). But history suggests that, like the "service" style police departments studied by James Q. Wilson during the 1960s (Wilson, 1968) — the Nassau County (NY) Police Department, for example — the Berkeley Police Department enjoyed such apparent success and exalted status largely because it was serving an ideal community that didn't need much from it.

When Vollmer was the police chief of Berkeley, the city was the fast-growing, prosperous, homogenous, and well-educated home to wealthy families who had been scared out of San Francisco by the crime, disorder, bawdiness, earthquake, and fire for which that bigger city on the Bay was best known at the time. Berkeley also was home to the first campus of the University of California, an industry of the type that did not draw employees or clients likely to cause the police much trouble. Indeed, if early twentieth-century Berkeley undergraduates sought to raise hell, it was easy enough for them to ferry across the Bay to the more exciting Sodom of San Francisco or to simply walk across the city line to the Gomorrah of Jack London's Oakland waterfront.

Wilson studied Nassau County, the Long Island suburb adjacent to New York City, when policing there was the same sort of cakewalk that Vollmer's staff had enjoyed a half-century earlier in Berkeley. Until World War II, Nassau County consisted largely of farms, a few small towns, and estates like those occupied by Fitzgerald's Jay Gatsby and friends. During the War, Long Island's expansion began with the growth of its defense industries and aircraft manufacturers. In the years immediately after the War, Nassau County became a booming suburb that, except for its larger population, was much like those that sprouted around Los Angeles at the same time. Generous GI financing, a new highway system, and quick construction methods combined with the desire for the good life—a patch of green away from mean city streets—overnight turned potato fields into tract housing. By the time Wilson observed its police department, the population of Nassau County had nearly doubled during the 1950s—to 1.3 million by 1960—and the county boasted a tax base larger than all but a small handful of U.S. cities. The non-white population in areas served by the county police (as opposed to the generally more exclusive towns policed by a few small independent departments) was 2.5%, and was located largely in a few small and long-established enclaves that had started as the homes for domestic help to the wealthy (Wilson, 1968:224). The county's homicide rate was less than one-sixth the national average and, despite the fact that its ratio of cars:population was far higher than the national norm, Nassau's vehicle theft rate was only one-third the national average (see Wilson, 1968:86–93). Like Vollmer's Berkeley Police Department, Nassau selected its officers carefully, paid and equipped them well, and asked them to give friendly service to a homogenous populace who sought to share peace, quiet, and stability with their neighbors.

Wilson's Nassau differed from Vollmer's Berkeley chiefly in size and by virtue of the high percentage of its population that wore blue collars at work. Both places enjoyed freedom from poverty, inequity, class and ethnic conflict, or social discord of any other type. Both had ideal police departments because both were populated by people of means who had chosen to move there from elsewhere in order to be part of an idyllic community.

In the years since Vollmer's tenure and Wilson's studies, both Berkeley and Nassau have changed. Neither has remained homogenous, uniformly prosperous, or untroubled by decay, conflict, social discord, homelessness, unemployment. Regardless of the quality and competence of its chief executives or what they may have accomplished since Vollmer's halcyon days, nobody in policing regards the Berkeley Police Department as *the* local American law enforcement agency that stands in a class by itself, *the* role model for professional policing. Nobody studies policing in Berkeley[4] and nobody in policing knows much about what may be going on there. Nor has any scholar recently studied police in Nassau County. There, while the number of residents has declined slightly over the last three decades, the population has grown much more heterogenous. The percentage of non-white residents has increased five-fold to 13.3 percent, and Hispanics — virtually unknown in the county at the time of Wilson's work — comprise another 3.3 percent (U.S. Department of Commerce, p. 72). In addition, crime rates have increased, closings of defense and aircraft manufacturers have severely hurt the economy, and even the most casual observer would not expect a replication of Wilson's work to come up with the same rosy picture he found a quarter century ago.[5]

Lessons Learned?

The two lessons of these experiences have not been easily digested by either the police or the public. The first of these lessons is that *neither the low crime rates during the golden years of J. Edgar Hoover and August Vollmer nor the great increases since then have had much to do with the police or law enforcement.* Despite Vollmer's good efforts, Berkeley boasted low crime rates during his years because it was a fast-growing, prosperous, homogenous, and highly-educated town in which the major employer was the state's flagship university. Around the country during the Depression years of Hoover's climb to fame, most people were concerned with putting bread on the table and were too beaten down to be aggressive. Thus, minor property crime was common but — except for a rash of well publicized kidnappings and one-man crime waves of the type he vigorously stifled — violent crime generally was not much of a concern.

With the exceptions of a few defense industry boomtowns, the home front remained quiet during World War II because most young men of crime-prone age were either in the military or busy working overtime to supply or fill in for the boys overseas. Crime remained low throughout the fifties, probably because the generation then at peak crime age (roughly 16–24) was small in number: it had been born in the Depression, when birth rates had dropped.

The sixties changed all this. Urban crime rates soared virtually everywhere regardless of whether police conformed to the ideal of professional-warrior-against-crime. The increase in crime was attributable to several converging forces, but two probably are most important. The huge baby-boom generation entered adolescence, so that an unusually large percentage of the population was in its most crime-prone years. In addition, cities changed. For years, blacks and Hispanics had steadily been replacing white city dwellers who had fled to suburbs like Nassau County, taking businesses, jobs, and the cohesiveness of their former neighborhoods with them. This pattern came to a head in the sixties: old communities broke up to be replaced by impersonal and densely populated projects. Racial, cultural, and class conflicts arose. Urban tax bases eroded, municipal services declined, and all the ills of the inner city flourished as they had not since the great waves of European immigration a half century earlier. Since the sixties, the death of Jim Crow, the increased mobility of the black middle-class, and cutbacks in social programs have aggravated these conditions. With few strong community institutions or positive role models for young people, inner cities have grown even more desolate and hopeless.

The fessional-warrior-against-crime, it is unrealistic to model the police on Hoover's FBI or, even, to think of the police as our first line of defense against crime. In large measure, the presence or absence of crime has nothing to do with the police. Indeed, even though many people continue to think of *police* and *law enforcement* almost interchangeably, the boom in scholarly studies of policing that began in the 1960s has shown with some consistency that only a small proportion of street police officers' time—in the neighborhood of a quarter—involves law enforcement or investigation of crime. Eric Scott, for example, studied more than 26,000 calls for police service in three urban areas. Two percent of these involved reports of violent crime; seventeen percent involved reports of nonviolent crime, and five percent concerned people or circumstances that had aroused citizens' suspicions. The remaining 76 percent concerned interpersonal conflict (seven percent); requests for medical assistance (three percent); traffic problems (nine percent); dependent persons in need of police care (three percent); noise and other public nuisances (11 percent); calls for miscellaneous assistance (12 percent); requests for information (21 percent); provision of non-crime-related information (eight percent); and various police internal matters (two percent) (Scott, 1981:28–30; see also, Reiss, 1971; Webster, 1970; Wilson, 1968). In short, the clientele of the FBI consists almost exclusively of criminal suspects and victims and witnesses to crime, but most of the people with whom the police interact need help with problems not related to crime.

The second lesson is that *policing can probably be regarded as ideal only in places that are themselves idyllic and untroubled.* This is a message with important implications for police reformers, many of whom currently urge adoption of new *community-oriented* and *community-based* policing models. According to the first of Trojanowicz and Bucqueroux's three-paragraph definition (1990:5–6):

> Community Policing is a new philosophy of policing, based on the concept that police officers and private citizens working together in creative ways can help solve contemporary problems related to crime, fear of crime, social and physical disorder, and neighborhood decay. The philosophy is predicated in the belief that achieving these goals requires that police departments develop a new relationship with the law-abiding people in the community, allowing them a greater voice in setting local police priorities and involving them in efforts to improve the overall quality of life in their neighborhoods. It shifts the focus of police work from handling random calls to solving community problems.

Trojanowicz and Bucqueroux go on to say that this new model requires the designation of some patrol officers as "Community Policing Officers." Each of these CPOs should be assigned on a continuing basis to the same small geographic area. There, from their patrol cars and the responsibility of responding to radio calls, CPOs can then develop collaborative relationships with community members. These relationships, in turn, will allow "people direct input in setting day-to-day, local police priorities, in exchange for their cooperation and participation in efforts to police themselves" (Trojanowicz and Bucqueroux, 1990:5).

While there certainly is room for greater and more imaginative police interaction with the communities they serve, it often is difficult to distinguish these new community-oriented models from Wilson's *service* style of policing and from such police arrangements as the democratic team policing alternative of John E. Angell (1971) and neighborhood team policing (see Sherman, et al., 1973). Indeed, I can find virtually nothing in descriptions of recent community policing models that differs from my own experience in two New York City police precincts that included Neighborhood Police Teams more than two decades ago.

But these prior attempts to rearrange police departments and their relationships with communities have either been discarded or, as in the case of Wilson's service style, apparently have been feasible only so long as there exists a monolithic community to which the police can become oriented.[6] Unfortunately, in the areas most in need of high quality police services — however such quality be defined — the *community* and its needs are neither readily identifiable nor monolithic.[7] Instead, as Wilson suggested, such neighborhoods are marked by great social, racial, and political cleavages, and by divergent views about law enforcement and order maintenance policies and practices (Wilson, 1968:288–89; see also, Greenberg and Rohe, 1986). As long as this is so, virtually every police policy or action will offend some interests in the community and near unanimous approval of the police, as in Vollmer's Berkeley or 1960s Nassau County, will remain unattainable. Further, as long as communities define the police role in the expectation that police will merely respond unquestioningly to their wishes, the police mandate will continue to be amorphous and unclear.

Consequences of Unclear Direction

Priority Setting

The consequences of vague definition of the police role and minimal police participation in specifying it are widespread. Police have not been given much direction for setting priorities among the melange of duties and responsibilities they have been assigned. The police are expected both to maintain order and to enforce the law but, in important instances, these two obligations may conflict. Uniformed officers assigned in response to citizens' complaints that specific streets have become open air drug markets, for example, usually are instructed by their superiors to enforce the law aggressively. But officers who follow such instructions by arresting the first minor offender they see may find themselves off the street and caught up in the booking and court processes for hours. While these officers are gone, their beats remain open territory, dealers do uninterrupted land-office business, and law-abiding citizens wonder what happened to the cops they had asked for. The final frustration in such cases usually comes when arrestees are slapped on the wrist by the courts, treated like public nuisances rather than as the purveyors of poison that officers and residents see.

A better alternative might be to direct officers to avoid making arrests except in major cases and, instead, to attempt to drive dealers off the street by maintaining as high a degree of presence as possible. If this were done, police officers might rid their beats of drug trafficking and restore order to lawless streets, just as they routinely have done in neighborhoods marred by street prostitution and other annoying public order offenses. Importantly, however, such a strategy would generate little of the enforcement "activity" so often used to justify police budget requests (Rubinstein, 1973).

Trying to Quantify Quality

Quantitative measures of police activity—numbers of tickets, arrests, calls for service, minutes and seconds required to respond to calls—often mislead. They say nothing about the vigor or quality of police service or, as in this street drug dealing example, about whether the numbers presented have had any substantial effect on the problem the police were marshaled to address (see, e.g., Rubinstein, 1973). But, regardless of their limited usefulness as a measure of police effectiveness—or their questionable accuracy—numbers are part and parcel of American policing. From the annual figures of the FBI's Uniform Crime Reports through the flashy charts and bar graphs that characterize police departmental annual reports to the monthly activity reports of patrol officers and traffic cops, policing revolves around numbers.

Herman Goldstein (1979) called this tendency to measure police performance in quantitative terms a "means-ends syndrome." It exists, he suggests, because of the ease of toting up the frequency and rapidity with which police use the tools available to them—arrests, tickets, response time—and the difficulty of sitting down and resolving Manning's dilemma by clearly defining police goals, measures of the extent to which they have been achieved, and some notion of whether the police actions involved in doing so may have created or aggravated other problems. From a desk in police headquarters, it is very easy and often very convincing to report to a concerned city councilperson that the police response to complaints about drug dealing on 25th Street has resulted in n arrests. It is not so easy to go out and measure the level of apparent drug activity on 25th Street, or to determine whether police presence has displaced it to 24th Street. Even when such measures are attempted, the absence of impressive arrest numbers often makes them less than convincing.

Prevention and Apprehension

This situation is a conundrum and a contradiction of the principles enunciated by Sir Robert Peel when he established the first modern urban police in Dublin and in London (Palmer, 1988). Before Peel's "Bobbies," police forces existed in continental Europe, but these generally focused their activities on political criminals and on after-the-fact investigations of crime; the notoriously persistent Javert of Hugo's *Les Miserables* is a case in point. But Peel, inspired by the Enlightenment view of man as a rational and ultimately redeemable creature, designed the London Metropolitan Police to be *preventive* rather than punitive. The widespread presence on the streets of police in distinctive but purposely nonmilitary uniforms, Peel reasoned, would convince potential criminals that successful crime was impossible. Accordingly, Peel also reasoned, the best measure of police success in crimefighting would be the *absence* of crime, disorder, and related police business, rather than the measures of law enforcement activity currently in vogue in the United States.

Certainly, police today also are expected to prevent crime. A considerable amount of research, however, suggests that their ability to do so, especially in sprawling, multicultural American cities, is more limited than Peel, Hoover, or Vollmer believed (Kelling, et al., 1974; Police Foundation, 1981). Further, the incentive to develop more sophisticated prevention strategies is diminished by news and entertainment media that grant police their greatest glory for arresting those whom they have failed to deter in the first place. *Cops 'n' robbers* make for spectacular headlines and sensational docudrama, but the work of police crime prevention officers has never been the focus of any movie or TV series. This emphasis and glorification of apprehension over prevention spills down to the lowest level of policing, where the greenest beat cops learn early in their careers that "important arrests" are enthusiastically counted and rewarded, while nobody knows—or seems to care—how many crimes did not occur because of officers' vigilance.

On occasion, the consequences of this apprehension-oriented incentive system are bizarre and certainly not what Peel intended. In some departments, instead of cruising by bars at closing time to make sure that drunks do not attempt to drive home, officers hide in darkened cars a block or two away to catch them after they have gotten into their cars and driven off. In using this technique to gain credit for arrests, these officers allow drunks to commit the very same life-endangering acts one might expect the police to prevent. In Los Angeles, an elite squad has for years refrained from intervening while, as its officers anticipated, armed burglars and robbers have victimized unsuspecting citizens. Instead of preventing these victimizations, officers have stood by and watched in order to confront their quarry—often with bloody results—after all doubt about their intentions has been removed. "Public safety is certainly a concern," the unit's commander told the *Los Angeles Times*, "but we have to look beyond that because if we arrest someone for attempt, the likelihood of a conviction is not as great" (Freed, 1988; Skolnick and Fyfe, 1993).

Accusations of Discrimination

At the same time that police are charged to enforce the law firmly and fairly, they also are expected to be judicious and selective in their enforcement efforts. Unfortunately, the police have received little guidance in establishment of criteria to distinguish between unfair discrimination and discretion that serves some legitimate social end. Consequently, "selective enforcement" often is little more than individual officers' *ad hoc* decisions about which driver should receive a ticket and which should not; which loudmouthed kid should be arrested, which taken home to his parents.

Regardless of how judicious a police department may be, the absence of meaningful decision-making standards dictates that any agency that polices a pluralistic constituency will be the subject of regular criticism and dissatisfaction on the part of one or more subpopulations. Further, the absence of such standards means that the best-intended police officers in such a department will be left confused and vulnerable to accusations of arbitrariness. Motorists know that cops do not issue tickets for all the traffic violations they witness. Consequently, every experienced cop has heard bitter motorists allege that the tickets they have just been handed were motivated by questions of race or class rather than by the need to enforce laws against traffic violations that so many others commit without punishment.[8]

Further, in a society in which race and class are as closely related as ours, it often is hard to draw a line between discretion and discrimination. The fundamental precept of the juvenile justice system—to *help and reform*, rather than to *punish* — generally dictates that police interventions into kids' minor delinquencies should be no more intrusive and formal than whatever may be necessary to accomplish two goals. First, the action selected — ranging anywhere from warning through arrest and booking — should give officers some sense that the youngsters involved have learned the errors of their ways. Second, officers should be assured that, after they leave the scene, responsible parties will carefully supervise the miscreants and keep them on the straight and narrow. But when cops act on these precepts, their dispositions of juveniles who have been involved in minor delinquencies result in numbers heavily skewed by class and, therefore, by race. Middle-class kids are skilled at ingratiating themselves to people who can affect their futures. When the police bring them home or to police stations after such kids have done wrong, the police meet concerned, stable families from nice neighborhoods. Most important, the police get convincing assurances from Moms and Dads that it will be a long time before Junior — who is by now teary-eyed and apologetic — has another opportunity to misbehave. Consequently, the police typically take no formal action, but leave such kids to the care of their parents.

Street kids learn early to challenge authority. In the ghetto, where life often includes no thoughts of the future beyond tomorrow, the middle class skill of ingratiating oneself to people who can affect one's future is meaningless and denigrated. Often, ghetto kids come from home environments in which no meaningful control is exercised over their conduct. In such circumstances, cops are likely to conclude that helping kids to find the straight and narrow can be accomplished only by invoking the formal juvenile justice system. This, of course, has two effects. First, it punishes these youngsters by attaching formal delinquent labels to them. Second, it generates statistics that can be used to put police on the defensive by those who claim that cops' decisions routinely are racist. In fact, the statistics may hide well-intended decisions to arrest or release juveniles that, like police and judicial decisions related to adults' bail and pretrial release, appropriately are driven by variables independent of the instant offense. Judges' bail decisions and police releases on adult suspects' own recognizance are based on assessments of the probability that defendants will be back in court on schedule. Cops' decisions about what to do with young violators often are based on officers' assessments of the probability that police will have no further contact with the youngsters involved. Thus, the goals of these decisions — to achieve the hope of seeing subjects again in the first case; to achieve the hope of never seeing them again in the second — are different, but the criteria used in making them should be similar. Unlike police and court discretion related to adult criminal defendants (see, e.g., Thomas, 1976; Institute for Law and Social Research, 1980), however, police decisions concerning juvenile offenders generally are unbounded by rules or guidelines and, therefore, remain subject to criticism.

Defining Good Policing

The discussion to this point suggests the overarching dilemma caused by the absence of a clear police mandate: beyond some prescriptions for specific field situations in which closure is rapid and clearly identifiable, we have yet to derive a widely accepted definition of police effectiveness. Within policing, the absence of such a definition reverberates at every level. The requirements for entry into an occupation, for example, should be those that best predict satisfactory job performance. But the absence of clearly articulated standards for assessing police effectiveness means that police entry requirements can be no more than guesses about which candidates are likely to be abusive, to beget scandals, or, through physical disability or acts that create legal liability, to impose great financial losses on those to whom they have applied for employment. Some police candidates are screened out on the basis of bizarre personal histories or criminal records. Others, however, survive this screening and demonstrate their lack of suitability for policing only after they have been locked into it by civil service tenure. Equally important, the imprecision inherent in searches to fill jobs that are not clearly defined undoubtedly results in the loss of fine candidates whose membership in policing would undoubtedly increase its representativeness of the population.

The Absence of the Satisfaction of a Job Well Done

Those who make it through this screening find that police work carries many rewards. Although no honest police officer ever becomes rich, policing in most parts of the United States pays a decent wage which, despite the last couple of decades' police layoffs in financially strapped cities, also is very dependable. In the busiest jurisdictions, the police workday goes very quickly and, in the words of a recruiting poster in use when I began my police career, often includes "a view of life your desk-bound friends will never see." Certainly, this view is not always pleasant or fulfilling: the things police see cause some to become chronically distrustful and hardened, ultimately leading to great problems in their private lives. Other officers, however, draw from their work greater appreciation of their own comparative good fortune. However trying, regular exposure to violence, exploitation, greed, madness, cruelty, poverty, hopelessness, addiction, and the rest of humankind's most serious ills puts into perspective and makes less insurmountable the annoyances of middle-class life.

Specific police actions — cracking a big case, pulling a driver from a burning car, talking an emotionally disturbed person out of a suicide attempt — also provide a great deal of satisfaction and official praise for police officers. But, absent the opportunity to engage in such heroics, cops may try their hardest to earn their salaries without ever knowing whether they are doing well or whether their work has made a difference, and without ever receiving formal acknowledgment of their efforts.

This issue involves much more than the salving of cops' tender egos. A quarter century ago, Arthur Neiderhoffer (1969:95–108) reported that New York City police patrol officers, the street cops who performed the most familiar but most ill-defined and least prestigious work in their department, had higher levels of cynicism than any other officers he studied. Over time, Neiderhoffer suggested, the intractability of patrol officers' work and their inability to get out of it and into more glamorous assignments may lead to a sense of frustration and victimization. These, in turn, may alienate officers—and, indeed, whole police departments— from the community, causing the dysfunctional *us and them* relationship between police and citizens found in many jurisdictions and manifested by incidents like the beating of Rodney King. It was no accident that the King incident involved the Los Angeles Police Department, the agency that, more than any other big city U.S. police department, had come to define itself as a beleaguered thin blue line that protects ungrateful and undeserving citizens from themselves (see, e.g., Gates, 1992).

Indeed, Carl Klockars (1980) suggests that the gap between what police are expected to achieve and what they can achieve encourages them to brutality, perjury, and other fabrications of evidence against guilty people who would otherwise go free. Anxious to achieve the noble end of seeing that offenders receive deserved punishment, good cops, asserts Klockars, become very frustrated by a criminal justice system that too often seems to dismiss cases for reasons that have nothing to do with whether arrestees actually committed the offenses of which they were accused. Then, like Clint Eastwood's movie character, "Dirty Harry" Callahan, some of these officers render a violent brand of street justice and/ or lie from the witness stand in order to assure that the guilty get what they deserve. The now famous videotape showing Los Angeles police beating Rodney King while he is on his hands and knees memorialized the first half of such an episode. Absent George Holliday and his videocam, the episode's second half would have been the prosecution the police had initiated against Mr. King before they knew they had been caught by George Holliday and his videocam. At this court proceeding, the police who arrested and beat King would undoubtedly have offered perjured testimony to the effect that King was standing upright and physically attacking them when they used no more than necessary force to subdue him.

Cops' Rules

Elizabeth Reuss-Ianni (1984) has written that police estrangement may extend to conflicting "street cop" and "management cop" subcultures within police departments. Where these exist, street cops see themselves as excluded from a management system that espouses lofty ideals and that employs meaningless statistics and other forms of smoke and mirrors in order to give the illusion that these ideals are being achieved. Consequently, street cops see their leadership as an illegitimate and naive obstacle that must be surmounted if *real* police work is to be accomplished.[9]

Like the values constructed and honored by lower class delinquent boys in response to rejection by middle class teachers (Cohen, 1955), however, street cops' definitions of admirable behavior are developed without input from above and, in addition to serving as guideposts to survival in a harsh world, often are antithetical to those publicly espoused by official police spokespersons. Reuss-Ianni's astute observations of New York City police led her to formulate a list of the rules that govern street cops' interactions with each other and with their supervisors and administrators:

> Watch out for your partner first and then the rest of the guys working the tour [shift];
>
> Don't give up another cop;
>
> Show balls [physical courage];
>
> Be aggressive when you have to, but don't be too eager;
>
> Don't get involved in anything in another guy's sector [car beat];
>
> Hold up your end of the work;
>
> If you get caught off base, don't implicate anybody else;
>
> Make sure the other guys [officers, but not supervisors or administrators] know if another cop is dangerous or "crazy";
>
> Don't trust a new guy until you have checked him out;
>
> Don't tell anybody else more than they have to know, it could be bad for you and it could be bad for them;
>
> Don't talk too much or too little;
>
> Don't leave work for the next tour;
>
> Protect your ass;
>
> Don't make waves;
>
> Don't give [supervisors] too much activity;
>
> Keep out of the way of any boss from outside your precinct;
>
> Don't look for favors just for yourself;
>
> Don't take on the patrol sergeant by yourself;
>
> Know your bosses;
>
> Don't do the bosses' work for them [e.g., let them discover miscreant officers without assistance];
>
> Don't trust bosses to look out for your interest. (Reuss-Ianni, 1984:14–16)

The adversarial relationship between "street cops" and "management cops" suggested by many of these rules has its roots in the pyramidal, military style of police organization that so sharply distinguishes between administrators and those on the front lines.[10] Thus, as we see over and over again in both examples of great heroism and officers' reluctance to expose the wrongdoing of colleagues (Christopher, et al., 1992; Daley, 1978; Maas, 1973), street cops' primary loyalties are to each other rather than to the bureaucracies in which they work or to the taxpayers who pay their salaries. In the absence of formal recognition of what street cops justifiably regard as good work, street cops' reward systems consist primarily of their peer groups' status rankings of their members, and the highest status in this system is the recognition that one is *a cop's cop*. The irony that those who win this high accolade from their peers often are regarded with antagonism and suspicion by police administrators is evidence of the depth of the cleavage between management and street cops.

What To Do

Several scholars have suggested solutions to all or part of this dilemma of the vague police mandate. Manning (1978:374) argues that police should focus on enhancing their ability as crime-fighters and on delegating to other agencies as many of their traffic control and other non-crime related service tasks as possible. However easy this proposal might appear to make police lives and evaluation of police performance, it is unrealistic. There is no evidence that any other agencies are anxious to fill the police role as round-the-clock-first-responders to the wide variety of non-enforcement tasks currently handled by police. Further, it is not easy to distinguish in advance between crime-fighting and police non-crime service tasks. Most police services are rendered in response to citizens' telephone calls for help of some kind or other. In some cases, 911 operators can determine very quickly that those who respond to assist must be authorized and equipped to use force and to enforce laws. In most cases, however, this is not possible, and officials must actually arrive at the scene to determine whether calls for services of the types currently handled by police require use of force, law enforcement, or both. Hence, it probably is wishful thinking to plan for police delegation to other authorities of such non-enforcement tasks as handling domestic calls, resolving neighbors' disputes, chasing noisy streetcorner groups, dealing with emotionally disturbed street people, and responding to vehicle accidents.

Klockars sees severe punishment of officers who use dirty means to achieve noble ends as the appropriate approach to the "Dirty Harry Problem." But, paradoxically, even he recognizes that this solution is unsatisfactory:

> In urging the punishment of policemen who resort to dirty means to achieve some unquestionably good and morally compelling end, we

recognize that we create a Dirty Harry problem for ourselves and for those we urge to effect such punishments. It is a fitting end, one which teaches once again that the danger in Dirty Harry problems is never in their resolution, but in thinking that one has found a resolution with which one can truly live in peace. (Klockars, 1980:47)

Klockars' realization that it would be difficult to live in peace with this resolution is correct, but for reasons he seems not to take into account. Punishment achieved by end runs around due process is no more an "unquestionably good and morally compelling end" than is family prosperity obtained by a breadwinner's thefts from his or her employer. In both cases, the most peaceful and satisfying resolution might be achieved not by punishing the wrongdoer, but by preventing the wrongdoing in the first place. This might be accomplished by demonstrating to the people on whose behalf the wrongdoing is likely to be conducted—the public in Klockars' case; the family in my analogy—that their desires are unrealistic and likely to impose other, unquestionably bad, costs.

Breadwinners usually can bring the desires of overly demanding families into line with reality by pointing out the limits of family resources and that the immorality and costs of stealing apply regardless of whether one is caught with a hand in the till. Public officials should make sure that their constituents know that the widespread desire to ignore constitutional limits so that *justice may be done* is oxymoronic and equally immoral and costly. Punishing wrongdoers without regard to the process that has been prescribed by 200 years of American experience weakens the entire society, perpetuates the myth that society can rely on the police as its primary defense against crime, and encourages society's policy makers to allow the continued festering of the social conditions that have turned our inner cities into crime factories. Unfortunately, in this era of concern over law and order and apparent resolve to address the crime problem by harshness alone, few public officials seem willing to bring forth this message.

Mastrofski's suggestions seem closer to the mark and are more strongly supported by the work and experiences of other scholars. He suggests that the broad and vague mandate of the police is here to stay. He indicates also that the extent to which it is accomplished is best assessed at close range, at the microlevel of the quality of police officers' daily encounters with citizens:

> . . . what police officers themselves know about good policing has to do with how officers respond to the particular circumstances they are called to handle. This is the craft of policing, about which a great deal is known, yet uncodified: making good arrests, deescalating crises, investigating crimes, using coercion and language effectively, abiding by the law and protecting individual rights, developing knowledge of the community, and imparting a sense of fairness by one's actions. (1988:63)

There is reason to believe that this is a feasible approach to the eventual derivation of a definition of *good policing*. As Bayley and Garofalo (1985) have reported, line police officers are excellent assessors of their peers' talents. These two researchers asked groups of street officers to identify the most outstanding of their number. Subsequently, Bayley and Garofalo observed both officers identified as outstanding and their colleagues at one of their most difficult police tasks, intervention in disputes. They report finding quantifiable differences between the manners and techniques employed by the *cops' cops* and the rest, most notably that the officers who had been identified as outstanding were less judgmental and more helpful than their peers in their dealings with disputants. Thus, even though the officers Bayley and Garofalo had asked to rate their peers had not been requested to specify *why* they thought some officers better than others, it appears that these officers had observed something different about the work of *cops' cops* that could subsequently be documented empirically.

Hans Toch and his colleagues (Toch, et al., 1975) had earlier approached much the same problem from a different angle (see article 28 of this volume). They identified a group of Oakland police officers who frequently were involved in on-the-job violence they seemed to provoke or manufacture. These violence-prone officers were themselves asked to analyze the problem of violence between police and citizens, and to develop solutions to it. The most intriguing result of this work was the creation by these officers of an officially approved Peer Review Panel, consisting mostly of violence-prone officers. This panel met regularly with officers whose apparent violent activities had been brought to light in incident reports or by supervisory referral, and was

> designed (1) to stimulate the subject to study his violence-related arrests over time and to help him tease out cues to his contributions to violent incidents and (2) to assist the subject to define and formulate alternative strategies for coping with violence-precipitating incidents. (Toch, 1980:60)

This program was, by all measures, a success. It allowed these most violent-prone street cops to diagnose their own problems, to analyze the more generic problem of police-citizen violence, and to devise solutions to it. It enhanced their analytic sophistication and helped to break down the adversarial relationship between street cops and management. Involvement in violent incidents by officers who participated in the program declined vis-à-vis that of other officers. Further, and just as important as substantive results, the Oakland work showed that:

> [p]rograms that are usually resisted as arbitrary interferences with the officers' autonomy can become experiments in whose outcome the officers have a proprietary interest and a substantial stake. (Toch, 1980:61)

This early exercise in what has since come to be known as *Problem-Oriented Policing* – identifying a problem and the most desirable outcome of attempts to resolve it; carefully analyzing the problem and devising appropriate means of resolving it (see, e.g., Goldstein, 1990)—was the basis for a project I subsequently directed in Dade County, Florida (Fyfe, 1988). There, a task force consisting of Metro-Dade Police Department street officers, trainers, investigators, and field supervisors was assembled and asked to analyze a random sample of reports of police-citizen encounters that had *gone wrong*, in the sense that they had resulted in citizens' complaints against officers, use of force by officers, or injuries to officers. The analysis required task force members to identify every decision and action of the officers in each encounter; to describe its effects (in terms of increasing or decreasing whatever potential for violence may have existed); and, where appropriate, to prescribe alternative decisions or actions that may have better served to defuse potential violence. The goals of this analysis were to identify the most satisfactory resolutions of several types of frequently encountered potentially violent encounters between police and citizens,[11] and to construct a detailed list of "Do's and Don't's" that would help officers to achieve these resolutions.

In other words, the project enlisted officers to define *jobs well done* in street cops' most challenging work, and to identify the steps most likely to help officers to do such jobs well. This project, conducted under rigid social science experimental conditions, eventually resulted in a five-day "violence reduction training program" that was delivered to all Dade County officers between February 1988 and February 1989. In the three years since then, Metro-Dade police records show that complaints against officers, use of force by officers, and injuries to officers all have declined between 30 and 50 percent.

All of this signals that street cops know more than anybody about what is *good policing* and who are the *cop's cops*. But, until the groundbreaking work of Toch, Grant, and Galvin, nobody had asked them. When they have been asked, street officers have responded with remarkable accuracy. In Oakland, street cops—notably, the *most violent* street cops—were empowered to address the problem of which they were the major part, and came up with solutions. Bayley and Garofalo asked street cops to identify the stars among themselves, and the answers appear to have been substantiated by observations of cops at work. I asked street cops, trainers, and supervisors below the policy making level to define *good policing* in a variety of challenging situations. The answers resulted in a course of training that has been followed by remarkable reductions in police-citizen violence in one of the country's most volatile policing environments.[12]

The implications seem clear. As Manning (1977) has noted, the police mandate is vague, internally inconsistent, and generally uninformed by the police themselves. If we are to derive a clear statement of the police mandate and how well it is accomplished, we should start by asking street cops to define *good policing* at the micro-level of their one-on-one interactions with citizens. Then, brick by brick, we will build meaningful macro-level definitions of the police mandate, good policing, good police department, and good cops.

Endnotes

[1] This definition owes much to the work of Egon Bittner and Herman Goldstein.

[2] Here, I distinguish between domestic disputes and domestic *violence*. In my view, the role of the police in situations involving violence of any kind is clear cut: to see that no violence occurs after the police have arrived on the scene, and to arrest those who have engaged in criminal violence before the arrival of the police.

[3] See, e.g., James Q. Wilson's description of "watchman" police agencies in *Varieties of Police Behavior* (Cambridge, MA: Harvard University Press, 1968).

[4] The most recent exception to my assertion apparently is a 1978 doctoral dissertation which compares dispositions of citizens' complaints in Berkeley, Contra Costa County (CA), Kansas City, Oakland, and San Jose (Perez, 1978).

[5] In addition to changes in Nassau County specifically, a more general trend to increased accountability for police actions has meant that activities regarded as acceptable at the time of Wilson's study would today be condemned as both indiscriminate and wasteful. Of Nassau County's special "burglary patrol," for example, Wilson noted:

> During 1965 this patrol, operating in high-risk areas of the county, stopped and searched over twelve thousand vehicles and questioned over fourteen thousand "suspicious persons." Eighty-six arrests resulted, but only nine were for burglary. (Wilson, 1968:204)

[6] The more successful of the two Neighborhood Police Teams in precincts where I worked was in Brooklyn Heights, a highly organized brownstone neighborhood populated largely by upper-middle-class residents who were very anxious to see that their community remained fashionable and expensive. The second NPT, in the tough Hell's Kitchen area of Manhattan's West Side, engendered considerably less interest and enthusiasm among residents.

[7] Monolithic community norms related to the police and their role in the community are not necessarily a good thing. In ethnically or racially changing neighborhoods, for example, the most powerful sentiment regarding the police may be a bigoted desire for their assistance in harassing the newcomers back to whence they came (Mastrofski, 1988).

[8] In my own 16 years of police experience, the specific race or class of the ticketed violator did not matter as much as the perception that police treated *others* with great leniency. I have heard whites claim that "you wouldn't give me this ticket if I were black" because, e.g., "you know they run this city," as often as I heard the converse claim from black violators. Similarly, obviously well-heeled violators bemoaned their tickets with claims that police enforcement efforts would be better directed at people driving dangerous "clunkers"; people in clunkers argued that enforcement should focus more heavily on luxury car drivers who "thought they owned the road" and could better afford tickets.

[9] Former Los Angeles police officer Mike Rothmiller has painted a similar picture of his department, where street officers used the pejorative term "pogues" to refer to their naive, and often venal, police supervisors and administrators (Rothmiller and Goldman, 1992).

[10] I have argued elsewhere that the military organizational model is a historical accident that probably is the single most inappropriate way to structure police organizations (Fyfe, 1992; Skolnick and Fyfe, 1993).

[11] The research showed that the most frequently encountered potentially violent encounters between Dade County police and citizens were routine traffic stops; responses to reports of crimes in progress or police investigations of suspicious persons; disputes; and "high-risk vehicle stops" of cars occupied by persons suspected of criminal activity (Fyfe, 1988).

[12] It is more than modesty that causes me to refrain from attributing this decline in police-citizen violence and tension exclusively to the project I directed. The training was part of

a wide variety of personnel, training, and administrative changes that began in the early 1980s and that has resulted in a major philosophical shift in the Metro-Dade Police Department. It is today a much more community-oriented and representative police department than was true a decade ago.

References

Angell, J. E., (1971). Toward an alternative to the classic police organizational arrangements: A democratic model. *Criminology, 9*, 185–206.

Bayley, D. H., & Garofalo, J. (1989, February). The management of violence by police patrol officers. *Criminology, 27*, 1–25.

Carte, G. E., & Carte, E. H. (1975). *Police reform in the United States: The era of August Vollmer, 1905–1932*. Berkeley: University of California Press.

Christopher, W., et al. (1991). *Report of the Independent Commission on the Los Angeles Police Department*. City of Los Angeles.

Citizens' Police Committee. (1969). *Chicago police problems*. Montclair, NJ: Patterson Smith (Reprint of 1931 original).

Cohen, A. K. (1955). *Delinquent boys: The culture of the gang*. New York: The Free Press.

Daley, R. (1978). *Prince of the city: The true story of a cop who knew too much*. Boston: Houghton-Mifflin.

Fogelson, R. M. (1977). *Big-city police*. Cambridge: Harvard University Press.

Freed, D. (1988, September 25). Citizens terrorized as police look on. *Los Angeles Times*, pp. 1, 3–5.

Fyfe, J. J. (1988). *The metro-Dade police/citizen violence reduction project: Final report*. Washington, DC: Police Foundation.

Fyfe, J. J. (1992, August). Lessons of Los Angeles. *Focus*. Washington, DC: Joint Center for Political and Economic Studies.

Fyfe, J. J., & Flavin, J. (1991, June). *Differential police processing of assault complaints*. Paper presented at Annual Meeting of Law and Society Association, Amsterdam.

Garner, J., & Clemmer, E. (1986). *Danger to police in domestic disturbances: A new look*. Washington, DC: National Institute of Justice.

Gates, D. F. (1992). *Chief: My life in the LAPD*. New York: Bantam Books.

Goldstein, H. (1979, April). Improving policing: A problem-oriented approach. *Crime and Delinquency, 25*, 236–258.

Goldstein, H. (1990). *Problem-oriented policing*. New York: McGraw-Hill.

Greenberg, S. W., & Rohe, W. M. (1986). Informal social control and crime prevention in modern urban neighborhoods. In R. B. Taylor (Ed.), *Urban neighborhoods: Research and policy* (pp. 79–118). New York: Praeger.

Institute for Law and Social Research. (1980). *Pretrial release and misconduct in the District of Columbia*. Washington, DC: Institute for Law and Social Research.

Kelling, G. L., Pate, T., Dieckman, D., & Brown, C. E. (1974). *The Kansas City preventive patrol experiment: Summary report*. Washington, DC: Police Foundation.

Klockars, C. (1980, November). The Dirty Harry problem. *Annals of the American Academy of Political and Social Science, 452*, 52.

Konstantin, D. (1984, March). Homicides of American law enforcement officers. *Justice Quarterly, 1*, 29–37.

Maas, P. (1973). *Serpico*. New York: The Viking Press.

Manning, P. K. (1977). *Police work: The social organization of policing.* Cambridge: MIT Press.

Margarita, M. (1980, November). Killing the police: Myths and motives. *Annals of the American Academy of Political and Social Science, 452,* 72–81.

Mastrofski, S. D. (1988). Community policing as reform: A cautionary tale. In J. R. Greene & S. D. Mastrofski (Eds.), *Community policing: Rhetoric or reality* (pp. 47–68). New York: Praeger.

Monkonnen, E. (1981). *Police in urban America, 1860–1920.* Cambridge: Cambridge University Press.

Neiderhoffer, A. (1967). *Behind the shield.* Garden City, NY: Doubleday.

Palmer, S. H. (1988). *Police and protest in England and Ireland 1780–1850.* Cambridge: Cambridge University Press.

Perez, D. (1978). Police accountability: A question of balance. Ph.D. dissertation, University of California, Berkeley.

Police Foundation. (1981). *The Newark foot patrol experiment.* Washington, DC: Police Foundation.

Reiss, A. J., Jr. (1971). *The police and the public.* New Haven: Yale University Press.

Reuss-Ianni, E. (1983). *Two cultures of policing: Street cops and management cops.* New Brunswick, NJ: Transaction Books.

Rothmiller, M., & Goldman, I. G. (1992). *L.A. secret police.* New York: Pocket Books.

Rubinstein, J. (1973). *City police.* New York: Farrar, Straus and Giroux.

Scott, E. J. (1981). *Calls for service: Citizen demand and initial police response.* Washington, DC: U.S. Government Printing Office.

Sherman, L. W., Milton, C. H., & Kelly, T. V. (1973). *Team policing: Seven case studies.* Washington, DC: Police Foundation.

Skolnick, J. H., & Fyfe, J. J. (1993). *Above the law: Police and the excessive use of force.* New York: Free Press.

Thomas, W. H. (1976). *Bail reform in America.* Berkeley: University of California Press.

Toch, H. (1980, November). Mobilizing police expertise. *Annals of the American Academy of Political and Social Science, 452,* 53–62.

Toch, H., & Douglas Grant, J. (1991). *Police as problem solvers.* New York: Plenum Press.

Toch, H., Douglas Grant, J., & Galvin, R. T. (1975). *Agents of change: A study in police reform.* Cambridge, MA: Schenkman.

Trojanowicz, R., & Bucqueroux, B. (1990). *Community policing: A contemporary perspective.* Cincinnati: Anderson Publishing Co.

United States Department of Commerce. (1991). *1990 Census of population and housing, summary of population and housing characteristics, New York,* CPH-1-34. Washington, DC: United States Government Printing Office.

Walker, S. (1977). *A critical history of police reform: The emergence of professionalism.* Lexington, MA: Lexington Books.

Webster, J. (1970). Police time and task study. *Journal of Criminal Law, Criminology and Police Science, 61,* 94–100.

Wilson, J. Q. (1964, March). Generational and ethnic differences among career police officers. *American Journal of Sociology, 69,* 522–528.

Wilson, J. Q. (1968). *Varieties of police behavior.* Cambridge: Harvard University Press.

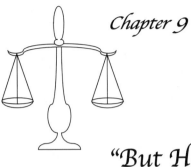

Chapter 9

"But How Can You Sleep Nights?"

Lisa J. McIntyre

Hardly anyone will take issue with the idea that everyone, guilty or innocent, is entitled to a fair trial. But beyond this, the views of lawyers and nonlawyers diverge. To the nonlawyer, a fair trial is one that results in convicting the defendant who is factually guilty and acquitting the defendant who is not. But it is the lawyer's job to do every possible thing that can be done for the defendant, even when that means getting a criminal off scot-free. Loopholes and technicalities are defense attorneys' major weapons. Lay people are inclined to feel that using legal tricks to gain acquittals for the guilty is at least morally objectionable, if not reprehensible. What many people want to know is how defense attorneys can live with themselves after they help a guilty person escape punishment.

It might be supposed that lawyers are unimpressed by what, to the rest of us, is the core dilemma of their profession—that is, how to justify defending a guilty person. It might be reasoned that lawyers escape this quandary because their legal training has taught them that it does not exist. In law school everyone learns that a defendant is innocent until proved guilty. Lawyers believe this—and can act on it—because they have been taught to "think like lawyers." Legal reasoning, "although not synonymous with formal reasoning and logic . . . is closely tied to them.

Lisa McIntyre, *The Public Defender: The Practice of Law in the Shadows of Repute*, pp. 139–170. Copyright © 1987 by the University of Chicago Press. Reprinted by permission of The University of Chicago Press.

Promotion of these skills encourages abstracting legal issues out of their social contexts to see issues narrowly and with precision" (Zemans and Rosenblum, 1981:205).

Simply put, legal reasoning depends on a closed set of premises; some propositions are legal, others are not. The nonlawyer can scarcely be expected to appreciate or understand the difference, for it takes "trained men" to "winnow one from the other" (Friedman, 1975:245). But lawyers, by virtue of this training, are expected to cope with complex issues, to detach themselves from difficult moral questions and focus on legal ones, to take any side of an argument while remaining personally uninvolved, and to avoid making moral judgments about their clients or their clients' cases. Thus—and this is a surprise to nonlawyers—the factual guilt or innocence of the client is *supposed* to be irrelevant. A lawyer is expected to take a point of view and argue it; a criminal defense lawyer is expected to put on a vigorous defense even when the client is known to be guilty.

On the other hand, however much their training sets them apart, there are some attorneys who cannot detach themselves, cannot overlook the social and moral meanings and consequences of their jobs. There are lawyers who in fact see the issues very much as nonlawyers do. Ohio attorney Ronald L. Burdge explained to columnist Bob Greene why he had given up defending criminal cases: "If your client is guilty and you defend him successfully, then you have a criminal walking the streets because of your expertise. I have a couple of children. I just didn't like the idea of going home at night knowing that I was doing something so— unpalatable. I found it difficult to look at my kids knowing that this was how I was making a living" (Greene, 1982:1).

A former assistant public defender who spent five years in the Cook County Public Defender's Office echoed Burdge when he explained his disenchantment with the job: "The public defender's cases are thankless: if you lose, society wins; if you win, society loses. I really began to feel as if I was doing a bad thing when I got someone off. They were dangerous people." Today, almost all of this attorney's clients are indigent, but criminal cases do not intrude into his practice.

In spite of their training, lawyers may find it difficult to focus only on the narrow legal aspects of their cases because they are rarely isolated from others who question the morality of the defense lawyer's job. Seymour Wishman, in his book *Confessions of a Criminal Lawyer*, says a chance encounter with one of these "others" marked a turning point in his career, made him rethink how he was spending his life. It happened in a hospital emergency room:

> Across the lobby, a heavy but not unattractive woman in a nurse's uniform suddenly shrieked, "Get that motherfucker out of here!" Two women rushed forward to restrain her. "That's the lawyer, that's the motherfucking lawyer!" she shouted.

I looked round me. No one else resembled a lawyer. Still screaming, she dragged her two restrainers toward me. I was baffled. As the only white face in a crowd of forty, I felt a growing sense of anxiety.

I didn't know what she was talking about. "Kill him and that nigger Horton!"

Larry Horton . . . of course. Larry Horton was a client of mine. Six months before, I had represented him at his trial for sodomy and rape. At last I recognized the woman's face. She had testified as the "complaining" witness against Horton. (1981:4)

Wishman remembered how he had humiliated this woman when she testified against his client, how by cross-examination he had undone her claim that she had been raped and had made her seem to be little more than a prostitute. Seeing her rage started him thinking that society—and, more specifically, the victims of those whom he had defended—were "casualties" of his skill as a defense lawyer. After years spent preparing for and practicing criminal law, Wishman believed that he had to change: "I had never turned down a case because the crime or the criminal were despicable—but now that would change. I could no longer cope with the ugliness and brutality that had for so long, too long, been part of my life."

Encounters between defense lawyers and those who question the ethics of their work are seldom as dramatic as the one experienced by Wishman. But it is certain that such encounters occur with great frequency in the lives of defense attorneys. All of the current public defenders with whom I spoke and nearly all (93 percent) of the former assistants interviewed in my research agreed that people "constantly" ask public defenders, "How can you defend those people?" But the disenchanted public defender quoted above seems to speak for only a minority of lawyers. The overwhelming majority (97 percent) of former public defenders interviewed agreed that they had believed that they were putting their legal skills to good use by working as public defenders. Only five (8 percent) said that they would not join the office if they had it to do over again.

Given that the public defender's goal is to zealously defend and to work toward acquittal for his or her clients (even clients whom they themselves believe are guilty of heinous crimes), how do these lawyers justify their work? As I explain below, it is not as if public defenders harbor any illusions about the factual innocence of the usual client; on the contrary, most will openly admit that the majority of their clients are factually guilty. If conventional morality has it that defending guilty people is tantamount to an obstruction of justice, how do public defenders justify their rebellion? How *do* they defend those people?

How can you defend people whom you know are guilty? Public defenders say that question is incredibly naive, that for the most part they have little patience with that question and little time for anyone who asks it. One suspects that they would like to answer with shock and outrage when asked how they do what they do — and sometimes they do answer like that. But usually they respond in a manner that is more weary than indignant:

> Oh God, *that* question! How do you represent someone you know is guilty? So you go through all the things. You know, "he's not guilty until he's proven guilty, until a judge or a jury say he's guilty, until he's been proved guilty beyond a reasonable doubt." I think everyone deserves the best possible defense, the most fair trial he can get. It's a guarantee of the Constitution, no more, no less.

> I tell them it's easy, and I give them a whole list of reasons why it's easy. . . . Everyone has a right to a trial, and with that right to a trial you have a right to a lawyer. I'm that lawyer. That's the American way.

> I get asked that all the time, even by my family, even by my wife! The only answer I can give is just that everyone deserves somebody to stand up for them; everyone deserves a trial, a fair trial. They aren't going to get a fair trial unless they have someone like me.

Without exception the public defenders whom I interviewed all had spiels prepared for that question — another testimony to the fact that answering it is part of their routine. As a reporter who interviewed public defender James Doherty in 1983 observed, "If you don't ask him soon enough, he'll preempt you" (Spencer, 1984:1). Some lawyers even had two spiels, one for people who phrased it *as* a question and another for those who made it an accusation: "I have developed a patter that depends on how aggressively I am asked. When asked aggressively, I respond aggressively — 'How can you possibly ask me such a question? Have you never read the Constitution?' It gets meaner. When I am asked, well, you know, in a relatively dispassionate way, a neutral sort of way, basically the response is, 'It makes no difference to me whether they are guilty or not, whether they have committed the offense or not, the person is entitled to have representation to protect his Constitutional rights.'" Simply put, public defenders believe that they come not to destroy the law but to fulfill it.

The sincerity of the public defenders' beliefs is compelling, but the persuasiveness of their arguments is less so. The litany of constitutional ideals rarely convinces the hearer any more (as I will suggest) than it emotionally empowers public defense lawyers to act zealously in the defense of their clients. Attorney Burdge, for example, states unequivocally that *he* still *believed* in the constitutional rights of defendants, that all he was abandoning was his personal protection of these rights: "I just think I'll let other lawyers defend them" (Greene, 1982:1).

Making a Case Defensible

Sociologist Emile Durkheim pointed out that conformity to and rebellion against conventional morality have much in common. The individual, he argued, can free him- or herself partially from the rules of society if there is a felt disparity between those rules and society as it is: "That is, if he desires a morality which corresponds to the actual state of society and not to an outmoded condition. The principle of rebellion is the same as that of conformity. It is the *true* nature of society which is conformed to when the traditional morality is obeyed, and yet it is also the true nature of society which is being conformed to when the same morality is flouted" (1974:65). If Durkheim is correct, public defenders who daily "flout" conventional morality by defending guilty people are perhaps no more focused only on the narrow legal issues than are those who are troubled by what public defenders do. In fact, if pursued (tactfully) beyond the obvious constitutional justifications, the question, How can you defend someone you know is guilty? uncovers the fact that other sorts of rationales are used. Although none of the lawyers went so far as to say, "Yes, I like putting guilty people back on the streets, and I am proud of myself each time I do it," they find justification for doing defense work precisely where Burdge and Wishman found justification for abandoning it—that is, in its social and moral (rather than simply legal) context. Of course, as one might expect, most public defenders stress a different kind of moral and social context than Burdge and Wishman emphasized.

Under some circumstances, mere empathy with the client's situation permits lawyers to feel justified when defending someone whom they know is factually guilty:

> Especially when I was in misdemeanor courts, I could see myself as a defendant. Sometimes you get angry enough at somebody to take a swing at them—if you had a gun, to take a shot at them. I could see myself doing that. . . . Just because somebody was arrested and charged with a crime doesn't mean they are some kind of evil person.

> Look, kids get into trouble, some kids get into serious trouble. I can understand that. In juvenile court our job isn't to punish, the result is supposed to be in the best interests of the minor. Here you've got to keep them with their family and give them all the services you can so they don't do this again.

Not unexpectedly, at some point the ability to empathize breaks down. This is especially true for public defenders who have passed through juvenile or misdemeanor assignments and into felony trial courts, where they are less able—or maybe less willing—to see themselves as being like their clients:

> They [the clients] are seedy and they tend to be, compared to the general population, they are seedier, dirtier, less intelligent, have less conscience, are more sociopathic, more inconsiderate of others, more violent, more poverty stricken and more schizophrenic.

> Your clients have no funds, they know witnesses who only have one name and not even an address because they all hang out on the streets. They don't have phones. They just don't have a life like the rest of us.

They don't make their appointments; they aren't articulate enough to take the stand. All those things make it hard.

While the differences between attorney and client mean that the attorney sometimes has a hard time understanding his or her client (and especially the client's motive), *it does not mean* that the client cannot be defended:

A guy hits somebody over the head and takes a wallet—no problem. A guy that gets into a drunken brawl—no problem. I understand that. Somebody that goes out in the street and commits a rape—I still don't know what goes on his mind. No, it doesn't make it harder to defend. There is *never* any excuse for a rape, but you don't have to understand what makes a rapist tick to defend him effectively.

Sometimes I would question their motives—if it [the crime] seemed senseless, if it seemed particularly brutal or something like that. Then I realized that those were really, for me, irrelevant questions. I still wonder, of course, but I don't ask anymore.

But the alien character especially of the crimes that their clients are alleged to have committed—and the sorts of attributions that they make about their clients because of their crimes—often mean that "you have to care more about your clients' rights than you can usually care about your clients."

A. The Moral Context of Public Defending

Why do I do it? I do it because the day that I start laying down and not doing my job is the day that people who aren't guilty are going to be found guilty, and that person might be you because the whole system will have degenerated to the point where they can arrest and convict you on very little evidence. So I am protecting you, I am protecting the middle-class.

On the surface, what a defense lawyer does is simply protect the client's rights. But many lawyers transform the nature of the battle. They are not fighting for the freedom of their client per se but to keep the system honest: "It doesn't mean that I want to get everybody off. It means that I try to make sure the state's attorneys meet up to their obligations, which means that the only way they can prove someone guilty is beyond reasonable doubt, with competent evidence, and overcoming the presumption of innocence. If they can do that, then they get a guilty. If they can't do that, then my client deserves to go home."

The lawyers' way of "bracketing" their role (Weick, 1979), of focusing not on the guilt or innocence of their client but on the culpability of the state, transforms circumstances of low or questionable morality into something for which they can legitimately fight. They do not defend simply because their clients have rights but because they believe that those rights have been, are, or will be ignored by others in the criminal justice system. That their adversaries often cheat is taken for granted by public defenders. As one put it, "I expected a fairly corrupt system, and I found one. Here I am representing people who cheat, lie, and steal, and I find the same intellect represented in the police who arrest them, in some of the prosecutors and some of the judges as well." Even when not asked to provide examples, every public defender with whom I spoke offered examples of cheating. There was cheating by the police:

> When I was [working] in the state's attorney's office, I would have cops walking up to me as I was preparing a case and I would say, "Officer, tell me what happened." And they would say, "Well, how do *you* want it to have happened?"

> The biggest form of police dishonesty was this street files thing. They were hiding evidence that would get people off — or get the correct person. But they had decided in their own minds, "This guy is the guy I'm going after," instead of letting the court system decide who was right.

And there was cheating by state's attorneys:

> Sometimes you know it; sometimes you just suspect that they are kinking the case. One guy, fairly high up in the state's attorney's office, described one of their lawyers as naive because he'd been shocked to find a state's attorney had kinked the case. He said of the lawyer, "He thinks this is for real?"

> Q: Kinked the case?

> R: You might call it suborning perjury; you might call it jogging the memory.

> Q: Are you saying that state's attorneys are sometimes a little unprofessional?

> R: Yes, yes, yes! Lying, having witnesses lie; they lie themselves on the record, they make inferences that I'm lying. It's just a basic matter of cheating, of not being professional. Because they feel they *must* win the case and will do anything to win the case. . . . Their obligation is *not* to win; it is to make sure the law is upheld — and to make sure that my client gets a fair trial. And to them, *that* is a fallacy.

> I remember in that case the prosecutor basically pulled every trick she could: she argued things that were outside the record; she told the jury that [my client] had a record, that he had put a contract out on the witness. She would stop at nothing to win.

This is not to say that one can walk into a Cook County courtroom and expect to see public defenders and state's attorneys at each others' throats. That does happen (at least verbally) on occasion (as I illustrate below), but most public defenders say that they try to maintain a good rapport with their opponents — if only because it helps them do their jobs. And I was cautioned by some lawyers not to listen to those who would condemn state's attorneys universally. As one lawyer told me, "Most of them are not unreasonable; most of them are not [pause] dirty. Most of them are just doing their jobs as best they can."

Yet, scratch the surface just a little and it is likely that a great deal of tension will be uncovered. It can be noted too that this is not unique to Cook County. A study conducted in Alameda, California, found that relations between public defenders and prosecutors were "often characterized by hostility, suspicion, and conflict" and that "relations between public defenders and judges were not much better" (Lydon, 1973; cited in Utz, 1978:215).

Actually, public defenders in Cook County seem to be of two minds about their judges. On the one hand, they seem willing to trust the judges to do the right thing.

> If the facts are on your side then you usually take a bench trial. Because you know if you take it before a decent judge, he'll give you a not guilty.

> We win most of our bench trials; at least we get what we think the case is worth in most of our bench trials.

> I think if you stand up there and talk like you know what you are talking about, judges who don't know the law tend to listen to you. If you can present it in a fair-minded way and not ranting and raving and saying, "You idiot, you can't do that and you can't do that!" Sometimes it doesn't work, but, for the most part, it is better if you rationally and calmly explain why you are right.

On the other hand, one gets a definite impression that what public defenders trust about judges is not their fair-mindedness and good-will, but rather, in many cases, the judges' desire not to get into trouble by being overturned by a higher court. In any case, many public defenders told me that they just do not trust the judges' instincts:

> Knowing legal theory is important, I guess, but it doesn't do any good in Cook County courts, because the question is not Does the law apply? but Can you get the judge to obey it, even though his instincts are to fuck you?

> Oh, I wised up real quick and found that judges don't care about the law; they don't always follow the law.

> Q: Do they know the law?

> R: Sometimes . . .

> Q: But there's always a public defender there to teach them?

> R: Yea [laugh], but they don't usually care.

> I view judges as another state's attorney. I see judges as essentially enemies I have to deal with . . . most of them are just bangers.

> Q: Bangers?

> R: Someone who gives heavy sentences — oftentimes regardless of the facts of the case.

The sort of cheating to which public defenders attribute their hostility toward police, prosecutors, and judges is something that public defenders say they see a lot. And though such cheating may be expected, public defenders find it unacceptable—and are not afraid to say so. It is ironic, but listening to public defenders talk about their cases and why they do what they do is like listening to someone who has just been mugged. Public defenders do feel as if they are often mugged—by the legal system. There is a lot of real and passionate anger: "Some people said I'd become cynical after a while. Well, I might be more cynical about some things, but I don't think I have really changed my attitude. If anything, I might have become a little more gung ho. You see that there really is an awful lot of injustice. It becomes very real and it's scary. I find myself becoming very angry in this job, all the time."

There is good evidence that the things that public defenders cite when they complain about police, prosecutorial, and judicial misconduct do happen (and not just in Chicago [see, e.g., Alschuler, 1972; Dershowitz, 1983; Dorsen and Friedman, 1973; Friedman, 1975]), but it would be difficult, of course, to determine just how widespread such behaviors actually are. Yet, the real frequency of misconduct is beside the point. The point is that most public defenders *believe* that such things do happen "all the time. It's something you really have to watch for."

Whether or not public defenders are correct in their assumptions that police lie, that prosecutors will often do anything to win, and that judges do not really care or know enough to be fair, it is quite clear that the way in which the public defenders see the world not only excuses their work but makes it seem important. Their rationales are enabling mechanisms for the public defenders. But what ultimately pushes the lawyer to do the job is, I believe, something even more personal—the desire to win.

B. "Adversariness"

Perspectives on the criminal justice system sometimes make use of two ideal type models: the classic adversarial model, which is "couched in constitutional-ideological terms of due process" (Blumberg, 1979:291), and the "dispositional" or "bureaucratic" model, which serves only "bland obeisance to constitutional principles. It is characterized by the superficial ceremonies and formal niceties of traditional due process, but not its substance" (Ibid., 145). (See also Eisenstein and Jacob, 1977; Packer, 1964.) The difference between the two models is the difference between the presumption of innocence and the presumption of guilt.

It is significant that social scientists who study public defenders tend to discuss their findings only in terms of the second model—the bureaucratic or plea-bargaining model. Never is the matter of how public defenders measure up as trial attorneys studied. The stereotype of the public defender as plea bargainer is, to put it mildly, firmly entrenched in the literature (see, e.g., Blumberg, 1967, 1979; Eisenstein and Jacob, 1977; Heumann, 1978; Jackson, 1983; Nardulli, 1978; Sudnow, 1965).[1]

It is a fact that most cases that come into the criminal trial courts are disposed of through pleas of guilty; many of these are negotiated—that is, based on a reduction of charges or sentences. Kalvin and Zeisel's (1966) estimate that 75 percent of total criminal prosecutions are disposed of through pleas is now seen as conservative; more often the estimate is between 85 percent and 95 percent (depending on whether misdemeanor cases are included in the count) (see Blumberg, 1979:168). The National Advisory Commission on Criminal Justice Standards and Goals (1974:42) has estimated that in many courts the rate of guilty pleas is 90 percent.

Public defenders do not deny the importance of plea bargaining in their work; they openly and easily acknowledge that the greatest majority of their cases are ultimately disposed of through pleas of guilty. But, they stress, plea bargaining is not their reason for being there but is just a tool:

> Q: Now here you are telling me that you are a "trial attorney." How can you say that? To be fair, isn't most of your work really plea bargaining?
>
> R: Plea bargaining is just part of procedure. Just like I wouldn't say, "I'm a procedural attorney." . . . It's part of what you go through, and it's one of the options available to my clients. You know, "If you in fact did this, and you want this deal, and you understand what you are offered, here is the deal."

In some cases, I was told, the structure that ostensibly exists to handle plea bargaining is used in the lawyer's trial strategy:

> In most courtrooms you have a conference before the trial and lay out your case and say what you are going to do. This happens before the judge. Part of this is a function of State's Attorney Daley's office. The state's attorneys are very rarely giving very reasonable offers. They are putting it all on the judges; they make the judge make the decision.
>
> So, in general what you do is ask for a plea conference. You go back with the state to the judge's chambers.
>
> Supposedly, you are there for the state to say their side, for you to say your side, and for the state to make an offer.
>
> What I'm finding though, is that you are trying your case that way—for the judge. We [public defenders] are stronger, better prepared. Even if I'm not getting an offer that my man is going to plead guilty to, I'm taking the case in front of the judge. It gives me an advantage in the trial.

The Role of Trials in Local Justice

The majority of their clients do plead guilty, but trials are not unimportant in the world of the public defender. They are important, on the one hand, because what happens during trials helps determine the outcome of cases that are plea bargained. For example, prosecutors wish to maintain a strong record of conviction at trial or else defendants who might otherwise opt for a plea bargain will seek acquittal at a trial. Rulings on evidence made by judges during trials also have an impact on the negotiating process. Attorneys from both sides will evaluate the strength of their positions by the standards evolved through trial court and appellate hearings; these rulings made by trial judges, as well as the sentences given to defendants found guilty, help parties in a plea bargain to determine what their respective cases are "worth" (Jacob, 1980:80).

But more fundamentally, trials are important in the public defender's world (and hence are stressed here) because, at least in Cook County, public defenders first and last define themselves as trial lawyers. Lawyers become public defenders primarily to gain trial experience; once they have become public defenders, performance at trial is much more crucial to attributions that they make about themselves and each other than one could ever guess given the relative frequency of these performances.

Public defenders often said that they like the trial work more than any other part of their job. Each one will admit, however, that there are some who do not feel that way.[2] These were pointed out to me as examples of bad public defenders or "kickers." "Sometimes we get a public defender that does not work. He'll force his guy to take a plea, finally on the last day before trial: 'Listen guy, you can take a plea which is the best thing you could do or you can go to trial. But I'm not prepared for trial and you're going to lose because you are *supposed* to lose this case — you know that too.'" Some public defenders are labeled as bad lawyers because they cannot hack it in the courtroom; the reason that they cannot hack it (it is said) is that they are afraid. As many pointed out, being "on trial" is scary. One veteran lawyer told me: "We lose a lot of public defenders because they can't handle being on trial."

But all of them, even the lawyers who love trial work, are ambivalent about it. Trial work, or so most of them acknowledge (in words, if not by deed), is as terrifying as it is exhilarating.

> You know [a lawyer who is now in private practice]? Now he is one of the better trial lawyers. But he used to throw up before final arguments. Once he did it right in front of the jury; he just went over to the wastebasket and threw up.

> Trials? *That's* when I can't sleep well at night; I'm too busy thinking. A trial is not one issue, it's many. It's win or lose; it's deadlines, organizing things, making sure your witnesses are ready, looking good in front of the jury, looking confident in front of the judge, watching everything you are doing, being alert, keeping a lot of things in your mind at once. And remembering that your client's freedom depends on your polish, how well you can bring it off.

Doing Trials

On television a defense lawyer confronts his clients with demands for the truth: "Okay, I'm your lawyer and you gotta trust me. If I'm going to do a good job I need to know exactly what happened. Don't be afraid to tell me, I can't defend you unless you are perfectly straight with me." The client is thus persuaded to tell all to his lawyer.

This sort of dialogue may appeal to the viewer's common sense — that is, of course the lawyer needs to know what happened and whether the client is guilty. But in real life, things do not happen that way — at least they do not happen that way when the lawyer is a public defender. Public defenders are quick to admit that they usually *do not* ask their clients whether they are guilty or innocent. Why not ask? The lawyers claimed that it was simply not relevant, that it was something that they did not need to know.

> I don't ask "Did you do it?" anymore. I realized it was irrelevant.

> I say to them first thing: "I don't care if you did it or not."

> I say: "I don't give a damn whether you did it or not. I'm not your judge, I'm not your priest, I'm not your father. My job is to defend you, and I don't care whether you did it."

It might be that public defenders do not ask because they know that their client is probably guilty and because, as one said, "they will all lie anyway." But there seems to be more to it than that. Many said that, when it comes down to it, they do not ask because they are afraid that the client will tell them the truth!

> Q: Don't you ever ask your clients if they are guilty or innocent?

> R: Never!

> Q: Why is that?

> R: Because, in the first place, it is irrelevant. It's not my role to decide whether they are guilty — in our sense of the term guilt.

> Q: What about the "second place?"

> R: Well, it is my role to fashion a defense and to be creative. If the person says to me "This is how I did it," it's pretty hard for me to come around and try to do something for them. In general, I fence around with some of my questions. I ask them about an alibi or something like that. But the more I think they are guilty, the less I will ask.

Public defenders do not begin their relationship with a client by asking awkward questions (e.g., Did you do it?) because once the client admits guilt, it limits what the public defender can ethically do:

> I don't ask them because you put them at a disadvantage if you ask them and they say they did it.

> I had a client once who was charged with battery, and he said, "Yea, I hit him, and I've been meaning to hit him for a long time. But it's just his word against mine, and I'm gonna say I didn't do it."
>
> And I said: "*Not* with me as your lawyer you're not! You are not going to say anything like that."
>
> So it's important to get the transcript [from the preliminary hearing] and look at the police reports and say "Look, this is the evidence against us" and then let him make up his own story. It's the only way to do it.

Being honest, ethical, and "scrupled" in a system that many of them believe is corrupt is very important to the lawyers with whom I spoke.[3] Although some (naive observers) may wonder at the fragility of this honesty, it is something in which the public defenders take pride:[4] "There aren't many public defenders—if any—that I can point to and say: 'that man is dishonest. He lied and distorted everything, just to get a client off.' That just doesn't happen. The same cannot be said for lawyers in the state's attorney's office.

You test the state's evidence, you doubt it, you put it into its worst light. But that is not dishonest. Quite the contrary, that is how you get at the truth!"

Public defenders learn quickly that the tell-me-the-truth approach will only help defend an innocent person—the exceptional client. Public defenders argue that it is not their job to decide who is guilty and who is not. Instead, it is the public defender's job to judge the quality of the case that the state has against the defendant. If the lawyer does decide that the state has a case that cannot be called into reasonable doubt, then the lawyer will probably try to get the defendant to admit guilt so that pleading is more palatable—but usually *only* then.

Bad Cases and Good Lawyers

> There is a saying in the office: "Good facts make good lawyers." A good lawyer, I think, is one who doesn't screw up a case. Someone who takes a case that's a winner—one that should be won—and wins it; gets a not guilty. A bad lawyer is a person who takes a case that should be won and loses it. A good lawyer isn't necessarily one that wins a loser case. You get lucky; you get a good jury and win a case that no one could possibly win. That doesn't prove anything; that is very often luck, and it doesn't mean anything.

In practice, a more diffuse yardstick is used: "competency is taking the right cases to trial and winning them." As I show below, the lawyers following this logic are in peril of succumbing to a painful tautological trap.

Public defenders try not to go into a trial with cases that cannot be won. Unfortunately, most of their cases are of this type—loser (or "dead-bang loser") cases, cut-and-dried situations in which the client was caught red-handed and "the state has everything but a video tape of the crime." In the face of overwhelming evidence, the lawyers will try to talk the client into taking a plea or "copping out." One reason for this is the knowledge that taking a loser case to trial will hurt the client:

> My philosophy is that if you are going down and you know it, you should get the best deal for your client that you can. And you should try and make your client see the wisdom of that. It's better for your client. I could say "Sure, I'll take this to trial, sure I can use the experience," but that doesn't do your client any good if he's going down for more time.

> I have a client who I have been dealing with just recently who, ah, I was his attorney and I told him he ought to plead guilty. I told him I got this *great* deal for him: I had packed up several cases he had pending in several courtrooms and got him two years. And he had been convicted before!

> But he didn't like it. He got himself a private attorney who gave him a guarantee of probation or something. He calls me up and said the private attorney had come back to him with an offer of *six* years. He said to me: "You were right!"

In large part, being competent is being able to convince a client that it is not in his or her best interests to insist on a trial that cannot be won. One lawyer explained how he had learned this lesson back when he was assigned to a preliminary hearing court:

> "Well, pal, listen. They caught you inside this guy's home, this guy held you down while his wife called the police. You are not going to get a chance to beat this case. You say you were drunk, but being drunk just isn't a good excuse anymore. It's up to you. The state is making you an offer and if you take it, you'll be better off than if you go upstairs [to the trial court]."

> Everybody told you to say things like that and sure enough, when I got up to the trial courts, I realized it was true. The offers *are* much better in preliminary hearing courts.

> But to confront those guys with that decision. It was incredible, it was so hard.

> Now I can do it fairly routinely because I have been doing it long enough to have confidence in what I'm saying. I know it is true. And I learned that you aren't doing anyone a favor when you bring a loser case upstairs—it's no good for the client, it's no good for the lawyer. But then I felt incredibly guilty.

Once it is decided that they have a loser case, different attorneys have different ways of trying to "cool out" clients who want to go to trial. However, all of the attorneys with whom I spoke and all of the public defenders that I observed with clients seemed uncomfortable with the idea of forcing anyone to take a plea.[3] Most emphasized that they always tried to reason with their clients:

> Most of our clients do feel that if you are a public defender you are not going to give it your all, because you have so many cases, or you just don't care, or whatever. They feel that you are just there to cop them out.

> But my partner and I sit down with a guy and say: "Look, we are lawyers, and we are paid to analyze facts. After we have analyzed the facts we might say to you, 'we don't think you have a good case and we think you should cop out.' If you don't feel that way, it's up to you."

> *We* let *them* make the decision.

> I always leave it up to the defendant. I lay it out for him what the risks are, and if he asks me I'll tell him what his chances of winning are. But just like I can't play God and say if he's guilty or not, I can't play God and tell a guy "You go to trial," or "You don't go to trial."

> I always tell them, "it's no skin off my nose whether you go to trial or not. I'll do the best job I can if you want to go to trial; I'll negotiate the best deal I can if you don't want to go to trial."

But, public defenders admitted, reasoning with a client does not always produce the desired result. One lawyer, now a supervisor, admitted that occasionally he would resort to a little "bullying."[6] What did he mean by that? "I would come in, and I would say things like, 'You know, you are a damn fool if you don't take this deal, because this is the best you are going to get. If you go on trial, in my opinion, you are going to be found guilty and you are going to get more time.' And then people would say — not often, but occasionally, the person would say — 'I don't care; I didn't do it, and I want a trial!' And I would say, 'Okay, okay. If *that's* your attitude, let's go to trial!'"

If public defenders resist taking loser cases to trial because it will hurt the client, they resist too because it will be painful for the lawyer. One of the worst things about being a public defender, said one former assistant, was "not the realization that most of your clients were in fact guilty" but the fact that "there was very little you could do to get the system to give them a not guilty" or that, as another said, "your clients never had any real obvious defense and you [the attorney] were just stuck."

Ask any public defender "What was your worst case?" and you may or may not hear about some horrible crime; you may or may not hear about the case that lasted the longest or took the most preparation. Chances are, however, you will hear about a case that was a loser. Understanding the nature of a loser case is crucial, for embedded in the concept — and in the distinctions that lawyers make between losers and other sorts of cases — is the clue to what makes public defenders tick.

The worst case is where the state has an overwhelming amount of evidence and there is nothing you can do with it. . . . It's a case where you are just overwhelmed by the state's evidence. It's a case where you get beat up in court. And that is just *no fun*.

You are so relieved when a guy pleads out on a case that you know you can't win, and you are going to get your head beaten on, and the jury is probably going to throw rocks at you when you make the closing argument.

My worst case was a very hopeless case, a rape and armed robbery, and the persons were captured by the police and they were contending that they were the wrong guys.

Q: Why was that your worst case? You've defended people accused of murder before.

R: The fact that the individuals were given reasonable offers and they should have copped pleas, because there wasn't a chance of their being acquitted. And they were going through the ordeal because they opted for a jury trial. It was just a very painful process; it was just an *absurd* situation.

Q: Was it a particularly awful crime?

R: No. Well, he just beat up his girlfriend; he didn't kill her or anything. The evidence was just overwhelming against him. He should have pleaded, and he wouldn't. He made me go to trial.

The opposite of a loser case is not necessarily a winner. It is a fun case, which in turn must be distinguished from a boring case.

I don't like armed robberies because they are boring. There are only one or two issues — either the guy did it or he didn't — and that doesn't make for very interesting work.

The case I am trying with _____ right now is a murder that is really a lot of fun.

Listen to me! "A murder is a lot of fun." How can I say that? [Laugh] It's a murder of a baby, and here I am with my two little kids and you would think that I would feel terrible about that, wouldn't you?

But it's an interesting case because the facts are such that they [the state] don't really have much evidence in the case — a lot of other people could have done it. It's all circumstantial evidence. That's fun. It's something for me to get excited about and get into, whereas a lot of cases — there are just no issues and that makes them boring.

I don't know if I have a favorite kind of case, there are some that are a lot more fun to do — if you just think of it in those terms. I may sound horrible, but, just because of the circumstances, usually murder cases are kind of fun.

Usually what kills you in a case is somebody is on the witness stand pointing a finger at your client, saying "that guy robbed me with his gun." Whereas in a murder case you don't have a victim.

Q: What you mean is that you don't have a victim who can come to testify in court, right?

R: Right, he's not there in court. And all the evidence—well, oftentimes you have a totally circumstantial case which gives you a lot to do.

And rape cases. I hate to say it, but there's a lot to play with in a rape case: identification, consent, much more so than in your average armed robbery. You never, for example, you never have the issue of consent in armed robbery.

It is shocking to hear the lawyers talk about their favorite cases, and they are not unmindful of this. But the point is important: a favorite case is the opposite of a loser—a loser is not a loser just because it is a case that will be lost. A case is a loser when it leaves the lawyer nothing to do for the client.

The lawyers are possessed by the very human desire, as they put it, not to make "assholes" of themselves or be perceived as "jerks" in court. The jury may not really throw rocks at them but, what is worse (or so the lawyers think), will think that they are naive or stupid for "falling for what the defendant told them."[7] A case is fun to the degree that it allows the lawyers to act in the way in which they think that lawyers ought to act; a case is interesting when it gives them an opportunity to "comport yourself in a professional manner, to be an advocate for your client without looking *ridiculous* in the process, when you can get across to the jury that there is, at least, a *respectable* difference of opinion here."

Loser cases put the lawyer-as-a-professional at a terrible disadvantage:

I had one case where the, one of the defendants shot the leg off a ten-year-old girl with a shotgun. You know, that's kind of rough.

What are you supposed to say in defense of that? But because the state wasn't offering us anything decent in the plea bargain and we offered some pretrial motions that we could only preserve by going to trial, we had to go to trial.

The worst case is one where you just don't have anything. And you know you are just going to go out there and lose, and there is *nothing* you can do.

Like, they will have two counts and one will be for aggravated battery and one will be for robbery and [the state] will toss the agg. batt., drop it down to plain battery, if you plead. But if you don't, and if you go to trial, you get a finding of agg. batt.

Well, I had to go to trial on this case because the kid swears up and down that he didn't do it. But I haven't got *anything*! They've got two eyeball witnesses, and all I have is the kid saying, "But I didn't do it!" *And what am I going to do with that?*

And it's a sure loser, but I am going to trial because the kid won't admit.

The lawyers feel that, with a loser case, it is hard — if not impossible — to look respectable. With a loser case it is often difficult to look as if you are doing *anything*.

Losing

In his look at the legal profession, sociologist Talcott Parsons (1954) commented that adherence to procedure (i.e., doing everything that can be done when it ought to be done and as it ought to be done) protects lawyers from being devastated when they lose: "The fact that the case can be tried by a standard procedure relieves [the attorney] of some pressure of commitment to the case of his client. He can feel that, if he does his best then having assured his client's case of a fair trial, he is relieved of the responsibility for an unfavorable verdict" (1954:380).

One of the attorneys with whom I spoke seemed to confirm Parsons's hypothesis, at least with respect to loser cases: "There is a certain consolation of going to trial with a loser case. If I lose, what the hell. I gave it my best shot. If I lose, *it was a loser*. If I win, it's amazing."

Most of the attorneys, however, were not so sanguine and could not detach themselves from the outcomes of their cases so easily. Even losing a loser case, most of them said, is incredibly hard on the attorney.

> It's hard, you know? You can tell someone the facts of the case, and they say, "What did you expect? It was a loser." But that doesn't make me feel any better when I lose a loser. I want to win.

> Ah, idealistically I've talked about why I'm a public defender, about how I want to keep the state on the straight and narrow. And I *could* go home and say, "Well, I forced the state to prove their case beyond a reasonable doubt," but, ah, I still, that isn't what I *really* feel when I lose. What I *really* feel is just that I lost this case and I wanted to win this case.

The attorneys are not much comforted by the fact that the client was guilty — or probably guilty, anyway.

> Q: When you feel bad about losing a case, doesn't it help to know that the client was probably guilty anyway?

> R: Yea [pause], maybe. But in the middle of the trial, it's you, you know? You are trying to make them believe what you are trying to sell them, and, if you don't win, it means that they don't believe *you*. That's probably one of the reasons that it doesn't help.

> There was a case, not too long ago, that I really came to believe that they had no evidence on my man, and I fought very hard for him. We lost, and I felt very bad about that.

> Afterward, he just fell apart, started screaming at me back in the lock-up. We had this big fight. And I yelled at him: "You know, I really put myself on the line too, and I did everything I could for you, and what are you doing yelling at me? Cause I really believed, and I worked hard."

And then I misspoke myself, because I said, "And I really believed that you didn't do this."

And he said, "Would it make you feel any better if I told you that I *did* do it?" [Laugh].

Q: How did you answer him?

R: [Laugh] I said, "I don't want to know; don't tell me!" I still don't want to know, and that's how it is.

Most telling is how these lawyers talk about doing trial work. They do not say, "I'm doing a trial now"; they do not ask, "Are you doing a trial this week?" They say, "*I'm* on trial"; they ask, "Are *you* on trial?"

Lawyers hate to lose because, although reason tells them a case is a loser, sentiment says that justice favors not the stronger case but the better lawyer. What makes losing any case, even a loser, so bad is their belief that, in the hands of a *good* attorney, there is really no such thing as a dead-bang loser case. One attorney told me: "Fewer and fewer of my cases are losers. . . . Because I am a better and better lawyer."

Most of the attorneys seemed to feel the same way:

One of the maxims I've learned is that the evidence is always better than the way it looks on paper. There is always some goof-up of a witness, something that comes up in the trial, so that you always have something to work with. Invariably that is so.

By the time I walk into the courtroom, even if rationally I sat down when I first heard the case and said "Well, there is no way I can win," by the time I walk into the courtroom I will figure out some way to argue to the judge or the jury that I think I can convince them. By that time, I believe I can win the case.

You start out thinking "I can't win this, no one can win this." Then you start to get a glimmer, a way out of it being a loser case. Then you think that, if only you can make the jury understand things the way you understand things, they will go along with you and give you a not guilty. Part of you knows — or at least that is what you tell yourself later — part of you knows you *can't* win, that you aren't going to win, but that gets lost in the part of you that wants so much to win this case for your guy — and to win this case for you.

Of course, you have to be good to take advantage of those goof-ups, those things that invariably come your way in the trial. Because of the suspicion that there is always something, when it cannot be found or when it does not work, the lawyer is apt to feel at fault. Even when they know that their client was factually guilty, public defenders are likely to feel, "I let my client down."

The most stressful time is on a difficult case and you realize that, well, some other lawyer could win this, why the hell can't I? I will do everything I can, but there will still be something I miss. And yet, maybe nobody in the courtroom, not even my client, knows about it. But it can destroy our case. Then, when you lose, you feel the weight of your client's sentence on your shoulders. When my client gets sentenced, part of me is going with him.

You go home and you have those "ah, shit! God damn, why didn't I? If I only would have, if I only would have spent ten more minutes, if I only would have asked him this, if I would have gone out and asked, or done more investigations.... Your mistakes? Your mistakes go to jail.

The stress of being on trial and the pain of losing are compounded on those rare occasions when the lawyer believes the defendant is innocent. For this reason, although the lawyers will say, "I don't care if he's guilty or innocent," their claim to neutrality is often a lie. When they say, "I don't care if my client is guilty," what they usually mean is, "I *prefer* my clients to be guilty."

Most defense attorneys would rather not have a client they think is innocent, because it's just irrelevant. Because it's your job to fight the state's case no matter what. You *hate* to lose, and you are worried about losing just because it's your job to win. And if you think he's innocent, you worry more. And that is just aggravation, which is really irrelevant to your job.

None of the current public defenders with whom I spoke said they preferred innocent clients, and all but two said they actually preferred representing defendants whom they believed were guilty.[8] Many of the attorneys did not want to talk about such cases, even hypothetically. Most of them just said something like, "In my own gut I know I have a harder time defending people I know are innocent than people I suspect are guilty — the pressure to win is so much greater then," or "it is just harder to defend an innocent person because there is so much pressure." Although no public defender said as much, given what they did say, I suspect that what makes defending an innocent client so stressful is the fact that if one should fail to win an acquittal, it would be difficult to avoid the conclusion that it was the lawyer's fault (although in theory, this may not be true). In such cases, the weight of the client's sentence really hangs on the defender. One lawyer told me how he protected himself from the possibility of that kind of "incredible stress." He explained that he "tried not to think about having innocent clients [pause], but it's academic since they are all guilty anyway."

Coping with Losing

Losing is one of the costs of being an attorney; losing a lot (I was told) is one of the costs of being a public defender:

You must try to convince the judge or the jury that what you are saying must be followed. But as a public defender, you get the realization that

> no matter how hard you do this, no matter how well you do this, you
> are probably not going to get it across. Or, even if you do, the judge or
> the jury is going to say no. You cannot be afraid to lose, because mostly
> it's a lost cause. You cannot have a personality where you must win or
> it's going to screw you.

> Sometimes it's just that you get rotten case after rotten case. It drives
> you crazy. What it does is it makes you think you can't win.

> When you lose a few in a row, you question yourself. And then it be-
> comes real hard to go back into court and try again.

Public defenders do not like to lose—but said that one must just
learn to accept it. Nevertheless, watching them try their cases and listening to them talk about their cases made it clear to me that the attorneys do
not just accept losing. In many instances, the attorneys seemed to try to
outwit defeat.

However it looks to the spectator—or, for that matter, to the defendant—public defenders can show you how a trial is not a zero-sum situation. Even when the lawyer does not win freedom for his or her client,
something may have been won: "I don't feel defeatist. There is a lot you
can do, even if you lose—like mitigate a person's involvement or partly
win by getting a guilty on one charge and not on another."

Even when there is no way to mitigate the client's guilt or to partly
win, there is such a thing as an almost win. Those count too—at least
they are counted by the attorneys, especially if the case had seemed to
be open and shut. There is a certain measure of satisfaction that can be
drawn, for example, from keeping the jury out longer than could have
been expected.

> It was a terrible case, a terrible case. It was a brutal, cold-blooded slay-
> ing of a ma-and-pa grocer. They had a witness, a flipper. The guy who
> drove the car flipped against them both. They found the guns in my
> guy's house; they had a dead-bang loser case against them.

> We tried to discredit the flipper and minimize the effect of the gun be-
> ing found, saying that they couldn't absolutely prove that it was the
> same gun that had been used.

> We lost. We kept the jury out for about ten hours or so, and that was
> something. But we ended up losing.

> We did a jury trial a few weeks ago—the case was a rape, a 14-year-
> old. Both my partner and I felt he would be found guilty and that he
> probably did it. But we tried that case *so* hard, then we lost it.

> But we kept the jury out almost three hours. And we thought it was
> going to be like a 15-minute guilty verdict.

Moreover, the lawyers are helped some by their ability to distinguish
a loss from a defeat. Even when they lose, public defenders search for evidence that they did a better job, that they "out-tried" the state's attorneys.

Out-trying one's adversaries can mean anything from simply acting more professional to forcing your opponent to commit reversible error. Sometimes it just means making him or her look silly in court.

During long or tough cases the level of exchange between defense and prosecuting attorneys can destroy all ideals that one might have about noble adversaries. Attorneys (as they themselves admit) will sometimes bait each other, trying to force their opponents to do something regrettable. The following are snatches of dialogue from a death-penalty case. All these exchanges took place on the record (I have, however, changed the lawyers' names). Mr. Buford and Mr. Petrone speak for the prosecution; attorneys Carney, Stone, and Richert appeared for the defense:

[Time One]

Richert: [To the court] During Mr. Carney's remarks, Mr. Buford came to me personally and pointed to Mr. Stone and said, "Do you realize your partner looks like Lenin?" I would appreciate if the prosecutor would avoid interfering with my participation in proceedings such as these.

The Court: Which prosecutor? Who is he talking about? Who looks like Lenin?

[Later that day]

Carney: [To Buford] Oh, put your foot down [off the table]. Act like an attorney. What is wrong with you?

Buford: Come on.

Carney: Take your foot off the table!

Buford: You don't tell me what to do!

Carney: It insults me as an attorney.

Buford: I may do that, but you don't tell me what to do!

The Court: We will take a recess.

[Time Two]

Petrone: Let's go. We have been wasting seven months for it.

Stone: That's unprofessional.

Petrone: That's as unprofessional as you, Mr. Stone.

Stone: Wasn't it enough that we showed you how to pick a jury?

Petrone: You showed us how to pick a jury? You pleaded him right into the electric chair!

[Time Three]

Buford [in chambers]: I am at this time requesting that we go out in the court and requesting that—I just did—that we go on the record, because once again, I am not going to put up with any more of this state's attorney baiting or this other bullshit that's gone on here in chambers.

Carney: *That's on the record!*

Buford: Right; exactly. That has gone on here for eight weeks. I request that we go out in open court. Let the record reflect [pause]. [To judge] Look at Mr. Carney!

Carney: And I am looking at Mr. Buford, Judge. And I have never heard *that* word said in a court of law in eight years, Judge, by a state's attorney or any defense lawyer, and I am *really* shocked!

Buford: Look at these faces that they are making. I am asking that you hold them in direct contempt!

The Court: All right, but I just wanted to know what witnesses are you calling?

The defense lost the case. They had hoped to "win" by getting a life sentence, but their client was sentenced to death. To any observer, it was a total loss. After listening to testimony for several weeks, the jury took less than an hour and only one vote to make the decision unanimous. Still, the attorneys (Mr. Carney, in particular) appeared to derive a great deal of satisfaction from their belief that they had not been "defeated," that they had caused their opponents (Mr. Buford, in particular) to "lose it" several times during the case. The night before the case ended, Mr. Carney recalled what for him had been a major highlight of the case. "Lisa, you know what Buford said to me that first day? He said, 'Carney, I heard you were a choker; I *collect* chokers, Carney.' When Buford said 'bullshit' in chambers, I leaned over and whispered to him: 'C-H-O-K-E.'" After the end of the last day in court, after hearing that their client would be sentenced to death, at a dinner that could more properly be called a wake, a deeply depressed Carney repeated several times: "We sure got that bastard Buford; we sure beat their asses, didn't we?" "Yes," he was assured again and again, "we *sure* did."

In retrospect the attorneys seemed a bit childish, their bickering like juvenile acting-out. Yet when one is trying to salvage something that is a lost cause, anyway, every little bit seems to help.

It should be noted too that the above exchanges are unusual, a result of the fact that, in the attorneys' minds, baiting the state's attorneys could not make things any worse for their client than it was inevitably going to be—and might, if they could push the prosecutor far enough, win him a mistrial. Normally, the attorneys are mindful of the fact that acting out will probably hurt one's client. Even in this case, the lawyers (the defense lawyers, anyway) never got totally out of control. It should be noted that while all of these exchanges (and others like them) took place on the record, they took place out of the hearing of the jury.

But even if the public defenders do not usually feel free to really mix it up with the prosecutor in court, there is still an important kind of anticipatory satisfaction that emerges from knowing that oftentimes the "only reason the state wins is because the facts are on their side." The satisfaction comes from knowing that *someday* most of those prosecutors are going to leave the state's attorney's office, and many of them are going to turn their hands to criminal defense work. That day, believe many public defenders, will be the day when these prosecutors will get what is coming to them. Public defenders sometimes sound almost smug when they talk about what is in store for prosecutors: "One of the ways I deal with [losing], with when I have to look over at the state's attorneys as they gleefully congratulate each other on their records of victory, when I know I have out-tried them on a case, well, you just say, 'chalk it up.' They are going to leave the office some day; they are going to find out that they are not such hot shit. That's a *big* satisfaction, a very big satisfaction."

Perhaps the most important way in which they cope with losing is knowing that they do not always lose. When I asked one attorney "How do you keep going when you lose?" he said: "Always remembering that there is a flip side of that—you feel great when you win. There is no feeling like it. And *that* wouldn't feel as good if it weren't so hard to win." In fact, the lawyers seem to go into each trial with great expectations of winning. The knowledge that the next case may be the one you win seems to keep them going.

Coping with Winning

I do not apologize for (or feel guilty about) helping to let a murderer go free—even though I realize that someday one of my clients may go out and kill again. Since nothing like that has ever happened, I cannot know for sure how I would react. I know that I would feel terrible for the victim. But I hope that I would not regret what I had done—any more than a surgeon should regret saving the life of a patient who recovers and later kills an innocent victim. (Dershowitz, 1983, xiv)

Doctors lose patients; lawyers lose cases. Failure is something with which every professional must cope. But implicit in the question, How can you defend those people? is the idea that public defenders ought to have trouble coping with winning.

The possibility of getting a guilty person off is not a specter that haunts public defenders, at least not to the extent that you would notice it. In misdemeanor and juvenile courts, the majority of defendants represented by public defenders are relatively innocent and/or harmless criminals accused of relatively innocent or harmless crimes. The lawyers are protected by the fact that they rarely win cases for clients who are horrible criminals; winning an acquittal for a burglar or even an armed robber is, for a public defender, hardly cause for intense introspective examinations of one's morality or personal guilt. It is not that they have lost all sense of proportion but that they have gained a new one—by the time that they get to felony courtrooms, the lawyers are, most of them, convinced that what they see happen to their clients in the jails or in the courts is as bad as or worse than most of what happens to victims out on the streets. There is, moreover, often a sense that the injustices perpetrated by the system are worse because they are committed by people who really ought to know better.

However rarely it occurs, the possibility of winning big someday and then having your client kill again exists in the future of every defense lawyer. It is not something that they seem to talk about very often. It is difficult to talk about it perhaps because there is so much emphasis on the importance of the defendant's right to a lawyer who will do everything possible to win a case. Moreover, in the tough, heroic world of the trial lawyer, it is perhaps difficult to conceive of feeling bad about winning.

A few years ago, an episode of the television show "Hill Street Blues" featured the story of a public defender who got a murderer freed on a "technicality." Some time later, the client murdered again. This time, the victim was a friend of the public defender, who, unable to deal with the guilt, quit the office.

At the time, many public defenders were avid fans of this television show, in large part (I thought) because the writers had created a very competent, tough, and sympathetic role for a public defender on the show. A few days after this particular episode aired, a group of lawyers in the office discussed the story-line and decided that it was unrealistic. I later asked one of them why. "Because the lawyer quit. That's just not the way it's done. You just move into the next case. As a lawyer you are very removed from the reality of it." Reflecting on his answer for a moment, I said, "I just can't believe that." "It's true," he assured me. I pushed him: "What would you do if it happened to you? What if you got a N.G. on a killer and he came around and killed again?" After a few moments he admitted that he "probably would move into another branch of law."

Most of the lawyers with whom I spoke said, as does Dershowitz, that it had not happened to them—and that while they hoped that it would not happen, they did not think that it would bother them. But one added: "As I say that, I am mindful of one public defender named _____, I think one of the reasons he left was that he managed to get a guy acquitted on a murder and the guy went out and committed another murder. That really got to him. And I watched him suffer with that, and I wondered if I would suffer like that, and I came to no conclusion."

A few of the lawyers admitted that they had come close to winning cases that, deep down inside themselves, they had not wanted to win: "I've never felt bad about winning a case. The last jury trial I did I almost won, and I was worried about that. It really bothered me. But all of it has to do with the relationship you have with your client. He was a real asshole and hard to deal with, and he was a mean son of a bitch."

Often it seemed that one of the things that helps the lawyer not to feel too bad about winning is one of the things that makes it so hard to lose—

that is, their relationship with the client. Most of the lawyers said that usually, especially when they go to trial, they end up liking their clients. In most cases, the lawyers spoke with some affection about their "guys."

> There is in any human being a soul you can reach. [Pause] Now I use language like this hesitantly, you know, people usually look at you like you're crazy when you talk like this. But if you are willing to take the risk and open up your heart and reach into their hearts, you will reach it.

> You need to do that for yourself. You need to do that too because if you are going to try the case for either a judge or a jury . . . you have to make that person human. They are not some black or brown face — or white face, for that matter. They are someone. And that is what costs. 'Cause everytime you do that you are giving something of yourself away. You get something sure, but you give away a lot.

> [At first] I was a little leery. You wonder, "Can I talk to a guy like this?" And you find out it's real easy [laugh], you find out that they are real people, just like you. Well [laugh], maybe not *just* like you, but real people. And you come to like most of your clients [laugh]. That surprised me, still does.

> A lot of criminals I have gotten to like. There are some real nice human beings even if they are in real serious trouble.

> [Recalling his first murder case] It was funny — I liked the shooter. He was a real nice guy.

The danger, of course, is in getting too involved with your client, getting to like him or her too much. That is when you lose your sense of proportion. As one lawyer told me, you "must always remember that he is a defendant, and you must treat him as a defendant."

Two of the lawyers with whom I spoke had experienced what one called the "defense lawyer's nightmare." One would not talk about it; one would:

> Once on a case with _____, he came up with a brilliant idea about collateral evidence, and I wrote a brilliant brief. It persuaded the judge to dismiss the indictment — just unheard of.

> And three months later he killed three other people. He participated in a gang killing — didn't actually do the killing, but he was definitely part of it. That, of course, is the defense lawyer's nightmare.

> There are people who can — for example, my partner — who can say, "that's not my concern," but that is bullshit. That is why he is losing his hair and I'm not. You feel bad. You *have* to feel bad.

> *However*, the constitutional proposition was correct, and it made some important law in Illinois; and I would do it again. But I would not represent [that client] again. Because we could not wholeheartedly represent him zealously, we were let off representing him.

"How can you live with that?" I asked. "You either leave, stay and repress it, or you stay and cope. Sure you feel bad, but you deal with it by knowing that hopefully you are doing enough good to make you feel good about what you are doing."

At the time, that did not seem like much of an answer—but perhaps it is the only one.

Concluding Remarks: Public Defenders and Their Society

Justifying the public defender's rebellion against society is, in fact, a strict adherence to important social values. They believe that it is right to defend "those people" because of the principle that everyone is innocent until proved otherwise and so everyone is entitled to a defense. More important, they also believe that it is right to defend even the guilty because their clients *need* someone to defend them against police, prosecutorial, and judicial abuse. Because of what they see happen in the system every day, public defenders would be the last to claim that defense lawyers are unnecessary luxuries for defendants (guilty or innocent) in our criminal courts.

Beyond these rationales, public defenders are motivated by the desire to legitimize themselves as professionals, to act as professionals, and, as final proof of their right to professional status and respect, to win. Their desire to win makes them look very closely at each client's case: Where has the state failed to make its case? Did the state make an error? Did the police mess up the arrest? Public defenders want to find those cases, because those are the kinds of cases that make them look good. The closer they look, the more they find, and this, in turn, reinforces their view that their work is essential.

In an important sense, then, there is a synergistic relationship between the public defenders' egoistic and altruistic concerns, their desire to win, and their view that they are needed. It is that synergy that no doubt accounts for the combative tone of most of their remarks. In theory this could spiral into a process that is out of all proportion to reality. In truth, the lawyers—especially when they are on trial—do seem to get carried away with what they do. But what prevents them from losing all touch with reality is, I think, the fact that they are not totally enclosed in the cognitive ghetto of public defending. Each is still a member of a society that suspects the morality of what they do; this attachment to society is shown in a process that some public defenders call "honking." By honking each other, public defenders remind one another how the rest of their society regards their work:

> There is a term that I didn't know until I came to this office, a thing called honking. And that is needling or giving someone a hard time,

ostensibly in a friendly manner—but it can be very pointed, very barbed. It goes on a great deal. People will get honked for their pretentiousness, for their actual performance on trial.

And people will get honked *mercilessly* for things over which they have *absolutely no control* — the quality of the client, the heinousness of the act with which the person is charged. And people get honked for trying to defend people who really have hopeless legal positions.

Endnotes

[1] Importantly, not all who study plea bargaining necessarily regard it as a nonadvocacy — or even a nonadversarial — process. Feeley, for one, has cautioned us that "preliminary hearings, probable cause hearings, and informal discovery may serve many of the functions of a trial—to obtain and test crucial evidence and challenge assertions of fact and law—which may in turn lead to nolles, dismissals, or pleas of guilty in the face of an overwhelming case. To infer the lack of an adversarial stance and the existence of bargained settlement—for the pure purpose of administrative convenience—from the absence of trials is to ignore altogether the importance of these other 'truthtesting' and highly combative processes" (Feeley, 1979:29; see also Maynard, 1984, chap. 5).

[2] At some level public defenders seem to understand clients who think that public defense lawyers are unwilling to go to trial, are just "penitentiary dispatchers" interested in making deals for clients. Appearances can sometimes be deceiving—even to some lawyers: "Now _____, he was to me the epitome of the worst kind of public defender. From a distance, I got the feeling that he was just there to cop people out, and to run through cases with no sense of the client, no empathy with the person. I know now I was making a childish sort of judgment. It's a show he puts on, maybe to protect himself. In reality he practically weeps when he loses, not for himself, but for his client."

[3] For discussions of such ethical positions see Freedman (1975, chap. 5) and Hazard (1978, chap. 9).

[4] On the other hand, most of the lawyers admitted that, as public defenders, they are relatively protected from temptations to cheat. Whenever I asked them about this, the typical response was "Who would want to bribe a public defender? Anyone who could afford to bribe someone would have a private lawyer."

   Once in private practice, these lawyers may not find it so easy to avoid what may be called the near occasions of sin that are apparently relatively common in Chicago. Recently, a former public defender was indicted for attempted bribery. He got a not guilty on a "technicality." Furthermore, five of the twenty lawyers alleged by the *Chicago Lawyer* magazine to be "Hallway Hustlers" were former public defenders. This label is applied to lawyers who hang out in misdemeanor courts and prey on unwary defendants—that is, take their money and render no or only dubious services.

[5] As a result of his nationwide survey of defense lawyers, Professor Albert W. Alschuler of the University of Chicago Law School noted that, in some measure, how the problem of the "innocent" defendant was handled helped to distinguish the strategies of public from private defense attorneys: "With only a few exceptions, public defenders refused to enter guilty pleas when their clients claimed to be innocent. Private defense attorneys, by contrast, were almost evenly divided between those who followed the same rule and those who maintained that 'guilt or innocence has nothing to do with it.'" (1975:1283).

[6] It should be noted that public defenders say that, when the occasion demands, they will work just as hard to convince a client with a good case that he ought to go to trial:
   Some will say, "I'm guilty, and I'm going to plead." And if I think they have a good case, I'll say to them, "Look, I think we can win this; you have a good case."

It takes something out of you when you have a case you think you can win and you want to try, but the guy pleads.

The *worst* situation, though, is when you have a young kid with no record who can't stand it any more, being locked up and raped and beaten in jail, and they offer him a way out and he takes it—probation, or time served, or something. And you can't get him to trial fast enough; it's living hell for him in there.

[7] Despite the lawyers' insistence that they do not want to know, they are careful to learn enough so they will not look silly in court. That is one of the first lessons that public defenders learn. Ronald Himel, a former public defender, in 1971 assured a reporter from *Newsweek* that one just cannot afford to believe everything one hears: "My first case out of law school, the guy told me he walked around the corner and found the TV set. So I put that on [in court]. The judge pushed his glasses down his nose, hunched up and said, 'Fifty-two years I have been walking the streets and alleys of Chicago and I have never, ever found a TV set.' Then he got me in his chambers and said, 'Are you f____ crazy?' I said, 'That's what he told me.' The judge said, 'And you believed that s____? You're goofier than he is!'" (8 March 1971:29).

[8] Consensus was not as high among former public defenders. When asked whether they agreed with the statement "Contrary to what you might expect, I preferred cases where I thought my client was guilty to cases where I believed my client was innocent," almost a third (32 percent) refused to answer, saying that it was irrelevant. Among those who did answer, about half (49 percent) agreed that they preferred guilty clients. When I compared the answers of those who had worked in felony courts with the answers of those who had not, there was a significant difference. Among those who only worked in misdemeanor, juvenile, or appeals divisions, only 21 percent agreed that they preferred guilty clients. Among those who had worked in a felony courtroom, 71 percent said that, as public defense lawyers, they preferred guilty clients.

References

Alschuler, A. W. (1972). Courtroom misconduct by prosecutors and trial judges. *Texas Law Review, 50,* 629.

Alschuler, A. W. (1975). The defense attorney's role in plea bargaining. *Yale Law Journal, 84,* 1179–1313.

Blumberg, A. S. (1967). The practice of law as a confidence game: Organizational cooptation of a profession. *Law and Society Review, 1,* 15–39.

Blumberg, A. S. (1979). *Criminal justice: Issues and ironies.* New York: New Viewpoints.

Dershowitz, A. M. (1983). *The best defense.* New York: Vintage.

Dorsen, N., & Friedman, L. (1973). *Disorder in the court.* New York: Pantheon.

Durkheim, E. (1974). *Sociology and philosophy.* New York: Free Press.

Eisenstein, J., & Jacob, H. (1977). *Felony justice: An organizational analysis of criminal courts.* Boston: Little, Brown and Co.

Feeley, M. M. (1979). *The process is the punishment: Handling cases in a lower criminal court.* New York: Russell Sage Foundation.

Freedman, M. H. (1975). *Lawyers' ethics in an adversary system.* Indianapolis: Bobbs-Merrill.

Friedman, L. M. (1973). *A history of American law.* New York: Simon & Schuster.

Friedman, L. M. (1975). *The legal system: A social science perspective.* New York: Russell Sage Foundation.

Greene, B. (1982, November 3). Lawyer closes the book on criminal defense. *Chicago Tribune,* sec. 4.

Hazard, G. (1978). *Ethics in the practice of law.* New Haven, CT: Yale University Press.

Heumann, M. (1978). *Plea bargaining.* Chicago: University of Chicago Press.

Jackson, B. (1983). *Law and disorder: Criminal justice in America*. Urbana: University of Illinois Press.

Jacob, H. (1980). *Crime and justice in urban America*. Englewood Cliffs, NJ: Prentice-Hall.

Kalvin, H., & Zeisel, H. (1966). *The American jury*. Boston: Little, Brown and Co.

Lydon, S. T. (1973). The public defender as an adversary: The Alameda County public defender revisited. In *Alameda County public defender, forty-sixth annual report*. Oakland, CA: Alameda County Public Defender.

Maynard, D. (1984). *Inside plea bargaining: The language of negotiation*. New York: Plenum.

Nardulli, R. F. (1978). *The courtroom elite: An organizational perspective on criminal justice*. Cambridge, MA: Ballinger.

National Advisory Commission on Criminal Justice Standards and Goals. (1974). *Report*. Washington, DC: Government Printing Office.

Packer, H. L. (1964). Two models of the criminal process. *University of Pennsylvania Law Review, 113*, 1–68.

Packer, H. L. (1954). A sociologist looks at the legal profession. In *Essays in sociological theory* (pp. 370–385). New York: Free Press.

Spencer, J. (1984, January 8). No glamour, no money: Public defenders still seek justice for all. *Chicago Tribune*, sec. 2.

Sudnow, D. (1965). Normal crimes: Sociological features of the penal code in the public defender's office. *Social Problems, 12*, 255–277.

Weick, K. (1979). *The social psychology of organizing*. Reading, MA: Addison-Wesley.

Wishman, S. (1981). *Confessions of a criminal lawyer*. New York: Penguin.

Zemans, F. K., & Rosenblum, V. C. (1981). *The making of a public profession*. Chicago: American Bar Foundation.

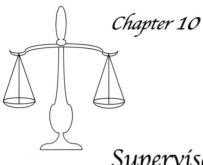

Chapter 10

Supervisory Styles of Patrol Sergeants and Lieutenants

Robin Shepard Engel

Introduction

Most scholars and practitioners agree that supervising patrol officers is a "challenging, and at times, insurmountable task" given the environmental constraints and general nature of patrol work (Tifft, 1971; Van Maanen, 1983). Although first-line supervision is critical to the success of police organizations, very little is known about the actual roles and activities street-level patrol supervisors perform. In addition, differences in supervisory styles have not been adequately described or examined. It is troubling that the policing community knows so little about the activities, roles, and styles of patrol supervisors, who are generally considered to be the backbone of American police organizations (Trojanowicz, 1980). In this era of community policing, as police departments are encouraged to move from traditional authoritarian bureaucratic models to flatter organizational structures with greater line-officer latitude, the importance of supervisory styles will increase. The promise of this research is that it identifies different supervisory styles that currently exist in policing and

Reprinted from *Journal of Criminal Justice,* Vol. 29, Robin Shepard Engel, "Supervisory Styles of Patrol Sergeants and Lieutenants," pp. 341–355, 2001 with permission from Elsevier.

addresses how supervisors with particular styles differ. Implications for policy and future research are also addressed.

Literature Review

Some general propositions can be reached from a review of the literature written about police supervisors' responsibilities, activities, and roles. First, it has been acknowledged that the performance of first-line supervisors is measured through the effectiveness of their subordinates' performance. This encourages supervisors and subordinates to engage in a reciprocity of informal "exchanges" (Brown, 1988; Manning, 1977; Rubinstein, 1973; Van Maanen, 1983). Furthermore, sergeants can use their specific daily tasks (e.g., scheduling of shifts, beats, assignments, etc.) to influence and control subordinate actions and behavior (Van Maanen, 1983, 1984). Finally, police sergeants are in a perceived position of conflict, caught between their responsibility *to* superior officers and their responsibility *for* subordinate officers. Faced with this conflict, individual sergeants adapt and define their roles differently (Trojanowicz, 1980; Van Maanen, 1983, 1984). Therefore, one would expect patrol supervisors to develop different supervisory styles, which influence their own behavior as well as the behavior of subordinate officers.

Several policing ethnographies have addressed the role of the police supervisor. Muir's (1977) work examining patrol officers' understanding of human kind and morality regarding the use of coercion suggested that patrol sergeants *could* have a fundamental influence on officers' development of both understanding and morality, and therefore on their behavior. Wilson (1968) also came to a similar conclusion, proposing that an administrator's preference has a varying influence on patrol officers' use of discretion in different types of citizen encounters. In contrast, Brown (1988:121) hypothesized that field supervisors and administrators have relatively little influence over patrol officers' behavior. His examination of survey responses of both patrol officers and supervisors indicated that "the routine actions of field supervisors have but a marginal impact on the way they [patrol officers] use their discretion." Other researchers have empirically tested the effects of supervision on patrol officer behavior (Allen, 1980, 1982; Allen and Maxfield, 1983; Brehm and Gates, 1993; Gates and Worden, 1989; Mastrofski, Ritti, and Snipes, 1994; Reiss, 1971; Smith, 1984; Tifft, 1971), but no firm conclusions have been reached. Much of this research has measured only the *quantity* of supervision (e.g., mere supervisor presence at police-citizen encounters, time spent at encounters, etc.) rather than the *quality* of supervision (e.g., styles of supervision, attitudinal and behavior differences among supervisors, etc.).

A handful of studies have examined different supervisory and leadership styles of patrol supervisors and administrators. Both Cohen (1980) and Pursley (1974) identified two types of police administrators based on survey data. Pursley's "traditionalist" and "nontraditionalist" police chiefs bear a striking resemblance to Cohen's "tradition-oriented" and "reform-oriented" commanders. Moreover, these classifications are similar to Reuss-Ianni and Ianni's (1983) identification of the "street cop" and "management cop" cultures. Van Maanen (1983, 1984) identified and described what he termed "street" sergeants and "station house" sergeants. His classification was based primarily on the activities of sergeants; active sergeants in the field who directly monitored subordinates (street sergeants) were contrasted with administrative sergeants who were more likely to remain in the station (station house sergeants). Van Maanen suggested that these two types of sergeants defined their roles differently.

In addition to these "police-specific" styles, leadership styles identified in the management literature have been applied to police supervisors. For example, the "consideration" and "initiating structure" styles of leadership developed through the Leader Behavior Description Questionnaire (LBDQ) (Halpin and Winer, 1957; Hemphill and Coons, 1957) have been applied to police supervisors (Aldag and Brief, 1978; Brief, Aldag, and Wallden, 1976; Pursley, 1974). Likewise, Blake and Mouton's (1978) managerial grid styles have been applied to police supervisors (Kuykendall, 1977, 1985; Swanson and Territo, 1982), as were Hersey and Blanchard's relations-orientation and task-orientation styles (Kuykendall and Roberg, 1988; Kuykendall and Unsinger, 1982). Furthermore, Jermier and Berkes (1979) have applied the supervisory styles developed in the path goal theory to police supervisors. Most of these studies sought to predict subordinate satisfaction and generally produced mixed results.

For a number of reasons, findings from this body of research should be interpreted with caution. First, the measures of supervisory styles are often based on subordinates' perceptions of their supervisors rather than supervisors' perceptions of themselves or their actual behavior (Aldag and Brief, 1978; Brief et al., 1976; Jermier and Berkes, 1979). It is also unclear if the subordinates were asked to, and were able to, answer the leadership questions about a particular supervisor, rather than simply describing supervision in general (Aldag and Brief, 1978; Brief et al., 1976). Many shifts are supervised by multiple supervisors, making it problematic to attribute subordinates' perceptions of supervision to a particular supervisor. Even studies that base measures of supervisory styles on behavior are limited because they use hypothetical vignettes rather than actual observed behavior (Kuykendall and Unsinger, 1982). Finally, while leadership questionnaires can generally be applied to most types of supervisors, they may not adequately capture the unique circumstances of supervisors in police organizations. Several scholars who applied these questionnaires to police populations reported findings that were somewhat different from results consistently reported in the management field (Aldag and Brief, 1978; Brief et al., 1976; Kuykendall and Unsinger, 1982).

In general, the police supervision literature is limited in scope and fails to answer many conceptual and empirical questions regarding field supervision. This is especially true of questions regarding differences in supervisory styles. As stated by Southerland and Reuss-Ianni (1992:177), "we need more broad-based research using a variety of methodological tools and conducted throughout a wide range of police agencies, not simply generalized from management studies conducted in business settings, to understand the current style and status of the police leadership and management." This article provides the first attempt to address this perceived need. The next section describes several underlying attitudinal constructs identified in the management and policing literatures that are combined to create four supervisory styles for a sample of patrol supervisors in two metropolitan police departments. These four styles are thoroughly described and their distribution among supervisors is explored.

Underlying Attitudinal Constructs

Since the 1930s, scholars focusing on leadership theories have described a variety of different leadership styles. Similarities among these theories are easily identified by examining their underlying attitudinal and behavioral constructs (Bass, 1990; Graham and Hays, 1993; Yukl, 1989). Indeed, there are strong similarities and one should expect a correlation between Lewin and Lippitt's (1938) "democratic" leaders, those leaders scoring high on the "consideration factor" created by the LBDQ (Hemphill and Coons, 1957), and Blake and Mouton's (1978) "concern for people" factor. The characteristics defining these types of leaders also correspond to Hersey and Blanchard's (1988) relations-oriented leader, McGregor's (1957, 1960) Theory Y managers, and Bass' (1985, 1990) transformational leader. Since many of the taxonomies of leadership behavior are similar, many of the leadership styles capture the same attitudes and behaviors. Yet, it is important to identify the actual individual constructs on which these leadership styles are based. Bass (1990) identified some individual attitudinal constructs underlying styles of leadership, each of which should be considered a continuum upon which leaders vary.

Rather than relying on styles identified in the management literature, this work identified underlying attitudinal constructs that were considered important for police supervision. Using Bass' (1990) work as a base, six underlying attitudinal constructs were identified and measured for a sample of police field supervisors: level of activity, decision making, power distribution, relations-orientation, task-orientation, and inspirational motivation. These constructs were later combined with three police-specific constructs (expectations for community policing, expectations for aggressive enforcement, and general views of subordinates), to create supervisory styles for police officers.

The first underlying construct, *level of activity*, examined the extent to which leadership was either avoided or attempted. This construct involved the relative distance and/or amount of supervision a leader employs. Early leadership research focused on three classic styles developed by Lewin and Lippitt (1938): authoritarian, democratic, and laissez-faire. One of the defining characteristics of these styles was the level of activity displayed by the leader. For example, laissez-faire leaders were described as inactive leaders that avoid or shirk their supervisory duties (Lewin, Lippitt, and White, 1939). In his discussion of Theory X and Theory Y management styles, McGregor (1960) compared close, controlling supervision to supervision that was more general and loose. Rather than simply identifying active or passive leadership as a dichotomy, a leader's motivation to manage can be measured along a continuum.

The second construct of leadership styles was based on *how leaders made decisions* (e.g., group decision-making, group input with one person deciding, one person deciding with no input, etc.). Tannenbaum and Schmidt (1958) examined how leaders made decisions and developed a continuum of autocratic and democratic behavior. Bass (1990) described the differences between directive decision-making and participative decision-making. The directive leader "plays an active role in problem solving and decision-making and expects group members to be guided by his or her actions," while participative leaders engage subordinates in the planning or decision-making process (Bass, 1990). Leaders have also been differentiated based on how they communicate the decisions they make to subordinates. Hersey and Blanchard (1988) have described four types of leadership styles — telling, selling, participative, and delegating — that are based in part on one-way and two-way communications between leaders and subordinates.

A third construct examined *how power is distributed* (i.e., who is in charge, how many share power, who makes the decisions, etc.). "Power" refers to the control of others, though it does not necessarily imply authority, or the legitimization of power in the eyes of followers (Graham and Hays, 1993). Authority is power that has been legitimized in the eyes of the follower. A leader may rely on other types of power that are not based on legitimate authority, for example, French and Raven (1960) identified five power bases that may be utilized by leaders: legitimate, reward, coercive, referent, and expert power.

The fourth and fifth underlying constructs, referred to as *relations-orientation* and *task-orientation*, involve the focus of the leader's attention (Hersey and Blanchard, 1988). These dimensions consider what needs are being met as determined by the particular focus chosen by the leader. Leaders who are more relations-oriented focus their attention on the well-being of their subordinates. These leaders pursue a human-relations approach and maintain supportive relationships with subordinates by building friendships and mutual trust. In contrast, task-oriented leaders are most concerned with the goals of the work group, means of achieving these goals, and the output produced. These leaders focus on production and achievement. Although these two dimensions share common elements, they are conceptually and empirically distinct. Therefore, a leader could simultaneously rank high (or low) on both dimensions. Relations-orientation and task-orientation are similar to the "consideration" and "initiating structure" dimensions identified through the use of the LBDQ (Halpin and Winer, 1957; Hemphill and Coons, 1957) and the "concern for people" and "concern for production" dimensions systematic arranged into the Managerial Grid (Blake and Mouton, 1978).

The final construct identified from the management literature, *inspirational motivation*, was a leadership dimension that refers to the potential range of team-building behavior that a leader may demonstrate. This dimension includes motivating and inspiring subordinates, arousing team spirit, and demonstrating commitment to goals and shared vision. Inspirational motivation is a form of transformational leadership (Bass and Avolio, 1994).

Research Sites

This empirical examination of supervision uses data collected for the Project on Policing Neighborhoods (POPN), a large-scale study of police behavior funded by the National Institute of Justice. Systematic observation of patrol officers and field supervisors (sergeants and lieutenants) was conducted during the summer of 1996 in the Indianapolis, Indiana Police Department and during the summer of 1997 in the St. Petersburg, Florida Police Department (see Parks, Mastrofski, DeJong, and Gray, 1999).

The Indianapolis Police Department serves the city of Indianapolis, which had an estimated population of 377,723 in 1995, including 39 percent minorities, 8 percent unemployed, 9 percent below the poverty level, and 17 percent female-headed households with children. The UCR Index crime rate in 1996 was 100 per 1,000 residents. During that year, the department employed 1,013 sworn officers—17 percent female, 21 percent minority, and 36 percent with a four-year college degree. The patrol division was divided geographically into four districts, all of which were studied during the project. Each district was unique in character, mission, and emphasis placed on community policing (for details see Mastrofski et al., 2000; Parks et al., 1999).

Supervisory structure and form differed across IPD districts and shifts. It was unclear if a direct supervisor-subordinate relationship actually existed because this department did not have a formal evaluation process in place. Each patrol officer in IPD was assigned one of three work schedules with rotating days off. On each shift in every district, a sergeant was assigned to a particular schedule. Therefore, each shift had three different squads supervised by different sergeants. This supervisory structure provided that sergeants work the same schedule as the group of officers (their squad) that they were responsible for. Officers working in specialized community policing units were directly supervised by one sergeant whose sole responsibility was to monitor and direct the activities of the officers in that unit. Three of the four observed districts had a community-policing unit, although the structure and emphases of these units differed. Finally, in the patrol division, one lieutenant was assigned to each shift in each district.

St. Petersburg, Florida is located at the southern tip of Pinellas County with a population of 240,318 in 1995, including 24 percent minorities, 5 percent unemployed, 6 percent below the poverty level, and 10 percent female-headed households with children. The UCR Index crime rate (per 1,000 residents) was 99 in 1996. During that year, the St. Petersburg Police Department had 505 sworn officers, 13 percent of whom were women, 22 percent minority, and 26 percent with a four-year college degree (Parks et al., 1999). The jurisdiction of this department was divided into three districts and forty-eight community policing areas (CPA) with a community policing officer assigned to each area.

The SPPD supervision structure had undergone tremendous change in recent years.[1] During the period of observation, it reflected a compromise between geographic deployment and a squad system. Sergeants were directly responsible for a "team" of officers on a particular shift working in a specific sector or geographic area (three sectors in each district), along with a handful of community policing officers assigned to a CPA. Each sergeant had responsibility for one or more CPAs (and the community policing officers working in those areas) within their sector. Sergeants were scheduled to work three "temporal" shifts (twenty-four hours) and then "flex" their schedule for the remaining sixteen hours each week. During a "temporal" shift, sergeants were responsible for the direct supervision of all patrol officers working that shift for the entire district, not just their sector. During "flex" shifts, sergeants were expected to work on problem-solving in their specific CPA, supervise their community policing officers, and complete administrative paperwork.

Methodology

Systematic observation was conducted in IPD with fifty-eight patrol supervisors (sergeants and lieutenants) during eighty-seven rides, totaling over 600 hours—78 percent of IPD patrol sergeants and lieutenants were observed at least once. In SPPD, systematic observation was conducted with twenty-six patrol sergeants, four patrol lieutenants, and eight patrol officers working as the acting temporal sergeant during seventy-two shifts—96 percent of patrol sergeants in SPPD were observed at least once. Data were also obtained through structured interviews with sixty-nine of seventy-four patrol supervisors in IPD and all twenty-seven patrol sergeants in SPPD. The interview captured demographic and background information along with supervisors' views in the following areas: perceived problems in their districts, training, subordinates, their role as supervisors, how they distribute and use power, patrol work, goals of policing, priorities of management, and problem-oriented and community-oriented policing.

In addition, field observation of patrol officers was conducted for over 5,700 hours in twenty-four neighborhoods across the two sites. In IPD, 194 patrol officers were observed during 336 shifts, while in SPPD, 128 officers were observed during 360 shifts. Combined, observers recorded information regarding encounters between officers and approximately 12,000 citizens (Parks et al., 1999).

The measures of supervision used in the following analyses are based on supervisors who were both interviewed and observed. Combining both sites, eighty-one supervisors are included in the analyses — seventeen lieutenants and thirty-nine sergeants from IPD and twenty-five sergeants from SPPD.[2] The demographic characteristics of these supervisors are displayed in table 1. The majority of supervisors in this sample were White (85 percent), male (85 percent), and with a four-year college degree (51 percent). The average supervisor was forty-four years old with nearly ten years of supervisory experience. Although supervisors reported receiving more *training* on issues related to supervision, management, and leadership compared to the concepts and principles of community policing, they reported having more *knowledge* about community policing issues.

In the following analyses, the substantive nature of supervision is measured using the underlying attitudinal dimensions of supervisory styles identified from the management and policing literatures. Individual items are extracted from the supervisor survey and are intended to represent the supervisors' beliefs and attitudes (for a complete list of these items, see appendix A). Six additive scales are created to represent the attitudinal dimensions previously described: power distribution, decision-making, activity level, relations-orientation, task-orientation, and inspirational motivation.[3] These scales are further described in table 2.

Any examination of supervisory styles of patrol officers must also take police-specific attitudinal constructs into consideration. In addition to the six dimensions previously described, three police-specific constructs were examined: supervisors' expectations for community policing by subordinates, expectations for aggressive enforcement by subordinates, and their general views of subordinates (see table 2 and appendix A). These police-specific dimensions were believed to be important underlying components of supervisory styles.

The attitudinal constructs do relate to one another in a meaningful and interpretable manner. As expected, some scales do have significant correlation coefficients. For example, supervisors who are strongly relations-oriented also appear to have positive views of subordinate officers.

Table 1   Supervisors' characteristics

Variables	Min	Max	Mean	Standard Deviation
Sup sex (1 =female)	0	1	0.15	0.36
Sup race (1 =nonwhite)	0	1	0.15	0.36
Supervisor age	31	70	44.07	7.99
Years experience as supervisor	1	33	9.94	7.13
Education (four-year college degree)	0	1	50.62	0.50
Amount training in concepts and principles of community policing	1	5	3.48	0.99
Amount knowledge of concepts and principles of community policing	1	3	1.72	0.60
Amount training in supervision, management, and leadership	1	5	3.70	1.07
Amount knowledge in supervision, management, and leadership	1	3	1.40	0.52

N = 17 IPD lieutenants, 39 IPD sergeants, and 25 SPPD sergeants.
Amount training: 1 (none), 2 (less than one day), 3 (one to two days), 4 (three to five days), and 5 (more than five days).
Amount knowledge: 1 (very), 2 (fairly), 3 (not very knowledgeable).

Table 2   Supervisors' attitudinal dimensions

Variables	Min	Max	Mean	Standard Deviation	Mean IPD Lieutenants	Mean IPD Sergeants	Mean SP Sergeants
Activity level scale	4	8	6.65	0.96	7.06	6.74	6.24
Decision-making scale	3	7	5.66	0.88	5.48	5.67	5.77
Power scale	17	32	24.38	3.12	25.65	24.51	23.32
Relations 1—friends	1	4	2.52	1.09	2.53	2.54	2.48
Relations 2—protect	1	5	2.68	1.46	3.00	2.74	2.36
Task-orientation scale	6	20	12.49	3.17	12.44	11.64	13.84
Inspirational motivation	1	5	4.09	1.23	3.94	4.33	3.80
Expect CP scale	20	36	27.21	3.90	27.41	27.51	26.60
Expect aggressive enforcement scale	4	13	8.62	2.32	8.82	8.05	9.36
View of subordinates scale	5	9	8.18	1.00	8.58	8.35	7.64

N = 81 supervisors.
Larger values represent higher levels of activity, more direct decision-making, more perceived power, and higher levels of relations-orientation, task-orientation, inspirational motivation, expectations for CP, expectations for aggressive enforcement, and more positive views of subordinates. Numbers reported in the table are unstandardized scores.

Likewise, supervisors who score high on the community expectation scale tend to score low on the aggressive enforcement expectation scale. Indeed, all of the constructs correlate in the expected directions (see Shepard, 1999).

Findings

These nine constructs[4] are analyzed using exploratory factor analysis to identify underlying latent styles of supervision. Based on the sample of eighty-one supervisors, factor analysis reveals four significant factors with eigenvalues greater than one, which collectively explain 63 percent of the variance.[5] The factor loadings for each attitudinal construct are reported in table 3. Each of the four factors is considered a different "style" of supervision. The factor scores indicate the strength of each underlying attitudinal construct for each style. The four styles of supervision that emerge are labeled *traditional, innovative, supportive,* and *active,* respectively. Supervisors are classified with a particular style based on their highest factor score.

"Traditional" Supervisors

The first factor is dominated by an expectation of aggressive enforcement and attitudes indicating high levels of task-orientation. To a lesser extent, these supervisors report being more directive in their decision-making and have lower expectations for subordinates to engage in community policing activities. Supervisors who score high on this factor may be considered more traditional in their approach to supervision. This traditional style of supervision is characterized by supervisors who expect subordinate officers to produce measurable outcomes—particularly arrests and citations, along with paperwork and documentation. Traditional supervisors expect officers to patrol aggressively, but they do not expect officers to handle situations that involve order maintenance or quality of life issues. They are more likely to make decisions because they tend to take over encounters with citizens or tell officers how to handle these incidents.

The traditional style of supervision is what many expect in police organizations. The supervisor who places importance on measurable outcomes of police activities and aggressive enforcement is representative of the "traditional" style of supervisor. They are concerned with controlling situations and the behavior of their subordinates. This control is maintained through relatively traditional means within the department—checking paperwork, measuring output based on arrest statistics, and making decisions themselves so subordinates will not have the opportunity to mishandle a situation.

It is important to recognize the differences between this style and other "traditional" labels of supervisors or officers from past research.

Readers may misinterpret traditional supervisors as shielding subordinate officers from punishment and being more tolerant of corruption. One aspect of traditional supervisors in this sample, however, is their no-nonsense approach to policing, along with their strict enforcement of rules and regulations. As an observer recounts about a traditional supervisor:

> S1 [the supervisor observed] was obsessed with the issue of respect. S1 expounded at length about the familiarity of the department and laxity of discipline. He blamed this initially on the academy training, then the demise of the military style, and societal erosion of respect for elders and authority. S1 cited the old-style policing when officers would never address their superiors by name but by rank and would hope against hope to not be called into a supervisor's office. Now, S1 claims that the officers seek out the district commanders personally instead of adhering to the chain of command (POPN).[6]

Just as traditional supervisors expect strict law enforcement on the street, they expect adherence to departmental rules including the chain of command. Emphasis of both discipline and respect are central to this style of supervision. As described by another supervisor:

> S1 [the supervisor observed] said that he will sanction individuals if necessary and that he has actually had someone fired for numerous small things that just seemed to add up. S1 noted that most other sergeants would not have sought action against this particular subordinate, but he believes that officers should follow the rules, and when given instructions, should follow those instructions. S1 said he was more upset that the officer in question did not submit to his authority than by his actual behavior. (POPN)

Traditional supervisors are also generally resistant to community-oriented policing or other new policing initiatives. They believe that com-

Table 3   Factor analysis—factor loadings

Variables	Factor 1 (traditional)	Factor 2 (innovative)	Factor 3 (supportive)	Factor 4 (active)
Power	− 0.102	0.640	0.124	0.250
Decision-making	0.261	0.008	− 0.002	0.279
Activity level	0.004	0.007	0.003	0.647
Relations-orientation (friends)	0.004	0.447	0.115	0.007
Relations-orientation (protect)	− 0.004	0.005	0.680	− 0.005
Task-orientation	0.617	− 0.204	− 0.402	0.007
Inspirational motivation	− 0.150	0.106	0.204	− 0.314
Expect community relations	− 0.328	0.608	− 0.184	− 0.004
Expect aggressive enforcement	0.980	− 0.167	0.008	0.002
View of subordinates	− 0.006	0.296	0.113	0.534

$N = 81$ supervisors.

munity policing involves duties that should not be the responsibility of patrol officers. The following explanation by a supervisor is typical of a traditional supervisor's view:

> S1 [the observed supervisor] is a self-described "traditionalist and dinosaur". . . . S1 felt that management has a real problem as a result of bending and swaying too much with whatever prevailing climate is in existence concerning the community, media and politics. In attempting to demonstrate change, initiative, and forward movement they have jeopardized efficiency, true policing, and proficiency. (POPN)

Traditional supervisors are more likely to be supportive of new policing initiatives if they are in the form of aggressive law enforcement. Of those classified as traditional, 61.9 percent "agree strongly" that "enforcing the law is by far a patrol officer's most important responsibility," compared to only 13.6 percent of innovative supervisors, 10.5 percent of supportive supervisors, and 10.5 percent of active supervisors. They expect and encourage the "traditional" goals of policing and demand strict adherence to rules and regulations.

The observed behavior of traditional supervisors also varied in expected ways. Traditional supervisors spend significantly less time per shift engaging in encounters with citizens (2.0 percent compared to 5.4 percent). This behavioral difference reinforces the characterization of traditional supervisors. One might speculate that they spend less time engaging with citizens simply because they emphasize their role as supervisor rather than doing patrol work. Although they may take over some incidents and make decisions, they are less likely to engage in direct citizen contact on their own. Furthermore, because traditional supervisors do not emphasize community policing, they may be less likely to engage in these activities themselves, which translates into less casual citizen contact, less contact with victims, fewer meetings with community representatives, etc.

Other observed behavior provides further support for classification. Traditional sergeants and lieutenants are more likely to give advice or instruction to subordinates (6.4 times per shift compared to 4.6 times), but less likely to reward them (0.9 times per shift compared to 2.4 times). Traditional supervisors may be less likely to reward officers because they are less relations-oriented. Rather, they are concerned with controlling situations and task-related behavior. Instructing subordinates is a behavior consistent with their desire for control.

"Innovative" Supervisors

The second factor represents supervisors who score high on the power and community-relations expectation scales. This factor is also characterized by high relations-orientation (have more officers they consider friends), low task-orientation, and more positive views of subordinates. These supervisors are "innovative" because they are generally more supportive of innovative changes in policing. They are defined by their expectations for community policing and problem-solving efforts by subordinates. Furthermore, they are less concerned with enforcing rules and regulations, report writing, or other task-oriented activities that characterize traditional supervisors.

Innovative supervisors are more receptive of new policing initiatives, and as a result, may encourage their officers to embrace these new philosophies as well. As one supervisor explained to an observer:

> S1 [observed supervisor] said that he is not resistant to change because he enjoys seeing the department strive to produce better quality services for the community. S1 said that some policies are certainly more effective than others but without change there is no way to make progress. (POPN)

Supervisors' support for innovative strategies appears to extend to expectations for their subordinates. Innovative supervisors' high scores on the expectation for community policing scale show that they expect subordinates to perform community-related tasks and insist on better relations with the community. One innovative supervisor describes his expectations for subordinates:

> S1 [the supervisor observed] said that he expects his officers to be fair with citizens and act in a morally defendable manner. S1 said that the people in the community are important to him and that officers often forget that they are employed by these people. S1 said that he expects his officers will treat all citizens with dignity and respect and act in a "courteous and respectful manner." S1 was very sensitive to matters of ethnicity, race, and gender. S1 said that every officer brings something different to the job and that a good officer is one who recognizes and accepts differences among groups of people. He said that he expects that officers will interact with citizens from different groups in appropriate though perhaps different ways. (POPN)

These expectations are further evident through innovative supervisors' responses to individual survey questions. For example, 95.5 percent of innovative supervisors reported that they "agree strongly" that "a good patrol officer will try to find out what residents think the neighborhood problems are," compared to only 47.6 percent of traditional supervisors, 68.4 percent of supportive supervisors, and 68.4 percent of active supervisors.

One of the goals of innovative supervisors is to provide subordinates with the support to implement community policing and problem-solving strategies. Scholars have noted that supervisors in an era of community policing should assume a new role, which includes coaching, mentoring, and facilitating officers. Innovative supervisors are more likely to embrace this new role. As one innovative supervisor explained to an observer:

S1 [supervisor observed] said that his role involves becoming a "teacher or educator" to the officers. S1 said that if nothing else, his many years of service have provided him with the opportunity to see a variety of situations. S1 said that this insight is only valuable if shared with other officers who may learn something from his experiences. S1 said that officers frequently come to him for advice or suggestions about how he would have handled a particular situation. He said that what he tries to teach officers is that every situation is different. S1 said that frequently officers will become so routinized in their responses to situations that they lump together as being identical. S1 said the key is to teach officers that although situations are similar, there are always different elements involved and that different ways to handle these situations may be appropriate. (POPN)

Unlike traditional supervisors, innovative supervisors generally do not tell subordinates how to handle situations or take over the situations themselves. Rather, they are more likely to delegate decision-making. Innovative supervisors have accepted a new supervisory role characterized by less control over subordinates' behavior and decision-making. They chose to guide and teach their policing philosophies rather than strictly control officers' behavior.

Some behaviors displayed by innovative supervisors differ significantly from behaviors observed for other supervisors. For example, innovative supervisors spend significantly more time per shift engaging in encounters with citizens (6.5 percent of the shift compared to 3.8 percent). Presumably, those supportive of innovative strategies would spend more time themselves engaging in community-policing types of activities, which include interacting with citizens. Innovative supervisors also spend more time engaging in other types of community policing activities, but these differences are not statistically significant.

Innovative supervisors also spend significantly more time per shift engaging in personal encounters (with citizens or other officers) than other supervisors (14.5 percent compared to 8.7 percent). This behavioral difference is also consistent with the descriptions of innovative supervisors. Those supervisors who emphasize and engage in community-oriented activities often have more unstructured time, and as a result, more time for personal activities.

"Supportive" Supervisors

The third factor is characterized by high scores on the "protect subordinates" relations-orientation scale and low scores on the task-orientation scale. Additionally, this factor is represented by higher levels of inspirational motivation. These supervisors support subordinates by protecting them from "unfair" discipline or punishment and providing inspirational motivation. Furthermore, supportive supervisors are less concerned with enforcing rules and regulations, paperwork, or making sure officers do their work.

Supportive supervisors show their concern for subordinates in a number of ways. They may provide a buffer between officers and management to protect against criticism and discipline. This gives their officers space to perform duties without constant worry of disciplinary action for honest mistakes. One example of this protective buffer is explained by a supervisor:

> S1 said that he also feels his role is to take care of his officers and be their advocate in front of the administration . . . S1 explained that it is almost like a plea bargain in court. S1 said that during administrative proceedings against his officers, he often concedes that they have done something wrong, but also tells the mitigating circumstances and tries to sell the officer's good points. (POPN)

Alternatively, supportive supervisors may simply encourage officers through praise and recognition, or show support by establishing good relations with subordinates, acting as counselors and showing concern for subordinates' personal well-being. Furthermore, supervisors can become "career counselors" in a sense, looking out for the well-being of subordinate officers within the organization.

In some cases, supportive supervisors do not have strong ties or positive relations with management. They often view the police administration as something that patrol officers need to be shielded against.

> S1 [observed supervisor] said that from management's point of view, the sergeant is the person that they will "hang out to dry" as an example and to rid themselves of responsibility. S1 said that his true role is to protect officers from the whims of management and also to make sure that the officers are doing their jobs and back up one another. (POPN)

As a result, some supervisors classified as supportive may actually function more as a "protector" than strictly a "supporter." Of the supportive supervisors, 68.4 percent reported that "protecting their officers from unfair criticism and punishment" is one of their three most important functions, compared to only 9.5 percent of traditional supervisors, 4.5 percent of innovative supervisors, and none of the active supervisors. These findings relate to Reuss-Ianni and Ianni's (1983) description of two predominate cultures in policing, street-cop culture and management-cop culture. Supportive supervisors appear to adhere to street-cop culture by aligning themselves with their subordinates against administrators. They are management cops only in the sense that their rank is higher than entry level.

This protector role adopted by some supportive supervisors has the potential to become problematic. As has been noted in recent history, shielding officers from accountability mechanism within the department often leads to police misconduct (Christopher Commission, 1991; Mollen Commission, 1994). Supervisory protection of officers has also been associated in other research with promoting police solidarity and secrecy, which cultivates an atmosphere where police abuse of power, misconduct, and corruption are tolerated (Crank, 1998; Kappeler, Sluder, and Alpert, 1998; Skolnick and Fyfe, 1993).

Systematic observation of supportive supervisors reveals only one significant difference in behavior. Supportive supervisors praise or reward subordinate officers significantly more often during an average shift than do other types of supervisors (3.0 times per shift compared to 1.7 times). Intuitively, one would expect this behavior from supportive supervisors who are concerned with relations-orientation and inspirational motivation.

"Active" Supervisors

The fourth factor is characterized by high levels of activity and positive views of subordinates. To a lesser extent, this factor is also represented by high scores on decision-making, high levels of perceived power, and low levels of inspirational motivation. The active supervisor can be compared to Van Maanen's "street" sergeant. These supervisors are often in the field, directive in their decision-making, and have a relatively positive view of subordinates.

One characteristic of active supervisors is working alongside their subordinates in the field. Among active supervisors, 94.7 percent report that they often go on their own initiative to incidents that their officers are handling, compared to only 23.8 percent of traditional officers, 54.5 percent of innovative supervisors, and 68.4 percent of supportive supervisors. Another goal of active supervisors is to control subordinate behavior, as shown with their high scores on the decision-making and power scales.

In addition, active supervisors also give importance to being in the field and engaging in police work themselves. The same supervisor explained:

> S1 indicated that he does not follow the popular opinion that "I got my stripes so I don't need to do patrol work anymore." S1 indicated that he still does traffic stops, takes his own calls, and goes on calls when he is not required. When I got in S1's car to begin the ride, he had two traffic tickets that he had written on his way to work. I also saw him stop two people on traffic violations. (POPN)

Active supervisors attempt to achieve a balance between being active in the field and controlling subordinate behavior through constant, direct supervision.

Even though active supervisors believe they have considerable influence over subordinate decisions, low scores on the inspirational motivation scale show they are less likely to help them work on problems. One possible explanation is their reluctance to be too controlling and therefore alienate subordinate officers. As one active supervisor explained to an observer:

S1 [supervisor observed] told me that he is the type of supervisor who likes to "get involved" and "be there" for his officers. S1 stated that he loves being on the streets. I asked S1 if he considered himself to be a "hands-on" manager. S1 thought about it for a moment, and then shook his head [no]. S1 commented that he associated "hands-on" with a supervisor who would get "too involved," not trusting his subordinates to do the job correctly or with a supervisor who was a control freak . . . S1 stated that he would describe himself as a sergeant who did his best to be available to his officers and as someone who was there to back them up. At this time, S1 told me that he would take calls and volunteer as backup, so his officers would know that he was not "above" working alongside them. (POPN)

As evident by this supervisor, there is a fine line between active supervisors and those who are perceived as overcontrolling or micromanagers by their subordinates.

Active supervisors spend more time per shift engaging in general motor patrol (33.0 percent of a shift compared to 25.7 percent) and traffic encounters (3.9 percent compared to 2.1 percent). Active supervisors are also less likely to engage in work-related discussions regarding crime or disorders with subordinate officers (4.7 times per shift compared to 8.0 times). This is probably due to the amount of time supervisors spend in the field and not in direct contact with officers in the station where most of these conversations are likely to occur. Again, the differences in behavior lend support to the classification of these supervisors.

Distribution of Supervisory Styles

The distribution of supervisory styles for this sample of sergeants and lieutenants is reported in table 4. There is a roughly equal distribution of each style, however, when the styles are examined for each department separately, significant differences emerge. Traditional supervisors are significantly overrepresented in SPPD, while active supervisors are underrepresented. Supervisors in IPD are evenly distributed across all styles, however, IPD lieutenants are slightly more likely to be classified as innovative and less likely to be classified as traditional.

Also reported in table 4 are the differences between male and female supervisors. Female supervisors represent a disproportionate number of traditional supervisors (50 percent of female supervisors are classified as traditional supervisors). With this exception, few other differences in classification are apparent. There are no statistically significant differences in classification with regard to the supervisors' race, rank, age, years of experience, or education. The four types of supervisors also do not differ from one another in their reported views of the importance of promotion or moving to a specialized unit, and their amount of training and general knowledge of the principles of community policing. Innovative supervisors, however, reported receiving significantly more training in supervision, management, and leadership.

Discussion

Using six underlying constructs identified from leadership theories and three underlying constructs identified from police ethnographic research, four different styles of police field supervisors are identified. These supervisory styles are evenly distributed among the sample of eighty-one supervisors, however, significant departmental differences exist. Nearly half of SPPD supervisors are traditional, compared to only 16 percent of IPD supervisors. Likewise, only 12 percent of SPPD supervisors are active, compared to 29 percent from IPD. Differences also emerge when the supervisor's sex is considered. Fifty percent of female supervisors are traditional supervisors, compared to only 22 percent of male supervisors. Furthermore, only 8.3 percent of female supervisors are innovative, compared to over 30 percent of males.

One explanation for these differences is the nature of the traditional supervisory style. Traditional supervisors are primarily concerned with controlling subordinate behavior. This is accomplished by demanding compliance with rules and regulations, monitoring work output measures, and using discipline. Van Maanen (1983) speculated that supervisors often focus on rules and regulations because they are concrete and can be controlled in a work environment that is unstable and difficult to regulate. Female supervisors, perhaps seeking to gain legitimacy in their supervisory roles, may be more likely to use rules and regulations as a means to control their officers. They rely on what French and Raven (1960) have termed a "coercive" power base (power taken from subordinates' perceptions of a leader's ability to mediate punishments given to them). In contrast, male supervisors are more likely to rely on "legitimate" power (based on subordinates' perceptions that the leader has a legitimate right to direct their actions) or "referent" power (based on subordinates' identification with leaders).

This explanation also accounts for the higher percentage of traditional supervisors in SPPD. Many of the SPPD supervisors complained that the supervisory structure and goals had changed several times in recent years due to administrative turnover and the implementation of innovative strategies. Many supervisors were unclear what their roles in the organization were, or what management expected of them. In fact, 72 percent of SPPD sergeants indicated during observation sessions that the structure of supervision and other departmental policies limited their ability to assess subordinate behavior and perform supervisory functions. Only 4 percent of IPD supervisors indicated similar feelings. It is likely that supervisors in organizations with changing structures, priorities, and strategies emphasize the one familiar element of their supervisory role—controlling subordinate behavior by enforcing established rules and regulations.

The implications for day-to-day operations and relationships with citizens for departments having a majority of supervisors with a traditional style are unknown. The present research has firmly established dif-

Table 4   Supervisory styles

Variables	Overall (n = 81)	Males (n = 69)	Females (n = 12)	White (n = 69)	Nonwhite (n = 12)	BA degree (n = 41)	IPD Lieutenants (n = 17)	IPD Sergeants (n = 39)	SPPD Sergeants (n = 25)
Traditional style	0.26	0.22	0.50	0.26	0.25	0.24	0.12	0.18	0.48
Innovative style	0.27	0.30	0.08	0.26	0.33	0.27	0.35	0.28	0.20
Supportive style	0.23	0.25	0.17	0.25	0.17	0.20	0.24	0.26	0.20
Active style	0.23	0.23	0.25	0.23	0.25	0.29	0.29	0.28	0.12

Numbers in the cells are means representing the percent of supervisors with that predominant style.

ferences in supervisors' attitudes and behaviors; however, whether or not these differences have an influence over subordinates' behavior on the street is an empirical question that should be explored. That is, to better assess the implications for policy and future research, the influence of these particular supervisory styles on *subordinates'* attitudes and behaviors need to be examined. Although most scholars and practitioners agree that one role of police field supervisors is to control the behavior their officers, the degree of control that supervisors actually have continues to be a matter of debate (Allen, 1980, 1982; Allen and Maxfield, 1983; Brehm and Gates, 1993; Gates and Worden, 1989; Mastrofski et al., 1994; Reiss, 1971; Smith, 1984; Tifft, 1971).

Based on their reported attitudes and observed behavior, one might expect that each of these four types of supervisors would have influences over subordinates' attitudes and behavior that differ significantly in form and substance. For example, one might speculate that officers with traditional or active supervisors would be more likely to engage in aggressive enforcement activities in an effort to produce measurable output (arrests and citations). As a result of this aggressive enforcement, officers might be involved in more conflicts with citizens and perhaps be more likely to use force. Analyses have shown that at least one supervisory style (active) has a significant influence on the increased likelihood of patrol officers' use of force. Analyses also show, however, that patrol officers with active supervisors spend significantly more time engaging in police-initiated and problem-solving activities, and have higher rates of arrest (Engel, 2000; forthcoming).

It will also be important to test whether or not innovative supervisors have an influence over the acceptance and utilization of community policing and problem-solving techniques. One might speculate that officers supervised by an innovative supervisor would spend more time on problem-solving activities. Alternatively, these officers might take their cues directly from innovative supervisors by spending more time conducting personal business or otherwise neglecting their duties. Finally, future research should examine the influence that supportive supervisors have over police misconduct. The protector role that some supportive supervisors embrace might be directly related to problematic subcultural norms including isolation, secrecy, and solidarity.

Although identifying supervisory styles and examining differences in supervisors' behavior have provided interesting findings, caution should be exercised when interpreting them. The data used in this study of police supervision were limited in several ways. The POPN utilized a data collection design created for systematic observation of encounters between patrol officers and citizens. The study of patrol supervision did not fit neatly into this scheme. Although systematic observation and surveys provided a descriptive slice of police work, they often did not provide detailed information about long-term patterns of police behavior or the effectiveness of long-term policies and strategies. The study of patrol supervision might be better captured by some type of modified ethnographic research design where detailed information about the actual patterns (especially the underlying rationales, objectives, etc.) of supervisory practices could be collected. While the POPN research design did have a partial ethnographic component with detailed information collected during each ride, the ability to describe long-term patterns of supervision and the structural, environmental, and political factors affecting these patterns was somewhat limited. Future research on police supervision should address these issues.

Nonetheless, the implications for policy were clear. Police administrators who wish to establish particular policies and procedures within their departments need to recognize the differences in first-line supervisors. None of the four supervisory styles identified in this research should be considered the "ideal" standard for police supervision. Each style was associated with both benefits and problems. The appropriate supervisory style for departments will differ based on their organizational goals. Police administrators should recognize the need for better training of first-line supervisors to achieve these organizational goals.

Appendix A:
Individual Survey Items

Decision-Making (2 items):

1. When you are on the scene of an incident with your officers, how frequently do you tell them how to handle the incident? Never [1], rarely [2], sometimes [3], or often [4]

2. When you are on the scene, how frequently do you take it over and handle the incident yourself? Never [1], rarely [2], sometimes [3], or often [4]

Power Distribution (11 items):

How much influence do you usually have over each decision: Hardly any or none [1], some [2], a lot [3].

1. Which officers are assigned to your unit.

2. The specific CPA or job assignments your officers receive.

3. Whether one of your officers is permitted to go out of service to do problem solving or other special tasks.

4. Whether your officers are disciplined for minor rule infractions.

5. Whether your officers receive assignments to specialist units when they ask for them.

6. Whether one of your officers is authorized to work overtime.

7. Whether one of your officers is approved for off-duty work.

8. Your officers' prospects for promotion to higher rank.

9. Department policies about patrol operations.

Never [1], seldom [2], sometimes [3], usually [4], always [5]

10. When you have asked for resources needed to do a job, how often have you been given what you requested?

11. When you have made decisions about how to do patrol operations, how often have your decisions been supported by higher-ups?

Relations-Orientation 1 (one item):

1. How many officers in your unit would you consider to be your friends? None [1], a few [2], about half [3], all or most [4].

Relations-Orientation 2 (one item):

Out of a list of ten items, indicate the three that you think are the most important for you to perform as a first-line supervisor [5], and three that are the least important [1].

1. Protecting subordinates from unfair criticism or punishment.

Task-Orientation (4 items):

Out of a list of ten items, indicate the three that you think are the most important for you to perform as a first-line supervisor [5], and three that are the least important [1].

1. Making sure that reports are properly completed.

2. Enforcing department rules and regulations.

Out of a list of seven goals indicate the two you believe are the most important for patrol officers with 911 assignments [5], and two that you think are the least important [1].

3. Handling calls for service to their assigned area.

4. Making arrests and issuing citations.

Level of Activity/Relative Distance of Supervision (2 items):
Never [1], rarely [2], sometimes [3], always [4]:

1. How frequently do your officers ask you to come to the incidents that they are handling?

2. Other than when it is required by department policy, how frequently do you go on your own initiative to incidents that your officers are handling?

Inspirational Motivation (1 item):
Out of a list of ten items, indicate the three that you think are the most important for you to perform as a first-line supervisor [5], and three that are the least important [1].

1. Helping officers to work on problems in their assigned areas.

Expectations for Community Policing (9 items):
Indicate your level of agreement with the following: Disagree strongly [1], disagree somewhat [2], agree somewhat [3], agree strongly [4]

1. Police officers have reason to be distrustful of most citizens [values reversed].

2. Assisting citizens is just as important as enforcing the law.

3. A good patrol officer will try to find out what residents think the neighborhood problems are.

How often should patrol officers with 911 assignments be expected to do something about each of the following situations: Never [1], sometimes [2], much of the time [3], always [4]

4. Public nuisances (loud parties, barking dogs)

5. Neighbor disputes

6. Family disputes

7. Litter and trash

8. Parents who don't control their kids

9. Nuisance businesses that cause lots of problems for neighbors

Expectations for Aggressive Enforcement (3 items):
    Indicate your level of agreement with the following: Disagree strongly [1], disagree somewhat [2], agree somewhat [3], agree strongly [4]

1. Enforcing the law is by far the patrol officer's most important responsibility.

2. A good patrol officer is one who patrols aggressively by stopping cars, checking out people, running license checks, and so forth.

Out of a list of seven goals indicate the two you believe are the most important for patrol officers with 911 assignments [5], and two that you think are the least important [1].

3. Making arrests and issuing citations.

Endnotes

[1] Supervision was previously organized as a "squad system," where one sergeant was directly responsible for a fixed group of officers who worked the same schedule. After a change in administrative personnel, SPPD implemented a supervisory structure that focused on geographic deployment. Each sergeant in the department was assigned to a particular geographic area (CPA) that they were directly responsible for. As a result, sergeants were responsible for supervising patrol officers and community policing officers who were assigned to their areas across every shift. After about a year, this structure of supervision was reorganized because of the unrealistic demands it placed on sergeants.

[2] Supervisors were excluded from the analyses if they were not both interviewed and observed (sixteen sergeants and lieutenants from IPD and three sergeants from SPPD). Also, eight patrol officers acting as temporal sergeants in SPPD were excluded as were all the lieutenants from this department. Lieutenants from SPPD did not engage in direct field observation of subordinate officers.

[3] Specific items with serious questions regarding their reliability or validity were eliminated from the composite scale measures. Where appropriate, a single item was used to represent an attitudinal dimension rather than an additive scale.

[4] The two relations-orientation items did not strongly correlate (Pearson's r = .11) and reliability analysis suggested that they do not belong in an additive scale (coefficient = .19). At face value, the items tap different issues. The number of officers that supervisors consider their friends does not appear to influence their reported importance of protecting officers from unfair criticism or punishment. As a result, these two items are entered separately in analyses, with both representing different aspects of the relations-orientation construct.

[5] This factor analysis is performed using the maximum likelihood extraction technique because its overall objective is "to find the factor solution which would best fit the observed correlations" (Kim and Mueller, 1978:23). An oblique rotation method (direct oblimin) is selected because "it does not arbitrarily impose the restriction that factors be uncorrelated" (Kim and Mueller, 1978:37). For a more detailed information on extraction and rotation methods, see Kim and Mueller (1978).

[6] For this and all subsequent quotes from supervisors, references to gender were reported in masculine form to further protect the identities of supervisors.

References

Aldag, R. J., & Brief, A. P. (1978). Supervisory style and police role stress. *Journal of Police Science and Administration, 6,* 362–367.

Allen, D. (1980). *Street-level police supervision: The effect of supervision on police officer activities, agency outputs, and neighborhood outcomes.* Ph.D. dissertation, Indiana University. Ann Arbor: University of Michigan Press.

Allen, D. (1982). Police supervision on the street: An analysis of supervisor/ officer interaction during the shift. *Journal of Criminal Justice, 10,* 91–109.

Allen, D., & Maxfield, M. (1983). Judging police performance: Views and behavior of patrol officers. In R. Bennett (Ed.), *Police at work: Policy issues and analysis* (pp. 65–86). Beverly Hills, CA: Sage Publications.

Bass, B. M. (1985). *Leadership and performance beyond expectations.* New York: Free Press.

Bass, B. M. (1990). *Bass and Stogdill's handbook of leadership: Theory, research and managerial applications* (3rd ed.). New York: Free Press.

Bass, B. M., & Avolio, B. J. (1994). *Improving organizational effectiveness through transformational leadership.* Thousand Oaks, CA: Sage Publications.

Blake, R. R., & Mouton, J. S. (1978). *The new managerial grid.* Houston, TX: Gulf.

Brehm, J., & Gates, S. (1993). Donut shops and speed traps: Evaluating models of supervision on police behavior. *American Journal of Occupational and Organizational Psychology, 67,* 69–78.

Brief, A. P., Aldag, R. J., & Wallden, R. A. (1976). Correlates of supervisory style among policemen. *Criminal Justice and Behavior, 3,* 263–271.

Brown, M. K. (1988). *Working the street: Police discretion and the dilemmas of reform.* New York: Russell Sage Foundation.

Christopher Commission. (1991). *Report of the independent commission on the Los Angeles Police Department.* Los Angeles, CA: The Commission.

Cohen, B. (1980). Leadership styles of commanders in the New York City police department. *Journal of Police Science and Administration, 8,* 125–138.

Crank, J. P. (1998). *Understanding police culture.* Cincinnati, OH: Anderson Publishing.

Engel, R. S. (2000a). Patrol officer supervision in the community policing era. *Journal of Criminal Justice* (forthcoming).

Engel, R. S. (2000b). The effects of supervisory styles on patrol officer behavior. *Police Quarterly, 3*(3), 262–293.

French, J., & Raven, B. (1960). The bases of social power. In D. Cartwright & A. F. Zander (Eds.), *Group dynamics* (2nd ed., pp. 607–623). Evanston, IL: Row, Peterson, and Company.

Gates, S., & Worden, R. (1989). *Principle-agent models of hierarchical control in public bureaucracies: Work, shirking, and supervision in police agencies.* 1989 Annual Meeting of the American Political Science Association, at the Atlanta Hilton and Towers, August 31–September 3.

Graham, C. B., Jr., & Hays, S. W. (1993). *Managing the public organization* (2nd ed.). Washington, DC: Congressional Quarterly Press.

Halpin, A. W, & Winer, B. J. (1957). A factorial study of the leader behavior descriptions. In R. M. Stogdill & A. E. Coons (Eds.), *Leader behavior: Its description and measurement* – 51). Columbus: Ohio State University, Bureau of Business Research.

Hemphill, J. K., & Coons, A. E. (1957). Development of the leader behavior description questionnaire. In R. M. Stogdill & A. E. Coons (Eds.), *Leader behavior: Its description and measurement* – 38). Columbus: Ohio State University, Bureau of Business Research.

Hersey, P., & Blanchard, K. H. (1988). *Management of organizational behavior* (5th ed.). Englewood Cliffs, NJ: Prentice-Hall.

Jermier, J. M., & Berkes, L. J. (1979). Leader behavior in a police command bureaucracy: A closer look at the quasimilitary model. *Administrative Science Quarterly, 24*, 1–23.

Kappeler, V. E., Sluder, R. D., & Alpert, G. P. (1998). *Forces of deviance: Understanding the dark side of policing* (2nd ed.). Prospect Heights, IL: Waveland Press.

Kim, J., & Mueller, C. W. (1978). *Factor analysis statistical methods and practical issues.* Newbury Park, CA: Sage Publications.

Kuykendall, J. L. (1977). Police leadership: An analysis of executive styles. *Criminal Justice Review, 2*, 89–100.

Kuykendall, J. L. (1985). Police managerial styles: A grid analysis. *American Journal of Police, 4*, 38–70.

Kuykendall, J. L., & Roberg, R. R. (1988). Police managers' perceptions of employee types: A conceptual model. *Journal of Criminal Justice, 16*, 131–137.

Kuykendall, J. L., & Unsinger, P. (1982). The leadership styles of police managers. *Journal of Criminal Justice, 4*, 311–321.

Lewin, K., & Lippitt, R. (1938). An experimental approach to the study of autocracy and democracy: A preliminary note. *Sociometry, 1*, 292–300.

Lewin, K., Lippitt, R., & White, R. K. (1939). Patterns of aggressive behavior in experimentally created social climates. *Journal of Social Psychology, 10*, 271–301.

Manning, P. K. (1977). *Police work.* Cambridge: MIT Press.

Mastrofski, S. D., Snipes, J. B., Parks, R. B., & Maxwell, C. D. (2000). The helping hand of the law: Police control of citizens on request. *Criminology, 38*(2), 307–342.

Mastrofski, S. M., Ritti, R. R., & Snipes, J. B. (1994). Expectancy theory and police productivity in DUI enforcement. *Law and Society Review, 28*, 113–148.

McGregor, D. M. (1957). The human side of enterprise. In J. M. Shafritz & A. C. Hyde (Eds.), *Classics of public administration* (3rd ed., pp. 217–223). Belmont, CA: Wadsworth Publishing.

McGregor, D. M. (1960). *The human side of enterprise.* New York: McGraw-Hill.

Mollen Commission to Investigate Allegations of Police Corruption. (1994). *Commission report.* New York: The Mollen Commission.

Muir, W. K., Jr. (1977). *Police: Street corner politicians.* Chicago: University of Chicago Press.

Parks, R. B., Mastrofski Muir, S. D., DeJong, C., Gray, M. K. (1999). How officers spend their time with the community. *Justice Quarterly, 16*, 483–518.

Pursley, R. D. (1974). Leadership and community identification attitudes among two categories of police chiefs: An exploratory inquiry. *Journal of Police Science and Administration, 2*, 414–422.

Reiss, A. J., Jr. (1971). *The police and the public.* New Haven, CT: Yale.

Reuss-Ianni, E., & Ianni, F. (1983). Street cops and management cops: The two cultures of policing. In M. Punch (Ed.), *Control in the police organization* (pp. 251–274). Cambridge: MIT Press.

Rubinstein, J. (1973). *City police.* New York: Ballantine.

Shepard, R. L. (1999). *Street level supervision: Styles of patrol supervisors and their effects on patrol officer behavior.* Ph.D. dissertation, University at Albany. Ann Arbor, MI: University Microfilms International.

Skolnick, J. H., & Fyfe, J. J. (1993). *Above the law: Police and the excessive use of force.* New York: Free Press.

Smith, D. (1984). The organizational context of legal control. *Criminology, 22,* 19–38.

Southerland, M. D., & Reuss-Ianni, E. (1992). Leadership and management. In G. W. Cordner & D. C. Hale (Eds.), *What works in policing? Operations and administration examined* (pp. 157–177). Highland Heights, KY: Academy of Criminal Justice Sciences and Anderson Publishing.

Swanson, C. R., & Territo, L. (1982). Police leadership and interpersonal communication styles. In J. Greene (Ed.), *Managing police work* (pp. 123–139). Beverly Hills, CA: Sage Publications.

Tannenbaum, R., & Schmidt, W. H. (1958). How to choose a leadership pattern. *Harvard Business Review, 36,* 95–101.

Tifft, L. (1971). *Comparative police supervision systems: An organizational analysis.* Ph.D. dissertation, University of Illinois at Urbana-Champaign. Ann Arbor, MI: University Microfilms International.

Trojanowicz, R. C. (1980). *The environment of the first-line police supervisor.* Englewood Cliffs, NJ: Prentice-Hall.

Van Maanen, J. (1983). The boss: First-line supervision in an American police agency. In M. Punch (Ed.), *Control in the police organization* (pp. 275–317). Cambridge: MIT Press.

Van Maanen, J. (1984). Making rank: Becoming an American police sergeant. *Urban Life, 13,* 155–176.

Wilson, J. Q. (1968). *Varieties of police behavior.* Cambridge, MA: Harvard University Press.

Yukl, G. A. (1989). *Leadership in organizations* (2nd ed.). Englewood Cliffs, NJ: Prentice-Hall.

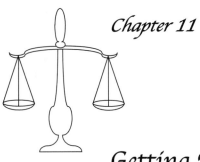

Chapter 11

Getting Rid of the Prima Donnas
The Bureaucratization of a Probation Department

John Rosecrance

The pervasive influence of bureaucracy in Western society is a central theme of twentieth-century social science. In the field of criminal justice, theorists have identified bureaucracy as the "single most important variable in determining the actual day-to-day functioning of the legal system" (Chambliss and Seidman, 1971:468). Criminological researchers have described the effects of bureaucratization upon probation recommendations (Hagan, 1977), juvenile court procedures (Tepperman, 1973), sentencing decisions (Reiss, 1974), police tactics (Littrell, 1979), plea bargaining (Rosett and Cressey, 1976), judicial processing (Blumberg, 1979), and parolee recidivism (McCleary, 1978). Bureaucratization of American criminal justice agencies typically involves shifting from a traditional authority system to a rational-legal one (Udy, 1959). Weber, a seminal source of modern bureaucratic concepts, observed that the bases of order and authority in traditional organizations are precedent and usage, while in rational-legal systems they are derived from formal procedure (Pugh, Hickson and Hinings, 1985:16–17). Although bureaucratization "is a somewhat nebulous concept" (Meyer, 1979:24), in this article it is the pro-

John Rosecrance, *Criminal Justice and Behavior*, Vol. 14 No. 2, pp. 138–155, copyright © 1987 by Sage Publications. Reprinted by permission of Sage Publications.

cess whereby authority based upon formal rules and discipline is imposed upon an informal organization where authority had depended upon technical expertise (Blau, 1974:33).

While the increasingly bureaucratic nature of criminal justice components has been well documented, employee reactions to shifts in authority structure have not been prominently identified. The expansion of bureaucracy invariably means the displacement of previously entrenched power bases, and is "always seen as a loss of prestige or actual power by both small and large groups of individuals" (Jacoby, 1973:14). The reactions and accommodations of criminal justice personnel to bureaucratic organization are an important but often overlooked phenomenon. The purpose of the present study is to describe and analyze the accommodations made by probation officers to the bureaucratization of their department. An understanding of this accommodation process, while of historical interest, can also provide valuable insight into organizational dynamics prevailing in contemporary probation practices. The types of employees who are able to adapt successfully to bureaucratic imperatives continue to shape the organizational milieu of today's probation departments. This article will also provide a glimpse of the real-world work experiences of white-collar correctional employees.

In the space of five years, the organizational dynamics prevailing in a California probation agency employing approximately 60 line officers and located in Pacific County (a pseudonym) were significantly altered by a change in administration. A new probation chief imposed a system of formal rules and central authority upon a department that had been run in an ad hoc, fragmented manner. In the process, probation officer discretion and individual decision making were restricted. Bureaucratic administrators were able to establish legal authority over work performance through the development and implementation of a department manual. Individualized work styles and expertise that officers had developed over the years were subordinated to formal procedures mandated by bureaucratic guidelines. Probation workers were discouraged from advocating controversial positions by an administration that emphasized smooth work flow and trouble-free relationships with other criminal justice agencies. Changes in the probation department authority structure occurred despite resistance from some of the existing probation staff. However, most of the probation officers satisfactorily adjusted to the bureaucratization of their department and relations between them and the administration were generally harmonious. The patterns of individual accommodation manifested by probation officers were similar to a tripartite typology identified by Presthus (1962). A delineation of these patterns will demonstrate how probation officers responded to a bureaucratic environment, and why certain types are well suited to such a setting.

The research methodology for this project involved a historical accounting based upon qualitative data drawn from probation sources and personal field notes. An ethnographic perspective was particularly suited to this type of analysis (Scott, 1965). The research data indicate that while bureaucratization can improve efficiency and lead to improved worker-organization relations, there can be problematic consequences. Those probation officers most adaptable to bureaucratic dictates are not likely to be sources of independent reporting or agents of change. This finding has import for those seeking to understand the reluctance of many probation departments to implement meaningful change in their operational practices (Glaser, 1985; Walker, 1985).

Methods

Much of the data for this research project was collected using a participant's perspective. For almost 15 years I was employed by Pacific County as a probation officer. I had worked there for seven years when the long-time probation chief, who had run the department on an informal basis, was replaced by an administrator who strongly advocated a formal hierarchical structure. For the next several years I witnessed the adjustments of probation officers to increasing bureaucratization. My particular adaptive pattern to bureaucratization, because of my interests outside of the work environment, was a passive noncontentious one. In the Presthus typology I would have been considered an "indifferent." By the time I left Pacific County the bureaucratic machinery was firmly in place and functioning smoothly. During this period of employment I kept field notes of my activities with the probation department. Subsequently these notes proved to be valuable in developing an accurate portrayal of events during the period of emerging bureaucratization.

When I began a historical accounting of this period I conducted interviews[1] with the current and former probation personnel (administrators, supervisors, and line officers) who were participants in the changing organizational structure. I had left the probation department under amicable conditions (to attend graduate school) and maintained generally good relations with both probation officials and line staff. During these interviews I queried probation sources on their views of and reactions to the formalized procedures instituted by the new administrators. I interviewed other criminal justice people such as judges, district attorneys, and public defenders regarding their recollections and observations of the events that occurred during the changing organizational structure of the probation department. Because of our common experiences, the respondents were generally candid and cooperative, and I was able to collect qualitative data unavailable to other researchers.

The method I used to analyze the data was similar to the grounded theory techniques of Glaser and Strauss (1967). I sought to develop analyses that were generated from the data. In the initial stages of the investigation I adopted a flexible and unstructured approach. As the data accumulated generalizations and propositions emerged; these were modified, compared, and, in turn, formed the groundwork for future data collection.[2]

Findings

An analysis of accumulated data revealed that accommodations by probation officers to bureaucratization tended to fall into one of three general patterns. These accommodations were similar to the ideal types posited by Presthus (1962): (1) upward mobile, (2) indifferent, and (3) ambivalent. A discussion of the three types will serve to clarify this finding. Since the Presthus typology is an empirical generalization with a sometimes accentuated set of criteria, the accommodation patterns of individual probation officers will vary from the type. However, each pure type can serve as a base line for gauging potential and actual deviations. In order to understand the responses of the probation officers it is necessary first to describe some procedures instituted by the bureaucratic administration. Several significant changes were brought about with the implementation of probation guidelines. The new administrators introduced a manual that eventually served to legitimate their actions in attempting to control dissension and divergence among the probation staff. From a Weberian standpoint the existence of written rules is the core of bureaucratic administration (Littrell, 1979:2). In this case the manual provided both instrumental and symbolic acceptance of rational-legal authority.

When the chief probation officer who had held the position for 20 years resigned under pressure, a judicial hiring panel charged his successor with the task of modernizing a probation department that was considered poorly managed, wasteful, inefficient, and "behind the times." The new chief probation officer had worked in a much larger and presumably more efficient probation department. He was given carte blanche (including the right to "kick ass") in his effort to improve Pacific County's probation department. Some probation workers were pleased with the change in leadership, as they had considered the former chief to have been capricious, unprofessional, and guilty of cronyism. The following quotes were taken from interviews with such probation officers:

> The old boy just wasn't consistent. He ran the place according to how he felt on that particular day.

> The chief got the job before civil service and he had no concept of professionalism.

> Chief _____ promoted only his buddies. He never paid attention to who was doing a good job; only to who was loyal to him.

The new chief probation officer took over an agency comprised of individual units such as adult supervision, adult investigation, juvenile intake, and juvenile supervision that had been functioning independently of departmental authority. Over the years probation officers had developed individual styles for managing their assignments. Those employees who had gained reputations for expertise were given wide discretion in handling probation cases and were subject to only minimal departmental supervision. Some officers had developed such credibility that their decisions were rarely questioned by supervisory staff. Characteristically, probation officers felt a greater responsibility to their individual units than to the department as a whole.

The new chief's first major undertaking was the centralization of authority, which meant breaking up the power bases that had developed under the traditional ad hoc system of his predecessor. The wide discretion and latitude that had been afforded individual officers were replaced with department regulations. Probation officers, regardless of their expertise, were required to adhere to the policies of the new probation administration. As the administration began to assert authority, it developed a rational justification for this action. Because there was no formal written policy governing employee job performance, the new chief probation officer developed a manual specifically delineating a department policy on this subject. Formal guidelines helped to temper criticism that the administration (consisting of a chief probation office, his appointed assistant chief, and four division heads left over from the previous administration) might be acting arbitrarily and set the stage for the curbing of individual discretion and decision making. During a staff meeting the assistant chief succinctly described the task facing the administration: "For the good of the department we've got to get rid of the prima donnas around here."

The new administration initiated two wide-ranging tactics as a first attempt to gain authority over the staff: transfers and mandatory staffing. Probation officers were transferred[3] "in the best interests of the department" and all pending court cases (that previously had been the responsibility of the individual officer) were to be staffed with supervisors. Buttressed by new departmental policies, wholesale transfers and innumerable case conferences commenced.

Probation officers who had worked in the same unit for several years were transferred to new and often unfamiliar assignments. Those who remained at their same job locations were patently aware that they too could be transferred. The staffing of every court case (holding a case conference) with supervisors enabled departmental authority to be reinforced on a continuing basis. Soon after mandatory staffing became a reality the administration indicated that in the future all court recommendations — the most visible aspect of probation work — were to be departmental rather than individual recommendations. In cases of disagreement between supervisor and officer it would be the supervisor's recommendation that was filed with the court. Individual officers were expected to subordinate their personal views in order to support departmental recommendations. The probation administration, through its supervisors, sanctioned adherence to prevailing sentencing guidelines and actively discouraged controversial court recommendations. Probation officers were expected to provide ballpark recommendations (Rosecrance, 1985) that, as one officer stated, "would not ruffle the feathers of judges or district attorneys." Officers who were reluctant to go along with the new administration's policies reported that they were transferred to unfavorable assignments or were not promoted.

When the new policies first took effect employees recalled that they had "chaffed" under regulations they believed severely limited their discretion. While there was a period of unrest, the department's authority came to be accepted as legal and binding through a combination of bureaucratic winnowing, attrition, and acquiescence. Eventually, employee relations with the administration improved as staff transfers slowed considerably, disputes over court recommendations gradually diminished, and department guidelines were rarely questioned. In most cases probation officers had accepted department policies to such a degree that the regulations now appeared logical and appropriate. The administration's noncontroversial stance also came to be accepted by the officers and discussions of divergent perspectives were rare. The completed department manual established formal regulations for the orderly operation of a probation department. After initial employee resistance to the administration ameliorated, there was little active dissension in the department. It was no longer necessary for the administration to assert its authority overtly on a staff that had embraced bureaucratic procedures. In effect, the bureaucratic system had become self-regulating. In order to understand how this occurred, it is necessary to describe the accommodation patterns of probation officers to a changing organizational structure.

Patterns of Accommodation [4]

Upwardly Mobile

According to Presthus (1978:182–183) the sine qua non of those who adopt an upwardly mobile pattern of accommodation to bureaucratization is their pragmatic willingness to accept organizational dictates. Upwardly mobile individuals are determined to make the most of opportunities for advancement in their organization (Terkel, 1975). This type of officer "does not need perfect causes" (Presthus, 1978:183) to support wholeheartedly organizational goals. Typically they find a bureaucratic setting congenial and the accommodation process is nonproblematic.

While the probation department was undergoing bureaucratization, some officers responded to the new procedures in a manner characteristic of Presthus's upwardly mobile type. This group of officers readily accepted central authority and were quick to adapt their work routines to the new guidelines. Their court reports generally adhered to the administration goal of noncontroversy and their recommendations were in line with informal judicial and prosecutorial expectations. Upwardly mobile types perceived their job as an extremely important part of their lives. They were concerned with maintaining stable employment and did not see themselves as agents of change. They generally had not been openly critical of the former chief probation officer. However, they were compatible with a bureaucratic structure and soon became strong supporters of the new administration. The following statement is representative of an upwardly mobile pattern of accommodation:

> I'm basically a team player. When the new chief took over I was a little nervous about the change. But when I could see the new administration was up-front about what it expected, I became a real fan. The new rules didn't bother me, some of them were long overdue. A few of the p.o.s had been getting out of hand. They were doing their own thing to such an extent that you hardly knew they worked for the probation department.

Officers who opted for this pattern of accommodation characteristically viewed the changing organizational structure as an opportunity to advance their careers. They were quick to scrutinize the new job requirements in order to render themselves promotable. The remarks of a probation supervisor are typical of this perspective:

> I sure like the changeover. Under _____ I never knew exactly what was expected of a p.o. But when the new job specifications and duties were clearly spelled out we all knew exactly what they wanted from us — and I liked that. I knew what it took to qualify for the supervisor's job, and I got the promotion. In the old regime I'd still be a p.o. wondering how to get ahead.

Since upwardly mobile probation officers frequently were rewarded with promotion, the bureaucratic nature of the probation department was maintained and strengthened.

Indifferent

The leitmotif of those who have adopted an indifferent accommodation pattern is "coming to terms with their work environment by withdrawal and by a reduction of their interests toward off-the-job satisfaction" (Presthus, 1978:186). When faced with bureaucratization, many probation officers in Pacific County decided the most appropriate course of action was acquiescence and compliance. While not wholeheartedly supporting the new organizational structure (as did the upward mobiles), they felt it was easier, as one officer put it, "to go along rather than swim against the current." In several instances the officers had manifested a similar pattern of disinterested compliance in dealings with the former administration. Their adjustments to a new organizational structure were a continuation of an established job outlook.

Indifferents tended to perceive their jobs as a necessary, but not the most fulfilling, aspect of their lives. They had developed interests or hobbies outside their work environment, and while demonstrating a superficial commitment to department regulations, they were not emotionally caught up in a changing department structure. The observation of an officer who chose an indifferent accommodation is representative:

> I saw a lot of dissension and scrambling resulting from the "new probation department." But to tell the truth it never really affected me. I just came in to work and did what they wanted me to do. I never took it all that seriously. You know I'm a real scuba nut—that's what turns me on. This job is not all that important. It pays the bills but it's not that big a deal for me.

Some in this category either were not concerned with occupational mobility or had become disenchanted with their promotion prospects and they were content to "draw a salary without working up too much sweat." Klockars (1972:551), in his typology of probation officers, labeled these types as "time servers." A probation officer who had been passed over for promotion (after the new administration had taken over) subsequently opted for an indifferent accommodation and indicated:

> I'll give them [the department] eight hours per day, but no more. I don't get worked up over the job anymore. I'll follow their rules; but I'm not going out of my way any more. I don't need the hassle. I already paid my dues and I'm sure not going to bust my ass.

For various reasons indifferents chose not to become actively involved in the bureaucratic process and adapted to the new regulations with resignation and while not embracing the new organizational dictates, neither did they oppose them. The opposition was to come from another group.

Ambivalent

One group of probation officers found it extremely difficult to adjust to increasing bureaucratization. Their patterns of accommodation were similar to the ambivalent type described by Presthus (1978:228):

> Creative and anxious, their values conflict with bureaucratic claims for loyalty and adaptability. While the upward mobile finds the organization congenial and the indifferent refuses to become engaged, ambivalents are a small residual category who can neither reject its promises of success and power nor play the roles required to compete for them. In the bureaucratic situation the ambivalent is a marginal person with limited career chances.

Under the informal policies of the former chief some probation officers had worked out accommodations whereby adequate job performance would allow them to have a good measure of independence. Officers with acknowledged expertise had the opportunity to individualize their reports and case recommendations without fear of department censure. They had been permitted relative freedom in handling their probation cases and in making recommendations to the court. It was generally understood "that as long as you got the job done, the chief didn't ask questions." A frequent observation among officers was "the chief didn't know much about probation but at least he left us alone."

The new regulations limiting discretion caused a small group of probation workers to question seriously administration dictates. These officers found the mandatory staffing of court cases particularly objectionable. They resented attempts by supervisors to influence the final court recommendation and balked at the administration's desire for noncontroversial reporting. These officers prided themselves on being independent and "telling it like it is." One ambivalent stated: "Those jerks in administration who didn't know shit about doing a probation report were trying to tell me how to do my work!" In the process of conducting investigations the officers often revealed information that, while germane to the case, raised questions about the appropriateness of plea bargaining agreements. Their recommendations, sometimes at odds with current sentencing guidelines, caused judicial questioning, and on occasion drew complaints from either prosecution or defense. Officers who strove to maintain independent reporting frequently caused problems for an administration bent on facilitating a routine, noncontroversial work flow. An administrator stated: "The prima donnas were a big pain in the ass. They pissed off the judges and caused everyone a lot of trouble. They only could see things their own way."

At first the dissatisfied officers took their complaints about the new procedures directly to the administration. Some examples of these confrontations with the administration included filing a union grievance over transfers, airing objections to mandatory case conferences at staff meetings, complaining to supervisors and unit heads about loss of discretion, and sending a delegation of officers to the chief probation officer to complain that the new policies were extremely unpopular. One of the rebellious officers summed up these efforts:

> By God, we tried to work within the department. We wanted to keep
> our bitches in-house. We did everything to convince them to change
> some of the new policies. But the administration turned a deaf ear. It
> was hopeless. They just ignored us. We had to take more direct action.

As their disagreement with the new administration worsened, the ambivalents openly rebelled against the new regulations by refusing to sign court recommendations with which they disagreed and by being contentious in dealing with supervisors during the staffing of cases. On occasion these officers complained to sources outside the probation department such as judges, public defenders, district attorneys, or members of the board of supervisors about the restrictive policies and loss of an objective perspective. Administration responded to these actions by quietly transferring the dissident officers to less visible assignments, such as juvenile hall counselors or supervisors of large write-in case loads. These jobs usually required little or no report writing, and the officers no longer had a viable work-related forum for expressing viewpoints differing from those sanctioned by the administration. The out-of-favor officers reported that they were watched carefully by their supervisors and indicated they frequently had been cited for minor violations of department regulations. None of the officers' names appeared on promotion lists. When questioned about these situations a supervisor replied:

> Of course they weren't promoted, and yes we did watch them carefully. What did they expect? Remember they were trying to wreck the department. What should we have done—rewarded them for being real assholes? No way! They got what they had coming to them. You can't have it both ways.

The rebellious officers exhibited ambivalence toward their employment by demonstrating both a strong liking for probation work and an impatient frustration with a system that (from their standpoint) made it difficult for them to perform their job responsibilities adequately. Other officers did not join or support the dissident officers. Gradually the protest lost its impact and administration policies were rarely challenged by probation staff. Eventually most of the group retired or left for other jobs while one member, frustrated by her inability to alter administration mandates, opted for noninvolvement and accommodated to bureaucracy through indifference. She recalled: "I got tired of beating my head against the wall. The administration wasn't going to change—regardless of our protests. So I said fuck it; I got a family to support. I stopped fighting and just did my job." Approximately one year after the abortive protest a probation administrator commented, "We finally got rid of the prima donnas in this department and everything's running smoothly."

Summary and Conclusions

In this article I have described the bureaucratization of a probation department. After initial employee protest was overcome the organization's rational-legal authority was established and bureaucratization proceeded smoothly until it became virtually self-regulating. While the study was concerned with a single, medium-sized probation department, the findings provide additional insight into the effects of organizational dynamics upon the behavior of probation personnel. My research has identified the fact that accommodations of probation officers to rational-legal authority help to maintain a bureaucratic structure. This factor has not been researched adequately and needs further study and clarification. However, preliminary indications from the present study reveal that prevailing accommodation patterns influence significantly the operations of probation departments.

I have demonstrated how the indifferent and upwardly mobile types of probation officers are able to survive and flourish in a bureaucratic setting. They adapt comparatively easily to organizational dictates by integrating their personal opinions with departmental goals. The ambivalents face a more problematic situation. They find it difficult to make necessary adaptations to organizational imperatives and inevitably are forced to leave probation work or to alter drastically their accommodation patterns. However, by actively discouraging the presence of ambivalents the probation bureaucracy has removed sources of balance, independence, and change.

In the absence of the balance provided by ambivalent officers who espouse varied and divergent perspectives, probation departments can be co-opted by more powerful organizations such as the court or district attorney. Probation officials and officers view judges as powerful figures who exert considerable influence upon their careers, and they have learned to "appreciate the importance of the breezes which blow from the judges' chambers" (Goldsborough and Burbank, 1968:109). Judges typically demand court reports that facilitate a smooth work flow, expect probation officers to sanction all pre-plea agreements, and favor recommendations that reflect their sentencing philosophies. Without officers who are willing to maintain differing viewpoints, many probation departments acquiesce to judicial demands and their court reports are structured accordingly (Blumberg, 1979).

Prosecuting attorneys can be an influential force in the decision making of probation officers (McHugh, 1973). Members of the district attorney's office frequently remain personally involved with criminal cases through sentencing and have few reservations about complaining to the probation administration concerning the way a particular case is being handled. Much of the information needed for court reports—for example, police reports, criminal records, and legal proceedings—is obtained from the district attorney's office, and provides an opportunity for prosecutors to influence probation officer investigations. While ambivalent officers often reject such influence, other types are more likely to be swayed. Frequently, overt and subtle attempts by prosecuting attorneys to influence probation officers result in court recommendations generally favorable to the prosecution (Hagan, Hewitt, and Alwin, 1979).

Ambivalents tend to put independence ahead of department loyalty. While this approach can be disruptive, it does have its place in probation work. In some situations the probation department is well served by officers who are willing to take a controversial stand. An administrator admitted to me that although the prima donnas were "no fun to be

around," they did provide sources of strength in the probation department. She indicated that many of the present probation officers "caved in
too easily" and could not be "counted on" to maintain firm convictions
about their cases. However, the ambivalent's desire for independence is a
crucial factor in the group's inability to survive in a bureaucratic milieu.
The remaining probation officer types (upwardly mobile and indifferent)
working with a departmental orientation, in the main, relinquish their
independence to expedite a routinized work flow.

Ambivalents provide an important ingredient in an organizational
structure by serving as agents of change. Those who have chosen
upwardly mobile and indifferent types of accommodation tend to be so
well integrated into the bureaucratic system that they cannot see the
need for flexibility. On the other hand, ambivalents have not conformed
fully to bureaucratic guidelines and are inclined to express criticism and
to seek changes in departmental policies. The very fact that some questioning occurs can be a positive organizational dynamic (Scott, 1981).
The need for flexible probation policies and procedures seems especially
salient in light of the generally accepted caveat that probation services
have failed to satisfy either public or organizational expectations (Conrad, 1985; Glaser, 1985; Petersilia, Turner, Kahan, and Peterson, 1985).

A retired supervisor described the dilemma facing many probation
departments: "Every department needs a few prima donnas—but not too
many. The trick is to find the right mix."

Endnotes

[1] My interview schedule included the following contacts:
  (A) Line officers: 27
      Current (still working at the department):   18
      Former (no longer working at the department):   9
  (B) Supervisors: 6
      Current: 3
      Former: 3
  (C) Administrators: 5
      Current: 3
      Former: 2
I also talked to four judges, three district attorneys, and two public defenders.
[2] An example of this process occurred early in my analysis when I tried to "make sense" of
the data. Originally I attempted to categorize adjustments to bureaucratization on the
basis of personality traits such as aggressiveness, passivity, or competitiveness. These
tentative generalizations and propositions proved invalid since I was unable to find traits
that were manifested in a regular pattern. Upon further observation I found that adjustments fell into three patterns and when I compared them to the Presthus typology there
was an obvious "fit."
[3] Several sources told me that the new chief probation officer frequently stated: "Transferring p.o.s keeps them off balance and easier for me to control."
[4] Out of the 60 officers in Pacific County during the reorganization I estimated that 17
could be classified as upwardly mobile, 28 as indifferent, 10 as ambivalent, and 5 who
didn't fit into these categories.

References

Blau, P. M. (1974). *On the nature of organizations*. New York: John Wiley.

Blumberg, A. S. (1979). *Criminal justice: Issues and ironies*. New York: New Viewpoints.

Chambliss, W., & Seidman, R. (1971). *Law, order, and power*. Reading, MA: Addison and Wesley.

Conrad, J. P. (1985). The penal dilemma and its emerging solution. *Crime & Delinquency, 31,* 411–422.

Glaser, B., & Strauss, A. (1967). *The discovery of grounded theory*. Chicago: Aldine.

Glaser, D. (1985). Who gets probation and parole: Case study versus actuarial decision making. *Crime & Delinquency, 31,* 367–378.

Goldsborough, E., & Burbank, E. (1968). The probation officer and his personality. In C. Newman (Ed.), *Sourcebook on probation, parole, and pardons* (pp. 104–112). Springfield, IL: Charles C. Thomas.

Hagan, J. (1977). Criminal justice in rural and urban communities: A study of the bureaucratization of justice. *Social Forces, 55,* 597–611.

Hagan, J., Hewitt, J., & Alwin, D. (1979). Ceremonial justice: Crime and punishment in a loosely coupled system. *Social Forces, 58,* 506–527.

Jacoby, H. (1973). *The bureaucratization of the world*. Berkeley: University of California Press.

Klockars, C. (1972). A theory of probation supervision. *Journal of Criminal Law, Criminology and Police Science, 63,* 550–557.

Littrell, W. B. (1979). *Bureaucratic justice: Police, prosecutors, and plea bargaining*. Newbury Park, CA: Sage.

McCleary, R. (1975). How structural variables constrain the parole officer's use of discretionary powers. *Social Problems, 23,* 209–225.

McCleary, R. (1978). *Dangerous men: The sociology of parole*. Newbury Park, CA: Sage.

McHugh, J. (1973). Some comments on natural conflict between counsel and probation officer. *American Journal of Corrections, 35,* 34–36.

Meyer, M. (1979). Debureaucratization? *Social Science Quarterly, 60,* 25–34.

Petersilia, J., Turner, S., Kahan, J., & Peterson, J. (1985). Executive summary of Rand's study, granting felons probation: Public risks and alternatives. *Crime & Delinquency, 31,* 379–392.

Presthus, R. (1962). *The organizational society: An analysis and a theory*. New York: Knopf.

Presthus, R. (1978). *The organizational society* (Rev. ed.). New York: St. Martin's.

Pugh, D. S., Hickson, D. J., & Hinings, C. R. (1985). *Writers on organizations*. Newbury Park, CA: Sage.

Reiss, A. J. (1974). Discretionary justice. In D. Glaser (Ed.), *Handbook of criminology* (pp. 679–704). Chicago: Rand McNally.

Rosecrance, J. (1985). The probation officers' search for credibility: Ball park recommendations. *Crime & Delinquency, 31,* 539–554.

Rosett, A., & Cressey, D. R. (1976). *Justice by consent*. New York: Lippincott.

Scott, W. R. (1965). Field methods in the study of organizations. In R. E. L. Fairs (Ed.), *Handbook of organizations* (pp. 485–529). Chicago: Rand McNally.

Scott, W. R. (1981). *Organizations: Rational, natural and open systems*. Englewood Cliffs, NJ: Prentice-Hall.

Shover, N. (1979). *A sociology of American corrections*. Homewood, IL: Dorsey.

Tepperman, L. (1973). The effect of court size on organization and procedure. *Canadian Review of Sociology and Anthropology, 10,* 346–365.

Terkel, S. (1975). *Working.* New York: Avon.

Walker, S. (1985). *Sense and nonsense about crime.* Monterey, CA: Brooks/Cole.

Udy, S. (1959). Bureaucracy and rationality in Weber's organizational theory: An empirical study. *American Sociological Review, 24,* 791–795.

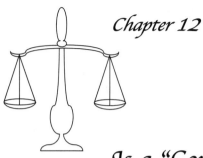

Chapter 12

Is a "Correctional Officer," by Any Other Name, a "Screw"?

Hans Toch

No one confuses professionalization with semantic sleights of hand. Sanitary engineers with mops are transparently janitors. The Blue Knight and Serpico are not "peace officers," and a person who empties bedpans is not a "therapeutic" staff person. We are rarely fooled by quasi-professional role labels, and we know that the role occupant is liable to be less fooled than the rest of us.

Does the advent of the "correctional officer" augur an emerging role in penology, or is such an officer a rebaptized Keeper of Cons? Are there attributes that distinguish the "new guard" from his precursors? Does he have expanded functions? A reshaped mission? More discretion? New tasks to perform?

In specific cases, we know the answer is "no." A correctional officer assigned to tower duty is a residue of the dark ages. He requires 20/20 vision, the IQ of an imbecile, a high threshold for boredom and a basement position in Maslow's hierarchy. For most officers—who are better than this—a tower assignment is palatable as an undiluted sinecure. The tower guard "does his time" because we offer him a paycheck

Hans Toch, "Is a 'Correctional Officer,' by Any Other Name, a 'Screw'?" *Criminal Justice Review*, Vol. 3 No. 2, 1978, pp. 19–35. Reprinted with permission of *Criminal Justice Review*.

for his presence. He is paid not only to be nonprofessional, but to be flagrantly non-contributing.

Other officers operate under roughly equivalent mandates. They must count, lock, unlock, escort, watch, stand by. They must complete forms certifying to the obvious or recording the unusual. They are enjoined to eschew communication with inmates, to invoke supervisors where real decisions are called for, to refer problems of consequence to colleagues of consequence.

There is little in the literature (either on prisons or on total institutions) that offers much hope to the officer. The guard, we are told, is the natural enemy of the inmates; client contacts corrupt guards, and are offensive to inmates of integrity. Guard-inmate links pinpoint politicians, rats, square johns; denote areas of staff compromise and marginality, of emasculation and bartering.

There are new facts to consider, however, new voices, new drummers to heed. Areas of inmate freedom have expanded, living conditions have been ameliorated. "Total" institutions are less total, more permeable to the outside. The guard is enjoined to be humane, respectful of cultural plurality, sensitive to client grievances. We try to recruit the officer from a broader — and presumably more responsive — pool. He is trained, or retrained, in human relations, crisis management and the social sciences generally.

If such contexts furnish a potential for new officer role, this potential should be evidenced, or should be presaged, among the officers themselves. We should see *some* officers responding in *tentative, experimental* ways, beginning to shape more contemporary roles for themselves. For where winds of change blow, they affect some of us first, and others later. It takes innovators to convince the more brave among us before the rest of us are swept along. Do innovators exist among correctional officers? Are there guards on the prison scene thinking and acting in non-traditional ways?

Innovation Ghettoes

In responding to this question, we must exclude the realm of "innovation ghettoes." These are settings in which roles are contextually arranged as components of experimental programs. A prison with therapeutic community units, for example, may train officers to be group workers. Elsewhere, special programs may have officers with roles redefined to conform with other innovative practices.

The roles of "experimental" officers are similar to those of tower guards. Role components are different from those of the "average" officer, and are circumscribed to their settings. Like localized growths, they carry the potential of dissemination, but the probabilities of metastases are small. Experimental programs tend to be admired and unemulated, like platoon commanders who charge up hills under the watchful eyes of tired men encamped at the bottom.

Nondissemination is not inevitable, "new" officers may be used to train "old" officers to arrange spread-of-effect. But such activity is different from spontaneous role changes among a rank and file. It is *spontaneous* change (if it exists) that is more directly relevant to our concerns. If non-special officers are playing new roles on the prison scene, others may follow. For such officers are caught under similar cross winds, stand on similar thresholds, live in similar worlds. It is the officers' worlds we must enter, to view the possibilities they offer in the face of traditions that restrain.

Pinpointing the Innovator

The vignettes we shall trace are excerpts of interviews.[1] The interviews from which the excerpts are drawn were aimed at one aspect of the guard role which is unambiguously non-traditional. This aspect relates to the officer as a dispenser of mental health services, as a person who resonates to adjustment problems of inmates-in-crisis, and seeks to respond to inmate suffering. Such activity falls into the human services realm and it is intrinsically non-custodial, though it may be clothed in a rationale of violence-prevention.

The interviews I shall use are representative in some respects, and atypical in others. They are representative because the samples are random and the officers are "mainline" guards in maximum-security settings. But the officers are not representative of the samples. Quotes are drawn from a subsample of officers (comprising 20% of the sample) whom we adjudged "liberal" along a helpfulness-nonhelpfulness dimension.

Our purpose in this paper is to explore the emergence of new officer role components. The vignettes we have selected are relevant to themes we have predefined as highlighting significant elements of the helping role. They are intended to stimulate our thinking about (1) what is possible, and (2) how and why it is possible.

The Humane Exercise of Discretion

A custodial officer is a figure of power and dispenser of authority. When we think of a man in these terms, his exercise of discretion becomes monothematic. If he is a purist, he retains his authority and exercises power; if he is selective, he compromises authority and relinquishes power. Viewed in power terms, a man who cuts corners is corrupt.

Sociologists have viewed prison guards as corruption-prone. The view is tempered — though not modified — by contextual issues. Contextual exculpations produce a patronizing portrait: a guard must become corrupt to get along, to buy loyalty and goodwill. This picture is not reassuring. It leaves the guard juggling the roles of blackmailer and blackmail victim, facing impotence or compromise. Survival as a shell of authority hinges on continuing corruptibility.

Whatever the new *correctional* officer may be, he must be more than a custodial officer. This means that new themes, themes beyond the exercise of authority, must enter into the definition of his role. The guard's behavior may subserve motives we have not encountered before, and these may have nothing to do with who's in charge, or who's running whom under what circumstances.

Among correctional officers, the power issue may emerge on its head. Power may be used on behalf of inmates rather than against inmates. Power may be used against superiors, or may be invoked to test their flexibility and resources. Where the custodial officer may give up power when he uses discretion, the correctional officer may stretch it. He manipulates power as a tool to get other (correctional) ends accomplished.

One correctional end is to provide support, to render assistance to inmates in need. This involves using guard power to supplement inmate power where the inmate is blatantly powerless. It involves testing resources, maximizing their "play" and flexibility, to get the job done.

Assistance-rendering is mobilized when there is a perception of need for assistance. Needs may take the form of manifest helplessness, misery, or anguish. The sufferer may request help, but (in prison) he may prefer not to. If there is no direct request from the person, his needs may emerge in symptomatic conduct. The officer diagnoses the man's symptoms by observing him. In doing so, the officer shows (1) "clinical" skill or sensitivity, and (2) empathy or willingness to care.

Where an officer is approached, he must assess the legitimacy of needs that underlay the inmate's overtures. If the officer is support-oriented, he is unlikely to dismiss help-bids as superficial or "attention-getting." He takes care to review conduct for evidence of suffering.

> **A 22:** He never mentioned the fact that he slashed his wrists. Just the fact that if he didn't get his sleeping pills, that was it. "And please help me to get them." And come right out and actually trembling, crying—he didn't break right down, he had a certain amount of composure. But he was choking up and tears started coming. And more or less pleaded with me to make sure that he got that pill. So when he came back from observation, he looked like a 90-year-old man. Drawn and pale, and he's grey-haired but it really stood out. He looked like he'd been a wino for 90 years with nothing to eat. Weight loss, the clothes he had on, he didn't care what he had on, how he looked, nothing.

> **GH 1:** I remember Timothy distinctly because he was the type of person that wanted to be helped, and he was asking for it in a way that you really had to look for it. You could see that he was asking for help, but I mean when you went by his cell he didn't say "listen, Mr. K., would you help me?" Or "would you do this?" But you could see, he would come to you, he would seek a conversation with you, he would encourage it,

stimulate conversation. And he would tell you things that he knew you would resent to get you into a conversation, so that he could—I think he felt so alone, so isolated from everyone else . . . he required so much attention that he used to do really strange things to gain attention. An awful lot like a child would. He would cut his hair off, I mean to the point where he'd shave his head . . . He would walk on the backs of his shoes, and he would put his slacks on and he wouldn't button them, he'd just kind of half-zip them so they hung on him. He was never an exhibitionist, he never exposed himself or suggested anything. But there was just a way about him, that you can tell it. Even if you weren't attracted to him, like keeping an eye on him security-wise, if he was just passing you in the corridor, you could tell there was something about Timothy that wasn't right.

I: I see. Now would he look to you like somebody that was depressed or confused or angry—what impression would he give you?

GH1: Timothy was very, very confused. Very confused.

I: His confusion sort of stood out?

GH1: It did. I think the thing about Timmy that really surprised me the most was the fact that I had taken such an interest in him.

Support-oriented guards not only respond to help-bids, but make independent determinations of needs. This means that the guard must be aware of inmate feelings, whether directly expressed, communicated to other persons, or revealed in conduct.

GH4: He doesn't know how to handle the relationship and the feelings that come in. Because I hear that he sits in the visiting room and everyone can see the love in them. And it's indescribable. It's hard to tell how their emotions are coming out. He can't hide it. It's flowing out of him.

I: You felt that he was fearful about going out in the free world? He wouldn't make this clear, but this is what you picked up?

GH 10: This is what I picked up. Myself and the other inmates. You take your lead from the inmates. Many times they can give you a lot of direction, but you have to listen closely to what they're saying.

I: And some of the suggestions they made about what they'd observed—

GH10: What they had observed, yeah.

I: Now did anyone give you an idea of what had happened to this guy over the two week period? Was it an overnight type shift or had this guy slowly fallen apart?

GH10: He slowly worked his way into it. And it was a very shocking thing, because at that time I ran the—of porters at that time, they cleaned up throughout the whole area. And we were a rather close-knit group. And any man of us received this sort of recognition, everybody rejoiced in a sense. This in turn, gave us all a good feeling. And now 12 years behind him and suddenly they open the door, he just couldn't take it.

CB: He was a little guy who was afraid of everything and everybody and then all of a sudden in a day's time he started standing up, which he knew was foolish—but he started standing up to some of the roughest guys in the division. And it just wasn't him. And I was afraid that he was going to get hurt because these guys don't take that kind of stuff. It was a complete reversal.

I: So it just stood out to you—here's a meek guy acting like a tiger.

CB: And plus it was all in a day's time. One day he was a meek guy and the next day he was on the move and he had just changed like that . . . The kid was actually serious. He wasn't putting it on. It was actually a serious thing. He actually, if it came right down to it, would have taken these guys on. Regardless of what the consequences would be. This is what I feel anyway and I knew he would get hurt.

Once an officer has diagnosed genuine needs, he is in a position to respond to these needs with supportive moves. Such moves can be routine practices, such as filing reports or making referrals. When an officer presses bureaucratic buttons, he is just doing his job. He exercises discretion where he transcends his mission.

Discretion may be exercised in a number of ways, including the exemption of inmates from obligations or restrictions. Such exemptions can be viewed as corrupt compromises, but they are really the very opposites. They are planned strategies of withholding pressure that is seen as stressful, and therefore as harmful to brittle inmates.

GM1: I have my clerk that I work with, he's the man in for murder, which means nothing to me, what he done out there. Now he's my clerk, I know he's a highly nervous person, he can't accept problems, he can't deal with them too fast. And he explodes, he doesn't mean to but he does. And a lot of times I tell him, "stay in your house, don't even bother coming out, just rest up."

I: You can see he's on the verge.

GM1: Yeah. "Don't do your work today." I can see when he's nervous or upset. I got him now so he'll come and tell me, somebody's bothering him, he wants to stay in for a couple of days, "go ahead, stay in," we pay him, it don't make no difference. And he'll come back around in a couple of days, he's all right, works good. Actually he's a good inmate, but if you didn't recognize his problems, you would have him in keep-lock, the next thing you know he'd be over in idle some-where, or segregation. He wouldn't want to be, but it would break him right down. He can't adapt to the situation.

I: So he's a guy that's easily made nervous and upset—

GM 1:   Yeah, and a lot of people try to make what we call a sweet boy or a punk out of him. He isn't that way, he actually is a very tough kid. As I say, he's in for murder, which doesn't help him any. And they pick on him, he's got a lot of time to do in jail.

I: So even though he's a tough kid, this sort of upsets him.

GM 1:   Yeah, right. All of our reliefs know him and if they see any-thing with him, they let him stay in. Like when I come on duty, they'll leave me a note and say so-and-so has had a rough night, he was hollering, somebody was hollering to him. And I'll say okay, and I won't bother him. Finally he'll come around and say "hi," or "you don't mind if I stay in today?" No, stay in, let me know when you want to come out."

A 23:   I had an inmate the other day, a big black inmate who is a known diabetic. He eats separate rations in the mess hall and he is a diabetic on a special diet here. He came out of the yard last week and went to C block to another officer and said "I've got to get to the hospital, I don't feel good." And it was about 35 degrees outside and he came in and he was totally saturated with perspiration. And they sent him back to the block and he said he didn't feel good, and I said "what's the matter?" And he said "I don't know. I think I'm having a spell." I knew the man was a diabetic, so I called the nurse, and I said "what can I do for him in the meantime?" And the nurse told me to give him about 5 teaspoons of sugar in a glass of warm water, mixed up and give it to him, and keep an eye on him for awhile, for at least an hour to make sure he doesn't have any reaction or anything. He may calm down, if he doesn't, give me another call. So I did, I gave the man the water and he said "thank you." And I told him to lay down. So I checked on him about every 15 minutes, and I said "are you sure you're going to be all right?" He said "yeah, I feel real good now." They were going to bring the medication later anyway, but he said he thought he would be all right. The man, the next day I was at work and he made a special point of breaking out of line for chow to thank me for giving him something to take care of his problem. . . . This man defi-nitely had a problem, he tried to get to a doctor. I talked to him afterward and told him that was the wrong thing to do, and he said he didn't know what to do. He didn't feel right. And you have to understand, you can't condemn a man for doing something wrong when he's in a position of feeling ill and he knows something could happen to him.

The officer may not only bend the rules on behalf of inmates-in-need, but he may explore the bureaucratic machinery for loopholes through which problems can be solved. This entails teaming up with other staff (who are problem-solving oriented) to find non-routine formulas or solutions.

> A X: And this goes back quite a few years and this fellow had done something like eight years on a 15-year sentence and he had a child that was nine. And whatever the case was, he had never spent Christmas with the child. And he met the board and he got an open date for six months and he did not have an approved program and he had promised the child that they would be spending Christmas together, buying him presents and right on down the line. And he did not get out in time for Christmas and he was really down in the dumps. He was real low, about as low as you can get. And this is right after Christmas and he was bitter about a lot of things and he was very disappointed with everything and he worked for me and I talked with Mr. so and so who was in charge of the service unit at that time—and I asked him if he would at least call the guy off the block and let him get it off of his chest and he did ... And something occurred to him that had occurred to nobody else and that was that the guy had worked in the plate shop for a good number of years and at that time he had saved half of his money. And so I asked the man how much they had in reserve for him and I told him and I said "let's take a chance and withdraw it and make a deposit in the bank in New York City and see if we can get you out on a reasonable assurance." And he did and he got it and he was out in ten days. And I think that it made an awful difference in that the man was let out and I think it could have been done before Christmas if someone had done more. If someone had taken the time.

Problem-solving conspiracies may not only involve the officer with other staff but also with inmates. The officer may combine forces with inmates to stretch prison rules on behalf of a troubled person.

> A 23: And the other inmate came to me and said "let's put everything aside, you're an officer and I'm an inmate, but let's think of him as a man," and he had a very good point. But the only solution that I could come up with was the fact that I had already put in an observation report and it came back with the man, there wasn't that much involved in it. The main thing was they didn't have an interpreter with them at the time, I don't believe. So what I did, I went around the system a little bit and I told this inmate, "explain to him that he has to go on sick call in the morning to see the psychiatrist, and what you do, you put a slip in for sick call in the morning

with the man. This way you'll both go to the psychiatrist together, you'll be there to interpret." I said "you may have a little bit of problems with the sergeant, but explain to the sergeant why you're there, if he has any questions, tell him to come to me because I'm the one that told you to do it." And he came back to me the next day and he thanked me, because they had moved the man out.

Discretion may border on advocacy where officers go out of their way to circumvent the system, or to fight it, on behalf of inmates. In the officer's eyes, the non-compliant bureaucracy is ritualistically and unreasonably obdurate, and he sees no point in conforming to it. This may cause resentment, and subject the officer to pressure.

A 22: There's times when the guys been out of pills, I don't have to do it, I could say piss on you, wait till fill-up day and get them yourself or go over and see the doctor and get them. I'll make the trip over and I'll go get them. One or two pills, whatever, to cover to hold the guy for the day. Because I've done it myself, I'm counting out pills or something and I'll drop them on the floor. I could shove it back in the bottle, but I destroy it, and I have to enter it in the book destroyed. There's times when the pharmacy will send over pills that says 28 in a bottle, there's 27, right off the bat I'm one short. So in the course of the week I have to go over and get that extra pill so that we're not short. Especially so that the night shift has got a pill to give the guy. Mainly this man with the sleeping problem and our epileptics. It's mandatory that they have the medication . . . You go over there to get some pills, they say "what the fuck you doing over here?" "I'm over to check this out." "That's what you got a hospital runner for." "Fuck it, I want to take care of it." . . . Four days ago, an epileptic, way down on the end, had fits, he hadn't been moved yet. So he come up, and he's given me static. This is the guy I was telling you, he's a Jew and he called me a Nazi and all this kind of shit. So I said "all right, I'll check into it." So I went over to the hospital, I was over there two hours, running this fucking thing down. Come to find out, the only thing that was holding it up was his job classification. You can't put a man on invalid company unless he's a grade four, no job. He can't work, he's medically unfit to work. That was all that was wrong, because they had him marked as a grade one. Grade one, you're going to work. And that was all that was holding it up, and they had to have a written order on it. That the man was changed from one to four, it took me two hours to get it. And I got static over that. So the guy will be moving today, everything's kosher.

I: So in the process of helping this guy out you have to put up with a lot of abuse.

A 22: Yeah. Fuck them, I don't need it.

The Building of Relationships

The custodial officer is not enjoined to be harsh or inhumane; he is presumed to be distant, vigilant, and firm-but-fair. Where an inmate gives the officer "no trouble," he is apt to be treated with nonintrusiveness; if the same inmate "acts up," he is dispassionately restrained and disciplined. In its positive stance, custody withholds negative power: it may even react with courtesy and politeness. It does not, however, get "chummy," because relationships complicate custodial functions. It is difficult to search, report or restrain an inmate tomorrow with whom one is personally involved today. If an inmate proves disruptive, the officer must react forcefully. He must do so because his principal function is to preserve order in prison.

The correctional officer may take a different view of inmates. He may see himself as "working" with inmates on a "person-to-person" basis. This may entail short-changing order maintenance to preserve or to create "working relationships."

A correctional officer has custodial assignments as part of his job. But he may give these assignments a human relations "twist." He may endeavor, for example, to de-escalate an impending officer-inmate confrontation to enable the inmate to establish reintegrative links. By taking a collaborative stance in a conflict situation, the officer may "defuse" an obdurate or rebellious inmate, and may establish a relationship with him.

> **GH 2:** The sergeant called me in and said "go upstairs and move a man downstairs." So right away I assumed that the man was causing some problems because we had all these other officers with us. So we approached the cell, we had about 5 or 6 officers plus the sergeant. The inmate was a young Puerto Rican about 62, very, very angry, obviously scared to death. The sergeant says "come on, we'll take you downstairs." He said "no man, I'm not going to come out, because as soon as I come out you're going to really kick my ass and I don't want anything to do with that." He says "I know I'm going to get hurt but I'm going to take some of you guys with me" ... I asked if I could speak to him. The sergeant says "yeah, go ahead." So I walked in and I said "hey, look, nobody wants to hurt you. I think I understand what your problem is." He says "what's that?" I said "you're putting yourself under a lot of peer pressure up here. Here you've been spouting off to all the other inmates in the gallery how tough you are. Now you want to prove something. You know and I know that we can take you out of here if we have to, but we don't want to hurt you. And why don't you just come along with me and I'll take you downstairs and nothing's going to happen to you." So after a few moments of saying I was lying to him and everything, I guess he really decided what the heck else did he have to lose? He says "you mean to tell me that you are

going to take me out of here and nobody else is going to lay a hand on me?" I said "yeah, you got my word. You'll go down to my area and I'll keep you down there and see how you behave yourself." So he agrees to do so. When we walked out of the cell naturally he's waiting for somebody to jump on him and romp around on him a little bit, but to his surprise nobody laid a hand on him. So his anger turned into making me more or less a father-image in his behalf. So on a daily basis I talked to this guy, anytime he had a problem he'd come to me. He started telling me that his problems were really not due to prison, there was an outside source between his wife and that sort of thing.

A non-custodial or de-escalating approach can help to reduce inmate resentments and can disconfirm assumptions about the guard role. This may make it possible for the inmate to react to the officer as a human (non-merely-custodial) agent, so that "correctional" work can take place. The vignette we have quoted has sequels.

GM 2: I talked to him several times in the yard. He said "what about this peer pressure thing, explain that to me." So I tried to sit down and tell him the term and just what it meant to him and everybody else and he said "gee, that's very interesting, I never looked at it that way." So then we got talking, and we'd sit down and talk about marriage and the problems he had with his children and that type of thing. We got along pretty good.

I: So this peer thing, he came to see it as one of his problems too?

GM 2: Yeah.

I: Did he ever admit to you that he was afraid and that's one of the reasons he put—

GM 2: Yeah, he said "I was scared to death. After all, you come to prison, you hear all kinds of stories." He said, "I've had a couple of occasions where they've kicked me around a little bit, I thought the same thing was going to happen to me." In fact he made a statement that surprised me the following day. He said "you know what, I'm afraid of you." I said "why are you afraid of me?" He said "you're too cool." I said "well, did I lie to you?" He said "no, I thought about that." He says "but you're either tough as hell or you got to be crazy." I said "why?" He said "well, you walked in the cell, obviously I was mad enough to hurt somebody." I said "well, I figured if you're going to hurt somebody you're not going to hurt me too bad because I had enough help there to back me up." But I said "I couldn't see you getting hurt from being stupid, and hurting somebody else." So he thought that was pretty good reasoning and we daily built a pretty good relationship.

I: Did he mention other things that had got him upset and made him act the way he was acting?

GM 2:   Well, he said he was lied to.

I: By who?

GM 2:   By other officers. I know another thing that upset him greatly too. I guess when he came in they took some personal property away from him he felt they shouldn't have taken. So I asked him what it was and I found that an officer made a mistake on two items and I got them back for him. So that sort of reassured him that everybody wasn't trying to be unjust to him.

I: He felt he was being treated unjustly.

GM 2:   Yeah.

The custodial officer may cultivate links with a few inmates (such as informers) to advance security ends. For the correctional officer, relationships may be the medium through which he works. Trust, loyalty, communication, friendship allow the officer to provide psychological support when it is needed. Such commodities also help the officer stimulate activity without recourse to power. The correctional officer may see himself as working "with inmates" rather than as insuring their compliance. The inmate the officer "works with" may be described in surprisingly personal terms, approximating language used for members of one's family.

GH 4:   He was pacing around and he didn't know where to turn. And I know more of the problem because when he has no one to turn to he turns to me. I don't know what he's in for. I don't know his crime. Although he has mentioned that one of these days he would like to sit and in length discuss it with me and he would like me to know. And we're very close, I'm his boss and his feeling for me is very close and he tells me almost every problem which he has. And we discuss it. And when he's uptight I talk about my own life and how my wife and I do this and that. And it kind of relaxes him and it's interesting for him. And how his feelings are for him he gets interested in the conversation. My aunt works here and we talk about the family all the time. And he was telling me about a dream the other night that he was on parole and he had married his girlfriend and she had gone to work and he was going out to have dinner and while he was out he ran into me and my wife and my aunt and her husband and we went out and he got his wife and the six of us went to Vegas just for the evening having a grand old time. And with a dream like this his feeling for me is more than just — we're very close friends.

Descriptions of this kind may strike us as strange, on two counts: first, our conceptions of officers may be custodial; second, we conceive of inmates as resistant to officers, except for rats (who inform) or square johns (who are subculturally discountable). We know it takes two persons to form a relationship. If the correctional officer does not find counterparts among inmates, his potency is circumscribed. He can render services and defuse crises, but in work situations he must be compliance-oriented.

We forget that inmates adjust to concrete officers. The squarest of johns may find some officers uncongenial, and the most militant inmate may find an officer he trusts. Officers sometimes facilitate relationships, while inmates often need relationships. Where such confluences occur, subcultures are no deterrent.

It may help to quote a young inmate whose divisional officer happens to conform to the correctional mold and enjoys a good "rep" among inmates generally.

> Cox V: When I first come to the division I had noticed that he was friendly toward the dudes that was on the floor, the tier boys. And he talked to them with respect, like you know, "how was your day today, did you do anything interesting?" It was different for a guard to ask inmates these questions. So when I got on the floor I started rapping to him about my main interest, which was cars, and he just happens to be another car freak, and we hit it off really good. And since then he's been a personal friend and not a guard to me . . . I talk to him about every problem. I go to him before I'll come to a chaplain or to a sergeant or something.
>
> I: And he's usually pretty helpful?
>
> Cox V: Very helpful. He's always got a suggestion. I mean it's not like "do this and this and this." He'll give me a suggestion and tell me the alternative, give me another suggestion and tell me another alternative . . . in June I had jumped in the silo and hurt my leg pretty bad. And they had left me up in the hospital for four whole days. That's about enough time for a cold to go away, and I had ripped all the muscles out of my leg, cracked a bone and so on. So they made me come back down to population and expected me to work. And I refused to work initially in the morning, but then I decided I'll go to work today and maybe I can talk to somebody tonight so I can get around it, get myself fixed up without getting locked up behind it. So I asked, "What should I do about this, these people want me to work, I can hardly walk." He said "who told you to go to work?" I said Sgt. so and so. He says "well listen, I'll get on the phone now and tell him you're having trouble with the leg, and I recommend you go up to reception. Because there's no sense you walking out of your limp a cripple because these people want you to go to work. We've got 700 inmates in here that can do your job." So he called up, talked to them and told the situation, right from the beginning, how I hurt it, how long I was up in the hospital and so on. The lieutenant personally called on the deputy

superintendents and got a direct order for me to stay up in reception until I was well enough that I could walk. This is from his personal interest.

I: Do you ever talk to this guy about very personal things, like your wife and your child, or what you think of the future, that type of stuff?

Cox V: Yeah, almost every night. We have a little chat session every night after lock-in. He stops by my cell, "hi, how you doing." And we start from there, you know. "Did you get a letter from your wife today?" Because he passes out the mail, he just asks as a joke type thing, you know. And I say "yeah, I got one." "What'd she have to say?" And I tell him this and this, and I won't hold nothing back. If she writes in there that she's having problems with the landlord or something like this, I'll tell it to him, he'll come up with either a suggestion or relate a story that happened to him and his wife, that would possibly help me out in my situation.

I: So this fellow really treats you as an equal?

Cox V: Right, he treats me as an individual, man, not as a group inmate . . . I believe out in the world most everybody's optimistic about what they want to do and so on. All right, when you come in jail, you're secluded from everything that's yours. Everything you love, everything you cherish, that you're used to doing, it's rough when you can't have it. And you figure "wow, I'm never going to get back out there again." And sitting in your cell and people bugging you, other inmates bugging you, this adds this much more badness on top of it. Losing hope is like just not even looking forward to getting back out there. I mean you're just institutionalized. And it's like every day is the same, it's just blah. You exist, you don't live. You eat your three squares a day, you take a shower at night and go to sleep and get up in the morning, and that's it. You don't think about ever getting back out there. No plans whatsoever. This happens I believe at one point to everybody who comes here.

I: And so when you say a guard shows concern for you, how does that give you that shot of hope?

Cox V: Well, it's like you remember like related incidents from the world to this man. Like if he says "hey look, when you get out there," you think back in the world, I remember a girl that used to say this, or my mother or father used to say this. And it brings you back closer to the world mentally. And when you're close to the world it makes you want to get back there because you remember the good things that happened. It's hard to explain . . . But it helps people, I don't know how, but when somebody's concerned about you, you've got the natural instinct to give them something back, whether it's affection or concern. You know, you've got to give them something back. And when you've got a contact like this, when you're concerned about somebody and he's concerned about you back, you've got a relationship going there that brings you above your environment. Brings you to be what you want to be. If you want to be back out in the world, you can put yourself to the point to remember when you were there. And how good it's going to be when you get back out there, not how long it's going to be, you know?

We have quoted our inmate at more length than seems necessary, (1) because of the "consumer" perspective the inmate can provide, and (2) because of his definitional or conceptual contribution.

The "traditional" officer is (in theory, at least) a custodial figure. As we meet new or emerging functions we see them first as departures from the custodial role, which tells us mainly about what they are not.

Our inmate defines the officer's role positively, because he highlights the concept "correctional" in "correctional officer." He tells us that the officer is helpful, but he also describes how he is being helped. His portrait deals with two major areas. The first is prison adjustment, which includes material assistance and stress-reducing counseling. The second entails enhancing the inmate's chances of reintegration into the community upon release. Our inmate includes the officer's contribution as a representative of the free world, with relevant experiences that help shape the inmate's expectations and attitudes. A custodial officer defines his job as order maintenance and this is a closed institution view. The corrections officer can deal with problems in the inmate's civilian past, in his links to the outside world, and in his future.

The Correctional Lag

Our "ideal type" portrait of officers is ideal in three senses: (1) the lines between "custodial" and "correctional" are less sharp than we have traced them: officers may be "mixed bags," and they may perform custodially in some situations, correctionally in others, and eclectically in others. Correctional goals may be custodially justified, or the other way around. (2) Thematic sequences are far from neat. Many officers were not "hacks" fifty years ago, and new men may play anachronistic roles more frequently than we like. (3) Contextual pressures qualify trends, and may stunt or snuff them. The innovator may be brave without being masochistic or suicidal. If he has no institutional supports, his innovativeness may languish, his idealism turn sour and his alienation may grow. In the absence of inmate appreciation, of peer reinforcement, of rewards from above, his new role may be abandoned after brief rehearsals.

While success stories exist, so do failures. The latter have consequences which are at times serious. They give rise to doubt, guilt, discouragement, and a mounting sense of impotence. They convert some officers into "closet counselors" and others into men who "once tried."

Failures can be produced by the custodial frame of the officer's role. This context is a source of tangible pressures, such as bureaucratic or personal resistances. The context also contains definitions and interpretations of acts which can tarnish the officer's self-image and undermine his self-esteem.

> **A 22:** And you have problems every once in awhile, like I have one man that during the noontime when everybody else is locked in, I let him out and he'll run a broom down the gallery. That's just a little extra, it keeps the dust down a little bit, cigarette butts and stuff. And he'll take a list at noontime for me and on weekends for movie, who's going to work, and it saves me from doing it because I've got a lot of other things to do. So I let him out. And he'll come up and maybe shoot the shit with me or go down and rap with somebody, and I had tabs dropped in on me that this guy is my pet, see.

> **A 22:** I had a case and it backfired on me. A man got locked up. The man was always on the floor while I was here, very respectful, no problems. You told him to lock in and before you finished saying it he locked in. He wanted to get water, he come out, got his water and locked back in. Yes sir, no sir, if he wanted something, you'd get, thank you. To me he was a model inmate. At the time I hadn't known what he was in for. I had heard rumors but unless I see it myself, piss on it, I ain't worrying about it. So the guy got locked up supposedly for assaulting an officer. He got locked up on my days off, so when I come back I seen he was locked up, Jesus Christ, what the hell did he do? He was the last guy I figured would get locked up. So I go down and he runs it all down to me, the officer harassed him all like this. And I said "you were supposed to have attacked this officer, took a swing at him." And I knew the guy knew a lot of the Japanese arts I guess you'd call them, kung fu, karate and all that. The man was fast, at times I'd seen him in the cell doing different jabs and stuff . . . And I knew the dude was fast and if he gets provoked enough where he takes a swing at a guy he's going to do a job on him because he's going to get busted one way or the other. So I said "all right, let me check." So come to find out that the officer more or less jived up the report a little bit to get this guy in the box. More or less "all right you cocksucker, you want to mouth off at me, I'm going to burn you good." So to make a long story short, when the guy came into court, I went to bat for him. Told him that the man was on my floor, he's all right, I can't understand. Plus the officer that wrote the report, he's wrote 90% of the reports that you get and they're all bum shit. He's a chronic report writer. And the reports are wrote like my son would write them. All busted up, nothing

> to the point, more or less hearsay, your word against mine. So this is the approach that I took, and I said I'm going to bat for the guy, I think he got a bum deal. Now they were all set to send this man right up to special housing. Anyway, they said all right, we're going to put it under investigation and I got to take care of it. "Do your end of it and we'll put a sergeant on it. Oh man, here we go." So I got static from my people. "What are you sucking his ass for and making another officer look like an asshole?" So the guy come to find out, I got set up. The inmate figured what my reaction would be, that I might stick up for this dude, so he played on it. And I took the bait. And I went to bat for the guy and I got burned. I got shit from both ends of the deal. And it's hard, because you want to do your job, yet you still don't want to look like a pansy-ass asskisser.

The correctional officer's frustrations also have another source. While the officer faces resistances from traditionalists, "progressive" elements may refuse to accept him. They may question his judgment, challenge his right to act, relegate him to ancillary roles, doubt his integrity, and stereotype him.

When the officer discovers he is isolated and friendless, he may question his own judgment, contribution and efficacy. He may dwell on his lack of credentials, his academic unpreparedness. He may see himself as having transcended his appropriate function.

GH1:   I went to the parole board personally and I spoke to one of the parole officers who was responsible for Timothy, and he in turn got in touch with his superior. He made his superior available to me and I discussed the possible stopping of Timothy's conditional release. Now normally this is unusual. But Frank and myself and Herbie discussed this, and we felt that it was the wrong move . . . the input that we have is respected to the point where if we say "look, we really feel this," they'll consider it. They'll look into the possibility. Number one, we found out that he was going out to a YMCA. On his own program, in other words a reasonable assurance type thing. Timothy was in no condition to go out to a YMCA unsupervised. Number two, he didn't have a job. Nobody was going to hire Timothy, not in the condition he was in. So we figured he would go out there, somebody would take advantage of him or he would get himself in a position where he'd get locked up again, or shot, and we couldn't see this happening. We just felt that after six months or so, even though we knew it was wrong what we were doing, keeping him locked up like this, it was existence, you know? And it beat being shot. So I intervened and they canceled his conditional release as a result of my going up there. Then about a month later I noticed that two ladies came, one from the Department of

Social Services in New York City and one from the Civil Liberties Union. Both very, very well-read, very professional people. One was a lawyer, one was a lady, I think she had a psychologist's degree, something like this, but she was from the Department of Social Services. And they were working on a program for Timothy. Now where they became interested in Timothy I don't know. They had like a bulldog determination to get this kid out of Green Haven and into the street. I told them, I explained to them what the past had been like. They didn't feel that we had observed him properly and they felt that him going out there on the street he was going to be O.K. . . . even though I was keeping him incarcerated, which is really a rotten thing, I hate it myself, being here incarcerated eight hours a day,

I still think that had he gone out there Frank and I and Herbie would have been the ones that pulled the trigger on him had he gotten hurt. We really felt that way, and that's why we did it. Even though I tangibly went upstairs and said "look, do this," we had discussed it. I don't know if I was trying to spread the guilt a little bit, but anyhow we had discussed it and I said "look, let me be the spokesman," and I went ahead and did it . . . and I think a big factor involved in Timothy's not relating that well with us—although we felt that he did, he obviously didn't do that well with us, because he left in worse condition than he came—was the idea that we had to wear two hats with Timothy. I think if we would have shook the uniform, and it had been a lot more informal. Even though we would have lost the security, and we would have lost the respect that the security gave us, I think we would have gained somebody that was worthwhile and we could have helped. I really do believe that.

I: You think you could have reached him if you could have gotten away from the role of guard?

GH 1: I think, naturally I really don't know. But I'm sure it would have helped. I felt very insecure inasmuch as I didn't have the education or the knowledge to be able to say to him "listen, I want to help you," and know what I was going to do, know where to start and in which direction to go in. I don't know what work I'm looking for but I just didn't feel, I wished that I would have had an education or a degree in psychiatry at the time because Timothy wanted to be helped and it was something that we experienced on a daily basis, and it was almost like a waste, you know, that we just sat there and watched him regress to the point where there was nothing else we could do after his maximum term expired, we went ahead and got in touch with the psychiatrist, we had a 3PC civil commitment put on him. Even at the end, it seemed so cruel what we were doing, but we just felt that after so many months as Timothy had been with us, and by that I mean on the tier, we just couldn't see throwing him to the dogs. So we got him a commitment in a civil hospital. Which isn't the best thing in the world, but at least it was a structured environment where if he wanted the help it would have been available to him.

"Corrections officer" is not a sterile label. Men fit under the label, in ways that make sense. We admit that there are few such men. Some day there may be more. On the other hand, there may not be. The corrections officer role is tender, the soil is arid, and it is infested by the custody ethic. New life needs nurturance. It needs strong support from its setting.

Men at the top of prisons often talk corrections and act custodially. Their formula is "humane custody." But humane custody is a myth, because it is a paradox. Where custody thrives, humaneness does not. Security defines a staff-inmate gap which widens, and makes men obdurate and difficult. A man usually bites the hand that reluctantly feeds him.

Our new "keeper" (if he survives) will be a "brother's keeper." He will be a man who cares and relates and helps. If we want such a man, we must care in turn. Officers must be appreciated, rewarded, assisted and their work disseminated. We must build our own ethic of support. Such an ethic builds bridges across human gaps — such as those between institutional staff and their clients.

Endnotes

[1] The interviews were conducted as part of a research program entitled "Interventions for Inmate Survival." This project was funded as Grant No. 77N-99-0030 by the National Institute of Law Enforcement and Criminal Justice. Officers were interviewed in five maximum-security institutions operated by the New York State Department of Correctional Services. We are grateful to the officers and their supervisors for making these interviews possible.

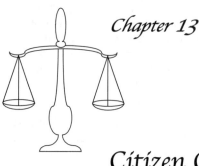

Chapter 13

Citizen Complaints and Problem Officers
Examining Officer Behavior

William Terrill
John McCluskey

Introduction

The police, as a public institution, relies on a grant of legitimacy rooted in public trust and confidence. Citizen complaints of police misconduct represent a weakening of that foundation. Complaints that become news events can erode confidence among an even wider audience. Incidents such as the Abner Louima brutality case in New York grab headlines and reverberate throughout the popular, academic, and policy-making environments.

Systematic research on police misconduct suggests most citizen complaints are generated by a handful of officers. In 1991, the Christopher Commission released its review of the Los Angeles Police Department in the aftermath of the Rodney King riots (Independent Commission on the Los Angeles Police Department, 1991). From its investigation, the Commission reported that a small group of officers were responsible for a disproportionate number of citizen complaints. Forty-four officers who had six or more allegations of excessive force or improper tactics were identified and subsequently labeled "problem officers." It stands to reason that

Reprinted from *Journal of Criminal Justice,* Vol. 30, William Terrill and John McCluskey, "Citizen Complaints and Problem Officers: Examining Officer Behavior," pp. 143–155, 2002, with permission from Elsevier.

officers who repeatedly receive citizen complaints will be looked upon with suspicion, reflecting the adage — "where there's smoke there's often fire." Police departments throughout the country have exerted much effort in recent years to identifying potential problem officers through the use of citizen complaint data. Several departments (e.g., Chicago and Detroit) have even experimented with computerized early warning systems to identify officers with a high number of citizen complaints (Kappeler, Sluder, and Alpert, 1994).[1]

Using data collected as part of an observational study of the police in St. Petersburg, FL, this article examines the relationship between citizen complaints and officer behavior in day-to-day encounters with the public. More specifically, do officers identified as problem officers (via their citizen complaint history) engage in physical force and discourteous behavior, stop suspected criminals, and engage in less inhibiting behaviors more often than those identified as non-problem officers? Previous studies concerning citizen complaints have most often concentrated on the complaint process (Dugan and Breda, 1991; Wagner and Decker, 1997). Others have examined officer characteristics, such as race, gender, and attitudes, in an attempt to identify patterns or differences between "problem officers" and their nonproblem counterparts, or rates of sustained complaints (Hudson, 1970; Lersch and Mieczkowski, 1996). What is lacking in this debate is an empirical examination of the relationship between citizen complaints and actual officer behavior. Equating complaints with behavior requires a leap of faith that is premature at this juncture.

Politicians, police administrators, and the public, whether fairly or unfairly, look upon those with extensive complaint histories as *potential* problem officers. Officers who are consistently identified as alleged violators merit attention, whether guilty of wrongdoing or not, whether being productive or not. Simply, it is these officers who pose the greatest risk to police departments in terms of public perception and financial liability. On the other hand, one has to question the validity of the "where there's smoke there's often fire" approach since there is little supporting evidence. The problem lies in the fact that it is difficult to uncover if there really is any fire beneath all that smoke, since most allegations of police misbehavior are rarely confirmed (Lersch and Mieczkowski, 1996).

This article provides the unique opportunity to combine citizen complaint data with actual observations. It examines the behavior of identified problem officers, as well as those who are not labeled as such. If there is fire under the smoke, one would expect differences in behavior between these two groups of officers. Do citizen complaint data truly identify problem officers who behave differently than their colleagues? What is it about these "potential problem officers," from a behavioral standpoint, that results in a high rate of repeat complaints from the public? Do these officers differ in how they discharge their duties?

Perspectives on Citizen Complaints and Problem Officers

The police-citizen encounter represents a special case of humans engaging in social interaction. The potential for conflict between actors is naturally heightened when individual actors battle for a differential outcome. This is not to say that overt conflict arises whenever this is the case. Most social interaction occurs without conflict. As Goffman argues, in most social interactions, a working consensus develops because "participants are sufficiently attuned to one another so that open contradictions will not occur"(1959:9). Generally, this type of peaceful scenario plays out even in the case of highly adversarial situations such as police-citizen interactions (Bayley and Garofalo, 1989). Most police-citizen encounters occur without conflict because of the "willingness of the actors to agree on the definition of the situation and to permit each actor to play out the role he has chosen for himself" (Hudson, 1970:180).

Nonetheless, as a result of the often adversarial nature of the police-citizen relationship, situations arise in which avoidance of conflict is not an option. Not every citizen willingly accepts an officer's definition of a situation; instead, he or she may choose to rebel against or challenge the authority of the police officer. Van Maanen (1978) noted that this type of citizen, termed the "asshole" by police, was likely to receive street justice in the form of a "thumping." Though Van Maanen's fieldwork took place three decades ago, police continue to confront citizens they label as "assholes" who challenge their authority (Mastrofski, Reisig, and McCluskey, 1999). Use of force against such suspects is, however, now receiving more careful scrutiny due to the aforementioned legal and financial implications. More precisely, "thumping" an "asshole" has garnered an increasing amount of both departmental and public attention (Skolnick and Fyfe, 1993).

When force is applied in conflict situations, the process or management of conflict becomes the focal concern (Mastrofski, 1999). It is one thing for an officer to use force, but another if such force is not delivered properly or legally (Klockars, 1995; Terrill, 2001; Toch, 1995). Legitimacy of the police institution is threatened when officers are unable or unwilling to resolve conflict situations in an appropriate manner (Kerstetter, 1995; Tyler, 1990). As a result, various mechanisms exist to restore legitimacy. For example, a citizen may bring a lawsuit against an officer or the police department alleging wrongdoing, letting the courts settle the issue, but this is expensive, time consuming, and realistically available only in cases where severe physical or monetary damage has resulted.

Another option is to file a complaint with the police department itself. Complaints indicate that citizens perceive something as "wrong," and they have a grievance requiring redress. This could be some noxious officer behavior (e.g., a racial epithet aimed at the complainant), it could be that the officer was perceived as rude or condescending, or it could be that the officer was alleged to have used excessive force. Regardless of the underlying source, a citizen complaint represents citizen frustration arising from an incident involving the named officer. Thus, if we know how many complaints officers have, *what exactly do we know?*

At least three different perspectives on the meaning of citizen complaints are possible. First, it may be that citizen complaints tell us little to nothing because they are unreliable or invalid indicators of officer behavior. Two arguments can be made in this respect. First, a citizen complaint is just that—a "citizen" complaint. It is the citizen's view or perception that the officer acted illegally or improperly, which is unlikely to be informed by rules and procedures promulgated by police departments for establishing uniform operating standards.[2] Second, a complaint is solely an allegation of wrongdoing and may have less to do with improper police behavior and more to do with the fact the citizen was the subject of an officer behavior (e.g., arrest, search) that the citizen simply does not like, thereby prompting a grudge on his or her behalf. These two points undermine the reliability of a noninvestigated complaint as a performance measure. One can presume that complaints that are subsequently sustained hold merit, but due to stringent evidentiary requirements, the ratio of sustained complaints to the total number of complaints is often extremely low in general, and even more so concerning serious complaints such as excessive force.

Second, it may be that complaints help to identify potential problem officers. Toch (1995) notes that complaints are subject to interpretation, but they may be a rough indicator of an officer's "propensity" for malpractice. Thus, officers with a high complaint rate, in particular, should be identifiable through variation in some behaviors when compared to nonproblem counterparts (Toch, 1995). To the extent that citizen complaints represent these behavioral propensities, they should be predictors of police behavior in encounters with citizens.[3]

Third, citizen complaints may actually be an indicator of officer productivity. It has been argued (Lersch and Mieczkowski, 1996; Wagner and Decker, 1997) that officers who receive repeated complaints may not actually be so-called problem officers, but rather productive officers. The surest way not to receive a complaint is to do little or no police work; or, to avoid probing or dealing with situations where conflict is likely (e.g., chasing drug dealers) (Muir, 1977; Willing, 1999). It is difficult to support or deny the merits of these arguments since all are rooted in plausible assumptions. Each perspective calls into question the inherent "meaning" of a complaint or what complaints actually represent.

These varying perspectives, and the fact police departments are increasingly relying on citizen complaints as a performance measure, illustrate the need to unpack the underlying meaning of citizen complaints.[4] This article examines whether a group of officers with identified complaint problems behaves differently in field contacts with citizens when compared with nonproblem counterparts. In particular, three domains of officer behavior are examined.

Physical Force and Discourtesy

The most serious complaints logged against an officer are those of excessive force and discourtesy. Excessive force complaints have long been a hot button topic, and departments engaged in community policing are increasingly sensitive to the issue of police discourtesy. Unfortunately, such complaints are also some of the most difficult to substantiate, and internal affairs investigations traditionally result in a finding of unfounded or not sustained.[5] Given the importance placed on these behaviors, do officers who received a high number of force and discourtesy complaints engage in such behaviors at a rate higher than their counterparts with few to no complaints?

Agitators

In addition to analyzing use of force and discourteous behaviors, various officer behaviors that may increase the likelihood of a complaint are examined. Officers with a high number of complaints may not necessarily engage in improper behavior, but they may be more apt to use tactics that tend to anger or frustrate the citizen. For instance, officers who receive complaints for force or discourtesy may have a tendency to order or threaten citizens more often, rather than negotiating or attempting to persuade. They may also be inclined to rely more heavily on interrogation and search tactics to gather information. Similarly, officers that are more proactive may prompt more complaints since they are placing the responsibility upon themselves to intervene in the lives of citizens, unlike a dispatched call for service. Previous studies of complaint data have shown that a disproportionate number of complaints stem from officer-initiated stops (Hudson, 1970; Lersch and Mieczkowski, 1996). This finding lends credence to those who argue that complaints correspond with productivity.

There is reason to question the productivity argument since the data from previous studies have often been taken only from the number of citizen complaints filed, which is akin to the problem of sampling on the dependent variable. For instance, two officers may each have ten complaints, with officer one having four complaints from officer initiated stops while the other has two. Advocates of the productivity argument may argue that officer number one is being more productive by getting involved in more problem situations, which increases his or her chance of a complaint. The unknown is: How many of each officer's self-initiated stops lead to a complaint? By relying on complaint data as the source for a rate of proactivity there is no way to determine this. With observational data, a rate of officer proactivity can be ascertained more adequately. For example, by looking at observed proactivity for these two hypothetical officers, one may find that each made twenty proactive stops. If this were the case, they would have equivalent levels of productivity, yet, officer one is receiving twice the number of complaints. The argument could be made that it is not officer productivity that leads to an increased number of complaints, but is something about *how* he or she is handling proactive stops.

Inhibitors

While officers may use tactics that tend to agitate citizens, it is also plausible that some officers engage in inhibiting behaviors more readily. These behaviors are characterized as those that can soothe or tone down the encounter. For instance, offering comfort or reassurance may positively affect citizens who officers encounter, even when such an encounter is inherently negative. An officer placing a citizen under arrest may explain the subsequent booking process and reassure the suspect that the procedure will be carried out as expediently as possible. Similarly, satisfying citizen requests can possibly affect citizen satisfaction and reduce the probability of a citizen complaint. For example, a suspect being taken into custody may request a shirt or shoes to wear. Failure to fulfill such a request may set the tone for the rest of the encounter and eventually lead to a complaint. The force used in taking the suspect into custody may be completely appropriate, but a decision to further degrade the citizen by sending him or her to lockup without shoes may prompt a complaint stating the officer used force improperly.

In summary, three questions are posed—do officers with a high number of physical force/discourtesy complaints:

- use physical force or display discourtesy at a *higher* rate than those with a low number of complaints?

- command and threaten, interrogate, search, or initiate activity at a *higher* rate than those with a low number of complaints?

- offer comfort/reassurance or satisfy citizen requests at a *lower* rate than those with a low number of complaints?

Examining physical force and discourtesy provides a picture of the degree to which these behaviors occur on the street and how well citizen complaint data corresponds with such behavior. Analyzing various tactics that could "agitate" citizens may provide clearer insight on what might provoke a citizen to file a complaint against an officer. If problem officers have a propensity for misbehavior, they are expected to have engaged in more agitating behaviors than their nonproblem counterparts. Inhibitors represent a third set of behaviors that may distinguish high-complaint officers from their colleagues. It is hypothesized that inhibiting behaviors are most likely to leave a citizen "satisfied" with the police-citizen encounter, thereby reducing the likelihood of a complaint. Officers who are non-problem officers should engage in these behaviors at a higher rate than their problem counterparts. Looking at possible agitating and inhibiting behaviors allows for a more comprehensive understanding of why some officers may be more complaint prone.

Data/Method

Data were collected during the summer of 1997 in St. Petersburg, FL as part of the Project on Policing Neighborhoods (POPN).[6] For the purpose of this article, two data elements from POPN were utilized: citizen complaint records and observation sessions. In reference to citizen complaints, POPN researchers were able to collect data on each officer dating back five years with the help of senior police officials and members of the internal affairs division. Contained in the complaint data is the type of case, including such categories as incompetence, inefficiency, conduct unbecoming, discourtesy, harassment, unnecessary force, as well as numerous minor violations.

Using these data, high-complaint officers were first identified. Complaints were restricted to those involving force and verbal harassment (arguably noxious and antisocial behaviors). An alternative approach would have been to use all citizen complaints to identify problem officers. Prior evidence suggests that officers engaged most often in forceful behavior are also most likely to receive citizen complaints for all types of behavior. For instance, as stated by Adams (1995), referring to identified problem officers in the Christopher Commission report on the Los Angeles police department, "[i]t is interesting to note that these officers received a large number of citizen complaints that did not necessarily involve use of force issues, suggesting the possibility that officers who are physically aggressive are associated with a wide variety of problems" (Adams, 1995:65). Despite support for such an approach, it was decided to take a more conservative approach and restrict the identification of problem officers to only those involving physical force and discourtesy complaints.[7] Table 1 shows that ninety-four officers were responsible for 181 citizen complaints.

Prior analysis of complaint data has generally grouped officers into two categories: problem officers and non-problem officers. To do so, an arbitrary cutoff point is made to place officers into one of these two groups (e.g., the 1991 Independent Commission on the Los Angeles Police Department report identified those officers with five or more complaints). A similar approach was applied here, but only after first standardizing the number of complaints received based on time in service (up to the five-year limit complaint data were available). To just count the number of complaints per officer and then place each officer into one of the two categories fails to account for how long each officer has actually been on the job, and, hence, the rate at which he or she receives com-

Table 1 Total number of complaints—force and discourtesy

Number of Complaints	Number of Officers
0	30
1	23
2	15
3	10
4	5
5	3
6	3
7	1
8	2
9	1
13	1
$N = 181$	$N = 94$
Mean = 1.93	
S.D. = 2.35	

plaints. An officer with three complaints and one year on the department is quite different than an officer with the same number of complaints who has been working for five years. Therefore, officers with a rate of one or more complaints per year were placed in the problem officer category while those with less than .21 per year were designated to the non-problem officer category.[8] While it is more customary to just split officers at a designated cutoff point and place them into problem and nonproblem groups, it was decided that the most powerful comparisons could be drawn by eliminating those officers with rates between 0.21 and one complaint per year.[9] Table 2 shows the rate of complaints per year for the ninety-four officers, which range from 0 to 2.6.

One threshold concern regarding the complaint data was whether the St. Petersburg Police Department was typical of other city police agencies. Data collected by Pate and Fridell (1994) concerning the number of excessive force complaints across a number of departments were examined to determine whether St. Petersburg had a similar excessive force complaint rate when compared with other agencies. These data, when filtered to include only municipal agencies serving more than 50,000 people (arguably the group most similar to St. Petersburg), were used to make a department level comparison. The complaint rate generated by dividing excessive force complaints by the number of total sworn officers is 0.06 for St. Petersburg during 1996. This rate puts them squarely in the middle third of municipal departments reporting data to Pate and Fridell. Thus, it can be argued that, at the organizational level, the department under study does not vary significantly from other agen-

Table 2   Rate of complaints per year—force and discourtesy

Rate of Complaints	Number of Officers
0.00	30
0.20	16
0.25	2
0.33	1
0.40	9
0.50	3
0.60	8
0.67	2
0.80	5
1.00	6
1.20	3
1.40	1
1.50	1
1.60	2
1.80	1
2.00	2
2.50	1
2.60	1
$N = 94$	
Mean = 0.488	
S.D. = 0.582	

cies in terms of excessive force complaints generated per sworn officer. This provides some confidence, in terms of the generation of complaints within the St. Petersburg Police Department, that this department is typical of similar municipal agencies.

The core element of POPN involved observing patrol officers in their natural setting.[10] Hence, the second core data element used here is taken from the observational database generated as part of POPN. Prior to beginning fieldwork, a team of observers (field researchers) underwent an intensive four-month training program on how to conduct Systematic Social Observation (SSO) of police (Mastrofski et al., 1998). Observers were a combination of undergraduate and graduate students from Michigan State University and the State University of New York at Albany who took a semester long class specifically on SSO protocol. Observers were criminal justice majors, none of which were former law enforcement officers. During the classroom portion (a total of forty-five hours) of the training phase, each student was trained on the specifics of SSO (see Mastrofski et al., 1998 for a detailed description). Observers also pretested the protocol in the field while conducting five training rides with a local department willing to permit observation. In addition to the training received at the home universities, observers conducted a training ride once arriving on site to acclimate them to the city, beat boundaries, and the organizational structure of the department.[11]

Field researchers accompanied patrol officers throughout a sample of work shifts in selected beats throughout the city.[12] Beat selection was biased toward beats where POPN researchers expected to observe higher levels of police activity than the average in the city (i.e. areas that had higher levels of social and economic distress than characteristic of the entire city).[13] Officers observed within these neighborhoods serve as the unit of analysis.

While on patrol, observers took brief field notes indicating when various activities and encounters with the public occurred, who was involved, and what happened.[14] According to POPN protocol, an *encounter* involved a face-to-face communication between officers and citizens that took over one minute, involved more than three verbal exchanges between officer and citizen, or involved significant physical contact between the officer and citizen. The day following the ride, observers transcribed their field notes into detailed narrative accounts and coded them according to a structured protocol. One hundred and twenty-six officers were observed in St. Petersburg, covering 360 shifts and consisting of approximately 3300 encounters.[15]

To compile the behaviors of interest (e.g., force, discourtesy) from the observational data, the total number of encounters observed was pared down to only those involving suspect/disputants ($N = 1487$), since it is in these encounters that one would expect such behaviors to be most prevalent (as opposed to encounters involving witnesses or victims). Tables 3–5 present the number of times each behavior (e.g., force, discourtesy) was observed during these encounters.

For analyses purposes, as discussed in the Results, a rate was then given to each officer (per number of suspects observed) according to the selected behaviors of interest. These data were then matched with the complaint data. Finally, since interest lies in comparing the differences between two groups — problem officers with non-problem officers (the rate at which each group displays the behaviors of interest noted), a two-sample t test of differences was used.

Results

Physical Force/Discourtesy

The initial set of comparisons involved physical force and discourtesy. Physical force involved any physical act a citizen was subjected to by an officer. This included restraint techniques (e.g., firm grip, grasp, wristlock), striking with the body (e.g., punch, kick, takedown maneuvers), or striking with an external weapon (e.g., baton, flashlight, mace).

Table 3 Observed physical force and discourtesy (police-suspect encounters) (N = 1487)

Number of Forceful Acts	Number of Officers	Number of Discourteous Acts	Number of Officers	Number of Forceful/ Discourteous Acts	Number of Officers
0	16	0	43	0	11
1	17	1	16	1	13
2	10	2	19	2	10
3	11	3	7	3	12
4	9	4	5	4	10
5	5	5	1	5	3
6	6	6	2	6	4
7	5	7	0	7	5
8	4	8	0	8	2
9	1	9	0	9	5
10	4	10	0	10	6
11+	6	11+	1	11+	13
N = 369		N = 125		N = 494	
Mean = 3.93		Mean = 1.33		Mean = 5.25	
S.D. = 3.92		S.D. = 1.90		S.D. = 4.87	

Table 4 Observed agitators (police-suspect encounters) (N = 1487)

Number of Command/ Threats	Number of Officers	Number of Suspect Searches	Number of Officers	Number of Suspect Interrogations	Number of Officers	Number of Proactive Encounters	Number of Officers
0	2	0	35	0	0	0	4
1	3	1	21	1	1	1	13
2	5	2	19	2	5	2	5
3	7	3	8	3	7	3	10
4	7	4	5	4	5	4	13
5	3	5	2	5	11	5	14
6	9	6	0	6	8	6	4
7	2	7	1	7	7	7	1
8	4	8	0	8	8	8	5
9	8	9	2	9	5	9	2
10	4	10	0	10	5	10	2
11+	40	11+	1	11+	33	11+	21
N = 1089		N = 150		N = 925		N = 633	
Mean = 11.58		Mean= 1.59		Mean = 9.84		Mean = 6.73	
S.D. = 10.24		D. = 2.11		S.D. = 6.79		S.D. = 6.17	

Table 5 Observed inhibitors (police-suspect encounters) ($N = 1487$)

Number of Suspects Offered Comfort/ Reassurance	Number of Officers	Number of Suspect Requests Satisfied	Number of Officers
0	37	0	22
1	28	1	19
2	10	2	12
3	7	3	12
4	7	4	12
5	2	5	7
6	0	6	3
7	0	7	1
8	2	8	2
9	0	9	0
10	0	10	0
11+	1	11+	4
$N = 134$		$N = 266$	
Mean = 1.42		Mean = 2.82	
S.D. = 7.94		S.D. = 3.39	

Given the subjective nature of trying to determine excessive force, there was no attempt to make any assertions that the observed force behavior was excessive.[16] The focus was to determine the extent to which, if at all, potential problem officers use force at a greater rate. If they engage in forceful tactics at a significantly higher rate, then one could infer a potential increased probability of having a citizen complaint logged against them. Police discourtesy was defined as calling the citizen names, making derogatory statements about the citizen or the citizen's family, belittling remarks, slurs, cursing, shouting, or ignoring the citizen (except in an emergency), making obscene gestures toward the citizen, or spitting (Mastrofski et al., 1999).

A combined measure of physical force and discourtesy (rate per suspect) was used to first test for a difference between the two groups.[17] As table 6 shows, there was no statistically significant difference between problem officers and non-problem officers when comparing the rate in which they engage in physical force and discourtesy. In fact, their average rate of using one of these forms of behavior is almost identical, 0.28 for non-problem officers and 0.29 for problem officers.

In addition to combining physical force and discourteous behavior together, each was also examined separately. Police "forcefulness" was analyzed in two different ways in an attempt to adequately measure this

Table 6   Comparisons of means—force and discourtesy

Observed behavior	Officer Grouping	Mean	Standard Deviation
Rate of physical force and discourtesy used on suspects ($P = .431$)	Low complaints High complaints	0.279 0.288	0.192 0.146
Rate of physical force used on suspects ($P = .055$)	Low complaints High complaints	0.149 0.225	0.114 0.179
Rate of frequency of physical force used on suspects ($P = .049$)	Low complaints High complaints	0.209 0.309	0.180 0.290
Rate of discourteous behavior used on suspects ($P = .356$)	Low complaints High complaints	0.070 0.082	0.130 0.071
Rate of frequency of discourteous behavior used on suspects ($P = .498$)	Low complaints High complaints	0.090 0.090	0.227 0.079

behavior. First, the rate of suspect encounters where officers used force at least once (prevalence) was compared. Second, the number of forceful tactics used in each encounter where force was used at least once (incidence) was examined. This second measure was used since force complaints are for "unnecessary" force, and it was conceived that officers with a high complaint rate may use force on the same number of suspects as low-complaint officers, but may use force more times during a given encounter, arguably a more accurate measure to capture the "excessive" aspect of police force.[18]

When looking at the difference between groups using rate of force per number of suspects (prevalence measure) as the dependent measure, there was not a statistically significant difference between groups (0.15 compared to 0.23, $P = .055$). Using rate of number of forceful tactics per suspect (incidence measure) as the dependent measure, high-complaint officers did apply force at a significantly greater rate than their low-complaint counterparts. On average, low-complaint officers used force at a rate of 0.21 compared to 0.31 for high-complaint officers ($P = .049$). It appears that while high-complaint officers do use a significantly greater number of forceful tactics against suspects, they do not apply force against a greater number of suspects. In looking at the P values for these two comparisons, only .006 separate the two ($P = .049$ vs. $P = .055$). In essence, regardless of the measure used, in only about five in one hundred cases would this finding be had by chance, thereby offering a fairly strong assurance (95 percent) that the difference between the problem and non-problem groups, in terms of physical force, is, in fact, real. Following conventional protocol calls for an outright rejection of the prevalence measure. From a substantive standpoint, however, it is difficult to reject one measure that six in one hundred times would be had by chance, yet accept the other that five in one hundred times would be had by chance.

The final two comparisons found in table 6 involve officer discourtesy. Regardless of whether rate of suspects (0.07 vs. 0.08) or rate of frequency (0.09 vs. 0.09) was used, no statistically significant difference between the two groups in terms of discourteous behavior emerged. This is not surprising given such similar average rates. High-complaint officers are no more likely to be discourteous than low-complaint officers.

Agitators

The first agitating behaviors analyzed were commands and threats. Commands involved "strong directive language" where an officer made it clear that he or she was not asking or requesting compliance, but rather ordering it (e.g., "drop the knife, don't move"). Threats were explicit statements made to the citizen, which signified a consequence if the command was not carried out (e.g., "don't move or I'll mace you").

As shown in table 7, while high-complaint officers did rely on commands and threats at a rate greater than low-complaint officers (0.48 vs. 0.42, respectively), the difference between the two did not reach statistical significance. Again, like physical force and discourtesy, a measure of the number of times officers used commands and threats within individual encounters was also tested. In this instance, there was no statistically significant difference between the groups (0.82 vs. 0.73).

The second agitating behavior analyzed was searching.[19] Searches were classified as any time an officer searched a suspect's person, his personal belongings, or premises. With respect to this behavior, no differences between the groups were uncovered. Low-complaint officers

Table 7 Comparisons of means—agitating behaviors

Observed behavior	Officer Grouping	Mean	Standard Deviation
Rate of commands and threats used on suspects ($P = .138$)	Low complaints	0.426	0.175
	High complaints	0.480	0.181
Rate of frequency of commands and threats used on suspects ($P = .224$)	Low complaints	0.731	0.438
	High complaints	0.823	0.415
Rate of searches used on suspects ($P = .125$)	Low complaints	0.081	0.089
	High complaints	0.128	0.163
Rate of interrogations used on suspects ($P = .023$)	Low complaints	0.576	0.200
	High complaints	0.688	0.197
Rate of proactive encounters with suspects ($P = .012$)	Low complaints	0.359	0.235
	High complaints	0.511	0.242

searched 8 percent of suspects encountered while high-complaint officers did so in 12 percent of suspect encounters.

Interrogation was defined as those instances when an officer questioned a suspect in order to gain information that would establish whether the suspect or his/her colleagues were involved in wrongdoing. Table 7 shows officers in the problem group used interrogation tactics at a significantly higher rate that their counterparts. On average, identified problem officers used some form of interrogation in 69 percent of suspect encounters, while non-problem officers used it 58 percent of the time.

Proactivity was distinguished by whether an officer self-initiated a suspect encounter as opposed to being summoned to one via dispatch or a citizen on-scene. The strongest effect was found on proactivity. As seen in table 7, officers in the high-complaint group, on average, initiated 51 percent of their suspect encounters. Conversely, non-problem officers were only involved in 36 percent of self-initiated encounters. This finding seems to support earlier studies showing that officers involved in more self-initiated activity tend to be at greater risk of garnering complaints.

Inhibitors

In contrast to potential agitating behaviors, it was believed that officers may also engage in inhibiting behaviors. More specifically, it was hypothesized that officers who offer comfort or reassurance to citizens are likely to lessen the likelihood of a complaint. As shown in table 8, however, no significant difference was uncovered between the two groups of officers in terms of comforting and reassuring suspects. The nonproblem group offered comfort or reassurance in 10 percent of suspect encounters while the problem group did so in 6 percent of suspect encounters.

Rate of fulfilling citizen requests was the second inhibiting behavior examined. A variety of citizen requests were combined to form this measure including: requests for physical help, requests for information, and requests that police advise or persuade another citizen. A suspect request was considered fulfilled if the officer fulfilled it outright or explained why the request could not be addressed at that time. As shown at the bot-

Table 8 Comparisons of means—inhibiting behaviors

Observed behavior	Officer Grouping	Mean	Standard Deviation
Rate of comfort given to suspects ($P = .101$)	Low complaints	0.101	0.118
	High complaints	0.062	0.082
Rate at which officers grant requests of suspects ($P = .114$)	Low complaints	0.890	0.233
	High complaints	0.766	0.382

tom of table 8, there was no significant difference in the rate at which citizen requests were granted (0.89 for low-complaint officers compared to 0.77 for high-complaint officers).

Discussion

When comparing officers with relatively high complaint rates to those with relatively low complaint rates in terms of force and discourtesy at least one (and arguably two) significant difference was found. Those officers in the high rate or problem group were more likely to use physical force than their nonproblem colleagues. While this supports the view of complaints as predictors of propensity for using force, the remaining comparisons—rate of physical force and discourtesy behavior combined, rate of discourtesy behavior, and rate of frequency of discourtesy behavior, proved insignificant. At first glance, this appears to undermine the utility of complaints as indicators of officer propensity for using force.

Two *agitators* occurred at significantly higher rates among the problem officer group: proactive stopping and interrogation. These represent a partial affirmation that productivity (a self-directed effort at stopping individuals and performing field interrogations) is related to complaints. Officers who had higher complaints were more active in terms of proactively confronting suspects and attempting to gather information in field interrogations.

These results do not provide bedrock support to the productivity hypothesis, nor do they indicate that police scholars or administrators are necessarily incorrect in asserting that complaints are a measure of officer propensity to use force in encounters with citizens. The inferences that can be drawn from this research serve only to temper the two perspectives. It appears here that, in some respects, both conceptions of the citizen complaint (as a productivity indicator and as an indicator of behavioral propensity) are partially supported.

It is likely that some officers are very productive and generate high rates of complaints because they actively engage the public. These officers might benefit from developing their ability to leave citizens as satisfied customers. Wiley and Hudik's (1974) research indicates that citizens would be more satisfied with encounters when they are made aware of the police's purpose. Stressing the treatment of citizens as coproducers rather than adversaries might transform the "productive officer" into a non-problem officer.

Similarly, the fact that the "problem officer" group was significantly more likely to use force against a suspect than a nonproblem colleague cannot be dismissed lightly. This indicates that officers with high complaint rates are resorting to force more often. It is possible that the identified problem officers represent two distinct groups. The first could be those who are unable to master the use of persuasion and negotiation and too quickly resort to force (Muir, 1977). The second could be those who are "gung-ho" and produce complaints because they are overly productive and fail to adopt an appropriate exit strategy (e.g., explaining why they have engaged a suspect) to leave the citizen satisfied with their interaction. With respect to this it was proposed that police might exhibit *inhibiting* behaviors such as comforting citizens or satisfying citizen requests, which, though not statistically significant, were behaviors that the low-complaint group *did* exhibit at a higher rate than their high-complaint counterparts.

Overall, the St. Petersburg Police Department offers only a conservative test of Toch's (1995) theory. The department is not large ($N = 512$ officers) and the cross-section of officers observed further restricted that number to ninety-four. If a larger number of officers were observed, it is likely that an even sharper contrast between high- and low-complaint officers would have emerged. It could also be argued that the use of a one complaint per year cut off is too low to distinguish problem officers from non-problem officers. Furthermore, the low complaint rate that existed in general in the St. Petersburg Police Department may indicate that the administration judiciously weeds out those officers who have high complaint levels or appear to be on a behavioral trajectory that will injure the department's standing in the community.

An alternative conception of citizen complaints would integrate them into the molding of a police officer. The ruminations in the previous paragraphs conceive of officers as static beings. Those with low complaint levels are permanently "good" officers and those with high complaint levels are "bad" officers. That is an oversimplification of reality since humans have the capacity to learn from mistakes, and if the citizen complaint is conceived of as a "lesson learned," it is not surprising that so much similarity between the two groups was found. Officers with high complaint rates may have internalized the lesson of the complaint and approach their work from a new perspective. One could appeal to Muir's (1977) discourse on the career of Tom Hooker, who had much difficulty early in his career but eventually developed into a "professional" as an example of a "made" officer. The extent that officers can adjust behavior to avoid future complaints is unknown, but it could explain, for example, why rates of officer discourtesy do not vary between the two groups.

This research began with the assumption that equating citizen complaints with officer behavior required a leap of faith that was premature given the lack of prior research. The findings presented here offer a first step in better understanding complaints relative to officer behavior. Future research should examine the individual level police-citizen encounter as a unit of analysis. It is possible that high-complaint officers act differently from their counterparts when confronted with various stimuli such as disrespectful citizens, evidence of citizen misbehavior, or citizen resistance. The present research was an aggregated snapshot of two groups of officers, which may mask variation among these individuals and their response patterns to citizen actions.

Endnotes

[1] A 1997 review article written for Law Enforcement News concerning developments in the policing field refers to this as one of the year's most notable trends (Rosen, 1997).

[2] A suspect being handcuffed for having a warrant issued against him for unpaid traffic tickets may feel like the officer is being unduly harsh in his treatment, but department procedures may call for handcuffing all suspects being taken into custody regardless of the crime. Nonetheless, the citizen may file a complaint alleging excessive force.

[3] Officers who have developed defective routines for handling "the family beef" might be likely to consistently adopt different tactics when compared to counterparts who have developed more effective methods of resolving conflicts (Muir, 1977).

[4] In St. Petersburg, Darrel Stephens, former Chief and well-known advocate of community policing, along with current Chief Goliath Davis, has contributed considerable effort to bridge the gap between the police and community. The department has developed an international reputation as a leader in the implementation of community policing. Within this framework, citizen complaints have become an important performance measure for determining how well officers go about managing conflict.

[5] In 1996, there were thirty-two cases alleging unnecessary force with zero sustained (St. Petersburg Police Department, Internal Affairs Annual Report, 1996).

[6] This study was funded by the National Institute of Justice. The intent of POPN was to provide a comprehensive picture of everyday policing in the 1990s and was a follow-up to the Police Services Study (PSS) from the 1970s and the Black/Reiss observational study from the 1960s.

[7] It is important to note the issue of *assignment hazard* with respect to citizen complaints, which may be defined as "the risk of getting complaints as a function of opportunity." In this regard, it is reasonable to assume that the probability of receiving a complaint is increased for officers working the street as opposed to those working in administrative positions. Unfortunately, data on officer assignments over the period of time (1992-1997) when complaints were generated was not available. The authors were restricted to those items recorded by internal affairs investigators and made available under the Florida State Sunshine Law on public records, which contained little more than basic types of information regarding the complaint (e.g., type of complaint and officer number, gender, race, length of service, etc.). Hence, a determination cannot be made as to the type of assignment for officers at the time of complaints. Nonetheless, it is important to note that assignment hazard is not an issue with respect to the observational component of the study. All officers (both those in the high complaint and low complaint group) during the observation period were part of the patrol division. POPN did not observe any special high-risk entry warrant teams, vice or narcotics units, or administrative personnel. Hence, all observed officers were exposed to the same degree of opportunity during the observation time period, at least with respect to being assigned to the same sort of duties — in this case, patrol duties. While this levels the playing field in that all officers are assigned the same type of duties, it still leaves open the question of whether some patrol officer assignments have an increased chance of "opportunity" for forceful or discourtesy behavior. It may be argued that an officer assigned a low crime beat as opposed to a high crime beat would have a decreased opportunity for such behavior because he or she rarely deals with suspected offenders. As a result, to account for this issue, behavior was standardized by the number of suspects encountered.

[8] While no specific number of complaints officially designates an officer in St. Petersburg as a "problem officer" or "non-problem officer" according to department policy (every case is analyzed on a case by case basis), officials stated that the rate of one or more complaints per year is the general standard used by supervisors to warrant additional attention.

[9] Models were also generated using numerous grouping strategies (everyone with less than one complaint per year compared to everyone with more than one, as well as those with less than 0.33 complaints per year compared to those with greater than 0.79).

Regardless of the grouping strategy applied, findings remained consistent with those presented in the Results.

[10] Field observation allows for "a direct, detailed account of what happens on patrol by someone whose sole job is to provide a *disinterested* account. Such detail, thoroughness, and accuracy are not available through popular social science methods of surveys (of the police or public) and official records" (Mastrofski, Parks, Reiss, and Worden, 1995:20; see also Mastrofski et al., 1998).

[11] As part of the training program, observers were trained extensively in what to look for, how to note it in the field, and how to record it for data analysis. POPN Principal Investigators included Albert Reiss Jr., Stephen Mastrofski, Roger Parks, and Robert Worden, three of which have extensive experience with designing and carrying out large-scale police observational studies. Reiss (1966) conducted one of the first large-scale police observational studies. In the 1977 Police Services Study (PSS), Parks was one of the three principal investigators and Mastrofski served as site director. In 1993, Mastrofski conducted a pilot study in Richmond aimed at perfecting the techniques used for POPN. For additional description on observer training and reliability issues, see Mastrofski et al., 1998.

[12] A quota sample was used that: (1) covered all work shifts for each beat, (2) included the diversity of patrol units that worked the study beats and larger areas that covered those beats, and (3) included both slow and busy days of the week. The study did not seek a strictly representative sample of patrol shifts because it needed a sufficient number of observations of certain patrol units and encounters with the public (more likely to occur during some shifts). Consequently, busy days (Thursday through Saturday) were oversampled, as were shifts and units where problem-oriented activity was more likely.

[13] This bias was intentional. POPN directors wished to observe large numbers of encounters between police and citizens. The bias is consistent with neighborhood selection in the earlier Police Services Study (1977) and by Reiss (1966).

[14] Field researchers accompanied their assigned officer during all activities and encounters with the public during the shift, except on those rare occasions when the officer instructed the researcher not to do so because of danger or because it would impede police business. Field researchers were instructed to minimize involvement in police work (except for minor assistance or emergencies) and to refrain from expressing views about police work in general or what was observed on the ride. The researcher's function was not to judge the officer, only to note what happened during the observation session and to note how the officer interpreted situations he or she encountered—officer interpretation of the situation was conducted through a "debriefing" session where the observer would inquire as to the officers' thoughts and motivation for handling the encounter (see Mastrofski and Parks, 1990 for explicit protocol on this technique).

[15] Although 126 total officers were observed, only officers observed on five or more suspect/disputant encounters ($N = 94$) were included in analyses in an attempt to prevent the rare occasion where an officer might be "out of character."

[16] According to POPN protocol, observers were only asked to document use of force behaviors not make a determination as to whether such behavior was excessive or unnecessary.

[17] A one-tail t test is used to compare groups since one-way direction is hypothesized.

[18] Additionally, given such similarity found in the combined measure of force and discourtesy used against suspects, both forms of behavior were broken down to ensure effects were not being masked in some manner by only looking at the rate of the combined behaviors on suspects.

[19] Unlike the previous measures on officer behavior, which examines a rate for the number of suspect encounters the behavior was present at least once, as well as the number of times within individual cases, all of the remaining behavioral measures are based solely on the former. A count on the number of times officers engaged in these behaviors during individual encounters was not coded by observers, only whether they engaged in the behavior at least once.

References

Adams, K. (1995). Measuring the prevalence of police abuse of force. In W. A. Geller & H. Toch (Eds.), *And justice for all: Understanding and controlling police abuse of force* (pp. 61–97). Washington, DC: Police Executive Research Forum.

Bayley, D. H., & Garofalo, J. (1989). The management of violence by police patrol officers. *Criminology, 27*, 1–26.

Dugan, J. R., & Breda, D. R. (1991). Complaints about police officers: A comparison among types and agencies. *Journal of Criminal Justice, 19*, 165–171.

Goffman, E. (1959). *The presentation of self in everyday life.* New York: Doubleday Anchor Books.

Hudson, J. (1970). Police-citizen encounters that lead to citizen complaints. *Social Problems, 18*, 179–193.

Independent Commission on the Los Angeles Police Department. (1991). *Report of the independent commission on the Los Angeles police department.* Los Angeles, CA: International Creative Management.

Kappeler, V. E., Sluder, R. D., & Alpert, G. P. (1994). *Forces of deviance: Understanding the dark side of policing.* Prospect Heights, IL: Waveland Press.

Kerstetter, W. A. (1995). A "Procedural Justice" perspective on police and citizen satisfaction with investigations of police use of force: Finding a common ground of fairness. In W. A. Geller & H. Toch (Eds.), *And justice for all: Understanding and controlling police abuse of force* (pp. 223–232). Washington, DC: Police Executive Research Forum.

Klockars, C. B. (1995). A theory of excessive force and its control. In W A. Geller & H. Toch (Eds.), *And justice for all: Understanding and controlling police abuse of force* (pp. 11–29). Washington, DC: Police Executive Research Forum.

Lersch, K. M., & Mieczkowski, T. (1996). Who are the problem-prone officers? An analysis of citizen complaints. *American Journal of Police, 15*, 23–44.

Mastrofski, S. D. (1999). *Policing for people.* Washington, DC: Police Foundation.

Mastrofski, S. D., & Parks, R. B. (1990). Improving observational studies of police. *Criminology, 28*, 475–496.

Mastrofski, S. D., Parks, R. B., Reiss, A. J., Jr., & Worden, R. E. (1995). Community policing at the street level: A study of the police and the community. Proposal submitted to the National Institute of Justice, Washington, DC.

Mastrofski, S. D., Parks, R. B., Reiss, A. J., Jr., Worden, R. E., DeJong, C., Snipes, J. B., & Terrill, W. (1998). *Systematic observation of public police: Applying field research methods to policy issues.* National Institute of Justice Research Report, NCJ 172859.

Mastrofski, S. D., Reisig, M. D., & McCluskey, J. D. (1999). [Unpublished manuscript.] Police disrespect toward the public: An encounter-based analysis. East Lansing: Michigan State University.

Muir, W. K., Jr. (1977). *Police: Streetcorner politicians.* Chicago, IL: Chicago University Press.

Pate, A. M., & Fridell, L. A. (1994). *Police use of force: Official reports, citizen complaints, and legal consequences, 1991–1992* [Computer file]. Ann Arbor, MI: Inter-University Consortium for Political and Social Research (ICPSR).

Reiss, A. J., Jr. (1966). Police observation report instructions. *Internal document of the Center for Research on Social Organization.* Ann Arbor: University of Michigan.

Rosen, M. (1997). Policing moves along parallel tracks of introspection and outreach. *Law Enforcement News, 480.*

Skolnick, J. H., & Fyfe, J. J. (1993). *Above the law: Police and the excessive use of force.* New York: Free Press.

St. Petersburg Police Department. (1996). *Internal Affairs Annual Report.*

Terrill, W. (2001). *Police coercion: Application of the force continuum.* New York: LFB Scholarly Publishing.

Toch, H. (1995). A theory of excessive force and its control. In W. A. Geller & H. Toch (Eds.), *And justice for all: Understanding and controlling police abuse of force* (pp. 99–112). Washington, DC: Police Executive Research Forum.

Tyler, T. R. (1990). *Why people obey the law.* New Haven, CT: Yale University Press.

Van Maanen, J. (1978). The "asshole." In P. K. Manning & J. Van Maanen (Eds.), *Policing: A view from the street.* Santa Monica, CA: Goodyear Publishing.

Wagner, A. E., & Decker, S. H. (1997). Evaluating citizen complaints against the police. In R. G. Dunham & G. P. Alpert (Eds.), *Critical issues in policing* (3rd ed., pp. 302–318). Prospect Heights, IL: Waveland Press.

Wiley, M. G., & Hudik, T. L. (1974). Police-citizen encounters: A field test of exchange theory. *Social Problems, 22,* 119–129.

Willing, R. (1999, June 15). Community policing passes the "Fort Apache" test. *USA Today,* p. 15A.

Group Behavior in Criminal Justice Organizations

One of the most fascinating areas within criminal justice administration is group behavior among employees. Much has been written about the power of socialization among officers within police departments, the influence of a "courtroom work group" on the court setting, and the ways in which correctional employees learn the ways of doing business within prisons. The extant literature has documented the nefarious side of criminal justice organizations with very little examination of how and why employee behaviors are tied to the structural makeup of their organizations and influenced by group norms and values.

Marquart, Barnhill, and Biddle examine the incidence of correctional employee boundary violations in a southern state prison during the latter part of the 1990s. By examining data on these boundary violations, the

authors note the inherent difficulties in maintaining an appropriate professional demeanor and distance between correctional staff and the prisoners they have been charged to supervise and control. The article notes
that boundary violations must be understood within the context of prison
security and the attendant problem of maintaining control within correctional institutions when the "defects of power" are so evidenced. While
the incidence and prevalence of very serious boundary violations was
small in comparison to more usual incidents of boundary violations, the
implications for prison administrators and managers are serious. Managing a correctional institution requires that correctional employees have a
clear demarcation between themselves and the prisoners, yet oftentimes,
this line is blurred when prison officials provide very little or poor training or do not hold people accountable for their actions. Yet, according to
Marquart et al., boundary violations within prisons may be just another
example of the pathology of imprisonment and a defect of total power.

In the second article of this section, Pogrebin and Poole explore
group dynamics within police organizations; they explore the lighter side
of policing by analyzing the role that humor plays within police work.
Humor, according to the authors, relieves the stresses associated with the
police occupation. Pogrebin and Poole place humor within a strategic and
functional role: humor serves the purpose of revealing the "distinctive
nature of patrol work." Such a revelation allows humor to be understood
within the context of police operations, but more importantly, it has specific effects regarding relations between supervisor and subordinate. The
humor defines both acceptable and unacceptable behaviors on the part of
officers while simultaneously affording the immediate supervisor, e.g.,
the sergeant, a reality perspective concerning the demands of patrol officers. The importance of sergeants to the delivery of services becomes critical for police administrators since they are the nexus between the rank
and file and commanders. This connection between administrators and
employees is of central concern to criminal justice managers, yet oftentimes changes and reform efforts gloss over the importance of maintaining open communication between managers and their employees.

Current efforts to "modernize" criminal justice operations run into a
myriad of problems due to poor communication. Instead of communicating clear expectations to employees, it is not uncommon for criminal justice administrators to demand absolute loyalty from their subordinates
when it is not clear what the consequences and benefits are from such
loyalty, either to the employee or to the agency. Souryal and Diamond
elevate the discussion on communication and relationships between
superiors and subordinates by examining the dimension of loyalty in
criminal justice organizations. They highlight the negative effects that
uncritical forms of loyalty produce within criminal justice agencies. They
discuss, most importantly, the necessity of having a clear distinction
between superior loyalty and the obligation and duty to perform the

tasks necessary for agencies to fulfill their mandates and missions. Blind loyalty to superiors will ultimately fail according to the authors and must be replaced with a duty-based model guided by some predetermined principles and expectations.

Kalinich and Stojkovic provide an analysis of prison contraband systems and their functional utility to prison organizations in the fourth piece in this section. The authors document how formal systems of control within prisons are, for the most part, an illusion and are to some degree dependent on the workings of an informal economy. They further suggest that greater control of the prison requires a conscious understanding of how important the underground economy is to prison stability. This understanding is learned and accepted by prison officials but very rarely expressed and formally condoned. The underground economy represents the "underbelly" of the prison; its recognition is informally understood but formally denied. For the prison administrator, it may be a reality of prison that is better left known to very few people, yet such a position denies its importance to the functioning of the prison. It is the awareness of the informal side of the prison that buttresses the formal components of the prison. This symbiotic relationship, in many areas, defines the context for correctional administration.

Gilbert, in the final piece in this section, describes the illusion of control within the traditional classical model of prison organization. Viewing prisons as places where discretionary authority is ubiquitous among officers, he suggests that the traditional approach to managing prisons is ineffective and insufficient to produce desired results. His critique points out that empowering traditional bureaucratic structures within prisons without being cognizant of the role and demands of correctional officers is pure fantasy. Correctional officers make the prison bureaucracy real; they enforce the rules and they negotiate with themselves and prisoners. Officer behavior is more influenced by group norms and the perception among them of what works and what does not work in the prison. Simply generating more rules without this fundamental awareness makes the classical model of management illusory and potentially dangerous to all in the prison environment.

Chapter 14

Fatal Attraction
An Analysis of Employee Boundary Violations in a Southern Prison System, 1995–1998

James W. Marquart
Maldine B. Barnhill
Kathy Balshaw-Biddle

Over 40 years ago, Gresham Sykes (1958:42) stated, "[F]ar from being omnipotent rulers who have crushed all signs of rebellion against their regime, the custodians are engaged in a continuous struggle to maintain order — and it is a struggle in which the custodians frequently fail."

Prison employees maintain only a theoretical dominance over inmates. Three institutional influences corrupt their authority. First, the staff cannot physically coerce the prisoners into total submission, and therefore must make deals with inmates wherein they let some things slide to secure compliance elsewhere. This has been termed the "norm of reciprocity," whereby employees exercise power over inmates by giving them "freedom" in return for good behavior. Second, the custodians rely on prisoners to perform numerous institutional chores (e.g., bookkeeping); such reliance cedes power to the kept. Third, the prison staff works closely with the kept; this situation increases the desire to get along with

James W. Marquart, Maldine B. Barnhill and Kathy Balshaw-Biddle, "Fatal Attraction: An Analysis of Employee Boundary Violations in a Southern Prison System 1995-1998," *Justice Quarterly*, Vol. 18 No. 4, December 1996, pp. 877–910. Reprinted by permission of the Academy of Criminal Justice Sciences.

the inmates. Pressures to get along blur the boundary between employees and prisoners. As a result of their constant interaction with inmates, staff members often redefine inmates as "people in prison" rather than as dangerous offenders.[1] In the present paper we focus on this latter aspect of the corruption of authority.

Proximity fosters personal bonds between prison employees and inmates, encouraging favoritism and selective rule enforcement (Crouch and Marquart, 1989). Worse, such proximity can facilitate romantic relationships, "consensual" love affairs, or even criminal sexual involvement (Baro, 1997; Hanson, 1999). In general, correctional occupational deviance refers to inappropriate work-related activities in which correctional employees participate (Kappeler, Sluder, and Alpert, 1994:22). We define actions that blur, minimize, or disrupt the professional distance between correctional staff members and prisoners as boundary violations; such activities represent one form of correctional occupational deviance. Boundaries are violated when the managerial desire to maintain formality and distance between keepers and kept erodes in the face of the operational realities of institutional life (i.e., the norm of reciprocity). Correctional staff members' violation of traditional boundaries through the formation of friendships, romantic relationships, or sexual involvement with inmates constitutes a major compromise of correctional work ethics and values. Such violations represent an extension of Sykes's (1958) concept of the corruption of authority.

Before the advent of sex-segregated prisons in 1870, female prisoners often were housed in separate wings of male prisons; accommodations set the stage for sexual victimization by male custodians (Dobash, Dobash, and Gutteridge, 1986; Rafter, 1985). Even sex segregation, however, did not eliminate sexual encounters between staff and prisoners. Zedna (1995:310) reported that "undue intimacy" between female prisoners and their female warders occurred with "surprising frequency" in Victorian prisons. The National Women's Law Center (1996) suggested that correctional employee sexual abuse of prisoners is widespread. United Nations researchers contend that guards' sexual involvement "is common in women's prisons" in America (Day, 1998; Olson, 1999). As Amnesty International (1999:1) noted, "[M]any women in prisons and jails in the USA are victims of sexual abuse by staff." In 1999, 11 male jail officers were indicted for sexually assaulting female prisoners in the Travis County (Austin, Texas) Jail between 1998 and 1999 (Phillips, 1999). Most recently, the notorious child killer Susan Smith admitted to sexual contact with a male security officer (Geier, 2000). Sexual misconduct, primarily by male staff members against female prisoners, has prompted lawsuits against 23 prison systems and jails (Hanson, 1999; Siegal, 1999; "Virginia Governor," 1999). In light of this problem, 42 states, the District of Columbia, and the federal government have enacted laws prohibiting staff members' sexual misconduct with inmates (National Institute of Corrections, 2000).

These reports imply that sexual misconduct involves only male staff and female prisoners. Inmate sexual contact, however, is only one form of occupational deviance resulting from prison personnel's close association with, and proximity to, inmates. Other forms of boundary violations, such as excessive familiarity, friendships, and romantic relationships, are probably much more common than overt sexual contact. Three other gender combinations also are possible in contemporary prisons: male staff-male prisoner, female staff-male prisoner, and female staff-female prisoner.

Until quite recently, prisons and jails were sex-segregated by both correctional staff and inmates (Jacobs, 1983; McDonald, 1997). Sex segregation, however, severely restricted women's employment and promotional opportunities in corrections (Jacobs, 1983). Title VII of the Civil Rights Act of 1964 banned sexual discrimination and gave women a foundation for seeking legal remedies (Martin and Jurik, 1996). Female correctional employees filed lawsuits[2] and won the right to work in male prisons (Pogrebin and Poole, 1997). In 1998, women constituted 22 percent of the American correctional officer workforce. Currently, eight female officers in 10 work in male prisons. Men accounted for 78 percent of the correctional officer workforce in 1998, but only 4 percent were assigned to female institutions (Camp and Camp, 1998).

Sexual integration of the correctional workforce has expanded the employment possibilities for women. Ironically, it also has facilitated female prison staff members' opportunity to engage in occupational deviance, especially boundary violations (forming personal relationships with male prisoners). We currently know little about gender differences in boundary violations among prison staff members: prison administrators customarily have regarded this matter as taboo (Mooney, 1995). Sykes's (1958) discussion of the corruption of authority centered on male officers and male prisoners, and modern prisons are far different places than he described decades ago. Despite recent media attention to male prison employees' sexual exploitation of female inmates in Florida, Georgia, and Michigan (Rivers, 1999), as well as anecdotes' (Mooney, 1995) and testimony from court cases (Elliot, 1999), the research literature on deviance in prison organizations lacks systematic inquiry into prison boundary violations (Stewart, 1998).

Building on Sykes's (1958) concept of the corruption of authority, we develop the rudiments of a general theory of boundary violations in prisons. We employ Goffman's (1974) model of social frames to examine gender differences in a group of prison staff members investigated for establishing personal relationships with prisoners. Our perspective helps us to understand gender differences in boundary violations, and illustrates how the processes that pull male and female prison employees into boundary violations may differ (Steffensmeier and Allan, 1996).

Boundaries and Social Frames

Boundaries demarcate areas where we are welcome or forbidden. Epstein (1994:15) states, "The concept of personal boundaries employs a spatial metaphor that helps us describe and define our relationships with other beings and objects in the external world." Social and psychological boundaries demarcate space and protect our individuality. Boundaries and their maintenance are essential to the survival of human communities; without them, social organization would be impossible (Erikson, 1966).

Social Frames and Boundary Maintenance

Erving Goffman (1974) defined social frames as principles of organization that govern social events and our subjective involvement in those events. At any level of human discourse, whether loving intimacy, group processes, business dealings, or sporting events, we tend to maintain a basic set of expectations and rules to comprehend reality. Goffman (1974) stressed that nearly every interpersonal situation included frames, or "ways of doing," that delineate the purpose and meaning of the relationship. Social frames organize involvement by providing participants with a sense of what is going on, as well as limiting how deeply the individual is to be carried into the activity. Involvement and a sense of purpose are critical aspects in fiduciary relationships, wherein one party has a professional obligation to care for or provide service to another (Friedman and Boumil, 1995).

Conceptualizing the Custodial Frame

In keeping with Goffman's (1974) notion of social frames, we conceptualize the custodial frame as a set of expectations that organize and give meaning to staff inmate interactions. It is commonly understood that prison systems differ greatly as to how far inmates can and should be trusted, the causes of criminality, the role of treatment, and the proper scope of prisoners' rights. Prison personnel share the "keeper" philosophy, which guides staff behavior (DiIulio, 1987). In their encounters with prisoners, prison employees are expected and trained to be firm but fair, nonabusive, impersonal, dispassionate, and nonconfrontational. These interaction rules are gender-neutral; they constitute the "custodial frame" that legitimizes and enforces the boundary between superordinates (staff) and subordinates (inmates). The custodial frame also facilitates cohesion among the staff members.

Throughout the history of prisons, employees have been forbidden from becoming personally involved with prisoners. The "no friendship" rule in prisons is akin to the incest taboo. Contemporary prisons ban interaction beyond the custodial frame, and have established disciplinary procedures to punish employees who engage in inappropriate relationships with prisoners (National Institute of Corrections, 2000). The custodial frame is maintained through physical barriers such as uniforms, grooming standards, and a variety of duty posts (e.g., gun towers, perimeter patrol cars, catwalks) and shift work. At the social level, formal modes of address (Sir, Mrs., Ms., Mr., Officer, Boss) have been institutionalized to enforce a polite but firm impersonal boundary between prison employees and prisoners. Inmates are expected to be polite, docile, nonthreatening/nonconfrontational, and impersonal in their interactions with staff.

Sometimes, however, the well-established and historic boundary or custodial frame between staff and inmates is broken. Staff members may denigrate inmates, ignore inmates' requests for assistance, physically abuse inmates, or bring contraband such as drugs or weapons to prisoners (Crouch and Marquart, 1980, 1989; Marquart, 1986). In his discussion of the corruption of authority, Sykes (1958) described how prison staff members bend the rules to secure inmates' compliance. The custodial frame is not absolute, nor can it govern every staff inmate interaction.

Breaking the Frame

Social frames can be broken, as in cases of child abuse, theft by employees, and situations where doctors or therapists victimize their patients (Epstein, 1994; Eschholz and Vaughn, 2000; Rutter, 1989; Sapp, 1997). Breaking a social frame constitutes a boundary violation, a well-researched topic in psychology, psychiatry, and health care (Gabbard, 1995; Gabbard and Lester, 1995; Gonsiorek, 1995). This body of research on power imbalances posits that boundary violations encompass an array of activities and behaviors. Most important for the present paper is Strom-Gottfried's (1999) research on the violation of therapeutic boundaries by social workers or therapists with their clients. She reviewed 894 ethics complaints submitted to the National Association of Social Workers over an 11-year period.

Strom-Gottfried uncovered three types of ethical transgressions: general blurring of roles (i.e., discussing personal information with clients, meeting with clients after hours); dual or overlapping relationships (i.e., dating, pursuing joint hobbies and social activities with clients); and sexual contact. One hundred and forty-seven cases went to formal hearings and resulted in affirmative findings of boundary violations. Of these cases, 107 involved some form of sexual violation, 62 entailed dual relationships, and 70 involved general breaches. Moreover, Strom-Gottfried found that each boundary violation, or frame break, consisted of a series of steps or a sequence of actions committed by the clinician. Further, a minority of cases involved a "slippery slope": clinicians began with a general blurring of roles, which progressed into sexual contact (Strom-Gottfried, 1999).

In the present paper we apply to the prison Strom-Gottfried's (1999) typology of boundary violations among social workers and their clients.

Our goal is to extend current theorizing to inform future research. We strongly suggest that the typology of boundary violations presented here is not exhaustive, but is a first pass at an unexplored problem in prisons.

Applying the Boundary Violation Perspective to Penal Organizations

In our application of Strom-Gottfried's (1999) continuum to the prison, general boundary violations constituted "unserious" framebreaks committed by employees who accepted from inmates, or exchanged with inmates, items such as soft drinks, food, and craftwork or materials, or wrote letters to prisoners whom they had known before incarceration.

Dual relationships occurred when employees blurred the boundary between themselves and inmates, and established romantic relationships with prisoners through excessive flirting and disclosure of personal information. These employees pursued an inmate's attention or affection, and fell in love. Staff members who engaged in dual relationships committed one or more of the following behaviors:

Discussed their personal life in detail with a prisoner (including sexual life, social life, marital status, spouse and/or children, experiences with domestic abuse);

Exchanged letters and/or personal photographs (including nude photos) with a prisoner;

Exchanged erotica (pornographic poems and letters) with an inmate;

Placed money in an inmate's trust fund;

Used aliases and post office boxes in nearby towns or cities to hide the relationship;

Contacted an inmate's family to relay information about the prisoner;

Established a relationship with an inmate in prison and then lived with the inmate upon his or her release from prison;

Moved in with an inmate's family member;

Provided a cellular phone to a prisoner, or took collect calls to facilitate off-duty conversations with an inmate;

Engaged in on-the-job subterfuge to hide the relationship.

We realize that placing money in an inmate's trust fund and/or exchanging "dirty" letters certainly stretch the definition of dual relationships. In our view, however, dual relationships encompass diverse behaviors up to, but not including, sexual contact. It is possible that the exchange of erotica may constitute another behavioral type suggesting eventual sexual contact. Additional research in other prisons (based on more cases) may further clarify the differences among dual relationships.

Staff-inmate sexual contact is the most serious boundary violation. In keeping with the research literature on sexual contact between patients and therapists (Wincze et al., 1996), we defined employee-inmate sexual contact as vaginal and/or anal intercourse, fondling, masturbation, genital exposure, and/or any oral-genital contact. Sexual boundary violations had to be observed or corroborated by a third party (another employee), and/or the employee under investigation must have admitted to the act (in written statements or under oath during a polygraph session).[3] Momentary kisses, hugs, and hand holding were not considered sexual contacts. For example, one employee admitted to investigators that she loved inmate X and had delivered 30 letters and 11 photos of herself to this inmate. She admittedly had kissed inmate X, had deposited $700 in his trust fund, wanted to have a "quickie" with him, and "fantasized about having sex" with him. These incidents were not considered sexual contact. Our criteria for sexual contact yielded 42 incidents (involving 18 males and 24 females) of reported employee-inmate sexual contact.[4] Additional acts of sexual contact in the same period probably went unreported (Day, 1998).

Some scholars and practitioners will argue that, because the relationship between staff and inmates is coercive, the kept cannot refuse a sexual relationship with employees. We suggest, however, that under certain circumstances it may be possible for the keeper and the kept to establish a consensual sexual relationship. The organizational links (e.g., a culture of silence) and the legal implications (e.g., consent) of sexual contact between prison employees and inmates are complex, and merit additional scholarly inquiry.

What kinds of employees had sexual contact with inmates? Where did this behavior occur? Where were the supervisors when the behavior took place? Answers to these questions will have important policy implications for prison management. Rather than simply developing a "kinds of people" explanation, we also examined the situational aspects of correctional employees' framebreaks. To this end, our research was guided by the research conducted over the past 25 years by Phillip Zimbardo and his colleagues, who emphasized the surprising and ironic power of institutional environments over the participants. Their research illustrates clearly how situational dynamics can distort an individual's judgment so far as to defy all individual expectations (Haney and Zimbardo, 1998:710).

In keeping with this line of research, we expect to find that certain situations and places in the prison will be conducive to staff-inmate framebreaks. We expect to find that such framebreaks will be more prevalent where supervisors and colleagues are absent. The lack of authority figures to exert formal control over an employee's contact with prisoners should be conducive to boundary violations. These violations will be more prevalent in unstructured employee-prisoner situations (i.e., choir practice, recreational activities) than in structured work-intensive situations such as supervising inmates on industrial work details (Osgood et al., 1996). Unstructured activities involving staff and inmates (one-on-one situations away from the supervisors' view) set the stage for blurring the line between staff and inmates, disrupting formal relations, and weakening the custodial frame.

Methodology

Data for this inquiry were obtained from the personnel files of 549 employees of the Texas Department of Criminal Justice, Institutional Division (TDCJ-ID). These employees were investigated by Internal Affairs and were formally disciplined between January 1, 1995 and December 31, 1998: They were punished for violating Rule 42 of the "Employees' General Rules of Conduct."[5] Originally the data set consisted of security officers, parole staff, health services staff, clerical staff, teachers, chaplains, and other members of the support staff. We focused on the prison staff members (security personnel, mail room clerks, secretaries) who had daily interactions with inmates. We eliminated 41 employees (parole officers and health services staff)[6] to reduce the data set to 508 "investigated" prison employees.[7]

Data and Contents of Personnel Files

Personnel files included employee applications, background investigations, and in-service work records. The employment application and background investigation contained demographic, educational, employment, military, and criminal history information. In-service records contained prison unit assignments, academy test scores, promotions, annual performance evaluations, initial interview and evaluation scores, records of sick and injured leave, disciplinary actions, dispositions of complaints, and all official correspondence or records. Each file contained the case and investigation history surrounding the circumstances and actors and/ or actions leading to the employee's investigation for violating Rule 42.

We content-analyzed each case history, searching for themes in the employees' version of the events (87 data categories emerged from this examination). We developed a coding instrument to capture relevant variables. (Employees' and inmates' names used in this paper are pseudonyms.)

We readily acknowledge that our analysis is employee centered and that we have lost a great deal by not incorporating the inmates' perspective. The inmate's voice is critical but it lies beyond the present paper's scope; we will deal with it in subsequent papers. Currently we are obtaining records and interviewing inmates who were investigated for inappropriate relationships with staff members.

Sample of "Successful" Employees

At the request of human resources administrators, we conducted a comparative analysis of "successful" and "unsuccessful" employees to determine, for recruiting purposes, whether significant demographic differences existed between the two groups. We were provided with a random sample of 585 prison employees hired between 1995 and 1998, who were still employed as of December 31, 1999. These individuals had undergone no Internal Affairs investigations and were considered successful employees. In the comparative analysis we explored differences between investigated and noninvestigated employees, based on the same data elements as gathered from the employment application and background investigation and from in-service records.

Interviews With Supervisors and Internal Affairs Investigators

Finally, to obtain personal insights into inappropriate employee-inmate relationships, we interviewed 12 employee supervisors (lieutenants, majors, and wardens) from five Huntsville-area prisons, as well as four internal affairs investigators. We asked the supervisors and investigators to explain the process by which employees become involved in inappropriate inmate relationships, why and how such relationships develop, and whether or not improved hiring standards and training could deter such relationships and improve retention of employees. We also asked the interviewees about the impact of recent organizational growth on staff recruitment, retention, and inappropriate relationships. The 20-question interviews averaged 60 minutes each; we carefully noted and later content-analyzed all responses.

Background Characteristics of the Investigated Employees

At the time of the investigation, the average age of the 508 prison employees was 36 years (31 at initial employment), and their tenure averaged slightly less than four years (46 months on the job). Fifty-four percent were Anglo, 30 percent were African-American, and 16 percent were Hispanic. Over two-thirds (68 percent) had a high school diploma. Thirty-eight percent reportedly were attending college, and three subjects claimed to be criminal justice majors. Most subjects (85 percent) had no prior military experience, and 86 percent reported performing service work or manual labor before their prison employment.

Seventy-seven percent of the investigated employees were females. This skewed proportion (or sex ratio) must be interpreted cautiously, however. In 1978, Texas prisons were sexually segregated workplaces for security staff members. In 1988, 17 percent of all female security staff worked in male units. By 1998, this proportion had increased to 80 percent. On the other hand, 95 percent of all male security officers worked in male prisons (Camp and Camp, 1998). Thus a larger proportion of female employees were exposed to male prisoners.

Raw percentages can be misleading, however. Table 1 presents employment data on male and female security officers between 1995 and

Table 1 Employment Figures for Security Staff Members by Year and Rate of Disciplinary Actions

Year	Total	Males	Females	Females in Male Institutions	Number of Females Disciplined	Rate of Female Violations	Males in Female Institutions	Number of Males Disciplined	Rate of Male Violations
1995	18,920	14,067	4,853	3,941	98	2.40	348	12	3.50
1996	22,846	16,655	6,191	5,332	115	2.10	542	12	2.40
1997	26,894	19,229	7,665	6,317	100	1.60	540	9	1.60
1998	27,509	19,009	8,500	6,616	54	.80	571	4	.70

1998. In 1995, 3,941 females worked in male prisons. In the same year, 98 female security employees (in our data set) were investigated for engaging in inappropriate relationships with male prisoners (a rate of 2.4 per 100 officers). In comparison, 348 male officers worked in female prisons; 12 were investigated for engaging in inappropriate relationships with female prisoners (a rate of 3.5 per 100 officers). Our analysis, although preliminary, shows that the overall rates of inappropriate relationships per 100 officers between 1995 and 1998 for male and female employees in sexually integrated settings were roughly the same.

Yet despite the similarity in rates of boundary violations, we suggest that the risk for deviance is far greater for female than for male employees in sexually integrated prisons. A male-dominated work environment, especially a prison, is characterized by a sexual ambiance and by the expression of male sexuality (Carroll, 1974). Women employed in male-dominated settings are more likely to experience social-sexual behaviors (e.g., invitations to sex, innuendo, harassment), a point underscored by research on sex and the workplace (Statham, 1996). We strongly suggest that sex-role spillover (the carryover into the workplace of gender-based expectations about behavior) also helps to explain the higher proportion of employee boundary violations by females (Gutek, 1985:149). It was highly likely that male prisoners perceived the women security officers as females first and employees second. Thus male prisoners, in keeping with sex-role behaviors, may have planned and initiated relationships and sexual interaction. (Research on the inmates' version of the events will help to clarify this process. Male prisoners also may "hit on" female employees to advertise and validate their heterosexuality to themselves and their peers.)

The sexual ambiance, sex-role behaviors, and expectations surrounding male employees in female prisons are different and deserve separate analysis. Although the rates of deviance may appear on the surface to be similar, the dynamics involved in male and female employees' boundary violations are probably very different, making any comparison difficult and subject to interpretational error.

Boundary violations occurred quickly, often within the first year of employment. Fifty-seven employees were investigated for engaging in inappropriate relationships with inmates after less than one month of employment, 161 employee.s were investigated after one to 12 months of employment, 99 between 13 and 24 months, and 64 between 25 and 36 months. In all, 381 subjects were investigated within 36 months of employment.

Most (71 percent) investigated employees were hired between 1994 and 1998, in part because of rapid ID growth in the mid-1990s. During that period many existing criminal laws were enhanced, and new laws mandating longer sentences were enacted. Texas spent $1 billion on prison construction in the early 1990s, and thousands of individuals were hired to manage the influx of new prisoners (Robison, 1991). Between 1995 and 1998, the ID prison population increased from 118,386 to 140,718, and the number of prisons jumped from 69 to 108. Between 1995 and 1998, TDCJ-ID also increased its annual operating budget from $1.5 to $2 billion, increased the number of employees from 35,458 to 39,418, and increased its total security force from 18,920 to 27,509 (Camp and Camp, 1995–1998). Roughly equal numbers of subjects were assigned to "old" prisons (1989 and earlier) and to "new" prisons (1990 and later). Fifty-five percent were terminated or dismissed, 23 percent resigned, and 31 percent received disciplinary probation.[8] Employees who resigned did so after they were confronted with the prospect of an investigation. Those who resigned were allowed to leave the prison service without any negative comments or blemishes in their personnel file. We also realize that some unknown number of employees simply quit to avoid formal investigation when they felt they were under suspicion.

Eligible applicants undergo an interview and take five pre-employment tests.[9] A final evaluation score is computed from the combination of pre-employment tests, along with nine dimensions evaluated by interviewers. Applicants with high school diplomas, no felony convictions, and evaluation scores of 60 and above are offered positions. Human resource managers review applicants with scores of 59 and below; depending on the factors that caused the low score and on the needs for facility personnel, some applicants may be offered employment. The average evaluation score for investigated employees was 63; 119 (23 percent), however, scored 59 or less, and one scored 38.

In summary, the "average" employee investigated for establishing an inappropriate relationship with an inmate was a 31-year-old white female with a high school diploma and a history of service and nonmilitary work, who was employed by the prison system in the mid-1990s as a uniformed security officer. These employees typically established an inappropriate inmate relationship within 36 months of employment.

Findings

In this section we compare the "investigated" employees with the "successful" employees, and apply Strom-Gottfried's (1999) continuum of boundary violations to the data from the Texas prison system. We then discuss the importance of situational dynamics as a possible explanation for inappropriate relationships in prisons.

Investigated versus Non-investigated Employees

As stated above, prison human resource administrators wanted to know, for recruiting and training purposes, whether significant demographic differences existed between successful and unsuccessful employees. Accordingly we gathered relevant background and ID employment data from a random sample of 585 noninvestigated employees to compare with the investigated employees (see table 2). A comparative analysis uncovered several important differences between the two groups. Investigated employees were significantly more likely than nondisciplined employees to be Anglos and females. In addition, they were significantly more likely than successful employees to have a general equivalency degree instead of a high school diploma, were significantly less likely to have military experience, and scored significantly lower on the pre-employment application (with average scores of 63 versus 68). Another important and statistically significant difference involved prior

Table 2 Investigated Staff Members Compared with Sample of Successful Staff Members, 1995–1998

Variable	Investigated Staff (N = 508)	Successful Staff (N = 585)
Race/Ethnicity*		
White	54%	51%
African-American	30	27
Hispanic	16	22
Gender***		
Male	23%	68%
Female	77	32
Education***		
GED	32%	14%
High school diploma	68	86
Marital Status		
Married	50%	52%
Single	50	48
Military Experience***		
Yes	15%	26%
No	85	74
Employment History		
Service	86%	93%
Supervisory	14	7
Prior Disciplinary Violations***		
Yes	45%	31%
No	55	69
Application Score***		
59 or less	24%	11%
60 and above	76	89
Average Application Score***	63	68
Average Age at Employment	31	31

* $p < .05$; *** $p < .001$

disciplinary problems: 45 percent of the investigated employees had at least one disciplinary write-up, compared with 31 percent of the noninvestigated employee group.

Analyses of Three Kinds of Boundary Violations

Using Strom-Gottfried's (1999) categorization scheme, we found that 38 employees (8 percent) had committed general boundary violations, 428 (80 percent) had engaged in dual relationships, and 42 (12 percent) had had sexual contact with prisoners (see table 3). A significant relationship emerged between gender and the type of boundary violation: female employees were more likely than males to commit a boundary violation, and 80 percent of nonsexual dual relationships involved female employees. Minor breaks typically resulted in disciplinary probation, while more serious boundary violations led to severe punishment. Employees investigated for dual relationships were significantly younger (average age 30) than employees investigated for the other boundary violations. In 1998 the average age of an ID prisoner was 35; this age differential (35 to 30) may be related in some way to dual relationships.

General Boundary Violations.   Among the 38 employees who committed general boundary violations (e.g., accepted or exchanged food products or craft work/materials with prisoners, or wrote letters to prisoners), most were Anglo (53 percent) and female (63 percent), had high school diplomas, and were 36 years old when hired by the ID. Most (79 percent) were hired between 1994 and 1998, and were investigated (66 percent) between 1997 and 1998. Slightly more than three-quarters (76 percent) were punished with disciplinary probation and received a second chance. All admitted their offense and expressed some degree of remorse.

The following vignettes (taken from the case files) illustrate common themes involved in general boundary violations:

> *Case 1.* In April 1998, Officer Daly admitted that she corresponded with Inmate Y and submitted a written statement that she was writing the inmate. She also stated that she had known Y before his current incarceration and did not realize that corresponding with former inmate friends was a violation of policy. She freely admitted that they were friends and that she wrote all the letters.

> *Case 2.* In a written statement, Officer Jones admitted that he corresponded with Inmate A. He wrote: "I have known A since we was kids. His mom used to baby sit me. We have been friends before I became a CO [correctional officer]. I wasn't thinking when I wrote him. I did not mean to break policy. I thought I would write to give an old friend some advice."

> *Case 3.* In July 1997, a unit investigation found that Officer Bailey deposited $20 in Inmate B's trust fund in return for a leather watchband.

When confronted, Bailey admitted to the actions and further stated, "I deeply regret this and apologize for my actions and want disciplinary actions. I didn't think this was a big deal."

Table 3   Investigated Staff Members' Background Characteristics, 1995–1998

| | Type of Boundary Violation | | |
| | General Boundary Violations (*n* = 38) | Dual Relationships (*n* = 428) | Sexual Involvement (*n* = 42) |
Variables			
Race/Ethnicity			
African-American	29%	30%	36%
White	53	55	50
Hispanic	18	15	14
Gender***			
Male	37%	20%	40%
Female	63	80	60
Education			
GED	32%	32%	31%
High school diploma	68	68	69
Marital Status			
Married	43%	49%	66%
Single	57	51	34
Year Hired			
1977–1987	8%	5%	4%
1988–1993	13	25	17
1994–1998	79	70	79
Year Investigated			
1995	21%	26%	19%
1996	13	31	45
1997	32	27	24
1998	34	16	12
Case Outcome**			
Terminated/dismissed	16%	57%	62%
Probation	76	19	5
Resigned	8	24	33
Unit Opened 1989 and Before	37%	48%	45%
Unit Opened 1990 and After	63	52	55
Application Score			
59 or less	24%	24%	17%
60 and above	76	76	83
Mean Application Score	64	63	65
Average Age at Employment*	36	30	34
Average Age at Termination	38	35	39
Mean Number of Months on Job	35	57	36

* $p < .05$; ** $p < .01$; *** $p < .001$

Most (63 percent) general boundary violations occurred in "newer" prisons. This finding suggests four possible explanations. First, it is plausible that the new units were flooded with rookies who failed, through ineffective training and supervision, to internalize the boundaries between themselves and inmates. When new employees enter a new prison, they may not know the organizational cultural taboos. The rapid expansion of the workforce may have weakened the organizational culture, as well as overwhelming the institutional norms that govern inmate-staff relationships. White (1995) states:

> During periods of organizational turbulence, there is a weakening of organizational culture and values. The organization loses its power to shape, monitor, and self-correct boundary problems within worker-client relationships. Weak organizational cultures lose the capacity to define boundaries of appropriateness in service relationships. Weak organizational cultures exert little influence or control on individual practitioners. Rapid staff turnover or growth opens up the possibility of new workers and emergent subcultures that deviate from an organization's historical values. Turbulence within organizational systems, just as in family systems, marks a period of great vulnerability for role boundary violations. (p. 189)

Second, organizational pressure to recruit staff may have led to the erosion of standards, compromising hiring practices between 1995 and 1998. Similarly, the rapid expansion of police forces in New York, Washington, Miami, Houston, and Detroit led to careless screening and hasty training, which contributed to increases in police corruption and brutality (Krauss, 1994). The recent Board of Inquiry into the Rampart area corruption incident in the Los Angeles Police Department attributed the criminal activity of several officers to accelerated hiring practices (in the late 1980s and early 1990s) and to the erosion of hiring standards (Board of Inquiry, 2000).

The interviewees maintained that massive prison expansion eroded hiring standards: in the rush to build prisons and attract "warm bodies" to staff the new prisons, hiring standards declined. As one supervisor stated:

> The hiring standards were loosened up to staff the units. They had to hire whoever they could. Look, this prison system is so big now that I believe we have exhausted the labor pool of decent applicants. They hired anybody that was warm and could walk. Inappropriate relationships? The reason for these things is due to a lack of standards. It only stands to reason that when you lower the standards you get a lower-quality employee. Poor employees translate into management problems.

Third, it is possible that new units were staffed with new or inexperienced supervisors, who enforced employee rules and regulations aggressively. General boundary violations may have been the form of misconduct most visible for remediation.

Fourth, some of the post-1990 prison units are new-generation prisons, with an open design, which could reduce the supervisors' span of control and facilitate staff-inmate deviance. In short, new prison architecture may be associated with inappropriate relationships.

All four explanations underscore the unintended consequences of organizational growth on employees' misconduct, and require further research. In addition, organizational growth represents a serious historical effect that could confound the internal validity of the present inquiry (Cook and Campbell, 1979). The data presented here clarify the effects of system expansion on personnel recruitment and boundary violations.

Dual Relationships. As stated above, the analysis found 428 employees who broke the custodial frame by becoming personally involved with an inmate. Each of these employees was both a friend and a supervisor of an inmate. Dual relationships commonly involved Anglos (55 percent), females (80 percent), security officers (91 percent), and male prisoners. These relationships involved one employee and one prisoner, and appeared to be consensual. Most of the employees had high school diplomas (68 percent), were hired between 1994 and 1998 (70 percent), and were investigated in 1996 and 1997 (58 percent); more than half were terminated (57 percent). Their average age was 30 at employment, and they were on the job for roughly five years at the time of investigation.

We failed to determine whether inmates or employees initiated these custodial framebreaks. The employees' accounts of the events, however, suggest that inmates initiated the relationship for a variety of reasons such as companionship, loneliness, money, desire for favoritism, sex, contraband, boredom, and competition with other inmates. It is possible, for example, that male inmates engaged in "fox hunting" and manipulated the employees to violate policy (Sapp, 1997). The employees' version of the events revealed no instances in which the inmate forced the staff member into a relationship. The staff members allowed the relationships to develop despite their training.

Dual or overlapping relationships involved a process or series of steps. Glances were exchanged; notes, photographs, and rings were passed; smiles and friendly conversations were offered. Typically an inmate engaged an employee in small talk (e.g., on the weather or current events). If an employee reciprocated, then other topics (such as personal likes and dislikes or home and social life) were broached incrementally until the employee disclosed sensitive personal information (e.g., marital status, friends, and off-duty interests). In other cases, an inmate passed a "hook letter" (see below) to an employee and waited for a response. Employees who corresponded with the prisoners were approached and engaged in additional small talk. Sometimes an employee requested a duty assignment near his or her inmate "friend."

Dear Officer Jones:

Commit thy works unto the Lord, and thy thoughts shall be established. (Proverbs 16:3)

Giving all praises an [sic] honor to the Lord and Savior, Jesus Christ. I'm praying that this small note becomes a long lasting friendship based on truth and honesty. To let you know that I am a honest man from the heart. Just searching for someone to relate to on verious [sic] issues of life. Most of all, life itself and what it truly means. To let you know a few things about me; I'm 36 years of age and I have a 30 yr. sentence. This is time that has no true meaning. I'm from Houston's North side. I'm a quiet type of guy and I stay to myself most of the time. So if this grabs you or even suits your fancy. Let me know, and of course let me know what turns you on and makes you happy. Just maybe I'm that friend you've been looking for.

"Looking to hear from you!"

Ricky

Dual relationships were typified by "lovesickness" (Gonsiorek, 1995) — situations in which employees became infatuated and then fell in love with inmates. These employees desired a soulmate. The two typically exchanged letters detailing their life histories, goals, aspirations, and devotion to each other. Many letters contained erotic themes and a desire for marriage when the inmate was paroled. Dual or overlapping boundary violations often involved romantic love and idealization of the inmate. Some employee-inmate correspondence revealed that female employees were drawn to male offenders to "straighten them up" or to tame a "rowdy man." In other cases, the employees were so consumed with romantic love that they identified (like Patty Hearst) with the prisoners rather than with the staff. The following vignettes from employees' letters or cards to inmates illustrate the intense emotions at work in dual relationships:

Dear Jay, As I lay here alone, listening to music, all I can think of is you. Do you realize that in such a little time we developed a love that is undescribable. In my heart I have so many feelings, we have a bond that will last forever. I need you at home with me so that I can love you right, you're my dreams, love, and you being locked up is the ultimate test of our friendship and love. (Female employee to male inmate)

I love you, I need you. I want you. Forget the past, I only wanna hear about the future. I dream about you every night. Please don't leave. I would marry you now. (Female employee to male inmate)

I love you as always. I have you in my thoughts and dreams. Girl you will always have a special place in my heart. I love you, and your whole body. God just made you so beautiful — I can't resist you. Oh yeah, never argue with the officers for It's bad news. (Male employee to female inmate)

I love you and I love this feeling also, the desire, the anxiety and excitement. I can't wait to get to work. (Female employee to male inmate)

Look darling, We've been through a lot together. We've risked a lot together and Today we came together to be man and wife. I am not only your friend and lover, or girlfriend anymore. I am your partner in life. I will always be there for you until the end of time. This is my solemn vow to you. PS. They are watching all the female officers because of that shit with that boss on the first shift, be careful. (Female employee to male inmate)

Remember I love you. My heart is yours forever. I know there is an age difference between us, but that does not matter to me because I love you, I live for the time that we can be together. (Male employee to female inmate)

These letters voiced obsession, excitement, romantic love, and a desire for a life together beyond the penitentiary. These employees were eager to come to work and to overlook the prisoner's criminal past. In eight dual relationships, the employee fell in love with an inmate gang member. Many married employees caught up in dual relationships appeared to be personally vulnerable.

Employees investigated for this violation often went to great lengths to keep the relationship secret. When we examined employee-inmate messages and letters, we often found employees instructing inmates to "keep a low profile," "lay low, they're [security staff] watching us," or "keep away for now, let things cool down." Security staff members often accidentally discovered the relationship during cell/property searches, after finding the employee's artifacts (e.g., love letters, poems, cards, photos) in the inmate's possession. In four incidents, inmate property searches unearthed an employee's cellular telephone. In one case, an inmate informed unit supervisors of an employee-inmate dual relationship "because everybody knows about it and it was causing friction on the wing." In two cases, employee-inmate relationships were discovered when the employee's name was found boldly tattooed, one on an inmate's stomach and the other on an inmate's leg. In six cases, the employee's spouse uncovered love letters in the employee's possession and informed unit supervisors. In four cases, investigated employees spoke of their relationships to their colleagues, who then informed investigators.

Where were the supervisors? The Mollen Commission, which investigated police wrongdoing in the New York City Police Department, reported that supervisors had a "willful blindness" to police misconduct (Commission to Investigate, 1994). The supervisors did not want the bad publicity and scandal that would follow if it was discovered that employees under their watch were engaged in misconduct. As a result, they looked the other way and refused to take action against officer wrongdoing. It is possible that the prison supervisors in Texas knew of dual relationships but practiced "willful blindness" to avoid scandal and embarrassment to the agency.

Sexual Contact. Forty-two acts of employee-inmate sexual contact occurred between 1995 and 1998, accounting for 8 percent of all boundary violations. Similarly, Strom-Gottfried (1999) found that over an 11-year period, 12 percent of all ethics complaints submitted by clients to the National Association of Social Workers dealt with sexual violations. Half of the prison employees were Anglos, 60 percent were women, and 79 percent were hired between 1994 and 1998. Over two-thirds had high school diplomas (69 percent), and nearly all were security staff members (90 percent) in their early thirties (average age 34) at the time of employment. These employees averaged three years on the job when they were investigated for sexual contact. Two-thirds were married; we had no information on the quality of the spousal relationship, however. Forty incidents involved heterosexual contact; two (5 percent) were same-sex pairings (male-male). A similar percentage (4 to 5 percent) was found in the literature on sexual contact between male therapists and male clients (Gonsiorek, 1995). Most of the employees investigated for sexual contact were terminated (62 percent) or resigned (33 percent) from employment. The National Institute of Corrections (2000:10–11) recently reported that in fiscal year 1998, more than 115 officers were discharged for substantiated incidents of sexual contact with inmates, and 20 were prosecuted. (Data were taken from 37 agencies.)

The following vignettes illustrate "typical" acts of employee-inmate sexual contact:

> *Case 1.* In a written statement, Officer Flanigan stated that I was working the night shift and doing my rounds in a dormitory and I saw inmate J masturbating in her bunk. I walked up to her and told her to stop but she unzipped my pants and rubbed my penis and placed it in her mouth. Well after that she demanded $40 from me and then $80. I didn't pay and she turned me in. I admit to the whole thing and I know I was wrong.

> *Case 2.* In a written statement, Officer Adams admitted that she loved inmate D and was involved in a personal relationship with D going on two years. Adams stated that she got to know D through casual conversations, which eventually grew into the present relationship. Adams also stated that she was in love with D and had discussed marriage and life together after he was released. Adams admitted that the two had engaged in acts of sexual intercourse in the chapel. She also admitted that she placed $350 in D's trust fund.

> *Case 3.* In written statements, Lieutenant Tan and Sergeant Green stated that they witnessed Officer Hays [female employee] stroking and fondling inmate H's penis in the dayroom. Officer Hay was also kissing inmate H and stroking his buttocks. When confronted by unit supervisors, Officer Hays, who was married and had two children, admitted the acts were true.

Case 4. In a written statement, Officer Toms observed Officer Fun-worth [female employee] being fondled by inmate A. The inmate had his hands under the shirt of Officer F and was fondling her breasts and she did nothing to stop it. When confronted, inmate A and Officer F admitted the act and Officer F resigned in lieu of termination.

Sexual contact typically occurred away from supervisory staff, a finding that parallels the police literature (Kappeler et al., 1994). Kitchen, chapel, closets, laundry, library, bathrooms, and offices were the primary locales for sexual contact. Discovery by coworkers was usually acciden-tal. In eight incidents, unit supervisors staked out the employee by cap-turing the incident on film, on microphone, and/or through "wired" inmates. In the other cases, suspected employees under investigation for dual relationships admitted to the relationship and sexual contact when confronted by investigators.

The employees' version of sexual contact illustrates the strong gender differences in this form of occupational deviance. Male employees typi-cally were sexual predators. The male prison officers' uniform (as a symbol of power and authority) and their custodial access to female prisoners were conducive to exploitation (Kraska and Kappeler, 1995). Female prison employees' motivation for sexual contact with prisoners involved love and postprison commitments. We found no evidence that female employees used sex as a mechanism (a commodity or a quid pro quo) to exploit inmates for personal gain. The inmates' perspective, when examined, will support or negate the female employees' interpretation of the situation.

Comparison of Boundary Violations by Situations

Four general types of situation led to official punishment. The employees did not simply violate policy in a vacuum; various situational dynamics must be accounted for or explained. Table 4 presents the find-ings from a comparative analysis of the three boundary violations by the four situations. We found a statistically significant relationship between boundary violations and situations.

Rescue Situations. In these situations, an employee felt sorry for a prisoner and then broke the rules to aid or assist him or her. We found only five rescue situations, but they involved unusual contexts worthy of separate treatment. In one instance, an employee placed money in the inmate's trust fund after the inmate told the employee of his dire situa-tion, "now that he had AIDS." In another instance, a male employee wanted to "save" an inmate from a lesbian relationship, and counseled her on religious proscriptions against homosexuality. Rescue situations typically involved employees who violated organizational policies to save inmates from a "life-threatening" situation. Rescuers expressed no remorse about their actions and insisted that they were providing "ther-apy" to the inmate.

Table 4 Boundary Violations Compared with Situations, 1995–1998

Type of Situation	Type of Boundary Violation***			
	General Boundary Violations	Dual Relationships	Sexual Acts	Total
Rescuer	.00% (0)	1.00% (4)	2.00% (1)	5
Naïveté/Accidents	84.00% (32)	16.00% (67)	2.00% (1)	100
Lovesick	13.00% (5)	75.00% (326)	60.00% (25)	356
Predators	3.00% (1)	7.00% (31)	36.00% (15)	47
Count	38	428	42	508

NOTE: Numbers are given in parentheses.
*** $p < .001$

Naïveté or Accidents.   One hundred employees were involved in situations that we defined loosely as naïveté or accidents: situations in which the employees appeared to be naïve or socially unaware about the professional relationship between themselves and inmates (Gabbard and Lester, 1995). The employees apparently were poorly prepared for correctional work, and/or had failed to internalize or understand) the custodial frame. We found several employees who tried to place money in an inmate's trust fund after purchasing craftwork from the inmate. The hallmark of these naïve situations or accidents was remorse; the employees all expressed profound self-reproach for not knowing the rules, and regretted their transgression. Further, 69 of these situations occurred in newer prison units; this finding suggests a link between expansion, organizational culture, and the internalization of professional boundaries by employees and supervisors. Additional preservice training may be needed to prepare new employees to work in new units.

Lovesickness.   We found 356 employees enmeshed in lovesick situations. These involved "romantic idealism," in which the employee disregarded the offender's personal history, placed the inmate on a pedestal, and fantasized about life together when the inmate was released. Their love was regarded as so extraordinary that employee policies and ethical codes were irrelevant (Gabbard, 1995). In dual or overlapping boundary violations and lovesick situations, romantic love and idealization of the inmate were often combined.

Seventy-five percent of all dual/overlapping relationships involved lovesick situations. Additional data analysis found that 268 (75 percent)

of these relationships involved female employees: The employee perceived the inmate as a person, a boyfriend, or a soulmate. These employees actively fostered a relationship with an inmate, typified by the letters
presented above. Some married employees had experienced a cata-
strophic traumatic event before or during employment: their correspondence to inmates mentioned domestic violence, sexual frustration,
marital strife or discord, boredom, ruptured dreams, or separation from
their spouses. Others felt at a loss because their children had left the nest,
or someone close to them had passed away. This personal vulnerability
then was sensed by the inmates, who seized upon the employees' troubles to manipulate the situation.

Personal vulnerability coupled with institutional vulnerability
(proximity to and manipulation by inmates) fostered or enhanced
employees' deviance. Gabbard and Lester (1995) noted a similar phenomenon among therapists who fell in love with their patients, in which infatuation occurred in connection with extreme stress in the analyst's life
(e.g., divorce, separation, disillusionment with their own career or marriage). The prison employees willingly accepted the inmates' attention
and violated policy.

The combination of dual relationships and lovesick situations
unfolded in duty posts such as the laundry, commissary, issue room,
kitchen, library, chapel, dormitories, and mailroom. These situations
often involved one employee (in an out-of-the-way location) and one or
more prisoners. We realize that prison employees, regardless of gender,
are assigned to a variety of duty posts on the basis of need. Lovesick situations, however, develop in institutional areas where supervisory contact
is minimal and where employees and offenders can interact with each
other as males and females, eroding the boundary between employee and
offender. Not all female employees who work (for example) in ID stew-
ards' departments succumb to prisoners' advances; our data simply suggest that specific hot spots exist in the units and bear close supervision.

Subsequent data analysis led us to conclude that the combination of
dual relationships and lovesick situations led to sexual encounters: 60
percent of the sexual contacts involved lovesick situations. These data
suggest a slippery slope, in which some employees (at least those who
were caught) who develop a romantic relationship with an inmate have
sexual contact. The progression from nonsexual to sexual contact has
been found as well among psychotherapist-patient relationships (Stake
and Oliver, 1991; Strasburger, Jorgenson, and Sutherland, 1992).

Predators.   We found 47 predatory situations in which employees
sought out and manipulated prisoners, and thought they could get away
with it for personal or private gain (Friedman and Boumil, 1995). In these
situations, the employee actively preyed on an inmate for money, property, and/or sex. One employee, for example, established relationships
with offenders and then cased their possessions and stole their property

(e.g., watches, necklaces, rings) under the cover of cell searches. Male employees were more likely to become involved in predatory situations.

Kraska and Kappeler (1995; see also Horswell, 2000; Vaughn, 1999) demonstrated that police sexual violations ranged from unobtrusive behavior (e.g., viewing photographs of victims) to criminal behavior (e.g., sexual assault). We found two primary types of correctional employee-inmate sexual contact.

First, as stated above, 25 cases (60 percent) involved lovesick situations: 22 employees were females and three were males. Similarly, Gartrell and colleagues (1986) found that 65 percent of psychiatrists who were sexually involved with a patient described themselves as in love with the patient. Among the prison employees, we found many letters filled with declarations of love, infatuation, lifetime commitment, and plans beyond the penitentiary. Some employees and inmates even exchanged vows and rings, and referred to themselves as married couples.

The employees' stories suggests that staff members took their first small steps down the slippery slope of boundary erosion, and ended up much farther down than they ever could have imagined (Strasburger et al., 1992). Our findings support those of Strom-Gottfried (1999), who found that clinicians who "break frame" often proceed from minor to major transgressions. How many dual relationships culminate in sexual contact is unknown.

In addition, we found 15 cases (all male employees and female prisoners) of employee-inmate sexual contact that involved predatory situations. In 14 of these cases, male employees used their position and power to procure sexual favors from female prisoners, such as sex in exchange for preferential treatment or marriage upon release. Sex becomes a commodity, and an underground economy evolves between male staff and female prisoners; this situation encourages female prisoners to prostitute themselves in exchange for preferential treatment and to avoid punishment or harm. Such behavior institutionalizes a form of exploitation and sexual slavery (Jolin, 1994). The predatory situations we researched paralleled Sapp's (1997:146) discussion of "sexual shakedowns" committed by police officers.

Currently it is unknown whether or not these 14 employees have been criminally prosecuted or have been served with civil lawsuits. All were terminated from prison employment. In one case of sexual contact, a male employee cohabited with a female parolee, whom he met while she was incarcerated. Upon questioning, both admitted to sexual activity. Under current Texas law, it is a second-degree felony (sexual assault) for a public servant to coerce another individual to participate in sexual activity (Texas Penal Code, 2000). The data suggest that male prison employees, like police officers, may be engaging in sexual activity with female prisoners simply because they can. The presence of numerous potential partners in routine encounters with inmates provides the opportunity for seduction (Crank, 1998:145).

Female prisoners, like women in the wider community, are at risk of victimization by coercive sexual strategies simply because of their gender (Finkelhor and Asdigian, 1996; Pogrebin and Poole, 1997). The data displayed in table 4 illustrate that employees' boundary violations were linked conceptually to certain situations. Our findings indicate the need to view each boundary violation and the specific situation as part of a process rather than as an isolated deviant episode. For example, employees might begin by asking inmates about their life and how they arrived in prison. An inmate might respond to this concern by writing the employee a note of thanks. If the employee reciprocates, the inmate receives a "mixed message" and assumes that the employee wants a relationship.

Inappropriate employee-inmate relationships often involved a mixture of situations, behaviors, emotions, needs, and human desires. Breaking the custodial frame entails an array of actions that must be considered in combination with various situational determinants. Our analyses of boundary violations and situational contexts illustrate the complexity of such inappropriate relationships.

Additional analyses (not reported in table 4) revealed a significant finding when we examined the relationship between incidents and the average number of months on the job at time of punishment. Employees involved in predatory situations averaged nearly 11 years of tenure at punishment. Predator situations are probably difficult to detect because employees take great care to cover their actions. It also appears that rescue situations occur quickly, illustrating how readily prisoners can manipulate receptive employees. Oddly, employees caught in naïveté or accident situations averaged 44 months of tenure at punishment. We expected these situations to unfold more quickly and cannot account for this finding, unless it relates to the difficulty of detection and the need for thorough investigation. Employees caught in lovesick situations averaged 37 months at punishment.

Why would seemingly normal employees become romantically (and even sexually) involved with prisoners? Haney, Banks, and Zimbardo (1973) posed a similar question when they asked why bright, emotionally stable young male college students (most of whom were in the peace movement) would abuse their fellow students in a prisonlike environment. Their answer to this question emphasized the surprising power of institutional environments over the participants (Haney and Zimbardo, 1998:710). As Haney and colleagues (1973:90) suggested, "[T]he abnormality here [the mock prison] resided in the psychological nature of the situation and not in those who passed through it." Over the past 27 years, these researchers have generated a body of research that clearly illustrates how "mind altering social psychological dynamics" can bend and twist human behavior (Haney and Zimbardo, 1998:710). If one accepts the situational explanation, then complex issues such as consent become difficult to define and comprehend. The inmates' version must be researched if we are to fully ascertain how and why these dual relationships develop.

Discussion and Conclusions

This paper represents the first study of boundary violations between correctional employees and inmates. It is based on four years of data, 1995–1998, a period of substantial organizational expansion that could affect the validity of our findings (Cook and Campbell, 1979). Also, our formulation of the continuum of boundary violations and situational dynamics is incomplete. Clearly the types of boundary violations overlap, and it is not possible to arrange a linear relationship among these behaviors (Strom-Gottfried, 1999). We suspect that each combination of boundary violation and situation contains subsets of other violations, as in the case of dual relationships and lovesick situations.

With these warnings in mind, we produced several important findings with implications for correctional personnel management, training, theory, and research on occupational deviance in penal settings.

First, the most important finding from our analysis was that inappropriate employee-inmate relationships must be understood as boundary violations. Custodial framebreaks involved various behaviors and activities. In this way, Strom-Gottfried's (1999) conceptualization of boundary violations (general, dual/overlapping, and sexual) enhances our understanding of this phenomenon in prisons. Dual/overlapping relationships were the most frequent form of deviance; typically they involved female employees who became romantically involved with prisoners. Boundary violations, especially dual relationships, involved a process or sequence of behaviors that transpired over weeks and months.

Second, our comparative analysis found that employees who broke the custodial frame were significantly more likely than not to be Anglos and females who had a GED and no military experience. Investigated employees received significantly lower pre-employment evaluation scores than successful employees; lower scores were risk markers for boundary violations. Investigated employees also were more likely than successful employees to have a history of rule violations.

Third, inappropriate employee-inmate relationships unfolded in specific situations. The most common context involved lovesick female employees who, through manipulation by inmates or their own volition, negated the role differences between themselves and the inmate. These employees viewed the inmate as a soulmate, a boyfriend or girlfriend, a pen pal lover, or a future spouse. The most important aspect of these situations was the employee's recasting of the offender as a nonprisoner or a "person who just happens to be in prison." In some cases, the employee identified with the prisoner. Ironically, inmates, rather than being powerless in their dealings with the staff, exert some control over interested employees. Naïveté/accident situations often occurred at newer prison units; thus it is possible that organizational expansion may precipitate these situations as a result of an unsettled organizational culture.

Fourth, most custodial framebreaks occurred within 36 months of employment. The first 12 months of tenure represent an at-risk period in which some employees (e.g., those with low application scores and with general equivalency diplomas) have not bonded to the organization, and perceive offenders to be "just other people." Perhaps seasoned employees could conduct additional on-the-job training, stressing the pitfalls and consequences of boundary violations to strengthen the new employees' ties to the organization. The interviewees strongly suggested that prison organizations should use "field training officers" (like their police counterparts) to guide and mentor new employees in the critical first few months on the job. Under the rubric of employee survival skills, the Texas prison system recently has expanded its pre-service training from one hour on "games inmates play" to nearly eight hours. This change in training underscores the agency's sensitivity to employees' vulnerability, and to the need for tools to forestall further problems.

Fifth, sexual violations represented 8 percent (or 42 cases) of all violations, a figure paralleling the research on sexual contact in other occupations. Most sexual contacts involved lovesick female employees; these situations suggest the escalation of an employee-inmate relationship from nonsexual to sexual contact. We found 14 male employees who used their position to procure sexual favors from female prisoners. Sexual contact is the most serious violation of professional conduct: currently, in 42 states, legislation prohibits sexual contact between correctional employees and inmates. Since 1996, 20 departments of corrections have developed or revised their policies regarding sexual misconduct (National Institute of Corrections, 2000).

Sixth, research is needed on the effects of sex-role spillover in prisons. Females employed in male prisons and males employed in female prisons work in nontraditional jobs, and sex-role spillover can be studied empirically as an underlying factor contributing to employees' boundary violations. Such research also will clarify the changing and complex nature of the corruption of authority.

The deviant employees studied here violated policy voluntarily. To suggest that there was something wrong with them initially implies that improved recruitment, proper screening measures, psychological tests, and incentives (i.e., merit raises) can eliminate inappropriate personal contact between employees and inmates. Osgood et al. (1996:639), however, suggest that "most people have the potential for at least occasionally succumbing to an opportunity for deviant behavior." Future prison researchers, like their police counterparts (Sherman, 1980), must examine the individual, situational, and organizational correlates of boundary violations in prisons. Such violations, and the situations in which they unfold, are an ironic aspect of the pathology of imprisonment, as well as an eternal defect of total power.

Endnotes

[1] We interviewed one of the first women employed as a security officer in a male Texas prison. She said she interacted with a notorious male prisoner who worked in the front office with her. Shortly after the inmate was paroled, he was killed while robbing a 7-11. Upon hearing of the inmate's death, the officer became upset. She remembered saying to a coworker "Who would want to kill Bill [an alias]? He was just trying to make it." This employee assumed that Bill was working in the store, not that he was trying to rob it. This story illustrates how staff members sometimes see inmates as people who happen to be in prison rather than as dangerous felons.

[2] See Coble v. Texas Department of Corrections (1983); Dothard v. Rawlinson (1977); Griffin v. Michigan Department of Corrections (1982); Grummett v. Rushen (1985).

[3] Eighty-eight employees had alleged or inferred sexual contacts, and 32 engaged in non-sexual contacts (e.g., hugging, hand holding).

[4] Studies of psychologists have yielded rates of sex misconduct between 5 percent and 12 percent for males, and 1 percent and 3 percent for females (Stake and Oliver, 1991). Research on male psychotherapists revealed that 7 percent had reported sexual contact with female clients (Pope and Bouhoutsos, 1986). Kardener, Fuller, and Mensch, (1973) found that between 5 percent and 13 percent of therapists had engaged in erotic behavior with their patients. We found that 5 percent of the female officers and 4 percent of the males engaged in sexual misconduct with inmates.

[5] Rule 42, Employee-Inmate/Client Relationships (association or correspondence): Employees are prohibited from continuing or establishing any personal relationships with inmates/clients or with family members of inmates/clients which jeopardizes, or has the potential to jeopardize the security of the Agency or which compromises the effectiveness or the employee. Employees are required to report to agency officials any previous or current relationships between: (1) the employee with an inmate/client; (2) the employee with a family member of an inmate/client; (3) a family member of the employee with an inmate/client; or (4) a family member of the employee with a family member of an inmate/client.

[6] Parole/health services staff members work for separate agencies. We lacked access to these records.

[7] We began in 1995 because these personnel files represented the most recent and most accessible files for individual review, coding, and analysis.

[8] Internal Affairs investigators informed us that employees who resigned would have been terminated in most cases. Therefore we decided to keep resignation in the database.

[9] The criteria are as follows: (1) eligible to work in the United States; (2) at least 18 years old, with no age maximum; (3) high school diploma or GED; (4) males age 18 to 25 must be registered with the Selective Service; (5) not on active duty in the military; (6) no felony or convictions for drug-related offense; (7) no convictions for offense involving domestic violence; (8) no Class A or B misdemeanor convictions within the last 5 years; (9) not on probation for any criminal offense or pending charges; and (10) pass TDCJ pre-employment test and drug test.

References

Amnesty International. (1999). *Sexual Abuse, International Women's Day, 1999*. London, UK: Amnesty International.

Baro, A. (1997). Spheres of consent: An analysis of the sexual abuse and sexual exploitation of women incarcerated in the State of Hawaii. *Women and Criminal Justice, 8*, 61–84.

Board of Inquiry. (2000, March 1). Rampart area corruption incident, Los Angeles police department. Bernard C. Parks, Chief of Police, Executive Summary.

Camp, C., & Camp, G. (1995–1998). *Corrections yearbook, 1995–1998.* Middletown, CT: Criminal Justice Institute, Inc.

Carroll, L. (1974). *Hacks, blacks, and cons: Race relations in a maximum security prison.* Lexington, MA: Lexington Books.

Commission to Investigate. (1994). The report of the commission to investigate allegations of police corruption and the anti-corruption procedures of the New York City police department. New York: City of New York.

Cook, T., & Campbell, D. (1979). *Quasi-experimentation: Design and analysis issues for field settings.* Boston, MA: Houghton Mifflin.

Crank, J. (1998). *Understanding police culture.* Cincinnati, OH: Anderson.

Crouch, B. M., & Marquart, J. (1980). On becoming a prison guard. In B. M. Crouch (Ed.), *The keepers: Prison guards and contemporary corrections* (pp. 63–106). Springfield, IL: Thomas.

Crouch, B. M., & Marquart, J. (1989). *An appeal to justice: Litigated reform of Texas prisons.* Austin: University of Texas Press.

Day, A. (1998). Cruel and unusual punishment of female inmates: The need for redress under 42 U.S.C. 1983. *Santa Clara Law Review, 38,* 555–587.

DiIulio, J. (1987). *Governing prisons.* New York: Free Press.

Dobash, R., Dobash, R., & Gutteridge, S. (1986). *The imprisonment of women.* Oxford: Basil Blackwell.

Elliot, J. (1999, October 4). Former parole officer liable in civil suit. *Texas Lawyer,* 9–12.

Epstein, R. (1994). *Keeping boundaries.* Washington, DC: American Psychiatric Press.

Erikson, K. (1966). *Wayward Puritans.* New York: Wiley.

Eschholz, S., & Vaughn, M. (2001). Police sexual violence and rape myths: Civil liability under section 1983. *Journal of Criminal Justice, 29,* 389–405.

Finkelhor, D., & Asdigian, N. (1996). Risk factors for youth victimization. *Violence and Victims, 11,* 3–19.

Friedman, J., & Boumil, M. (1995). *Betrayal of trust: Sex and power in professional relationships.* Westport, CT: Praeger.

Gabbard, G. (1995). The early history of boundary violation in psychoanalysis. *Journal of the American Psychoanalytic Association, 43,* 1115–1136.

Gabbard, G., & Lester, E. (1995). *Boundaries and boundary violation in psychoanalysis.* New York: Basic Books.

Gartrell, N., Herman, J., Olarte, S., Feldstein, M., & Localio, R. (1986). Psychiatrist-patient sexual contact: Results of a national survey. *American Journal of Psychiatry, 14,* 690–694.

Geier, A. (2000). Smith says she had sex with a guard. Associated Press. Retrieved August 31, 2000 (http://www.Charleston.net).

Goffman, E. (1974). *Frame analysis.* Boston, MA: Northeastern University Press.

Gonsiorek, D. (1995). *Breach of trust: Sexual exploitation by health care professionals and clergy.* Thousand Oaks, CA: Sage.

Gutok, B. (1985). *Sex and the workplace.* San Francisco, CA: Jossey-Bass.

Haney, C., Banks, W., & Zimbardo, P. (1973). Interpersonal dynamics in a simulated prison. *International Journal of Criminology and Penology, 1,* 69–97.

Haney, C., & Zimbardo, P. (1998). The past and future of U.S. prison policy. *American Psychologist, 53,* 709–727.

Hanson, E. (1999, October 27). Prisoner who said deputy raped her wins suit. *Houston Chronicle*, p. 3, sec. 2.

Horswell, C. (2000, February 17). Patrol man resigns amid sex scandal. *Houston Chronicle*, p. 35A.

Jacobs, J. (1983). Female guards in men's prison. In J. Jacobs (Ed.), *New perspectives on prisons and imprisonment* (pp. 178–201). Ithaca, NY: Cornell University Press.

Jolin, A. (1994). On the backs of working prostitutes: Feminist theory and prostitution policy. *Crime and Delinquency, 40*, 69–83.

Kappeler, V., Sluder, R., & Alpert, G. (1994). *Forces of deviance*. Prospect Heights, IL: Waveland Press.

Kardener, S., Fuller, M., & Mensch, I. (1973). A survey of physicians' attitudes and practices regarding erotic and non-erotic contact with patients. *American Journal of Psychiatry, 130*, 1077–1081.

Kraska, P., & Kappeler, V. (1995). To serve and pursue: Exploring police sexual violence against women. *Justice Quarterly, 12*, 85–111.

Krauss, C. (1994, September 18). The perils of police hiring. *New York Times*, p. 3, sec. 4.

Marquart, J. (1986). The use of physical force by prison guards: Individuals, situations, and organizations. *Criminology, 24*, 347–366.

Martin, S., & Jurik, N. (1996). *Doing justice, doing gender*. Thousand Oaks, CA: Sage.

McDonald, M. (1997). A multidimensional look at the gender crisis in the correctional system. *Law and Inequality, 15*, 505–546.

Mooney, T. (1995, April 3). In prison, sex, abuse prevalent. *Providence Journal-Bulletin*, A4.

National Institute of Corrections. (2000). *Sexual misconduct in prisons: Law, remedies, and incidence*. Longmont, CO: Information Center, U.S. Department of Justice.

National Women's Law Center. (1996). *Fifty-state survey on state criminal laws prohibiting the sexual abuse of female prisoners*. Washington, DC: National Women's Law Center.

Olson, E. (1999, March 31). U.N. panel is told of rights violations at U.S. women's prisons. *New York Times*, p. A16.

Osgood, D., Wilson, J. K., O'Malley, P. M., Bachman, J. G., & Johnston, L. D. (1996). Routine activities and individual deviant behavior. *American Sociological Review, 61*, 635–655.

Phillips, R. (1999). Jail sex scandal nets twelve indictments. Retrieved December 17, 1999 (APBnews.com).

Pogrebin, M., & Poole, E. (1997). The sexualized work environment: A look at women jail officers. *Prison Journal, 77*, 41–57.

Pope, K., & Bouhoutsos, J. (1986). *Sexual intimacy between therapists and patients*. New York: Praeger.

Rafter, N. (1985). *Partial justice*. Boston, MA: Northeastern University Press.

Rivers, G. (1999). Women in prison: Nowhere to hide. Retrieved September 10, 1999 (www.msnbc.com.news/geraldorivera.front.asp).

Robison, C. (1991, November 7). Prison OK'd by voters may never be built. *Houston Chronicle*, p. A21.

Rutter, P. (1989). *Sex in the forbidden zone*. Los Angeles, CA: Jeremy Tarcher.

Sapp, A. (1997). Police officer sexual misconduct. In P. Cromwell & R. Dunham (Eds.), *Crime and justice in America* (pp. 139–151). Upper Saddle River, NJ: Prentice-Hall.

Sherman, L. (1980). Causes of police behavior: The current state of quantitative research. *Journal of Research in Crime and Delinquency, 17*, 69–100.

Siegal, N. (1999). Stopping abuse in prison. *The Progressive, 63*, 31–33.

Stake, J., & Oliver, J. (1991). Sexual contact and touching between therapist and client. *Professional Psychology, 22*, 297–307.

Statham, A. (1996). *The rise of marginal voices: Gender balance in the work place.* Lanham, MD: University Press of America.

Steffensmeier, D., & Allan, E. (1996). Gender and crime: Toward a gendered theory of female offending. *Annual Review of Sociology, 22*, 459–487.

Stewart, C. (1998). Management response to sexual misconduct between staff and inmates. *Corrections Management Quarterly, 2*, 81–88.

Strasburger, L., Jorgenson, L., & Sutherland, P. (1992). The prevention of psychotherapist sexual misconduct: Avoiding the slippery slope. *American Journal of Psychotherapy, 4*, 544–554.

Strom-Gottfried, S. (1999). Professional boundaries: An analysis of violations by social workers. *Families in Society, 80*, 439–449.

Sykes, G. (1958). *Society of captives.* Princeton, NJ: Princeton University Press.

Texas penal code (14th ed.). (2000). Eagan, MN: West Publishing Company.

Vaughn, M. (1999). Police sexual violence: Civil liability under state tort law. *Crime and Delinquency, 45*, 334–357.

Virginia governor orders prison sex-abuse inquiry. (1999, October 13). *New York Times*, p. A22.

White, W. (1995). A systems perspective on sexual exploitation of clients by professional helpers. In J. Gonsiorek (Ed.), *Breach of trust: Sexual exploitation by health care professionals and clergy* (pp. 220–244). Thousand Oaks, CA: Sage.

Wincze, J., Parsons, J., Richards, J., & Bailey, S. (1996). A comparative survey of therapist sexual involvement between an American state and an Australian state. *Professional Psychology, 27*, 289–294.

Zedna, L. (1995). Wayward sisters: The prison for women. In N. Morris & D. Rothman (Eds.), *The Oxford history of the prison* (pp. 295–324). New York: Oxford University Press.

Cases Cited

Coble v. Texas Department of Corrections, 568 F. Supp. 410 (1983)

Dothard v. Rawlinson, 433 U.S. 321 (1977)

Griffin v. Michigan Department of Corrections, 654 F. Supp. 690 (1982)

Grummett v. Rushen, 779 F. 2d 491 (1985)

Chapter 15

Humor in the Briefing Room
A Study of the Strategic Uses of Humor Among Police

Mark R. Pogrebin
Eric D. Poole

Within various occupational groups humor represents a symbolic resource through which social meanings are created (Zijderveld, 1968). Certain types of humor actually come to characterize members of these groups. As part of the group subculture, humor entails a set of joking relations that support group values, beliefs, and behaviors.

First, through humorous exchanges group members find that they share common experiences and that they can raise a variety of both individual and group concerns that could not otherwise be addressed (Fine, 1983). Humor represents a strategic tool in testing the attitudes, perceptions, or feelings of other group members. By exploring some issue or concern through humor, people can gauge others' positions without having to take a stance themselves (Emerson, 1969).[1]

Second, humor promotes social solidarity. Through mutual ribbing, teasing, or pulling pranks, group members recognize that they can laugh at

Mark R. Pogrebin and Eric D. Poole, *Journal of Contemporary Ethnography* (formally *Urban Life*), Vol. 17 No. 2, pp. 183–210, copyright © 1988 by Sage Publications. Reprinted by permission of Sage Publications.

each other with no ill intent since they share a communal relationship (Coser, 1959, 1960). Shared laughter reflects a social benchmark of the group's common perspective. Joking relations among peers generate feelings of implicit understanding and camaraderie, thus strengthening group norms and bonds. Similarly, solidarity may be enhanced by directing humor at out-group members. This "laughter of inclusion" (Dupreel, 1928) affirms the group's social boundaries and moral superiority (Davies, 1982).

Third, groups utilize humor as a coping strategy in managing a variety of forces beyond their direct control. For example, gallows humor represents an attempt to transform crises or tragic situations into ones that are less threatening and thus more tolerable (Orbdlik, 1942). Although the humor may be morbid and cynical, group members are able to laugh at their plight, demonstrating *communities* and reinforcing group cohesion. Humor also helps to normalize crises by couching the threatening situations as routine occurrences; that is, as just part of the job. In this way humor fosters a sense of confidence that these problems can be handled (Holdaway, 1984).

In this article we extend the previous works on the role of humor in groups by exploring how police patrol officers incorporate humor as a strategic activity to ensure the integrity of their occupational work group. We seek to identify how various types of humor are used to define situations salient to police work; that is, we attempt to show how humor is situationally grounded in the social construction of reality of the police occupation. First, we describe our research methods. Second, we examine the strategic uses of four types of humor among patrol officers. Third, we discuss the role of institutionalized humorous communication in maintaining organizational relationships.

Methods

We collected data for the project during a year-long ethnographic study of a medium-sized metropolitan police department in Colorado. Our study began in June 1985 and ended in June 1986. Our objective was to examine the nature of interpersonal relations among patrol officers. We focused on humor and joking relations as complex, patterned constructions of interpersonal behavior and as strategic activities serving various functions for the group. We attempted to interpret and assign meaning to police humor by identifying how it was both responsive to a specific contextual situation and consistent with normative properties of the more general occupational structure.

Research Setting

The police department we observed is located in a community of approximately 90,000, part of the Denver Metropolitan Statistical Area.

During the study there were 135 sworn personnel on the force, with 83 officers attached to uniformed street patrol. Patrol officers were assigned to one of three shifts for a 12-month tour, working a 10-hour day and a 4-day week. At the end of that time, a complex bidding process, based on seniority, was used to reassign officers across the three shifts; moreover, departmental policy prohibited any officer from serving more than two consecutive years on the same shift.

Every month we each took a different shift, rotating through all three shifts during the year. This procedure allowed us to return to the same shift every three months and provided the opportunity for both of us to spend four full months on each shift. It also ensured a more representative sampling of police activities across shifts and patrol assignments throughout the 12-month study. As observers, we kept field diaries, reviewed daily police logs, and conducted informal interviews. Our monthly rotating shift procedure provided the means by which we crosschecked our independent observations and field notes.

Our daily observations began in the briefing room, where all patrol officers met at the beginning of their shift. Based on officer deployment plans, we implemented a procedure whereby we rode with a different patrol officer every other day. Since we covered each shift on a three-month rotation, we were able to schedule our ride-along assignments so that both of us spent time on patrol with every officer during the year. On many occasions we spent the entire shift with the assigned patrol officer; on others, we were able to spend only a few hours on patrol. Our daily observations concluded with the debriefing sessions when the officers returned to the station house to complete their reports. Since our emphasis was on the role of humor among patrol officers, we focused our attention on the group interactions during the briefing and debriefing sessions.

Field Relations. We made an intensive effort to get to know all patrol officers during the study. First, we sought to earn their respect through our personal commitment of time and energy in their organization. Second, we sought to gain their acceptance through our sustained collegiality and professional relations. As confidants, many officers kept us informed about the latest organizational rumor or personnel gossip, offered their personal views and assessments, and provided a wealth of "war stories"; others sought us out for information. While we gratefully acknowledged receipt of information, we were insistent that the code of ethics that governed our research prohibited our divulging any information that we received in confidence. This explanation was generally satisfactory to most officers; moreover, it reinforced the trust element that we worked hard to ensure in our field relations.

During the project we developed a working camaraderie with the officers, so that our presence on patrol or in the station house was taken for granted. We were viewed as part of the social organization of the department, having personally participated in the "routine" experiences of police work. Our personal acceptance in the police organization also led to our being invited by officers to off-duty social gatherings. The extension of these social relationships allowed us access to the private lives and personal histories of the officers. The mutual rapport and understanding that arose from such associations further supported our position in the police organization as "insiders." As a result, we feel confident that our observations and interpretations are reliable and valid representations of the phenomena under study.

Backstage Behavior in the Briefing Room. While we were able to ride with and observe each officer on patrol, it was in the social context of the briefing room that groups of officers routinely exhibited the types of humor we focus on as part of the police occupation. The briefing room served as the primary setting where officers engaged in backstage behavior, that is, where the officers were not performing to a public or providing stereotyped scripts to outsiders (Goffman, 1959; Punch, 1979).

The briefing room represented what Lyman and Scott (1967:270) have defined as a "home territory . . . where regular participants have a relative freedom of behavior and a source of intimacy and control over the area." Ardrey (1966) has argued that control of territory is associated with maintaining identity. Backstage behavior reflects the subcultural group identity in contrast to the frontstage identity managed in public. As Goffman (1959) has noted, backstage identities are revealed in territories that are separated from public view.

In the station house a formal reception area served as a staging place where police appearance was managed for the public. It represented a screen or barrier for the backstage area where police could act in an uninhibited manner and not concern themselves with outside scrutiny. For each shift of officers, the briefing area offered a collective arena where they could talk about their street experiences to others who understood and appreciated their feelings and perceptions. Still, as members of a paramilitary bureaucracy, officers had to be careful to ensure that their manner of expressing these experiences was organizationally acceptable or tolerable. Humor provided a wide range for creative expressions within such organizational constraints.

The Briefing Room Routine. When police officers arrived at the station house, they usually went directly to the locker room to change into their uniforms. The officers working a particular shift then proceeded to the briefing room for roll call and patrol assignments. During the 15-to-20-minute briefing session, officers also received current information on previous shift activities and communications on policy from the command staff. At times the shift sergeant cautioned the officers about some present dangers in the community, praised officers for their exceptional performance or related accomplishments, or called attention to particular problems officers might be experiencing.

At the end of a shift, officers returned to the station house briefing room to complete their paperwork. During this debriefing session, the sergeant reviewed the officers' reports, cleared up any questions that might arise, and offered officers constructive advice. The time required for debriefing all shift officers could range from a few minutes to over an hour, with officers leaving when their reports were filed and approved; however, officers typically remained in the briefing room long after their official duties were completed.

This informal period of officer interaction came to serve as a forum for officers to swap stories about individual work experience, allowing officers to "cool out" from a rough shift, to vicariously experience the highlights of fellow officers' calls, or to wind down before going home. It also provided an opportunity to discuss department policies, politics, and personalities. Rumors made their rounds at this time—with a few being squelched, several being started, and many being embellished. As Hannerz (1969) has observed, such informal gatherings of police officers foster highly stylized exchanges of information and forms of communication.

Like most groups characterized by informality, patrol officers have developed a set of joking references that require "insider" knowledge to be fully understood and appreciated as humorous.[2] After several weeks of riding with patrol officers and attending briefing and debriefing sessions, we began to discern distinct functions of joking relationships. The forms of humor we have identified are grounded in the natural work experiences of policing. We have classified police humor into four types: jocular aggression, audience degradation, diffusion of danger/tragedy, and normative neutralization.

Strategic Uses of Humor Among Police

In this section we will explore the strategic uses of the four types of humor. We begin our assessment of each type with a view of its functions in general; we then illustrate and examine the way each manifests itself within specific contexts of police work.

Jocular Aggression

Jocular aggression represents a humorous attack against supervisory or management personnel. It is a way subordinates in a group can collectively denounce departmental policies and regulations or the directives and orders of superiors in an acceptable manner. Jocular aggression thus avoids a direct confrontation with a superior that could lead to organizational sanctions.

Blau (1955) has contended that within bureaucracies individual complaints are often expressed and explored through joking relations in an informal work group. Jocular aggression reflects this type of joking relation in which discontent can be vented in a safe manner; that is, individuals are able not only to get their complaints out in the open but also to displace latent frustration and aggression via humorous expressions. In addition, jocular aggression serves to translate an individual concern into a group issue. In the group context the expression of an individual concern brings to bear the collective experience and advice of fellow workers. Individual problems may then be viewed from the perspective of the group.

The following problem incident involved a shift lieutenant who persisted in stopping drunk drivers and then calling for a patrol officer to respond to the scene and make the arrest. Such action involved the administration of a breathalyzer test, forced the officer to wait at the station until someone could come and take the drunk driver home, and required the completion of a lengthy offense report.

> Did you hear our favorite lieutenant on the radio tonight? He tied the fucking thing up so long we couldn't get through to anyone. Here we got both DUI cars tied up and that nut is running around catching four DUIs. It's dangerous to leave him out on the street. Why doesn't he sit on his ass in the station and pretend he's busy like the rest of the lieutenants do?

Another problem incident arose from the chief's new policy concerning relations with the minority community, whose spokespersons had met with the chief to complain about their treatment by patrol officers. The chief videotaped his new policy on minority-police relations and had it played for all shifts during briefing sessions. At one of the shift viewings, we observed the following. The officers were all seated, waiting for the tape to be played. One officer yelled out, "It's the Chief Marty Show; let's get some popcorn." As the tape played, officers made wisecracks, hissed, booed, and laughed; moreover, several officers threw paper airplanes at the screen. At the end of the video presentation, there was sporadic applause, and one policeman yelled out:

> This show was boring. . . . They should have sex flicks and make the Chief's show more interesting. Hell, I almost fell asleep.

Another officer joined in the chorus of criticism with a rather sarcastic observation:

> Now that was really a useful piece of shit. We all need to improve our community relations skills. Next thing they'll have us doing is asking a suspect for his permission before we can arrest him.

Jocular aggression reinforces the solidarity of the individuals within the group because it is based on shared experiences of the membership. Like jokes, it causes a collectivity of laughter that strengthens the group's social cohesion (Martineau, 1972). One such incident: An officer saw a young woman's car stuck in the snow and, after attempting to push her out, told the woman that he could do no more for her. After a short discussion in which the woman berated the officer for refusing to use his patrol car to pull her car from the snow drift, the officer told the woman to calm down and call a tow truck.

The woman subsequently filed a formal complaint against the officer with the department. Even though departmental policy prohibits the use of a police vehicle to remove a civilian's car (unless the car is impeding traffic), the officer received a three-day suspension without pay for the way he handled the incident. In assessing the implications of this administrative action, a fellow patrol officer presented his position to the shift:

> The next time it snows I'm going to help every goddam person stuck. Then when the dispatcher calls me on a case, I'm going to just say the chief wants us to help citizens get their cars out of the snow. I really have no time for the call.

Another officer followed up on this statement:

> And don't forget to tell them how grateful you are that you could be of help. You wouldn't want to leave a poor citizen stranded two blocks from home with groceries to carry.

The stories told in the briefing room tend to mediate the hierarchy of authority within the bureaucratic structure of the department. Such stories relate the patrol officer's perception of what "real" police work is all about. These humorous tales often reflect frustrations experienced by officers who must rely on their own common sense in working patrol and then have their decisions second-guessed by a supervisor later on. Jocular aggression affirms the patrol officer's perceived superiority to management personnel who are far removed from the realities officers face on the street.

Because they must often deviate from administrative policies and procedural regulations in order to perform order-maintenance functions, patrol officers guard their autonomy and discretionary decision making. New sergeants have to adjust to this informal work norm. For these supervisors, learning the nuances of the shift's personality is critical to their success in effectively managing the officers' activities on patrol (Van Maanen, 1984).

Officers want and expect the sergeant to act in a consultative manner. They feel that because of the nature of their front-line work, they should initiate the bulk of their contacts with a supervisor as they deem necessary. As the following example reveals, supervisors must learn to accept and support the autonomy and discretion so valued by patrol officers. A new sergeant had been assigned to the swing shift (4 P.M. to 2 A.M.). Because he had worked for the preceding five years in the detective bureau, he had limited contact with those working patrol. Thus, the new sergeant was known to patrol officers only by reputation, although there were a few veteran officers who had worked with him when he was on the street in uniform.

Most officers contend that new supervisors have a tendency to become involved in too many radio-dispatched calls to patrol. On a busy night it is not uncommon for a rookie sergeant to be running from one side of town to another for what he believes to be necessary supervision of his shift. Since officers resent close scrutiny, they attempt to socialize new shift sergeants to the patrol norms stressing laissez faire supervision.

An example of this process took place in the briefing room after a busy Saturday night of calls for service. The new sergeant was obviously fatigued from attempting to be with his patrol officers at every call. He was seen as constantly invading officers' territory and interfering with the tactics each officer had developed for handling interactions with suspects and citizens. Jocular aggression was abundant that night, as evidenced in the remarks of one officer during debriefing:

> Hey, Sarge! Where were you when I got that call on those bikers' loud music complaint over on the East Side? I figure you could have made it there if you used your lights and siren. It was only about five miles from where you were. Hell, if you ran hot at 90 miles an hour, you could have been there to help me.

A veteran officer also raised the issue of the sergeant's intrusion into patrol work during that shift. He described an incident in which a male suspect placed under arrest for possession of an illegal weapon was refusing to come peacefully with his younger partner. The rookie sergeant arrived, took charge of the scene, and tried to convince the suspect to come to the station. All attempts by the sergeant failed to resolve the situation, and the suspect became more agitated. At this point the veteran officer decided to intervene. He simply picked up the suspect and carried him back to the sergeant's car for transport to the station. At the debriefing, the officer gave the sergeant some friendly advice:

> Well, Sergeant, the reason I picked up that asshole at the apartment house and carried him to your car was that the bullshit that guy was giving you would have gone on forever. I figured you and Sam had talked enough; I just got tired of that runt's smartass manner. We got better things to do than listen to pukes like him. . . . Now don't you think I was professional?

In the following remark, we see how jocular aggression is used to address the larger issue of the new sergeant's attempts to supervise shift officers at every call:

> Now we all know that the city wants us to cut down on our driving time to save on gas expenses. Sarge, you must have put on over a thousand miles tonight. You better be careful or the city manager is going to get on your ass. You know you've got to help the city save money in these times of cutback management.

In short, jocular aggression provides a means by which subordinates can express dissatisfaction with superior officers or with the organization itself. However, those in subordinate positions must maintain the lines of authority that define the police structure. They must be careful not to cross the communicative boundary where jocular aggression becomes directly offensive to a superior, lest they suffer the consequences for violating organizational status (e.g., being perceived as insubordinate and sanctioned).

Audience Degradation

As we noted earlier, debriefing sessions present the opportunity for discussion of problems officers faced during the shift and feedback on how they were handled. Swapping stories about citizen encounters offered officers a chance to exploit the humor in the troubles and foibles of the public in general. Because the police saw themselves frequently called to intervene in conflicts between equally disreputable parties, they came to view the public in rather cynical terms. That is, they often failed to differentiate citizens in need of police services from individuals suspected of criminal involvement.

"Naming" refers to the process by which police classify people as social objects having certain stereotypical attributes and then act toward them on the basis of the identifying label (Lindesmith et al., 1977). Such standardized characterizations provide a common argot among police for conjuring up the appropriate images (e.g., demeanor, dress, speech, attitude) of individuals encountered. There is no need for further explanation when an officer refers to various persons contacted during the shift as "scumbag," "asshole," "puke," "bimbo," or other equally graphic appellations. One officer described his contact with a drunk couple as follows:

> I had a real good DUI tonight. I pulled behind a couple parked on the side of the road and they were drunk as well. When the driver got out, this bimbo also got out of the car and started yelling at me to leave the driver alone. There she is yelling at me about harassment, shit-faced and all, with her dress wide open. When I finally pointed this out to her, she sure as shit quieted down.

The use of the disparaging reference to the female suspect in this incident also reflects the frustration that officers experience in trying to protect citizens from themselves. Similarly, humorous remarks are used to belittle those individuals who create the "dirty work" that officers are called upon to perform. For example, one officer described the following encounter:

> A mental starts talking to me outside the station when I was coming to briefing. I can't understand what he's saying, but the next thing I know he pulls his pants down and exposes himself. At the same time all these women are coming out of city hall leaving work. . . . Hell, I don't know why he did that; there wasn't that much to show.

While most opportunities for backstage humor occur in the briefing room, many humorous stories about citizen encounters are told during slow times of a shift when patrol officers know that the supervisor is at the station or otherwise indisposed. These exchanges usually take place in isolated areas secluded from public view. A favorite spot for patrol officers to, as they put it, "shoot the shit" is behind shopping centers late at night. Usually two or three patrol cars will be parked parallel to one another, and officers will converse without leaving the vehicles. Such impromptu meetings of a few officers allow for more individualized sharing of work experiences that would not be suitable for collective discussion in the briefing room; moreover these brief storytelling sessions help break up the routine of a tedious shift. Comic relief provided by these occasions is illustrated in the following exchange among three officers:

> Officer Able: What was that call for over at the Sandstone apartments? It sounded like a good one.

> Officer Baker: There were some teenagers swimming naked in the pool, raising a lot of hell. When we rolled up, the boys ran but the chicks stayed. They came over stark naked and began to talk with Brewer and me; shit, they didn't bat an eye. It was hard not to look, believe me. . . .

> Officer Cruz: Damn, I never get good calls like that. If I did, by the time I was on the scene they'd probably be dressed.

The access the police had to individuals' personal problems caused them to make moral judgments on a regular basis. They were more often called on to perform social-service functions than law enforcement duties. They had to be counselors, mediators, arbitrators, referral agents, power brokers, and all-purpose consultants. To patrol officers oriented to "real" police work, many citizens calls for service seemed trivial, mundane, or unfounded. Officers came to view complainants as people who were too weak or ineffectual to handle their own problems. Responding to their calls was viewed as a waste of time and effort. In order to manage such distasteful situations, police recounted their encounters with citizens in humorously degrading ways, often poking fun at complainant misfortunes. As Goffman (1959:175) has pointed out, "Backstage derogation of the audience is another strategy that performance teams employ in order to maintain morale." Humorous putdowns of complainants served to promote the police sense of moral superiority and to maintain the dichotomy between police and policed.

Diffusion of Danger/Tragedy

Police are expected not to show fear in dangerous situations. Even to admit being afraid after threatening encounters is taboo. Displays of fear, although quite understandable under such conditions, are viewed as a sign of weakness. It is through humor that police can empathize with each other's feelings of fear and vulnerability. Joking relations concerning dangerous interactions provide a way for officers to express their emotions without damaging their professional image as confident and fearless. As Fine (1983:175) has argued, such humor fosters "a sense of social control for the participants on how to deal with these threatening or embarrassing topics."

In the following example, an officer conveyed the fear brought about by a highly threatening situation using joking references implicitly understood by other members of the group. The incident involved five patrol officers and one lieutenant who responded to a residential burglary-in-progress call. The six officers positioned themselves around the perimeter of the house and waited for the suspect to exit. An account of what occurred was provided by one of the patrol officers during the shift's debriefing session:

> There were six of us on the scene. The perpetrator is in the house and we've got the area covered. Everyone is in position waiting for the thief to come out. I'm in some bushes about 10 feet behind the lieutenant, who's standing behind a tree. The dude comes running out the back door, and the lieutenant is in the firing position and yells at the top of his lungs, "Hit the ground or I'll blow your fucking head off!" I thought the lieutenant was going to come in his pants right there. I couldn't tell who was more afraid—the bad guy or the lieutenant.

Every police officer is aware of the danger inherent in such incidents; moreover, apprehension is heightened by the possibility that the suspect is armed. The following incident illustrates how officers humorously reflect upon their own vulnerability in precarious situations. The call involved an officer dispatched to a residence for what was thought to be a minor domestic disturbance. Upon his arrival at the residence, the officer was met by a highly agitated male suspect wielding a shotgun. The officer immediately radioed for backup, took his shotgun from the cruiser, and positioned himself behind a tree in the front yard of the residence. The suspect demanded that the officer "get the hell off my property"; the officer ordered the suspect to put down his weapon. Neither complied, but the officer continued to talk to the suspect in an effort to calm him down. The backup officers arrived within minutes and assumed tactical positions behind their cars. After a 10-minute standoff, the suspect finally dropped his shotgun and surrendered to the first officer. At the debriefing one of the backup patrolman began gibing his officer:

> I thought you were going to be behind that tree all goddam night. That asshole didn't give a shit if you blew him to hell. I was going to bet Alex that you would shoot first. But you know him, he never carries more than a quarter when he's on duty.

Another backup officer joked about what could have happened:

> It's a good thing Wayne didn't have to shoot that scumbag, because we haven't qualified with the shotgun for I don't know how long. He

would have shot and probably hit the front window, and that son of a bitch would have opened up on all of us.

This example reveals the importance of the officer maintaining control over his emotions; for had he "lost it" and overreacted, the consequences could have been disastrous. Yet the reality of such threatening situations cannot be denied, and the intense emotions must eventually be dealt with. Jokes can be used to focus on the uncomfortable topic of fear, allowing the group to deal collectively with an emotion that could not be expressible otherwise. When a fellow officer has confronted a life-threatening situation, the backstage humor of the briefing room promotes shared understanding of the experience and identification with the feelings of the officer. In this way, humorous debriefings help to manage the danger that is a part of police work.

Similarly to the way humor is used to diffuse emotions accompanying dangerous situations, joking relations also serve to temper tragic events experienced on the job. As trained professionals, police officers are expected to maintain a poised presence even under the most tragic circumstances. Their authority and effectiveness in handling such events would be compromised if officers could not control their own emotions. In the face of tragedy (e.g., victims of child abuse, rape, accidents), officers must maintain their composure, distancing themselves from the intense emotional reactions evoked in such encounters. To an outsider, the jokes that are told to diffuse tragedy may not seem humorous at all. In fact they can be perceived as cruel and insensitive; however, for patrol officers the callousness of such jokes actually helps lessen the emotional intensity elicited by tragic events. In this way humor allows the police to handle situations that would emotionally paralyze others.

One tragic event that occurred during our observational study involved the arrest of a middle-aged, white male suspect for driving under the influence of alcohol. After being brought to the police station and given a breathalyzer test, the suspect requested to see his "good friend" on the force, Lieutenant Williams. Although it was 2 A.M., the lieutenant was called to the station. When the lieutenant arrived, he briefly talked with the suspect, explaining the procedures to be followed in DUI cases, then drove the suspect home. A few hours later the suspect committed suicide.

When the graveyard shift came off the street at 8 A.M., Lieutenant Williams was in the briefing room and the discussion focused immediately on the suicide. It was soon learned that the suspect was not the lieutenant's close friend; rather, he was at best a casual acquaintance whom the lieutenant saw infrequently at a local stable where they both kept their horses. Once the relationship had been clarified, the patrol officers saw the opportunity to diffuse the tragic elements of the case for the lieutenant:

> I saw the guy in here when he was waiting to blow in the machine. He didn't look depressed. What the hell did you say to him to depress him

to the point he blew himself away? You didn't bore him to death with all those horse stories you always tell?

After a few more speculative gibes concerning the role of the lieutenant in the suspect's demise, one officer offered the lieutenant some final advice:

> I tell you, Lieutenant, you really have to pick your friends more carefully in the future. You know, you could give the department a bad name.

In another tragic incident we observed during our study, a middle-aged white man walked into the police station around 3 A.M. on a Saturday and reported that he had just murdered his live-in girlfriend. When the graveyard shift returned for debriefing later that morning, the officers shared what they had learned about the bizarre event:

> The guy comes into the station, hardly anyone is around, and tells the desk clerk he needs to see a cop. I happen to pass the front desk and am told . . . that there is a man here who wants to speak to an officer. I take him back to the briefing room and he tells me he murdered his girlfriend and gives me the details. Then he says as calmly as hell he wants to speak to a priest, not a lawyer, but a priest! That's when I figure this guy's for real. Hell, it's too late to get religion.

One of the officers dispatched to the crime scene then described what he found:

> The door to the house was open and there to the left of the front door was the .22 [caliber] rifle, just like we were told by dispatch. We know right away this guy was not a mental. We go to the master bedroom and there is this broad with covers over her. We pull them back and, man, there are about five holes in her chest. She's deader than hell. Looks like the guy was trying to make her look like Swiss cheese.

The casual observer is likely neither to understand nor to appreciate the humorous social meanings created by these stories. But the appropriateness of joking depends on the situation; that is, there are contextual rules for joking that are often not explicit or even consciously recognized. They represent intricate functions of group processes. It is through the shared experiences of group activity that the standards by which humor is judged and interpreted evolve.

For police, backstage humor represents a strategic means of managing the consequences of tragic events. First, jokes allow officers to vent feelings in an acceptable manner. Second, joking relations provide for a collective diffusion of emotional responses (e.g., outrage, disgust, horror) to tragedies. Third, the humorous treatment of tragedy promotes its normalization as just part of the job. Humor thus supports emotional distancing, allowing officers to perform their jobs regardless of the situation.

Normative Neutralization

According to Reuss-Ianni (1983), the street-officer culture supports bending formal rules and procedures that may impede officers from doing their job as they deem necessary. Sometimes the law itself is seen by the police as getting in the way of the administration of justice (Skolnick, 1966); thus legislative and judicial constraints may have to be sidestepped by officers. When police "know" a suspect is guilty (i.e., factual guilt), they feel justified in violating procedural rules in order to obtain evidence that may better ensure a conviction. Similarly, if police perceive that a suspect who they feel deserves punishment is unlikely to be prosecuted or convicted, they may impose "street justice" (e.g., verbal or physical abuse). Street justice is also administered to belligerent suspects whom the police lack probable cause to arrest but whom the police feel need to be taught a lesson in proper respect for police authority.

We found patrol officers quite candid in describing street justice incidents to their peers. They often swapped humorous stories about these encounters during debriefing sessions, although they were discreet in the presence of certain supervisors. Such humorous accounts help to define the working ideology of patrol officers, providing examples of informal standards and expectations for behavior by which officers may be judged.

The following example shows how legal guidelines were compromised by one officer in adhering to the principle of street justice. This incident involved a veteran officer who was dispatched to a residence for a family disturbance call. After restraining the couple involved in the dispute, the officer learned that the wife had just returned home, having left her husband and two small children for a two-month hiatus with another man. This man had accompanied the wife to the home and was present when the officer arrived. The situation was further aggravated by the woman's agitated state and violent demeanor, a condition the officer judged to be drug-induced. Demanding that the officer arrest her husband, the woman then produced a court order awarding her temporary custody of the children, enjoining the husband to leave the home, and denying him child visitation rights until a subsequent court hearing was held.

The officer felt that the judge who issued the injunction was not fully cognizant of all the facts in the case; consequently he decided to ignore the court order. Instead, he lectured the woman on parental responsibility, told her and her boyfriend to leave the house without the children, and advised her to get an attorney. The officer then warned the woman that if she caused any more trouble that night, he would have her arrested for suspected drug use. The next day the woman filed a formal complaint against the officer at police headquarters.

When questioned about the incident by his fellow officers during the debriefing session, the veteran officer provided the following insight to his application of street justice:

No sooner do I arrive on the scene when this hysterical asshole starts screaming at me to get her husband out of the house. There she is waving a court order in my face, screaming the judge wants him out. Then I heard from her old man that she returned after deserting the family for two months, leaving the two small kids at home with him and never leaving a note to explain where she was going and never contacting her husband while being gone. I told her what she could do with the court order. Then she gets real loud and starts cussing me out, all the while threatening to sue my ass. "Lady," I said, "you're high on drugs and I'm going to haul your ass in if you don't shut up and get out of here now." She saw I was pissed and she leaves with her boyfriend. No way I was going to throw that guy out and let that bitch stay with the kids, especially not in her condition. I just can't believe the judge knew what this case was about. But what the hell do they know anyway. When was the last time you saw a judge handle a domestic?

The working ideology of patrol officers is premised on the inherent superiority of their decision making and commonsense understandings that determine the appropriate course of action to be taken. By humorously degrading the demeanor of the wife and the wisdom of the judge, the officer justified both his negative assessment of her moral character and his refusal to abide by the court order. In this case, ensuring street justice was more important than abiding by the law. The legal constraints were thus neutralized by an appeal to higher loyalties (Sykes and Matza, 1957).[3] Although every shift member knew the officer would be subject to departmental disciplinary action, his example reinforced the preeminence of autonomy and discretion within the occupational ideology.

In addition to their resentment of legal constraints, patrol officers express frustration in following operational policies and procedures formulated by police administrators. Patrol officers often assert that management has lost touch with the realities of real police work and complain that many administrative directives are either intrusive or useless. Because officers view certain managerial policies as obstacles preventing them from being effective, they bend the rules and follow those procedures that have worked best for them.

In the following example one officer administered street justice to a suspect in direct contradiction to departmental policy concerning the handling of intoxicated individuals. The incident involved a routine investigation of a suspicious vehicle parked on the shoulder of a major thoroughfare early on a Saturday morning. The officer described the circumstances to the shift at the debriefing session:

It's almost 2 A.M. and I came across this '85 Olds Cutlass on the side of Sheridan. The dome light is on and the driver's door is open, with a guy's legs hanging out. I wake up the dumb shit who's been sleeping one off and order him out of the car. Immediately he starts mouthing off, and really goes bat shit when I tell him I'm taking him to detox. . . .

I told the asshole three times to shut up, but he keeps running his mouth. Fuck it. The puke goes to the county jail. . . . After I checked his license, I noticed it was his birthday and started feeling a little sorry for the guy. But I'm sure some of the inmates will have a few surprises for him this weekend.

In almost all cases when a person is found to be intoxicated but not driving a vehicle, departmental policy instructs that suspects be taken to the detoxification center, a county facility that holds drunken individuals for 24 hours and provides treatment on a voluntary basis. The policy calls for the use of the detoxification center in such situations in order to prevent the individual from getting injured or harming others.

In this case, the officer felt that the suspect had exceeded the bounds of acceptable demeanor to be exhibited in such encounters. He thus decided to arrest the suspect on a drunk and disorderly charge and have him jailed. In taking this action, the officer ensured a punishment more commensurate with the seriousness of the suspect's disregard for police authority. The officer's humorous account of the incident at the debriefing session served to justify his discretionary street justice superseding the departmental policy. Through humor the police reinforce their work perspective and organizational status, promoting a collective self-confidence conducive to the maintenance of group autonomy and the exercise of individual discretion.

Discussion

The four types of humor we have examined—jocular aggression, audience degradation, diffusion of danger/tragedy, and normative neutralization—reflect rather serious issues in policing. In considering the strategic uses of humor, we must address why officers choose to express such serious content in unserious forms. As noted above, joking relations provide a socially acceptable means to test the feelings of group members, one that allows denial of the serious implications of the humorous message if challenged. But the expression of serious concern in a humorous form may ensure more than a defensible posture in gauging others' sentiments.

First, a serious theme expressed in jest, rather than in earnest, may actually dramatize its message. The humorous expression, by providing amusement and eliciting overt reactions of smiling or laughter, symbolically commits the group to the position of the humorist. The impact of the message is also increased with the weight of consensual acknowledgment implicit in group laughter. If an overtly serious comment is offered, the group's response may be concealed by ambiguous silence or equivocally impassive faces.

Second, humor provides a forum for presentation of concerns without directly threatening the system that fosters them; that is, unlike the formal repercussions that could result from taking a serious position on an issue, humor affords expression (or even diffusion and defusion of concerns) without changing the terms of the organizational relationships. To this extent, then, the medium is the message. Humor is communicated and interpreted within the existing subcultural context (e.g., ideology, power, status, morality, norms, and values) of the police organization. Both the individual officers and the police organization benefit from institutionalized humorous communication. The status quo is preserved.

A final consideration of our findings deals with the use of jocular aggression aimed at superiors. We focus on this type of humor since previous studies have indicated that jocular aggression is directed either laterally or downwards through the organizational hierarchy; that is, individuals jokingly attack their equals or subordinates, but not their superiors. In two observational studies of joking relations in work settings, both Bradney (1957) and Coser (1959, 1960) reported no instance in which a subordinate worker used humor to express aggression or hostility to a superior face-to-face; humorous derision of superiors occurred only in their absence. In contrast, superiors publicly as well as privately, ridiculed subordinates for their failings or inadequacies.

The similarity of these findings, obtained in markedly different work settings (Bradney studied interactions of department store staff; Coser observed psychiatric staff meetings), supports the notion of asymmetrical access to jocular aggression. As the object of the hostile joking by subordinates, superiors have the authority to make reprisals. Subordinates subjected to humorous derision by superiors do not. Yet, in our observations of jocular aggression among police we have noted numerous occasions on which nonranking patrol officers directly ridiculed their first-line supervisors, the shift sergeants. To account for this joking relationship, we must examine the nature of the sergeant's position in the police organization.

Observational studies of police work have revealed that the exercise of authority in law enforcement agencies is primarily based on personal relationships with subordinates (Rubinstein, 1973; Muir, 1977; Van Maanen, 1984). This is because all supervisory personnel must rise from line-level positions in the police organization. The common occupational socialization experiences in the street culture of patrol work provided the basis for group solidarity and informal relations across departmental ranks.

At the same time, Van Maanen (1984) has pointed out that senior police administrators seek to promote individuals who are less likely to bring the "patrolman's mentality" to the supervisory role. The purpose of this selection strategy is to ensure that supervisors will supervise from a formal administrative, rather than an informal line-level perspective. Success in rising through the ranks is dependent, in part, on shedding the "street-cop" mentality. This promotional process thus serves to increase tension and social distance between supervisory and line staff.

Police sergeants, as first-line supervisors, occupy rather incongruous positions in the police organization. First, they are at the bottom of the supervisory hierarchy where policy and procedures developed from above must be implemented at the line level. But the ability of sergeants to implement policies and procedures is largely determined by the actions of line officers (Van Maanen, 1984). Sergeants have to earn the respect of their subordinates; it is not granted on the basis of rank alone.

Second, the relations between sergeants and patrol officers reflect a structured ambiguity. There is a mixture of camaraderie and antagonism, identification and rejection, and trust and suspicion. This ambiguity lends itself to a mutual testing of the boundaries of acceptable behavior in the roles of superior and subordinate. Under these conditions, subordinates are provided greater latitude in the expression of jocular aggression. For example, Radcliffe-Brown (1940) has argued that such joking relations are premised on institutionalized social ambiguity. That is, jocular aggression arises among individuals whose relationship is simultaneously conjunctive and disjunctive—having grounds for both solidarity and separation and reflecting "a peculiar combination of friendliness . . . [and] hostility" (Radcliffe-Brown, 1940:195). The terms of the joking relation allow a person to make fun of another who, in turn, is expected to take no offense. Since the police organization provides an analogous relation between sergeants and line officers, we can account for why, contrary to previous research, the subordinates in our study could direct jocular aggression at their superiors.

In this article we have explored the strategic uses of humor among patrol officers. We have emphasized the contextual aspect of humor; that is, we have focused on specific types of humor in relation to the distinctive nature of patrol work. It is hoped that future ethnographic research will build upon our efforts and move toward identifying the roles of individuals in the social organization of humor and the role of groups as humor repositories. In this way, a better understanding of the rules governing humorous interaction, communication, and transmission of group culture may be obtained.

Endnotes

1 If the humorous remarks produce a positive response, one may assume that others share, or at least sympathize with, one's own viewpoint. On the other hand, if the humor is rejected, one may suffer the embarrassment of having told a bad joke but risk very little else, since the joker was, after all, only kidding.

2 This is particularly important in relation to humor premised on an understanding of historical events within the department. Subtle or indirect remarks linking past experiences to present situations would be unrecognizable to those outside the work group. During the debriefing sessions, oral histories of the department are passed along to successive cohorts of police officers. Much of the localized culture is embodied in humorous stories and jokes that capture different aspects and reflect various versions of the department's history.

[3] One may argue that the officer also employed another technique of neutralization, denial of victim harm, in ignoring the court order; that is, the officer felt that the wife deserved the kind of street justice meted out because she had acted so irresponsibly.

References

Ardrey, R. (1966). *The territorial imperative.* New York: Dell.

Blau, P. M. (1955). *The dynamics of bureaucracy.* Chicago: University of Chicago Press.

Bradney, P. (1957). The joking relationship in industry. *Human Relations, 10,* 179–187.

Coser, R. L. (1959). Some social functions of laughter. *Human Relations, 12,* 171–182.

Coser, R. L. (1960). Laughter among colleagues. *Psychiatry, 23,* 81–95.

Davies, C. (1982). Ethnic jokes, moral values and social boundaries. *British Journal of Sociology, 33,* 383–403.

Dupreel, E. (1928). Le problème sociologique du rise. *Revue Philosophique, 106,* 213–260.

Emerson, J. P. (1969). Negotiating the serious import of humor. *Sociometry, 32,* 169–181.

Fine, G. A. (1983). Sociological approaches to the study of humor. In P. E. McGhee & J. H. Goldstein (Eds.), *Handbook of humor research* (Vol. 1, pp. 159–181). New York: Springer-Verlag.

Goffman, E. (1959). *The presentation of self in everyday life.* Garden City, NY: Anchor.

Hannerz, U. (1969). *Soulside: Inquiries into ghetto culture and community.* New York: Columbia University Press.

Holdaway, S. (1984). *Inside the British police.* Oxford: Basil Blackwell.

Lindesmith, A. R., Strauss, A. L., & Denzin, N. K. (1977). *Social psychology.* New York: Holt, Rinehart & Winston.

Lyman, S. M., & Scott, M. B. (1967). Territoriality: A neglected sociological dimension. *Social Problems, 15,* 236–249.

Martineau, W. H. (1972). A model of the social functions of humor. In J. H. Goldstein & P. E. McGhee (Eds.), *The psychology of humor* (pp. 101–125). New York: Academic Press.

Muir, W. K. (1977). *Police: Streetcorner politicians.* Chicago: University of Chicago Press.

Orbdlik, A. J. (1942). Gallows humor: A sociological phenomenon. *American Journal of Sociology, 47,* 709–716.

Punch, M. (1979). The secret social service. In S. Holdaway (Ed.), *The British police* (pp. 102–117). Beverly Hills, CA: Sage.

Radcliffe-Brown, A. R. (1940). On joking relationships. *Africa, 13,* 195–210.

Reuss-Ianni, E. (1983). *Two cultures of policing.* New Brunswick, NJ: Transaction Books.

Rubinstein, J. (1973). *City police.* New York: Farrar, Straus & Giroux.

Skolnick, J. H. (1966). *Justice without trial.* New York: John Wiley.

Sykes, G. M., & Matza, D. (1957). Techniques of neutralization: A theory of delinquency. *American Journal of Sociology, 22,* 664–670.

Van Maanen, J. (1984). Making rank: Becoming an American police sergeant. *Urban Life, 13,* 155–176.

Zijderveld, A. C. (1968). Jokes and their relation to social reality. *Social Research, 35,* 268–311.

Chapter 16

The Rhetoric of Personal Loyalty to Superiors in Criminal Justice Agencies

Sam S. Souryal
Deanna L. Diamond

> When an organization wants you to do right, it asks for your integrity; when it wants you to do wrong, it demands your loyalty.
> Author Unknown

> Employment is a specific contract calling for a specific performance and for nothing else. . . . An employee owes no loyalty, he owes no attitudes — he owes performance and nothing else. (Drucker, 1974:424)

Introduction

One of the most perplexing issues in public service in general, and in criminal justice institutions in particular, is that of loyalty and loyalties. On the one hand, practitioners are required to be loyal to the Constitution, state laws, and professional values, yet they must be *personally* loyal to their supervisors and superiors and, of course, to one another. While this may sound commonsensical, in reality, it may be exhaustively problematic. The unexamined assumptions here are: First, personal loyalty at the workplace is essential. Second, practitioners are intuitively capable of figuring

Reprinted from *Journal of Criminal Justice,* Vol. 29, Sam S. Souryal and Deanna L. Diamond, "The Rhetoric of Personal Loyalty to Superiors in Criminal Justice Agencies," pp. 543–554, 2001, with permission from Elsevier.

out where their primary loyalty lies at all times. Third, if a loyalty conflict arises, it is the practitioners' responsibility to resolve it at their own risk.

These are difficult assumptions, especially since nothing is offered to prepare public workers to handle them. As a result, a great number of practitioners continue to agonize over these issues, perhaps more than any others. Ironically, however, if workers and superiors were loyal to constitutional and departmental values, they would, by natural association, be loyal to one another, making the need for personal loyalty irrelevant.[1]

In the objective reality of criminal justice organizations, concern for loyalty enters into *every* decision the practitioners make. Subconsciously, but only humanly, the practitioners ask themselves if they do this or that, whom will they please and whom will they offend, who will support them, and who will penalize them, and, inescapably, will their careers prosper or suffer. To articulate this point, consider, for example, this scenario: a police officer pulls over a young lady suspected of speeding and who, upon questioning, turns out to have violated state law and was also the police chief's daughter. How will the majority of officers handle this situation? No one knows for sure since no pertinent research exists. What is characteristically human, however, is that officers will agonize, at least to some measure, over the possibility of negative reaction by the chief (even if the ticket issued was perfectly legitimate), whereas in most other situations they would not. What makes this situation particularly stressful is the unspoken sentiment of personal loyalty — to whom and at what price? Obviously, the officers' decisions to issue a ticket will depend entirely on their moral fortitude, discretion, and trust in their department's sense of fairness. While this scenario is fairly benign, it exemplifies the dangers of personal loyalty to superiors — the officers' inability to do what they know ought to be done for fear of retaliation or criticism by their superiors. More serious scenarios also occur. They include shootings by police, beating up of inmates by correctional officers, "testifying" in court by probation officers, covering up misfeasance, or violating the constitutional rights of citizens.

The purpose in this article is *not* to scandalize criminal justice agencies. Far from being so, the authors are loyal practitioners of criminal justice. The purpose, nevertheless, is to call attention to the dangers of the unexamined issue of *personal* loyalty to superiors whereby the practitioners are compelled to offer loyalty to the superior's person (rather than the office) at the price of undermining the public good.

Examining this issue becomes even more important when, upon further scrutiny, one discovers that the practice of personal loyalty to superiors is both unnecessary and potentially dangerous. It is self-evident that if both the workers *and* the superiors are equally loyal to the Constitution, the laws, and agency rules and regulations, they should by association be loyal to one another. Anything else must be contradictory or redundant. Critics, on the other hand, view the practice as an excuse to legitimize official oppression by superiors. It allows them to degrade (and when necessary get rid of) workers who disagree with them by accusing them of disloyalty, a charge so irrational that it required whistle-blowing legislation to provide protection from its arbitrariness (Blamires, 1963; Denhardt, 1987; Souryal, 1998).

Focus

Lest the authors be misread, this article does not question the original sentiment of loyalty to God, country, family, friends, or even superiors under enlightened conditions. Indeed, in these settings, loyalty can be instrumental in promoting sociability and reaffirming evolutionary values (Wilson, 1993). Furthermore, the authors also believe that agency rules and regulations should be maintained, respect to superiors rendered, and professional discipline observed, yet an examination of the facts reveals that personal loyalty to superiors *is not* an official obligation, is irrational, is organizationally problematic, and can cause undue harm to the unsuspecting public.[2] The authors reason that personal loyalty to superiors has a "coercive tendency" that makes practitioners either unable or unwilling to serve public good as they professionally know they ought. As a result, in the name of loyalty to superiors, criminal justice practitioners may find themselves justifying untruth, impeding justice, supporting cover-ups, and lying under oath.

If this basic argument is plausible, then personal loyalty to superiors should be neither offered nor expected, and workers should be loyal only to the dictums of law and conscience. Failure to support this view may reveal a management system that favors power and status over reason and obligation. In criminal justice agencies, that would be especially disheartening since the practitioners' original attachment is to the principles of justice, due process, equal protection, and democracy. Finally, while the authors' views are not meant as a blanket indictment of all criminal justice agencies, the civility of each such agency will have to be measured by the "moral agility" of its members and the "moral courage" of its leaders.

Some *Exploratory Questions*

To accentuate the debate over personal loyalty in public agencies, the *Journal Criminal Justice Ethics* (Winter/Spring 1993) devoted the entire issue to examining the hermeneutics of loyalty and loyalties. While this issue renewed interest in the subject, it challenged some of the most rudimentary assumptions of loyalty. Some of the more significant questions raised are: First, why should personal loyalty be an issue, at all? If each practitioner (including superiors) is assigned an official duty, why should anyone have to owe personal loyalty to another? Second, if personal loyalty to superiors is such a great virtue, why is it not stated in agency rules and regulations? Third, are all superiors, as a class, assumed to be worthy of loyalty? If they are, why are so many disciplined for acts of misfeasance or malfeasance? If they were not, would it not mean that some practitioners are required to be loyal to unworthy superiors? Fourth, is absence of loyalty to superiors the moral equivalent of organizational disloyalty? Is it not legitimate that practitioners can act independently without being disloyal to the agency? Finally, what specifically are loyal workers supposed to do beyond carrying out their duties to the best of their abilities? If there is anything, then what is it? If there is nothing, then what difference can personal loyalty make (Souryal and McKay, 1996)?

With these questions in mind, one may wonder whether personal loyalty to superiors is justified or is it, as the critics argue, another "organizational drama" designed to intimidate subordinates into submission to unreasonable demands by a "ruling class" that is more motivated by personal power than promoting the agency's mission (Manning, 1985).

The Workplace View

Criminal justice practitioners, perhaps because of the nature of their functions, are keenly aware of the hierarchy of loyalties. Each time they make an arrest, lock up an inmate, or revoke a probationer, they ponder where their primary loyalty lies: the Constitution, the community, public good, agency rules, the boss, the partner, or self? While several of these loyalties overlap, and even clash, a *primary* loyalty should not; it must always remain first and foremost.

While politicization can make public officials unable to figure out this quandary of loyalties, criminal justice practitioners seem reluctant to do so. This may be due, in part, to the fact that they serve at the pleasure of their superiors, are organized along paramilitary lines, perform under extraordinary conditions (i.e., police and correctional officers), and operate under traditional cultures. As a result, they somehow seem united in the belief that personal loyalty to superiors is a central ethic and that deference to the superiors' wishes is an organizational requirement. Consequently, if they want their careers to prosper, they should comply with their superiors' desires without *much* concern for rightness or wrongs.

The continuance of this seemingly routine practice may be more harmful than originally thought. It "unofficially" commits criminal justice practitioners to uphold allegiance to certain persons for a durable period of time where such allegiance may compete with more legitimate loyalties. Such loyalties include one's obligation to the truth, to due process, to probable cause, to equal protection, to agency mission, and to ethical values. Since these are *sovereign* obligations (while personal loyalty to superiors is not even administratively recognized), it must follow that the latter is a questionable tradition. The incoherence of this tradition can be more easily discerned when the picture is compounded and the superior in question is known to be dishonest or corrupt. What complicates issues of personal loyalty to superiors in criminal justice agencies is that they are never discussed in preservice or in-service training. By design or by default, criminal justice academy instructors do not discuss the subject for fear of offending the superiors who assigned them to teach in the first place. If so, it should be safe to conclude that criminal justice practitioners learn this questionable tradition solely from organizational culture. Through real or fictitious experiences, they are made to believe that the practice is intrinsically good and that any inclination to the contrary would constitute disloyalty. So ingrained is this belief in the practitioners' psyches, it appears that they use personal loyalty to superiors as a "crutch" to success; it can make their careers prosper or dwindle, produce a promotion or a demotion, or somehow make their lives more or less "miserable." Due to this misguided logic, perhaps, it is no accident that so many police, corrections, and community supervision practitioners are attracted to "browning" and overtly flattering their superiors (Klockars, 1999:23), yet, unknown to them, the more they do so, the more entangled they get in competing loyalties and the more vulnerable their careers can be.

What further complicates issues of loyalty and disloyalty in criminal justice agencies is the ghastly silence that surrounds them, chiefly out of fear. Criminal justice practitioners, even when attending management seminars, seem afraid to comment on the issue. Especially in police and correctional departments, bringing up the subject, even in the best of intentions, can be considered a regrettable mistake. Not unlike joking about bombs when walking through airport metal detectors, many criminal justice practitioners believe that discussing the subject can get them in trouble for "suspicion of disloyalty."

At this point, it may be necessary to explain that while personal loyalty to superiors in unionized criminal justice organizations may likely have different dimensions than in nonunionized organizations, the principle remains the same. This is basically because the objects of loyalty and the incentives for acting loyally are the same. A practitioner's willingness to comply with personal wishes in unionized organizations is no less attractive than in nonunionized organizations. Also, because of the wide variety of unionization models (i.e., hard trade unions, police associations, fraternity unions, etc.), criminal justice practitioners may feel that they owe more or less loyalty to their unions. In general terms, however, criminal justice practitioners are not nearly as intimidated by their unions as they are by their superiors. There are two reasons for that. First, as unionists, they stand to benefit or suffer collectively rather than individually. Second, unions are always seen far away while superiors are always right here and now. In some cases, however, the rewards for personal loyalty to superiors in unionized organizations may be more gratuitous and durable than in nonunionized organizations. For example, a promotion to a managerial position in a nonunionized organization is more likely to be rescinded once the agency's CEO leaves office, while in unionized organizations, such a promotion is more likely to be permanent. This is especially the case in organizations fashioned along the strong civil service model. A critical difference exists between unionized and nonunionized organizations. In unionized organizations, practitioners invariably have legal protection provided to them by the "Due and Fair Representation" clause if they are threatened by dismissal or made to pay monetary fines. In nonunionized organizations, the practitioners may have to forge for legal protection and pay for it. Ironically, that critical difference may have been the strongest motivation for practitioners to embrace personal loyalty to superiors in the first place.

The Goliath of Disloyalty

Throughout history, disloyalty has been recorded as the most shameful of defections. Kleinig (1995:74) describes disloyalty as "the forsaking of an object of loyalty for self-serving and individualistic or self-assertive reasons." The authors define it as an act of social or occupational betrayal. Disloyal practitioners, especially in police and prison institutions, are considered pariahs whose chances for survival are demonstratively low; however, it does not take much reflection to realize that "the loyalty of a Gordon Liddy or a John Mitchell generates about as much admiration as the honor amongst thieves, and that for all their soul-stirring qualities, [loyalties] are frequently jingoistic and exclusionary" (Kleinig in Souryal and McKay, 1996:53).

An accusation of disloyalty at the workplace is one of the most misunderstood and least researched issues in organizational literature. This may be due, in part, to the common misuse of the dichotomous rule. As in love, patriotism, or religiosity, the opposite of loyalty is *not* disloyalty but the absence of loyalty, and the opposite of disloyalty is *not* loyalty but the absence of disloyalty. This clarification can be better understood by the following example: for one not to support organized religion, one should not necessarily want that it be discontinued or destroyed. Similarly, an accusation of disloyalty to a superior may have little or nothing of disloyalty to the department. Indeed, it may be manifestation of a higher departmental loyalty — "safeguarding lives and property, protecting the innocent against deception, or the weak against oppression or intimidation," to quote the Law Enforcement Code of Ethics (2000).

To better understand issues of loyalty and disloyalty at the workplace, the dichotomous rule should be replaced by a continuum. This creates a new category of practitioners who are neither loyal nor disloyal, but *aloyal*, if you will. These individuals should neither be considered disloyal since they may be loyal to higher obligations (i.e., duty, professionalism, compassion or humanity) nor be blamed for wanting to disassociate themselves from unwise or prejudiced superiors. The increasing number of aloyal police and correctional officers who report violations by colleagues is a case in point. In the absence of any counter-reasoning, it should be safe to believe that aloyal officers are motivated by a different set of loyalties and that they only differ from others by how they identify their primary loyalties.

To avoid the perception of disloyalty, most criminal justice practitioners play the "personal loyalty card." Particularly when workers find themselves in conditions of perceived unfairness or unkindness, they tend to "fall into a self-protective mode. Like turtles, they crawl into their shells and hide" (Morris, 1997:123). They act subserviently to their bosses (or at least pretend that they do) and, not infrequently, allow their allegiance to devolve into a master and slave relationship, causing humiliation to themselves and embarrassment to their profession (Denhardt, 1987). Deputy sheriffs often react this way toward their chief deputy, probation officers toward their chief, and correctional officers toward their captains. Even on the academic side of criminal justice, it does not take many scruples to notice that untenured instructors tend to more overtly offer personal loyalty to chairpersons and deans.

Subservience to superiors, especially when unjustified, can undermine the public interest, promote mediocrity, reduce productivity, and demoralize workers (Souryal, 1999:874). Police and correctional officers are often pressured to mete out selective justice in a rough neighborhood or a prison cellblock simply because a racist sergeant may so direct them. By the same token, probation officers may have to include negative comments in a PSI report simply to allow their judges to demonstrate "toughness" on crime. In response to such pressures, public service may be undermined and "ethical" practitioners demoralized. As a high-profile illustration, yet without overdramatizing the point, it was during the Iran-Contra Affair that Bud MacFarland, the foreign policy advisor to the President, attempted to commit suicide, and during the Whitewater Affair that Vincent Foster, Assistant to the President, succeeded in taking his own life (Souryal and McKay, 1996).

The following cases articulate the dysfunctional view of personal loyalty to superiors: the first in a police department and the second in a correctional institution.

Case No. 1: A Police Situation

On April 27, 2000, Miami Mayor Joe Carollo fired City Manager Donald Warshaw over a disagreement pertaining to Police Chief William O'Brien. Following the raid on the home of Elian Gonzalez's Miami relatives, Carollo demanded that Warshaw fire O'Brien for failing to inform the Mayor's Office of the raid and allowing a Miami police officer to participate in the action after the Mayor had announced that the Department would not assist federal agents if such a raid was conducted. When Warshaw, the former Miami chief of police, refused to fire O'Brien (his successor at the department), Carollo dismissed Warshaw, although the city charter does not grant the Mayor the authority to do so. Sixteen hours later, O'Brien announced his resignation, stating, "I refuse to be chief of police when someone as divisive and destructive as Joe Carollo is mayor" (Bridges, 2000:1A).

Carollo defended his dismissal of O'Brien, claiming that he had "lost all confidence" in the chief for refusing to warn him of the raid by the federal authorities (LaCorte, 2000:5A). O'Brien defended his decision not to inform the Mayor of the raid, calling it "a police issue and not a political issue" (LaCorte, 2000:5A). The Immigration and Naturalization Service, which led the raid, requested that the Department keep plans for the action confidential and not disclose the purpose of the federal search warrant. An INS agent later called O'Brien "a hero" (Bridges, 2000:18A).

Case No. 2: A Corrections Situation

In 1997, Wayne Garner, the commissioner of corrections in Georgia, allegedly authorized a mass beating of inmates at Hays State Prison in northwestern Georgia. He reportedly watched while the inmates, some handcuffed and lying on the floor, were punched, kicked, and stomped until blood streaked the walls. When the officers implicated in this beating were later interrogated, they stated, "We were all under the impression that it was OK to do it." Furthermore, Ray McWhorter, the highest-ranking prison official participating in the assault, allegedly covered up the entire affair, "denying that any abuse had occurred" (Prison Commissioner is Implicated in Abuse, 1997).

Discussion

These two cases articulate the dangers of personal loyalty in the workplace, the first at the executive level and the second at the operational level. Dialectically, they also demonstrate the need for moral fortitude in the practice of criminal justice. In the first case, the police chief resigned in protest, and in the second, the correctional officers helplessly succumbed to the illegal and arrogant whim of their superiors. These cases also show the vulnerability of public good when left unprotected from the whims of superiors by watchful subordinates. On the one hand, it was the seemingly disloyal act of Chief O'Brien that carried the day by making the INS raid successful. On the other hand, it was the seeming abdication of professional judgment by the correctional officers that allowed illegal and unjustified physical assault to be inflicted on the inmates.

The moral of these two cases is both complex and troubling, yet they call attention to the hierarchical nature of loyalties in criminal justice agencies and the imperative that every practitioner be faithful to the *summum bonum* of all loyalties—the public good. To Carollo, O'Brien's cooperation with INS agents constituted an act of disloyalty of the most egregious kind, but by choosing to keep the INS raid confidential and by allowing his second in command to participate, O'Brien accomplished a much higher good. The raid's objectives were accomplished, America's honor was preserved, and no one was hurt in the process. By so doing, O'Brien remained loyal to constitutional provisions and his obligation to protect the lives of his officers on duty. By the same token, by failing to fire O'Brien, Warshaw demonstrated loyalty to higher values (almost loyalty to loyalty) by halting disruption in city government following the raid, rather than feeding Carollo's agenda. The circumstances of both men aptly demonstrate for organizational ethicists the need to reexamine the misguided practice of personal loyalty to superiors.

In the second case, another unhealthy phenomenon is clear—the occupational culture of personal loyalty to superiors. It is far less plausible to believe that the participating correctional officers were naturally evil or that they were suddenly confronted with a situation they had never experienced during training. It is much more plausible to believe, on the other hand, that they submitted to the commissioner's desire because "it was the way it is always done" at the unit. Organizational culture seemed to make the officers believe that thinking for themselves and contemplating operational options, even when matters went out of hand, was forbidden. Evidence of such a culture was much more evident when McWhorter (the highest-ranking prison official participating in the assault) covered-up the entire affair, denying that any abuse had occurred. It seemed clear that personal loyalty to the commissioner and his men was the overriding reason for the brutal assault. If that was not the case, one would have expected that at least a few officers would have questioned the extent of applied force or would have reported the episode later. Since that did not happen, it becomes compelling to believe that the participating officers selected to "suspend their own judgment about right and wrong and act on the basis of unsubstantiated sentiments" (Fletcher, 1991:61). The fact that the commissioner led the assault must have triggered the officers' "personal loyalty effect," prompting them to act under a "veil of ignorance" without much concern to legality or propriety. It also seems plausible to assume that prior to the attack, the officers were well aware of their primary obligation not to use excessive force, yet in deference to the commissioner's desire, they manufactured a "mental reservation" that allowed them to engage in unlawful activities, all with a minimal amount of guilt.

Three ethical lessons can be learned from these cases. First, all criminal justice practitioners, superiors as well as subordinates, are equally responsible for accomplishing their official duties legally and ethically, each at his or her level. Second, subordinates, while inferior in rank, are not inferior in professional judgment. Third, superiors cannot allow the ends to justify the means unless the means are themselves legitimate.

Finally, superiors cannot take advantage of subordinates by coercing them into pacts of personal loyalty.

The Paradoxes of Personal Loyalty to Superiors

Based on the previous discussion, and to articulate the conceptual incoherence of personal loyalty to superiors in criminal justice agencies, the following paradoxes associated with the practice need to be presented.

First, despite the emotional support for the practice, there is no mention of it in agency rules and regulations. Except in small sheriff departments, perhaps, no criminal justice agency *requires* that practitioners be personally loyal to superiors. This paradox compels one to reason: "If personal loyalty to superiors is such a great virtue, why are agency rules and regulations so silent about it?" On the other hand, if personal loyalty to superiors is supposed to be optional, yet it is so generously rewarded, should it not raise suspicion concerning the integrity of the organization, the profession of criminal justice, and the integrity of its leaders?

Second, superiors usually make demands for personal loyalty when the agency is under attack (i.e., a state audit, an Internal Affairs investigation, a charge of misappropriation of funds, the disappearance of criminal evidence, etc.). By contrast, no loyalty demands are usually made when an agency is stable and business is conducted "as usual." As an illustration of this paradox, consider the undocumented story of a state governor who had just lost a favorite bill in the legislature by a single vote and who, upon knowing who the legislator responsible was, accused him of disloyalty. In bewilderment, the legislator responded "but Governor, I have always been loyal to you when you are right." At that moment, the governor rudely interrupted the legislator saying: "but . . . I do not need you when I am right!" Even if this illustration is fictitious, it can show how harmful personal loyalty to superiors in public service can be.

Third, personal loyalty to superiors ignores the fact that some superiors are not worthy of loyalty. Dialectically speaking, if it can be shown that all superiors are worthy of loyalty, it cannot be shown that some are not. Since hundreds of supervisors and administrators are fired or disciplined each year for violating agency rules, it must be assumed that at least some superiors are unworthy of loyalty. In such a case, it would be inappropriate to expect criminal justice practitioners to be loyal to unworthy superiors and hypocritical if they were compelled to be so. By contrast, if one concedes the view that unworthy superiors should not receive personal loyalty from subordinates, would not one indeed be granting employees the right to choose to whom they offer (or do not offer) personal loyalty? If this was the case, one would be giving credence to the proposition that personal loyalty to superiors is not mandatory.

Fourth, the rationale that personal loyalty to superiors is a *reflex action*, one akin to saluting commanders on military bases, is misleading.

While saluting military commanders is required by military rules, personal loyalty to superiors, especially in criminal justice agencies, is not. Furthermore, while no harm to third parties would occur if military commanders were saluted, serious harm to third parties can occur if criminal justice practitioners are expected to thoughtlessly comply with their superiors' desires. On the other hand, if personal loyalty to superiors was really intended as a reflex action, the fundamental argument for loyalty would be pointless because it would be bereft of sociability and meaningful association.

Fifth, the tendency of superiors to treat personal loyalty as a one-way-street relationship (i.e., the superiors need not return the loyalty) destroys the essence of loyalty. In a free society, any one-sided relationship can be suspect and potentially abusive. Since institutional effectiveness requires that superiors and subordinates trust one another, the practice of a one-way-street loyalty may well destroy this trust. Furthermore, because criminal justice practitioners are particularly skeptical of how they are treated by superiors (Barker and Carter, 1994; Delattre, 1996; Herzberg, 1976; Souryal, 1998; Souryal and McKay, 1996), the practice of not returning loyalty by superiors can be seen as evidence to the farcical nature of personal loyalty to superiors.

Instead of Personal Loyalty, What?

To adequately explain the hierarchical nature of loyalties, the authors must admit that balancing one's loyalties to God, family, friends, and community is a complicated endeavor that can be either gratifying or distressing. Balancing one's loyalties at the workplace can be more complex because, more often than not, one has to work with total strangers. Workplace loyalties, therefore, should not be seen as "fair weather commitments"; they have a self-sacrificing dimension, which can preserve the organization from self-assertion and self-diminishment (Kleinig, 1995). For that reason alone, perhaps, it is important to discuss the *grammar* of workplace loyalties.

The term grammar is here used to mean the skillful manipulation of three types of loyalty, which, though not interchangeable, overlap at the workplace with varying degrees of intensity. The ethical "conjugation" of these loyalty types by both practitioners and superiors is critical to the conduct of public service. These types will be here rank-ordered from that of the least value to that of the highest ethical conjugation.

First, *personal loyalty* is the lowest level of loyalty at the workplace. It is mechanical in nature and constitutes the subordinate's unexamined obligation and desires of a specifically identified superior. Examples include the obligation of deputy sheriffs to be loyal to their sheriffs and school teachers to their principals. The moral of personal loyalty is "from each to each immediate superior."

Second, *institutional loyalty* is the next level of loyalty at the workplace. It is organizational in nature and is constituted by the obligation of each agency member, including subordinates and superiors, to accept, comply with, and support the agency's mission and its ends-means strategy. Examples include the obligation of correctional officers or probation officers to be loyal to agency policies, rules, and regulations. The motto of institutional loyalty is "from each to the collective essence of the agency."

Third, *integrated loyalty* is the highest and most virtuous level of loyalty at the workplace. It is idealistic in nature and constitutes genuine concern by each worker to the values and ideals of the profession. It transcends the previous loyalties by honoring the ideals of accountability, rationality, fairness, and good will. Examples include the obligation to respect the constitutional rights of all individuals, to protect the innocent against oppression, and to preserve the principle of equal protection. The moral of integrated loyalty is "from each to all professional ideals and values."

These loyalty types may also be characterized in terms of their durability. Personal loyalty is transient; it seldom outlives the subordinate-superior relationship. Institutional loyalty is organizationally oriented; it is expected to last for the worker's entire association with the organization. Integrated loyalty is transcendental; it is expected to last throughout the worker's organizational life, regardless of the organization where the work takes place.

The conjugation of these loyalty types at the workplace requires special care since they can overlap in the organizational setting, causing considerable distortion as to whom or what should be the first object of loyalty. The authors propose the following conjugation rules: (1) personal loyalty, being the most volatile and temporal, may never replace institutional loyalty; (2) institutional loyalty, being the most supportive and durable, should be positioned ahead of loyalty to superiors; and (3) integrated loyalty, being the *summum bonum* of all workplace loyalties, should be the cornerstone of all workplace loyalties and pursued before any institutional loyalty. Failure to accept this conjugational proposal is detrimental to the moral integrity of public agencies.

Three Explanatory Assumptions

Before presenting the main arguments for and against personal loyalty to superiors, three preliminary assumptions must be made. They are essential to the theoretical construct of personal loyalty in the organizational setting.

Clear and Distinct Difference

The purpose of personal loyalty to superiors must be distinct from that of organizational control, discipline, or effectiveness. The difference is as clear as expecting school children to bring the teacher an apple (under the tacit risk of being treated differently if they do not) and requiring them to study hard to graduate. It would be naive to expect, for instance, that when police or correctional officers put their lives in danger, they do so because of personal loyalty to any superior. It is much more plausible to believe that when they so do, they are motivated by a professional sense of devotion that calls on their inner strength to overcome "impossible" odds.

Concerns for organizational control, discipline, or effectiveness, on the other hand, are *contractual obligations*. They are embedded in organizational theory and enforced through agency rules and regulations. Contractual obligations are *primary relationships* that are complete in themselves; they possess the *necessary connection* to work objectives and are not contingent upon any kind of loyalty to make them legitimate. Drucker (1974:424) states, "An employer has no business with a man's personality. Employment is a specific contract calling for a specific performance and for nothing else. . . . An employee owes no loyalty, he owes no attitudes—he owes performance and nothing else."

Primacy of Loyalty to Public Service

Criminal justice is not just another field of public service; it is critical to societal survival. It embodies the *intrinsic* values of liberty, justice, democracy, and ideals that are inextricably connected to the primacy of public service, but if personal loyalty to superiors were to be the most important, then loyalty to public service would be of lesser importance. If that was the case, then accommodating the *instrumental* desires of superiors (who may or may not be worthy of loyalty) would subject the virtues of public service to the ideology of organizational convenience.

Concerns to Institutional Integrity

Any culture that condones unrestricted submission to superiors, whether they be kings, rulers, or administrators, undermines institutional integrity. While the Nazi culture in Germany and McCarthyism in the United States were extreme cases, the principle, nevertheless, applies to all public agencies. Consider, for example, the public embarrassment law enforcement officials had to endure because of the Rodney King case, the Ruby Ridge case, or the Branch Davidians case. Moreover, in each of these cases, it seems safe to assume that justice would have been better served had the practitioners been loyal to the obligation of duty rather than the pleasure of their superiors.

The Personal Loyalty Debate

Proponents of personal loyalty to superiors in criminal justice agencies argue that it is essential because of six considerations. First, it motivates the practitioners into producing above and beyond duty. Second, it bolsters institutional responsibility. Third, it increases productivity. Fourth, it makes work more meaningful. Fifth, it inhibits organizational disloyalty. Finally, it insures institutional integrity. The authors' view is that each of these considerations is questionable, if not logically inaccurate.

Personal Loyalty to Superiors Fosters Supererogation

According to this view, such loyalty obligates workers to perform above and beyond the call of duty. The idea of supererogation lies in Christian theology, particularly the story of the Good Samaritan, who paid the innkeeper "over and above for taking care of the robbed and wounded man" (Heyd, 1982:18). Paradigmatically, supererogatory acts have been characterized as "saintly and heroic, those in which people make sacrifices to achieve a morally good end" (Heyd, 1982:118). Perhaps with the exception of police and prisons, most supererogatory deeds in criminal justice are relatively low-level acts, such as staying after hours and finishing something for the boss or performing extra tasks that are not specified in the work contract (Souryal and McKay, 1996).

Although supererogation is an admirable virtue, no evidence supports the view that supererogatory acts by criminal justice practitioners are products of personal loyalty to superiors. It is implausible to suggest, for instance, that when police officers risk their lives to disarm a bomb or subdue a dangerous felon, they do so because of personal loyalty to any supervisor. It would be much more plausible to argue that when police officers or correctional officers act heroically, they do so because they are confronted with a professional situation that calls forth a response of extraordinary courage. On further reflection, one may legitimately view supererogatory acts in criminal justice as having nothing to do with personal loyalty and everything to do with professional commitment.

Furthermore, not all supererogatory acts may be good; some may be arbitrary and even foolhardy (Souryal and McKay, 1996). The others can be praiseworthy or blameworthy depending on the reasoning behind them. Consider, for instance, General Custer's Last Stand. Was his decision to fight until death an act of supererogation or was it simply motivated by military duty? Was it more consistent with proper military strategy or with personal egoism? Finally, was it worth doing? With these questions in mind, criminal justice practitioners should be able to debate the supererogatory nature of acts such as those claimed by correctional officers who risk starting a prison riot by beating a recalcitrant inmate.

Personal Loyalty to Superiors Bolsters Institutional Responsibility

This view suggests that loyalty to superiors enhances discipline by maximizing compliance with agency rules and regulations. This practice, in turn, can reduce rule violations and acts of misfeasance.

Although this assumption sounds logical, compliance with agency rules and regulations hinges essentially on an effective system of quality supervision. If that is the case, then failure to comply with rules and regulations is totally unrelated to matters of loyalty to superiors. It would be even more plausible to argue that failure to comply with rules and regulations can only be minimized when supervisors dutifully watch for errors, set quality controls, and enforce disciplinary actions impartially, yet these activities are antithetical to the tradition of personal loyalty to superiors. When superiors and workers enter into loyalty pacts, the natural implication is that they will, by virtue of such pacts, "take care of each other"; the former will act as "guardian angels" for the latter. This implication suggests that errors will be overlooked, support will be always offered, and misbehaviors will be forgiven. Indeed, the effectiveness of discipline in many criminal justice agencies seems to be undermined by the existence of loyalty pacts between workers and superiors. In the name of loyalty, the workers underreport the "seriousness" of their violations and the supervisors, interested in keeping these pacts, disingenuously oblige.

Personal Loyalty to Superiors Increases Productivity

According to this view, productivity is improved when the workers, "united" by personal loyalty to superiors, act as an organic social group (McGregor, 1960; Merton, 1938; Williams, 1982). In this sense, Japanese workers have been hailed as a showcase. Despite the romanticism of this view, American workers do not embrace it. On the contrary, it appears that a more pragmatic feature motivates American workers, a spin-off of the relationship between business owners and expert workers (Souryal and McKay, 1996). This feature has been regarded as more conducive to employees' satisfaction and agency productivity (Herzberg, 1976; Simon, 1997).

In criminal justice agencies, affinity among workers does not seem to arise from loyalties to revered objects and it is more likely to develop as "a byproduct of shared experiences and thought" (Schaar, 1957:6). Furthermore, despite the increasing use of liberal management styles, workers seldom choose those for whom they work or those who work for them. As a result, especially in police and correctional institutions, it is more likely that relations between first-line officers and ranking officers will be characterized by conflict, contention, and distrust, despite public claims to the contrary. Herein lies one of the most difficult tests of personal loyalty to superiors, having to offer unearned allegiance to a person in a position of power despite the justified negative sentiments one may hold toward such a person (Souryal and McKay, 1996). This contradiction may well demonstrate that what may casually be perceived as personal loyalty to superiors is nothing other than a temporary pact of mutual protection.

Personal Loyalty to Superiors Makes Work More Meaningful

This view suggests that personal loyalty to superiors promotes a healthy environment conducive to collaboration and harmony. Without such an environment, according to this theory, workers would be unwilling or unable to achieve "the hard goals of community integration, social coherence, or civic wholeness" (Haughey, 1993:31). In a Herzbergian sense, Haughey (1993) advocates job enrichment as a means of minimizing bureaucratization and petty management procedures. As a remedy, he proposes a more sympathetic environment, one that is typically supported by an abundance of loyalty sentiments. Only in such an atmosphere, Haughey claims, can "meaningfulness" be restored and workers' self-worth reasserted.

Despite the sentimentality of this view, unsympathetic work environments are invariably products of inconsiderate management; they are either caused or tolerated by managers, who alone are able to restore their "meaningfulness." If this is the case, then no amount of personal loyalty to superiors can make a difference, since changing the work environment is ostensibly the function of a caring, deliberate management. In the absence of such a management style, further offers of loyalty to superiors would be pointless.

Personal Loyalty to Superiors Inhibits Organizational Disloyalty

In this view, it is assumed that if workers had no loyalty to their superiors, they would, by implication, have no loyalty to their organization. This logic is incorrect for two reasons. First, superiors are only tools for achieving organizational ends, withholding loyalty from the former is not the equivalent of denying loyalty to the latter. Second, sentiments of loyalty and disloyalty are (as mentioned earlier) not mutually exclusive. The essence of loyalty is offering unwavering personal support and the essence of disloyalty is committing professional betrayal; however, aloyal criminal justice workers (whom the authors argue are a majority) cannot be characterized as individuals totally without loyalty (Souryal and McKay, 1996). Indeed, they may have higher institutional or integrated loyalties than do loyal workers. This assertion may well explain the "whistle-blowing" phenomenon whereby aloyal workers can publicly switch their loyalty to what they proclaim is a higher loyalty. As a case in point, Frederic Whitehurst, a FBI forensic scientist, blew the whistle in 1995 on the problems of the FBI crime lab. When he was later accused of disloyalty, he defended himself by invoking loyalty to professional practices, an ideal he accused his superiors of abandoning. In the final analysis, however, Whitehurst's act of aloyalty may have been a supererogatory act; because of his alleged disloyalty, the crime lab has undergone monumental reforms.

Personal Loyalty to Superiors Ensures Institutional Integrity

This view suggests that establishing an unbroken chain of personal loyalty to superiors can enhance institutional integrity. Again, while this argument may sound plausible, it is flawed for two reasons. First, it is doubtful that any chain of loyalty can exist in any but the smallest of criminal justice agencies. Even if this was possible, loyalty chains invariably break when power arrangements change from within or from outside the agency. For example, when a correctional lieutenant is promoted to assistant warden, creating a situation in which her former captain serves under her command, the existing chain of loyalty changes. Loyalty chains also break when supervisors are hired laterally or professional jealousy and conflict permeate the ranks.

Second, even if a perfect chain of loyalty existed, the agency's institutional integrity would not be any stronger than the integrity of its weakest link. Furthermore, if the "chain" argument is pushed to its limit, there can be no room for acts of disloyalty by middle managers, deputy directors, or assistant bureau heads, but such acts routinely occur without any noticeable loss of agency efficiency (Souryal and McKay, 1996).

The Organizational Imperative: The Duty-Based Thesis

Instead of personal loyalty to superiors in criminal justice agencies, the authors propose loyalty to duty and public service ideals. Dutifulness is the *workers' obligation to do the best they possibly can in the service of their publics, rather than themselves or each other* (Souryal and McKay, 1996). In Kantian terms, dutifulness is a *categorical imperative*, since it is consistent with ideals that are abstract, objective, and universal. Since dutifulness commits practitioners to carrying out their assignments as official contracts, they would, by virtue of such commitment, be disinterested in compromising themselves by seeking personal gain.

The duty-based thesis is a module consisting of two "lungs," one representing commitment to professional accountability and the other organizational identification. The former reinforces compliance with agency rules and regulations, the latter to individual responsibility; the former focuses on procedural matters, the latter on substantive matters; the former signifies policy decisions, the latter discretionary decisions. Use of the word lungs here is significant because it emphasizes unison of action—no lung can function separately from the other. In criminal justices agencies, public service requires that *both* commitments to professional accountability and organizational identification be synchronized like lungs. Together, they can maximize productivity without incurring the risk of personal loyalty to superiors. To incorporate this module effectively into criminal justice agencies, three countercultural changes should be made.

The Use of the Term Loyalty Should be Avoided in the Context of Relations between Superiors and Subordinates

Like the use of the term war (as on crime or on drugs), it is too emotionally charged; it implies "taking sides," "offering one's all," "supporting one's camp at any price," and, in extreme cases, engaging in a *jihad*. Although the mental faculties associated with these terms can enable workers to separate acceptable from unacceptable behavior, they can also lead them to irrational conclusions (Zerubavel, 1991). Workers may perceive a crevasse between those "in the social cluster" and those "outside its confines," those to be favored "regardless of what they do," and those to be disfavored "despite the great services they do" and possibly between those who "deserve justice" and those "who deserve it not." By contrast, the essence of criminal justice must be always seen as spiritual. Although it can be violent at times, it is fundamentally embedded in the principles of veracity, impartiality, tolerance, and good faith.

In lieu of the loyalty, criminal justice agencies should consider concepts such as collaboration, cooperation, and support. Such concepts have a sociological tendency to bind workers and superiors in a social reality that transcends obsessions with occupational boundaries, antipathies, salutations, and betrayal. In the final analysis, they may be able to experience the beatitude of criminal justice as a field of the reasonable, the legal, and the moral.

Dutiful Supervision Should be Strengthened

When criminal justice workers make procedural decisions, they should be held accountable to agency rules and regulation, yet for this to occur, a system of "dutiful supervision" must be in place. Supervisors should impose reasonable standards, apply ethical sanctions, and, when necessary, terminate "uncooperative" workers. Dutiful supervision, nevertheless, cannot be performed in a Kantian context; it requires a Wilsonian context, whereby it stimulates the sentiments of sympathy, self-control, responsibility, and good faith (Wilson, 1993). A system of dutiful supervision cannot succeed without fairness, the absence of which may have precipitated the need for protection by practicing personal loyalty to superiors in the first place.

Professional Accountability Should be Institutionalized

When criminal justice practitioners make discretionary decisions, they should be motivated by professional accountability before any other value. Their determination of what is reasonable, legal, or moral must reflect both institutional and integrated loyalties. Although they should be encouraged to seek guidance from superiors, acquiescence must be voluntary. The relationship between practitioners and superiors should be civil: one that is characterized by maturity and not subservience, respect and not fear, strength and not feebleness, and optimism and not dejection. If these traits are cultivated and nourished, both workers and superiors will defer to organizational identification—the institutional imperative of serving the public interest before any other.

When professional accountability and organizational identification are operative, it would only be natural to expect criminal justice practitioners to develop a philosophical conviction of justice and a contextual understanding of themselves. The more they learn, the more they would wish to pursue the public good. Workers eventually would be able to support their superiors when they are right and correct them when they are wrong. Superiors, in return, would be able to transcend the need for personal loyalty and respond with *noblesse oblige*, a fundamental sentiment that emphasizes understanding, appreciation, and patience. Finally, with the growth of mutual trust, the workers would be able to see their superiors as philosopher-kings, role models, mentors, and (when mutually agreeable) friends.

Policy Implications

Loyal to the scholarly tradition, the authors are tempted to recommend that each prescription advanced in the duty-based thesis be incorporated in departmental policy, but consistent with the "integrated loyalty" view, the authors recommend not to do so. There are three reasons for that. First, ethical issues should be separated from legal issues because the latter can always be rescinded, reversed, or modified. Since the issue of loyalty and loyalties at the workplace is an ethical issue, it should be differentiated from policy. Second, like discretion, the exercise of loyalties at the workplace lends itself to reasoning rather than obeying, understanding rather than believing, and justifying rather than complying. As such, while the conjugation of workplace loyalties may vary from one practitioner to another, it would be legitimate as long as it is morally justified. Third, ethical issues can be countercultural. Requiring criminal justice practitioners to change their immutable view of loyalty to superiors may not only be antithetical but also disturbing. If so, the organization as a whole will be confused.

In the final analysis, criminal justice practitioners, both superiors and subordinates, will have to be reeducated in the exercise of workplace loyalties by learning more about the sanctity of public service, liberation ethics, and the obligation to maximize public good. When they learn and act in good faith, these sanctities will be intrinsically honored.

Endnotes

[1] While the roles of supervisors and superiors in the organizational setting can be considerably different, from a loyalty standpoint, this article will arbitrarily treat them as one and the same. To avoid redundancy, furthermore, both will be referred to as "superiors."

[2] For a proposition on how the practice of personal loyalty to superiors can be replaced, see Personal Loyalty to Superiors in Criminal Justice Agencies, *Justice Quarterly*, Vol. 16, No. 4, December, 1999.

References

Barker, T., & Carter, D. L. (Eds.). (1994). *Police deviance*. Cincinnati, OH: Anderson.

Blamires, H. (1963). *The Christian mind*. London, England: Society for Promoting Christian Knowledge.

Bridges, T. (2000, April 29). Elian fallout topples second Miami official. *The Houston Chronicle*, pp. 1A, 18A.

Delattre, E. (1996). *Character and cops: Ethics in policing*. Washington, DC: American Enterprise Institute.

Denhardt, R. B. (1987). Images of death and slavery in organizational life. *Journal of Management, 13*, 529–541.

Drucker, P. F. (1974). *Management: Tasks, responsibilities, and practices*. New York: Harper & Row.

Fletcher, G. P. (1991). *Loyalty: An essay on the morality of relationships*. New York: Oxford University Press.

Haughey, J. C. (1993). Does loyalty in the workplace have a future? *Business Ethics Quarterly, 3*(1), 1–16.

Herzberg, F. (1976). *The managerial choice: To be efficient and to be human*. Homewood, IL: Dow Jones-Irwin.

Heyd, D. (1982). *Supererogation*. New York: Cambridge University Press.

Kleinig, J. (1995). Loyalty. *Criminal Justice Ethics, 13*(1), 34–36.

Klockars, C. B. (1999). The rhetoric of community policing. In S. Stojkovic, J. Klofas, & D. Kalinich (Eds.), *The administration and management of criminal justice organizations* (pp. 19–36). Prospect Heights, IL: Waveland Press.

LaCorte, R. (2000, April 28). Miami mayor dismisses official who refused to fire police chief. *The Houston Chronicle*, p. 5A.

Law Enforcement Code of Ethics. (2000). (Online). Available at: http://www.co.riverside.ca.us/sheriff/general/law-code.htm.

Manning, P. K. (1985). The police: Mandate, strategies, and appearances. In W. C. Terry III (Ed.), *Policing society: An occupational view* (pp. 133–154). Newark, NJ: Wiley.

McGregor, D. M. (1960). *The human side of enterprise*. New York: McGraw-Hill.

Merton, R. (1938). Social structure and anomie. *American Sociological Review, 3*, 672–682.

Morns, T. (1997). *If Aristotle ran General Motors*. New York: First Owl Books.

Prison commissioner is implicated in abuse. (1997, July 1) *The Houston Chronicle*, p. 5A.

Schaar, J. (1957). *Loyalty in America*. Berkley, CA: University of California Press.

Simon, H. (1997). *Administrative behavior*. New York: The Free Press.

Souryal, S. (1998). *Ethics in criminal justice: In search of the truth* (2nd ed.). Cincinnati, OH: Anderson.

Souryal, S. (1999). Personal loyalty to superiors in criminal justice agencies. *Justice Quarterly, 4*(16), 871–895.

Souryal, S., & McKay, B. W. (1996). Personal loyalty to superiors in public service. *Criminal Justice Ethics, 15*(2), 41–58.

Williams, J. D. (1982). *Public administration: The people's business.* Boston, MA: Little, Brown.

Wilson, J. Q. (1993). *The moral sense.* New York: Free Press.

Zerubavel, E. (1991). *The fine line: Making distinctions in everyday life.* New York: Free Press.

Chapter 17

Contraband
The Basis for Legitimate Power in a Prison Social System

David B. Kalinich
Stan Stojkovic

The traditional approach to prison organization and management has been the application of bureaucratic authority over guards and inmates. Control over inmates is based on a lengthy set of institutional rules and regulations. Threats of coercion are used for noncompliance, with institutional rules and rewards, such as "good time," being offered to inmates for conformance. The preponderance of research literature on prison organizations points out, however, that a great deal of leakage of administrative control exists, and prison rules and regulations are readily circumvented both by guards and inmates (Sykes, 1958; Sykes and Messinger, 1960; Cloward, 1960). This understanding of prison organizations is supported by literature and research in organizational theory, which suggests that control over subordinates, especially in large bureaucratic agencies, is difficult to achieve, and leakage of control is normal for such organizations (Downs, 1966; Warwick, 1975). Yet prisons are rela-

David B. Kalinich and Stan Stojkovic, *Criminal Justice and Behavior*, Vol. 12 No. 4, pp. 435–451, copyright © 1985 by Sage Publications. Reprinted by permission of Sage Publications.

tively stable, with disturbances and rioting occurring with no more frequency than civil disturbances and rioting.

The popular question posed after a riot or disturbance is, "why do prisoners riot?" This question is ultimately posed visibly after a prison riot by the establishment of a blue ribbon committee appointed by the executive branch of the government empaneled to investigate the causes of the riot. Given that the traditional bureaucratic approach to prison is a weak form of management fraught with leakages of control and inmates seemingly without a normative commitment to the system to which they are unwilling subordinates, the more perplexing question that should be addressed is why prisons are relatively stable. It seems that addressing this question will provide insights into periods of instability. The purpose of this article is to examine the phenomenon of stability in prison organizations, and how this is augmented, in part, by the prison contraband marketplace.

Stability in a prison environment is dependent to a great extent upon the need most inmates have for stability, certainty, and safety. Most inmates attempt to find a niche in the prison community, serve their time unobtrusively, and earn their release at the earliest possible time (Toch, 1977). Prison guards similarly desire certainty, stability, and safety. Guards attempt to establish a working relationship with inmates by using their discretion in enforcing rules, which becomes the basis for cooperation with the inmates, as well as providing the guards with a reputation among inmates as being fair (Lombardo, 1981). It is these interactions between officers and inmates that help ameliorate the stressful conditions of prison life. As described by Lombardo (1982), when adaptation by inmates to the stress-producing situations of prison is unsuccessful, then individual and collective violence supersede control and stability as predominant elements in the prison social setting.

The literature on informal prison social structure suggests that order and stability in prison are provided through accommodative and exchange relationships between inmates and custodial staff. Sykes (1958) provides the earliest systematic analysis of the leakage of formal control over the prison environment and the development of the informal social system based on the accommodation of inmate needs. He suggests that the systematic deprivation that inmates suffer provides them with the incentive to develop an identifiable social system that provides mechanisms that help alleviate the pains of imprisonment. The inmate social system includes the development and selection of leaders who facilitate and support the inmate culture.

The leaders are appropriately referred to as "politicians" in prison jargon as they are capable of developing favorable interpersonal relationships with inmates, guards, and treatment personnel and gaining the trust of individuals with whom they deal. Leaders are typically older than other inmates, have spent considerable time in the institution, and are serving long sentences. They have usually been involved in criminal behavior that gives them status with their peers, and sometimes they have been important members of criminal gangs or organizations on the outside (Irwin, 1970). By and large, inmate leaders hold key administrative or clerical positions and have access to avenues of communication and influence in administrative decision making through relationships of trust and the power of persuasion (McCleery, 1960).

Inmate leaders and guards form exchange relationships and share a common concern for a smoothly running prison. Inmate leaders, who gain relatively more from the informal social system, have a vested interest in a status quo posture within the prison environment, and will assist guards in keeping an orderly and smooth-running cell block by exerting influence and pressure on potentially disruptive inmates. As a result, inmate leaders and prison administrators share the goal of maintaining an orderly institution (Cloward, 1960). It is at this focal point where guards and inmate leaders develop compromises that the formal system interacts with, and that facilitates the informal power structure, as both systems have the same organizational objectives—order maintenance and social control in the environment.

It has been pointed out that guards could not control the inmate population and keep order (the criteria by which they are ultimately judged) without the assistance of key inmate leaders (McCorkle and Korn, 1954; McCleery, 1960). However, there is a cost to the institution for assistance from inmates in maintaining its system. The basis of power wielded by influential inmates who facilitate order maintenance is their ability to alleviate the systematic pains of imprisonment imposed upon their fellow inmates. To allow inmate leaders to maintain their leadership and influence roles, the prison staff must give inmate leaders autonomy to circumvent and manipulate the formal oppressive system of control and operate a system that minimizes inmate deprivations. A major facet of that informal system is the contraband market, which provides (a) material goods and services to inmates that they otherwise would not have access to, and (b) a sense of psychological satisfaction, both from seeing the formal system "beat" and from feeling they have at least some control over their lives. In effect, inmates have created their own system of governance, one that they accept and legitimize at the informal level.

In this informal social system, rules and norms are promulgated and imposed, at least through influence, by inmate leaders. These rules can provide the basis for a stable environment—an output that administrators can accept. What is developed at the informal level is a legitimate form of governance for inmates that is based, in part, on the contraband marketplace and, as such, is at odds with bureaucratic prison authority. It is this legitimate form of governance, we posit, that ultimately enhances stability in prisons. Ironically, this form of legitimate governance evolves naturally out of the contradiction between the rigid control orientation of prison and the inherent inability of the traditional bureaucratic system to achieve control. Therefore, the stability of a prison is contingent upon the strength of the informal inmate social system, which is linked inexorably to the contraband market system.

The social system within prisons is defined relative to the patterns of social interactions of inmates (Sykes, 1958). These interactions are predicated on a separate system of values, beliefs, and attitudes among inmates. These attributes promulgate an informal hierarchy, with the presence of specific roles by inmates, including leaders within the inmate corp. Strength within an inmate social system is defined as the degree of consensus, commitment, and acquiescence on the part of inmates to the rules of the informal system and to those who are given leadership roles — in other words, the formation of a legitimate form of governance.

Current literature suggests that a cohesive inmate social system does not exist to any great extent in contemporary prisons, as some prison societies are divided by race (Carroll, 1974), dominated by "super-gangs" (Jacobs, 1977), organized along loosely connected cliques (Irwin, 1980), and are torn internally because of the rising politicalization of the typical inmate (Stastny and Tyrnaurer, 1982). The heterogeneity of the prison society clearly is an impediment to the development of a universally accepted informal inmate social structure, and, as such, limits the development of an informal form of legitimate governance; this creates the potential for instability (Lombardo, 1982). In fact, conflict between inmates or groups of inmates is sometimes based on feuds over marketing territories and rights of more profitable forms of contraband (Davidson, 1977). However, coalitions are formed, and compromises are often struck in deference to the survival of the marketplace and the individual buyers and sellers involved.

The Contraband Marketplace: The Basis of the Informal Social System and Informal Legitimate Governance

The position of this article is that the contraband marketplace is a factor that is instrumental to the development of a legitimate form of inmate governance.[1] Contraband is defined as materials that are unauthorized by the formal prison administration. Common examples of contraband are the following: drugs, alcohol, gambling and gambling paraphernalia, real money, and a host of other assorted commodities and services. The demand for contraband is created by the institution's formal goals: the control and punishment of inmates. The supply of contraband products comes about due to the inability of the organization to achieve its primary goal.

The organization cannot totally control its inmate body for a variety of reasons: low officer-to-inmate ratio, lack of normative commitment to the organizational rules by inmates, and the inability to implement an efficient reward/punishment system to gain compliance among inmates. Thus administrators emphasize that which is obtainable: relatively quiet and clean cell blocks that are free of visible violence. This obtainable goal is achieved through a series of relationships developed between guards and influential leaders. It is at this focal point that the formal system erodes and the inmate social structure begins.

Much activity in the inmate social structure evolves around the maintenance of the contraband marketplace. A vast amount of inmate time is dedicated to the contraband marketplace; inmates are dependent upon the marketplace for material and psychological well-being, and inmates who are influential and are cast in leadership roles are those who contribute to the maintenance of the contraband marketplace (Kalinich, 1980; Stojkovic, 1984).

One of the earliest works on the black market in prison was written about a prisoner of war (POW) camp for American soldiers in Germany during World War II; the work described a flourishing contraband system that included a system of trade between prison camps (Radford, 1945). Since then, a great deal has been written about prisons, particularly in relation to the informal inmate social structure. Although most of the literature does not focus on the contraband marketplace, almost all of it makes reference to contraband flow, with some of the literature describing that phenomenon in detail. McCleery (1960) and Davidson (1977) describe active and prosperous contraband market systems that were controlled by powerful inmate leaders. Irwin (1970) depicts the links between inmates' street behaviors and their behaviors in the prison contraband market and the tenuous connection contraband provides among prison gangs. As a result of his research in a Federal Prison, Guenther (1975) concluded that contraband was rather common, and guards attempted to control dangerous contraband (weapons, escape equipment) whereas they, in effect, turned their backs on contraband that was considered a nuisance (drugs, gambling material, homemade alcohol). Shoblad (1972), describing his life as an inmate, discusses with some detail the sophisticated nature of the contraband marketplace and the ease with which inmates provided unauthorized goods and services to the prison population.

Research focusing on the contraband marketplace in a maximum security prison described the existence of a thriving marketplace in which most inmates participated with a great deal of frequency and with an array of goods and services available to them (Kalinich, 1980). The major categories of goods and services available were the following: drugs, alcoholic beverages, gambling, appliances (TV sets, hot plates, radios, and so on), clothing, buying of institutional privileges and reports, weapons, food and snack services, and prostitution. Each of these categories included a number of subcomponents, with complex or simple interactions, and the system was found to be based on a complex monetary operation that included the use of a regular banking system, organized loan sharking in

the institution, inmates' prison accounts, inmate script, and real money—
"green"—and cigarettes. Similar to Guenther's (1975) research, this study
showed that some forms of contraband were considered dangerous
byguards—and inmates—such as weapons, whereas much of the contraband was considered a thorn in the side of guards. However, this study
found that certain forms of contraband were considered beneficial by custodial staff and were allowed to exist with the tacit but rather open
approval of the majority of the staff.

A common and approved contraband service was the "inmate
store." Each cell block had one or two inmates who kept a large stock of
snacks, pop, instant coffee, and so on, that they purchased at the inmate
commissary—the authorized outlet—and resold to inmates in the eve-
nings after the commissary was closed. This form of "convenience store"
was found beneficial by the custodial staff as it gave the inmates a
method to help structure their free evening time. This was harmless
though unauthorized and added to the smooth running of the cell block.
Guards' views on drug use by inmates were mixed, even though administrators saw drugs as a definite threat to the security of the institution.
Whereas older guards viewed drugs as dangerous, but alcoholic beverages brewed in the institution harmless, younger guards viewed marijuana use as a method of pacifying inmates (Kalinich, 1980).

Other research in a maximum security prison has concluded that
narcotics and its distribution are extremely important in controlling the
institutional environment (Stojkovic, 1984). When inmates were asked to
describe the influence of drugs within the facility, they stated the importance of the sub-rosa drug market in stabilizing the environment. The
consensus among inmates was that the providing of illegal goods and
services by pivotal inmates in the inmate social system provided control
for correctional officers and comfort to inmates in coping with their incarceration. In effect, the distribution of specific contraband items—differing
types of narcotics—was essential for both custodial staff and key inmates
in the control of the environment.

What was produced was a situation in which institutional capital
was concentrated and power centralized with a few inmates. The short-
term effect was that the inmate society was pacified until the next supply
of drugs was delivered. In the interim, inmates attempted to cope with
imprisonment using illegal means. It was at this juncture that inmate violence, assaults, and robberies surfaced. More important, this is where the
value of inmate leaders is pivotal. When institutional violence surfaces, it
becomes incumbent upon these leaders to develop compromises among
the warring factions to ensure "domestic tranquility." In this way, not
only is the institution stabilized through the influence of inmate politicians but the market structure remains intact.

Thus it becomes clear that the contraband marketplace is an important focal point for inmates, around which they focus a great deal of their

activities as well as structure their behaviors and interactions with each other and the prison staff, especially custodial staff.

Power of Inmate Leaders, Legitimacy, and Stability

The link between inmates and staff is through the inmate leaders. One of the major roles of inmate leaders is to facilitate the flow of contraband. In doing so, they gain the backing and support of those inmates who value contraband and, thus, can influence them and their behaviors.

The use of formal rewards and punishments to control inmates' behavior is limited. Guards often overlook rule violations by inmates who are not troublemakers and tend to be cooperative over all. As stated earlier, guards depend on more influential inmates' cooperation in keeping the cell blocks clean and relatively peaceful. In return for their cooperation, guards will overlook the manipulations of the influential inmates as long as the order of the cell block is facilitated and not disrupted by those manipulations.

There are three elements that are common to inmate leaders. First, they have had extensive knowledge of the informal institutional structure from past experience and are serving long sentences. Second, they have jobs that permit freedom of movement from one area within the institution to another. Third, they have a large number of contacts with fellow inmates who will work for or with them, and some may have criminal contacts outside the institution that can help coordinate the inflow of contraband into the prison black market (Kalinich, 1980). In addition, they are skillful at developing good relationships with inmates and guards. They can usually gain a relationship of trust with inmates and guards, giving both groups the appearance of allegiance to them. In most cases, the inmate leaders have a vested interest in the status quo and the stability of the institution (Cloward, 1960) and, therefore, share the guards' interest in an orderly cell block. They have resources, "business" expertise, are sensitive to the needs of both inmates and prison staff, and can negotiate with the two groups who may otherwise be in constant conflict. In effect, they can contribute to the sense of control and order of the custodial staff, and they can control their constituents—the inmates—through overt and covert means and help keep order in the prison community.

It was found to be a common practice for inmates who were politicians to be selected by prison staff for work assignments, involving some responsibility and trust, such as a clerical position working under a supervisor or counselor. The selection is made on the inmate's potential as a "politician" as staff look for inmates who "know how the prison really works." These inmates, though not expected to be informants, have their finger on the pulse of activities in the institution, and can help legitimize the authority of the staff member they are working for through their

influence over other inmates. Staff members enter this employment relationship usually knowing the inmate will use the position for his own
benefit. The trade-off of bureaucratic control for stability is considered a
rational choice at the operational level (Kalinich, 1980).

The label "politician" suggests that inmate leaders hold legitimate
power over their fellow inmates. Their ability to supply contraband goods
and services directly and facilitate the behavior of others who are active in
the contraband marketplace provides them with the ability to influence and
lead their fellow inmates. They nurture and sustain a system that inmates
have a normative commitment to in that it concurs with their values, and it
provides a material and psychological payoff. Thus a system exists upon
which a set of acceptable rules are readily promulgated that reify the system. Inmate leaders are expected to support the rules and system developed at the sub-rosa level and to enforce the rules when necessary and
possible. Inmates who inadvertently fall into positions of potential influence with the staff through job assignments or personal interactive skills are
expected to become politicians and support the sub-rosa system by facilitating the contraband flow. If they do not take on politician roles and leadership responsibilities as defined by the inmate subculture, other inmates will
bring pressures to bear to influence that inmate into accepting at least a partial role as a politician, or will manipulate that person out of the position
(Kalinich, 1980). Within this framework of legitimacy, inmate leaders have
access to specific forms of power to influence inmate behaviors.

These kinds of power are everchanging within the prison environment. These forms of power vary depending upon the individual and the
situation. Past research has suggested that inmate leaders express these dis-
parate forms of power dependent upon how well they influence their peers
(Stojkovic, 1984). Accordingly, there are five types of power exercised by
politicians: coercive, referent, providing of resources, expert, and legitimate.

Coercive power is defined as the threat of force or the actual application of punishment to gain conformity among inmates. This type of
power has been documented as the primary method inmate leaders
employ as a control strategy (Jacobs, 1977; Irwin, 1980). Referent power
can be defined as the identification inmates have with a group or gang,
and conformity is achieved through a commitment to group norms. This,
too, is quite common in our prisons and usually is advanced by various
religious groups and "super gangs" in the institution.

Third, providing resources is a particularly important form of
power. This kind of power is predicated on the ability of the leader to
access goods and services. This type of power is the most relevant to the
contraband system. Fourth, expert power is rooted in the knowledge an
individual possesses. Typically, leaders who understand the legal system
are able to gain much power in the inmate social world and can influence
many other prisoners. Finally, legitimate power can be identified; this
power base is dependent upon an internalization process, where inmates

follow the rules and regulations prescribed by leaders because they perceive them as justified and in the best interest of inmates. We found that those inmate leaders who focused their efforts on facilitating the flow of contraband had access to all of the above-mentioned social bases of power and were the strongest stabilizing force within the informal system. Therefore, conformity is accomplished through a consensus among inmates that adherence to the rules furthers the inmates' needs vis-à-vis the formal administration (Stojkovic, 1984).

Therefore, a loosely defined but strong form of governance develops at the informal level. This promotes stability in that a set of rules is created that inmates can accept; leadership is denied by inmate values, and leaders will develop who contribute to the maintenance of the accepted system. Disturbances in the contraband marketplace will cause similar disturbances in the inmate legitimate governance system. If the contraband system is suppressed through tightening of administrative controls, the basis of legitimate governance is also suppressed. This will, in turn, disrupt the basis for stability in the prison environment.

Implications

What we have attempted to convey is that contraband market systems in our prison environments establish legitimacy among often alienated bodies of inmates. In this way inmates tacitly approve of the social organization of the prison through a shared and agreed upon operation of prescribed rules and regulations. Furthermore, these separate and identifiable roles played by inmate politicians foster a subtle form of control, which ironically stabilizes the prison setting. However, if legitimacy is sought after as an end by prison officials, fostering illegal contraband markets among prisoners only further separates keepers from kept. The pivotal question, therefore, becomes the following: Can a formal sense of legitimacy be developed among antagonistic groups of inmates in our prisons by administrators?

Irwin (1980) states: "Thus, in order for these organizations to obtain and hold the commitment of a number of leaders and thereby to begin supplanting the violent, rapacious group structures, they will have to have some power in decision making." Fogel (1975) arrives at the same conclusion when he suggests that prisoners should be allowed to "wield lawful power" within the institutional environment. Other writers have suggested this approach through the development of participatory models of management within prison settings (Baker, 1977; Baunach, 1981).

As described by Stastny and Tymauer (1982), however, the movement for more inmate self-governance has been ineffective in reorganizing the internal structure of our prisons. They state that "the trend toward a less isolated prison milieu, toward the detotalization of the prison culture, which had its beginnings in a very different era, appears to be inching slowly forward." Although movement in the direction of more inmate input into the day-to-day operations of the prison remains slow, it is still essential in trying to form a consensus among inmates that their incarceration is justified.

What we have shown is that there is agreement among prisoners today, and that it is contingent upon, in part, the contraband market. Although prison social groupings are not as integrated and cohesively bound today as in the past, what we are suggesting is that the violence and fragmentation of the more modern inmate social milieu is relative to the operation and control of sub-rosa activities. As mentioned by Jacobs (1977), the old, traditionally oriented con power structure was replaced by more violent and racially motivated gangs. He describes the role these gangs play in the distribution of goods and services:

> The gang in prison serves important economic and psychological functions. To some degree the gang functions as a buffer against poverty. Each organization has a poor box. Each of the six cell-house chiefs in each gang collects cigarettes from his members and stores them for those who are needy. When a member makes a particularly good "score," he is expected to share some of the bounty with the leaders and donate to the poor box.

The gang or group in the contemporary prison serves the same purpose as the old inmate organization: the fulfillment of psychological and physical needs and desires. In this way, the gang develops normative symbols, rules, and regulations that support the structure of the gang, while fulfilling the basic needs of its members. Thus the strong identification of members is what binds individuals to the group and, at the same time, the unifying theme of the gang is the collection and distribution of contraband items. It is at this focal point that violence reaches its zenith; each gang competes for scarce resources, which helps the individual collective cope with the incarceration process. This provides material comfort and status to the group. Therefore, the group's physical and psychological needs are met by the informal contraband market operation.

However, this process promotes more manipulation and dishonesty among prisoners and staff, causing a situation in which stability is dependent upon informalities and illegalities within the prison environment. In addition, the contraband market system may lead to direct violence and hidden hostilities. The most salient problem is the use of individual or gang violence to take over lucrative contraband markets. Recently in the Michigan system, a drug dealer was burned to death by a competitor who resented the victim's intrusion into his territory. (The gasoline used in the murder was purchased as contraband.) In a flourishing prison contraband market system, an economic class structure emerges, with those willing and able to participate as dealers gaining relatively greater wealth and status than other inmates.

It is not uncommon for inmates with relatively limited wealth to feel even more alienated and deprived within the system than they otherwise might feel. Inmates in the "low economic class" found the class difference a ready rationalization to steal from fellow inmates who had accumulated some material wealth, whether the accumulation was from contraband dealing or legal sources (Kalinich, 1980). Finally, the opportunity and temptation for staff to become corrupted exists in the delivery of contraband goods that are highly profitable. It would seem demoralizing to conscious staff to think certain inmates are making large sums of money by continuing their criminal careers while in prison. Although contraband organization and distribution enhances a tenuous form of stability, what is required is a more formalized sense of legitimacy among inmates. It is our contention that this could be accomplished through a more direct relationship between inmate bodies and the prison hierarchy in the decision-making processes of the organization.

As posited by Baunach (1981), although participatory approaches have been implemented in various prisons throughout the country over the years, there has been no long-term incorporation of the concept within our correctional institutions. What we are suggesting is that the operation of our prisons requires some form of legitimacy among those being incarcerated; at present, that is being provided by the supply of goods and services via the sub-rosa market structure. The power that such a system exhibits is tremendous, and if administrators would seek more control over their institutions, they need to alter the structural arrangements within the environment to promote more legitimate forms of power among inmates. If not, they will continue to operate on the symbiotic relationships endemic to the contraband system and be subject to its many uncertainties. Having looked at contraband as a major determinant of stability, we need to return briefly to the more popular question of what causes prison riots. Factors that disrupt the contraband economic system will destabilize the normative system developed by inmates. One observable factor that can disrupt the delicate economic system is an aggressive prison administration that on occasion may impose its goal of bureaucratic control effectively and interfere with the contraband flow. Ironically, effective administration of a prison in the classic bureaucratic sense may cause prisoners to riot.

Endnotes

[1] In the way we are employing this term, we mean "legitimate" as something that is accepted and agreed upon by a majority of inmates. On the other hand, we do not intend the reader to perceive "legitimate" as something that is "legal" and formal in nature, such as the rules and regulations of the institution. See French and Raven (1968) for a further discussion and clarification of legitimate power.

References

Baker, J. E. (1977). Inmate self-government and the right to participate. In R. M. Carter et al. (Eds.), *Correctional institutions* (2nd ed.). Philadelphia: J. B. Lippincott.

Baunach, P. J. (1981). Participatory management: Restructuring the prison environment. In D. Fogel & J. Hudson (Eds.), *Justice as fairness: Perspectives on the justice model*. Cincinnati, OH: Anderson.

Carroll, L. (1974, reissued 1988). *Hacks, blacks, and cons*. Prospect Heights, IL: Waveland Press.

Cloward, R. A. (1960). Social control in prison. In L. Hazelrigg (Ed.), *Prison within society*. New York: Doubleday.

Davidson, R. T. (1977). The prisoner economy. In R. M. Carter et al. (Eds.), *Correctional institutions* (2nd ed.). Philadelphia: J. B. Lippincott.

Downs, A. (1967). *Inside bureaucracy*. Boston: Little, Brown.

Fogel, D. (1975). *We are the living proof*. Cincinnati, OH: Anderson.

French, J. R. P., & Raven, B. (1968). The bases of social power. In D. Cartwright & A. Zander (Eds.), *Group dynamics* (3rd ed.). New York: Harper & Row.

Guenther, A. L. (1975). Compensations in a total institution: The forms and functions of contraband. *Crime & Delinquency, 21*, 243–254.

Irwin, J. (1970). *The felon*. Englewood Cliffs, NJ: Prentice-Hall.

Irwin, J. (1980). *Prison in turmoil*. Boston: Little, Brown.

Jacobs, J. B. (1977). *Stateville: The penitentiary in mass society*. Chicago: University of Chicago Press.

Kalinich, D. B. (1980). *The inmate economy*. Lexington, MA: D. C. Heath.

Lombardo, L. X. (1981). *Guards imprisoned: Correctional officers at work*. New York: Elsevier.

Lombardo, L. X. (1982, reissued 1988). Stress, change, and collective violence in prison. In R. Johnson & H. Toch (Eds.), *The pains of imprisonment*. Prospect Heights, IL: Waveland Press.

McCleery, R. (1960). Communication patterns as bases of systems of authority and power. In *Studies in social organization of the prison* (pp. 49–77). New York: Social Sciences Research Council.

McCorkle, L., & Korn, R. (1954). Resocialization within the walls. In S. Johnson & Wolfgang (Eds.), *The sociology of punishment and corrections*. New York: John Wiley.

Radford, R. A. (1945). The economic organization of a prisoner of war camp. *Economics, 12*, 258–280.

Shoblad, R. (1972). *Doing my own time*. Garden City, NY: Doubleday.

Stastny, C., & Tymauer, G. (1982). *Who rules the joint: The changing political culture of maximum-security prisons in America*. Lexington, MA: D. C. Heath.

Stojkovic, S. (1984). Social bases of power in a maximum-security prison: A study of the erosion of traditional authority. Unpublished doctoral dissertation, Michigan State University.

Sykes, G., & Messinger, S. L. (1960). The inmate social system. In R. Cloward et al. (Eds.), *Theoretical studies in social organization of the prison* (pp. 5–19). New York: Social Science Research Council.

Toch, H. (1977). *Living in prison: The ecology of survival*. New York: Free Press.

Warwick, D. P. (1975). *A theory of public bureaucracy: Politics, personality, and organization in the state department*. Cambridge: Harvard University Press.

Chapter 18

The Illusion of Structure
A Critique of the Classical Model of Organization and the Discretionary Power of Correctional Officers

Michael J. Gilbert

Early studies of correctional officers did not recognize the rich diversity of work behaviors that these officers possess. Correctional officers were often portrayed in stereotypic terms as if they were part of a monolithic work force characterized by shared traits. Philliber (1987) showed that these characterizations consisted mainly of negative stereotypes. Correctional officers were presented as having limited intelligence, a high threshold for boredom, low self-esteem, a high level of cynicism, extreme alienation, a hostile attitude toward inmates, a willingness to quickly use physical force, and a propensity for the use of excessive force. Recent studies have recognized wide variation in the work behaviors and discretionary power displayed by line correctional officers. These studies have emphasized diversity, complexity, job stress, and individual discretion (Cheek and Miller, 1982; Cullen, Lutze, Link, and Wolfe, 1989; Jurik, 1985; Kauffman, 1988; Lombardo, 1989; Meyerson, 1992; Whitehead and Lindquist, 1989).

Michael J. Gilbert, "The Illusion of Structure: A Critique of the Classical Model of Organization and the Discretionary Power of Correctional Officers," *Criminal Justice Review*, Vol. 22 No. 1, Spring 1997, pp. 49–64. Reprinted by permission of *Criminal Justice Review*.

Line correctional officers control or deliver services to inmates. These officers strongly influence the lives of the inmates they supervise. Whether a confinement experience is constructive or destructive is largely determined by the actions of line correctional officers. "On the job" behaviors of line officers often determine whether new programs or policies are implemented faithfully or are subverted (Hall and Loucks, 1977; Mazmanian and Sabatier, 1983). There is broad recognition among scholars that the discretionary power of line officers is crucial to policy implementation. However, there is disagreement over the question of how that discretionary power should be guided and managed.

The purpose of this paper is to provide a conceptual framework for understanding the nature and extent of correctional officer discretionary behavior. The primary vehicle for accomplishing this task is Muir's typology of discretionary behavior of police officers (1977). Police officers are viewed as political actors who must exercise individual discretion as an inherent part of their job. Muir describes four work styles:

1. The professional[1] is open and nondefensive, makes exceptions when warranted, prefers to gain cooperation and compliance through communication, but is willing to use coercive power or force as a last resort.

2. The reciprocator wants to help people, assists them in resolving their problems, prefers clinical or social work strategies, may be inconsistent when making exceptions, prefers to "go along to get along," and tends not to use coercive authority or physical force even when it is justifiable.

3. The enforcer practices rigid, "by the book," aggressive enforcement, actively seeks out violations, rarely makes exceptions, has little empathy for others, takes unreasonable risks to personal safety, sees most things as either good or bad, and is quick to use threats, verbal coercion, and physical force.

4. The avoider minimizes offender contact, often does not "see" an offense, avoids confrontation and coercion, views interpersonal aspects of the job as not part of the job, often backs down from confrontation, and blames others.

Theoretical Foundations

Brown (1981:34) identified a set of common organizational conditions that heighten the discretionary power of employees in public sector organizations as "intense political conflict over what [the organization] does, and [pressure to] provide satisfactory solutions to intractable social problems, [while faced with] immense difficulties in rationalizing organizational decision making. Consequently, the latitude for discretion is rather broad and the criteria used to judge different events may be a manifestation of the personal values of the decision maker as much as the priorities and expectations of the administrators." Correctional systems face precisely these conditions. Prisons are embroiled in political conflicts regarding questions of who should be incarcerated, appropriate sanctions, conditions of confinement, resource allocation, overcrowding, site location, operational problems, inmate rights, and many other politically charged issues. Crime is a truly "intractable social problem." There is little public consensus about the social purpose of imprisonment (Durham, 1994; Irwin and Austin, 1994).

While the appropriate role and function of our prisons may be debated, correctional officers have a job to perform. On a daily basis they must translate vague philosophical notions into concerted actions and specific work behaviors. The lack of clarity as to the purpose, role, and function of prisons, the variations between institutions and systems, the inability of correctional managers to communicate consistent philosophical principles and values, and the autonomy that is given to line officers broaden their individual discretionary power. The public image of correctional officers as part of a tightly controlled, paramilitary work force is inconsistent with the discretionary power that these officers possess and exercise; it is assumed that hierarchical and rigid organizational structures afford line officers little independence of action or decision-making authority (Weber, 1971; Wilson, 1941), but this assumption is simply wrong.

The intellectual foundations for understanding the discretionary behavior of correctional officers are found in many of the seminal works on political theory, justice, discretion, organizational behavior, and implementation. Machiavelli (1513/1980), Hobbes (1651/1981), and Locke (1690/1980) provided much of the political theory that guided the formation of modern civil societies. Their works also provided the rationale for the bounded use of coercive power by governments against citizens. The unlimited use of discretionary power by sovereigns gradually gave way to a more circumscribed understanding of the legitimate uses of coercive political power to enforce laws, create police forces, and operate confinement facilities for the common good.

Beccaria provided the conceptual foundation for Western criminal justice, by which legitimately established criminal laws can be enforced by acknowledged political authority (government and public officials) using the coercive powers of the state to maintain social order, peace, and public safety (Beccaria, 1764/1963:87). He recognized that criminal sanctions are political instruments used for social control. Beccaria would also have recognized that correctional officers are employed in a political enterprise serving political interests. However, this perspective was first articulated in 1918 by Max Weber (cited in Gerth and Mills, 1946:77–128) when he argued that public functionaries (i.e., all governmental workers) were employed in a "political vocation" and possessed inherent discretionary power. In this way Weber applied the rationale for bounded use of discretionary power by sovereigns to governmental workers who serve the state.

Muir's Typology

Muir's typology of police discretionary behavior is based on these underlying philosophical and theoretical foundations (Muir, 1977). Muir's typology is shown in table 1.

One of the strengths of Muir's typology is that the characteristics used were derived from Weber's 1918 speech "Politics as a Vocation": In order for political actors to function effectively in a political vocation they need (a) passion for a cause in the interest of public welfare, (b) responsibility to that cause, and (c) a sense of proportionality that enables an actor to calmly and objectively reflect on a situation apart from the people and things involved in the circumstances (Weber, cited in Gerth and Mills, 1946:115). Weber's work serves as a link between earlier philosophical notions of bounded discretionary power and Muir's work styles in its recognition that public officials, at any level, are practitioners of a political vocation with inherent and irrevocable discretionary power.

One of the determinants of an officer's work style preference (i.e., the manner in which he or she exercises discretionary power) is the ability to resolve the ethical or moral dilemma concerning the use of coercion—a socially negative attribute—to protect public safety and personal property and maintain order (Muir, 1977). The use of coercive authority may be seen as the attainment of "just ends through dubious means." Officers who are able to resolve this quandary are said to have an "integrated morality" that allows them to use coercion appropriately in their professional role without damaging their self-image. Those officers who cannot resolve this quandary are said to have a "conflicted morality" that prevents them from using coercion without damaging their self-image.

Table 1   Muir's typology of discretionary working styles.

	Human Relations Perspective	
	Tragic	**Cynical**
Integrated morality (Able to use coercion without damage to self-image or values)	*Professional* (Reasonable, innovative, able to make exceptions)	*Enforcer* (Aggressive, by the book, unable to make exceptions)
Conflicted morality (Unable to use coercion without damage to self-image or values)	*Reciprocator* (Counseling orientation toward enforcement duties)	*Avoider* (Defines tasks out of the job to limit enforcement activities)

Muir's second determinant is the officer's ability to develop a "tragic sense" of the human condition in which offenders find themselves. An ability to have empathy, sensitivity, and compassion for others permits an officer to view human nature (in all its forms) as part of a single continuum encompassing the officer as well as others. Thus most behavioral deviations and aberrations may be viewed as exceptions rather than the norm. Officers with a "tragic sense" usually see deviations in behavior, including their own, as circumstantial abnormalities.

The inability to develop a tragic sense is termed a "cynical perspective" and is characterized by officers who view human nature in dualistic terms (e.g., the good and the bad, victim and victimizer, weak and strong). Such officers tend to focus on extremes of behavior and have difficulty making reasonable allowances for exceptional behavior in anyone, including themselves. From the cynical perspective, once a criminal always a criminal, once a bad cop always a bad cop. Such an officer often sees himself as good and offenders as evil. This dualistic orientation makes empathy for the human condition of others, especially offenders, nearly impossible. Officers with a cynical perspective may deal with offenders in a demeaning, hostile, or aggressive manner.[2]

Lipsky (1973:104) acknowledged the broad discretionary power of line employees in governmental bureaucracies with his definition of "Street Level Bureaucrats" as "government workers who directly interact with citizens in the regular course of their jobs, whose work within the bureaucratic structure permits a wide latitude in job performance, and whose impact on the lives of citizens is extensive." Correctional officers deal directly with citizens who are incarcerated as convicted offenders. The prisons they work in are chronically understaffed and provided with limited resources. Consequently, "wide latitude in job performance" is afforded to these line officers.

It is difficult to define what corrections officers do, let alone assess how well they have done it. Nevertheless, it is clear that the direct work product that these officers produce is not security, control, or safety but personal interactions between themselves and inmates. The affective nature of these interactions directly influences the level of tension between officers and inmates and indirectly influences the safety, security, and control within the prison. The intensely personal nature of 24-hour-a-day supervision and the strong influence of correctional supervision on the daily lives of inmates have been widely noted (Johnson, 1996; Johnson and Price, 1981; Kauffman, 1981, 1988). The importance of the interpersonal aspect of the correctional officer's role in maintaining control of inmates has also been recognized by Gilbert and Riddell (1983:34), who wrote, "Correctional officers must manage the prisoner population, through face to face interactions, in a way that assists in the development and maintenance of a stable, orderly prison in which the living and working environment is safe, secure, and humane; and, where survival with dignity and

respect is ensured so that personal growth and self change is possible."
From this perspective safety, security, and control may be viewed as
byproducts of the personal interactions between officers and inmates that
characterize the prison environment. This feature of the job for correctional officers is often unrecognized but is highly consistent with Muir's
model of discretionary behavior.

Although the work of both correctional officers and police officers
involves the use of state-authorized coercive power and affords officers
considerable discretion, these occupations are not identical. The occupations have different job dimensions, and consequently the nature of their
discretionary behavior is different. For example, correctional officers are
focused on delivery of correctional services to offenders held in confinement, whereas police officers are focused on order maintenance and
delivery of law enforcement services to free citizens. Correctional officers
also have less opportunity than police officers to pursue interests or initiatives that take them away from their area of responsibility. Patrol officers may retreat to their patrol car and ride. Police officers may also use
the patrol car to avoid situations by simply "not seeing them" and driving past them. Consequently, the behavioral descriptors used in Muir's
typology for police officers must be modified when applied to correctional officers. Table 2 provides a comparison of behavioral descriptors
for police and correctional officers.

As early as 1982 the Arizona Department of Corrections formally
recognized the discretionary power of correctional officers in their training documents. The values-based ends to which correctional officers
could appropriately apply their work style preferences were characterized as the following objectives:

1. To maximize cooperation among all participants in the correc-
    tional setting—inmates and staff alike.

2. To promote interaction between inmates and staff which demon-
    strates how individuals should interact in their communities and
    homes.

3. To harmonize, as much as possible, the need for security with
    respect for human dignity.

4. To develop a consistent scheme of rewards and deterrents which
    lead inmates to view the use of your [the officer's] discretion as fair
    and just. By "fair and just" we mean that the use of rewards and
    deterrents requires that you balance fitting rules and regulations to
    the individual with assurance that like situations receive the same
    response. (Arizona Department of Corrections, 1982:4.

The same document goes on to clarify the meaning of "human concern"
and provide values-oriented parameters to guide officers in the
appropriate use of their discretionary power:

Table 2 Discretionary work style descriptors for officers based on Muir's typology

Style type	Police Officers	Correctional Officers
Professional	Develops the beat	Develops the housing unit
	Takes educated risks	Takes educated risks
	Provides citizens advice on law and government	Provides inmates advice on rules and regulations
	Increases pressure over time to correct behavior	Increases pressure over time to change behavior
	Uses arrest as a last resort	Uses the "write-up" as a last resort
	Tries to preserve the dignity of citizens through the use of non-demeaning behaviors and attitudes	Tries to preserve the dignity of inmates through the use of non-demeaning behaviors and attitudes
	Views offenders as not much different from self	Views offenders as not much different from self
	Empathizes with the human condition of citizens and offenders	Empathizes with the human condition of inmates
	Allows for exceptions in his/her own behavior and that of others	Allows for exceptions in his/her own behavior and that of others
	Uses coercion and force judiciously	Uses coercion and force judiciously
	Calm and easygoing	Calm and easygoing
	Articulate and open	Articulate and open
	Focuses on attaining justice for individuals	Focuses on ensuring the due process and decency in security and control tasks
	Views most other officers as being enforcer-oriented	Views most other officers as being enforcer-oriented
Reciprocator	Allows local "toughs" to keep citizens in line, a mutual accommodation	Allows inmate leaders to keep the unit quiet, a mutual accommodation
	Uses clinical/social work strategies to help people "worthy" of assistance	Uses clinical/social work strategies to help inmates "worthy" of assistance
	Rationalizes situations	Rationalizes situations
	Attempts to educate, cure, or solve the citizen's problems	Attempts to educate, cure, or solve the inmate's problems
	Low tolerance for rejection of offered assistance	Low tolerance for rejection of offered assistance
	Easily frustrated	Easily frustrated
	Often does not use coercion when it should be used	Often does not use coercion when it should be used
	Inconsistent job performance	Inconsistent job performance
	Irrational behavior by citizens stymies the officer	Irrational behavior by inmates stymies the officer
	Often displays a superior attitude toward others	Often displays a superior attitude toward others
	Highly articulate	Highly articulate

continued

Table 2 Discretionary work style descriptors for officers based on Muir's typology (continued)

Style type	Police Officers	Correctional Officers
Enforcer	Aggressive law enforcement	Aggressive rule enforcement
	Makes many arrests	Issues many "tickets"
	Actively seeks violations	Actively seeks violations
	Frequently uses force or excessive force	Frequently uses force or excessive force
	Tends to view order maintenance and service functions as not a part of police work	Tends to view treatment functions as what "others" do with or for the inmates
	Strict enforcement orientation, limits service and order maintenance duties	Strict security and control orientation, limits service delivery duties
	Little or no empathy for the human condition of citizens/offenders	Little or no empathy for the human condition of inmates
	Citizens often complain about this officer's behavior	Inmates often submit grievances over this officer's behavior
	Rigid, rule-bound, makes few exceptions even when appropriate	Rigid, rule-bound, makes few exceptions even when appropriate
	Maintains a dualistic view of human nature (good/bad, cop/criminal, strong/weak)	Maintains a dualistic view of human nature (good/bad, officer/inmate, strong/weak)
	Dislikes management	Dislikes management
	Postures for effect	Postures for effect
	Crazy/brave "John Wayne" behaviors, takes unnecessary risks	Crazy/brave "John Wayne" behaviors, takes unnecessary risks
	Views other officers as "soft" or "weak" if not like him/her	Views other officers as "soft" or "weak" if not like him/her
	Views officers like him/her as being the majority of officers	Views officers like him/her as being the majority of officers
Avoider	Often leaves situations as quickly as possible	Often leaves situations as quickly as possible
	Tends to view most functions as not being "real" police work or part of the job	Tends to view human communications with inmates as not being part of security and control
	Uses the patrol car to reduce contact with citizens	Uses the mechanical aspects of security and control to reduce contact with inmates
	Often the last to arrive in response to an emergency	Often among the last to arrive at an emergency scene
	Likely to seek refuge from the street in the patrol car	Likely to select tower duty/isolated positions away from inmates
	Plays the "phony" tough and frequently backs down	Plays the "phony" tough and frequently backs down
	Tends to blame others for avoidance behaviors or inadequacies	Tends to blame others for avoidance behaviors or inadequacies
	Structures the work to reduce chances of observing offenses and use of coercion	Structures the work to avoid observing infractions and use of coercion
	Avoids confrontations and interactions with offenders and citizens	Avoids confrontations and interactions with inmates

> While it is important for you to develop a sense of human concern for your clients [inmates], you must direct this concern to situations rather than to creating favorites. In short, it is legitimate for you to show human compassion for particular situations (e.g., inmates receiving dear john letters from home), and therefore use your *discretion* [italics added] to work with any inmate who finds himself (herself) in such a situation. However, using your *discretion* [italics added] to make life easier for those inmates you personally like and hard for those who you dislike is not the appropriate way to express your human compassions. (Arizona Department of Corrections, 1982:4)

Prisons are complex organizations that use the symbolic threat of force as the visible means of control to retain inmates within the institution (Etzioni, 1975). They are also "total institutions." Prisoners live, work, sleep, and play within the same general area and under the same authority. All prisoners are treated alike and their activities are preplanned, structured, and strictly scheduled (Goffman, 1961). In short, life in a prison tends to be highly regimented. Controls are placed upon the totality of life for those who are confined and upon the work life of employees.

In order to maintain this regimentation, prisons have typically used paramilitary structures similar to those adopted by police. The military model has historically been viewed as the most appropriate model for the management of formal social control agencies like police forces and prisons (Stinchcombe, 1980). Criminal justice organizations are still characterized by paramilitary structure with strict chains of command, vertical management, centralization, emphasis on formal communication, top-down decision making, written rules for internal control, detailed policies and procedures, limited autonomy, and a view of employees as unwilling workers in need of constant supervision. These features are consistent with Weber's (cited in Gerth and Mills, 1946:196–264) and Wilson's (1887/1941) conceptualization of the "classical model of organization" and are readily observed in most prisons.

Paramilitary organizational structures emphasize strict compliance to orders issued by superiors. Almost every aspect of the paramilitary organization is used in an attempt to reduce or eliminate individual discretion held by employees. The rules, regulations, and policies created are explicitly intended for this purpose. Such efforts are based on faulty assumptions rooted in the classical model of organization. Hierarchy, rules, and regulations do not limit discretionary power; they simply make it more dangerous for employees to openly exercise their discretionary power. Workers who continue to make independent decisions in spite of threats to their careers retain their discretionary power. Each correctional officer must supervise inmates in a wide variety of situations and circumstances that cannot be fully prescribed by formal policies and procedures. Consequently, full 100% enforcement of all rules is impossible. Under these conditions officers are placed in a no-win situation.

Attempts to attain full enforcement are among the surest ways to increase hostility, tension, and danger within a prison, because they sharply increase the number of daily confrontations between inmates and staff. On the other hand, selective enforcement exposes officers to censure, discipline, or termination if their decisions backfire and become known to formal authorities (Johnson, 1996:206).

Security and control in prisons are attained mostly through interpersonal communication skills and discretionary application of coercive authority. The line officer's objective is to gain inmate compliance with as little confrontation as possible. Every correctional officer must learn to enforce rules, regulations, and policies in reasonable and appropriate ways given the situations encountered. Officers must also learn to use human relations skills in ways that are appropriate to both the human condition of inmates and the seriousness of the situation.

The classical model of organization used in most prisons ignores the discretionary power held by line officers. Classical organizations also fail to recognize the importance of discretionary decisions by officers to the attainment of a stable, secure, and safe prison. Instead managers in these organizations insist that officers "go by the book." This exhortation is problematic because line officers are greatly outnumbered by the inmates at all times. If inmates decide en masse not to obey these rules, there is little that officers can do about it. The quandary faced by line officers is that rigid enforcement of rules drives up the incentives for inmates to act out in disruptive ways and decreases both officer safety and the security of the institution. When officers are denied authority to decide how and when to exercise their coercive power and prohibited from making reasonable exceptions to rules, there are increased tensions between the reality of their job and the expectations placed upon them by management. Under these conditions officers are likely to become highly frustrated, rule-bound, hostile, demeaning, antagonistic, abusive, neglectful, or avoidance-oriented when dealing with inmates. The negative impacts of such behaviors are exacerbated when officers also have poor interpersonal communication skills. The rigid and unrealistic management expectations imposed by the classical model foster negative discretionary behaviors and attitudes among officers and threaten security and control by undercutting the interpersonal aspects of inmate management performed by correctional officers.

Consequently, the absolute power of the officer is more fiction than reality (Johnson, 1996; Kauffman, 1988; Sykes, 1980). An officer's control over inmates does not depend on strength, imposing stature, threat of force, or rigid application of rules. Rather, as Muir's typology suggests, control over inmates depends on well-developed verbal skills of persuasion, appropriate use of coercive authority, human relations skills, and leadership ability to gain voluntary cooperation of inmates (Johnson, 1996).

Correctional agencies, like other classical organizations, overrely on formal structures such as hierarchy and regulations to control individual discretion. Change is often imposed without direct connection to or commitment from correctional officers. In many cases the philosophy, rationale, and values behind these changes have not been explained or discussed with line officers. In addition, correctional managers tend to view line correctional officers with suspicion similar to that with which line officers view inmates (Johnson, 1996:204–206). As a result, enmity and distrust are easily fostered between managers and line officers. Staff resistance is especially common when formal management controls or operational changes are viewed as being at odds with the values and interests held by line officers. For these reasons, formal bureaucratic controls are unlikely to be effective as a guide for individual discretionary behavior. By default, classical management in a prison leaves the discretionary behavior of correctional officers almost totally unguided under the paramilitary guise of rigid control. Establishing boundaries that structure discretionary behavior among line correctional officers will require that managers provide clearly defined values and ethical structures, establish widely understood and broadly accepted linkages to the values, interests, and concerns of line officers, and hold frequent discussions of the moral and ethical dilemmas regularly faced by line officers.

Correctional organizations are not military organizations. They are primarily social service organizations. In contrast to military organizations, the most important correctional decisions are made by the lowest-ranking members of the institution through their routine and daily interaction with inmates. The meaning of confinement for inmates is determined at the face-to-face level between the line officer and the inmate by the nature of their interpersonal relationships. Effective supervision of inmates depends mostly on the interpersonal communication skills of line correctional officers rather than rank, uniform, military bearing, command voice, or other militaristic attribute. Furthermore, the personal safety of correctional officers depends on their ability to supervise inmates without creating or escalating confrontations with inmates unnecessarily.

The concern of correctional officers for their personal safety provides the underlying rationale for the "passion" dimension needed to apply Muir's model to correctional officers. Uncaring, rigid, and rule-bound enforcement behaviors by officers jeopardize everyone's safety and make voluntary cooperation by inmates unlikely. Furthermore, cynicism, threats, intimidation, physical force, abuse, or neglect by officers toward inmates makes unnecessary enemies among the inmate population, inflames their fears, fosters increased hatred for correctional staff, and drives up the incentives for inmates to attack officers, destroy property, assault each other, and escape. Each of these outcomes is a direct threat to institutional security and control and to the safety of officers. The intuitive but often unstated awareness of officers that their safety depends largely on constructive professional relationships with inmates is the foundation for genuine concern for the human condition of inmates. Such relationships are highly controlling because they are based on human decency, honesty, directness, respectful treatment, and consistent actions that demonstrate the genuineness of an officer's concern for the welfare of inmates. Constructive professional relationships between officers and inmates lead to voluntary cooperation by most inmates.

There will always be some distrust and tension between line officers and inmates because of the officers' rule enforcement responsibilities and the con games that inmates play. Nevertheless, some level of human interaction between officers and inmates beyond that of keeper and kept is an essential aspect of inmate management. It is the collective force of thousands of daily and hourly personal interactions between inmates and officers that drives up tensions and hostilities or quells them, fosters resistance or compliance, and engenders confrontation or cooperation in any prison. The 24-hour-a-day treatment provided inmates by routine interactions with line officers should be recognized as the primary and most influential treatment program offered by any prison. The nature and quality of these interactions will largely determine the extent to which prison security, control, and safety are attained. The character of these routine interactions may also determine the effectiveness of formal treatment programs.

Factors such as classification systems that maintain separation of inmates, grievance systems that resolve inmate complaints, programs and services that reduce idleness and provide treatment opportunities, and adequate resources that minimize conflicts due to scarcity, as well as policies and procedures, are all important elements of prison security and control that are provided or directed by correctional managers. However, these inmate management strategies may be rendered ineffective by a cadre of indecent, disrespectful, insensitive, and rigidly rule-bound correctional officers or by concerted resistance by officers. The effectiveness of formal inmate management strategies is highly dependent on the discretionary power of line officers to either carry them out as envisioned by management or quietly subvert them in subtle ways.

Simon (1976) identified the power of the informal organization within every formal organization. The informal organization is composed of social and professional support networks among employees (e.g., "the locker room") and under some conditions may have more power than the established hierarchy to control the actions of line workers. Therefore, the discretionary power of line workers can be used to oppose as well as support management directives. In prisons, the informal organization of line officers controls inmate movement and therefore inmate access to programs and services. If these officers wish, they can discourage inmate participation in various programs and services simply by retarding the movement of inmates or otherwise "hassling" inmates who do participate.

New employees are socialized to varying degrees into the informal organization during their probationary period as coworkers and supervisors model the work behaviors that they are expected to emulate. As the values, attitudes, and behaviors of new employees increasingly approximate those of coworkers and supervisors, acceptance by their colleagues improves and they are progressively socialized by the informal organization. However, the values, attitudes, and behaviors advocated by the informal organization may not be consistent with those desired by the management team (McGregor, 1978; Simon, 1976).

The policy process by which formal rules are generated is dynamic and fraught with implementation problems. Implementation is dependent on line-level employees who convert written policy and procedure into concerted actions and services delivered. Faithful implementation by line officers (i.e., the informal organization) becomes less likely when a new policy or program is perceived as a confrontation to the values, interests, beliefs, and experiences of line officers (Hall and Loucks, 1977; Mazmanian and Sabatier, 1983). Nevertheless, the paramilitary model of organization has traditionally assumed that policy will automatically be followed by faithful implementation; if not, then faulty employees will be removed and replaced by those who will implement the policy. There is ample theoretical basis to conclude that line correctional officers exercise extensive discretionary power in their professional roles. This power may be exercised in a manner that is either constructive or destructive to inmates, staff, and official policy. The traditional assumptions of faithful and deliberate implementation by line correctional officers are highly questionable.

Conclusions and Implications

Correctional officers, like police officers, are social service personnel. They are required to take independent actions and make independent decisions that affect the lives of clients. They are also expected to use control behaviors that are consistent with both the human conditions of their clients and the enforcement situation. These circumstances require flexibility, reasonable judgment, sensitivity to others, responsible actions, appropriate use of coercion, and, at times, exceptions to formal policy. Unfortunately, the autocratic, authoritarian, and militaristic style used by most correctional organizations attempts to suppress the ability of correctional officers to make reasonable and effective decisions. The militaristic management style also forces officers to make decisions that are not recognized by formal policy and procedure. This structural quandary places line correctional officers in an untenable position. On the one hand, if their decisions turn out well, no one really cares. On the other hand, if their decisions turn out badly, officers may be disciplined or terminated. The inconsistency between such management expectations and the reality of the job for line officers creates tension or conflict that has been linked by some researchers to alienation and cynicism among correctional officers (Cheek and Miller, 1982; Poole and Regoli, 1981).

Correctional supervisors and managers often ignore the critical role that individual decision making by line officers plays in correctional practice. They usually rely on written rules and regulations as the means to structure officer behavior and ignore the underlying values and assumptions that actually guide officer behavior. Rarely do these organizations formally acknowledge that the exercise of discretionary power by line officers is inherent to their occupation and is used to resolve many minor problems before they accumulate to become major management problems. It is therefore ironic that the control-oriented paramilitary structure of prisons should result in line officers being provided little or no guidance for the exercise of their discretionary power over the lives of inmates. In this sense the realities of prison work for line correctional officers are not consistent with the classical (paramilitary) structure of most prisons.

Muir's typology of police discretionary behavior can theoretically be adapted to the study of correctional officers and provide a conceptual framework for understanding their discretionary power. This suggests that correctional executives may need to change the way they have conceptualized prison management if they hope to guide the discretionary power that is applied by those officers who work for them. Correctional managers and supervisors need to formally recognize that full enforcement of prison rules, policies, and procedures is an impossibility and communicate this understanding to line officers. They must also allow correctional officers to make discretionary decisions in complex situations where policy is absent, vague, or inconsistent with the circumstances encountered. Executives, middle managers, and supervisory personnel should also expect variation in work style among line officers. Finally, these managers need to recognize that the discretionary power held by correctional officers is guided less by formal rules and hierarchy than by an explicit understanding of the shared operational values and ethical principles that govern correctional practice (Pollock, 1994).

The development of an ethical framework to guide officers in the application of their discretionary power requires frequent discussion and debate (i.e., formal training experiences) of the operational and ethical quandaries that are found at all levels of prison work. Although managers must allow and expect correctional officers to make ethically defensible exceptions to rules as a routine part of an officer's job, managers are responsible for helping these officers understand the appropriate boundaries of their discretionary power. When the decisions and behaviors of line officers are reasonable (given the situational context they face), consistent with a common set of values and ethical parameters, and legal, they should be supported by those in leadership positions. As a general principle, employees should not be disciplined for making reasonable exceptions to formal rules in complex situations. This is especially important where strict adherence to the rules and regulations would make little sense or would endanger security, control, or safety. Improvements in decision making should be attained through training rather than by disciplinary actions by supervisors and managers.

If future research confirms the efficacy of Muir's typology of discretionary behavior when applied to correctional officers, there will be a need for less rigid models of organization for prisons. Operational policies and procedures and hierarchical supervision are insufficient guides for discretionary behavior because these structures only make it more risky for officers to make discretionary decisions when formal rules do not fit the situations they face. In the absence of values-based ethical principles consistent with management intent, individual discretionary power is largely unguided by management concerns. In classical organizations such as prisons, the discretionary power of line officers is structured mostly by the extent to which officers understand and internalize the values of the formal and informal organization. Because the values of the formal organization are typically vague, abstract, or unstated, it is the values of the informal organization that most influence the work behaviors and attitudes of correctional officers. When the values of the formal organization are perceived to be at odds with those of the informal organization, there are often increased conflicts between management and line officers and greater operational inconsistencies between shifts, work groups, and individual officers. Such outcomes usually conflict with the objectives established by the official hierarchy. Unfortunately, the illusion that the discretionary behavior of line officers is highly structured by the classical organization of prisons persists and will probably continue as long as correctional executives believe it to be the only organizational model suitable for prison management.

Endnotes

[1] Neither police officers nor correctional officers are full professionals in the classical sense of that term. Instead they are something less than full professionals (i.e., paraprofessionals), who earn their living applying a specific body of knowledge and skill. Muir's use of this term refers only to a categorization of officers viewed as recognizably different from other types.

[2] Testimony in the 1995 trial of O. J. Simpson revealed similar behaviors among Los Angeles police officers in their efforts to "fight crime" by any means possible.

References

Arizona Department of Corrections. (1982). *Channeling discretion in the correctional environment.* Phoenix, AZ: Author.

Beccaria, C. (1963). *On crimes and punishment.* Indianapolis, IN: Bobbs-Merrill Educational Publishing. (Original work published 1764.)

Brown, M. (1981). *Working the street.* New York: Russell Sage Foundation.

Cheek, F., & Miller, M. (1982). *Prisoners of life: A study of occupational stress among state correctional officers.* Washington, DC: American Federation of State, County and Municipal Employees, AFL-CIO.

Cullen, F. T., Lutze, F. E., Link, B. G., & Wolfe, N. T. (1989). The correctional orientation of prison guards: Do officers support rehabilitation? *Federal Probation, 53*(l), 33–42.

Durham, A. M. (1994). *Crisis and reform: Current issues in American punishment.* Boston, MA: Little, Brown & Company.

Etzioni, A. (1975). *A comparative analysis of complex organizations – On power and their correlates.* New York: The Free Press.

Gerth, H., & Mills, C. (1946). *From Max Weber: Essays in sociology.* New York: Oxford University Press.

Gilbert, M. J., & Riddell, J. (1983). Skills for achieving security, control, and public protection. In American Correctional Association (Ed.), *Correctional officers: Power, pressure, and responsibility* (pp. 31–36). College Park, MD: American Correctional Association.

Goffman, E. (1961). *Asylums.* Garden City, NY: Anchor Books.

Hall, G., & Loucks, S. (1977). A developmental model for determining whether a treatment is actually implemented. *American Education Research Journal, 14,* 263–276.

Hobbes, T. (1981). *Leviathan.* New York: Penguin Books. (Original work published 1651.)

Irwin, J., & Austin, J. (1994). *It's about time: America's imprisonment binge.* Belmont, CA: Wadsworth Publishing Company.

Johnson, R. (1996). *Hard time: Understanding and reforming the prison* (2nd ed.). Belmont, CA: Wadsworth Publishing Company.

Johnson, R., & Price, S. (1981). The complete correctional officer: Human service and the human environment of prison. *Criminal Justice and Behavior, 8,* 343–373.

Jurik, N. (1985). Individual and organizational determinants of correctional officer attitudes toward inmates. *Criminology, 23,* 523–539.

Kauffman, K. (1981, July). Prison officers' attitudes and perceptions of attitudes – A case of pluralistic ignorance. *Journal of Research in Crime and Delinquency, 18,* 272–294.

Kauffman, K. (1988). *Prison officers and their world.* Cambridge, MA: Harvard University Press.

Lipsky, M. (1973). Street-level bureaucracy and the analysis of urban reform. In G. Frederickson (Ed.), *Neighborhood control in the 1970s* (pp. 103–115). New York: Chandler Publishing.

Locke, J. (1980). *Second treatise of government.* Indianapolis, IN: Hackett Publishing Company. (Original work published 1690.)

Lombardo, L. (1989). *Guards imprisoned: Correctional officers at work* (2nd ed.). Cincinnati, OH: Anderson Publishing Company.

Machiavelli, N. (1980). *The prince.* New York: The New American Library of World Literature. (Original work published 1513.)

Mazmanian, D. A., & Sabatier, P. A. (1983). *Implementation and public policy.* Dallas, TX: Scott, Foresman and Company.

McGregor, D. M. (1996). The human side of enterprise. In J. S. Ott (Ed.), *Classic readings in organizational behavior* (2nd ed., pp. 57–62). Belmont, CA: Wadsworth Publishing Company.

Meyerson, B. A. (1992). Role definition for the practitioner of correctional supervision: Transcending the role conflict in theory and practice. In C. A. Hartjen & E. E. Rhine (Eds.), *Correctional theory and practice* (pp. 82–96). Chicago: Nelson-Hall Publishers.

Muir, W. (1977). *Street corner politicians.* Chicago: University of Chicago Press.

Philliber, S. (1987). Thy brother's keeper: A review of the literature on correctional officers. *Justice Quarterly, 4*(l), 9–37.

Pollock, J. M. (1994). *Ethics in crime and justice: Dilemmas and decisions* (2nd ed.). Belmont, CA: Wadsworth Publishing Company.

Poole, E., & Regoli, R. (1981, August). Alienation in prison: An examination of the work relations of prison guards. *Criminology, 19,* 251–270.

Simon, H. (1976). *Administrative behavior* (3rd ed.). New York: The Free Press.

Stinchcombe, J. B. (1980). Beyond bureaucracy: A reconsideration of the "professional" police. *Police Studies, 3,* 49–61.

Sykes, G. M. (1980). The defects of total power. In B. M. Crouch (Ed.), *The keepers: Prison guards and contemporary corrections* (pp. 225–246). Springfield, IL: Charles C. Thomas.

Weber, M. (1971). Legitimate authority and bureaucracy. In D. S. Pugh (Ed.), *Organization theory* (pp. 15–30). New York: Penguin Books.

Whitehead, J. T., & Lindquist, C. A. (1989). Determinants of correctional officer's professional orientation. *Justice Quarterly, 6*(l), 69–87.

Wilson, W. (1941, December). The study of administration. *Political Science Quarterly, 56,* 481–506. (Original work published 1887.)

Section 4

Processes in Criminal Justice Organizations

Section four explores the processes found within criminal justice organizations. Two important processes are decision making and organizational effectiveness. Criminal justice administrators are keenly aware of these processes since it is these processes that bring them under public scrutiny and criticism. How criminal justice officials make decisions and are able to defend them against severe criticism is a true test of their overall effectiveness. In addition, both decision making and organizational effectiveness are related. Perceived patterns of decision making define, in part, how effective a criminal justice organization is viewed by the public. As a result, it is problematic as to which processes are being evaluated and understood since many processes are inextricably intertwined and difficult to separate. Nevertheless, criminal justice administrators understand outcomes and invariably processes have both general and specific effects. It is these effects that they attempt to control as a critical part of criminal justice administration.

Dalton describes a process whereby police, prosecutors, and community groups got together to address one of the most difficult problems faced by criminal justice officials today—urban homicide. By examining the Strategic Approaches to Community Safety Initiative (SACSI), Dalton provides a blueprint for how criminal justice officials and communities can reduce homicides. The central message of such efforts is to have criminal justice administrators at the local level make more prudent decisions on how they allocate resources and address the homicide problem within urban communities. By pulling together all relevant parties in a concerted effort to address homicide, Dalton believes that many lessons can be learned to effectively impact the homicide problem. She notes the relative success the city of Boston had in reducing homicides by applying the principles, practices, and processes found in SACSI.

In a similar way, Smith, Novak, Frank, and Travis III describe how some criminal justice organizations have attempted to work together and make better decisions on addressing the nation's drug problem. The authors examine the efficacy and effectiveness of multijurisdictional drug task forces by exploring the impact that they have had on drug-related outputs and outcomes in the state of Ohio. Unlike the positive findings offered by Dalton through a collaborative approach such as SACSI, the authors of this piece do not find the types of outputs that would justify the practices of multijurisdictional drug task forces. In fact, this research shows the difference between the outputs produced by multijurisdictional drug task forces and locations that do not have multijurisdictional task forces is virtually nonexistent. This research calls into question the utility of addressing the country's drug problem through such task forces.

The final three articles in this section explore decision making by focusing on the exercise of discretion among actors within the criminal justice system. All three articles are considered classic explorations of the importance of discretion in criminal justice decision making.

Waegel shows how "case routinization" is essential in detective work. By offering an explanation as to the nature of "interpretive activities" among detectives, Waegel documents how they handle the pressures of their positions while effectively dealing with the uncertainty of tasks and the many demands of both victims and other actors in the criminal justice system. His analysis highlights the importance of recognizing a confluence of factors that affect the exercise of discretion among detectives.

Matheny applies a similar logic to the practice of plea bargaining. By offering a specific model of plea bargaining, he develops an understanding predicated on how plea bargain decisions are contextually made and constrained by a number of organizational dictums. First and foremost, he urges for a recognition of the importance of uncertainty in the process of plea bargaining. His analysis takes us beyond purely formalistic descriptions of plea bargaining and suggests other directions to pursue for those interested in reforming the plea bargaining process.

Finally, Rosecrance suggests that probation presentence reports represent a typification process whereby some factors are more important than others in determining sentencing recommendations for criminal offenders. The factors of current offense and prior criminal record are so strong in the final sentencing recommendation that Rosecrance questions whether or not probation departments can really individualize justice. The critical question becomes: Why even ask for other relevant information, such as social history or work history, regarding the offender if the information has very little effect on the final recommendation?

All three articles have serious implications for our understanding of criminal justice processes and, more importantly, how we reform the administration and management of criminal justice organizations. It is this topic the final section of articles addresses.

Chapter 19

Targeted Crime Reduction Efforts in Ten Communities
Lessons for the Project Safe Neighborhoods Initiative

Erin Dalton

The Strategic Approaches to Community Safety Initiative (SACSI) starts with the simple but powerful notion that law enforcement has the power to prevent the next homicide. This concept was not uniformly embraced at the SACSI sites at the onset. Prosecutors, police officers, and probation officers wondered: "Could the decisions we make really affect who will get shot tomorrow night or next week?" This provocative question was eventually answered with a "yes," but only after considerable hard work by many people. This article presents the main lessons from SACSI problem-solving efforts with the hope that the Project Safe Neighborhoods Initiative (PSN) sites will learn from what SACSI has accomplished.

The SACSI sites realized that the question posed could not be answered by a single person or a single agency. They needed a team. They also realized that the question had to be split into more answerable inquiries. For example: "What if we could identify the most violent individuals and most violent groups on the street?" "What if we could follow, document, and map the feuds among these criminally-involved individuals and groups?" These and many other questions were asked and

United States Attorneys' Bulletin, Vol. 50 No. 1, January 2002

answered in a deliberative way by the SACSI sites, requiring information from both traditional and non-traditional sources.

Next, the SACSI sites learned that they needed strategies designed to deal with the specific opportunities presented by the data. The working groups considered the following: "What if we established an early warning system to monitor assaults and shootings among these individuals/groups and intervene before they became homicides?" "What if we communicated clearly to these individuals/groups that violent behavior would not be tolerated and that if they behaved violently, all of the resources of the community would be brought against them?" "What if we actually made good on our word?"

The question "how can the decisions we make change who will get shot tomorrow night or next week?" became answerable and was answered—although with different strategies in each community. The days of discussing random homicides, of knowing that an individual was at risk to kill or be killed and not being able to intervene in time, became rare events.

SACSI sites efforts to develop the strategic partnerships, to collect and analyze the information needed to answer the questions raised above, and to design and evaluate strategies aimed at preventing the next homicide, demonstrate that large-scale, problem-solving efforts can be rewarding. They also demonstrate the difficulty and challenges associated with problem-solving.

How It Started

In the early 1990s, in the midst of youth homicide epidemics plaguing our nation's major cities, the National Institute of Justice funded Harvard University's Kennedy School of Government to achieve a simple but extremely challenging goal: Stop the violence in Boston. The efforts of Kennedy School's researchers and their partners, which became known as Operation Ceasefire, were extraordinarily successful. Youth homicides, which averaged forty-four per year between 1991 and 1995, fell to twenty-six in 1997 and to fifteen in 1998. A thoughtful and rigorous evaluation that describes and validates the team's work is available from the National Institute of Justice. [David M. Kennedy et al., Developing and Implementing Operation Ceasefire, Reducing Gun Violence, U.S. Dept. of Justice, National Institute of Justice (September, 2001). NCJ 188741. Anthony A. Braga et al. Measuring the Impact Operation Ceasefire, Reducing Gun Violence, U.S. Dept. of Justice, National Institute of Justice (September, 2001). NCJ 188741.]

Even before a formal evaluation was completed, Boston's Operation Ceasefire was hailed in the media as an unprecedented success. Other major cities started calling and visiting Boston in the hope of replicating its miracle. At the same time, the Department of Justice sought to replicate the *process* Boston used to achieve significant reductions in youth homicide. The replication was called SACSI. The SACSI sites were funded in two phases. The first phase was funded in 1998 and included: Indianapolis, Indiana; Memphis, Tennessee; New Haven, Connecticut; Portland, Oregon; and Winston-Salem, North Carolina. The second phase was funded in 2000 and included: Albuquerque, New Mexico; Atlanta, Georgia; Detroit, Michigan; Rochester, New York; and St. Louis, Missouri.

The process involved the following elements:

- Develop a strategic partnership.

- Use research and information to assess the specific nature and dynamics of the targeted problem.

- Design a strategy to have a substantial near-term impact on that targeted crime problem.

- Implement the strategy.

- Evaluate the strategy's impact and modify the strategy as indicated.

This process is not dissimilar to the Project Safe Neighborhoods (PSN) Initiative model in which U.S. Attorneys will:

- Develop partnerships with federal, state, and local law enforcement and others.

- Develop strategic plans which include crime analysis and strategic enforcement, suppression, and prevention activities.

- Publicize their law enforcement successes to the community.

- Measure the impacts of their efforts.

While the specifics may vary somewhat, both initiatives begin with collaboration, rely on data and information-driven strategies, seek near-term results, and hold themselves accountable for their efforts by measuring the results. This article reviews the (1) organizational structures that seemed most effective under SACSI; (2 & 3) problem-solving approaches that evolved; (4) tactics that emerged; and, (5) their effectiveness at reducing violence with the hope that the PSN communities will learn from SACSI's lessons and take problem-solving to the next level.

Developing an Effective Partnership

Partnerships represent a key aspect of success for many recent criminal justice initiatives (including SACSI and PSN). Yet partnerships are often assumed to exist when they do not, are difficult to achieve, and are rarely studied. Preliminary assessments of SACSI sites partnerships provide some useful insights.

Key issues in developing partnerships included membership, partnership structure, leadership, and project management. Two especially important and difficult issues in the SACSI sites were (1) whether to, and how to, involve the community and (2) how to balance the need for high-level leadership and support with the need for line-level law enforcement knowledge and know-how.

Establishing the Team

Almost as important as deciding who to include as partners is how to invite them to join, how large the partnership should be, and at what organizational level (leaders or line-practitioners) the partnership operates. Race, gender, and culture were also important to the SACSI sites as they developed the composition of their working groups.

After two years of working together, the SACSI sites identified the following partners as most critical to the success of their problem-solving efforts: U.S. Attorney's Office, police department, research partner, district attorney's office, probation/parole agencies, and the Bureau of Alcohol, Tobacco, and Firearms. Most also mentioned a community-based organization or representatives of the clergy as critical to their success.

The consensus that emerged obscures the variation in team memberships and organization. At the beginning of the SACSI initiative, participation ranged from a small team consisting of a core of law enforcement and criminal justice officials without social service and community participation (as in New Haven), to a large and broad team comprised of officials and leaders from law enforcement, criminal justice, social service, and community-based organizations (as in Portland).

Which partnership structure was more successful? There is no easy answer to this question. Partnerships that started small and were relatively homogenous seemed more mobile and quicker to make key decisions. Small groups of law enforcement officials were more likely to trust one another and to share — and be legally permitted to share — sensitive information. However, these smaller partnerships sometimes lacked the diversity of opinions, approaches, and perspectives that characterized larger groups with more nontraditional partners. Also, larger groups may have been better protected from negative community, media, or political reactions.

Several SACSI sites combined these two distinct approaches. They started with a working group made up primarily of law enforcement and criminal justice representatives. The working group remained small until the team had a detailed understanding of the crime problem they were targeting. At that point, the group presented their findings to community and clergy groups and social service agencies, some of whom were subsequently included in the partnership and involved in shaping and implementing the strategies that followed. A benefit of waiting until the initial problem identification and analysis is complete before involving these other groups is that the working groups were able to identify the right groups and affected communities, and their roles were much more apparent than in sites that involved a larger group before a focus for the project was established.

Leadership

One of the most important dimensions of SACSI partnerships is leadership. The U.S. Attorney's Office played a significant role in leading the SACSI partnerships. As the highest ranking law enforcement officer in the community, the U.S. Attorney's status brought local law enforcement leaders, to the table. In addition, because the U.S. Attorney's Office had a distance from the everyday local law enforcement business that most police departments, district, attorneys offices, and even mayor's offices cannot claim, the U.S. Attorney was usually seen as more neutral in local law enforcement circles. The U.S. Attorney's leadership sometimes helped bring local law enforcement leaders to SACSI partnerships with an open mind. Lessons from the SACSI sites suggest that problem-solving partnerships often fall apart, or never come together, in the absence of a powerful, neutral convener.

Management

If we learned one thing from the SACSI initiative, it was the necessity of having a project director responsible for the hands-on management of problem-solving efforts. This critical team member managed the daily process, facilitated the conversation, moved the group toward the collective goal, ensured that different components of the partnerships worked effectively, held the group to task, and worked with the research partner to think through the nexus of operational capacities, local data analysis, and crime control theory. A successful project director balances the managerial need to keep the project on task while building the capacity of the other partners to shoulder essential tasks and responsibilities. Like effective leadership, problem-solving partnerships cannot succeed, in the absence of effective project management.

The Power of Including Front-Line Practitioners in the Partnership. Successful SACSI partnerships used knowledge and information gleaned from nontraditional sources. Typically, police chiefs and agency heads are asked about their most serious crime problems. Officers who are out on the streets everyday are rarely asked these same questions. The experiences of the SACSI sites indicate this is a glaring omission. Front-line practitioners are uniquely immersed in the problem. Their knowledge is essential to understanding the dynamics of targeted crime problems. While others may have a solid understanding of the outlines of a problem (e.g., they may know there is a gang component to the violence problem), front-line practitioners typically know the contours and vital details of the problem (e.g., they know who the gang leaders are, which gangs are most violent, and which are currently feuding). To achieve the balance between the need for leadership and the need for front-line practitioner knowledge, some of the sites established a working group with two levels—one with management representatives that met every six weeks or so—and one with line-level representatives that met more frequently.

The Significance of Involving the "Community" in the Partnership. The partners in the SACSI sites debated a great deal about the necessity and importance of involving the "community" in problem-solving efforts. Some participants argue that the work of the Ten-Point Coalition or gang outreach workers in Indianapolis or Winston-Salem played a major role in achieving crime reductions in those cities. Other participants consider their role less critical, and even potentially disruptive, to information sharing and development of trust within the partnership. Some issues to consider when deciding whether to involve the community can be articulated: Will the community groups or individuals provide intelligence or perspectives not contained elsewhere in the partnership? Will their participation help craft more effective law enforcement approaches, as well as provide buy-in, that can temper community disapproval for aggressive law enforcement strategies that may be included as part of the initiative? Do they have a unique connection with the offender population? Are they likely to put limits on the trust that can be developed within the group? What issues are presented to the functioning of the partnership if law enforcement information needs to be shared when these individual/groups are present? These and other questions should help guide the decision about whether to, and how to, include the "community" in the partnership.

The Importance of an Outside Perspective in the Partnership. Having someone from outside the operational world who can see practitioners' work from a different perspective, frame operational efforts in a broader context, and validate law enforcement efforts to management and policymakers, make research partners a critical part of the problem-solving team. In addition, having someone trained in research methods and criminological theory has been significant in the SACSI partnerships. These partners helped develop the fullest possible understanding of the targeted crime problem, as well as a strategy that was based on the data and was measurable.

Understanding the Targeted Crime Problem

For SACSI sites, the process of identifying the specifics of a problem often began with a review of the formal crime and community safety data, and usually progressed to include interviews, focus groups, and incident reviews. A closer look at two sites—Indianapolis, Indiana and Rochester, New York illustrate the processes. [For a full examination of the Indianapolis Violence Reduction Partnership see Edmund F. McGarrell, and Steven Chermak, Problem Solving to Reduce Gang and Drug-Related Violence in Indianapolis. Forthcoming *Gangs, Youth Violence and*

Community Policing, S. Decker and E. Connors (eds.). For more information on the Rochester SACK project, contact Lori Gilmore, Western District of New York, (716) 263-6760.]

Indianapolis and Its Violence Problem

Indianapolis is a city with just over 800,000 residents in a metropolitan area of approximately one and one-half million. It has long ranked in the mid-range among the nation's larger cities in rates of crime generally and violent crime in particular. However, during the mid-1990s, Indianapolis experienced a significant increase in homicides, reaching a peak level of 157 in 1997. The doubling of the homicide rate, from 10 in 1990 to 20 in 1998, was attributed by local law enforcement to the late arrival of crack cocaine in this mid-western city. Some officials also thought that a gang problem fueled violence on the streets.

The working group used existing information systems (police incident reports, GIS crime mapping, court records) to analyze Indianapolis homicides. The 1997 and 1998 homicides looked similar to those in most urban, U.S. cities. They involved young men, using firearms, in concentrated geographic areas. Many of the victims and suspects had very similar personal characteristics—age, race, and gender—and many had prior criminal history. The most common age for victims was twenty-eight. Suspects were even younger, peaking from ages seventeen to twenty-six with a median of twenty-three. Nearly 80 percent of victims were male and more than 80 percent of suspects were male. Two-thirds of victims and 72 percent of suspects were African-American. At least 63 percent of the victims and three-quarters of the suspects had either an adult or juvenile criminal record. Firearms were used in about three-quarters of the homicides.

Crime mapping indicated that homicides were concentrated in particular neighborhoods in three of the five Indianapolis Police Department districts. The specific police beats tended to be the same ones with the most violent crime and the ones receiving the most citizen complaints about drug activity.

The analysis of official crime reports helped paint a picture of the overall patterns, but the picture was not detailed enough to craft interventions. For example, the official reports indicated that very few homicides involved either gangs (one in 1998) or drugs, (six in 1997, seven in 1998). Nevertheless, investigators and line-level officers strongly suspected that gangs and drugs were involved in many, perhaps most, of the homicides.

To get a detailed picture of homicides, the working group decided to follow the approach taken in Boston, Minneapolis, and Baltimore. They brought together Indianapolis law enforcement officials with street-level intelligence on homicides and violence to participate in an examination of every homicide incident occurring in 1997. Participants included detectives and officers from the Indianapolis Police Department and Marion County Sheriff's Department, prosecutors, probation officers, corrections officials, and federal law enforcement (approximately seventy-five representatives from ten agencies). The intent was to move beyond the basics contained in official records and tap into the extensive knowledge available from the law enforcement professionals working these cases and areas of the city. Specifically, the working group sought information about motive and events leading up to the homicide, networks of chronic offenders involved in homicides, and whether and how homicides were related to drug use and distribution.

The incident review revealed that approximately 60 percent of the homicides involved suspects or victims who were described as being part of a group of known chronic offenders, or loosely organized gangs. Additionally, more than half the homicides had some type of drug connection involving known users and dealers, as well as incidents tied to drug sales, retaliations, and drug turf battles. The working group, armed with a problem analysis that enabled them to consider interventions, decided to concentrate their efforts on group and drug-related homicides.

Rochester and Its Violence Problem

Rochester is a city of about 217,000 people with a metropolitan area of just under 1.1 million. The metropolitan area has grown over the past thirty years, but the city itself has lost over one-third of its population since its peak in 1950. Rochester has averaged about fifty murders a year. While relatively small in absolute numbers, Rochester's homicide *rate* is the highest in New York—higher than New York City, 30 percent higher than Buffalo, and nearly 60 percent higher than Syracuse and Albany. It is also higher than cities such as Indianapolis and Los Angeles.

After reviewing the official data, Rochester found much the same general pattern as Indianapolis and other U.S. cities. Homicides involved young, African-American men, using firearms, in concentrated geographic areas, and many of the victims and suspects had prior involvement in the criminal justice system.

Like Indianapolis, the review of the official records was helpful in understanding basic crime patterns, but it left the Rochester SACSI team with little idea of how to reduce homicides. Much of what the analysis of the official records revealed was already widely known by the police and the general public. It was also clear that interventions already underway in this city were not having the desired effect.

The Rochester team decided that a homicide incident review would help give specificity to the problem. As in Indianapolis, the team wanted to develop a deeper understanding of the motives behind the murders and to see if there were patterns or individuals associated with multiple events that could lead to intervention strategies.

The review of all homicides in 2000 proved to be effective. It highlighted motives, weapons, and even individuals common across cases. Analysis of the data gained from the incident review revealed three types of murder in Rochester: (1) A small portion (13 percent) involved people who simply found themselves at the wrong place at the wrong time; (2) About half involved disputes and arguments; (3) About 40 percent involved murder associated with illegal business — almost all drug sales, robberies or robbery assassinations.

The homicide review also revealed that 40 percent of the homicides were connected with more than one assailant. The consensus among the group was that these were not highly organized gangs, but rather small groups of friends, involved in drug-related disputes and drug rip-off assassinations.

Before proceeding to interventions, the working group wanted to know more about the genesis and dynamics of drug houses and drug-house robberies, and needed additional information about the nature and frequency of disputes on the street. This led SACSI researchers to the Monroe County Correctional facility where they conducted lengthy focus groups with inmates.

The focus groups revealed valuable insights into the criminal lifestyle in Rochester. On the whole, the focus group members felt they lived in a very dangerous world. They believed they could run into conflicts anywhere: and that most people in their neighborhoods had experienced, or were experiencing, serious "beefs" with others. Furthermore, they believed that weapons carrying and violence were common in their neighborhoods. They talked about "flash and respect" and reported that wearing expensive clothing or jewelry in their neighborhood may lead to envy by other young men. "Too much flash" seemed to be at the root of many conflicts and drug robberies.

In addition to providing invaluable insights into the criminal lifestyle, the focus groups also provided important information about the extent, supply, and reasons for gun carrying; the frequency, nature, and causes of disputes; and the history, operations, and dynamics of drug houses and drug house robberies. Further, the focus groups provided insights into the effectiveness of current law enforcement actions and on-going prosecution strategies such as Project Exile, as well as the level of intrusion and effect sanctions, including probation and parole, had on their lifestyle. From these focus groups, the Rochester SACSI group concluded that they had enough information to start thinking about strategies.

Observations About the Problem Specification Process

The precise nature and flow of the problem-specification process was unique to each of the SACSI sites. However, two generalizations can be made. First, the targeted crime problems were not necessarily what they seemed initially. On the surface, Indianapolis and Rochester (and many other cities) have the same violence problem. After a much closer look, it became clear that the gang and drug-market dynamics were very different in different communities, as were the reasons behind the homicides. Indianapolis had semi-organized gangs engaged in drug turf battles. Rochester had drug-house robberies and disputes among individuals and groups. Second, the process demonstrates the importance of qualitative and nontraditional sources of data. Official data were critical to outlining the problems, but systematic questioning of line practitioners, community groups, outreach workers, and even offenders, proved much more revealing of the motives and nature of the events. It is in the underlying patterns where opportunities for intervention were to be found.

Developing a Strategy

Many of the SACSI sites struggled to move from specifying the problem to developing an intervention strategy. In some sites, it may have been difficult to develop a strategy because of an insufficient understanding of the problem—suggesting that the working group needed to continue gathering data. In others, it may have been an absence of leadership at a pivotal time. Often, it was simply the difficulty of matching the resources and assets of the working group to these difficult problems. Reflecting on the Boston experience, David Kennedy, one of the designers of the Boston Gun Project, urges patience. He reminds us that the types of problems likely to be addressed by sustained, large-scale, problem-solving exercises are typically difficult ones—otherwise, lesser efforts would have been sufficient to deal with them. The Boston Gun Project Working Group spent more than a year designing Operation Ceasefire. The SACSI sites took at least that long to design and implement their strategies.

Kennedy's Decision Rules

While there is no cookbook of lessons that will tell you how to innovate or give you the solution to the targeted crime problem, the Boston and the SACSI experiences offer the outline of a process for strategy development. They also offer effective ways of deciding whether the solutions and tactics suggested to address the targeted crime problem will meet their goals.

In the SACSI sites, the working groups took their problem analysis to community groups, line-level officers, social service agencies, and affected neighborhoods, in an attempt to solicit solutions. Most also looked at similar problems and solutions in other communities, and considered ways to apply criminological theory and practice to identify possible solutions to the problem.

Common suggestions included:

- Reducing poverty in high crime neighborhoods;

- Eradicating drug demand;

- Federal prosecution of all illegal gun carriers;

- Offering parenting classes; and,

- Supporting conflict resolution training and anti-gang programming in the schools.

All of these solutions were plausible ones in many of the SACSI
communities. Reducing poverty and other root causes in high-crime
areas would likely have an effect on violence in those neighborhoods.
Eradicating drug demand would likely eliminate drug markets and the
violence associated with them. Federally prosecuting all gun carriers
would likely remove many potentially violent offenders from the community. Offering parenting classes and supporting positive training in
schools might lead to healthier and less violent at-risk kids.

To narrow down the possible solutions, the SACSI sites applied
Kennedy's decision rules to each one:

1. How big of an impact can we anticipate?

2. How long will it take?

3. Can we do it?

4. Do we want to?

As simple as they are, these questions set a very high standard.
Most of the potential tactics suggested by SACSI working groups failed to
meet at least one of the four rules. Two of the above mentioned examples — eradicating drug demand and federally prosecuting all illegal gun
carriers — illustrate the point.

Eradicating Drug Demand

If drug demand were eradicated, illegal drug markets and the violence associated with them would dissipate. Thus, this strategy would
pass rule #1 by yielding significant impacts on violent crime. All members of the working groups would have happily eradicated drug demand,
and many members desperately wanted to do it (passing rule #4). However, eradicating drug demand would take longer than the working
group had (failing rule #2) and was not something the working group
had resources, know-how, or capacity to accomplish (failing rule #3).
Thus, this strategy was discarded.

Federal Prosecution of all Illegal Firearms Carriers

This was clearly something the working group could accomplish
(passing rule #3), and, the results were likely to be almost immediate
(passing rule #2). However, when working groups carefully examined
the impact this strategy will have and the number of resources required
to sustain it over any duration, most groups concluded that this tactic
was not targeted enough and did not offer enough "bang for the buck"

(failing by rule #1). Further, when working groups considered the desirability of this action, most concluded that a good number of these offenders came from impoverished, addicted, and broken families, and not all of them deserved to be treated as hardened criminals, particularly if something better could be offered. Working group members also knew that many communities would not support federal prosecutions for all firearms carriers. For these, and other reasons, this strategy was not appealing (failing by rule #4). The strategy was discarded.

The SACSI sites had to keep searching until they found tactics that were both doable and effective in the short-run. The tactics that eventually passed the test were more often enforcement-focused than some working groups would have preferred. Thus, some sites developed a parallel track in which longer-term interventions were implemented and assessed.

Common Tactics

SACSI sites rarely settled on a single tactic as the immediate best answer. Rather, they used a variety of integrated tactics (which came together as a single strategy) aimed at identified causes. While every strategy was different, a few tactics were common to many of the sites and to Boston. Common tactics are described below.

The List

The goal of "the list" is to identify the most serious, violent offenders in the city and increase the arrest, prosecution, and incarceration of these offenders. If you can identify the most serious offenders, those responsible for most of the violence, and put them away, you will reduce violence and fear on the street. How the offenders for this list are identified is critical to success. Some cities relied solely on criminal history data, and thus sometimes identified older offenders who were not necessarily the most likely to commit homicide. Other cities combined criminal history data with a monthly version of the incident review process. In incident reviews, practitioners examined recent homicides, as well as other types of incidents (including shootings, shots fired, assaults, and/or robberies) to bring ongoing violent events to bear in developing the list.

Once the list was developed, efforts were made to increase the arrest, prosecution, and incarceration of these offenders. In some sites, part of the effort involved establishing a team that screened all firearms and/or violence cases to determine the appropriateness of local or federal prosecution. This tactic is referred to in Richmond and other cities as "Project Exile." Some cities also increased the enforcement of bench warrants and increased probation/parole scrutiny on individuals on the list. In some communities, the list became something that was feared on the street.

This tactic was not used by all of the SACSI sites. Working groups that did not have strong community support feared being accused of "profiling" if they were to develop or use a tactic such as the list. On the other hand, working groups that were supported by community coalitions stood behind the list as strategic enforcement which sought to rid communities of the "worst of the worst," the offenders everyone wanted off the street.

Lever-Pulling

The lever-pulling strategy attempts to: (1) increase the perception among high-risk individuals that they were likely to face criminal sanctions if they continued to engage in violence; (2) make high-risk individuals aware of, and provide access to, legitimate opportunities and services; (3) communicate clearly and directly to them; and, (4) be credible by following through on the threat of sanctions when violence occurs and by making services and opportunities available as an alternative to criminal activities.

The lever-pulling strategy starts by selecting a narrow target category of illegal behavior (for example, gang violence in Boston or adult offenders who involved juveniles in crimes as in Winston-Salem). The working group then delivers a direct and explicit message to a relatively small, targeted group regarding what kind of behavior will elicit a special response from law enforcement and what that response will be. Then the working group monitors the targeted group and the targeted behavior closely and follows-through when individuals or groups step out of line.

When individuals or groups commit targeted acts, the reaction must be immediate and certain. The working group must make good on its word, and "pull levers" on those who have engaged in violence. The working group should then communicate the results of the crackdown with others they are trying to effect. In other words, the working group should tell the targeted group (for example, Gang B) why members from Gang A are being prosecuted federally for their violent acts and what will happen to them if they behave similarly.

The primary method for delivering the lever-pulling message in the SACSI sites was a series of forums (or highly formalized meetings) with the target audience. The targeted audience of criminally involved individuals was most commonly identified through a combination of ongoing incident reviews and the use of the list. Federal and local prosecutors, accompanied by local, state, and federal law enforcement, explained the sanctions (levers) that would be applied to individuals and groups participating in violence. At the same forum, clergy and community leaders expressed their concerns about violence in the neighborhoods and the number of young men being victimized and incarcerated. The meetings also offered descriptions of available services and support opportunities available from providers, community, and clergy participants.

While this was the general format for the forums, the message, messengers, and precise format for the meetings varied across sites. Letters or phone calls to offenders, billboards, and posters may also serve as primary or secondary ways of notifying offenders of the message. What is critical is not necessarily how the offender is notified, but that the message reaches the *right* people, and that the message is clear, direct, and, most important, *credible*.

Home Visits

Another key tactic in the SACSI sites were unannounced visits to the homes of probationers and parolees by teams of probation/parole officers, police, and in some cities (like Winston-Salem) clergy representatives. The home visits reinforced the message that the criminal justice community was united and serious about ensuring that targeted offenders were not committing violent offenses. Often these teams met not only with the offender, but also with the offender's family and neighbors, to let others know what was going on. Some of the visits ended with drug tests and some ended with distribution of resource information and contact sheets for services for the offenders and their families.

Measuring Outcomes

The SACSI sites are using multiple techniques to determine if their interventions are having the intended effect. Most sites took careful pre-intervention measures of key violence indicators such as homicide, shootings, robbery, and aggravated assault, especially in the neighborhoods where the problems were concentrated and the solutions were implemented. All sites continued to monitor the indicators monthly, and where appropriate, by neighborhood to determine the impact. If key indicators showed an effect, SACSI site researchers sought to determine whether the effects could be replicated and predicted over time. They also attempted to identify alternative interventions or other dynamics (for example, economic or demographic changes) that could have caused these effects. Because some of the sites (for example, Winston-Salem) applied their strategies in several neighborhoods, they were able to compare the "test" areas with the "control" areas — those that experienced comparable violence but had not received the resources of the working group. The comparison of test and control areas was done to determine whether targeted crime was being displaced to other areas of the city.

In addition to these measures, several sites sought to determine how the strategies were affecting the city at large. For example, researchers in Indianapolis examined data over time from NIJ's Arrestee Drug Abuse Monitoring (ADAM) program, which regularly tracks drug use by arrestees by asking questions about their drug use history. The researchers used ADAM to assess offender awareness of SACSI tactics, to learn more about the perceptions of criminal justice system effectiveness, and to determine if perceptions have changed on the street due to the strategies. Similarly, researchers in New Haven conducted pre- and post- intervention surveys of fear of crime in neighborhoods where the interventions were most acutely focused. SACSI sites have also attempted to determine whether the notified group has taken advantage of services and opportunities provided, and what effect these resources have had on offenders.

SACSI Site Results

The University of Illinois-Chicago is conducting an evaluation of all of the SACSI sites. The initial findings from the first five SACSI sites funded in 1998 (the sites funded in late 2000 have not begun implementing interventions yet) are promising. For example, in Indianapolis, targeted crimes were down 11 percent from the 1999 level and 46 percent since 1998. Memphis has also seen its targeted crime (sexual assault) rates decline 26 percent over the course of intervention. Winston-Salem's statistics indicate a steep decline in the use of firearms in violent crimes in targeted areas. SACSI publications should be available in the coming year.

Conclusion

The lesson from Boston Ceasefire and SACSI is that law enforcement can prevent the next homicide. To do so, they need to build the right team and to ask the right questions. More often than not, the answers to these questions come from crime incident reviews, focus groups, and interviews with practitioners, in addition to administrative criminal justice system data. Only once the team has asked and answered all of these questions, can they design strategies to deal with their unique and precise problem. Over time, the team learns to assess their strategies and modify their approaches until they can predictably prevent homicides. These steps sound easy but each one contains many pitfalls. The lessons from SACSI are offered with the hope that the problem-solving model will continue to be improved upon by the Project Safe Neighborhoods Initiative.

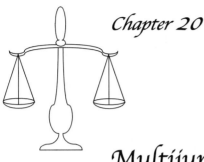

Chapter 20

Multijurisdictional Drug Task Forces
An Analysis of Impacts

Brad W. Smith
Kenneth J. Novak
James Frank
Lawrence F. Travis III

Introduction

Over the past decade, the growth in law enforcement task forces aimed at controlling drug crime has been nothing short of phenomenal. Coldren and Sabath (1992) estimated that over 1000 such task forces existed in the United States over five years ago. Currently, nearly half of all federal Edward M. Byrne Memorial Fund grant money is dedicated to supporting these task forces. Yet, Sherman (1997:8–40) contended that these task forces have never been "subjected to a published impact evaluation." The research reported here examined the effect of membership in a drug enforcement task force on police agency production of drug enforcement outputs and perceptions of effectiveness.

Since the 1980s, there has been increased emphasis on drug crime and drug enforcement. Law enforcement organizations have employed a variety of strategies aimed at arresting drug offenders and disrupting drug markets (Manning, 1980; Branham, 1986; Lyman, 1987; Kleiman, 1988; Moore and Kleiman, 1989; Fagan, 1992; Hillsman, 1992; Weisburd

Reprinted from *Journal of Criminal Justice,* Vol. 28, Brad W. Smith, Kenneth J. Novak, James Frank, and Lawrence F. Travis III, "Multijurisdictional Drug Task Forces: An Analysis of Impacts," pp. 543–556, 2000, with permission from Elsevier.

and Green, 1995; Bynum and Worden, 1996). Traditionally, these drug enforcement strategies were developed and implemented by officers within one police agency or members of a single department's drug unit (Hayeslip and Weisel, 1992). In the early 1980s, police recognized that drug markets and drug law offenders often operate across jurisdictional boundaries, and that single agency enforcement efforts were limited by the cross jurisdictional nature of drug crime and drug markets.

The most common reform proposed to address this limitation was the consolidation and coordination of police services within identified areas. In theory, coordinated law enforcement efforts overcome jurisdictional limits and result in greater efficiency and economy of scale. Efforts at the coordination of drug enforcement have produced formal interagency drug enforcement collaborations known as multijurisdictional drug task forces. The federal initiative against drugs and drug-related crime in 1986 and 1988 made substantial financial resources available to states for enforcement efforts. A significant portion of these funds has gone to support multijurisdictional drug enforcement task forces (McGarrell and Schlegel, 1993; Dunworth et al., 1997; Sherman, 1997).

Research that has examined drug task forces to date has been primarily descriptive (Coldren et al., 1993). The few available impact studies have been limited in scope (Schlegel and McGarrell, 1991) and the available evidence on the impact of drug task forces is equivocal at best. Participants in these cooperative ventures believe them to be beneficial in combating drug crimes, but task force agencies have not been shown to be more productive in drug enforcement than non-task force efforts. The essential question remains: Are agencies participating in these joint ventures more effective than their counterparts?

The issue of effectiveness is multidimensional. Most assessments of criminal justice program impacts seek to determine whether programs achieve instrumental goals such as reductions in crime, lower recidivism, increased arrests, and the like. From the perspective of the organizations involved in these programs, however, participation can have process and organizational benefits regardless of impact on any target problem. In the case of multijurisdictional drug enforcement task forces, the availability of external funding may be the primary goal of program participation for police agencies. Thus, an assessment of effectiveness should consider both impact and process components of organizational goals. This research examined the effectiveness of drug enforcement task forces in terms of both their impact on drug enforcement products and agency perceptions of the benefits of participation.

Organizational Effectiveness and Task Forces

The measurement of organizational performance is exceedingly difficult and quite complex (Whitaker and Phillips, 1983; Damanpour and Evan, 1984). There are a variety of problems associated with measuring performance. For instance, due to the complexity of the construct, there is no single best measure or set of measures for effectiveness (see Duffee, 1980; Whitaker and Phillips, 1983; Klofas et al., 1990). Furthermore, effectiveness studies, like all evaluation research involves political decisions about the criteria to be used as the standard for organizational success (Klofas et al., 1990:255–256). To overcome these and other problems, various models and evaluation criteria have been utilized by researchers and theorists to assess organizational effectiveness, including goal attainment models, system or process models (i.e., participant satisfaction and system resource models), and structural models (Etzioni, 1975; Hall, 1991; Scott, 1987; Klofas et al., 1990). These different models suggest that organizations can derive different types of benefits from their activities. In the case of drug law enforcement, a police agency can increase its efficiency in closing drug cases, increase arrests, increase fine and forfeiture revenues, and the like. So, too, the agency might receive increased funding, develop better relations with other agencies, or increase member satisfaction with how the agency operates. Organizational goals include both transitive (or production) goals and reflexive (system maintenance) goals (Mohr, 1973). Goal attainment models focus on the transitive elements of the organizational goal while system resource models emphasize the reflexive elements. The following sections outline these two different models of organizational effectiveness.

Goal Attainment Model

Most researchers have contended that measuring effectiveness requires that organizational goals be defined and that whether they are realized determines the extent to which an organization has been successful in achieving its objectives (Simon, 1945; Etzioni, 1960, 1975; Scott, 1975; Thompson and McEwen, 1980; Damanpour and Evan, 1984; Hall, 1991). Most evaluation research on the effectiveness of criminal justice agencies has used the goal attainment model. For example, the examination of whether there is congruence between an observed outcome and stated or implicit goals of organizations continues to be the most prevalent means of evaluating prison performance (Marsden and Orsagh, 1983). Similarly, Smith and Klein (1983:92) stated that a "measure of police performance must be related to some set of objectives or goals." The use of defined goals as a standard against which to measure organization performance may be especially critical for criminal justice agencies, and task forces in particular, since there is no market mechanism to assess the value of goods and services provided to the consumers of public safety.

While the goal attainment model appears quite simple (i.e., have the goals of the organization been met?), operationalizing its concepts is not so straightforward. First, specification of the goals of an organization is not an easy task, especially if they have not been explicitly stated by the organization. Second, organizations often have multiple and conflicting goals (Mohr, 1973; Duffee, 1980; Wycoff and Manning, 1983; Hall, 1991), which make it virtually impossible to satisfy all of the goals. Third, goal realization may depend on factors external to the organization and, in fact, may be highly dependent on environmental constraints (Whitaker and Phillips, 1983; Hall, 1991). Fourth, the goal attainment model posits a completely rational model of organizations in which decision makers direct organization activities and efforts solely toward attainment of organization objectives. In actual practice, however, "conflicting goals, inadequate information, and the need to 'satisfyce' rather than optimize limit organizational rationality" (Klofas et al., 1990:255).

In accordance with a goal model of performance evaluation, and after noting a lack of research on the effectiveness of multijurisdictional drug task forces, Sherman (1997:8–40) stated that "It does not seem inappropriate, however, to specify measurable goals for the program, and to design an impact evaluation to test the effectiveness of the Task Forces in accomplishing those goals." Measurable goals may be retrieved from the grant applications of task forces and they may be used to assess whether task force agencies are attaining their stated goals.

Process Model

Partially in response to problems associated with determining proper outcome measures and goals, some researchers turned to measures of the processes internal to organizations to assess effectiveness (Scott, 1975). These measures generally focus on the relationships among the elements of an organization's system which are often thought to enhance the ability of the organization to meet its objectives (Etzioni, 1975), or activities internal to organizations that are believed necessary for organization success. For instance, Wycoff and Manning (1983) suggested there is a need to focus on the processes that translate inputs into outputs (see also Ostrom et al., 1978).

Within this model, the internal processes of the system and the organization participants take on critical importance. Internal processes that transform inputs into outputs are examined to determine if they are operating smoothly and with as little internal strain as possible (Ostrom et al., 1978; Wycoff and Manning, 1983). Relatedly, individual assessments of effectiveness are examined because they may be associated with participant decisions to continue to work and survival of the organization. As such, measures of worker judgements about the quality of the organizations' products and beliefs about organizational success are often utilized to examine dimensions of effectiveness (Hall, 1991). Assessments of effectiveness might also explore the processes that are believed to be associated with increased production.

Multijurisdictional organizational arrangements should foster trust among participants and be a catalyst for increasing the cooperation and communication among task force members. Under optimum conditions, these organizational arrangements should also increase member agency perceptions of the quality of their outputs, namely, drug cases. Past research on task forces suggested that increased communication and cooperation among task force member agencies is a benefit associated with task force membership (Coldren et al., 1990; Ruboy and Coldren, 1992; McGarrell and Schlegel, 1993), while the findings on quality of drug cases are quite limited (Schlegel and McGarrell, 1991).

The determination of the proper criterion for assessing task force effectiveness and, ultimately, determining whether they are successful may depend on the model and standards utilized in the study. Objective and subjective performance indicators that relate to different performance criteria are used to assess whether task force members differ from nonmember law enforcement agencies on the achievement of these performance criteria. This allows an examination of task force effectiveness within the context of the two effectiveness models outlined above: goal attainment model and process model.

Multijurisdictional Drug Task Forces

At the national level, indications are that drug task forces have been effective at making drug arrests and seizing drug-related assets. Between 1988 and 1991, BJA-funded drug task forces averaged over 86,000 yearly drug arrests nationwide and were responsible for seizing more than US$100 million in assets (Justice Research and Statistics Association, 1992). Concurrent successes were also reported at the state level. For example, shortly after implementation of the Anti-Drug Abuse Act of 1988, Ohio's 33 BJA-funded task forces were credited with increasing the number of drug arrests from 1014 in 1988 to 1983 in 1990 (Justice Research and Statistics Association, 1992). While these data indicate successful task force implementation in the aggregate, they tell us little about the impact of task force membership on individual agencies.

Multijurisdictional drug task forces are formed to increase the effectiveness of law enforcement agencies as they attempt to regulate the sale and use of drugs. If task forces enhance the capacity of participating agencies to curb drug-related activities, then it would be expected that agencies participating in task forces will perform at a higher level than single agencies when products of drug investigations are examined. Specifically, task force agencies should experience more inter-agency communication, drug-related cases should be of higher quality, and they should make more arrests for both the sale and possession of drugs than non-member agencies.[1]

Inter-Agency Communication

In the limited research on the performance of drug task forces, inter-agency communication has received substantial attention. The focus of this research has been on member perceptions of the effects of task force membership on communication. For example, Coldren et al. (1990) surveyed grant administrators in all 50 states and six U.S. territories and found that increased communication was one of the stated benefits of task force membership. In addition, they reviewed 19 task force case studies and concluded that task force members perceive increased inter-agency communication after joining the cooperative drug unit. Ruboy and Coldren (1992) reviewed the results of state-sponsored task force evaluations and reached similar conclusions. Namely, agencies perceived increased communication after becoming members of a task force.

In their study of two Indiana task forces, McGarrell and Schlegel (1993) examined not only perceptions of increased communication, but also attempted to measure the extent of inter-agency communication. They compared two regions that each operated a task force with two comparison sites that were each without a funded task force. Similar to other research, officials in the two task force regions perceived that the task force had increased communication. Responses to the questions regarding the extent of inter-agency communication, however, did not yield statistically significant differences between the two task force and two non-task force regions. This finding may have resulted because members perceived an increase even though there really was no difference in the extent of communication of task force and non-task force jurisdictions. Alternatively, aggregating the data to a regional level of analysis may have masked differences that existed had the task force region included only task force agencies.

Products of Drug Enforcement Activity

Drug enforcement activities, whether engaged in by single police agencies or drug task forces, are intended to produce certain immediate outputs. Specifically, arrests of drug market participants and the development and prosecution of quality arrests are all anticipated effects of drug control efforts. Apart from the aggregate level findings on drug task force products (Justice Research and Statistics Association, 1992; Office of Criminal Justice Services, 1994), there is a dearth of research on the products of individual task forces and member agencies.

For example, research on the impact of drug task force arrests is limited to Schlegel and McGarrell's (1991) analysis of arrest practices in two task force regions and two comparison regions in Indiana. They found that arrests increased in task force regions as well as the control locations after implementing the task forces. Further, the number of offenders arrested on more serious charges (sale of drugs and arrests for cocaine vs. other drugs) also increased in the study locations. When only the task force regions were examined, it appeared that the increases in arrests and charge seriousness were the result of the activities of the task force in one of the task force regions, though the authors noted that "task forces are not necessary conditions for such increases" (Schlegel and McGarrell, 1991:422).

In contrast, there is a substantial body of research that has delineated the outcomes of drug law enforcement activity. The effectiveness of traditional narcotics enforcement activities is often measured by the number of arrests for drug offenses and the nature of prosecuted drug cases (Kleiman, 1988; Zimmer, 1990; Mastrofski and Wadman, 1991; Hillsman, 1992; Gajewski, 1993; Green, 1996).

Ohio Task Force Characteristics

Ohio task forces differ along several dimensions. For example, task forces in Ohio vary by, among other things, the type of agency which assumes the role of implementing agency, the geographic region or working environment, number of counties served, and the number of agencies participating. The implementing agency is often the primary agency responsible for coordinating task force operations, including budgetary resources and often assignment of the task force commander. The implementing agency for a majority (51 percent) of the Ohio task forces is a county sheriff's office followed by municipal police departments (31 percent) and county prosecutor's offices (13 percent).

An examination of the geographic locations of the task forces indicated that 38 percent of the task forces served jurisdictions that were a mixture of rural and urban areas. This is not surprising considering that, with few exceptions, task forces generally cover entire counties which are usually a mixture of rural and urban areas. The second most common type of region served by Ohio task forces was rural. The number of counties served by a task force ranges from between one and eight, with the modal number of counties being one. Finally, the number of agencies in a task force ranged from five to thirty-seven, with a mean number of agencies of almost twelve (see Jefferis et al., 1998 for a more detailed discussion of the organizational structure and operations of Ohio drug task forces).

The task forces are generally decentralized with the day to day operations directed by a task force commander. Tactical decisions are somewhat idiosyncratic to specific task forces; however, there are some commonalities in operations. By and large, the Ohio task forces use traditional methods of drug enforcement with the added benefit of information sharing between agencies, increased resources, and the ability to cross jurisdictional boundaries (for a discussion of traditional drug operations, see Moore and Kleiman, 1989).

Information concerning drug activity is usually obtained from confidential informants, citizen tips or from other officers. In most cases, officers are given wide discretion to obtain information and make decisions regarding if and how to proceed on information. In some cases, task force commanders are consulted by officers prior to proceeding with any case.

In general, task forces claimed to focus on both street-level and upper-level traffickers and dealers. Most, however, place a greater emphasis on upper-level traffickers and dealers. Officers are given wide latitude regarding if and how to proceed in most cases, with decisions generally based on a number of factors. First, the severity of crimes, including type and quantity of drugs, is considered. Generally, crack is believed to be associated with violence and thus considered more serious. Second, whether those involved in the drug-related behavior are a problem beyond drugs is also explored. Third, whether violence is associated with the drug activity is investigated. And fourth, if there is an organizational structure (i.e., gang) or connection to higher dealers is also considered. Last, the amount of information or likelihood of success is considered prior to proceeding. Other factors are also often considered and different task forces may place greater emphasis on certain criteria over others, but overall, task force commanders and officers point to these factors when making decisions regarding whether and how to investigate (for a more detailed discussion of the operations and structure of Ohio task forces, see Frank et al., 1998).

Methods

The main questions addressed in the present study are: Do agencies participating in drug task forces produce more drug enforcement products and are they more effective than non-task force members? Or in other words: Do task force members outperform agencies that do not participate in task forces and therefore are they more successful? In an attempt to answer these related questions, we compared rates of inter-agency communication and the volume of drug law enforcement products of agencies that participated in drug task forces in Ohio with agencies that did not participate in task forces. Three research questions directed our analysis: (1) Do task force jurisdictions have more frequent inter-agency communication? (2) Do task force jurisdictions make more drug-related arrests? (3) Do task force jurisdictions rate the quality of their drug arrests higher than non-task force agencies?

Data Sources

Data for the present study were obtained from three different sources (survey of law enforcement agencies in Ohio, the FBI, and the U.S. Bureau of Census) as part of a larger evaluation of the organization and effectiveness of Ohio's multijurisdictional drug task forces that was funded by the Ohio Office of Criminal Justice Services (OCJS). Because of idiosyncrasies associated with each of the data sets, a brief discussion of the data collection methods follows.

First, surveys were sent to law enforcement agencies in Ohio, and were constructed by the research team to resemble those previously used in a study of Indiana drug task forces (see McGarrell and Schlegel, 1993). The survey tapped, among other things, task force membership, inter-agency communication and cooperation, and perceptions of drug enforcement in the region. The sampling frame for this study consisted of 950 law enforcement agencies in Ohio including municipal police and county sheriffs.[2] Overall, a total of 539 usable law enforcement agency surveys (56.7 percent) were completed and returned. Usable surveys were returned by 266 agencies that were members of drug enforcement task forces and 273 non-member agencies.

Second, monthly Ohio agency arrest data for the sale and possession of drugs were obtained from the FBI for 1995. Reporting to the FBI is voluntary. Unfortunately, only 244 (24.7 percent) different agencies reported arrest data in 1995 and most of these 244 agencies did not report during all twelve months of every year. Due to the quantity of missing data, only eighty agencies could be included in the regression analyses performed on drug arrests.[3]

Finally, Bureau of Census data were collected for use as indicators of agency environment. These data were collected for each jurisdiction in the sample (members and non-members). Once collected, the data were used to create four indicators of population complexity.

Dependent Variables

In accordance with Sherman's comment, three dependent variables were constructed that would allow the authors to examine whether task forces in Ohio were successful in achieving their stated output and process goals. To accomplish this, all funded Byrne program multijurisdictional drug task force grant applications in Ohio for the period between 1987 and 1996 were examined. Applications for Byrne funds must include a statement concerning the goals the task force hopes to achieve if funded. The review of these applications indicated that a substantial majority of the drug task forces listed four objectives. The most frequently mentioned goal was to increase the level of communication between task force agencies and other agencies within the criminal justice system. Second, task forces noted the goal of increasing the number of arrests of drug sellers and users, with an emphasis on investigating people within the drug distribution chain. Third, task forces included the goal of increasing the number of drug-related forfeitures. Finally, task forces listed the goal of improving the quality of drug investigations and cases forwarded for prosecution. As such, the dependent variables examined in this study included measures of inter-agency communication, organizational outputs (number of arrests for the sale and possession of drugs and total drug arrests) and perceptions of the quality of drug cases. Table 1 presents a description of the dependent variables.

That organizational goals are comprised of both reflexive and transitive elements suggests that the notion of effectiveness is at least two-dimensional. Any measures of effectiveness should assess the impact of task force membership on organizational health as well as on drug law enforcement production. To that end, this research included two categories

Table 1   Description of dependent variables

Item	n	Mean	SD
Communication—five-item scale tapping inter-agency communication	514	9.68	3.64
Quality of drug cases—single survey item asking respondents to rate the quality of drug cases in jurisdiction (1 = very low, 2 = low, 3 = moderate, 4 = high, 5 = very high)	529	3.73	1.05
Log of sale arrests—natural logarithm of sale arrests	87	2.14	1.20
Log of possession arrests—natural logarithm of possession arrests	87	4.04	1.74
Log of arrests—natural logarithm of total number of drug arrests	87	4.23	1.08

of dependent variables: process goals which tap the reflexive dimension of the organizational goal, and output goals that reflect the transitive element.

Dependent Variables: Process Goals

Communication Scale.   Five questions from the survey of both task force participants and non-member agencies were used to construct a communication scale. Survey respondents were asked about the amount of communication their agency had with other criminal justice agencies (e.g., local, federal, state, and out of state law enforcement, as well as courts and prosecutors) regarding drug enforcement during the previous 6 months. These questions were designed to measure communication directly related to drug enforcement activities (i.e., communication regarding enforcement rather than communication regarding attendance at a task force meeting). Response options included "None," "1–5 Times," "6–10 Times," and "More than 10 times." The scale was constructed by simply summing the values for all five questions with the resulting scale ranging from 5 to 20 with a mean of 9.72.[4] Higher values indicate greater communication within the past six months. The total item intercorrelation suggests that there is internal consistency with these five items (Cronbach's alpha = 0.835).

Perceived Quality of Drug Cases.   Agency perception of the quality of drug cases was a second dependent variable. Agency responses to a survey question asking respondents to " . . . rate the quality of drug cases (i.e., likelihood of prosecution) in your jurisdiction?" were used to operationalize this variable. Response options included "Very High," "High," "Moderate," "Low," and "Very Low." Admittedly, this is a subjective measure of the quality of drug investigations. A comparison of actual arrest charges with convictions, the more common measure of arrest quality, was not possible.

Dependent Variables: Output Goals

Drug Arrests. Agencies in Ohio report separately to the FBI the number of arrests for the sale and possession of drugs. Since task forces are not recognized as law enforcement agencies for record keeping purposes, individual law enforcement agencies record arrests made by task forces within their jurisdiction. The quantity of sale and possession arrests were each used as dependent variables. A third arrest variable was created by summing the number of sale and possession arrests. An examination of the distribution of drug arrests revealed that arrests were highly skewed (towards fewer arrests). As a result of a relatively small sample and the concern with the statistical significance of the independent variables (see Berry and Feldman, 1990), the natural logarithms of all three arrest variables (sale, possession, and total arrests) were computed.[5]

Independent Variables

The present study was primarily concerned with the impact of membership in a drug task force on the ability to produce drug-related outcomes. In addition, the analyses, controlled for agency size and certain population characteristics within member and non-member jurisdictions. See table 2 for a description of the independent variables.

Task Force Membership. Task force membership was represented by a dummy variable (1 = task force member, 0 = nonmember) taken from the survey of law enforcement agencies. Respondents were asked if their agency was involved in a task force and, if so, to identify the task force. Two hundred sixty-six (49.4 percent) of the 539 agencies used in the sample reported membership in a task force.

Agency Size. Agency size refers to the total number of full-time sworn personnel within each department. This measure of size has been used in research exploring the impact of police agency size on organizational structure (Langworthy, 1986; Crank, 1989; see also Blau, 1971; Scott,

Table 2   Description of independent variables

Item	*n*	Mean	SD
Task force membership—whether an agency participates in a task force (1 = yes, 0 = no)	538	0.49	0.50
Agency size—number of full-time sworn personnel	532	31.60	120.23
Heterogeneity—proportion of non-White population	530	0.05	0.09
Mobility—proportion of renter-occupied housing units	530	0.29	0.12
Poverty—proportion of persons below poverty level	530	0.10	0.07
Density—persons per square mile	522	1767.15	1516.06

1975). A number of plausible hypotheses can be derived concerning the relationship between task force size and productivity. First, it could be expected that as the number of full-time sworn personnel increases, so too does the number of officers working drug investigations and other investigations that result in drug arrests. These officers may be communicating with other agencies and producing drug-related organizational outputs. In other words, large organizations are more likely to possess the human resources necessary to acquire control over drug markets. At the same time, it is also possible that as the size of the organization increases, so too does the opportunity for participants to "loaf or "free ride" (Olson, 1971; Gooding and Wagner, 1985). As such, one would likely anticipate that the relationship between size and productivity may be positive, but at a decreasing rate. Data for this measure were also obtained from the survey of law enforcement agencies.

Population Characteristics. Population characteristics of jurisdictions served by law enforcement agencies were used as control variables in the regression analyses. Prior research suggests that contextual characteristics of jurisdictions served may influence rates of offending, and, by implication, the number of drug users and sellers. As such, environmental factors may constrain or increase the number of drug targets and opportunities to engage in drug law enforcement (Pennings and Goodman, 1977; Hall, 1991). Research has shown a positive association between illicit drug abuse and trafficking and indicators of poor socioeconomic conditions and social disorganization (Johnson et al., 1990; Uchida and Foist, 1994). As such, in certain jurisdictions, there are likely to be more opportunities to make drug-related arrests than in other locations.

Four indicators of population complexity were created that tap factors associated with rates of drug law offending. The creation of these measures follows those used by Shaw and McKay (1942), Bursik (1986), Sampson (1986), and Sampson and Groves (1989). These four population characteristic variables were created from 1990 U.S. Census data on population and housing. First, racial heterogeneity was measured as the proportion of non-White persons that live within each jurisdiction. Second, population mobility was operationalized as the proportion of all living units within a jurisdiction that were classified as rental dwelling units. Third, poverty represented the proportion of persons within the jurisdiction that live below the poverty level. Finally, density consisted of the number of persons per square mile.

Analysis

In order to assess whether there are differences between agencies participating in task forces and agencies that do not participate in task forces, the authors estimated a series of regression equations with perceptions of the extent of communication, the perceived quality of drug cases, the total number of drug arrests, and the number of sale and possession arrests as dependent variables. As previously noted, the sample of agencies for each analysis presented in the following tables varies depending upon the dependent variable being examined. Ordinary least squares (OLS) regression was used to estimate the relationships between the dependent variables and task force membership. With each estimated equation, the influence of agency size, population mobility, heterogeneity, poverty, and density were controlled for.[6]

Findings

Subjective Outcomes: Process Goals

Communication Scale. Table 3 presents the results of the OLS regression analysis utilizing the communication scale as the dependent variable. The main independent variable in the model—task force membership—was statistically significant. Furthermore, the direction of the coefficient was as expected. In other words, task force member agencies reported communicating with other criminal justice agencies a greater number of times over a six-month period than did nontask force agencies. Agency size was also significantly related to the communication scale. This finding suggests that when controlling for the size of the agency, task force membership is still significantly related to the communication scale. The beta for the task force membership variable, however, indicates that it exerted less of an influence on the communication scale. Also significantly related to the communication scale was the contextual variable population heterogeneity.

Perceptions of the Quality of Drug Cases. Increased prosecutions as a result of better cases and more communication were among the stated

Table 3 Regression analyses of process goals

	Communication Scale (N = 490)			Drug Case Quality (N = 504)		
	Coefficient	b	Significance	Coefficient	b	Significance
Task force membership	0.719	0.098	0.023	0.398	0.190	0.000
Agency size	0.008	0.223	0.000	4.320	0.042	0.372
Heterogeneity	6.801	0.163	0.001	1.390	0.128	0.010
Mobility	1.878	0.060	0.268	0.416	0.493	0.399
Poverty	−1.762	−0.035	0.494	−2.040	0.745	0.007
Density	−7.861	−0.003	0.947	6.440	3.320	0.053
Constant	8.422		0.000	3.440		0.000
R^2	0.140			0.087		
F	13.162*			9.04*		

* Probability < 0.001

goals of drug task forces. As noted, data on outcomes of actual drug cases could not be obtained for the present study. As such, perceptions of the quality of drug cases were used as a proxy for quality of arrests. Table 3 shows that task force membership was significantly related to the ratings of the quality of drug cases. Further, agencies located in more heterogeneous areas and agencies in areas with a smaller proportion of persons below the poverty level were also more likely to rate the quality of drug cases higher.

Objective Outcomes: Output Goals

Drug Arrests. All three logged arrest variables (total, sale, and possession arrests) were regressed on the same independent variables and the results are presented in table 4. Model 1 indicates that task force membership was not a significant predictor of total drug arrests. The beta for population heterogeneity indicates that this variable was the strongest predictor of total drug arrests with the poverty level of the jurisdiction also significantly related to the total number of drug arrests. Task force membership was also not significant in model 2 (possession arrests). Population heterogeneity was again statistically significant and accounted for the majority of the explained variation in the dependent variable.

In model 3, population heterogeneity of the jurisdiction was the only significant predictor of drug arrests. Task force membership was not a significant predictor of arrests for the sale of drugs. The three models suggest that two population variables were the strongest predictors of drug arrests. Surprisingly, neither task force membership nor agency size is a significant predictor of arrests for drug offenses.

Discussion and Conclusion

In accordance with Sherman's (1997) comments regarding the lack of research on drug task forces and his suggestions for evaluating drug task forces, the present study operationalized the most commonly stated goals of Ohio task forces using three dependent variables (communication, quality of drug arrests, and arrests for drug offenses). Agencies participating in drug task forces were then compared with agencies not participating in drug task forces on these three indicators of task force effectiveness, controlling for agency size and contextual characteristics. Table 5 summarizes the results from the multivariate analyses.

The underlying premise of drug task forces is that increased cross jurisdictional communication and cooperation will ultimately increase the quantity and quality of drug arrests (Levine and Martin, 1992). Our findings, however, indicate that task force members did not generally produce more drug enforcement outputs than non-members of task forces. Specifically, task force membership was not related to the number of drug possession or sale arrests. In other words, law enforcement agencies that were members of task forces were not more likely to attain their stated drug output goals.

Table 4 Regression analyses of output goals: arrests ($N = 80$)

Item	Model 1 - Total Drug Arrests[a]		
	Coefficient	b	Significance
Task force membership	0.340	0.135	0.106
Agency size	7.68	0.144	0.240
Heterogeneity	8.30	0.699	0.000
Mobility	0.345	0.037	0.757
Poverty	−4.21	−0.261	0.037
Density	−3.26	−0.049	−0.554
Constant	3.71		0.000
R^2	0.448		
F	13.70*		

Item	Model 2 - Possession Arrests[a]		
	Coefficient	b	Significance
Task force membership	0.297	0.131	0.130
Agency size	5.76	0.120	0.345
Heterogeneity	7.51	0.702	0.000
Mobility	2.88	3.46	0.999
Poverty	−3.61	−0.248	0.055
Density	−2.79	−0.047	0.613
Constant	3.66		0.000
R^2	0.448		
F	11.84*		

Item	Model 3 - Sale Arrests[a]		
	Coefficient	b	Significance
Task force membership	0.481	0.132	0.101
Agency size	8.45	0.111	0.354
Heterogeneity	10.72	0.628	0.000
Mobility	2.85	0.214	0.070
Poverty	−4.55	−0.196	0.105
Density	−4.96	−0.052	0.548
Constant	0.637		0.115
R^2	0.516		
F	15.20*		

[a] Natural logarithm of the variable.
* $p < 0.001$

At the same time, task force members perceived that they were successful, e.g., task force members rated the quality of their drug arrests higher than non-task force members. In addition, task force members reported higher levels of communication with other criminal justice agencies about drug investigations than did agencies not participating in drug

Table 5   Summary of results

	Communication	Quality of Arrests	Total Drug Arrests	Possession Arrests	Sale Arrests
Task force membership	+	+			
Agency size	+				
Heterogeneity	+	+	+	+	+
Mobility					
Poverty		−	−		
Density					

task forces. This finding is consistent with prior research (see Coldren et al., 1990; Ruboy and Coldren, 1992; McGarrell and Schlegel, 1993). Task forces therefore seem to be successful at meeting their system goals when member perceptions are utilized as the measure.

The findings also indicate that certain characteristics of the population served by the task force and agency size are more powerful predictors of drug outputs than membership in a task force. The dependent variable, inter-agency communication, was significantly correlated with agency size. Further, when both agency size and task force membership were statistically significant, the standardized regression coefficients indicated that agency size exerted a greater effect on the dependent variable. With the dependent variables concerning quantity of arrests, population heterogeneity was a consistent predictor and population poverty levels were also significantly related to the quantity of total drug arrests. It therefore appears that environmental factors, and not necessarily membership in a task force, influence drug enforcement output and process goals.

Overall, it is unclear whether joining a task force and investing agency resources will produce a good return in terms of drug enforcement outputs for agencies. Task force members, however, perceived greater levels of communication and better quality drug arrests than non-task force agencies. This disjuncture between outcome and process measures of task force effectiveness may be due to differences in the foci of the measures being utilized. The traditional production measures of effectiveness did not indicate that membership in a task force was related to success, while members perceived that the task force process positively influenced their exchange of drug-related information and that the task force system was effective in developing higher-quality drug cases.

This research study began with a discussion of different definitions of organizational effectiveness: the goal attainment model and the process model. At this point, the authors return to an assessment of these two perspectives. Proponents of the goal attainment model suggest that the effectiveness of an organization can be determined by assessing whether the organizational goals have been met. This study suggests that task force members do not produce significantly more outcome goals than agencies not participating in task forces. Therefore, an evaluation of drug task forces using the goal attainment model would suggest that these organizations are not effective. On the other hand, the process model of organizational effectiveness suggests that the actual attainment of goals is of secondary importance compared to the activities and operations of participants within the organization. This study finds that process outcomes, such as inter-agency communication and perceived quality of drug arrests, are positively influenced by membership in task forces. These perceptions might explain organizational survival and continued participation of members. It is also assumed, however, that increased efficiency of the internal task force operation should influence output production. In other words, increased communication and cooperation should result in "better" cases and more drug arrests. Based on our evidence, this does not appear to be the case.

The results of the present study may lead some to reconsider the investment of resources in drug task forces. The present study suggests that task force members do not produce more drug enforcement outputs than non-members; however, it must also be remembered that the influence of task forces on cross-jurisdictional cases or on cases within the category of arrest for the sale and possession of drugs (e.g., sale of cocaine vs. sale of marijuana) is unknown. Further, it is unknown if task force member agencies are now producing more than they did before joining a task force. It is possible that agencies involved in task forces do not produce more than non-task force agencies; however, they may still be producing outputs at a higher level than prior to joining the task force. Future research should consider the use of time series analysis to determine if agencies produce more outputs after joining a task force.[7]

Drug task forces, although they may not be increasing the quantity of drug arrests, may be having an influence on specific types of cases. For example, task forces may be influencing the types of dealers arrested for drug sales or they may be having an impact on cross jurisdictional drug cases. An in-depth examination of the specifics of drug task force cases may be able to shed some light on these issues. Future research should also attempt to examine the quality of drug arrests with both objective and subjective measures to determine if task force members actually do produce better quality drug arrests. Researchers might look at charge and conviction records of task force agencies, for example. There is another potential explanation for the finding that task force members do not produce more drug enforcement outputs than non-members. Law enforcement agencies involved in a task force may cease or decrease independent drug enforcement and allow the task force to act as a specialized unit handling drug investigations for the agency. Thus, the task force may be doing what the participating agencies once did without the task force.

Lastly, future research should examine task force membership vs. task force participation; i.e., the benefits of task force membership may differ depending on the quality and quantity of participation by agencies. Some agencies may simply provide written agreements of cooperation, but contribute little in the way of tangible resources or assistance. On the other hand, an agency may provide resources and information and, in turn, receive more substantial benefits than less active members.

The lack of research directed toward this area of law enforcement in which substantial federal, state, and local resources are devoted is lamentable. It is unfortunate that these cooperative ventures have not been adequately evaluated and that criminal justice practitioners and policy makers must continue to devote resources to such costly ventures without knowledge of their impacts on drug enforcement.

Endnotes

[1] Drug task forces in Ohio are not recognized as separate law enforcement entities; i.e., they must be associated with a law enforcement agency to receive such things as law enforcement powers and insurance. Similarly, they do not report data to the Federal Bureau of Investigation (FBI). Individual law enforcement agencies participating in task forces report arrests made within their jurisdictions by task forces to the FBI. Thus, task force arrests are reflected in agency arrest data.

[2] For the present study, university police departments and special purpose police were excluded from the analysis. University police and special purpose police do not report arrests to the FBI.

[3] Of the 244 Ohio law enforcement agencies reporting data to the FBI in 1995, the majority (164) failed to report at least seven months of data. Only eighty-seven agencies reported at least eight or more months of data. Mean replacement was used for the agencies failing to report 1–4 months of data. Thirty-two agencies had data missing for one or two of the twelve months reported. Twenty-seven agencies had data missing for three or four of the twelve months.

[4] In constructing the communication scale, cases with missing communication questions were excluded from the analysis.

[5] Since some agencies reported no possession arrests and the natural logarithm of zero is undefined, one was added to all cases prior to calculating the natural logarithm. Upon examination of the logged values, a more normal distribution on the dependent variable was observed (mean = 4.23, SD = 1.08) and thus, these logged values were utilized in subsequent analyses.

[6] Prior to any analyses, a check for multicolinearity between the independent variables was conducted. Bivariate correlation matrices were estimated for the independent variables. Significant relationships with a Pearson's correlation of 0.70 or greater would suggest that multicolinearity might be present in the model. No correlations above 0.70 between the independent variables were found. In addition, colinearity diagnostics using variance inflation factors was conducted. A variance inflation factor of ten or above suggests multicolinearity between variables (Freund and Wilson, 1998). No variance inflation factor was above three; thus, multicolinearity was not considered a problem in the current study.

[7] A time series analysis was initially proposed using FBI arrest data for a sample of agencies involved in Ohio drug task forces. Unfortunately, adequate data were only available for a limited number of agencies. The joining date for the task force was used as the intervention point. Time series analysis revealed no relationship between joining a task force and quantity of drug arrests.

References

Berry, W. D., & Feldman, S. (1990). Multiple regression in practice. *Sage university paper series on quantitative applications in the social sciences, 07-050.* Beverly Hills, CA: Sage Publications.

Blau, P. M. (1971). A formal theory of differentiation in organizations. *American Social Review, 35,* 201–218.

Branham, J. E. (1986). New Orleans, LA: Undercover operations. *Police Chief, 53,* 42–44.

Bursik, R. J., Jr. (1986). Ecological stability and the dynamics of delinquency. In A. J. Reiss, Jr. & M. Tonry (Eds.), *Communities and crime* (pp. 35–66). Chicago, IL: University of Chicago Press.

Bynum, T. S., & Worden, R. E. (1996). *Police drug crackdowns: An evaluation of implementation and effects.* Washington, DC: National Institute of Justice.

Coldren, J., McGarrell, E., Sabath, M., Schlegel, K., & Stolzenberg, L. (1993). *Multijurisdictional drug task force operations: Results of a nationwide survey of task force commanders.* Washington, DC: Criminal Justice Statistics Association.

Coldren, J. R., Coyle, K. R., & Carr, S. D. (1990). *Multijurisdictional drug control task forces 1988: Critical components of state drug control strategies.* Washington, DC: Bureau of Justice Assistance.

Coldren, J. R., & Sabath, M. J. (1992). *Multijurisdictional drug control task forces 1988-1990: Critical components of state drug control strategies.* Special Analysis Report of the Consortium for Drug Strategy Impact Assessment for the Bureau of Justice Assistance.

Crank, J. P. (1989). Civilianization in small and medium police departments in Illinois, 1973–1986. *Journal of Criminal Justice, 17,* 167–177.

Damanpour, F., & Evan, W. M. (1984). Organizational innovation and performance: The problem of organizational lag. *Administration Science Quarterly, 29,* 392–409.

Duffee, D. E. (1980). *Explaining criminal justice: Community theory and criminal justice reform.* Prospect Heights, IL: Waveland Press.

Dunworth, T., Haynes, P., & Saiger, A. J. (1997). *National assessment of Byrne Formula Grant Program. National Institute of Justice research in brief.* Washington, DC: U.S. Department of Justice.

Etzioni, A. (1960). Two approaches to organizational analysis: A critique and a suggestion. *Administrative Science Quarterly, 5,* 257–278.

Etzioni, A. (1975). *Complex organizations: On power, involvement, and their correlates.* New York: The Free Press.

Fagan, J. (1992). Drug selling and licit income in the distressed neighborhoods: The economic lives of street level drug users and dealers. In A. V. Harrell & G. E. Peterson (Eds.), *Drugs, crime, and social isolation: Barriers to urban opportunity* (pp. 99–146). Washington, DC: Urban Institute.

Frank, J., Smith, B., Novak, K., Travis, L., & Langworthy, R. (1998). *Ohio multijurisdictional drug law enforcement task forces: Final report.* Columbus, OH: Office of Criminal Justice Services.

Freund, R., & Wilson, W. (1998). *Regression analysis: Statistical modeling of a response variable.* San Diego, CA: Academic Press.

Gajewski, F. (1993). The drug market analysis program: A participant observation study. Unpublished Master's Thesis, Seton Hall University.

Gooding, R. Z., & Wagner, J. A. (1985). A meta-analytic review of the relationship between size and performance: The productivity and efficiency of organizations and their subunits. *Administrative Science Quarterly, 30,* 462–481.

Green, L. (1996). *Policing places with drug problems.* Thousand Oaks, CA: Sage Publications.

Hall, R. H. (1991). *Organizations: Structures, processes and outcomes* (5th ed.). Englewood Cliffs, NJ: Prentice-Hall.

Hayeslip, D., & Weisel, D. (1992). Local level drug enforcement. In G. W. Cordner & D. C. Hale (Eds.), *What works in policing? Operations and administrations examined* (pp. 35–48). Cincinnati, OH: Anderson Publishing.

Hillsman, S. (1992). *The community effects of street-level narcotics enforcement: The study of the New York City Police Department's tactical narcotics teams.* New York: Vera Institute of Justice.

Jefferis, E., Frank, E., Smith, B., Novak, K., & Travis, L. (1998). An examination of the productivity and perceived effectiveness of drug task forces. *Police Quarterly, 1,* 85–107.

Johnson, B., Williams, T., Dei, K. A., & Sanabria, H. (1990). Drug abuse in the inner city: Impact on hard drug users and the community. In M. Tonry & J. Q. Wilson (Eds.), *Drugs and crime.* Chicago, IL: University of Chicago Press.

Justice Research and Statistics Association. (1992). *Multijurisdictional drug enforcement task forces: Accomplishments under the state and local formula grant program.* Washington, DC: Office of Justice Programs.

Kleiman, M. A. R. (1988). Crackdowns: The effects of intensive enforcement on retail heroin dealing. In M. Chaiken (Ed.), *Street-level drug enforcement: Examining the issues* (pp. 3–34). Washington, DC: National Institute of Justice.

Klofas, J., Stojkovic, S., & Kalinich, D. (1990). *Criminal justice organizations: Administration and management.* Belmont, CA: Brooks/Cole Publishing.

Langworthy, R. H. (1986). *The structure of police organizations.* New York: Praeger.

Levine, M., & Martin, D. (1992). Drug deals have no boundaries: Multijurisdictional narcotics task forces. *Law Enforcement,* 34–37.

Lyman, M. D. (1987). *Narcotics and crime control.* Springfield, IL: Charles C. Thomas.

Manning, P. K. (1980). *The narc's game: Organizational and informational limits on drug law enforcement.* Cambridge, MA: MIT Press.

Marsden, M. E., & Orsagh, T. (1983). Prison effectiveness measurement. In G. P. Whitaker & C. D. Phillips (Eds.), *Evaluating performances of criminal justice agencies* (pp. 211–236). Beverly Hills, CA: Sage Publications.

Mastrofski, S. D., & Wadman, R. (1991). Personnel and agency performance measurement. In W. Geller (Ed.), *Local government police management* (pp. 364–397). Washington, DC: International City Management Association.

McGarrell, E. F., & Schlegel, K. (1993). The implementation of federally funded multijurisdictional drug task forces: Organizational structure and interagency relationships. *Journal of Criminal Justice, 21,* 231–244.

Mohr, L. (1973). The concept of the organizational goal. *American Political Science Review, 67,* 470–481.

Moore, M. H., & Kleiman, M. A. R. (1989). *The police and drugs.* Washington, DC: U.S. Department of Justice, National Institute of Justice.

Office of Criminal Justice Services. (1994). *Ohio 1994 state annual report: Byrne Memorial State and Local Law Enforcement Assistance Act.* Columbus, OH: Office of Criminal Justice Services.

Olson, M. (1971). *The logic of collective action.* Cambridge, MA: Harvard University Press.

Ostrom, E., Parks, R. B., Whitaker, G. P., & Percy, S. L. (1978). The public service production process: A framework for analyzing police services. In R. Baker, Jr. & F. A. Meyer (Eds.), *Evaluating alternative law enforcement policies* (pp. 65–73). Lexington, KY: DC Heath.

Pennings, J. M., & Goodman, P. S. (1977). Toward a workable framework. In P. S. Goodman & J. M. Pennings (Eds.), *New perspectives in organizational effectiveness* (pp. 146–184). San Francisco, CA: Jossey Bass.

Ruboy, M. A., Jr., & Coldren, J. R. (1992). *Law Enforcement task force evaluation projects: Results and findings in the states.* Washington, DC: Bureau of Justice Assistance.

Sampson, R. J. (1986). Crime in cities: The effects of formal and informal social control. In A. J. Reiss, Jr. & M. Tonry (Eds.), *Communities and crime* (pp. 271–313). Chicago, IL: University of Chicago Press.

Sampson, R. J., & Groves, W. B. (1989). Community structure and crime: Testing social disorganization theory. *American Journal of Sociology, 94,* 774–802.

Schlegel, K., & McGarrell, E. F. (1991). An examination of arrest practices in regions served by multijurisdictional drug task forces. *Crime Delinquency, 37,* 408–426.

Scott, W. R. (1975). Organizational structure. In A. Inkeles (Ed.), *Annual Review of Sociology* (Vol. 1, pp. 1–20). Palo Alto, CA: Annual Reviews.

Scott, W. R. (1987). The adolescence of institutional theory. *Administration Science Quarterly, 32,* 493–511.

Shaw, C. R., & McKay, H. D. (1942). *Juvenile delinquency and urban areas.* Chicago, IL: University of Chicago Press.

Sherman, L. W. (1997). Policing for crime prevention. In L. W. Sherman, D. Gottfredson, D. MacKenzie, J. Eck, P. Bushway, & S. Bushway (Eds.), *Preventing crime: What works, what doesn't, what's promising.* Washington, DC: U.S. Department of Justice (Chapter 8).

Simon, H. A. (1945). *Administrative behavior: A study of decision-making processes in administrative organization.* New York: The Free Press.

Smith, D., & Klein, J. (1983). Police agency characteristics and arrest decisions. In G. P. Whitaker & C. D. Phillips (Eds.), *Evaluating performances of criminal justice agencies* (pp. 63–98). Beverly Hills, CA: Sage Publications.

Thompson, J. D., & McEwen, W. J. (1980). Organizational goals and environment. In A. Etzioni & E. W. Lehman (Eds.), *A sociological reader on complex organizations* (3rd ed., pp. 136–143). New York: Holt, Rhinehart and Winston.

Uchida, C. D., & Forst, B. (1994). Controlling street-level drug trafficking: Professional and community policing approaches. In D. L. MacKenzie & C. D. Uchida (Eds.), *Drugs and crime: Evaluating public policy initiatives* (pp. 77–94). Thousand Oaks, CA: Sage Publications.

Weisburd, D., & Green, L. (1995). Policing drug hot spots: Findings from the Jersey City DMA experiment. *Justice Quarterly, 12,* 711–736.

Whitaker, G., & Phillips, C. D. (1983). *Evaluating performances of criminal justice agencies.* Beverly Hills, CA: Sage Publications.

Wycoff, M. A., & Manning, P. K. (1983). Police and crime control. In G. P. Whitaker & C. D. Phillips (Eds.), *Evaluating performances of criminal justice agencies* (pp. 15–32). Beverly Hills, CA: Sage Publications.

Zimmer, L. (1990). Proactive policing against street-level drug trafficking. *American Journal of Police, 9,* 43–44.

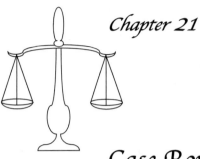

Chapter 21

Case Routinization in Investigative Police Work

William B. Waegel

Discretionary decision making and the nature of the processes by which legal agents structure and manage their handling of persons and events have become central concerns in recent studies of the criminal justice system. Much traditional research on this system has focused on discretion in the context of race and class discrimination. The image is often that of one-person legal units making decisions, but this individualistic conception appears to be substantially misleading. A recent study by Swigert and Farrell (1977) highlights the inadequacy of the use of ostensibly objective criteria of race and class in the analysis of legal processing: they found that social and demographic attributes are filtered through stereotypic conceptions held by legal agents. Their work suggests that conventional research strategies will continue to produce a mass of contradictory findings regarding legal decision making.

Discretion is an irreducible element in the behavior of legal agents. In police work, as in other socially organized activities, members do not always have a set of formal rules which provide an adequate decision-making base for organizing their conduct. Bittner put this succinctly:

> The domain of presumed jurisdiction of a legal rule is essentially open-ended. While there may be a core of clarity about its application, this

William B. Waegel, "Case Routinization in Investigative Police Work," *Social Problems,* Vol. 28 No. 3, February, 1981, pp. 263–275. Reprinted by permission of The University of California Press.

core is always and necessarily surrounded by uncertainty. . . . No matter how far we descend on the hierarchy of more and more detailed formal instruction, there will always remain a step further down to go, and no measure of effort will ever succeed in eliminating, or even meaningfully curtailing, the area of discretionary freedom of the agent whose duty it is to fit rules to cases. (1970:4)

Police investigators, prosecutors, public defenders, and presentence caseworkers typically must process a steady stream of cases or clients under rather rigid time constraints. In their normal day-to-day activities, these agents do not generally proceed by following a set of codified rules and procedures. However, their discretion is not unlimited nor are their decisions most usefully viewed as individualistic "free choices." The organizational setting in which the work is performed places distinctive constraints and demands on legal agents, producing a specific orientation to case handling and a set of largely shared formulas for dealing with different types of cases.

A more promising approach for understanding legal decision making assigns central importance to occupational typifications and common social stereotypes. Under pressure to observe court schedules or meet paperwork deadlines, and in an effort to reduce problematic features of their tasks at hand, legal agents typically rely on shorthand methods for reaching required decisions.

Typical or "normal case" conceptions have been found to act as a central basis for client treatment in a variety of organizational settings. Sudnow's (1965) study of case processing in a public defender's office found that attorneys did not handle clients and cases in terms of their unique features, but rather used typifications of the normal offense and normal offender as a basis for understanding particular cases and deciding how to handle them. For cases reasonably conforming to a familiar pattern, specific plea bargaining formulas were routinely employed. Stereotypic conceptions have been found to act as guiding imageries for action in the treatment of skid-row residents by patrolmen (Bittner, 1967), in police encounters with juveniles (Piliavin and Briar, 1964) and a "suspect population" (Skolnick, 1967), and in responses to shoplifters (Steffensmeier and Terry, 1973). Swigert and Farrell's (1977) study of the processing of homicide defendants found that critical legal decisions regarding bail, the assignment of counsel, and plea bargaining were based upon the extent to which the person involved conformed to popular criminal stereotypes.[1]

The theoretical implication of these studies is that the decisions made in dealing with a person or event are based not so much on specific features of the actor or situation at hand, but upon the recognition of the person or event as properly belonging to a familiar and typical category and the taken-for-granted understandings built into that category. Stokes and Hewitt (1976) argue for a reflexive relationship between such social constructions and conduct. While meaning structures are a *product* of social action, it is also the case that:

> A great many of the objects that constitute the human world have a "preexisting" meaning, in the sense that people confront such objects with a set of assumptions about them — with a particular preparedness to act in routine, familiar and unquestioned ways. (Stokes and Hewitt, 1976: 841)

Typifications of others and events serve to structure interaction in a provisional way, rendering it more predictable, minimizing its problematic character, and enabling the actor to better manage an ambiguous social environment. Typificatory schemes are used as resources from which to construct a practical solution to the problem at hand.

The corresponding implication for research is that conventional research strategies focusing on decision-making variations between individuals and between functionally similar organizations have severe limitations. A more fruitful approach for studying processing outcomes takes as its focus the shared categorization schemes used by members in organizing their day-to-day activities.

Working Cases: An Overview

In the police department studies,[2] detectives face two practical problems which substantially shape the manner in which cases are handled. They must satisfy the paperwork demands of the organization (referred to as "keeping the red numbers down") by classifying each case and producing a formal investigative report within two weeks after the case is assigned. Sanctions may be applied to those who fail to meet deadlines and who thus accumulate too many "red numbers." At the same time, the detectives are under the same pressure as other employees: they must produce. Specifically, detectives believe they must produce an acceptable level of arrests which will enhance their chances of remaining in the detective division and gaining promotion. While no arrest quota is formalized in the division, there is a shared belief that one should produce roughly two to three lock-ups per week. This arrest level is a practical concern for the detective because most wish to remain in the division and avoid transfer "back to the pit" (i.e., back into uniform in the patrol division). Moreover, the position of detective holds the highest status of any assignment in the department, and a transfer, therefore, generally entails a loss of status.

For the vast majority of cases handled, no explicit procedures exist to indicate what must be done on the case and how to go about doing it. As detectives go about the ordinary business of investigating and processing cases, they can select strategies ranging from a *pro forma* victim interview comprising the total investigative activity devoted to the case, to a full-scale investigation involving extensive interviewing, physical evidence, the use of informants, interrogation, surveillance, and other activities. The selection of a particular handling strategy in most cases is an informal process and not the direct result of formal organizational policy or procedure. This process of selection is grounded in practical solutions to concrete problems faced by the detective; it consists of an assignment of meaning to persons and events in ways that are regarded as proper because they have "worked" in previous cases.

A great deal of actual detective work may thus be seen as a process of mapping the features of a particular case onto a more general and commonly recognized *type* of case. The present work suggests that a detective's interpretation, classification, and handling of cases are guided by a set of occupationally shared typifications. The categorization schemes used by detectives center around specific configurations of information regarding the victim, the offense, and possible suspects. Information pertaining to these three elements constitutes the meaningful unit that detectives deal with: the case.

The most basic dimension of case categorization is that of the routine versus the nonroutine. Where a particular configuration of information regarding the victim, the offense, and possible suspects appears, the competent detective understands the case as a routine one—as an instance of a familiar type—and particular handling strategies are deemed appropriate. Such cases contrast with those which are viewed as nonroutine: that is, where no general type is available to which the case reasonably corresponds, and where the case is vigorously investigated and the detective attends to the unique features of the case. Case routinization is most characteristic for burglaries, which comprise the bulk of cases handled by detectives, but it is also exhibited in the handling of many assault, robbery, rape, and homicide cases.

The categorization schemes used by detectives are derived from concrete experiences in working cases and are continually assessed for their relevance, adequacy, and effectiveness in handling one's caseload. It is because typificatory schemes serve as a solution to practical problems commonly faced by all detectives that they learn to share most of the content of these schemes. Both through direct experience in working cases and through interaction with other members, the detective learns to categorize and handle cases in ways that are regarded as proper by other detectives.

Routine case imageries serve as resources upon which detectives may draw to construct a solution to their problem of interpreting, investigating, and resolving their cases. The features of a specific case are compared with routine case imagery in a process of interpretive interplay. In some instances a correspondence is readily apparent, in others a fit is forced by the detective, and in still others the features of a specific case render the use of the typical imagery inappropriate. The interpretation and handling of a case may also change over the case's history; a routine case may come to be treated as nonroutine upon the receipt of additional information, and vice-versa.

The Organizational Context of Case Routinization

In the department studied, detectives have no formal guidelines for allocating time and effort to different cases and there is little effective monitoring of daily activities by supervisors.[3] In conducting their work, detectives are, however, guided and constrained by two organizational imperatives: 1) the requirement to submit investigative reports, and 2) the requirement to produce arrests. In other words, the work is not organized by formal rules, but rather by the kinds of outcomes that are expected. Both of these expected outcomes generate practical problems leading to routinized solutions.

An investigative report must be produced for each case assigned, and its submission within the prescribed time limit is viewed as a fundamental constraint on how vigorously different cases can be investigated. Departmental policy indicates that each investigative report submitted must be reviewed and signed by a supervisory lieutenant. However, in practice, these reports are often given only a cursory glance, and seldom is the content of a report questioned or challenged by a lieutenant. The primary concern of the supervisor is that the submission of reports complies with time deadlines.

The potential a case appears to hold for producing an arrest also has an important impact on how the case will be handled. Most detectives believe that the number of arrests they produce will be used as a basis for evaluating performance and, therefore, will affect decisions regarding promotions and transfers. Attempts to cope with the practical problems of meeting paperwork demands, while at the same time producing a satisfactory number of arrests, creates a situation in which one burglary case involving a $75 loss may receive less than five minutes investigative effort, yet another case with an identical loss may be worked on exclusively for two or three full days. These two concerns constitute central features of the work setting which structure case handling.

Paperwork

Formal organizational procedure demands that a case be investigated, classified, and a report produced within a specified time period after it is assigned. Detectives experience paperwork requirements and deadlines as central sources of pressure and tension in their job, and stories abound concerning former detectives who "could handle the job but couldn't handle the paperwork."

Most cases are assigned during the daily roll-call sessions. At this point, the information about the incident consists of an original report written by a patrol officer and any supplemental reports submitted by personnel in the evidence detection unit. Each case is stamped with a "red number" which supervisors use to monitor compliance with report deadlines.

Ordinary cases require the submission of two reports within specific time periods. A brief first-day report, consisting essentially of an interview with the victim, is formally required the day after the case is assigned. However, this deadline is generally ignored by supervisors and first-day reports are seldom submitted. The more meaningful deadline for detectives is the fourteen-day limit for the submission of an investigative report. Here, the detective must provide a detailed accounting of the activities undertaken in investigating the incident and assign an investigative status to the case. Compliance with this second deadline is closely monitored: every Sunday a lieutenant draws up a list of each detective's overdue red numbers, and this list is read at the next roll call along with a caution to keep up with one's paperwork.

In the investigative report, the detective must classify the status of the investigation as suspended, closed arrest, or open. The ability to manipulate information about cases to fit them into these categories is of the utmost importance to detectives, for it is through such strategic manipulations that they are able to manage their caseloads effectively.

Of the total cases handled by a detective, a substantial majority are classified as suspended. This means that the steps already taken in the investigation (which may consist merely of a telephone interview with the victim) have not uncovered sufficient information to warrant continued investigation of the incident. Any number of acceptable reasons for suspending a case may be offered, ranging from a simple statement that the victim declines to prosecute up to a fairly elaborate report detailing contacts with the victim, the entry of serial numbers of stolen articles into the computerized crime files, the usefulness of evidence obtained from the scene, and a conclusion that the case must be suspended because there are no further investigative leads. Over 80 percent of the burglary cases assigned in the city are suspended; this percentage drops considerably for robbery cases and even more for assault, rape, and homicide cases.[4]

An investigation is classified as closed when one or more arrests have been made pertaining to the incident and the detective anticipates no additional arrests. A case is classified as open when an investigation extends beyond the fourteen-day limit but it is expected that an arrest eventually will be made. Generally, only major cases may remain classified as open after the fourteen-day investigative period.

Producing Arrests

As organizations become more bureaucratized and their procedures more formalized, there evolves a general tendency to develop quantitative indices or measures of individual performance. In the department studied, most detectives believe that the crude number of lock-ups they make is used as a basis for assessing their performance and competence in doing investigative work. Every arrest a detective makes is entered into a logbook, which is available for inspection by superiors and from which they can compare each detective's arrest level with that of others.

Ambitious detectives in particular are very conscious of producing a steady stream of arrests, feeling that this is an effective way to achieve recognition and promotion. One young detective boasted:

> I've made over forty lock-ups since the beginning of the year and eleven in April alone. Since I don't really have a godfather in here, I gotta' depend on making good lock-ups if I'm gonna' make sergeant.

This detective's use of the term "godfather" reveals a widely shared belief that some individuals are promoted not because of their performance but because they have a friend or relative in a position of power within the department.

Skimming off selected cases from one's workload is widely practiced as a means of achieving a steady stream of arrests. The practice of skimming refers to 1) selectively working only those cases that appear potentially solvable from information contained in the original report, and 2) summarily suspending the remainder of one's ordinary cases. Supervisors are certainly aware of both aspects of this practice, but they recognize its practical value in producing arrests. Moreover, supervisors, to a greater extent than working detectives, find their performance assessed in crude quantitative terms, and they are likely to be questioned by superiors if arrest levels begin to drop sharply. Supervisors support the practice of skimming even though they recognize that it ensures that a majority of ordinary cases will never receive a thorough investigation. The pragmatic work orientation of detectives is further revealed in the lack of attention given to conviction rates both by detectives and supervisors. Competence and productivity are judged by the arrests made, not by the proportion of cases which survive the scrutiny of the judicial process.

The recognition of potentially productive cases and of their utility in effectively managing one's caseload are among the earliest skills taught to the neophyte in the detective division. Moreover, newcomers are taught that their work on burglary cases is the primary basis upon which their performance will be judged. In a sizeable percentage of crimes against persons, the perpetrator is readily identified from information provided by the victim. Since no great investigative effort or acumen is involved, the same credit is not accorded an arrest in this type of case as in burglary cases. Detectives are expected to produce a steady flow of "quality" arrests: that is, arrests involving some effort and skill on the part of the investigator. Straightforward assault cases involving acquainted parties, for example, are often handed out by supervisors along with a remark such as "Here's an easy one for you. "

Interpreting Cases

The preceding observations have suggested that detectives are constrained in their conception and handling of cases not by the formal organization of their work or by supervisory surveillance, but rather by the bureaucratic pressure of writing reports and producing the proper number and quality of arrests. The process of interpreting cases in accordance with these pragmatic concerns may now be considered.

Data derived from observation of detective-victim interviews and from written case reports provide a basis for examining the interpretive schemes used by detectives. In the victim interview, the kinds of questions asked and the pieces of information sought out reveal the case patterns recognized as routine for the different offenses commonly encountered.[5] However, in attempting to make sense of the incident at hand, detectives attend to much more than is revealed in their explicit communications with the victim. Interpretation of the case is also based upon understanding of the victim's lifestyle, racial or ethnic membership group, class position, and possible clout or connections—especially as these factors beat upon such concerns as the likelihood of the victim inquiring into the progress of the investigation, the victim's intentions regarding prosecution, and the victim's competence and quality as a source of information.

The interpretive schemes employed also receive partial expression in the written investigative reports which must be produced for each case. These reports contain a selective accounting of the meaning assigned to a case, the information and understandings upon which this interpretation is based, and the reasonableness of the linkage between this particular interpretation of the case and the handling strategy employed.[6]

Several important features of the process of interpreting cases as routine or nonroutine may be seen in the following incidents.

Case 1: Attempted Homicide

A radio call was broadcast that a shooting had just occurred on the street in a working-class residential area. The victim, a white male, was still conscious when the detectives arrived, although he had been severely wounded in the face by a shotgun blast. He indicated that he had been robbed and shot by three black males, and provided a vague description of their appearance and clothing. This description was broadcast, an area search was initiated, the crime scene was cordoned off, and a major investigation was begun.

The following morning, the victim's employer brought into question the account of the incident that had been provided. He indicated his belief that the incident involved a "lover's triangle" situation between the victim, a male acquaintance of the victim, and a woman. All three were described as "hillbillies." The three parties were interviewed separately and each denied this version of the incident. After further questioning, the victim finally admitted that the story concerning three black males was false, but would say nothing more about the incident. Articles of the woman's clothing believed to show bloodstains and a weapon believed to have been used were obtained, but crime lab analysis would take at least three weeks. The case was now interpreted as a routine "domestic shooting" and little additional effort was devoted to it.

Case 2: Burglary

A detective parked his car in front of an address in a public housing project and pulled out the original burglary report. A new member of the prosecutor's office was riding along to observe how detectives work. The detective read over the report, and after hesitating for awhile decided to go into the residence. He explained to the prosecutor that the loss was an inexpensive record player and added, "This one's a pork chop, like most of the burglaries we get. But we gotta' go and interview the victim before suspending it." The detective asked the victim if she knew who might have committed the burglary or if she had heard about anyone committing burglaries in the area. Negative replies followed both questions. The entire encounter with the victim lasted less than two minutes.

Case 3: Assault and Robbery

A robbery squad detective was waiting for two victims to come in the hall to be interviewed. Both were black, middle-aged, center-city residents who were described by the detective as "dead-end alcoholics." They had been robbed in their residence by a young male who had forced his way in, taken $20 from the pair, and cut the female victim on the hand with a knife. The victims were able to provide the detective with the name of their assailant, and they both picked his photograph out of a number of pictures they were shown. Several minutes later the detective handed them a photograph of a different individual, asking, "Are you sure this is the guy who robbed you?" After inspecting the picture they replied that they knew this person as well but he had not been the one who robbed them. At this point, the detective sat down and took a formal statement from the victims.

When the victims had left, the detective explained his views and usual handling of such "ghetto robberies": "In a case like this, what can we do? To tell you the truth, the only way this kind of thing is going to stop is for the victims or somebody they know to kill this guy off. My involvement in this case is minimal. If the two victims, those two old drunks, if they sober up and if they show up in court, we'll see how they do there. It's up to them here and not up to me."

Case 4: Burglary

A detective entered the center-city residence of a burglary victim in a block where about one-fourth of the row houses were vacant. He examined a large hole in a basement wall that had been made to gain entry, and then sat down to compile a list of articles that had been stolen. The victim had literally been cleaned out, losing every easily transportable item of value she had owned. The woman explained that she worked during the day, that this was the fifth time she had been burglarized in the past four years, and that her coverage had been dropped by the insurance company. She added that she lived in the house for 21 years and was not about to move, and then asked, "What can I do to keep this from happening again?" The detective replied:

"Ma'am, I don't know what to tell you. You're the only white family on this block. Most of the people around here work during the daytime and a lot of these people, even if they saw somebody coming out of your house with some of your stuff, they're not going to call the cops anyhow. That's the way it is around here. It's a shame, but that's the way it is." The detective entered the serial numbers of some of the stolen articles into the computerized stolen property files, "to cover myself, just in case." The written report indicated that the pawnshop sheets had been checked but in fact this step was not taken. When the report deadline approached, the case was suspended.

Case 5: Homicides

Two homicides had occurred over the weekend. On Monday morning two detectives who were working on the different cases were discussing the status of their investigations. One detective, who was investigating a shooting death that occurred in a crowded bar in the presence of 100 persons noted that he was on the verge of making a lock-up even though none of the witnesses present had voluntarily come forward. The other detective was investigating a bludgeoning death of a male homosexual whose body had been found by firemen called to extinguish a small fire in the victim's residence. There were as yet no suspects in the case. The second detective took offense to remarks made by the other comparing the lack of progress in the second case to the nearly completed investigation in the barroom case. The second detective remarked, "Anybody can handle a killing like you've got. What we've got here is a murder, not a killing."

The above incidents illustrate detectives' use of a body of accumulated knowledge, beliefs, and assumptions which lead to the interpretation of certain case patterns as common, typical, and routine. Cases are interpreted primarily using conceptions of 1) how identifiable the perpetrators seem to be; 2) the normal social characteristics of the victims; and 3) the settings involved, and behavior seen as typical in such settings. A detective's initial efforts on a case tend to focus on these three aspects, in the process of assigning meaning to the case and selecting an appropriate strategy for handling it.

1. Conceptions of how different kinds of offenses are typically committed—especially how identifiable the perpetrators seem to be—are routinely used in interpreting incidents. These imageries are specifically relevant to a detective's practical concerns. The ordinary burglary (cases 2 and 4) is seen as involving a crude forced entry at a time of day or at a location where it is unlikely that anyone will witness the perpetrator entering or exiting. A burglary victim's ability or inability to provide information identifying a probable perpetrator constitutes the single feature of burglary cases which is given greatest interpretive significance. In roughly ten percent of these cases, the victim provides the name of a suspected perpetrator (commonly an ex-boyfriend, a relative or a neighboring resident), and vigorous effort is devoted to the case. For the

remaining burglary cases, the initial inclination is to treat them as routine incidents deserving of only minimal investigative effort. In these routine cases the victim's race and class position have a decisive impact on whether the case will be summarily suspended or whether some minor investigative activities will be undertaken to impress the victim that "something is being done."

On the other hand, assault, rape, and homicide cases commonly occur in a face-to-face situation which affords the victim an opportunity to observe the assailant. Further, detectives recognize that many personal assault offenses involve acquainted parties. The earliest piece of information sought out and the feature of such cases given the greatest interpretive significance is whether the offense occurred between parties who were in some way known to one another prior to the incident. The interpretation and handling of the shooting incident in case 1 changed markedly when it was learned that the victim and suspect were acquainted parties and that the offense reasonably conformed to a familiar pattern of domestic assaults. Where the victim and perpetrator are acquainted in assault, rape, and homicide cases, the incident is seen as containing the core feature of the routine offense pattern for these cases. In such incidents a perfunctory investigation is usually made for the identity of the perpetrator generally is easily learned from the victim or from persons close to the victim.

The barroom homicide in case 5 was termed a "killing" and viewed as a routine case because the victim and perpetrator were previously acquainted and information linking the perpetrator to the crime could be easily obtained. The term "murder" is reserved for those homicides which do not correspond to a typical pattern.

A somewhat different pattern follows in the category of incidents which detectives refer to as "suspect rapes." Victims having certain social characteristics (females from lower-class backgrounds who are viewed as having low intelligence or as displaying some type of mental or emotional abnormality) are viewed as most likely to make a false allegation of rape. Where a victim so perceived reports a sexual assault by a person with whom she had some prior acquaintance, the initial orientation of the detective is to obtain information which either negates the crime of rape (the complainant actually consented) or warrants reducing the charge to a lesser offense. Where the victim and assailant were not previously acquainted, the case receives a vigorous investigative effort. The level of police resources devoted to the case varies according to the race and social standing of the victim.

2.   Conceptions of the normal social characteristics of victims are also central to case routinization. Victims having different social characteristics are regarded as being more or less likely to desire or follow through with prosecution in the case, to be reliable sources of information about it, and to inquire as to the outcome of the investigation.

The treatment of the assault and robbery in case 3 illustrates how a case may be interpreted and handled primarily in terms of the victim's class position, race, and presumed lifestyle and competencies. The case was cleared by arrest on the basis of information provided by the victims, but the handling of this "ghetto robbery" involved little actual police effort. No attempt was made to locate witnesses, gather evidence from the crime scene, or otherwise strengthen the case against the accused.

Poor and working-class people who are regarded as unlikely to make inquiries regarding the handling and disposition of the case are seen as typical of victims in the category of routine burglaries. Case 2 illustrates how the interpretation of an incident may be accomplished solely on the basis of information contained in the patrol report and prior to an actual interview with the victim. The interview was structured in this case by the detective's expectation of its outcome.

Case 4 illustrates how inconsistent elements in an otherwise routine pattern (in this instance the victim's social status and apparent interest in the handling of the case) are managed to suit the purposes of the detective. Detectives speak of a case "coming back on them" if a respectable victim contacts superiors regarding progress in the case when the incident has received little or no investigative effort. Informing the victim that the case was not solvable largely because of her neighbor's attitudes enabled the detective to suspend the case with minimal problems.

3.   Routinization formulas, finally, contain conceptions of the settings in which different kinds of offenses normally occur and the expected behavior of inhabitants of those settings. While assumptions about victims and perpetrators are derived in part from the nature of the offense involved, the physical and social setting where the incident occurred also contributes to a detective's understanding of these parties. The fact that the burglary in case 2 occurred in a particular public housing project told the detective much of what he felt he had to know about the case. It should be noted that none of these perceptions were communicated to the prosecutor observing the detective work; they were part of the taken-for-granted background upon which the detective based his handling of the case.

With regard to actual and potential *witnesses*, however, a detective's assumptions and beliefs are based primarily on the offense setting, if the witness is seen as a normal inhabitant of that setting. (This latter qualification simply recognizes that detectives attribute different inclinations and sentiments to social workers or salesmen who may have witnessed an incident than to residents of the area who may have witnessed a crime.)

The impact of territorial conceptions may be seen in the handling of case 4. Routine burglaries occur mainly in low-income housing projects, residences in deteriorating center-city areas or, less frequently, in commercial establishments in or near these locations. Residents of these areas are considered unlikely to volunteer that they have witnessed a crime.

Although official investigative procedure dictates that neighboring residents be interviewed to determine whether they saw or heard anything that might be of value to the investigation, this step was not undertaken in cases 2 or 4 because it was assumed that the residents would be uncooperative.

Routine cases, then, may be seen as having two components, one at the level of consciousness and cognition, and the other at the level of observable behavior. A detective's interpretation of a case as routine involves an assessment of whether sufficient correspondence exists between the current case and some typical pattern to warrant handling it in the normal way. The criterion of sufficient correspondence implies that not all the elements of the typical pattern need be present for a detective to regard a case as a routine one. Common elements are viewed and used as resources which may be drawn upon selectively in accordance with one's practical concerns and objectives. Further, when certain elements in a case appear inconsistent with the typical pattern, there is a tendency to force and manage a sufficient fit between the particular and the typical in ways that help detectives deal with their caseload management problems and constraints.

These features of the interpretation process mean that the assessments of the routine or nonroutine nature of a case take on more of the character of a dichotomy than a continuum. Once an assessment is made, the case will be handled by means of prescribed formulas unless additional information changes the interpretation. It must be emphasized that the routinization process is not a matter of automatic or unreflective mapping of case features onto more general conceptions of criminal incidents. The interpretation of any particular case is shaped by a detective's understandings of what is required and expected and of how to manage these concerns effectively.

Case Handling

Case handling normally proceeds in accordance with informal understandings shared among detectives. Routine case patterns are associated with prescribed handling recipes. It is critical to an understanding of investigative police work that interpretation of criminal incidents as routine or nonroutine largely determines which cases will be summarily suspended, which will be investigated, and how vigorous or extensive that investigation will be.

The characteristic behavioral element of a routine case is an absence of vigorous or thorough investigative effort. Two distinct sets of circumstances are ordinarily encountered in routine cases which lead to such a superficial or cursory investigative effort. The first, most common in burglary and robbery cases, is that the available information concerning the incident is seen as so meager or of so little utility that the possibility of making a quick arrest is virtually nonexistent. Viewing the case as non-productive, and not wishing to expend effort on cases for which there are no formal rewards, the detective produces a brief investigative report detailing the routine features of the incident, concludes the case summary with "N.I.L." (no investigative leads were found), and classifies it as a suspended case.

The second set of circumstances associated with an absence of vigorous investigative effort involves assault, rape, and homicide cases which require some investigation because of their seriousness and the possibility of scrutiny by the judicial process. However, in many such incidents the facts of the case are so obvious and straightforward that little actual investigative work needs to be done. In these three types of offenses the victim and perpetrator are often known to one another, and it is not at all uncommon for the victim to name the assailant as soon as the police arrive. Cases in which a spouse or lover is still standing by the victim with weapon in hand when the police arrive, or in which the victim names the perpetrator before expiring, are not unusual. In essence, such cases are solved without any substantial police investigation. The detective is obligated to produce a comprehensive report on the incidence, and the investigation is generally classified as closed in this report if the perpetrator has been apprehended. Indeed, in such obvious and straightforward cases the detective's only difficult task may be that of locating the perpetrator.[7]

Handling recipes associated with routine cases have a practical and instrumental character, reflecting the objective circumstances surrounding the investigation of many criminal events. After all, in the great majority of burglary cases the probability of ascertaining the identity of the perpetrator is rather small. Yet, handling recipes reflect certain *beliefs* and *assumptions* on the part of detectives concerning such matters as a victim's willingness to cooperate fully in the case, whether persons in particular sections of the city are likely to volunteer information about a crime, or the kind of impression a victim or witness would make in court. Such beliefs and assumptions constitute integral features in the construction of cases as routine or nonroutine, and they represent a pivotal linkage between specific features of cases and particular handling recipes.

The following incident illustrates the extent to which case handling may be guided by the detective's beliefs and assumptions about the nature of an incident and the parties involved:

Case 6:

A detective was assigned a case in which a man had stabbed his common-law wife in the arm with a kitchen knife. The patrol report on the incident indicated that the woman had been taken to City Hall to sign an arrest warrant, while the man had been arrested by patrol officers on the charge of felony assault and released on his own recognizance. Nominally, the detective was required to collect additional information and evidence relating to the incident and to write a detailed and comprehensive report which would be used in prosecuting the case.

However, the detective's interpretation of the incident, based on his understanding of the area in which it occurred and the lifestyles of the persons involved, led him to view any further investigative effort on his part as futile. He remarked: "These drunks, they're always stabbing one another over here. Then you see 'em the next day and they're right back together again. She won't show up in court anyhow. Why waste my time and everybody else's on it." The handling of the case involved only the production of a brief report which concluded: "The victim in this complaint wishes no further investigation by the police department. This complaint is to be classified as closed."

The interpretive schemes used by detectives are not based solely on their experiences as police investigators, but also on their accumulated experiences as everyday social actors; they thus reflect commonsense social knowledge. Categorizations made by detectives about race, class, ethnicity, sex, and territory parallel wider cultural evaluations of morality and worth. None of the features of the formal organization of detective work substantially reduce this reliance on commonsense knowledge and its typical biases, prejudices, and interpretations.

Summary and Implications

Some general features of case routinization may now be noted in an attempt to clarify the interpretive activities through which detectives achieve order and predictability in their handling of cases and their encounters with victims and other relevant actors.

1. Shortly after receipt of a case, specific pieces of information are sought out and attended to for use in assessing the typicality of the incident. That is, the fundamental case-working orientation of detectives involves an attempt to establish commonalities between an actual case and typical case patterns. Incidents having typical features are interpreted and constructed as some variety of routine case. The orientation to typify and routinize cases is partly traceable to bureaucratic pressures and constraints to meet paperwork deadlines and produce a certain quantity and quality not of convictions but of arrests.

2. The interpretation of an incident is accomplished by attending to case features having commonly recognized utility as indicators of the type of case at hand. Detectives use such routinization schemes unless some problematic feature of an actual case brings into question their applicability and appropriateness. The interpretation of a case as routine or nonroutine essentially determines whether the case will be quickly closed or suspended or whether it will receive a more vigorous and extensive investigation. However, this initial assignment of meaning is provisional and subject to revision or modification upon receipt of additional information. Most importantly, the handling of cases is directed by these informal categorization schemes, and is not the result of formal

organizational policy or procedures. These schemes constitute a taken-for-granted background of decision making.

3. The interpretive schemes shared by detectives represent "successful" solutions to common practical problems, based on experience and shared understandings about the nature of urban crime and about types of urban residents, lifestyles, and territories. These understandings are rooted in socially distributed as well as role-specific knowledge, for both provide a basis for constructing solutions to work problems. Occupationally specific knowledge provides a set of instructions for interpreting case patterns in ways which enable a detective to successfully manage organizational constraints and demands. Commonsense social knowledge provides an understanding of the typical characteristics, attitudes, and action patterns of persons encountered. Identities may be readily assigned to persons by drawing on this stock of knowledge. Such identity assignments structure case handling along race, class, age, sex, and territorial lines in ways that are intended to minimize case handling problems. Because of this reliance on general social knowledge, the treatment of different types of urban residents tends to reflect wider cultural evaluations of social worth.

4. The essential nature of these interpretive processes is phenomenological rather than mechanical or rule-guided. In formulating a particular case, the operative process involves a determination of whether sufficient correspondence exists between the actual case and the paradigmatic case to warrant handling the incident in routine, low-effort ways. Sufficient correspondence assessments are accomplished in ways that serve the practical purposes of detectives, especially those of paper-work compliance and productivity.

5. Accordingly, routine cases are not constituted as a single determinant pattern. A variety of combinations of case features may result in routine handling of the case. For each offense, a core feature or set of features gets maximum interpretive significance. When a core feature is recognized in a particular case, other features which are ambiguous or even contradictory tend to be interpreted in a manner consistent with the identified core feature. Additional interpretive features, particularly the social status of the victim, are used as resources in selecting a safe and workable handling strategy.

6. In highly routinized case patterns, there is a tendency to squeeze great indicativeness out of a few case features. Detectives often rely upon assumptions to add detail to a case rather than actually gather information to further specify the type of case at hand. In other words, it is frequently taken for granted that certain investigative procedures will have predictable outcomes. Frequently, this process manifests itself in the fudging, doctoring, and manipulation of formal organizational reports.

It is likely that interpretive schemes having similar features will be found in all bureaucratically organized enterprises where large numbers of clients or cases are processed (e.g., social service centers, public hospitals, and other agencies in the criminal justice system). Whenever we find an organizational setting where members deal with similar events time and again, and where there are no features in the formal organization of the work which act to counter stereotyping, we may expect to find routinization schemes in use. These schemes will be used to categorize the population and apply standard patterns of treatment to each category.

These observations have significant implications for the study of decision making by legal agents. Decision making by bureaucratic agents inevitably involves discretion on the part of the agent who must fit general rules to particular cases. This discretionary latitude will be reflected in different forms of decision making in different kinds of organizational settings. The work of Roth (1977), Scheff (1978), Sudnow (1965), and others suggests that caseload size, amount of information readily available about the person or event, the nature of the body of knowledge used, and the expectation of future interaction with the person are crucial features governing the nature of the decision-making process. Where caseloads are high, continued interaction is not anticipated, minimal information is available, and the body of knowledge used by the agent is imprecise — stereotypes tend to become the operative and binding basis for decision making. Accordingly, detective work, presentence casework, public defender work, and medical practice in clinics or emergency rooms may be seen as lying toward the end of a continuum where typifications act as essentially final judgments.

At the other end of the continuum are settings where caseload sizes are smaller, more detailed information about the person is available, future interaction is anticipated, and decision making is grounded in a more substantial body of knowledge. In such settings, typificatory schemes are likely to be used only as provisional hypotheses, to be amplified and modified over the course of the encounter. Thus in probation work, some types of social service work, and the practice of general medicine, we might expect to find interaction only tentatively structured by stereotypic understandings. As interaction proceeds in these latter settings, typifications will begin to fade in importance as the basis for decision making.

Endnotes

[1] The use of shared typificatory schemes to make required decisions appears to be a pervasive phenomenon not only in social control organizations, but in other organizations which process large numbers of people as well. Roth (1977) observed the same basic process in the evaluation, categorization, and treatment of patients by hospital personnel. The differential treatment of clients of public service bureaucracies was likewise found to be rooted in occupational typifications (Gordon, 1975).

[2] The description and the analysis presented here are based on nine months of participant observation fieldwork in a city police detective division. Further, information about access agreements, characteristics of the city and department, the field role adopted, and problems encountered during the research is available from the author.

[3] An exception to this general observation occurs where a supervisor imposes a "major case" definition on an incident. In highly publicized or nonroutine homicide or rape cases, especially those involving higher status victims, a supervisor frequently takes an active part in the investigation and more closely monitors and directs the activities of detectives. With regard to the influence of the victim's social status on case handling, see Wilson's (1968:27) analysis of police perceptions of the legitimacy of complaints made by middle-class versus lower-class victims.

[4] Official nationwide clearance rates are listed as 17.6 percent for burglary, 27.3 percent for robbery, 63.4 percent for felonious assault, 51.1 percent for rape, and 79.9 percent for homicide (Hindelang et al., 1977).

[5] Cf. Sudnow's (1965) argument that public defenders use their first interview with a client to gain an initial sense of the defendant's place in the social structure as well as the typicality or lack thereof of the offense with which the person has been charged.

[6] Garfinkel (1967:186–207) argues that organizational records are not to be treated as accurate or mirror reflections of the actual handling of a client or case by organizational members. However, these records can be employed to examine how members go about constructing a meaningful conception of a client or case and use it for their own practical purposes. Any valid sociological use of such records requires detailed knowledge on the part of the researcher regarding the context in which the records are produced, background understandings of members, and organizationally relevant purposes and routines.

[7] Reiss (1971) makes a similar observation. He found that a great deal of detective work in the department studied merely involves attempting to locate identified perpetrators. The Rand survey of investigative practices in 153 police departments draws conclusions similar to those presented here. It was found that substantially more than half of all serious reported crimes receive no more than superficial attention from investigators (Greenwood and Petersilia, 1975).

References

Bittner, E. (1967, October). The police on skid row: A study of peace keeping. *American Sociological Review, 32,* 699–715.

Bittner, E. (1970). *The functions of the police in modern society.* Chevy Chase, MD: National Institute of Mental Health.

Garfinkel, H. (1967). *Studies in ethnomethodology.* Englewood Cliffs, NJ: Prentice-Hall.

Gordon, L. (1975). Bureaucratic competence and success in dealing with public bureaucracies. *Social Problems, 23*(2), 197–208.

Greenwood, P. W., & Petersilia, J. (1975). *The criminal investigation process* (Vol. 1). Santa Monica, CA: The Rand Corporation.

Hindelang, M., Gottfredson, M., Dunn, C., & Parisi, N. (1977). *Sourcebook of criminal justice statistics.* Washington, DC: National Criminal Justice Information and Statistics Service.

Piliavin, I., & Briar, S. (1964). Police encounters with juveniles. *American Sociological Review, 70,* 206–214.

Reiss, A. (1971). *Police and the public.* New Haven: Yale University Press.

Roth, J. (1977, October). Some contingencies of the moral evaluation and control of clients. *American Journal of Sociology, 77,* 830–856.

Scheff, T. (1978). Typification in rehabilitation agencies. In E. Rubington & M. S. Weinberg (Eds.), *Deviance: The interactionist perspective* (pp. 172–175). New York: Macmillan.

Skolnick, J. (1967). *Justice without trial.* New York: Wiley.

Steffensmeier, D., & Terry, R. (1973). Deviance and respectability: An observational study of reactions to shoplifting. *Social Forces, 51*, 417–426.

Stokes, R., & Hewitt, J. (1976). Aligning actions. *American Sociological Review, 41*, 838–849.

Sudnow, D. (1965). Normal crimes: Sociological features of the penal code in a public defender's office. *Social Problems, 12*(3), 255–276.

Swigert, V., & Farrell, R. (1977). Normal homicides and the law. *American Sociological Review, 42*, 16–32.

Wilson, J. Q. (1968). *Varieties of police behavior.* Cambridge, MA: Harvard University Press.

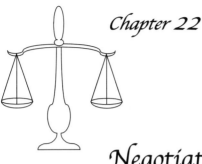

Chapter 22

Negotiation and Plea Bargaining Models
An Organizational Perspective

Albert R. Matheny

Plea bargaining seems eminently compatible with the assumptions involved in economic models of resource allocation and decision-theory models of negotiation One can easily picture the choices between trial and negotiated settlement of criminal charges as a matter of utility calculation within the resource constraints of prosecution and defense (Landes, 1971; Forst and Brosi, 1977). Similarly, the settlement itself can readily be interpreted as an "equilibrium point" between competing negotiation strategies based upon the defendant's and prosecutor's expectations of trial outcome (Nagel and Neef, 1976a, 1976b; Fried, 1974). It is no wonder, then, that scholars from several disciplines have recently focused their efforts on "modeling" the plea bargaining process (Lachman and McLauchlan, 1977). A common characteristic of these modeling efforts has been their emphasis on the behavior of individual participants in the criminal process, stressing the "rationality" of that behavior, consistent with the classic assumption of micro-economic theory.

The analysis of the criminal process, and particularly plea bargaining, in terms of economic and decision-theory models, has contributed some powerful insights to our understanding of the actual operation of

Albert R. Matheny, "Negotiations and Plea Bargaining Models: An Organizational Perspective," *Law and Policy Quarterly*, Vol. 2, No. 3, 1980, pp. 267–284. Reprinted with permission of Basil Blackwell.

the criminal justice system and has inspired several empirical efforts aimed at demonstrating the efficacy of a few derivatives from these models (e.g., Landes, 1971, 1974; Forst and Brosi, 1977). Of course, the models are based on a set of simplifying assumptions which necessarily sacrifice descriptive specificity for theoretical generality.

This essay assesses the appropriateness of the dominant models of plea bargaining by introducing certain organizational assumptions into their equations in an attempt to reconcile individual-level behavior of the participants in the criminal process with the collective, administrative demands arising from the peculiar organization of the American criminal justice system. Specifically, we employ "contingency theory" (Thompson, 1967, Thompson, 1973; Carter, 1974a) in order to introduce the concept of *uncertainty*[1] into the plea bargaining equation. Out intent is to temper the economic and decision-theory models with an "organizational model" which can incorporate a broader range of the available empirical information into the practice of plea bargaining. The direction of our analysis is toward greater "descriptive specificity" about plea bargaining, and, as a result, the reasoning used here will be less elegant than that employed by the formal modelers of plea bargaining. Nonetheless, our assertions should enable us to test empirically some of those formal assumptions with available criminal justice data on dispositions and sentencing.

Uncertainty and the Administration of Justice

At the outset, we must conceptualize the criminal process in terms compatible with the language of organization theory. Initially, it is helpful to consider the adversary process as the formally prescribed "technology" of the criminal justice system, used to determine the guilt or innocence of the accused and to establish appropriate punishment.[2] An organization's integrity vis-à-vis its environment depends primarily upon its ability to maintain and enhance the predictability of its technical operations by insulating them from uncertainty in the environment.

The criminal justice system as an organization confronts a peculiar problem. Its formally prescribed technology itself contains elements of uncertainty which contribute to unpredictability in its operation. As noted by Packer (1968), the outcome of a criminal trial is the product of a system of challenge which resists a priori rationalization. The skepticism inherent in the "due process" model of criminal adjudication, replete with its presumptions favoring the defendant, restrictive rules of evidence, and the participation of a lay jury (when requested), injects an essential unpredictability into the determination of guilt or innocence.[3] Because the criminal justice system processes cases despite their unpredictable content, the analyst must explain how the system manages uncertainty in processing criminal cases.

The first step is to examine how the organization actually treats the accused, independent of legal ideals and the formal prescriptions of due process. Then one must describe the way organizational actors make decisions in light of administrative realities and the formal procedures involved in applying criminal sanctions.

Several observers have commented that the actual transformation process of the criminal justice system resembles Thompson's (1967) description of an "intensive technology" (Carter, 1974a; Dill, 1973; Nardulli, 1979).[4] This type of technology refers to an organizational "treatment" strategy in which treatment is determined by the needs of the typically human "input object." Its distinctive feature is that specific treatments cannot be specified a priori; rather, the choice of various treatment techniques must await diagnosis. In other words, initial treatment depends upon perceived characteristics of the input; subsequent treatments depend upon the perceived outcome of initial treatment. The knowledge or "expertise," of organizational actors consists of an ability to apply a treatment from among techniques available to the organization. "Success" in treatment at all stages of the process is indicated by "appropriate" response from the input object. Obviously, an intensive technology is highly discretionary. Decision makers are usually endowed with professional credentials and given relative autonomy in exercising the discretion necessary for an intensive technology to work.

The criminal process displays many properties of an organization that uses an intensive technology.[5] But the discretionary decision-making in the criminal process is complicated considerably by two factors: (1) *expectations of rationality*, both in terms of procedural rules for establishing guilt or innocence and in terms of consistency in processing defendants; and (2) the *existence of uncertainty* surrounding such decisions as the determination of charges, the development of evidence, the determination of guilt or innocence, and the selection of punishment alternatives. According to Thompson's theory of organizations,[6] intensive technologies are most suitable in decentralized organizations whose actors have a good deal of autonomy, placing them in intimate association with the relevant input so that they can better *monitor* the input, facilitating "diagnosis" and "feedback" Such an arrangement would presumably enable the criminal justice system to attain what Thompson calls "bounded rationality" (1967:76–77).

However, such an organization is incompatible with the "due process" requirements of a criminal justice system based on an adversary model. The criminal trial itself directly conflicts with the tenets of discretionary decision-making by autonomous experts. The defendant's right to trial invokes procedural rules designed to limit the discretionary power of the prosecution, defense, and judge. A system of challenge and potential appellate review further reduces the autonomy, decentralization, and flexibility of these actors, who nevertheless must operate within an intensive technology. In addition, resort to trial increases the risks associated with making decisions about the defendant's guilt and subsequent punishment, well summarized in the following statement:

> No matter how strong the evidence may appear and how well prepared and conducted a trial may be, each side must realistically consider the possibility of an unfavorable outcome. At its best the trial process is an imperfect method of factfinding; factors such as the attorney's skill, the availability of witnesses, the judge's attitude, jury vagaries, and luck will influence the result. (President's Commission on Law Enforcement and the Administration of Justice, 1967:10.)

In response to the conflict between procedural prescriptions and administrative necessities, participants in the criminal process routinely resort to plea bargaining. While officially tolerated as an alternative to trial (*Santobello v. New York*, 1971), the practice of plea bargaining enables the participants to establish localized and conditionally autonomous decision-making units consistent with the achievement of bounded rationality in the administration of criminal justice. These plea bargaining units, called "courtroom workgroups" by Eisenstein and Jacob (1977), accommodate nicely the intensive nature of criminal justice operations under conditions of uncertainty.

The Impact of Uncertainty on Models of Plea Bargaining

So far we have only sketched an organizational explanation of plea bargaining and have only addressed tangentially the important concept of uncertainty as it applies to the administration of justice. However, by applying the insights gained from our organizational "model" to the economic and decision-theory models of plea bargaining, we hope to elaborate upon our assumptions, while at the same time strengthening the descriptive reality of the economic and decision-theory models of plea bargaining. The first step is to interpret the concept of uncertainty in the terms of these models.

The Calculus of Uncertainty

Economic and decision-theory models of plea bargaining assume that uncertainty in criminal justice decision-making can be accounted for simply through the adjustment of conditional probabilities of conviction and/or length of sentence. However, Mack (1971) has pointed out that decisions are amenable to rational analysis only if specific attributes of the decisions are consistent with the assumptions of the models involved. Modeling the decision-making process in criminal justice is reasonable only if the goals of that process are clearly defined, if the utilities of the parties to decisions can be identified, and if information on outcomes of the process is available to the parties.

Two models of plea bargaining will be examined here in light of the above discussion. The first is Landes's (1971) economic model of plea bargaining, which attempts to explain the choice between trial and negotiation of criminal charges. The second is Nagel and Neef's (1976a, 1976b) decision-theory model which poses, among other things, a rationale for predicting sentence outcomes resulting from negotiation.

Landes's model assumes that the prosecution and defense maximize their expected utility within respective resource constraints, as they choose between negotiated settlement and trial. Conceptually, that choice is said to depend upon the probability of conviction at trial, the severity of the crime, the availability and productivity of respective resources, trial versus settlement costs, and attitudes toward risk. Crucial assumptions in Landes's model are that the probabilities of conviction entertained by prosecution and defense can be estimated by each and that these probabilities are directly affected by the amount of resources each employs, such that an increase in prosecution resources will increase the probability estimates for both and an increase in defense resources will decrease those estimates. The prosecutor's decision rule is to maximize the expected number of convictions weighted by the severity of the offense, subject to budgetary constraints. The defendant's decision rule is determined by subtracting the costs of obtaining an acquittal from the costs of being convicted at trial, including the transaction costs associated with trial relative to those of a negotiated settlement.

This sketch of Landes's model provides a compelling rationale for why so few criminal cases actually go to trial. Applying the model to actual cases, those few going to trial would be characterized by: (1) relatively serious charges; (2) relatively high levels of resource commitment by both prosecution and defense; (3) differential assessments of conviction probabilities, with the defendant's assessment considerably lower than the prosecutor's; and/or (4) a defendant predisposed to gambling with his future.

Nagel and Neef's model addresses the choice between negotiation and trial in a fashion consistent with Landes's approach, except that their model has the prosecutor maximizing the sentence expected from each conviction, regardless of the severity of charges. Our examination focuses primarily upon Nagel and Neef's efforts to model the dynamics of the plea bargaining process itself. On the assumption that prosecution and defense have opted for negotiation and that both have: (1) an idea of what could have been the outcome at trial and (2) an idea of their respective bargaining limits, Nagel and Neef argue that negotiations will proceed along a stepwise pattern of convergence, characterized by "bluffing" in the exchange of offers and counteroffers. Negotiated settlement occurs only if the bargaining limits of the parties "overlap"; otherwise, the case goes to trial.

The assumptions of both Landes's model and Nagel and Neef's model can be criticized for their failure to recognize the full effect of

uncertainty on decision-making in the criminal process. From empirical observation (Carter, 1974a; Mather, 1973; Heumann, 1978), it is
obvious that prosecutors do not articulate precisely or consistently the
decision rules for choosing between trial and negotiation. The disagreement between the two models (see also Forst and Brosi, 1977) on
decision rules of the prosecution is evidence enough on this score. Further, the very unpredictability of the trial process, discussed earlier,
makes it extremely unlikely that prosecutors and defendants can
develop precise enough estimates of the probability of conviction and
sentence length at trial to make a rational choice between trial and settlement or to form a cogent strategy for negotiation. Finally, neither
model seems to appreciate the entirely different positions of prosecution and defense with regard to the risk, or personal investment, in the
eventual outcome of a given case. For the prosecutor, the outcome of a
given trial is simply an individual occurrence in a long series of events
to which probabilities might reasonably be attached and used in the
development of decision rules governing the choice between trial and
settlement. In contrast, the defendant is faced with a "one-shot" outcome involving, at worst, the severest personal consequences, for
which probabilities of acquittal offer little comfort or guidance. The
defendant's predicament, called "non-seriability" by decision-theorists
(Mack, 1971), reflects a fundamental asymmetry in the positions of
prosecution and defense (Galanter, 1974). Perhaps this explains why
defendants are so often willing to engage in plea bargaining even
though empirical evidence demonstrates that, in most cases, no real
sentence concessions result, based upon several comparisons of sentencing following plea bargaining and following conviction at trial
(Rhodes, 1979; Uhlman and Walker, 1977; Shin, 1973).

By ignoring the effects of uncertainty on criminal justice decision-
making suggested above, the two models of plea bargaining project a false
precision as well as an illusion of symmetry in accounting for the negotia-
tive strategies of defense and prosecution. While each presents a plausible
argument for the prevalence of plea bargaining in the system, an organizational approach achieves the same end with less demanding and more
empirically relevant assumptions. Using the presence of uncertainty as a
guide, we can easily grasp, in organizational terms, why prosecutors and
defendants avoid the trial process and favor negotiation in its place. Uncertainty generally begets conservatism in decision-making. Prosecutors
faced with only vague estimates of the probability of conviction at trial will
very likely set their bargaining limits unnecessarily low. Likewise, defendants, faced with the same vagueness, compounded by the non-seriability
of their decisions, will very likely set unnecessarily with high bargaining
limits, thus enhancing the likelihood of "overlap" and the attractiveness of
negotiation. Conceptually, of course, this interpretation of the impact of
uncertainty on criminal justice decision-making could still be accommo-

dated in the models described above, and, to that extent, these models further our understanding of the criminal process. But these models fail in their precision to grasp the richness of the organizational context of the criminal process and its relevance to the decision to settle or try cases.

Uncertainty and Reciprocity

When it occurs, plea bargaining involves the defendant and members of the "courtroom workgroup," mentioned in our earlier discussion of the organization of the criminal justice system. To understand the dynamics of the plea bargaining process, we must examine the ongoing relationships between the members of the courtroom workgroup, particularly the prosecutor and defense attorney. Bargaining under uncertainty forces prosecution and defense to make exchanges or concessions which are difficult to weigh for their equivalence. Rarely are they simple, balanced, quid-pro-quo deals. Doubts are likely to linger about who is "indebted" to whom when an individual case is resolved through negotiations. Gouldner (1960) has argued that, in general, a "norm of reciprocity" is likely to be invoked to guard against the exploitation of ambiguity by one of the two parties to negotiation. Insofar as the prosecution and defense functions can be characterized as an "exchange relationship" (Cole, 1973) which exists over many cases, the norm of reciprocity is likely to be extended and become generalized into what Carter (1974a:29) calls a "bond of reciprocity":

> These [reciprocal bonds] are built on candor, honesty, and "being realistic." . . . Indeed, instead of depending on exchange of favors — "I'll let you plead X to a reduced charge if you plead Y to the given charge" in the case where a defense attorney represents two clients — the reciprocal bond may facilitate the opposite, the capacity to deny the requests of another or to concede the justness of his position, because each member trusts the other's judgment and can afford to insist or concede without becoming further obligated or threatened.

Under conditions of uncertainty, the mutuality of the exchange relationship between prosecution and defense is likely to be enhanced, as each is particularly vulnerable in negotiations and must rely on trust in the other simply to define the case they are dealing with. This mutuality militates against bluffing, or what might be called "strategic negotiation," and replaces it with a sort of epistemic negotiation, or what Scheff (1968) calls "the negotiation of reality." Within this interpretation, plea bargaining cannot be considered simply haggling in the sentence marketplace between a buyer-defendant and a seller-prosecutor, as characterized by Nagel and Neef (1976b:1). Rather, plea bargaining must be seen as a cooperative venture between two parties, each with limited knowledge, attempting to piece together an acceptable picture of criminal reality.

Ethnographic studies of the American criminal process contribute additional insights to this interpretation of plea bargaining. The gist of these studies is that individual case disposition must be placed within the context of previous dispositions and the ongoing expectations of workgroup members. Rather than bluffing ad hoc about sentence length in a particular case, the parties to negotiation may be engaged in a mutual search for an acceptable way to *categorize* that case among other cases. This categorical bargaining produces "normal crimes," first noted by Sudnow (1965:262):

> Over the course of their interaction and repeated "bargaining" discussions, the P.D. [public defender] and the D.A. [district attorney] have developed a set of unstated recipes for reducing original charges to lesser offenses. These recipes are specifically appropriate for use in instances of normal crimes and in such instances alone. "Typical" burglaries are reduced to petty theft, "typical" ADW's [assaults with a deadly weapon] to simple assault, "typical" child molestation to loitering around a schoolyard, etc.

The plea bargaining recipes represent charge and/or sentence reductions which have proved sufficient in the past to induce the defendant to plead guilty, while at the same time satisfying the prosecution's demands that the defendant "get his due."

Sudnow's approach casts plea bargaining in a new light. It becomes the key to a *learning process* by which the courtroom workgroup as a decision-making unit can reduce uncertainty about the appropriate response to its case input through reliance on past experience with similar cases and on mutual expectations about how each member of the workgroup will react to any given case. Mather (1973) noted such a process in the Los Angeles criminal courts, where defense attorneys and prosecutors implicitly categorize cases in a two-by-two matrix defined by an evidentiary dimension (from "dead-bang" cases to "reasonable-doubt" cases) and a seriousness dimension (from "nonserious" to "serious"). The mode of disposition followed by the Los Angeles prosecutors and defenders depends largely upon the initial, intuitive categorization of each case.

For the individual members of the courtroom workgroup, socialization to workgroup norms is the prerequisite for effective participation. In his study of New Haven criminal courts, Heumann (1978) found that "newcomers" to the plea bargaining process, whether defense attorneys, prosecutors, or judges, were at a distinct disadvantage until they gained a "feel for a case," learned exclusively through experience in negotiation. Battle (1973) found that learning workgroup norms was just as important for private defense attorneys as for public defenders in Denver.

Negotiation as uncertainty reduction rather than convergence through simple haggling and bluffing in a sentence marketplace clearly reveals itself in this summary comment by Eisenstein and Jacob (1977:61):

> Workgroup characteristics heavily influence the techniques used to dispose of cases. When members are familiar with one another, many more cases will be disposed of by negotiation than when they [workgroups] are composed of strangers. Familiarity permits work-group members to reduce uncertainty through bargaining. They know each

other well enough to predict reactions to proposals and to achieve some control over outcomes through bargaining.

It should be evident that, from an organizational perspective, plea bargaining enables the decision-making unit of the courtroom workgroup to develop over time the expertise necessary for the operation of an implicit intensive technology in the criminal process. Through something closely akin to "organizational learning" (Cyert and March, 1963), the workgroup develops a diagnostic capacity (with regard to the defendant) and maintains a "repertoire of treatment techniques" which it can apply routinely to transform the defendant's status and to attach an appropriate sanction, while avoiding entirely the inherent uncertainties of the trial process.

Empirical Findings: A Brief Summary

The economic and decision-theory models discussed above suggest that the choice between trial and settlement depends primarily upon the characteristics of the individual cases involved, and, thus, patterns of dispositional choice should remain fairly constant across jurisdictions with similar patterns of criminal activity and prosecution. In their research on urban felony jurisdictions, Eisenstein and Jacob (1977) discovered, on the contrary, a great diversity of disposition rates in different jurisdictions. Using their data for Baltimore and Chicago, we can compare those rates. Table 1 reveals that, aside from dismissals, Baltimore relies most heavily on bench trials for dispositions, while Chicago handles the bulk of its cases through guilty pleas.

Table I Disposition Rates for Baltimore and Chicago[a]

Mode of Disposition	Baltimore		Chicago	
	N[b]	Rate	N	Rate
Dismissals, etc.[c]	1107	50.5%	188	22.1%
Guilty Pleas	293	13.4	487	57.4
Bench Trials	662	30.2	124	14.6
Jury Trials	130	6.0	50	5.9
Total:	2192	100.1%[d]	849	100.0%

[a] SOURCE: Statistics are based upon original data from the survey by Eisenstein and Jacob (1977).

[b] From analysis of original data.

[c] From *weighted* sample to approximate randomness; the Chicago sample is unweighted and considered random. "Dismissals, etc." includes all cases screened out of the system prior to resolution by one of the other three modes of disposition.

[d] Rounding error.

The description of the organizational characteristics of the two juris-dictions provides an explanation for the differences in dispositional choice consistent with our organizational "model" of plea bargaining. At the time of Eisenstein and Jacob's analysis (1972), Baltimore had a high turnover among prosecutors, judges served only one-year rotations in given courtrooms, and public defenders were assigned to defendants rather than to courtrooms, on a "man-to-man" basis. All of these factors contributed to the low workgroup stability found there by the authors. In contrast, Chicago's prosecutors held office for longer periods and, with judges, were assigned indefinitely to particular courtrooms, as were pub-lic defenders (a "zone" arrangement). In addition, retained counsel were able to direct cases to courtrooms with which they were familiar. These arrangements established very stable workgroups in Chicago (see Eisen-stein and Jacob, 1977:224–252).

Data from these two jurisdictions are presented here to illustrate the apparent influence of organizational context upon guilty plea rates. This is not to say that other contextual factors, such as office policies guiding prosecutorial discretion or concerted efforts by a given community's defense bar, have no effect on a jurisdiction's rates of trial and settlement. In fact, data gathered by Brosi (1979) reveal extraordinary variation in the rate of guilty pleas per cases filed, ranging from a low of 28 percent in one jurisdiction to a high of 77 percent in another,[7] suggesting the influence of a variety of factors on plea rates. We are isolating only one of these factors.

A reanalysis of the Eisenstein and Jacob data reported elsewhere (Matheny, 1979) employed discriminant function analysis to examine fur-ther the differences in patterns of dispositional choice in Baltimore and Chi-cago. Using variables crucial to the Landes and Nagel and Neef models, such as charge seriousness, evidentiary strength, and extent of defendant resources, it found that, in fact, cases going to bench trials in Baltimore were similar in terms of these variables to ones resolved by guilty pleas in Chi-cago.[8] Apparently, because of workgroup instability, bench trials were nec-essary in Baltimore for disposing of cases that would have been resolved as guilty pleas by the more stable workgroups in Chicago. This interpretation is corroborated by Eisenstein and Jacob's (1977:250) observation:

> In Baltimore, bench trials became a functional equivalent to the guilty plea; they were sometimes called a slow plea. Prosecutors and defense counsel presented their evidence to the judge hastily; the formal trial was interspersed with off-the-record remarks which presaged the out-come. Such slow pleas helped reduce uncertainty in the same way ne-gotiations did in Chicago and Detroit, though to a lesser degree.

In support of the economic and decision-theory models, relatively serious cases were, in fact, more likely to be tried before a jury in both jurisdictions. But, with regard to evidentiary strength, cases with rela-tively weak evidence against the defendant were more likely to go to jury trial in Baltimore, while, in Chicago, evidentiary strength had little or no discriminating effect on the different modes of disposition. While we can only speculate, it appears that evidentiary uncertainties were less problematical for the more stable Chicago workgroups, and could be overcome through informal agreement based upon more well-developed bonds of reciprocity and a richer catalog of normal crimes.

Conclusions

The results from this brief empirical analysis indicate only partial support for the substantive assertions of economic and decision-theory models of choice behavior in negotiating and disposing of criminal cases in two urban felony jurisdictions. A more complete explanation of the *differences* in disposition patterns between jurisdictions requires recognition of contextual factors surrounding the choice behavior of prosecution and defense. We have focused on the structural characteristics of the criminal process to develop a complementary organizational "model" explaining plea bargaining. Our model refines the concept of "uncertainty" and introduces other concepts, such as "technology" and "organizational learning," which, I feel, more accurately describe the operating realities of the criminal justice system than do the formal models discussed above. In addition, our model stresses the significance of key organizational attributes (e.g., courtroom workgroup stability), which may be shown to have an effect on patterns of case disposition across jurisdictions.

The formal models discussed above may mislead those interested in reforming the practice of plea bargaining by creating an illusion of precision surrounding a decision-making process that is, in fact, overwhelmingly uncertain. As models of behavior, they confuse the distinction between calculation and speculation and, thereby, ignore the structural consequences of uncertainty. These are the consequences that must be faced if the operating reality of the criminal courts is to be understood. The "intensive" nature of the criminal process's implicit technology must be appreciated before any effective reform of plea bargaining can be staged. The formal theories of dispositional choice must be tempered by an acknowledgment of organizational factors impinging upon their assumptions. Otherwise, they will be of little practical help in contributing to our understanding of criminal justice decision-making.

Endnotes

[1] As defined in contingency theory, organizational uncertainty is an organization's inability to bring "system-closure" to its operations and is the product of the following conditions:

 (a) inadequate linkage in causal sequence of all variables relevant to the processing of input through the organization

 (b) unpredictable behavior of elements within the organization's environment — elements which vitally affect the organization's operations

(c) ambiguous standards of evaluation for judging the "quality" of the organiza-
    tion's operations and output vis-à-vis some stated abstract objective

(d) incomplete decision-premises surrounding the roles of individual decision mak-
    ers within the organization, such that organizational incentives are incompatible
    with individual rationality in decision-making.

[2] Basically, an organization's technology is a process of transformation derived from a the-
    ory of cause-and-effect relationships which makes assertions of predictability about the
    organization's output, given certain knowledge about its input (Thompson, 1967).

[3] Max Weber (1958:216–221) emphasized unpredictability as the key feature distinguishing
    the "empirical" quality of Anglo-American criminal justice from the "rational" quality of
    Continental criminal jurisprudence. Compare this with the "matter-of-factness" of Conti-
    nental criminal procedure and its relatively heavy reliance on expertise (Rosett, 1972).

[4] Thompson (1967:17) describes three basic varieties of technology: the *long-linked* technol-
    ogy used in assembly-line mass production processes; the *mediating* technology used in
    organizations which "pool" resources for the purpose of connecting suppliers and con-
    sumers; and the *intensive* technology. In general, organizations employing an intensive
    technology determine "the selection, combination, and order of application" of elements
    in the process of transforming input into output on the basis of "feedback" from the input
    object itself. It is a customized technology.

[5] This is clearly illustrated if one considers what the criminal process actually *does* to the
    defendant. First, the prosecutor "labels" the defendant by filing criminal charges (the ini-
    tial treatment) using characteristics of the accused and his or her alleged criminal act as
    guides. Then, he or she assembles evidence in support of those charges in order to iden-
    tify subsequent treatments (e.g., defining the elements of the crime for establishing culpa-
    bility). The defendant is monitored for signs that the treatment is appropriate (e.g.,
    anticipating the arguments in defense of the accused), and adjustments are made on the
    basis of this information (e.g., through pretrial and trial defense challenges of the prose-
    cutor's case). Virtually any criminal case can be seen as a mutual feedback and adjust-
    ment process which culminates explicitly in the selection and application of a form of
    punishment deemed appropriate for "correction" of the convicted criminal.

[6] Space limitations make it impossible to provide a full development of Thompson's prop-
    ositional analysis as applied to the organization of criminal justice. For a full treatment of
    this, see chapter three of my dissertation (Matheny, 1979; see also Carter, 1974a).

[7] Figures are from a nationwide, twelve-jurisdiction sample. The jurisdiction with the 28
    percent plea rate was the Florida second circuit; the one with the 77 percent plea rate was
    Cobb County, Georgia. Taken as a percentage of convictions, the plea rates for these two
    jurisdictions were 68 percent and 100 percent, respectively (Brosi, 1979:5).

[8] The similarity of Baltimore bench trials and Chicago guilty pleas was indicated by the
    proximity of the group centroids of the two types of disposition when plotted in discrim-
    inant space. For details, see chapter five of my dissertation (Matheny, 1979).

References

Battle, J. B. (1973). Note: Comparison of public defenders' and private attorneys'
    relationships with the prosecutor in the city of Denver. *Denver Law Journal,*
    50(1), 101–136.

Blumberg, A. S. (1967). *Criminal justice.* Chicago: Quadrangle Books.

Brosi, K. B. (1979). *A cross-city comparison of felony case processing.* Washington, DC:
    Institute for Law and Social Research.

Carter, L. H. (1974a). *The limits of order.* Lexington, MA: D.C. Heath.

Carter, L. H. (1974b, Autumn). Flexibility and uniformity in criminal justice. *Policy*
    Studies Journal, 3, 18–25.

Cole, G. F. (1973). *Politics and the administration of justice.* Beverly Hills, CA: Sage.

Cyert, R. M., & March, J. G. (1963). *A behavioral theory of the firm.* Englewood Cliffs, NJ: Prentice-Hall.

Dill, F. D. (1973). Bail and bail reform. Ph.D. dissertation, University of California, Berkeley.

Dolbeare, K. M. (1967). *Trial courts in urban politics.* New York: John Wiley.

Eisenstein, J., & Jacob, H. (1977). *Felony justice.* Boston: Little, Brown.

Feeley, M. M. (1973, Spring). Two models of the criminal justice system. *Law and Society Review, 7,* 407–425.

Fried, M. (1974). A decision theoretic model of plea bargaining. Paper presented at the meeting of the Midwest Political Science Association, Chicago.

Forst, B., & Brosi, K. B. (1977). A theoretical and empirical analysis of the prosecutor. *Journal of Legal Studies, 6*(1), 177–191.

Galanter, M. (1974, Fall). Why the "haves" come out ahead. *Law and Society Review, 9,* 95–160.

Gouldner, A. W. (1960, April). The norm of reciprocity: A preliminary statement. *American Sociological Review, 25,* 161–178.

Heumann, M. (1978). *Plea bargaining.* Chicago: University of Chicago Press.

Lachman, J. A., & McLauchlan, W. P. (1977). Models of plea bargaining. In S. Nagel & M. Neef (Eds.), *Modeling the criminal justice system.* Beverly Hills, CA: Sage.

Landes, W. M. (1974, June). Legality and reality: Some evidence on criminal procedures. *Journal of Legal Studies, 3,* 287–337.

Landes, W. M. (1971, April). An economic analysis of the courts. *Journal of Law and Economics, 14,* 61–107.

Mack, R. P. (1971). *Planning on uncertainty.* New York: John Wiley.

Matheny, A. R. (1979). Plea bargaining in organizational perspective. Ph.D. dissertation, University of Minnesota.

Mather, L. M. (1973, Winter). Some determinants of the method of case disposition. *Law and Society Review, 8,* 187–216.

Mohr, L. B. (1976, Summer). Organizations, decision, and courts. *Law and Society Review, 10,* 621–642.

Nagel, S. S., & Neef, M. (1976a, Summer). Plea bargaining, decision theory, and equilibrium models: Part I. *Indiana Law Journal, 51,* 987–1024.

Nagel, S. S., & Neef, M. (1976b, Fall). Plea bargaining, decision theory and equilibrium models: Part II. *Indiana Law Journal, 52,* 1–61.

Nardulli, P. F. (1979). *The courtroom elite.* Cambridge, MA: Ballinger.

Packer, H. L. (1968). *The limits of the criminal sanction.* Palo Alto, CA: Stanford University Press.

Posner, R. A. (1973, June). An economic approach to legal procedure and administration. *Journal of Legal Studies, 2,* 399–458.

Posner, R. A. (1977). *Economic analysis of law.* Boston: Little, Brown.

President's Commission on Law Enforcement and the Administration of Justice. (1967). *Task force report: The courts.* Washington, DC: Government Printing Office.

Rhodes, W. M. (1979). Plea bargaining: Its effect on sentencing and convictions in the District of Columbia. *Journal of Criminal Law and Criminology, 70*(3), 360–375.

Rosett, A. I. (1972, February). Trial and discretion in Dutch criminal justice. *UCLA Law Review, 19,* 353–396.

Scheff, T. J. (1968). Negotiating reality: Notes on power in the assessment of responsibility. *Social Problems, 16*(1), 3–17.

Shin, H. J. (1973). Do lesser pleas pay?: Accommodations in the sentencing and parole processes. *Journal of Criminal Justice, 1*, 27–42.

Sudnow, D. (1965). Normal crimes: Sociological features of the penal code in a public defender's office. *Social Problems, 12*, 255–276.

Thompson, J. D. (1967). *Organizations in action.* New York: McGraw-Hill.

Thompson, V. A. (1973). Organizations as systems. *University Programs Modular Studies.* Morristown, NJ: General Learning.

Trubek, D. M. (1977, Winter). Complexity and contradiction in the legal order. *Law and Society Review, 11*, 529–569.

Uhlman, I. M. & Walker, D. (1977). Pleas no bargains: Criminality, case disposition and defendant treatment. Presented at the meeting of the American Political Science Association.

Weber, M. (1958). *From Max Weber: Essays in Sociology* (Ed. C. W. Mills, Trans. H. H. Gerth). New York: Oxford.

Cases Cited

Santobello vs. New York (1971). 404 U.S. 257.

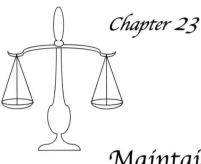

Chapter 23

Maintaining the Myth of Individualized Justice
Probation Presentence Reports

John Rosecrance

The Justice Department estimates that over one million probation presentence reports are submitted annually to criminal courts in the United States (Allen and Simonsen, 1986:111). The role of probation officers in the presentence process traditionally has been considered important. After examining criminal courts in the United States, a panel of investigators concluded: "Probation officers are attached to most modern felony courts; presentence reports containing their recommendations are commonly provided and these recommendations are usually followed" (Blumstein, Martin, and Holt, 1983). Judges view presentence reports as an integral part of sentencing, calling them "the best guide to intelligent sentencing" (Murrah, 1963:67) and "one of the most important developments in criminal law during the twentieth century" (Hogarth, 1971:246).

Researchers agree that a strong correlation exists between probation recommendations (contained in presentence reports) and judicial sentencing. In a seminal study of judicial decision making, Carter and Wilkins (1967) found 95 percent agreement between probation recommendation and sentence disposition when the officer recommended pro-

John Rosecrance, "Maintaining the Myth of Individualized Justice: Probation Presentence Reports." *Justice Quarterly,* Vol. 5 No. 2, 1988, 235–256. Reprinted by permission of the Academy of Criminal Justice Sciences.

bation and 88 percent agreement when the officer opposed probation. Hagan (1975), after controlling for related variables, reported a direct correlation of .72 between probation recommendation and sentencing. Walsh (1985) found a similar correlation of .807.

Although there is no controversy about the correlation between probation recommendation and judicial outcome, scholars disagree as to the actual influence of probation officers in the sentencing process. That is, there is no consensus regarding the importance of the presentence investigator in influencing sentencing outcomes. On the one hand, Myers (1979:538) contends that the "important role played by probation officer recommendation argues for greater theoretical and empirical attention to these officers." Walsh (1985:363) concludes that "judges lean heavily on the professional advice of probation." On the other hand, Kingsnorth and Rizzo (1979) report that probation recommendations have been supplanted by plea bargaining and that the probation officer is "largely superfluous." Hagan, Hewitt, and Alwin (1979), after reporting a direct correlation between recommendation and sentence, contend that the "influence of the probation officer in the presentence process is subordinate to that of the prosecutor" and that probation involvement is "often ceremonial."

My research builds on the latter perspective, and suggests that probation presentence reports do not influence judicial sentencing significantly but serve to maintain the myth that criminal courts dispense individualized justice. On the basis of an analysis of probation practices in California, I will demonstrate that the presentence report, long considered an instrument for the promotion of individualized sentencing by the court, actually deemphasizes individual characteristics and affirms the primacy of instant offense and prior criminal record as sentencing determinants. The present study was concerned with probation in California; whether its findings can be applied to other jurisdictions is not known. California's probation system is the nation's largest, however (Petersilia, Turner, Kahan, and Peterson, 1985), and the experiences of that system could prove instructive to other jurisdictions.

In many California counties (as in other jurisdictions throughout the United States) crowded court calendars, determinate sentencing guidelines, and increasingly conservative philosophies have made it difficult for judges to consider individual offenders' characteristics thoroughly. Thus judges, working in tandem with district attorneys, emphasize the legal variables of offense and criminal record at sentencing (see, for example, Forer, 1980; Lotz and Hewitt, 1977; Tinker, Quiring, and Pimentel, 1985). Probation officers function as employees of the court; generally they respond to judicial cues and emphasize similar variables in their presentence investigations. The probation officers' relationship to the court is ancillary; their status in relation to judges and other attorneys is subordinate. This does not mean that probation officers are completely passive; individual styles and personal philosophies influence their reports. Idiosyncratic approaches, however, usually are reserved for a few special cases. The vast majority of "normal" (Sudnow, 1965) cases are handled in a manner that follows relatively uniform patterns.

Hughes's (1958) work provides a useful perspective for understanding the relationship between probation officers' status and their presentence duties. According to Hughes, occupational duties within institutions often serve to maintain symbiotic status relationships as those in higher-status positions pass on lesser duties to subordinates. Other researchers (Blumberg, 1967; Neubauer, 1974; Rosecrance, 1985) have demonstrated that although judges may give lip service to the significance of presentence investigations, they remain suspicious of the probation officers' lack of legal training and the hearsay nature of the reports. Walker (1985) maintains that in highly visible cases judges tend to disregard the probation reports entirely. Thus the judiciary, by delegating the collection of routine information to probation officers, reaffirms its authority and legitimacy. In this context, the responsibility for compiling presentence reports can be considered a "dirty work" assignment (Hagan, 1975) that is devalued by the judiciary. Judges expect probation officers to submit noncontroversial reports that provide a facade of information, accompanied by bottom-line recommendations that do not deviate significantly from a consideration of offense and prior record. The research findings in this paper will show how probation officers work to achieve this goal.

In view of the large number of presentence reports submitted, it is surprising that so little information about the presentence investigation process is available. The factors used in arriving at a sentencing recommendation, the decision to include certain information, and the methods used in collecting data have not been described. The world of presentence investigators has not been explored by social science researchers. We lack research about the officers who prepare presentence reports, and hardly understand how they think and feel about those reports. The organizational dynamics and the status positions that influence presentence investigators have not been identified prominently (see, for example, Shover, 1979). In this article I intend to place probation officers' actions within a framework that will increase the existing knowledge of the presentence process. My research is informed by 15 years of experience as a probation officer, during which time I submitted hundreds of presentence reports.

Although numerous studies of probation practices have been conducted, an ethnographic perspective rarely has been included in this body of research, particularly in regard to research dealing with presentence investigations. Although questionnaire techniques (Katz, 1982), survey data (Hagan et al., 1979), and decision-making experiments (Carter, 1967) have provided some information about presentence reports, qualitative data, which often are available only through an insider's perspective,[1] are notably lacking. The subtle strategies and informal practices used routinely in preparing presentence reports often are hidden from outside researchers.

The research findings emphasize the importance of *typing* in the compilation of public documents (presentence reports). In this paper "typing" refers to "the process by which one person (the agent) arrives at a private definition of another (the target)" (Prus, 1975:81). A related activity, *designating*, occurs when "the typing agent reveals his attributions of the target to others" (Prus and Stratten, 1976:48). In the case of presentence investigations, private typings become designations when they are made part of an official court report. I will show that presentence recommendations are developed through a typing process in which individual offenders are subsumed into general dispositional categories. This process is influenced largely by probation officers' perceptions of factors that judicial figures consider appropriate; probation officers are aware that the ultimate purpose of their reports is to please the court. These perceptions are based on prior experience and are reinforced through judicial feedback.

Methods

The major sources of data used in this study were drawn from interviews with probation officers. Prior experience facilitated my ability to interpret the data. Interviews were conducted in two three-week periods during 1984 and 1985 in two medium-sized California counties. Both jurisdictions were governed by state determinate sentencing policies; in each, the district attorney's office remained active during sentencing and generally offered specific recommendations. I did not conduct a random sample but tried instead to interview all those who compiled adult presentence reports. In the two counties in question, officers who compiled presentence reports did not supervise defendants.[2]

Not all presentence writers agreed to talk with me; they cited busy schedules, lack of interest, or fear that I was a spy for the administration. Even so, I was able to interview 37 presentence investigators, approximately 75 percent of the total number of such employees in the two counties.[3] The officers interviewed included eight women and 29 men with a median age of 38.5 years, whose probation experience ranged from one year to 27 years. Their educational background generally included a bachelor's degree in a liberal arts subject (four had degrees in criminal justice, one in social work). Typically the officers regarded probation work as a "job" rather than a profession. With only a few exceptions, they did not read professional journals or attend probation association conventions.

The respondents generally were supportive of my research, and frequently commented that probation work had never been described adequately. My status as a former probation officer enhanced the interview process greatly. Because I could identify with their experiences, officers were candid, and I was able to collect qualitative data that reflected accurately the participants' perspectives. During the interviews I attempted to discover how probation officers conducted their presentence investigations. I wanted to know when a sentencing recommendation was decided, to ascertain which variables influenced a sentencing recommendation decision, and to learn how probation officers defined their role in the sentencing process.

Although the interviews were informal, I asked each of the probation officers the following questions:

1. What steps do you take in compiling a presentence report?
2. What is the first thing you do upon receiving a referral?
3. What do you learn from interviews with the defendant?
4. Which part of the process (in your opinion) is the most important?
5. Who reads your reports?
6. Which part of the report do the judges feel is most important?
7. How do your reports influence the judge?
8. What feedback do you get from the judge, the district attorney, the defense attorney, the defendant, your supervisor?

In addition to interviewing probation officers, I questioned six probation supervisors and seven judges on their views about how presentence reports were conducted.

The procedure I used to analyze the collected data was similar to the grounder theory method advocated by Glaser and Strauss (1967). This method seeks to develop analyses that are generated from the data themselves (Blumer, 1979). Thus in the beginning of the study I maintained a flexible and unstructured approach. This flexibility was particularly important because I wanted to ensure that my years in the field had not left me with a preconceived conceptual model and that my research was not an attempt to justify conclusions already reached. By facing the issue of possible subjectivity at each stage of the investigation, I let the data lead me rather than the other way around. As the data accumulated and as theories and propositions emerged, they were modified and compared, and in turn formed the groundwork for further data collection. Initially, for example, I attempted to frame the presentence process in the context of factors related to the individual officer (reporting style, experience, or criminal justice philosophy). I could no discern a regular pattern, however, so I analyzed other factors.

Findings

In the great majority of presentence investigations, the variables of present offense and prior criminal record determine the probation officer's final sentencing recommendation. The influence of these variables is so dominant that other considerations have minimal influence on probation recommendations. The chief rationale for this approach is "That's the way the judges want it." There are other styles of investigation; some officers attempt to consider factors in the defendant's social history, to reserve sentencing judgment until their investigation is complete, or to interject personal opinions. Elsewhere (Rosecrance, 1987), I have developed a typology of presentence investigators which describes individual styles; their types include self-explanatory categories such as hard-liners, bleeding-heart liberals, and team players as well as mossbacks (those who are merely putting in their time) and mavericks (those who strive continually for independence).

All types of probation officers, however, seek to develop credibility with the court. Such reputation building is similar to that reported by McCleary (1978) in his study of parole officers. In order to develop rapport with the court, probation officers must submit reports that facilitate a smooth work flow. Probation officer; assume that in the great majority of cases they can accomplish this goal by emphasizing offense and criminal record. Once the officers have established reputations as "producers," they have "earned" the right to some degree of discretion in their reporting. One investigation officer described this process succinctly: "When you've paid your dues, you're allowed some slack." Such discretion, however, is limited to a minority of cases, and in these "deviant" cases probation officers frequently allow social variables to influence their recommendation. In one report an experienced officer recommended probation for a convicted felon with a long prior record because the defendant's father agreed to pay for an intensive drug treatment program. In another case a probation officer decided that a first-time shoplifter had a "very bad attitude" and therefore recommended a stiff jail sentence rather than probation. Although these variations from normal procedure are interesting and important, they should not detract from our examination of an investigation process that is used in most cases.

On the basis of the research data, I found that the following patterns occur with sufficient regularity to be considered "typical." After considering offense and criminal record, probation officers place defendants into categories that represent the eventual court recommendation. This typing process occurs early in the course of presentence inquiry; the balance of the investigation is used to reaffirm the private typings that later will become official designations. In order to clarify the decision-making processes used by probation officers I will delineate the three stages in a presentence investigation: 1) typing the defendant, 2) gathering further information, and 3) filing the report.

Typing the Defendant

A presentence investigation is initiated when the court orders the probation department to prepare a report on a criminal defendant. Usually the initial court referral contains such information as police reports, charges against the defendant, court proceedings, plea-bargaining agreements (if any), offenses in which the defendant has pleaded or has been found guilty, and the defendant's prior criminal record. Probation officers regard such information as relatively unambiguous[4] and as part of the "official" record. The comment of a presentence investigator reflects the probation officer's perspective on the court referral:

> I consider the information in the court referral hard data. It tells me what I need to know about a case, without a lot of bullshit. I mean the guy has pled guilty to a certain offense—he can't get out of that. He has such and such a prior record—there's no changing that. So much of the stuff we put in these reports is subjective and open to interpretation. It's good to have some solid information.

Armed with information in the court referral, probation officers begin to type the defendants assigned for presentence investigation. Defendants are classified into general types based on possible sentence recommendations; a probation officer's statement indicates that this process begins early in a presentence investigation.

> Bottom line; it's the sentence recommendation that's important. That's what the judges and everybody wants to see. I start thinking about the recommendation as soon as I pick up the court referral. Why wait? The basic facts aren't going to change. Oh, I know some POs will tell you they weigh all the facts before coming up with a recommendation. But that's propaganda—we all start thinking recommendation right from the get-go.

At this stage in the investigation the factors known to probation officers are mainly legally relevant variables. The defendant's unique characteristics and special circumstances generally are unknown at this time. Although probation officers may know the offender's age, sex, and race, the relationship of these variables to the case is not yet apparent.

These initial typings are private definitions (Prus, 1975) based on the officer's experience and knowledge of the court system. On occasion, officers discuss the case informally with their colleagues or supervisors when they are not sure of a particular typing. Until the report is complete, their typing remains a private designation. In most cases the probation officers type defendants by considering the known and relatively irrefutable variables of offense and prior record. Probation officers are convinced that judges and district attorneys are most concerned with that part of their reports. I heard the following comment (or versions thereof) on many occasions: "Judges read the offense section, glance at the prior record, and then flip to the back and see what we recommend." Officers indicated that during informal discussions with judges it was made clear that offense and prior record are the determinants of sentencing in most cases. In some instances judges consider extralegal variables, but the officers indicated that this occurs only in "unusual" cases with "special" circumstances. One such case involved a probation grant for a woman who killed her husband after she had been a victim of spouse battering.

Probation investigators are in regular contact with district attorneys, and frequently discuss their investigations with them. In addition, district attorneys seem to have no compunction about calling the probation administration to complain about what they consider an inappropriate recommendation. Investigators agreed unanimously that district attorneys typically dismiss a defendant's social history as "immaterial" and want probation officers to stick to the legal facts.

Using offense and prior record as criteria, probation officers place defendants into dispositional (based on recommendation) types. In describing these types[5] I have retained the terms used by probation officers themselves in the typing process. The following typology is community (rather than researcher) designated (Emerson, 1981; Spradley, 1970): (1) deal case, (2) diversion case, (3) joint case, (4) probation case with some jail time, (5) straight probation case. Within each of these dispositional types, probation officers designate the severity of punishment by labeling the case either lightweight or heavy-duty.

A designation of "lightweight" means that the defendant will be accorded some measure of leniency because the offense was minor, because the offender had no prior criminal record, or because the criminal activity (regardless of the penal code violation) was relatively innocuous. Heavy-duty cases receive more severe penalties because the offense, the offender, or the circumstances of the offense are deemed particularly serious. Diversion and straight probation types generally are considered lightweight, while the majority of join cases are considered heavy-duty. Cases involving personal violence invariably are designated as heavy-duty. Most misdemeanor cases in which the defendant has no prior criminal record or a relatively minor record are termed lightweight. If the defendant has an extensive criminal record, however, even misdemeanor cases can call for stiff penalties; therefore such cases are considered heavy-duty. Certain felony cases can be regarded as lightweight if there was no violence, if the victim's loss was minimal, or if the defendant had no prior convictions. On occasion, even an offense like armed robbery can be considered lightweight. The following example (taken from an actual report) is one such instance: a first-time offender with a simulated gun held up a Seven-Eleven store and then returned to the scene, gave back the money, and asked the store employees to call the police.

The typings are general recommendations; specifics such as terms and conditions of probation or diversion and length of incarceration are worked out later in the investigation. The following discussion will clarify some of the criteria for arriving at a typing.

Deal cases involve situations in which a plea bargain exists. In California, many plea bargains specify specific sentencing stipulations; probation officers rarely recommend dispositions contrary to those stipulated in plea-bargaining agreements. Although probation officers allegedly are free to recommend a sentence different from that contained in the plea bargain, they have learned that such an action is unrealistic (and often counter-productive to their own interests) because judges inevitably uphold the primacy of sentence agreements. The following observation represents the probation officers' view of plea-bargaining deals:

> It's stupid to try and bust a deal. What's the percentage? Who needs the hassle? The judge always honors the deal — after all, he was part of it. Everyone, including the defendant, has already agreed. It's all nice and neat, all wrapped up. We are supposed to rubber-stamp the package — and we do. Everyone is better off that way.

Diversion cases typically involve relatively minor offenses committed by those with no prior record, and are considered "a snap" by probation officers. In most cases, those referred for diversion have been screened already by the district attorney's office; the probation investigator merely agrees that they are eligible and therefore should be granted diversionary relief (and eventual dismissal of charges). In rare instances when there has been an oversight and the defendant is ineligible (because of prior criminal convictions), the probation officer informs the court, and criminal proceedings are resumed. Either situation involves minimal decision making by probation officers about what disposition to recommend. Presentence investigators approach diversion cases in a perfunctory, almost mechanical manner.

The last three typings generally refer to cases in which the sentencing recommendations are ambiguous and some decision making is required of probation officers. These types represent the major consequences of criminal sentencing: incarceration and/or probation. Those categorized as joint (prison) cases are denied probation; instead the investigator recommends an appropriate prison sentence. In certain instances the nature of the offense (e.g., rape, murder, or arson) renders defendants legally ineligible for probation. In other situations, the defendants' prior record (especially felony convictions) makes it impossible to grant probation (see, e.g., Neubauer, 1974:240). In many cases the length of prison sentences has been set by legal statute and can be increased or decreased only marginally (depending on the aggravating or mitigating circumstances of the case).

In California, the majority of defendants sentenced to prison receive a middle term (between minimum and maximum); the length of time varies with the offense. Those cases that fall outside the middle term usually do so for reasons related to the offense (e.g., using a weapon) or to the criminal record (prior felony convictions or, conversely, no prior criminal record). Those typed originally as joint cases are treated differently from other probation applicants: concerns with rehabilitation or with the defendant's life situation are no longer relevant, and proper punishment becomes the focal point of inquiry. This perspective was described as follows by a probation officer respondent: "Once I know so-and-so is a heavy-duty joint case I don't think in terms of rehabilitation or social planning. It becomes a matter of how long to salt the sucker away, and that's covered by the code."

For those who are typed as probation cases, the issue for the investigator becomes whether to recommend some time in jail as a condition of probation. This decision is made with reference to whether the case is lightweight or heavy-duty. Straight probation usually is reserved for those convicted of relatively innocuous offenses or for those without a prior criminal record (first-timers). Some probation officers admitted candidly that all things being equal, middle-class defendants are more likely than other social classes to receive straight probation. The split sentence (probation and jail time) has become popular and is a consideration in most misdemeanor and felony cases, especially when the defendant has a prior criminal record. In addition, there is a feeling that drug offenders should receive a jail sentence as part of probation to deter them from future drug use.

Once a probation officer has decided that "some jail time is in order," the ultimate recommendation includes that condition. Although the actual amount of time frequently is determined late in the case, the probation officer's opinion that a jail sentence should be imposed remains constant. The following comment typifies the sentiments of probation officers whom I have observed and also illustrates the imprecision of recommending a period of time in custody:

> It's not hard to figure out who needs some jail. The referral sheet can tell you that. What's hard to know is exactly how much time. Ninety days or six months—who knows what's fair? We put down some number but it is usually an arbitrary figure. No one has come up with a chart that correlates rehabilitation with jail time.

Compiling Further Information

Once an initial typing has been completed, the next investigative stage involves collecting further information about the defendant. During this stage most of the data to be collected consists of extralegal considerations. The defendant is interviewed and his or her social history is delineated. Probation officers frequently contact collateral sources such as school officials, victims, doctors, counselors, and relatives to learn more about the defendant's individual circumstances. This aspect of the presentence investigation involves considerable time and effort on the part of probation officers. Such information is gathered primarily to legitimate earlier probation officer typings or to satisfy judicial requirements; recommendations seldom are changed during this stage. A similar pattern was described by a presentence investigator:

> Interviewing these defendants and working up a social history takes time. In most cases it's really unnecessary since I've already decided what I am going to do. We all know that a recommendation is governed by the offense and prior record. All the rest is just stuffing to fill out the court report, to make the judge look like he's got all the facts.

Presentence interviews with defendants (a required part of the investigation) frequently are routine interactions that were described by a probation officer as "anticlimactic." These interviews invariably are conducted in settings familiar to probation officers, such as jail interviewing rooms or probation department offices. Because the participants lack trust in each other, discussions rarely are candid and open. Probation officers are afraid of being conned or manipulated because they assume that defendants "will say anything to save themselves." Defendants are trying to present themselves in a favorable light and are wary of divulging any information that might be used against them.

It is assumed implicitly in the interview process that probation officers act as interrogators and defendants as respondents. Because presentence investigators select the questions, they control the course of the interview and elicit the kind of responses that serve to substantiate their original defendant typings. A probationer described his presentence interview to me as follows:

> I knew what the P.O. wanted me to say. She had me pegged as a nice middle-class kid who had fallen in with a bad crowd. So that's how I came off. I was contrite, a real boy scout who had learned his lesson. What an acting job! I figured if I didn't act up I'd get probation.

A probation officer related how she conducted presentence interviews:

> I'm always in charge during the interviews. I know what questions to ask in order to fill out my report. The defendants respond just about the way I expect them to. They hardly ever surprise me.

On occasion, prospective probationers refuse to go along with structured presentence interviews. Some offenders either attempt to control the interview or are openly hostile to probation officers. Defendants who try to dominate interviews often can be dissuaded by reminders such as "I don't think you really appreciate the seriousness of your situation" and "I'm the one who asks the questions here." Some defendants, however, show blatant disrespect for the court process by flaunting a disregard for possible sanctions.

Most probation officers have interviewed some defendants who simply don't seem to care what happens to them. A defendant once informed an investigation officer: "I don't give a fuck what you motherfuckers try and do to me. I'm going to do what I fuckin' well please. Take your probation and stick it." Another defendant told her probation officer: "I'm going to shoot up every chance I get. I need my fix more than

I need probation." Probation officers categorize belligerent defendants and those unwilling to "play the probation game" as dangerous or irrational (see, e.g., McCleary, 1978). Frequently in these situations the investigator's initial typing is no longer valid, and probation either will be denied or will be structured stringently. Most interviews, however, proceed in a predictable manner as probation officers collect information that will be included in the section of the report terms "defendant's statement."

Although some defendants submit written comments, most of their statements actually are formulated by the probation officer. In a sociological sense, the defendant's statement can be considered an "account" (Scott and Lyman, 1968). While conducting presentence interviews, probation officers typically attempt to shape the defendant's account to fit their own preconceived typing. Many probation officers believe that the defendant's attitude toward the offense and toward the future prospects for leading a law-abiding life are the most important parts of the statement. In most presentence investigations the probation investigator identifies and interprets the defendant's subjective attitudes and then incorporates them into the report. Using this procedure, probation officers look for and can report attitudes that "logically fit" with their final sentencing recommendation (see, for example, Davis, 1983).

Defendants who have been typed as prison cases typically are portrayed as holding socially unacceptable attitudes about their criminal actions and unrealistic or negative attitudes about future prospects for living an upright life. Conversely, those who have been typed as probation material are described as having acceptable attitudes, such as contriteness about the present offense and optimism about their ability to lead a crime-free life. The structuring of accounts about defendant attitudes was described by a presentence investigator in the following manner:

> When POS talk about the defendant's attitude we really mean how that attitude relates to the case. Naturally I'm not going to write about what a wonderful attitude the guy has—how sincere he seems—and then recommend sending him to the joint. That wouldn't make sense. The judges want consistency. If a guy has a shitty attitude but is going to get probation anyway, there's no percentage in playing up his attitude problem.

In most cases the presentence interview is the only contact between the investigating officer and the defendant. The brevity of this contact and the lack of post-report interaction foster a legalistic perspective. Investigators are concerned mainly with "getting the case through court" rather than with special problems related to supervising probationers on a long-term basis. One-time-only interviews rarely allow probation officers to become emotionally involved with their cases; the personal and individual aspects of the defendant's personality generally are not manifested during a half-hour presentence interview. For many probation officers the emotional distance from offenders is one of the benefits of working in presentence units. Such an opinion was expressed by an investigation officer: "I really like the one-shot-only part of this job. I don't have time to get caught up with the clients. I can deal with facts and not worry about individual personalities."

The probation officer has wide discretion in the type of collateral information that is collected from sources other than the defendant or the official record. Although a defendant's social history must be sketched in the presentence report, the supplementation of that history is left to individual investigators. There are few established guidelines for the investigating officer to follow, except that the psychiatric or psychological reports should be submitted when there is compelling evidence that the offender is mentally disturbed. Informal guidelines, however, specify that in misdemeanor cases reports should be shorter and more concise than in felony cases. The officers indicated that reports for municipal court (all misdemeanor cases) should range from four to six pages in length, while superior court reports (felony cases) were expected to be six to nine pages long. In controversial cases (to which only the most experienced officers are assigned) presentence reports are expected to be longer and to include considerable social data. Reports in these cases have been as long as 30 pages.

Although probation officers learn what general types of information to include through experience and feedback from judges and supervisors, they are allowed considerable leeway in deciding exactly what to put in their reports (outside of the offense and prior record sections). Because investigators decide what collateral sources are germane to the case, they tend to include information that will reflect favorably on their sentencing recommendation. In this context the observation of one probation officer is understandable: "I pick from the mass of possible sources just which ones to put in the report. Do you think I'm going to pick people who make my recommendation look weak? No way!"

Filing the Report

The final stage in the investigation includes dictating the report, having it approved by a probation supervisor, and appearing in court. All three of these activities serve to reinforce the importance of prior record and offense in sentencing recommendations. At the time of dictation, probation officers determine what to include in the report and how to phrase their remarks. For the first time in the investigation, they receive formal feedback from official sources. Presentence reports are read by three groups important to the probation officers: probation supervisors, district attorneys, and judges. Probation officers recognize that for varying reasons, all these groups emphasize the legally relevant variables of offense and prior criminal record when considering an appropriate sentencing recommendation.[6] Such considerations reaffirm the probation officer's initial private typing. A probation investigator described this process:

> After I've talked to the defendants I think maybe some of them deserve to get special consideration. But then when I remember who's going to look at the reports. My supervisor, the DA, the judge; they don't care about all the personal details. When all is said and done, what's really important to them is the offense and the defendant's prior record. I know that stuff from the start. It makes me wonder why we have to jack ourselves around to do long reports.

Probation officers assume that their credibility as presentence investigators will be enhanced if their sentencing recommendations meet with the approval of probation supervisors, district attorneys, and judges. On the other hand, officers whose recommendations are consistently "out of line" are subject to censure or transfer, or they find themselves engaged in "running battles" (Shover, 1974:357) with court officials. During the last stage of the investigation probation officers must consider how to ensure that their reports will go through court without "undue personal hassle." Most investigation officers have learned that presentence recommendations based on a consideration of prior record and offense can achieve that goal.

Although occupational self-interest is an important component in deciding how to conduct a presentence investigation, other factors also are involved. Many probation officers agree with the idea of using legally relevant variables as determinants of recommendations. These officers embrace the retributive value of this concept and see it as an equitable method for framing their investigation. Other officers reported that probation officers' discretion had been "short-circuited" by determinate sentencing guidelines and that they were reduced to "merely going through the motions" in conducting their investigations. Still other officers view the use of legal variables to structure recommendations as an acceptable bureaucratic shortcut to compensate partially for large case assignments. One probation officer stated, "If the department wants us to keep pumping out presentence reports we can't consider social factors — we just don't have time." Although probation officers are influenced by various dynamics, there seems little doubt that in California, the social history which once was considered the "heart and soul" of presentence probation reports (Reckless, 1967:673) has been largely devalued.

Summary and Conclusions

In this study I provide a description and an analysis of the processes used by probation investigators in preparing presentence reports. The research findings based on interview data indicate that probation officers tend to de-emphasize individual defendants' characteristics and that their probation recommendations are not influenced directly by factors such as sex, age, race, socioeconomic status, or work record. Instead, probation officers emphasize the variables of instant offense and prior criminal record. The finding that offense and prior record are the main considerations of probation officers with regard to sentence recommendations agrees with a substantial body of research (Bankston, 1983; Carter and Wilkens, 1967; Dawson, 1969; Lotz and Hewitt, 1977; Robinson, Carter, and Wahl, 1969; Wallace, 1974; Walsh, 1985).

My particular contribution has been to supply the ethnographic observations and the data that explain this phenomenon. I have identified the process whereby offense and prior record come to occupy the central role in decision making by probation officers. This identification underscores the significance of private typings in determining official designations. An analysis of probation practices suggests that the function of the presentence investigation is more ceremonial than instrumental (Hagan, 1985).

I show that early in the investigation probation officers, using offense and prior record as guidelines, classify defendants into types; when the typing process is complete, probation officers essentially have decided on the sentence recommendation that will be recorded later in their official designation. The subsequent course of investigations is determined largely by this initial private typing. Further data collection is influenced by a sentence recommendation that already has been firmly established. This finding answers affirmatively the research question posed by Carter (1967:211):

> Do probation officers, after "deciding" on a recommendation early in the presentence investigation, seek further information which justifies the decision, rather than information which might lead to modification or rejection of that recommendation?

The type of information and observation contained in the final presentence report is generated to support the original recommendation decision. Probation officers do not regard defendant typings as tentative hypotheses to be disproved through inquiry but rather as firm conclusions to be justified in the body of the report.

Although the presentence interview has been considered an important part of the investigation (Spencer, 1983), I demonstrate that it does not significantly alter probation officers' perceptions. In most cases probation officers dominate presentence interviews; interaction between the participants is guarded. The nature of interviews between defendants and probation officers is important in itself, further research is needed to identify the dynamics that prevail in these interactions.

Attitudes attributed to defendants often are structured by probation officers to reaffirm the recommendation already formulated. The defendant's social history, long considered an integral part of the presentence report, in reality has little bearing on sentencing considerations. In most cases the presentence is no longer a vehicle for social inquiry but rather a typing process which considers mainly the defendant's prior criminal record and the seriousness of the criminal offense. Private attorneys in growing numbers have become disenchanted with the quality of probation investigations and have commissioned presentence probation reports privately (Rodgers, Gitchoff, and Paur, 1984). At present, however, such a practice is generally available only for wealthy defendants.

The presentence process that I have described is used in the great majority of cases; it is the "normal" procedure. Even so, probation officers are not entirely passive actors in this process. On occasion they will give serious consideration to social variables in arriving at a sentencing recommendation. In special circumstances officers will allow individual defendants' characteristics to influence their report. In addition, probation officers who have developed credibility with the court are allowed some discretion in compiling presentence reports. This discretion is not unlimited, however; it is based on a prior record of producing reports that meet the court's approval, and is contingent on continuing to do so. A presentence writer said, "You can only afford to go to bat for defendants in a few select cases; if you try to do it too much, you get a reputation as being 'out of step.' "

This research raises the issue of probation officers' autonomy. Although I depict presentence investigators as having limited autonomy, other researchers (Hagan, 1975; Myers, 1979; Walsh, 1985) contend that probation officers have considerable leeway in recommendation. This contradictory evidence can be explained in large part by the type of sentencing structure, the professionalism of probation workers, and the role of the district attorney at sentencing. Walsh's study (1985), for example, which views probation officers as important actors in the presentence process, was conducted in a jurisdiction with indeterminate sentencing, where the probation officers demonstrated a high degree of professionalism and the prosecutors "rarely made sentencing recommendations." A very different situation existed in the California counties that I studied: determinate sentencing was enforced, probation officers were not organized professionally, and the district attorneys routinely made specific court recommendations. It seems apparent that probation officers' autonomy must be considered with reference to judicial jurisdiction.

In view of the primacy of offense and prior record in sentencing considerations, the efficacy of current presentence investigation practices is doubtful. It seems ineffective and wasteful to continue to collect a mass of social data of uncertain relevance. Yet an analysis of courtroom culture suggests that the presentence investigation helps maintain judicial mythology as well as probation officer legitimacy. Although judges generally do not have the time or the inclination to consider individual variables thoroughly, the performance of a presentence investigation perpetuates the myth of individualized sentences. Including a presentence report in the court file gives the appearance of individualization without influencing sentencing practices significantly.

Even in a state like California, where determinate sentencing allegedly has replaced individualized justice, the judicial system feels obligated to maintain the appearance of individualization. After observing the court system in California for several years I am convinced that a major reason for maintaining such a practice is to make it easier for criminal defendants to accept their sentences. The presentence report allows defendants to feel that their case at least has received a considered decision. One judge admitted candidly that the "real purpose" of the presentence investigation was to convince defendants that they were not getting "the fast shuffle." He observed further that if defendants were sentenced without such investigations, many would complain and would file "endless appeals" over what seems to them a hasty sentencing decision. Even though judges typically consider only offense and prior record in a sentencing decision, they want defendants to believe that their cases are being judged individually. The presentence investigation allows this assumption to be maintained. In addition, some judges use the probation officer's report as an excuse for a particular type of sentence. In some instances they deny responsibility for the sentence, implying that their "hands were tied" by the recommendation. Thus judges are taken "off the hook" for meting out an unpopular sentence. Further research is needed to substantiate the significance of these latent functions of the presentence investigation.

The presentence report is a major component in the legitimacy of the probation movement; several factors support the probation officers' stake in maintaining their role in these investigations. Historically, probation has been wedded to the concept of individualized treatment. In theory, the presentence report is suited ideally to reporting on defendants' individual circumstances. From a historical perspective (Rothman, 1980) this ideal has always been more symbolic than substantive, but if the legitimacy of the presentence report is questioned, so then is the entire purpose of probation.

Regardless of its usefulness (or lack of usefulness), it is doubtful that probation officials would consider the diminution or abolition of presentence reports. The number of probation workers assigned to presentence investigations is substantial, and their numbers represent an obvious source of bureaucratic power. Conducting presentence investigations allows probation officers to remain visible with the court and the public. The media often report on controversial probation cases, and the presentence writers generally have more contact and more association with judges than do others in the probation department.

As ancillary court workers, probation officers are assigned the dirty work of collecting largely irrelevant data on offenders (Hagan, 1975; Hughes, 1958). Investigation officers have learned that emphasizing offense and prior record in their reports will enhance relationships with judges and district attorneys, as well as improving their occupational standing within probation departments. Thus the presentence investigation serves to maintain the court's claim of individualized concern while preserving the probation officer's role, although a subordinate role, in the court system.[7]

The myth of individualization serves various functions, but it also raises serious questions. In an era of severe budget restrictions (Schumacher, 1985) should scarce resources be allocated to compiling predictable presentence reports of dubious value? If social variables are considered only in a few cases, should courts continue routinely to require presentence reports in all felony matters (as is the practice in California)? In summary, we should address the issue of whether the criminal justice system can afford the ceremony of a probation presentence investigation.

Endnotes

[1] For a full discussion of the insider-outsider perspective in criminal justice see Marquart (1986).

[2] In a few jurisdictions, officers who prepare investigations also supervise the defendants after probation has been granted, but, this procedure is becoming less prevalent in contemporary probation (Clear and Cole, 1986). It is possible that extralegal variables play a significant role in the supervision process, but this paper is concerned specifically with presentence investigations.

[3] There was no exact way to determine whether the 25 percent of the officers I was unable to interview conducted their presentence investigations significantly differently from those I interviewed. Personal observation, however, and the comments of the officers I interviewed (with whom I discussed this issue) indicated that those who refused used similar methods in processing their presentence reports.

[4] On occasion police reports are written vaguely and are subject to various interpretations; rap sheets are not always clear, especially when some of the final dispositions have not been recorded.

[5] I did not include terminal misdemeanor dispositions, in which probation is denied in favor of fines or jail sentences, in this typology. Such dispositions are comparatively rare and relatively insignificant.

[6] Although defense attorneys also read the presentence reports, their reactions generally do not affect the probation officers' occupational standing (McHugh, 1973; Rosecrance, 1985).

[7] I did not discuss the role of presentence reports in the prison system. Traditionally, probation reports were part of an inmate's jacket or file and were used as a basis for classification and treatment. The position of probation officers was legitimated further by the fact that prison officials also used the presentence report. I would suggest, however, that the advent of prison overcrowding and the accompanying security concerns have rendered presentence reports relatively meaningless. This contention needs to be substantiated before presentence reports are abandoned completely.

References

Allen, H. E., & Simonsen, C. E. (1986). *Corrections in America*. New York: Macmillan.
Bankston, W. B. (1983). Legal and extralegal offender traits and decision-making in the criminal justice system. *Sociological Spectrum, 3*, 1–18.
Blumberg, A. (1967). *Criminal justice*. Chicago: Quadrangle.
Blumer, M. (1979). Concepts in the analysis of qualitative data. *Sociological Review, 27*, 651–677.

Blumstein, A. J., Martin, S., & Holt, N. (1983). *Research on sentencing: The search for reform*. Washington, DC: National Academy Press.

Carter, R. M. (1967). The presentence report and the decision-making process. *Journal of Research in Crime and Delinquency, 4*, 203–211.

Carter, R. M., & Wilkins, L. T. (1967). Some factors in sentencing policy. *Journal of Criminal Law, Criminology, and Police Science, 58*, 503–514.

Clear, T., & Cole, G. (1986). *American corrections*. Monterey, CA: Brooks/Cole.

Davis, J. R. (1983). Academic and practical aspects of probation: A comparison. *Federal Probation, 47*, 7–10.

Dawson, R. (1969). *Sentencing*. Boston: Little, Brown.

Emerson, R. M. (1981). Ethnography and understanding members' worlds. In R. M. Emerson (Ed.), *Contemporary field research* (pp. 19–35). Boston: Little, Brown.

Forer, L. G. (1980). *Criminals and victims*. New York: Norton.

Glaser, B., & Strauss, A. (1967). *The discovery of grounded theory*. Chicago: Aldine.

Goldsborough, E., & Burbank, E. (1968). The probation officer and his personality. In C. L. Newman (Ed.), *Sourcebook on probation, parole, and pardons* (pp. 104–112). Springfield, IL: Charles C. Thomas.

Hagan, J. (1975). The social and legal construction of criminal justice: A study of the presentence process. *Social Problems, 22*, 620–637.

Hagan, J. (1977). Criminal justice in rural and urban communities: A study of the bureaucratization of justice. *Social Forces, 55*, 597–612.

Hagan, J. (1985). *Modern criminology: Crime, criminal behavior, and its control*. New York: McGraw-Hill.

Hagan, J., Hewitt, J., & Alwin, D. (1979). Ceremonial justice: Crime and punishment in a loosely coupled system. *Social Forces, 58*, 506–525.

Hogarth, J. (1971). *Sentencing as a human process*. Toronto: University of Toronto Press.

Hughes, E. C. (1958). *Men and their work*. New York: Free Press.

Katz, J. (1982). The attitudes and decisions of probation officers. *Criminal Justice and Behavior, 9*, 455–475.

Kingsnorth, R., & Rizzo, L. (1979). Decision-making in the criminal courts: Continuities and discontinuities. *Criminology, 17*, 3–14.

Lotz, R., & Hewitt, J. (1977). The influence of legally irrelevant factors on felony sentencing. *Sociological Inquiry, 47*, 39–48.

Marquart, J. W. (1986). Outsiders as insiders: Participant observation in the role of a prison guard. *Justice Quarterly, 3*, 15–32.

McCleary, R. (1978). *Dangerous men*. Beverly Hills: Sage.

McCleary, R., Nienstadt, B., & Erven, J. (1982). Uniform crime reports as organizational outcomes: Three time series experiments. *Social Problems, 29*, 361–373.

McHugh, J. J. (1973). Some comments on natural conflict between counsel and probation officer. *American Journal of Corrections, 3*, 15–32.

Michalowski, R. J. (1985). *Order, law and crime*. New York: Random House.

Murrah, A. (1963). Prison or probation? In B. Kay & C. Vedder (Eds.), *Probation and parole* (pp. 63–78). Springfield, IL: Charles C. Thomas.

Myers, M. A. (1979). Offended parties and official reactions: Victims and the sentencing of criminal defendants. *Sociological Quarterly, 20*, 529–546.

Neubauer, D. (1974). *Criminal justice in middle America*. Morristown, NJ: General Learning.

Petersilia, J., Turner, S., Kahan, J., & Peterson, J. (1985). Executive summary of Rand's study, granting felons probation. *Crime and Delinquency, 31,* 379–392.

Prus, R. (1975). Labeling theory: A statement on typing. *Sociological Focus, 8,* 79–96.

Prus, R., & Stratten, J. (1976). Factors in the decision-making of North Carolina probation officers. *Federal Probation, 40,* 48–53.

Reckless, W. C. (1967). *The crime problem.* New York: Appleton.

Robinson, J., Carter, R., & Wahl, A. (1969). *The San Francisco project.* Berkeley: University of California School of Criminology.

Rodgers, T. A., Gitchoff, G. T., & Paur, I. (1984). The privately commissioned presentence report. In R. M. Carter, D. Glaser, & L. T. Wilkins (Eds.), *Probation, parole, and community corrections* (pp. 21–30). New York: Wiley.

Rosecrance, J. (1985). The probation officers' search for credibility: Ball park recommendations. *Crime and Delinquency, 31,* 539–554.

Rosecrance, J. (1987). A typology of presentence probation investigators. *International Journal of Offender Therapy and Comparative Criminology, 31,* 163–177.

Rothman, D. (1980). *Conscience and convenience: The asylum and its alternatives in progressive America.* Boston: Little, Brown.

Schumacher, M. A. (1985). Implementation of a client classification and case management system: A practitioner's view. *Crime and Delinquency, 31,* 445–455.

Scott, M., & Lyman, S. (1968). Accounts. *American Sociological Review, 33,* 46–62.

Shover, N. (1974). Experts and diagnosis in correctional agencies. *Crime and Delinquency, 20,* 347–358.

Shover, N. (1979). *A sociology of American corrections.* Homewood, IL: Dorsey.

Spencer, J. W. (1983). Accounts, attitudes and solutions: Probation officer-defendant negotiations of subjective orientations. *Social Problems, 30,* 570–581.

Spradley, J. P. (2000 [1970]). *You owe yourself a drunk: An ethnography of urban nomads.* Prospect Heights, IL: Waveland Press.

Sudnow, D. (1965). Normal crimes: Sociological features of the penal code. *Social Problems, 12,* 255–276.

Tinker, J. N., Quiring, J., & Pimentel, Y. (1985). Ethnic bias in California courts: A case study of Chicano and Anglo felony defendants. *Sociological Inquiry, 55,* 83–96.

Walker, S. (1985). *Sense and nonsense about crime.* Monterey, CA: Brooks/Cole.

Wallace, J. (1974). Probation administration. In D. Glaser (Ed.), *Handbook of criminology* (pp. 940–970). Chicago: Rand-McNally.

Walsh, A. (1985). The role of the probation officer in the sentencing process. *Criminal Justice and Behavior, 12,* 289–303.

Section 5

Change in Criminal Justice Organizations

No other topic has generated more discussion and debate among citizens, politicians, and criminal justice administrators over the past decade than change and reform. Initiatives have been proposed across the country to address a myriad of criminal justice problems. Whether the issue is jail overcrowding, the police use of force, or appropriate sentencing schemes, both critics and reformers have proposed some interesting and controversial reforms for the criminal justice system. The primary concern for criminal justice administrators is how these change efforts will affect their organizations. History is replete with examples of how intended consequences are very rarely realized in criminal justice reform movements. Instead, what has been produced is a host of unintended consequences and bad results. While reformer intentions generally have been good, the aphorism that the road to hell is paved with good intentions is no more accurate than in criminal justice reform and change platforms.

The first article in this final section explores the dangers of criminal justice reform. Doleschal provides an excellent analysis of how reforms tend to fall into circularity. Today's reforms, over time, resemble the practices of the past; in some cases the reforms actually do more harm than good. Criminal justice administrators are aware of this unavoidable consequence, yet in many cases they are impotent or powerless to do anything about reforms, particularly those reform efforts that are externally imposed and politically charged. Doleschal warns both the criminal justice administrator and the reformer that all change programs have consequences and that if reform is to have any real and long-lasting impact, the implementation process should be based more on circumspection rather than zeal.

Allen in the second piece in this section examined the impediments to changing police organizations from a traditional, top-down hierarchy to the more flexible and open organizational structure found within a community policing model. She documents not only the impediments to change within police organization, but more importantly, those factors that seem to facilitate change. Of particular importance to the change process within police organizations are individual attitudes and pressure to change. Police administrators have the ability to influence both of these variables if they desire change within their organizations. The process of change is enhanced by the commitment of police administrators to the change process and the influence they can engender toward accepting change among police officers in the rank and file. Planning for change is a long-term process and a commitment. If this is not recognized by administrators, then the possibility of promoting and instituting significant change within criminal justice organizations is drastically reduced.

Employing a case study approach, Zupan analyzes the effects of improper planning on a jail environment. Her examination is in tune with what the sociologist Charles Perrow refers to as gross-malfunctioning analysis. The insightful examination shows how county officials, in their zeal to make some money by filling spare beds in their jail, produced a situation where the institution became unsafe and unmanageable. Poor planning and poor communication fostered an environment where correctional officers, inmates, and jail administrators were constantly at odds with one another. The article's value, however, lies in its realization that change and reform initiatives must be understood within the context of an organization's mission and purpose. In this case, it may be that a jail is not and can never be a prison. The former is designed to house short-term inmates, while the latter is meant for long-term prisoners. Not recognizing the primary purposes of criminal justice organizations is what plagues many reform efforts. In fact, the attempt in the 1990s to "privatize" and economize correctional matters may be one of the most pressing issues facing jail administrators and prison officials. Moreover, such attempts may also have adverse consequences when imposed upon criminal justice organizations in a haphazard or ill-conceived manner.

Shichor examines the effects of one such attempt by exploring penal policy and the movement toward "three strikes and you're out" laws. Shichor shows how the "new penology" has refocused the crime discussion by stressing the control of crime in the aggregate and, more importantly, has adopted the buzz words and practices of the private sector: efficiency, predictability, and control. Three-strikes laws are consistent with these practices, yet it is not clear that through the implementation of such laws there has been a reduction in the crime problem. Shichor, in fact, argues the exact opposite. He shows the deleterious effects of such laws—more irrationalities than rationalities. Through metaphor, Shichor reveals how the new penology is part of a larger trend toward the commodification and "McDonaldization" of American society. Questions for both reformers and criminal justice administrators, however, remain. As with earlier articles, Shichor suggests that such reform efforts are difficult to evaluate and to implement.

Schafer continues this line of reasoning in her examination of judicial reform at a local jail. Her analysis points to the problems of gaining compliance among criminal justice system actors. The most important contribution lies in the discussion of the timeline of the reform efforts. Change ultimately occurred, but it was slow in coming. On the one hand both internal and external constituent groups were parties to change, yet on the other hand, obstinate and resistant to change. Even though federal court intervention was present, the parties were ever vigilant in advancing their positions. Schafer's presentation clearly brings home an obvious point when discussing criminal justice reform: Individual interests are instrumental to any reform program and criminal justice administrators must be sensitive to these concerns.

Beyond individual and organizational interests, change must be understood within the context of a developing body of scientific knowledge. Ferguson provides an interesting and compelling justification for the use of research in correctional organizations. She notes how in the correctional treatment literature there have been many scientifically documented successful interventions with offender populations. How a correctional administrator incorporates this knowledge into the organization becomes another matter. Ferguson notes the importance of understanding knowledge in the organizational context and framing change contingent upon the many factors that affect the implementation of knowledge within correctional organizations.

In the seventh piece of this section, Klockars discusses the many "circumlocutions" that have been presented by police reformers over the past one hundred years to justify the fact that the police are the only legitimate exerciser of nonnegotiable coercive force in a democracy. This unsettling reality has to be justified through a series of justificatory premises and rhetoric. In contemporary times, the newest circumlocution is community policing. Klockars suggests, as a circumlocution, community policing efforts are offered as part of a change agenda that alters the structure and functions of police, yet further analyses reveal that community policing efforts may be the "new" approach that attempts to mask the reality of police work that is rooted in the coercive power of the state to control criminal behavior. As a proponent of change, it has to be questioned if community policing efforts really change anything or are they just the latest police circumlocution.

Lovell concludes this section by expanding on the role of interests in reform by examining how research influences criminal justice organizations. He goes to the core of organizational analysis by looking at how information is collected and used by correctional organizations. In this case, his description is of how information serves the interests of prison administrators. Through a revealing analysis, Lovell demonstrates what many researchers are hesitant to face or discuss, namely that research must have some instrumental purpose for correctional administrators in order for it to be useful to them. By emphasizing bureaucratic and organizational constraints, Lovell informs the reader that research use and nonuse is highly structured and contingent upon specific demands in the work setting. He shows how research use and nonuse is critical to reformers who seek to change criminal justice organizations.

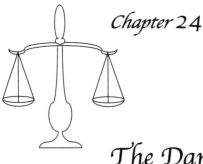

Chapter 24

The Dangers of Criminal Justice Reform

Eugene Doleschal

Several years ago, Robert Martinson startled the criminal justice community by presenting convincing evidence that "nothing works" — that no type of correctional effort is capable of reforming offenders, of reducing recidivism. Although he has had many critics, and volumes of comments on his main work[1] have been written, his basic point is driven home again and again. Almost every day, the Information Center of the National Council on Crime and Delinquency receives evidence from evaluative studies that Martinson was indeed correct. One solution to this discouraging and humbling finding was well expressed by Edwin Schur, in his *Radical Non-Intervention*: That is, people should be left alone as much as possible. They and society are better off if we intervene as little as possible and then only when absolutely necessary.[2]

Evidence is also accumulating about the effects of efforts to reform the criminal and juvenile justice systems. The highly disturbing findings of evaluations show that well-intentioned humanitarian reforms designed to lessen criminal justice penalties either do not achieve their objectives or actually produce consequences opposite those intended. In other words, it may be said that "nothing works" in criminal justice reform, as in offender rehabilitation. Worse than this, criminal justice

Eugene Doleschal, *The Dangers of Criminal Justice Reform*, pp. 133–152, copyright © 1982 by Sage Publications. Reprinted by permission of Sage Publications.

reforms tend to backfire, making things worse from the reformer's point of view, not better.

This review will examine some of the literature on the untoward effects of criminal justice reforms, draw on evidence from other disciplines exhibiting similar patterns, and attempt to point a way out of the dilemma.

Adult Criminal Justice Reforms

During the recent past an increasing number of criminal justice researchers and writers have expressed concern over the direction of diversion and similar "alternatives to incarceration." Those who helped develop pretrial diversion programs are deeply troubled by the way they have worked out. Programs have had a minimal effect on defendants, and judges and prosecutors are using them to widen the net of social control.[3]

The Vera Institute of Justice of New York studied the effects of the oldest and largest pretrial diversion program, New York's Court Employment Project. The report concluded that the project was accomplishing none of its goals: It was not reducing pretrial detention time; it was not reducing the number of stigmatizing criminal convictions; it was not having any effect on the behavior, employment, educational status, or life styles of its clients; and it was not reducing its clients' recidivism. Above all, almost half the diverted defendants, the report found, would not have been prosecuted had there been no court Employment Project.[4]

How local enforcement agencies responded to and influenced the direction of the San Pablo (California) Adult Diversion Project (SPAD) was examined in a study using randomly placed experimental and control groups. Both groups were followed for a 36-month period to test SPAD's effects on recidivism, costs, and social control.

Five distinct stages of reform were found to emerge during the SPAD experiment: (1) resistance, (2) accommodation, (3) transformation, (4) dissolution, and (5) rebirth. Each of these phases resulted in major change in the content and direction of the reform. Impact results show that SPAD had no effects in reducing recidivism, that it proved to be much more expensive than traditional processing, and that it failed to curb the level of criminal justice intervention.

The dismal results are explained by process analysis. Local officials interpreted diversion as a means of increasing control over misdemeanant defendants. Consequently, they selected defendants for the program unlikely to be severely sanctioned by the courts. Such a population was found to engage infrequently in criminal acts regardless of the court's intervention. By locating diversion at the pretrial stage and within the lower courts, the program diminished the potential for reducing social control. By working with such a population, the program diminished the potential for reducing crime and costs. More important, pretrial diversion placed the value of intervention and control ahead of a determination of the defendant's guilt or innocence, thereby compromising the basic values of a due process model of justice. Instead of correcting the deficiencies of the justice system itself, diversion extended an irrational system. As one writer has concluded in his review of such alternatives: "Instead of justice, there is diversion."[5]

Further similar evidence comes from a national assessment of restitution programs in the Untied States. The theme is the same: Restitution projects have been unable to divert substantial numbers of offenders from severe penalties; they, too, exhibit a tendency to increase the degree of social control exercised over offenders. Instead of helping to reduce rates of incarceration as intended, such projects increase the number of persons under custodial confinement.[6]

The results of a national evaluation of community service programs funded by the Law Enforcement Assistance Administration also demonstrated that community service is only marginally effective, if effective at all, as a means of reducing institutional overcrowding, correctional costs, recidivism, or probation caseload. The reader may be left wondering what it is good for except to widen the net of social control.[7]

A study of community correction programs in Saskatchewan found that a great expansion of such programs produced no corresponding decrease in the use of correctional institutions. On the contrary, the use of institutions increased steadily; thus, the establishment of community programs permitted the correctional system to expand at a tremendous rate, placing an ever larger proportion of the population under some form of state supervision. During the 18 years under study, the rate of persons under supervision nearly tripled.

It is clear that, had community programs not been introduced as humanitarian "reform," the cost of supervising an increasing volume of offenders would have been enormous. If the state had been unable or unwilling to sustain these additional expenditures, the correctional system could not have expanded, and some offenders would have been released outright without supervision. In effect, community programs have not been alternatives to incarceration but alternatives to release. Social control, once concentrated in the institutions is now being dispersed into the community.[8]

There is wide agreement among students of criminal justice that the trend during the first three-quarters of the twentieth century has been a consistent movement toward community programs in lieu of penal institutions as the mode of correction. A study aptly entitled "Alternatives to Incarceration: From Total Institutions to Total Systems" takes issue with this common perception of correctional history, using California as the focus of a time series analysis of correctional reform. California was chosen for many reasons, chiefly because that state has been a pioneer in criminal justice reform. It was in California that the substitution of other penalties for imprisonment reached its extreme, with the introduction of the probation subsidy program. Moreover, the state of California has made a greater investment in research than has any other state. Massachusetts was used as the control state. Unlike California, that state introduced very few correctional reforms after 1900; most criminologists and other experts, including those who served on the prestigious President's Crime Commission of 1966, regarded criminal justice in Massachusetts as "mediocre."

The study found the same pattern of reform effects: Alternatives to incarceration in California did not reduce prison populations, but they increased the control of populations previously left alone. Providing the first hint of what may be responsible for this development, the study found that California, the inventor of innumerable "alternatives" to incarceration, kept considerably more people in prisons, in jails, and on probation and parole than did "mediocre" Massachusetts, which did very little during the same 80 years under study, even if crime rates are taken into account. When declines in some measures of incarceration did occur in California, they did not follow the introduction of any particular new alternative: Declines in incarceration appear to have resulted from increases in control rather than from the process of substitution. Faster increases in other forms of control reduced the proportion of offenders incarcerated but there were no declines in the rates of offenders committed to institutions.

Overwhelming evidence was found in the comparison of the two states for the proposition that the twentieth century has witnessed a process of extension of control, whereby offenders have been shifted from mechanisms that exerted very little control, or no control at all, to mechanisms with more social control. Sharp increases in control immediately after the introduction of major alternatives, such as probation, the split sentence, and the probation subsidy, strongly suggest that active reforms are responsible for this development. After probation was introduced in California around 1900, the risk of incarceration did not decline, and a large group of probationers was simply added to the ranks of the controlled population. Similarly, split sentences legislation expanded probation and jail populations without reducing prison populations, and the probation subsidy program did more to enhance superior court probation populations than it did to decrease commitments to prisons.

The study is a powerful addition to the growing body of literature indicating a relationship between correctional innovations and reforms and the extension of criminal justice control over populations previously not controlled — through formalizing available types of control, and incorporating them into the criminal justice process. Early probation laws in California replaced several forms of informal control and suspended sentences. Split sentences led to increases in sentences to institutions as well as to probation. The California probation subsidy program was instrumental in the transition from traditional forms of incarceration to less traditional ones, while at the same time it led to a substantial increase in probation.

The study concludes that (1) new alternatives to incarceration will draw most of their clientele not from institutions but from populations not previously incarcerated, and (2) relatively successful alternatives that divert offenders from institutions involve some modified form of institutionalization, such as civil commitments and split sentences. Extension of control occurs in liberal systems more than in conservative ones, in innovative and activist states more than in those where change is slow.[9] In its conclusion, the study serves to remind us of the Netherlands, which is generally regarded as having the world's most humane criminal justice system, as well as the world's lowest rate of incarceration and the lowest average length of stay in prison among offenders worldwide — but which is absolutely without "innovative" correctional programs.

Criminal justice reform enthusiasts have argued that the widespread adoption of community-based programs would benefit the criminal justice system in a number of ways. The alternative programs, it is argued, are more effective than correctional institutions in rehabilitating offenders. Therefore, they will reduce crime rates and ease requirements for correctional programming. The literature is also replete with statements, as mentioned above, that such programs are an important means of coping with the mounting volume of offenders and that they provide a substitute for the institution.

A paper by John Hylton presents convincing evidence refuting arguments for the effectiveness, humaneness, and economy of community-based programs. Such programs, Hylton points out, have a range of highly undesirable effects on the justice system and on society — effects that have been largely ignored. The failure to reduce reliance on institutions is not restricted to the United States. No country in the world in which community-based programs have been widely adopted has experienced substantial reductions in imprisonment rates. This is equally true in those countries where elimination or curtailment of the use of institutions has been an explicit goal.[10]

There is also a substantial and growing body of evidence indicating that community programs have been associated with a variety of outcomes that can hardly be termed humane. A number of studies have shown that community programs, particularly those housing participants, tend to reproduce in the community the very features of the system they were designed to replace. They serve not only as alternatives to incarceration but rather as alternative forms of confinement. Community resistance to such programs is one reason why they are apt to reproduce institutional environments in the community. The community, Hylton stresses, is not necessarily a more humane environment than the correctional system; we may be in the process of creating a monster of a new system.

Modern correctional programming has blurred the boundaries between the institution and the community and left the community susceptible to entirely new strategies of supervision and control. The "correctional continuum" that extends from the institution to the community makes it difficult to discern where the social control apparatus begins and ends. This blurring is a natural outgrowth of the community correction philosophy. The dangerous system we are creating, a system that will be able to track and influence our activities at almost all times and places, may not seem to be an outgrowth of the "humane" community care movement until the significance of blurring the boundaries between the institution and community is recognized.[11]

If Hylton is right, if this is the cure we are devising, perhaps we should prefer the disease. The dream of criminal justice reform come true can readily become the nightmare of the benevolent state gone mad.

The phenomenon of untoward effects of reforms has been observed in other countries as well: The experience of foreign countries demonstrates convincingly that the criminal justice system has a life of its own, independent of and oblivious to the intent of administrative or legislative reform. In Britain, the suspended sentence of imprisonment was introduced in 1968 as a way to reduce prison populations. As in the United States, the effect was the opposite. Courts used suspended sentences not only in place of imprisonment but also in place of fines and probation, sentences that in Britain carry no threat of incarceration. In addition, courts imposed longer suspended sentences than sentences of actual imprisonment. As suspendees reoffended, they had their old sentences activated and served those and their new sentences consecutively instead of concurrently. England's prison population increased as a result of this reform, in direct contrast to what was intended.[12]

A similar phenomenon has been observed in state subsidies to local correction. Although promoted as a means of reducing prison populations and allowing countries and cities to supervise offenders in their own communities, the intent has not been fulfilled.

An official report on the Minnesota Community Corrections Act (CCA), a model adopted later by many states, sums up the experience of most of the states that introduced correctional subsidies. In 10 of 11 geographic areas analyzed in the evaluation, there was no evidence that the CCA had had an effect on the adult sanctions meted out. The CCA's failure to affect the diversion from prison of significant numbers of offenders is the major explanation for this finding. Costs increased compared with the costs of pre-CCA policy because of the development of 12 new organizational structures at the local level without corresponding decreases in the cost of state-level administration.

The major failure of the Minnesota program has been the inability of state correctional legislation to alter judges' sentencing policies. Judges responded to the reform by using local incarceration to a greater extent for types of offenders previously sentenced to the community. In addition, the alternative to state prison tended to the local jail.[13] Finally, in none of the areas was there improved public protection as measured by arrests of crime rates.

Of the various subsidies, none has been analyzed and evaluated more frequently than has the California probation subsidy. Perhaps the most thorough is an evaluation by Edwin Lemert and Forrest Dill. Under the California subsidy, probation departments built their strategies on the hope that careful use of special supervision caseloads would reduce commitments. Departments sought to bring about commitment reductions simply by opening their doors to more probationers. This strategy broke down early, and departments began to lean more on local institutions and quasi-institutional programs as methods of reducing commitments. While the California probation subsidy promoted somewhat liberalized use of probation, it also increased the use of facilities for local incarceration. As in all the other criminal justice "reforms," the program helped to augment the capacity of the correctional system in California.

With regard to reduced probation caseloads, the subsidy experiment confirmed earlier findings: They accomplish little, and officers accustomed to large caseloads do not know how to handle small caseloads. In some departments, particularly in Los Angeles, growth was measured by earnings from the state subsidy, and a great deal of entrepreneurial energy was applied to push them upward. This produced uneven development and disorganization in the sense that almost any means were deemed valid to reduce commitments.

A system of control based on rewards, the researchers conclude, presents great administrative difficulties. They draw a useful comparison between the California probation subsidy and the Stakhanovite movement in Soviet industry in 1935, which greatly increased productivity but reduced product quality, caused disruption among the workers, and distorted human values.[14]

In adult criminal justice reform, the phenomenon of the distortion and frustration of the original purposes of reforms is evident in the efforts to decriminalize victimless crimes, including such offenses as public drunkenness. Removal of victimless crimes from criminal justice jurisdiction and law enforcement scrutiny as advocated by the President's Crime Commission of 1966 and numerous criminal justice reform agencies is another example of a criminal justice reform that has not worked out as intended. In 1969, victimless crime arrests in the United States were 51.5 percent of all arrests; in 1980, they were 32.4 percent of all arrests. In 1960, 36 percent of all arrests nationally were for public drunkenness alone; in 1980, they were just over 10 percent. However, the law enforcement community was shifting its attention not from victimless crimes to (serious) index crimes, as reformers wanted them to do, but to the less serious part II crimes. Although victimless crime arrests declined from 51.5 percent of all arrests in 1969 to 32.4 percent of all arrests in 1980, part II crimes (minus victimless crime arrests) increased from 29.5 percent to 45.2 percent of all arrests, rising in almost the same proportion as the fall in victimless crime arrests. Arrests for the more serious index crimes remained relatively stable at around 20 to 22 percent of all arrests throughout this period.

As in so many other reforms, the decline in victimless crime arrests nationwide was accomplished through widening of the net in part II crimes and through "label switching" from one type of offense to another. For instance, public drunkenness or disorderly conduct can easily become simple assault. In addition, a substantial increase in arrests in "all other" category of offenses occurred: They increased from 12 percent of all arrests in 1970 to 17 percent in 1980.[15]

How the intent of the reform to decriminalize public drunkenness was frustrated is illustrated by two case studies, one in Massachusetts and one in New Mexico. Both states abolished the crime of public drunkenness in 1973, yet both experienced an increase in the number of drinking-related jail detention: While "arrests" were abolished, the same activity continued under the label "protective custody." In Massachusetts, protective custody detentions increased 19 percent, and disorderly conduct charges increased 27 percent after the reform.[16] In 1979, the city of Gallup, New Mexico, population 18,000, checked drunken persons into its jail for protective custody 26,000 times. An immense drunk tank was built in 1970 as part of a new jail after living conditions in the old one were declared unconstitutional by a federal court. Conditions in the new jail are worse: Gallup officials view the protective custody law as exempting them from minimum standards for the treatment of jail inmates because drunk tank inmates are not formally arrested and therefore technically not inmates. While the old jail provided inmates with mattresses and blankets, most drunks in the new jail sleep on cement floors.[17] The original intent of the reform that decriminalized drunkenness was for inebriates to be placed in a detoxification center, not in a jail under "protective custody."

The History of Reform

Our fathers and forefathers tried to reform criminal justice according to varying diagnoses of the system's problems. After almost 200 years of criminal justice reform, we should know what has to be done. This is not, however, the case. Historical analyses of criminal justice reforms provide substantial evidence of their ill effects, as well as of the circularity and repetitiveness of reform. The harmful consequences of good intentions are only now beginning to be understood.

Stanley Cohen notes that decarceration as a correctional policy is currently hailed with as much enthusiasm as was its opposite, the concept of asylum and of the penitentiary, when it was first introduced 150 years ago. On the surface, large-scale reaction against institutions may appear to stem from ideological opposition to state intervention. Yet ironically, the major results of the new movements toward "community" and "diversion" have been increases rather than decreases in the amount of intervention directed at many groups of deviants and offenders in the system, expanding rather than lowering the total number of persons brought into the system. "Alternatives" are not alternatives at all but new programs that supplement or expand the existing system by attracting new populations. The "new" move into the community, Cohen observes, is merely a continuation of the pattern established in the nineteenth century. It is only the scale of the operation and the technologies enabling the expansion of social control that are new. [18]

David Rothman, in his *Conscience and Convenience*, documents that notwithstanding the good intentions of reformers, convenience was a major factor in the implementation of their reforms; administrators used the reforms to their own advantage. Historically, all progressive reforms share one outstanding feature: They expanded the power of the state, thus enlarging the freedom of action of public officials. Rothman's basic finding is by now familiar: Innovations that appeared to be substitutes for incarceration became supplements to incarceration.[19]

Another characteristic of reform is its circularity. Two hundred years ago, much of criminal justice was community justice, and it was often brutal and inhumane. To counteract this inhumanity, Quakers invented the penitentiary in the early 1800s; this was quickly accepted as the model institution for correcting offenders in North America and Western Europe. Instead of being exposed to a vindictive and cruel community, the Quakers argued, criminals would be placed in a quiet cell of their own, there to engage in penance, mediation, and prayer, and through their actions to reform. It did not take the Quakers long to regret their invention. The penitentiary turned out to be no more humane than the pillory or the whipping post. Two hundred years later, the new reformers have discovered that the community has not become more humane, more accepting, or less vindictive toward its offenders, even though the physical expression of that vindictiveness is no longer tolerated.

The circularity of criminal justice reform is also documented in a study of women's prison reform. Nineteenth century women prison reformers proclaimed a sisterhood with the imprisoned woman, explicitly identifying with her plight inside prisons run by and for men. After a long and hard-fought campaign by nineteenth century feminists, a sexually segregated penal system was established with separate prisons run by and for women. The reformers clung to a definition of woman's separate nature that limited the reformers' own power and stifled the inmates they sought to aid. In the 1970s began an experiment with a "new" correctional reform: sexual integration of the prisons. The circle is complete.[20]

Juvenile Justice Reform

Evaluations of efforts to reform juvenile justice consistently yield results identical to those documented in criminal justice reform.

In a review of evaluations of juvenile diversion programs, Thomas Blomberg finds net widening reported again and again. Virtually all diversion projects expanded control by selecting the major proportion of their clients from a population never before adjudicated. The widening of control has had as its practical consequence double prosecution jeopardy, increased rearrest rates, intrusion into the family, and accelerated movement of youths into the justice system. Juvenile justice reform has resulted in a continuing sprawl of the correctional system.[21]

An analysis of a California juvenile court's implementation of a diversion program found that it expanded the organization and service function of the juvenile court, extending services beyond problem youths to include whole families. Data collected on five years of the court's diversion program showed it to produce expanded control as measured by larger numbers of youths receiving some form of juvenile court service, as well as accelerated control as determined by out-of-home placement of youths whose families were unable or unwilling to respond to family intervention. Diversion has enlarged the scope of the juvenile court and the proportion of the population under its control.[22] An evaluation of a Dade County (Florida) prevention and diversion program reported the familiar pattern of findings: The five programs, which provided counseling, recreational, educational, and employment services, widened the net of intervention and control without demonstrating any reduction in delinquency.[23]

An evaluation of 15 juvenile diversion projects funded by the California Office of Criminal Justice Planning found that, of all the clients served, 49 percent would not have been processed within the traditional juvenile justice system had the diversion projects not existed. The findings with respect to recidivism were mixed: Recidivism was not reduced for youths who had no or two or more arrests. Among youths with one prior arrest, clients did better than comparisons.[24]

Another interesting example of juvenile justice reform is the fate of Youth Service Bureaus (YSBs). YSBs were originally promoted by the President's Crime Commission in 1966 and by many agencies such as the National Council on Crime and Delinquency as a "key to delinquency prevention." The primary functions of YSBs were to be service brokerage, advocacy, resource development, and systems modification. YSBs were not to engage in direct service.

Three selected evaluations of YSBs (a national evaluation, an evaluation of two Illinois YSBs by the National Council on Crime and Delinquency, and a local evaluation of a YSB in Minneapolis) had similar results and led researchers to identical conclusions. Contrary to the original intent, YSBs provided direct service. The advocacy function was non-existent in all YSBs, and no YSB was engaged in systems change. In Minneapolis, diversion from juvenile justice via YSBs was negligible, as suburban communities had few youths to divert and central city police did not refer juveniles to YSBs.[25]

The development of the YSBs has been so contrary to their original purpose that, for the past five years, the literature has remained remarkably silent about this type of reform. No new evaluations are reported since 1977, and agencies such as the National Council on Crime and Delinquency long ago ceased advocating them as a means to reduce delinquency or reform juvenile justice.

By far the most revealing analysis of a juvenile justice reform concerns the effort to deinstitutionalize status offenders. The first example is a federally funded attempt to remove status offenders from institutions in ten states. The result was an easily documented and considerable widening of the net. In one site, enthusiastic practitioners were found to be canvassing neighborhoods for clients to populate the programs. Many youths who were "diverted" had had no contact with the law at all.

The second example of an effort to deinstitutionalize status offenders was in California, where legislation mandated the removal of all status offenders from locked institutions, a dramatic and uncompromising move. No youths officially labeled status offenders were found in public correctional institutions after the law went into effect. However, there was considerable circumvention of the mandate, through relabeling, which took three forms: from status offender to criminal offender, from status offender to neglected or dependent child, and from status offender to psychiatrically troubled youth. All three forms of relabeling enabled status offenders to be incarcerated in spite of the legislation. They were more stigmatized than would have been the case under the old law, and the seriousness of their official records in the system was increased.[26]

An evaluation of the Illinois Status Offender Services project (ISOS) also documents a pronounced widening of the net. Contact with ISOS increased the youths' penetration into the justice system and the public social service system. That is, it increased court processing of status offenders and their subsequent referral to the Illinois Department of Children and Family Services. The findings were that 10.3 percent of pre-program youths but 76.3 percent of ISOS program youths came to the attention of the department. Comparison of secure detention and the community-based program did not reveal differences in their effects on youths' subsequent contacts with the juvenile justice system.[27]

Edwin Lemert is generally credited with being the "father" of modern diversion. Yet Lemert, as well as others who have developed diversion programs, is deeply troubled by the way they worked out. A salient and unintended consequence of the diversion movement, Lemert maintains, has been its substantial preemption by police and probation departments, which, in many areas, have set up in-house programs, hired their own personnel, and programmed cases in terms of the departments' special needs and circumstances. This development is diametrically opposed to the main idea of diversion—that is, that movement should be away from the juvenile justice system. The effect has been little more than an expansion in the intake and discretionary powers of police and a shuffling of such powers from one part of their organization to another.

Cases selected for diversion include large numbers of youths who formerly would have been screened out. Diversion projects have included disproportionately large numbers of younger juveniles, those with trivial offenses, youngsters without prior records, females, and status offenders.

What began as an effort to reduce discretion in juvenile justice has become a warrant to increase discretion and extend control where there was none before.[28] Lemert reflects on the failure of the diversion movement he helped to create:

> The cooptation of the diversion movement by law enforcement leaves the rather sour impression that not only have the purposes of diversion been perverted but, moreover, police power has been extended over youths and types of behavior not previously subjected to control. . . . It may be argued that police never should have been involved in the programmatic aspects of diversion and that the way to make diversion work is to take it out of the juvenile justice system.[29]

James Austin and Barry Krisberg conclude that all the frantic activity in criminal and juvenile justice reform has resulted in an unchanged system or an extension of its reach. Reform movements have widened, strengthened, or created different nets of social control as organizational dynamics resist, distort, and frustrate the reform's original purpose. Reformers have ignored the surrounding political, social, economic, and ideological context in which their reforms occur. Future efforts at change, the authors recommend, must include detailed analyses of the larger political structure and its connections with the social control apparatus if more substantive results are to be realized.

Austin and Krisberg's explanation for the failure of reform emphasizes the interactive and dialectic nature of the criminal justice system as an organization. The system is interactive in the sense that changes in one part of it trigger reactions among others, reactions that may take the form of resistance, modification, or efforts to defeat the intended reform. Crime control ideology, agency values, power, and authority are sources of conflict among police, prosecutors, the courts, and correctional officials. Agencies compete with one another, and reactions to a given reform depend upon the perceived value of that reform to the agency's survival. In addition, the criminal justice system is dialectic in the sense that it is affected by contradictions in the larger society and is subject to the ideological currents that support the structure. Research on an earlier period of intense criminal justice reform shows that the interplay of ideology, social change, and reform in criminal justice today is an extension of previous patterns.[30]

Criminal Justice Statistics Creation of Illusions

So far in this paper we have examined the effects of liberal reform efforts designed to decrease penalties or reduce the number and the rate of persons incarcerated or under control by the criminal justice system, and we have noted their failure to do so. Readers of a review ("Social Forces and Crime") published in a previous issue of this journal will recall that it examined many studies of efforts designed largely to achieve the opposite, namely, an increase in penalties or an increase in the number or rate of persons to be subjected to criminal sanctions. Without exception, they, too, were failures: The evaluations showed that discretion removed from one point of justice simply reappears elsewhere; punishment increased at one point is nullified in practice at another point.[31] It was shown that juries might defeat or nullify the purpose of legislators, parole release the effects of plea bargaining, judges the intent of prosecutors, police the intent of a governor, and courts the purpose of a city council.

An example taken from the experience of the federal prison system deserves to be repeated here. Over the years, legislators at the federal level have passed ever more punitive criminal laws. Federal judges have reflected the increasingly punitive trend and increased the average length of prison sentences. In 1960, the average sentence to prison meted out to federal offenders was 29.6 months; in 1965, it was 33.5 months; in 1970, 41.1 months; in 1975, 45.5 months; in 1979, 49.0 months.

Charts in the federal prison system's latest annual reports graphically illustrate how flexible indeed a prison system can be, how instantaneous is its population-regulating mechanism, and how meaningless it is to use length of sentences as a tool for gauging reform: The charts trace the average sentence length of released inmates from 32 months in 1965 to 40 months in 1975, then following it to an apparently temporary drop back to 32 months during 1976 and 1977. As the chart traces the average length of sentence, it shows a *simultaneous* and *immediate* decline in the percentage time actually served of the average sentence from about 60.5 percent in 1965 to 46.5 percent in 1975. As sentence lengths declined in 1976 and 1977, the prison system adjusted immediately by simultaneously increasing the percentage of time served from 46.5 percent to about 50.1 percent. The overall result was a remarkable constancy in the average time served of roughly 19 months throughout the 12-year period. Unusual highs in average time served (21 months in 1967) were immediately followed by declines; unusual lows (15 months in 1976) were immediately followed by increases during the following year.[32]

The overall national patterns are not as easily traced and not quite as pronounced but nevertheless clearly discernible. Throughout the depression years of the 1930s the incarceration rate in the United States steadily increased until it reached a high of 137 per 100,000 population. It then sharply decreased during World War II to reach a low of 100 in 1946. The late 1940s and 1950s experienced a slow increase except for a slight dip during the Korean War. It reached a high of 121 in 1961, only to decline again during the Vietnam War years to a historic low of 94 in 1968. Beginning with 1973 the rate experienced its sharpest increase and is now about 150 per 100,000 population.

The national median time served to first parole is available for only a few years, but the data are enough to show a distinct pattern: During most of the period the National Prisoner Statistics report a typical median time served of around 21 months. But there are important exceptions: During World War II the median jumped to 25 months, and during the Vietnam War year of 1966 it was 26 months, 4 to 5 months longer than the norm. In 1977, 1978, and 1979, the national median dropped to its lowest level ever: 17 months, or 9 months less than during 1966.

The clear and logical pattern is that as the incarceration rate decreases the length of stay in prison increases, and as the rate of incarceration increases the length of stay in prison decreases. It is one of the many population-regulating mechanisms the system uses to deal with underpopulated or overcrowded prisons.[33] An additional mechanism is prison returns: According to the *Uniform Parole Reports* a smaller and smaller percentage of parolees are returned to prison for new convictions or technical violations. To the question, are we more punitive today than we were in the past, the answer is clearly yes and no: We incarcerate more offenders, but we keep them locked up for shorter periods and return fewer of them once they are released on parole.

The many examples cited in this paper and the previous review mentioned above lead to the conclusion that there is a dynamic equilibrium in criminal justice which prevents those attempting to reform criminal justice by reducing penalties or incarceration rates from succeeding. Conversely, the studies also support the conclusion that those who attempt the opposite, an increase in penalties, are also ultimately, if not immediately, frustrated in their efforts. Furthermore, an increase in one type of punitiveness (incarceration rates) is accompanied by a decrease in another type of punitiveness (time served). The powers of both groups are thus extremely limited, if not nonexistent. Although incarceration rates fluctuate from decade to decade to a greater or lesser extent, they have the tendency to return to previous highs or previous lows, not rising much beyond apparently predetermined limits or going much below them. When unusual highs or lows are reached, they are compensated for by other factors, such as inmates' increased or decreased lengths of stay in prison and increased or decreased returns to prison of released and paroled offenders.

Shooting the Wolves

Man and society are thus not exempt from the checks and balances that have been observed in many other disciplines. There is no reason why such an equilibrium should not work to man's advantage and for his survival, as it does in nature. Ecologists, to use one example, speak of a balance between predator and prey that assures neither will die out. They speak of an equilibrium in nature within which all living things exist.

Historians, to use another example, long ago discovered the balance of power that exists between nations. History is full of examples of its mechanism: When France emerged as Europe's superpower three centuries ago, alliances between unlikely partners, such as England and tsarist Russia, quickly nullified France's predominance. The balance was quickly restored. When Nazi Germany and Japan threatened the world's balance of power, the world quickly and automatically united to thwart the threat. After World War II, America stood on the pinnacle of unchallenged nuclear power, but the balance was soon restored by the rise of Soviet Russia and the Chinese power. Today, the Soviet Union seems to pre-dominate militarily, but its very success has triggered the balancing mechanism, which is tilting the world once again toward a restoration of the balance of power. In the process the two most unlikely societies, China and the United States, as have so many nations so many times before, find themselves drawn to one another. A Sino-American alliance grows closer with each new Soviet threat. Once again, the USSR's very success has caused the world to realign itself to nullify Russia's increased might: Now 900 million Chinese are added to the economic and technological power of the United States, Japan, and Western Europe.

A program on educational television showed herds of caribou that migrate north across Canada and Alaska during the summer and south again in the winter. Their steady companions are packs of wolves. While wolves reach a top speed of about 25 miles an hour and can run for short spurts only, caribou have a top speed of over 40 miles an hour and can maintain it for long distances. A healthy caribou thus has nothing to fear from the slower wolf, who has to wait patiently until a member of the herd becomes sick or is injured or too old. The constant presence of the wolf makes the caribou alert, his running away from his predator keeps him set on his journey and in shape to face the cold and the arduous trek.

Along comes man, who shoots the pack of wolves to protect the caribou. What happens to the herd? Since wolves no longer kill the caribou, the herd grows in size. Instead of a fast, merciful death, many caribou die a slow death of starvation and disease. Man has done the herd no favor. He has increased its suffering. Nature would maintain the balance, but man has intervened, disrupting a healthy exchange.

Eventually other wolves from other parts of Canada rejoin the herd and the ecological balance is restored. Man learns his lesson: The cruelty of the wolf is in fact merciful. His quick kill in eliminating the sick and the injured has a vital role in the survival of the herd and its fitness. The caribou *needs* the wolf as much as the wolf needs the caribou. They are in ecological balance.

The next point has already been hinted at. Man is not exempt from a system of balances. The Sierra Club and other organizations whose job it is to protect nature are hammering away at their theme: Man may study and observe, but he must leave nature alone; he must not upset the balance; he must not shoot the wolves. Science fiction writers and futurists speculate, in writing about visitors to earth from outer space, that if such visitors are beings of superior intelligence they will come only as observers, never intervening in anything we do, never taking sides. The same thought is expressed in many religions: If there is a God, He does not intervene in man's activities directly, but works indirectly, allowing man to make his mistakes and to learn from them; "God helps those who help themselves" is a proverb that expresses the same idea.

Accumulating evidence shows that crime and punishment are also in social balance, in an equilibrium assuring that neither can get out of hand in the long run, that both have their distinct limits. It means that "criminals" cannot expand their activities indefinitely, and neither can society increase its punishments without triggering counterforces which reduce crime and punishment to their former levels and keep them in balance. A new level of thinking in criminal justice is taking Schur's principle one step farther, urging that we leave the *system* alone and allow each society to find its own level of crime and punishment. *We are learning that that is in fact the most humane level.* Criminal justice reforms that ignore the balance of social, political, and economic forces in society make things worse, not better; they increase suffering, rather than diminishing it. You don't shoot the wolves.

In an essay written in 1894, sociologist William Sumner reflected on the "Absurd Effort to Make the World Over":

> If we puny men by our arts can do anything to straighten [the world] it will be only by modifying the tendencies of some of the forces at work, so that, after a sufficient time, [it] may be changed a little. . . . This effort, however, can at most be only slight, and it will take a long time. In the meantime spontaneous forces will be at work, compared to which our efforts are like those of a man trying to deflect a river, and these forces will have changed the whole problem before our interferences have time to make themselves felt. . . . The things that will change [the world] are . . . the new reactions inside the social organism. . . . The utmost [men] can do by their cleverness will be to note and record their course as they are carried along, which is what we do now, and is that which leads us to the vain fancy that we can make or guide the movement. That is why it is the greatest folly of which man can be capable, to sit down with a slate and pencil to plan out a new social world.[34]

In 1892, H. Spencer applied the idea of regressive effects to a variety of governmental programs. In his view, legislative intrusion into natural evolutionary processes almost always produces destructive results:

> Acts of Parliament do not simply fail; they frequently make worse. Moreover, when these topical remedies applied by statesmen do not exacerbate the evils they were meant to cure, they constantly induce collateral evils; and these are often graver than the original ones.[35]

There is no dearth of contemporary authors who are discovering "new reactions inside the social organism" and "forces that will have changed the whole problem before our interferences will have time to make themselves felt." Sam Sieber, in his book *Fatal Remedies – The Ironies of Social Intervention*, examines null effects, side effects, and reverse effects not only in criminal justice reforms but in innumerable other social reforms as well, noting that good intentions have very often made matters far worse for the very people for whom the help was intended. A wide variety of causes of ironic outcomes are analyzed, in education, political behavior, criminal justice, welfare, warfare, health care, public administration, and economic development. Sieber proposes a theory of "social devolution" as a counterbalance to Parsonian theory of social evolution.[36]

Similarly, Robert Merton refers to "unanticipated consequences as self-amplifying social problems in which efforts to do away with one social problem introduce other damaging problems."[37] And D. Bell has a profound message for social reform and criminal justice reform groups who demand to be heard or are encouraged to expect full participation in the social process:

> There is probably more participation today than ever before in political life, at all levels of government, and that very increase in participation leads to the multiplication of groups that "check" each other, and this to a sense of impasse. Thus increased participation paradoxically leads, more often than not, to increased frustration.[38]

The groups, in other words, "monitor" each other and are in antagonistic balance with one another.

That we should leave the system alone, intervening as little as possible and only when absolutely necessary, is an idea whose time has come, and an increasing number of authors are expressing it. A Canadian author, looking at Canadian and foreign data and experiences with diversion, concludes that formalized diversion will increase rather than decrease social control; in effect, he urges the Canadian Parliament not to pass pending legislation on diversion. If Parliament does decide to go ahead with the proposed legislation, it should at least acknowledge that doing nothing with an offender may be preferable.[39]

One of the strongest arguments for allowing the criminal justice system to operate in a marketlike fashion is aptly entitled "The Desirability of Goal Conflict within the Criminal Justice System." Radicals, liberals, and conservatives alike, it is observed, agree on the desirability of a unified, rational, and well-integrated system of criminal justice in which a common set of goals can be pursued through a compatible set of strategies and techniques. Taking a contrary point of view, the article argues that such positions ignore the political environment in which criminal justice operates. There are at least three reasons why goal conflict and fragmentation, rather than unification of the system, are advantageous to the system's processes and functioning: Conflict makes it possible to represent and protect different societal interests; conflict establishes a system of checks and balances; and conflict promotes a smoothly operating offender-processing system. The dynamic equilibrium of a fragmented justice system promotes a balance of power between antagonistic interests as it encourages adaptation and change. As social attitudes and values change, the system can make corresponding changes.[40] A study of a prosecutor's office found that it operated in a marketlike fashion and the decision to prosecute or not to prosecute was often based on the influence of a variety of officials and groups. Any system that exhibits high diversity, even in the form of fragmentation, allows conflicts to be played out and resolved on a continuing basis. Centralization and unification, on the other hand, promote rigidity and create a bureaucracy that is an inefficient structure for change.

Seen in this light, the principle of planned and judicious nonintervention in the operation of the criminal justice system assumes new meaning. Direct intervention and interference become the social equivalent of "shooting the wolves" by producing the kind of untoward consequences discovered by studies of the full effects of criminal justice reforms. The principle of nonintervention allows the system to make its mistakes because the social balance between antagonistic forces renders those mistakes relatively harmless and allows for evolutionary change.

By allowing small conflicts and confrontations to be resolved on a continuing basis society in effect maintains a healthy and steady equilibrium of forces and avoids major conflict and confrontation. The ritual of criminal justice thus becomes a useful, functional safety valve designed to prevent more violent conflict.

Endnotes

[1] Lipton, D., Martinson, R., & Wilks, J. (1975). *The effectiveness of correctional treatments.* New York: Praeger. Martinson's and two of his main critics' points of view were reprinted in a 1976 NCCD pamphlet entitled Rehabilitation, Recidivism, and Research.

[2] Schur, E. (1973). *Radical non-intervention.* Englewood Cliffs, NJ: Prentice-Hall.

[3] Potter, J. (1981). The pitfalls of pretrial detention. *Corrections Magazine, 7*(1), 5–7, 10–11, 36.

[4] Ibid.; U.S. National Institute of Justice. (1981). *Diversion of felony arrests: An experiment in pretrial intervention. An evaluation of the court employment project.* Washington, DC: Government Printing Office.

[5] Austin, J. F. (1980). *Instead of justice: Diversion.* Ph.D. dissertation, University of California, Davis.

[6] University of Minnesota, School of Social Development. (1980). *National assessment of adult restitution programs: Final report.* Duluth: University of Minnesota.

[7] Cooper, G., & Anita, S. (1981). *An evaluation of the community service restitution program: A cluster analysis*. Denver, CO: West University of Denver, Denver Research Institute.

[8] Hylton, J. H. (1980). *Community corrections and social control*. Regina, Saskatchewan: University of Regina.

[9] Miller, D. (1980). *Alternatives to incarceration: From total institutions to total systems*. Ph.D. dissertation, University of California, Berkeley.

[10] Hylton, J. H. (1981). *Rhetoric and reality: A critical appraisal of community correction programs*. Regina, Saskatchewan: University of Regina.

[11] Ibid.

[12] Bottoms, A. E. (1981). The suspended sentence in England, 1967–1978. *British Journal of Criminology, 21*(1), 1–26.

[13] Minnesota Corrections Department. (1981). *Minnesota community corrections act evaluation: General report*. St. Paul: Minnesota Corrections Department.

[14] Lemert, E. M., & Dill, F. (1978). *Offenders in the community: The probation subsidy in California*. Lexington, MA: Lexington Books.

[15] Doleschal, E. (1981). 1980 victimless crime arrests. Unpublished memorandum to National Council on Crime and Delinquency.

[16] Daggert, L. R., & Rolde, E. J. (1980). Decriminalization of drunkenness: Effect on the work of suburban police. *Journal of Studies on Alcohol, 41*(9), 819–828.

[17] Katel, P. (1980). Sleeping it off in Gallup, N.M. *Corrections Magazine, 6*(4), 16–23.

[18] Cohen, S. (1979). The punitive city: Notes on the dispersal of social control. *Contemporary Crises, 3*(4), 339–363.

[19] Rothman, D. J. (1980). *Conscience and convenience: The asylum and its alternatives in progressive America*. Boston: Little, Brown.

[20] Freedman, E. B. (1981). *Their sisters' keepers: Women's prison reform in America, 1830–1930*. Ann Arbor: University of Michigan Press.

[21] Blomberg, T. G. (1980). Widening the net: An anomaly in the evaluation of diversion programs. In M. W. Klein & K. S. Teilmann (Eds.), *Handbook of criminal justice evaluation* (pp. 572–592). Beverly Hills, CA: Sage Publications.

[22] Blomberg, T. (1977). Diversion and accelerated social control. *Journal of Criminal Law and Criminology, 68*(2), 274–282; Blomberg, T. (1978). *Social control and the proliferation of juvenile court services*. San Francisco, CA: R & E Research Associates.

[23] Dade County Human Resources Department. (1979). *An evaluation of the impact of five juvenile delinquency prevention/diversion programs*. Miami, FL: Dade County Human Resources Department.

[24] Palmer, T., & Lewis, R. V. (1980). *An evaluation of juvenile diversion*. Cambridge, MA: Oelgeschlager, Gunn and Hain.

[25] Minnesota Center for Sociological Research. (1974). *Evaluation of seven youth service bureaus in the Twin Cities region*. Minneapolis: University of Minnesota; National Council on Crime and Delinquency, Survey Services. (1973). *Youth services bureaus in Rock Island and Henry Counties, Illinois*. Austin, TX: National Council on Crime and Delinquency, Survey Services; U.S. National Institute of Law Enforcement and Criminal Justice. (1977). *National evaluation program youth service bureaus – Phase 1 assessment*. A. Schuchter & K. Polk (Eds.). Boston: Boston University.

[26] Van Dusen, K. T. (1981). Net widening and relabeling: Some consequences of deinstitutionalization. *American Behavioral Scientist, 24*(6), 801–810.

[27] Spergel, I. A., Reamer, F. G., & Lynch, J. P. (1981). Deinstitutionalization of status offenders: Individual outcome and system effects. *Journal of Research in Crime and Delinquency, 18*(1), 4–33.

[28] Lemert, E. M. (1981). Diversion in juvenile justice: What hath been wrought. *Journal of Research in Crime and Delinquency, 18*(1), 34–46.

[29] Ibid., p. 43.

[30] Austin, J., & Krisberg, B. (1981). Wider, stronger, and different nets: The dialectics of criminal justice reform. *Journal of Research in Crime and Delinquency, 18*(1), 165–196.

[31] Doleschal, E. (1978). Social forces and crime. *Criminal Justice Abstracts, 10*(3), 395–410.

[32] U.S. Federal Prison System. (1977). *Statistical Report, 1975 and 1977.* Washington, DC: Government Printing Office.

[33] Incarceration rates and median time served are taken from the National Prisoner Statistics published by various bureaus of the U.S. Justice Department for the past 40 years. Median time served since 1977 is taken from NCCD's annual Uniform Parole Reports.

[34] Sumner, W. G. (1919). The absurd effort to make the world over. In W. G. Sumner & A. K. Keller (Eds.), *War and other essays* (pp. 209–210). New Haven, CT: Yale University Press.

[35] Spencer, H. (1946). *The man versus the state.* Caldwell, ID: Caxton Printers.

[36] Sieber, S. D. (1981). *Fatal remedies: The ironies of social intervention.* New York: Plenum Press.

[37] Merton, R. K. (1978). Unanticipated consequences and kindred sociological ideas. Paper delivered at the annual meetings of the Society for the Study of Social Problems, San Francisco.

[38] Bell, D. (1973). *The coming of post-industrial society* (p. 469). New York: Basic Books.

[39] Trepanier, J. (1981). La déjudiciarisation des mineurs délinquants au Canada et les projets législatifs du gouvernement fédéral [The removal of juvenile offenders from juvenile court jurisdiction in Canada and legislative projects of the federal government]. *Canadian Journal of Criminology, 23*(3), 279–289.

[40] Wright, K. N. (1981). The desirability of goal conflict within the criminal justice system. *Journal of Criminal Justice, 9*(3), 209–218.

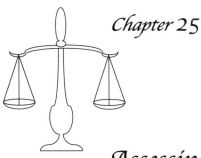

Chapter 25

Assessing the Impediments to Organizational Change
A View of Community Policing

Rhonda Y. W. Allen

Introduction

With the advent of reengineering, rightsizing, reorganizing, and reinventing government, one of the greatest challenges facing public organizations is the process of change. Change implies a fundamental difference or a substitution of one thing for another. Organizational change involves, by definition, a transformation of an organization between two points in time (Barnett and Carroll, 1995).

In the context of American policing, change is particularly difficult. Although the structures of most police departments conform to the quasi-military, hierarchical model of organization, police officers are not closely supervised (Blau, 1994; Sewell, 1986). This social arrangement in which the police work results in a highly fragmented, internalized, and isolated environment (Stamper, 1993). As a result, the police tend to band together and exclude outsiders. This tendency to close ranks develops into a police culture that makes it extremely difficult to make changes within police departments.

This study addressed the issue of impediments to organizational change within police agencies. More specifically, this research identifies

Reprinted from *Journal of Criminal Justice*, Vol. 30, Rhonda Y. W. Allen, "Assessing the Impediments to Organizational Change: A View of Community Policing," pp. 511–517, 2002, with permission from Elsevier.

and assesses the impediments to implementing community-oriented policing (COP) in three southwestern police departments. Identifying the impediments to change across departments provide a theoretical basis for informing the kinds of management decisions that will inevitably transform police departments into healthy productive organizations.

Background

Resistance to change has been discussed in the current organization development (OD) literature at great length (Damanpour, 1991; Delacroix and Swaminathar, 1991; Greenwood and Hinings, 1996). Many models and theoretical frameworks had been used to explore, describe, explain, and predict what will aid in the change process. The literature on organizational change examined several schools of thought about organizations' abilities to change and the characteristics that impede or assist in the change process (Halliday, Powell, and Granfors, 1993; Huber, Sutcliffe, Miller, and Glick, 1993; Kelly and Amburgey, 1991). A variety of insightful arguments has been advanced regarding characteristics that produce positive change. Little has been done, however, to compare the implementation of programs across departments and identify the major forms of resistance that remain constant across them. Largely missing are integrative models that have the ability to examine and explain the multidimensional phenomenon of organization change (Klein and Sorra, 1996). Therefore, by examining the underlying dimensions of change and ascertaining, if there are any impediments that remain constant across the various departments, the present study expands the current literature and opens the door for greater knowledge about resistance to change and impediments to program implementation.

COP-Designated Patrol Assignment

The concept of COP began with the community relations programs of the 1950s and 1960s, which developed in order to increase interaction between the community (especially the minority community) and the police, and continued through the 1970s with the team policing concept (Greene, 1987). Team policing was a patrol method from the late 1960s to the early 1970s. Team policing focused on efficient and effective policing, improved police-community relations, assigned patrol of police teams, and enhanced police officer morale (Sherman, 1973). Despite the failure of the team-policing concept in some organizations, the idea of a community context of policing remained strong.

More recently, the proliferation of community policing has been initiated as a result of the increasing evidence that the reactive model and conventional police practices have not been effective (Bayley, 1994; Goldstein, 1990; Greene, 1987; Rohe, Adams and Arcury, 2001; Smith, Novak and

Frank, 2001). Therefore, programs that focused on dealing with specific problems faced by communities and reducing community fear of crime continued to develop (Brown and Wycoff, 1987; Eck and Spelman, 1987; Goldstein, 1987; Skolnick and Bayley, 1987). Although community policing is widely believed to be important by those involved with or affected by community policing, the term means different things to different people (Bayley, 1988). For example, under the rubric of community policing, police departments are developing crime prevention seminars, storefront and mini-police stations, newly designed patrol beats, community advisory groups, neighborhood watch programs, increased foot patrols, patrol-detective teams, and door-to-door visits by police officers (Bayley, 1988; Rohe et al., 2001; Skogan, 1994).

Although the initial idea of COP was to institute programs that allowed the police to become familiar with people in the community, the definition has been expanded to include almost any program that serves as an instrument to improved police service and better community relations. This expansion of the community policing definition, however, has resulted in much confusion concerning what the term community policing actually means and how to implement it. Implementing community policing has many difficulties. As indicated previously, police organizations are inherently reluctant to accept and try new ideas (Scheingold, 1991). Thus, many police organizations resist the notion of community policing because it represents a change from the traditional reactive policing model.

This research examined the patrol assignment aspect of community policing. In police organizations where community policing is not the standard philosophy, police officers are assigned to a beat that covers an extensive area of the city. In police organizations that share in the community policing philosophy, police officers are often assigned to a small community area to allow officers to become familiar with the community (citizens) so that they can proactively solve problems together. Patrol assignment includes the selection and placement of officers in newly designed community policing areas, as well as the tasks assigned to them. Much of the success or failure of community policing efforts rests on the actions of the individual officers who translate community-policing philosophy into reality (Brown, 1989; Friedmann, 1992).

The cross-case comparison of the impediments to COP implementation revealed that COP is a complex and complicated philosophy and the methods used to implement COP programs will vary. Focusing on designated patrol assignment, however, has isolated key impediments to COP implementation.

Methodology

The agencies selected for study were three municipal police departments located in a large metropolitan area of Arizona: the Phoenix Police

Department (PPD), the Mesa Police Department (MPD), and the Tempe Police Department (TPD). The agencies selected were all self-defined as engaged in designated officer assignments to implement some form or variation of COP.

At the time of this study, the PPD had approximately 2,310 sworn police officers and served a population of 1,149,417. The MPD had approximately 634 sworn police officers and served a population of 338,117. The TPD had approximately 260 sworn police officers and served a population of 153,821. The three police departments had similar organizational structures in terms of personnel and operating units. Each department had slightly over 90 percent White, non-Hispanic, male officers.

In-depth interviews were conducted with 126 employees of the three municipal police agencies, including three different levels (executive, middle, and street-level) of police practitioners identified as being responsible for or involved with the specific aspects of the change program being studied — community-based patrol assignment. Interviews were conducted at the three different levels in order to collect data from different perspectives. The interviews included ninety street-level officers, twenty-six mid-level officers, and ten executive-level officers. Participants were assured of confidentiality and written permission was received from each agency. The interviews were in a structured, open-ended format and a comprehensive protocol ensured standardization of data collection across sites.

Interviews were conducted over a four-month period. Interviews were approximately one to three hours in length and extensive field notes were taken. The interview time varied depending on interviewees' availability and willingness to give information. The data collected from each interview was recorded with as much detail as possible; interviews were taperecorded when possible.

Each interview session began with a general set of questions regarding interviewees' length of time in the department, current and past positions, and overall length of time in the field of law enforcement. Police personnel were asked about the role they played in the change effort, major problems of program implementation, ease of implementation, most effective methods of implementing change, organizational attitude toward community policing, and the relationship between management and employees during the change process. In conjunction with the interviews, supporting data were gathered through observations while in the police stations, on patrol ride-alongs, and through police records and official documents.

The Study Variables

Dependent Variable

Resistance to organizational changes — more specifically, resistance to designated officer assignment for community policing. Resistance to change includes both the overt (obvious) and covert (subtle) actions that affect implementation of the change programs (Recardo, 1995).

Independent Variables

Based on the organizational change literature (Allen, 1999; Barnett and Carroll, 1995; Porras and Silvers, 1991), factors that impede or facilitate change fall into two general categories—structure or process. Structural variables deal with division of labor and the arrangements of organizational parts. Process variables relate to the way the transformation occurs—the speed, the planning, the sequence of activities, and the communication systems. Structural variables for this study included complexity, centralization, and formalization. Process variables included pressure, individual attitudes, departmental attitude, and communication.

Complexity referred to the number of structural components (horizontal differentiation, vertical or hierarchical differentiation, and spatial dispersion) that required coordination and control (Hall, 1996). A highly complex organization is characterized by many occupational roles, sub-units (division and departments), levels of authority (rank structure, i.e., chiefs, captains, lieutenants, and sergeants), and operating sites. Complexity is perceived as beneficial in the planning stage of change, but a problem for implementation. In short, complexity adds to the difficulty of implementing change.

Centralization described the locus of decision making within an organization (Hall, 1996). Centralization was measured by the level and variety of participation in strategic decisions by groups relative to the number of groups in the organization (Hage, 1980). Resistance to change is minimized when organizations involve employees in the decision-making process (Covin and Kilmann, 1990).

Formalization referred to the use of rules in an organization and involved organizational control over individuals (Hall, 1996). Formalization is also related to the number of new programs added in an organization. Formalization has been shown to be negatively associated with the adoption of new programs (Hall, 1996). In the more formalized organizations, there is likely to be less time, support, or incentive for involvement in change and innovation. Measures of formalization included job codification and rule observation.

Pressure described the perceived or real pressure for the change (reasons). The literature notes the concept of pressure as being an important factor in the implementation of change (Guyot, 1991; Slack and Sigelman, 1987).

Individual attitude described the respondents' (top-management, mid-management, and street-level officers) attitudes toward the underlying issues (i.e., the role of the police—COP) of the particular change programs. Attitudes toward COP have been reported as being related to the motives underlying individuals' resistance to change (Skogan, 1994).

Departmental attitude described the departments' (command staff) attitudes toward the underlying issues of the particular change programs. It should be noted that the individual attitude and departmental attitude variables were separated during the initial data collection stage. Respondents made clear distinctions between their individual attitudes and their department's overall attitude toward change.

Communication referred to the exchange of information and the transmission of meaning (Hall, 1996). Communication occurs in three directions: upward, downward, and horizontal; it also includes omission, distortions, and overload of information. Lack of organizational communication or poor communication can result in an unclear purpose of the program and misplacement of program responsibility (Covin and Kilmann, 1990).

Case Analysis

Miles and Huberman's (1994) pattern coding and case analysis strategy were used for this study. The names of the variables were used as categories (subject headings) to code and analyze the data collected from the open-ended interviews. This method initially organized data into separate categories that corresponded with the variable names. The coding scheme included complexity, centralization, formalization, pressure, individual attitudes, departmental attitude, and communication. During the course of the field research, however, the coding scheme was revised and subcodes were developed.

Coding was done after each wave of interviews by transcribing and reviewing the collected data and then tagging the most relevant pieces. Coded data were condensed (summarized) and categorized under the previous stated subject headings. The codes were used to retrieve and organize the data. This grouping assisted in identifying and clustering the segments related to the impediments of implementing COP. Clustering then set the stage for the analysis and conclusions.

The analysis was aimed at understanding both individual case dynamics and cross-site comparisons. First, recurring patterns and themes were noted (pattern coding). There was an expectation that patterns involving similarities and differences among categories and processes involving implementation would surface. The second stage of analysis pulled together the separate pieces of data. Once the data were clustered, they were reviewed to see which pieces of data went together and which did not. Clustering by similar patterns or characteristics assisted in gaining a better understanding of the factors affecting the change process.

Findings

This study revealed that centralization, complexity, and formalization (the structural variables) could be impediments to change. Themes related to the structural variable surfaced in all three police departments. For example, although the command staff of the PPD tried to push discretion and authority down to the street-level officers in an attempt to implement COP, it was met with skepticism and mistrust. This was also true with the MPD and the TPD. Street-level officers, in all three departments, reported being unable to trust that their departments would support their decisions, if and when something went wrong. Therefore, street-level officers did not take full advantage of their new level of authority and discretion. Command staff from each department believed that the many years of working under a quasi-military, bureaucratic structure made officers unable to accept a more decentralized departmental structure. The effects of the structural variables, however, were not strong and varied depending on the stage of implementation and size of the organization. This finding supported earlier literature that examined the effect of structure on organization change (Amburgey, Dawn, and Barnett, 1993; Delacroix and Swaminathan, 1991).

Although, in many cases, strong themes did not emerge related to the three structural variables, there was enough evidence to show that these factors may influence many of the process variables. For example, in the PPD, complexity affected communication. Within all three of the police departments, formalization affected departmental and individual attitudes. By influencing the process variables, the structural variables had a greater ability to affect organizational change.

Of the process variables, the pressure variable surfaced consistently as a major factor in facilitating the implementation of COP. All three levels of police practitioner responded to external pressure and reported that, without it, organizational change may not have occurred. Additionally, respondents from all three police departments and at all three levels did cite that environmental changes (change in crime rates and city demographics) acted as an impetus for change. This emerging theme was consistent with earlier studies that argued that organizational change occurs mainly through the adaptive responses of existing individual organizations to natural changes in technology and environment (Burt, 1992; DiMaggio and Powell, 1983; Zucker, 1983). Although the majority of these studies were directed at the private sector, the current study found that this was also true for the police organizations.

Of all the variables studied, individual attitudes were among the most important factors in COP implementation. Proponents of the COP philosophy, in all three departments, had embraced the concept, but reported that it was the opponents of COP who made implementation difficult. Mid-level managers who did not buy into the COP concept always found "other things" for their officers to do, instead of assignments related to community policing. Street-level officers, who were resistant to the change, went through the motions, but never put forth any real effort of implementing community-based programs. It was mentioned repeatedly by street- and mid-level officers that someone from the command rank must champion the COP concept to facilitate the change process.

As was found in the MPD, proponents still struggle with the initial phases of implementation because of the department's lack of strong support from the command staff. The TPD implemented COP throughout the department, and while no one openly resisted the change, covert resistance was rampant throughout the organization. The lack of overt resistance was reported as being the result of strong COP support from command staff.

Discussion

Police organizations are complex social systems that are grounded in democracy, operate within a "fishbowl," and are funded primarily by tax dollars. To use tax dollars more efficiently and effectively, it is imperative that police organizations understand the change process and the difficulties that they might encounter. This study identified several factors that could potentially impede the change process within complex settings.

To mobilize and motivate employees, trust must be established before managers can transfer the necessary decision-making authority. To establish trust, employees must exhibit competence and prove they are knowledgeable; that is, understand the assigned tasks and can do their job. There must also be managers who support employees and will not punish them if they voice their own opinions. Once trust is attained and authority transferred, employees must learn how to use their newly acquired power. There were several examples, within this study, where command staff had attempted to empower street-level officers, but officers did not trust or believe that they had discretion to make decisions. As a result, officers refused to accept the decision-making power and followed the standard hierarchy of decision-making. In these instances, command staff never asked why officers did not accept their new authority, nor did street-level officers communicate their concerns to the supervisors.

Clearly, communication must be honest and open. Anything less than sincere conversation will result in a false sense that progress is being made. Without clear understanding through open communication and training, change may not take place. It is, however, extremely important to note that public sector agencies have multiple constituents, thus complicating the process of change and making it more difficult to implement.

In terms of policing, it is important to understand that those who attempt to introduce change programs within police departments often fail to take into account the constant effects of the police setting and culture. That is, new programs are planned and implemented without a sufficient understanding of the effects of the context on the likelihood of successful change.

The police agencies used in this study were well aware of the potential benefits of employee participation in planning, organizing, and decision-making. The police departments understood that a lack of support from line officers, as well as upper- and mid-level managers, could slow down or, worse yet, stop the change process. The police agencies also knew the importance of training and clear communication throughout the organization. When it came time to getting the job done, however, they immediately fell back into their standard operating procedures: (1) command staff makes the decisions, (2) command staff delegates to middle management, (3) middle management orders rank and file to do the job. In sum, police organizations must apply their knowledge to their current practices.

The journey through organizational change is challenging and difficult, yet it is possible to achieve a balance between the goals of the organization and the needs of the employee. The best strategies of successful change are not only in the literature, but are in organizations that have tried and tested many approaches to making their organizations more effective and efficient. The goal is to continue finding successful change organizations in order to collect and disseminate their information that will assist other agencies in making positive change and eliminating the forces of resistance. This information will contribute to the knowledge and practice regarding organizational change.

Conclusion

The ability to plan for and identify impediments to change is an important issue for law enforcement administrators. In an attempt to use a more integrative model to examine and explain the phenomenon of organizational change, this study identified potential impediments to implementing COP. Results indicated that pressure and individual attitudes toward change were the factors that remained consistent across departments. Individual attitudes were impediments to implementing change, while pressure acted as a facilitator of change. Additionally, communication surfaced as a necessary factor when implementing change and was intertwined with all of the study variables.

By examining the underlying dimensions of change and ascertaining impediments that remained constant across departments, the present study expands the current literature and opens the door for greater knowledge about resistance to change and impediments to program implementation.

References

Allen, R. Y. W. (1999). Analyzing organizational change: Characteristics, structure and process. *Journal of Pubic Management and Social Policy, 5*, 1–17.

Amburgey, T., Dawn, K., & Barnett, W. (1993). Resetting the clock: The dynamics of organizational change and failure. *Administrative Science Quarterly, 38*, 51–73.

Barnett, W., & Carroll, G. (1995). Modeling internal organizational change. *Annual Review of Sociology, 21*, 217–236.

Bayley, D. (1988). Community policing: A report from the devil's advocate. In J. R. Green & S. D. Mastrofski (Eds.), *Community policing – rhetoric or reality* (pp. 225–237). New York: Praeger.

Bayley, D. (1994). *Police for the future*. New York: Oxford University Press.

Blau, T. (1994). *Psychological services for law enforcement*. New York: Wiley.

Brown, L. P., & Wycoff, M. A. (1987). Policing Houston: Reducing fear and improving service. *Crime and Delinquency, 33*, 71–89.

Brown, M. (1989). *Working the street: Police discretion and the dilemmas of reform*. New York: Russell Sage.

Burt, R. S. (1992). *Structural holes*. Cambridge: Harvard University Press.

Covin, T. J., & Kilmann, R. H. (1990). Participant perceptions of positive and negative influences on large-scale change. *Group and Organization Studies, 15*, 233–248.

Damanpour, F. (1991). Organizational innovation: A meta-analysis of effects of determinants and moderators. *Academy of Management Journal, 34*, 555–590.

Delacroix, J., & Swaminathan, A. (1991). Cosmetic, speculative, and adaptive organizational change in the wine industry: A longitudinal study. *Administrative Science Quarterly, 36*, 631–661.

DiMaggio, P. J., & Powell, W. W. (1983). The iron cage revisited: Institutional isomorphism and collective rationality in organizational fields. *American Sociology Review, 48*, 147–160.

Eck, J. E., & Spelman, W. (1987). Who ya gonna call? *American Journal of Police, 6*, 45–65.

Friedmann, R. (1992). *Community policing: Comparative perspectives and prospects*. New York: St. Martin's Press.

Goldstein, H. (1987). Toward community-oriented policing: Potential, basic requirements, and threshold questions. *Crime and Delinquency, 33*, 6–30.

Goldstein, H. (1990). *Problem-oriented policing*. Philadelphia: Temple University Press.

Greene, J. R. (1987). Foot patrol and community policing: Past practices and future prospects. *American Journal of Police, 6*, 1–15.

Greenwood, R., & Hinings, C. R. (1996). Understanding radical organizational change: Bringing together the old and the new institutionalism. *Academy of Management Review, 21*, 1022–1054.

Guyot, D. (1991). *Policing as though people matter*. Philadelphia: Temple University Press.

Hage, J. (1980). *Theories of organizations*. New York: Wiley.

Hall, R. (1996). *Organizations, structures, processes, and outcomes*. Englewood Cliffs, NJ: Prentice Hall.

Halliday, T. C., Powell, M. J., & Granfors, M. W. (1993). After minimalism: Transformations of state bar associations from market dependence to state reliance, 1918 to 1950. *American Sociology Review, 58*, 515–535.

Huber, G. P., Sutcliffe, K. M., Miller, C. C., & Glick, W. H. (1993). Understanding and predicting organizational change. In G. P. Huber & W. H. Glick (Eds.), *Organizational change and redesign* (pp. 215–263). New York: Oxford.

Kelly, D., & Amburgey, T. L. (1991). Organizational inertia and momentum: A dynamic model of strategic change. *Academy of Management Journal, 34*, 591–612.

Klein, K. J., & Sorra, J. S. (1996). The challenge of innovation implementation. *Academy of Management Review, 21,* 1022–1054.

Miles, M. B., & Huberman, A. M. (1994). *Qualitative data analysis.* Thousand Oaks, CA: Sage Publications.

Porras, J., & Silvers, R. (1991). Organization development and transformation. *Annual Review of Psychology, 42,* 51–58.

Recardo, R. (1995, Spring). Overcoming resistance to change. *National Productivity Review, 14,* 5–12.

Rohe, W. M., Adams, R. E., & Arcury, T. (2001). Community policing and planning. *Journal of the American Planning Association, 67,* 78–82.

Scheingold, S. A. (1991). *The politics of street crime — criminal process and cultural obsession.* Philadelphia: Temple University Press.

Sewell, J. (1986). Administrative concerns in law enforcement stress management. In Reese & Goldstein (Eds.), *Psychological services for law enforcement: A compilation of papers submitted to the National Symposium on police psychological services* (pp. 153–159). Quantico, VA: FBI Academy.

Sherman, L. (1973). *Team policing: Seven case studies.* Washington, DC: Police Foundation.

Skogan, W. G. (1994). The impact of community policing on neighborhood residents: A cross-site analysis. In D. P. Rosenbaum (Ed.), *The challenge of community policing* (pp. 167–180). Thousand Oaks, CA: Sage Publications.

Skolnick, J. H., & Bayley, D. (1987). *Community policing: Issues and practices around the world.* Washington, DC: National Institute of Justice.

Slack, J. D., & Sigelman, L. (1987). City managers and affirmative action: Testing a model of linkage. *Western Political Quarterly, 40,* 668–673.

Smith, B. W., Novak, K. J., & Frank, J. (2001). Community policing and the work routines of street-level officers. *Criminal Justice Review, 26,* 17–37.

Stamper, N. (1993). Workshop given at the International Association for Civilian Oversight of Law Enforcement (IACOLE) Eighth Annual Conference — Law Enforcement Issues, San Diego, CA.

Zucker, L. G. (1983). Organizations as institutions. In S. B. Bacharach (Ed.), *Perspectives in organizational sociology: Theory and research: Vol. 2* (pp. 1–14). Greenwich, CT: JAI Press.

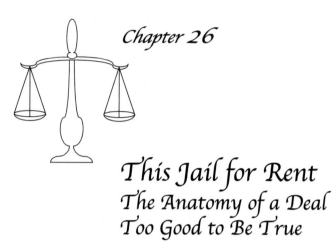

Chapter 26

This Jail for Rent
The Anatomy of a Deal
Too Good to Be True

Linda L. Zupan

In the early morning hours of December 15, 1988, 50 sentenced felons from the overcrowded Lorton Correctional Complex were shepherded aboard a chartered airplane at Dulles International Airport and flown over 3,000 miles to their new home—the Spokane County Jail in Washington State.[1] Their transfer came less than three weeks after the Spokane County Board of Commissioners signed a $1.1 million, one-year contract to house prisoners from District of Columbia Department of Corrections in the county jail.

The contract lasted only three months. During that time the D.C. prisoners threatened and assaulted correctional officers, set numerous fires, threw food trays, clogged toilets, destroyed jail property, and filed a slew of lawsuits against the county, alleging violations of their civil rights. Correctional officers, abused and assaulted by the D.C. prisoners and concerned about glaring deficiencies in the jail's safety systems, overwhelmingly voted to strike. A prominent local civil liberties attorney, angered by the heartless treatment of the D.C. prisoners, filed a lawsuit against the county to force their removal. The media, sensing a controversy of grand scale, printed article after article on the problems at the

Linda L. Zupan, "This Jail for Rent: The Anatomy of a Deal Too Good to Be True," *American Jails*, February 1993, pp. 22–32. Reprinted by permission of the American Jail Association.

jail. The public, exasperated by the goings-on at the jail, voiced its opinion in numerous letters to the editor of local newspapers. And finally, the District of Columbia forgot to pay its bill to the county.

In many respects, the Spokane County Jail is like every other jail in the United States. In times of scarce resources, it falls victim to budgetary belt-tightening due in no small measure to the less-than-deserving nature of its clientele. Understandably, some local officials will grasp at any alternative to defray or reduce the costs of expensive jail operations. Some will even consider turning the jail into a revenue-generating, rather than revenue-consuming, enterprise. In the case of Spokane County, the alternative was to fill the jail's empty beds with prisoners from the other end of the country. But like most "get-rich-quick" schemes, the hidden costs were immense. What began as a "too-good-to-be-true" deal turned out to be a gigantic boondoggle—one that wasted considerable money, effort, and public goodwill.

The primary purpose of this article is to relate the interesting, and perhaps rueful, account of Spokane County's unfortunate decision to house 50 D.C. prisoners in the jail and the unforeseen consequences of that decision. It also provides a forewarning to those who are contemplating a similar venture. While renting space to other state prison systems can provide jails with much-needed revenue, the costs of such an alternative may be prohibitive.

Why Did The County Enter Into the Contract?

At first glance, the reason Spokane County Commissioners entered into the contract with the District of Columbia appears simple and straight-forward. The jail was about to lose a lucrative contract with the state of Washington to house overflow populations from the state's prison system. The revenue from the District of Columbia was needed to compensate for this loss of these state funds. Closer examination reveals, however, that the County Commissioners' motivations were more complex.

Funding for construction of the new, 483–bed Spokane County Jail was provided by the state of Washington under the provisions of the City and County Jails Act of 1977. The state also provided Spokane County with a special grant of $6 million to construct an additional floor of the high-rise jail. In exchange for the special grant, Spokane County agreed to house up to 92 inmates from the state's overcrowded prison system and to be compensated at the rate of $1.67 per inmate hour.

At the time, Washington State was in critical need of additional incarceration space. Prison populations were on the rise and the state was forced to contract with local jails to house prisoners. The state's over-crowded prisons proved to be financially rewarding for Spokane County. In 1987, for example, Washington State paid the county over $620,000. The revenue comprised 20–25 percent of the jail's annual operating budget!

The county's good fortune was short-lived. By 1988, two years after the new Spokane County Jail opened, the state no longer needed additional space. The infusion of millions of dollars for the construction of additional prison beds as well as aggressive use of alternatives to incarceration produced a 16 percent reduction in the state's prison populations between 1985 and 1989. In fact, prison populations in Washington State had declined so significantly that the state offered to lease 1,000 beds to the federal government and other states, and was providing 200 beds for use by county jails. Spokane County officials were notified that the contract with the state would not be renewed in 1989.

This announcement by the state concerned county officials. Jail operating expenses had climbed steadily since the opening of the new facility, primarily due to increases in the number of jail personnel. The larger capacity of the new facility required more personnel to operate and with its direct supervision design, the jail could not function effectively when understaffed. The County Commissioners gave Sheriff Larry Erickson an ultimatum: locate alternative sources of revenue or decrease the operating budget of the jail by reducing the work force.

At the same time that Spokane County was grappling with the loss of state revenue, the District of Columbia was dealing with its own problem: too many prisoners and too little prison space. By 1988, overcrowding in D.C. prisons and jails had reached crisis proportion. Inmate populations in the District of Columbia were growing at the rate of nearly 150 inmates a month with no sign of abatement. At Lorton Reformatory Central the prison population regularly exceeded court-ordered caps by as much as 40 percent.

Under pressure from federal courts to comply with population caps set in a 1982 consent decree or pay $5,000 in fines per day, the District of Columbia Department of Corrections entered into contracts with any jurisdiction willing to temporarily house its prisoners. Among the jurisdictions accepting D.C. prisoners was the state of Washington.

Spokane County Sheriff Larry Erickson learned about the possibility of leasing jail space to the District of Columbia from his contacts in the Washington State Department of Corrections. In late fall 1988 he dispatched Jail Commander Don Manning to sell D.C. correctional officials on the jail. Although skeptical about such an arrangement, Manning nevertheless pitched the benefits of the Spokane County Jail. During the meeting Manning indicated that the jail was only prepared to handle medium custody, sentenced prisoners who had no litigation or legal matters pending. He also stipulated that the jail would only accept prisoners who voluntarily agreed to transfer. The D.C. officials nodded in agreement.

On November 29, 1988, against the recommendations of Jail Commander Manning, a resolution was passed by the Board of Spokane County Commissioners to house 50 D.C. prisoners in the jail. The contract between the two jurisdictions required that Spokane County "confine, care for, treat and rehabilitate inmates from the District of Columbia." For their effort, Spokane County would be paid a fee of $60.74 per inmate day or over $1.1 million per year to house the 50 prisoners. The contract allowed for renewal after one year. Less than three weeks after the contract was signed, the D.C. prisoners were transported to the Spokane County Jail.

Was it only the acute need for revenue that motivated the Spokane County Commissioners to enter into the contract with the District of Columbia? Probably not. In the years preceding the contract, Spokane County was operating in the black. In 1986, the county had a $3.2 million fund balance (profit). By 1987, the fund balance increased to $4.3 million and by 1988, the year of the contract with D.C., the fund balance was up to $6.1 million. The county was not in dire financial need.

Nor was the revenue generated by the jail significantly reduced by the loss of the state contract. Jail revenue from other sources (e.g., U.S. Marshals Service, city of Spokane, other counties in the state) increased 60 percent, or over $800,000, in 1989, the year after the loss of state revenue. This increase more than offset the loss of approximately $600,000 per year in state revenue. Ironically, Jail Commander Manning brought the projected increases in revenue to the attention of Sheriff Erickson *before* the County Commissioners signed the contract. Given the rather rosy financial situation, why did the Spokane County Commissioners threaten to penalize the jail by reducing its operating budget if alternative revenue was not found? Why did the County Commissioners welcome the contract with the District of Columbia without questioning the possible ramifications?

Commissioner Patricia Mummey had her own reasons. When asked why the county's considerable fund balance was not used to offset the projected loss of jail revenue, Mummey stated that she wanted the money to go to improving county services outside of criminal justice. She argued that a substantial and increasing proportion of the county's budget went to support the criminal justice function, and as a consequence, other county services were ignored and underfunded. Mummey got her wish. The fund balance was primarily used by the Commissioners to create new personnel positions within noncriminal justice county offices. (In an ironic twist, the county was operating at a deficit by 1991 and the Commissioners were considering a reduction in the county's operating budget, including the elimination of those positions created by the fund balance!)

Commissioner John McBride had his own reasons for supporting the contract. According to McBride, the jail was staffed and operated for full capacity, yet 25 percent of the beds were vacant. By the principle of "economy of scale," the jail was losing money. McBride reasoned that if the space and necessary staff were available, why not lease beds to any jurisdiction in need of incarceration space? What he failed to recognize was that the jail was not staffed at appropriate levels. High turnover among correctional officers, and timely lags in hiring and training personnel had resulted in chronic understaffing at the jail.

Finally, an answer to why the County Commissioners entered into the ill-fated contract with D.C. can be found in their collective attitude toward the jail. The County Commissioners resented the jail. After the new facility opened in 1986, it was found to be more personnel intensive than expected. The creation and funding of new staff positions was necessary to effectively operate the new facility. The County Commissioners considered the jail to be a "black hole" into which money was poured with very little payoff.

Why Did The Contract Fail?

The contract with the District of Columbia lasted only three months before the County Commissioners, upon the recommendation of Sheriff Erickson, voted to terminate it. Four factors contributed to the demise of the contract.

Factor 1: Type of Inmate Transferred to Spokane County

When Jail Commander Manning initially met with representatives from the District of Columbia Department of Corrections in the fall of 1988, he made three stipulations in regard to the type of prisoner that would be accepted by Spokane County. First, only prisoners classified for medium security would be accepted. Although the Spokane County Jail routinely housed high-risk, maximum-security prisoners, their number was usually small enough for the facility to house and effectively manage. Jail officials were concerned that the infusion of 50 maximum-security prisoners at one time would cause considerable housing and security problems for the jail. Second, the jail would only accept prisoners with no legal matters or issues pending. This stipulation was necessary to reduce the cost and security risks involved in returning prisoners to the District of Columbia for court dates. It was also meant to circumvent prisoner complaints concerning accessibility to the D.C. courts. A third and final stipulation was that only prisoners who volunteered for transfer from Lorton would be accepted at the jail. Jail officials believed that if prisoners came to Spokane voluntarily, they would be more likely to comply with jail programs and would be easier to manage than those who were moved to Spokane against their will.

While the contract between the two jurisdictions granted Spokane County the authority to screen "applications of each individual inmate proposed for confinement" it did not specify that only prisoners who met Manning's three qualifications would be referred. In consequence, the contract gave Spokane County very little control over the type of prisoner referred for screening. Furthermore, the contract didn't stipulate how the screening would be conducted. A request by Manning to personally interview prisoners was denied by the D.C. Department of Corrections.

Instead, the D.C. Department of Corrections sent prisoner files for jail officials to make their selections.

All of the prisoners "proposed for confinement" by the D.C. Department of Corrections were serious offenders, sentenced to long periods of incarceration and housed under maximum-security conditions in the Lorton Correctional Complex. The perception of Manning and others at the jail was that the D.C. Department of Corrections referred the "worst of their worst inmates" and expected Spokane County to select the most acceptable or, more appropriate, the least intolerable.

By all accounts, the "most acceptable" prisoners eventually selected were among the most serious offenders Lorton had to offer. They were the "hard cases" who, prior to their removal from the prison, were housed under maximum-security conditions. Twenty-three of the 50 prisoners had been convicted of murder or multiple murders and, as a group, were responsible for killing 40 people. The remaining 27 prisoners were serving time for other serious and multiple felonies such as rape, kidnapping, and robbery. Representatives of the Spokane County Jail correction officers' union claimed that 37 of the 50 prisoners were serving life or multiple-life sentences, but a spokesperson for the D.C. Department of Corrections maintained that only 25 of the prisoners were sentenced to life. Unbeknownst to jail officials, many of the 50 prisoners had pending legal matters including appeals on their criminal convictions and, ironically, civil suits filed against the D.C. Department of Corrections and other D.C. officials. Also unbeknownst to jail officials was that none of the 50 D.C. prisoners had volunteered for the move and, in fact, were unaware of their impending transfer until just hours before their flight and were ignorant of their destination until the plane landed in Spokane.

To the correctional officers at the jail, the D.C. prisoners were vastly different from the local inmates they routinely supervised. All of the prisoners were black and were born and raised on the inner city streets of D.C. Many of them were adherents to the Islamic religion and many were ardent jailhouse lawyers. All of them were sophisticated offenders with long criminal histories. By contrast, the correctional officers reflected the community from which they were recruited. They were white males and females who were born and raised in a rural or suburban environment populated by very few blacks or other minorities. Their upbringing and even their work experiences at the jail gave them little understanding of the D.C. inmates, their ethnicity, background, religion, level of sophistication, or savvy knowledge of the criminal justice system.

To the citizens of Spokane County, the D.C. prisoners represented their worst nightmare. The D.C. prisoners projected the "perfect image" of the sophisticated, "big city" black criminal who commits the most atrocious crimes. Although few of the individuals interviewed for this study were willing to link the community's eventual opposition to the presence of the prisoners to racism, *Spokesman-Review* reporter Jim DeFede believed that the ethnicity of the 50 D.C. prisoners certainly contributed to community opposition. Whether it was because they were black, from the "big city," or were perceived as sophisticated offenders, community members nevertheless expressed concern over their presence in the community. Some feared that once the D.C. prisoners were released from incarceration, they would want to remain in Spokane. Others feared that the prisoner's *families* would move to Spokane in order to be closer to their loved ones.

Factor 2: Treatment of the D.C. Inmates

By the time the 50 D.C. prisoners arrived in Spokane, they were in an explosive mood. According to one D.C. prisoner: "We're in a firecracker mood. This is a bunch of angry, frustrated men." Contributing to their ire were the suddenness and manner by which they were transferred from Lorton to Spokane. For security reasons, the prisoners were not notified about their impending transfer until just hours before the move. Nor were they told of their final destination. The prisoners were given neither the time nor opportunity to contact their families. And most were concerned that their families would not know what had happened to them. The prisoners felt that they had been shanghaied.

They were also told by Lorton officials that they could only take one box of property with them. Many of the inmates had to leave behind possessions that held great symbolic and sentimental value to them. They also had to abandon reams of paperwork important to their pending appeals and civil lawsuits.

At 2:30 A.M., the inmates, bound in handcuffs, shackles, and belly-chains, were transported from the prison to Dulles International Airport where they waited on the tarmac until 4:30 A.M. to board the chartered airplane. For many of the inmates, it was their first time on an airplane and the first time they had traveled beyond the D.C. area.

None of the prisoners were told why they were being transferred out of Lorton. Many believed that they were handpicked by the D.C. Department of Corrections for punitive reasons or because of their reputations as "jailhouse lawyers" who wrote numerous writs, tied up the court system, and were occasionally successful in the lawsuits they filed.

Also contributing to the hostility of the D.C. prisoners were the conditions under which they were to be confined. To many prisoners, jail incarceration is considered "hard time" marked by boredom and idleness, and the lack of personal freedoms, programs, and job opportunities commonly available in prisons. As the D.C. prisoners soon learned, the operations and physical design of the Spokane County Jail provided none of the comforts that they were accustomed to in Lorton.

No one would dispute that conditions within the Spokane County Jail were safer and far more physically comfortable than those in the Lorton Correctional Complex. In the newly constructed jail, the D.C. prisoners were housed in 48-man living units. Each prisoner had his own room, furnished with a bed, desk and chair, toilet, sink, and window. During the day, the prisoners had free access to a large carpeted dayroom that was furnished with soft, movable furniture and multiple televisions and telephones. They also had free access to an enclosed, concrete recreation area adjacent to the living unit. Conditions in the Spokane County Jail were certainly an improvement over the overcrowded, old, and decrepit physical plant of Lorton Correctional Complex.

Despite the luxury of their physical surroundings, the D.C. prisoners were unimpressed. What they missed were the "comforts" that Lorton provided and which made prison more bearable for those serving life sentences. In Lorton, prisoners had access to an extensive law library, a variety of exercise equipment, and an outdoor recreation yard. Also available were a wide array of academic and vocational classes as well as wage-earning job opportunities. Prisoners wore their own clothing and were allowed to have television sets, radios, boxes of legal research, and other personal items in their cells. Prisoners were not confined 24 hours a day to their cellblock but were allowed to move from program areas to the recreation yard to other areas of the prison compound. Given the proximity of the prison to their homes, prisoners could regularly visit with their families or call them without the expense of a long-distance telephone charge. Prisoners in Lorton also had access to illicit narcotics and other contraband items that were smuggled in by visitors or even correctional staff. In the transfer to the Spokane County Jail, the D.C. prisoners lost most of these comforts, they were required to wear uniforms, were allowed only one box of property in their cells (no televisions or radios), and were confined in the living units 24 hours a day. The only programs available to them were basic adult education, religious, and drug and alcohol classes. Visits by family were nearly impossible given the distance, and even telephone calls were limited due to the high cost of long-distance charges and the meager funds of most prisoners' families.

The D.C. prisoners were also subjected to a more extensive form of surveillance than they experienced in Lorton. With two correctional officers assigned 24 hours a day to directly supervise the living unit, there were few opportunities available for the prisoners to engage in behavior without observation. Finally, in the Spokane County Jail, the D.C. prisoners did not immediately have the connections and opportunities necessary for smuggling drugs and other contraband into the facility.

It did not take long for the D.C. prisoners to express their anger through actions. Less than three days after their arrival—long enough to sleep off the effects of the "red-eye" flight and to get their bearings—the prisoners staged their first demonstration. Several of the prisoners threw burning clothes through the slots in cell doors. Others threw food trays and clogged their cell toilets, causing minor flooding. The point of these and other incidents was clear. The prisoners wanted out of the Spokane

County Jail and they would do anything necessary to force their removal. After all, most of the prisoners were serving long-term or life sentences; they had little to lose and a lot to gain from their disorderly behavior.

Factor 3: Lack of Preparation

District of Columbia correctional officials wasted little time in transferring the 50 prisoners from the overcrowded Lorton Correctional Complex to the Spokane County Jail. Less than three weeks after the contract was signed the prisoners were winging their way to Spokane. The suddenness of the transfer gave jail officials little time to adequately prepare for the new arrivals. Special education, work, and visitation programs originally planned for the D.C. prisoners could not be fully implemented in such a brief period of time. Nor were the programs implemented after the arrival of the prisoners. Jail officials were so preoccupied dealing with the disruptive behavior of the prisoners that plans for special programs were all but abandoned.

More critical was the lack of staff preparation. Although jail officials originally planned to provide correctional officers with special training on how to manage the D.C. prisoners, the prisoners arrived before the training could be carried out. Nor were correctional officers informed about the D.C. prisoners until the day before their arrival. During this briefing, they were told that the prisoners were doing "short time" and that they had "nothing to be concerned about." The officers soon discovered that the D.C. prisoners were, in fact, serious offenders who were doing "long time."

Failure to adequately forewarn and prepare correctional officers exacerbated tensions between the officers and jail administrators that had been brewing for over a year. Through their union representatives, officers repeatedly voiced concern for their personal safety and demanded corrective action on the part of Sheriff's Department administrators. Five issues were of particular concern to officers. First, due to the architectural design of the jail and the absence of surveillance cameras in the living units, officers were almost totally dependent on two-way radios and body alarms to notify central control of problems in the units. Yet the body alarms had not been operational for at least one year prior to the arrival of the D.C. prisoners and the two-way radios constantly malfunctioned and could not be depended on in an emergency. Second, the jail had no emergency response team to deal with critical inmate incidents, nor was there a written policy or training for the handling of these situations. Third, the jail was severely understaffed. Although there were enough correctional officer positions allocated to adequately staff the facility, the jail was not functioning with a full staff of correction officers because of high turnover. To cope with the understaffing, a policy of mandatory overtime was instituted, but officers complained that under the haphazard policy they were not assured of their days off or vacation. Fourth, the booking area of the jail was chronically understaffed. At times, there would be as many as 30 inmates waiting to be booked and only two officers in the area. The fact that the Spokane County Jail has an "open booking" system makes this area particularly hazardous for officers.[2] Finally, appropriate fire safety equipment was lacking. Common garden hoses were used in place of fire hoses, and there were no air packs in the jail. The behavior of the D.C. prisoners after their arrival demonstrated the obvious deficiencies in equipment and policies and served to heighten correctional officers' concerns about their safety.

On January 12, 1989, almost one month after the arrival of the D.C. prisoners in Spokane, union representatives again presented a list of safety concerns to Sheriff's Department officials and demanded that immediate changes be made to improve conditions in the jail. The following day, on request by the correctional officers' union, representatives from the Washington State Department of Labor and Industries (WISHA) arrived at the jail to begin an investigation into correction officer safety. While WISHA refrained from ruling on the staffing or emergency response issues because they were out of its jurisdiction, it did find in favor of the officers on several of the other issues. Spokane County was ordered to install fire hoses and air packs, purchase new body alarms, and provide radios that functioned properly. In addition, WISHA found that the camera system used to monitor inmate transport throughout the jail was inadequate and that there were many blind spots in the jail where officers could be injured. Spokane County was ordered to install additional cameras. It was given up to 90 days by WISHA to make the necessary changes.

To ensure that it took their demands seriously, correction officers, on January 19, 1989, voted 95 to 3 to strike if the safety issues were not resolved within 30 days. To forestall the strike, the County Commissioners allocated $160,000 in emergency funds for safety equipment inside the jail. Although the correctional officers' union representatives were primarily concerned about improving safety conditions at the jail, they also objected to the presence of the D.C. prisoners and their continued threat to officer safety. Consequently, the union joined an injunction filed against Spokane County to force the removal of the D.C. prisoners from the jail.

Although the correctional officers had legitimate complaints about safety and about their lack of preparation for the D.C. prisoners, they were nevertheless blamed for the eventual failure of the contract. Soon after the contract was terminated, Commissioner John McBride stated in a local newspaper, "I am rather disappointed in our jailers; they claim to be jailers, but they don't want to take the responsibility." In an interview conducted over two years later, McBride was still blaming the correctional officers. He accused the officers of "dereliction of duty" and "mutiny," and of engaging in a "work slowdown" as a means to rid the jail of the D.C. prisoners. Although the jail's correctional officers made "top dollar" and were some of the "best trained officers in the nation,"

McBride claimed that they were basically "lazy" and "did not want to deal" with the D.C. prisoners. In many respects, the correctional officers were made the scapegoat for failure of the contract.

Factor 4: Legality of the Contract

Two months after the arrival of the D.C. prisoners, Carl Maxey, a prominent and influential civil rights attorney in Spokane, filed an injunction against Spokane County, the Board of County Commissioners, the Sheriff s Office, and the jail to force the removal of the D.C. prisoners from the jail. His suit alleged that the contract entered between Spokane County and the District of Columbia was illegal. Although it is not the purpose of this article to explore the legal issues raised by Maxey, it is informative to understand the history behind and rationale for the suit.[3]

Maxey first became involved in the controversy when some 20 D.C. prisoners contacted him soon after their arrival in Spokane to complain about the move and the jail's treatment of them. He also received several complaints from Spokane County inmates who were in jail for minor offenses and were "fearful" of the D.C. prisoners. Maxey wrote to the Washington State Attorney General's Office requesting that a taxpayer's lawsuit be filed against the county. When the Attorney General's Office declined, Maxey filed suit against the county under his own name and that of Lawrence S. Keciemba, a legal investigator for the Maxey law firm. On March 10, 1989, the Washington State Council of City and County Employees, the correction officers' union, joined the suit. Three days later, the American Civil Liberties Union also joined the suit.

In his suit, Maxey alleged that the contract between the D.C. Department of Corrections and Spokane County was invalid, primarily because the county lacked the authority under Washington State law and the Interstate Corrections Compact to enter such a contract. Because Maxey dropped his lawsuit against the county when the contract was terminated, it is open to debate whether or not his arguments on the legality of the contract hold merit.[4] Nevertheless, his lawsuit did have impact in that it compounded the considerable problems the county and jail officials were facing with the D.C. prisoners. First, the lawsuit added to the growing number of legal actions filed against the county in the matter. Collectively, the D.C. prisoners filed 11 lawsuits against Spokane County alleging numerous and varied violations of their civil rights. Several of the lawsuits were pending long after the contract was terminated and the prisoners were removed from the jail. Some of the lawsuits were eventually settled by the county. Second, the lawsuit garnered significant media coverage, thus adding to the already considerable attention the media was extending to the D.C. prisoner affair and, perhaps in part, inciting further community opposition to the contract. Certainly the presence of yet another lawsuit and even more negative press did little to engender community support for the contract or, in the long run, for the jail.

Concluding Remarks

On March 28, 1989, the Spokane County Commissioners voted unanimously to terminate the contract with the District of Columbia. Within a month, the last of the D.C. prisoners were removed from the jail and transferred to the authority of the federal prison system. For their effort, Spokane County received some $280,000 from the District of Columbia. It cost the county and jail much more in terms of strained labor relations, loss of public confidence, demoralization of staff, and erosion of reputation.

County officials contemplating similar contracts can learn much from the experiences of Spokane County. Many of the mistakes Spokane County made in the transfer of prisoners from the District of Columbia could have been avoided through careful planning, rigorous inmate screening and selection, and coordination with the sending jurisdiction. However, there still remain a number of inherent problems in such arrangements. Chief among these is the thorny moral issue of housing long-term prisoners in an institution designed for short-term incarceration.

Endnotes

[1] The information in this article was gathered from a number of sources, including: over 65 articles published in the *Spokesman-Review*, *Spokane Chronicle*, and *Washington Post*; complaints and affidavits from 12 lawsuits filed against Spokane County over this matter, correspondence from the correctional officers' union, Carl Maxey, and the County's Safety/Loss Control Manager; the contract between Spokane County and the District of Columbia; and Spokane County revenue and budget figures for 1986 through 1989. In addition, interviews were conducted with Spokane County's three Commissioners (John McBride, Patricia Mummey, Steve Hasson); Budget Director John Ogden; Attorney Carl Maxey; *Spokesman-Review* reporter Jim DeFede; correctional officer union representative Bill Keenan; and Spokane County Jail Commander Don Manning, now Chief Criminal Deputy, Spokane County Sheriff's Department. Although several attempts were made to interview Spokane County Sheriff Larry Erickson, he was unavailable.

[2] Unlike a traditional booking area where arrestees are secured in bare, concrete single- or multiple-occupancy cells until they are booked, in the open-booking design arrestees are free to mingle in a large lounge area equipped by a television, telephones, and soft, movable furniture. Arrestees are advised by booking officers that they can either await booking in the luxury of the lounge area or they can be locked in the bare concrete cells that surround the opening booking area.

[3] For a full discussion and analysis of the legal questions involved in transferring inmates from the District of Columbia Department of Corrections to the Spokane County Jail, see Linda L. Zupan and Frances P. Bernat, "The Legality of Interstate Prisoner Transfers to County Jail Facilities," a paper presented at the 1992 annual meeting of Law and Society in Philadelphia.

[4] Frances Bernat, a lawyer, Ph.D., and neutral party in the D.C. prisoner affair, conducted an analysis of Washington State law, the Interstate Corrections Compact, and relevant court decisions, and concluded that the contract was not legal.

She concluded that under Washington State law a county in the state does not have the authority to enter into a contract of this nature. Dr. Bernat points out that Spokane County also violated many of the provisions of the contract that required the jail to provide prisoners with the same services, programs, and reviews as provided by the D.C. Department of Corrections. At no point did Spokane County comply with these contract provisions, nor is it likely that the jail could have provided comparable services, programs, and reviews required by the contract. For a comprehensive analysis of the contract and relevant legal issues, see: Linda L. Zupan and Frances Bernat, "The Legality of Interstate Prisoner Transfers to County Jail Facilities," a paper presented at the 1992 annual meeting of the Law and Society Association in Philadelphia.

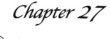

Chapter 27

Three Strikes as a Public Policy
The Convergence of the New Penology and the McDonaldization of Punishment

David Shichor

Introduction

Street crime has become one of the major public concerns in the United States during the past two decades. In response to it, several "war on crime" campaigns have been waged since the 1970s, and there is a growing public demand to get "tough on crime" and to get even tougher on violent and repeating criminals. The crime issue has become a focal point of almost all political campaigns and a rallying cry for politicians that fits into the general conservative political climate that has become prominent since the 1970s. Also, crime has become a dominant theme in the media, and, in turn, presentations of crime have influenced criminal justice policies (Sanders and Lyon, 1995; Surette, 1996). These trends led to the "war on drugs," more and longer prison sentences, the rapid

David Shichor, *Crime & Delinquency*, Vol. 43 No. 4, pp. 470–492, copyright © 1997 by Sage Publications. Reprinted by permission of Sage Publications.

growth of the prison population, the overcrowding of correctional facilities, and the steep increase in correctional costs. Irwin and Austin (1994) referred to these developments as the "imprisonment binge" and noted that, at the end of the 1980s, 39 states were under court order to "cap" their prison populations unless the holding capacities of their prisons were increased. In the spring of 1994, the U.S. prison population passed the 1 million mark and the nation gained the dubious honor of having the highest incarceration rate in the world. By 1996, the U.S. jail and prison population was around the 1.5 million mark.

In spite of the chronic problems of overcrowding and the bulging correctional costs and budget shortages, the pursuit of penal policies of deterrence-incapacitation continues unabated (Shichor, 1987). In 1994, as an incremental step toward increasingly punitive crime policies (Saint-Germain and Calamia, 1996), the Violent Crime Control and Law Enforcement Act, also known as the Federal Crime Bill, was enacted by Congress. Among other things, this law "mandates life in prison for criminals convicted of three violent felonies or drug offenses if the third conviction is a federal crime" (Lewis, 1994:6). It became labeled, using the popular baseball lingo, as the "three strikes and you're out" law. Several states followed suit and enacted similar measures.[1] One of those mentioned most often was the California mandatory sentencing law, which came into effect in March 1994 and prescribes that "felons found guilty of a third serious crime be locked up for 25 years to life." It stipulates the following:

> Although the first two "strikes" accrue for serious felonies, the crime that triggers the life sentence can be for any felony. Furthermore, the law doubles sentences for a second strike, requires that these extended sentences be served in prison (rather than in jail or on probation), and limits "good time" earned during prison to 20 percent of the sentence given (rather than 50 percent, as under the previous law). (Greenwood, Rydell, Abrahamse, Caulkins, Chiesa, Model, and Klein, 1994:xi)

It is not clear yet how the further implementation of the California law will be affected by the recent state supreme court ruling that judges have the discretion to overlook prior convictions in three-strikes cases (Dolan and Perry, 1996).

This article focuses on the "three-strikes" laws in general with particular emphasis on the California measure because that law has been the most scrutinized and quoted in the professional literature so far. Although there are differences in some of the details among the various three-strikes laws, their main aims and principles are similar.

Several scholars maintain that recent penal thinking and the ensuing policies have gone through a major paradigm change. According to them, a "new penology" has emerged shifting the traditional penological concern that focused on the individual offender to an actuarial model focusing on the management of aggregates. Feeley and Simon (1992) argued that this change "facilitates development of a vision or a model of a new type of criminal that embraces increased reliance on imprisonment . . . that shifts away from concern with punishing individuals to managing aggregates of dangerous groups" (p. 449).

The analysis to follow examines three-strikes laws in relation to the new penology and in relation to their connections to a more general socio-cultural orientation, identified by Ritzer (1993) as the "McDonaldization" of society, based on the rationalization process suggested by Max Weber (one of the pioneers of sociological thought), that is embodied in the model of fast-food restaurants (Weber, 1968). Although these two models have many similar and mutually supportive characteristics that define current criminal justice policies, they diverge in some of the details.

Three Strikes and the New Penology

In a widely cited article, Feeley and Simon (1992) claimed that the conservative turn in the social and penal ideology of the 1970s and 1980s led to a new trend in penology that involves changes in three major aspects:

1. The emergence of new discourses: In particular, the language of probability and risk increasingly replaces earlier discourses of clinical diagnosis and retributive judgment.

2. The formation of new objectives: [T]he increasing primacy [is] given to the efficient control of internal system processes in place of the traditional objectives of rehabilitation and crime control.

3. The deployment of new techniques: These techniques target offenders as an aggregate in place of traditional techniques for individualizing or creating equity. (p. 450)

Three-strikes measures are one manifestation of these changes. Their language employs terms such as "high-risk offenders" or "strikeable offenses," and their objectives center around efficient control of the operation of the criminal justice system.

Feeley and Simon (1992) contrasted the new trend with what they called the "old penology" based on American law focusing on individuals and in which penal sanctioning "has been aimed at individual-based theories of punishment." By contrast, the new penology is "concerned with techniques to identify, classify, and manage groupings sorted by dangerousness" (pp. 451–52). This approach is more concerned with responses to social harm "based on aggregations and statistical averages" than with the punishment and treatment tailored to individual perpetrators (Alschuler, 1990:15–16). Accordingly, certain subpopulations, which are identified by officials as "high-rate offenders," "career criminals," or "habitual offenders" and by social scientists as the "underclass" or the "truly disadvantaged," are to be singled out for special surveillance, aggregate management, and selective incapacitation (Hagan, 1995). This view has centered on criminal justice policies that are in accord with an orientation of penal administrators that is focused on managerial goals (Garland, 1990). As a consequence, "Sanctioning rates are determined by the ways in which official actors use strategic discretion to manage their domains of action and only indirectly by reform or socioeconomic imperatives" (Sutton, 1987:613). Henry and Milavonovic (1996) described this new penology as a "discourse based on utilitarian considerations rather than on moral ones" (p. 114).

In an earlier work, Cohen (1985) reviewed some of the results of this move toward "containment and coercion" (p. 108). Among other things, he foresaw "increasing rates of imprisonment," "increasing severity of punishment," "a widening net of criminalization," and "greater publicity given to street crimes." He pointed out that the new direction that abandoned rehabilitation as an objective in favor of the management of controlled groups has created a bifurcation of penal policies. The "hard" side of the control system became harsher, resulting in more incarceration, longer prison stays, and determinate and mandatory sentences for "hard core," "career," and "dangerous" offenders, whereas the less serious offenders (Cohen referred to them as "deviants") were to be handled by the "soft end" of the system, mostly in community settings under various surveillance practices often referred to as "intermediate sanctions." These measures are more severe than traditional probation but less restrictive than incarceration; they include home arrest and intensive probation often monitored by electronic surveillance systems, boot camps, and drug rehabilitation programs (Morris and Tonry, 1990). These policies have led to "net widening" because the extended use of intermediate sanctions has brought people who otherwise would have been handled informally under some type of supervision or into formal correctional programs.

The change from penal policies aimed at punishment and rehabilitation of individuals to the management and control of certain categories of people has followed the pessimism expressed about the criminal justice system's ability to change offenders, making them into law-abiding citizens (Gottfredson and Hirschi, 1990; Martinson, 1974). In this vein, Bottoms (1980) noted that "the abandonment of the rehabilitative ethic has led to a widespread abandonment of hope" (p. 20) because the idea of rehabilitation was an expression of optimism about human nature and about the ability of social organizations to bring out the positive in people. The new penology takes for granted that a high level of criminal behavior will continue to occur, and its concern is how to manage the criminal justice system efficiently rather than to effect major changes in crime rates or to bring about rehabilitation of a significant number of offenders.

The new penology has rekindled the historical notion of "dangerous classes" that traditionally has been linked to the urban poor.[2] Feeley and Simon (1992) claimed that the new penology is oriented toward the management of a "permanently dangerous population" (p. 463). Their description of this population parallels Wilson's (1987) depiction of the "underclass," which, because of the social realities of capitalist industrial societies in which production is based on a high level of technology and a reduction of manual labor, became a marginal population, unemployable, lacking in adequate education and marketable skills, and without any real prospects or hope to change its situation. This approach bears a similarity to the Marxist concept of the "lumpenproletariat," an exploited and potentially dangerous class whose members lack class consciousness and, instead of fighting the ruling class to change their inferior social and economic conditions, prey mainly on their poor working-class compatriots (Bonger, [1916] 1969).

The new penal approach, focusing on the control and management of specific aggregates, has made increasing use of actuarial methods that rely heavily on statistical decision theory, operations research techniques, and system analysis to devise and implement penal policies (Simon, 1988). These reflect the positivist orientation in criminology that concentrates on "methods, techniques, or rules of procedure" rather than on "substantive theory or perspectives" (Gottfredson and Hirschi, 1987:10).[3] This trend was reinforced in Alfred Blumstein's presidential address to the members of the American Society of Criminology in which he saw as one of the most important missions of criminological researchers "the generation of knowledge that is useful in dealing with crime and the operation of the criminal justice system (i.e., relevance) and then helping public officials to use that knowledge intelligently and effectively (rationality)" (Blumstein, 1993:1).

Three-strikes laws have historical roots in American penology (Feeley and Kamin, 1996; Zeigler and Del Carmen, 1996; Turner, Sundt, Applegate, and Cullen, 1995). They are based on the penal principle of incapacitation. The rationale behind this principle is that "some crimes are produced exclusively by exceptional people, as some commodities are. If some of these people are incapacitated, production is reduced" (Van den Haag, 1975:53). In theory, three-strikes laws were meant to target repeating violent and dangerous felons, similar to "selective incapacitation" strategies that "target a small group of convicted offenders, those who are predicted to commit serious crimes at high rates, for incarceration" (Visher, 1987:513). Implicitly, three-strikes laws also involve the probability and risk assessment of certain aggregates and the "management" (through long prison sentences) of those high-risk groups that are considered to be the most harmful to society.

In one respect, however, three-strikes laws do not seem to be in tune with the new penology, which, according to Feeley and Simon (1992), in addition to focusing on the management and control of "a permanently dangerous population," is concerned with "maintaining the system at a minimum cost" (p. 463). Three-strikes legislation does not put a major emphasis on dealing with the material consequences of its implementation.[4] In this regard, Simon and Feeley (1994) criticized the three-strikes measures, stating, "This spate of three-strikes laws as well as other types of mandatory sentences can easily be characterized as mindless 'spending sprees' or 'throwing money at a problem' without likelihood of benefit" (p. 13). However, advocates may claim that indirectly, through the reduction of serious crimes that is expected as a result of the implementation of these measures and the ensuing "bifurcation" according to which intermediate punishments, therapies, fines, or even release are applied to categories of offenders classified as less serious criminals (including many white-collar crime offenders), certain concern with correctional cost is implied.

The new penology's approach of controlling "permanently dangerous people," depicted as potentially habitual criminals often connected with the drug scene, is related to a sociocultural atmosphere in which phenomena similar to moral panics may easily emerge (Cohen, 1973). There is a pervasive public perception, reinforced by the mass media, that these dangerous offenders "pose a threat to the society and to the moral order. . . . Therefore, 'something should be done' about them and their behavior" (Goode and Ben-Yehuda, 1994:31). This "something" usually is the increased severity of punishment. One major reflection of this trend is the legislation of three-strikes laws. But in addition, the contention of this article is that these measures also are related to, and are characteristic of, the social control policies that may be derived from the McDonaldization model of society.

The McDonaldization of Punishment

In a recent book, Ritzer (1993) used the analogy of fast-food establishments to characterize and analyze the social and cultural ethos of modern technological societies, particularly that of the United States. He defined McDonaldization as "the process by which the principles of the fast-food restaurant are coming to dominate more and more sectors of American society as well as the rest of the world" (p. 1). This process also has a major impact on the social control policies of these societies. The theoretical underpinnings of the three-strikes measures, their definitions of strikeable offenses, and the wide-scale public support of these types of legislation are closely related to, and are influenced by, McDonaldization.

In this model, which is based on the Weberian concept of "formal rationality" (Weber, 1968), there are four basic dimensions of the fast-food industry: efficiency, calculability, predictability, and control. Efficiency refers to the tendency to choose the optimum means to a given end, calculability is identified as the tendency to quantify and calculate every product and to use quantity as a measure of quality, predictability has to do with the preference to know what to expect in all situations at all times, and control involves the replacement of human technology with nonhuman technology in a way that goods, services, products, and workers are better controlled. Ritzer (1993) suggested that there are various degrees of McDonaldization and that some phenomena are more McDonaldized than others. As mentioned previously, the contention of this article is that three-strikes laws are promoting punishment policies in accordance with this model.

Efficiency and Penal Policy

Efficiency in the context of three strikes can be defined as the achievement of the maximum possible incapacitation effect for dangerous offenders. Incapacitation can be seen as an indicator of efficiency because offenders are prevented during their prison sentences from causing harm in their outside communities. The issue of serious street crime is a valance issue, "one that elicits a single, strong, fairly emotional response and does not have an adversarial quality" (Fattah, 1986:3). There is general consensus that something has to be done about this major social problem, and this widely held public concern is exploited by politicians who want to show their commitment to fighting crime by proposing extreme punishments in order to be elected. Thus, the "solution" to the "growing" problem of "serious" crime is the adoption of incapacitation as the leading penal policy, that is, applying more and longer prison sentences to a larger variety of offenses and offenders. This policy is seen by many legislators, public officials, and large segments of the public as efficient because, if followed properly, it should deprive offenders of the opportunity to commit additional harm against innocent victims during their incarcerations. Three-strikes laws make incapacitation mandatory and long lasting; therefore, many consider them as a major step in the "search for a far better means to an end than would be employed under ordinary circumstances" (Ritzer, 1993:35), a hallmark of efficiency. One of this policy's major attractions is that, like the new penology, it focuses on a specific discredited group, the "dangerous" violent criminals who are mainly from lower-class backgrounds. Therefore, by incapacitating these offenders who are responsible for a disproportionately high percentage of violent crimes, this measure is seen as potentially very efficient. An additional expectation is that three-strikes laws will have an increased deterrent effect (both specific and general) as a result of the increase in the severity of punishment. Theoretically, the deterrence factor coupled with incapacitation should enhance preventive efficiency; thus, this measure carries the promise that a substantial reduction of crime rates can be achieved. Indeed, the RAND Corporation's analysis of the long-term impact of California's three-strikes measure predicts a 22 percent to 34 percent decline in serious felonies (Greenwood et al., 1994).[5] But a major question remains: At what price will this decline be achieved, if at all?

Calculability

According to commonsense thinking, three-strikes laws make punishment easily calculable. In a three-strikes sentence, as in other mandatory and determinate sentences, the release date is calculable at the time of the sentencing because only a limited good time range is stipulated in the law. The calculation of the sentence is based on the seriousness of the offense and the prior record of the offender. The "sentencing guideline grid" used in Minnesota often is mentioned as an example of calculable sentences. The Minnesota Sentencing Commission has "established a ten-category scale for ranking offenses and a seven-point scale measuring prior convictions. Combining these two dimensions provides a seventy-cell matrix. For each cell in the matrix, the commission established presumptive sentences" (Goodstein and Hepburn, 1985:77).

Zimring and Hawkins (1991) referred to this sentencing method as the "mechanical approach" (p. 161) to determining punishment. It severely limits judicial discretion and provides a sterling example of calculability both for policy makers and for the general public. Three-strikes measures work on the same principle as does the Minnesota grid with the addition of the mandatory component, which enhances the calculability of the punishment even more.

Calculability also implies that quantity becomes the indicator of quality.[6] In terms of punishment, the fact that three-strikes laws increase substantially the length of punishment for "dangerous" criminals is an indicator for many politicians, officials, and citizens that the "quality" of justice is improved. Also, the severe reduction of prisoners' good time included in these measures (e.g., for a second strike, offenders in California have to serve at least 80 percent of their sentences instead of 50 percent as before) increases the calculability of punishment by lessening the disparities of time served among inmates. This feature of three-strikes laws seems to satisfy often-voiced demands for "truth in sentencing" because the time convicted offenders will serve in prison is known from the beginning and supposedly will increase the deterrent effect of punishment by substantially lengthening the sentences.

Predictability

Prediction is one of the aims of science. The method of scientific inquiry, based on the principle of rationality that provides predictive ability, is highly valued in modern societies. In them, government authorities try to base public policies on rational foundations to be able to predict and control what is going to happen in the future. Thus, McDonaldization follows a highly rational model:

> Rationalization involves the increasing effort to ensure predictability from one time or place to another. In a rational society, people prefer to know what to expect in all settings and at all times. . . . In order to ensure predictability over time and place, a rational society emphasizes such things as discipline, order, systematization, formalization, routine, consistency, and methodical operation. (Ritzer, 1993:83)

The importance of prediction in criminal justice is underscored by Gottfredson (1987), who asserted that prediction is "often a requisite to control and is central to the application of scientific methods to understand and control crime. If one seeks to control crime behavior, one needs first [to] be able to predict it" (p. 6).

Three-strikes laws are assumed to provide a high level of predictability regarding the nature and extent of penal sanctions because, by curtailing judicial discretion, the punishment is known and, consequently, the variations in sentences among jurisdictions and among individual judges are reduced or eliminated. Thus, theoretically, these measures are in line with the retributive ideal of uniformity of punishment.

Control

McDonaldization involves the increased control over production and products, especially through the substitution of nonhuman for human technology (Ritzer, 1993). Three-strikes laws increase substantially the control over sentencing, especially when they use prepared formulas such as Minnesota's sentencing guidelines grid for the determination of punishment. This practice follows the formal legal theory of sentencing, which suggests that "sentencing is primarily determined by legal variables" (Dixon, 1995:1157). According to this model, imposition of a sentence can be accomplished easily by a computer program when relevant items of information such as the offense or prior criminal history are entered in the computer and the sentence is automatically meted out. The fact that upon conviction the sentence is mandatory and determined is supposed to give a great deal of control over the punishment into the hands of legislators and prosecutors and, as seen, is supposed to limit considerably the courts' discretion. This development is a major shift in the power structure of the criminal justice system. Many judges are frustrated by their loss of discretion and resent the fact that they have little say regarding the nature and amount of punishment. In most cases, their involvement in sentencing hardly amounts to more than a rubber stamp on law enforcement and prosecutorial decision making that determines the charges that will be leveled against defendants.

Mechanical control and nonhuman technology are applied not only to the determination of sentences but also to the location and conditions of punishment (e.g., the security level of prisons, the type of intermediate sentences). This is a part of the growing trend toward the application of nonhuman technology such as electronic surveillance, urinalysis, computer-based offender-tracking systems, or electronic monitoring as well as the use of other technical devices such as hydraulic doors or other automated security systems in prisons[7] in penal practice.

The extension of control by nonhuman technology started with the modernization of punishment and the emergence of the penitentiary.

Bentham's nineteenth-century Panopticon was planned to incorporate into its architectural design a mechanism for a "totalizing surveillance" (Simon, 1993:4) that allowed for the reduction of correctional personnel. Garland (1990) pointed out that in the Panopticon "the power relations involved are, in a sense, automated and objective. They are an effect of the distribution of places and visibility and do not depend upon the strength or intentions of those who occupy these positions" (p. 146). According to Foucault (1977), the major impact of the Panopticon was "to introduce in the inmate a state of conscious and permanent visibility that assure the automatic functioning of power" (p. 201). He used the term "panopticism" to refer to the mechanical maximization of surveillance in prison.

Stryker's (1989) analysis of the "technocratization of law" in modern capitalist societies has direct relevance to the issue at hand. She emphasized the reliance of the modern state on science and predicted that the "advanced capitalist state will increasingly incorporate scientific-technical expertise" (p. 341). Furthermore, she pointed out that the reliance on technological methods has a depoliticizing effect and converts questions of policy goals to questions of efficacy of means. This development is characteristic of the McDonaldization process including the penal policies that have culminated in the legislation of three-strikes laws.

The Irrational Consequences of McDonaldization in Penology

Three-strikes laws and McDonaldization are phenomena of modernization that put a high value on rationality. However, although McDonaldization represents rationalism (i.e., scientific approach, positivism, modernity), it also leads to irrational consequences. Borrowing from Weber's (1969) concept of the "iron cage of rationality," Ritzer (1993) referred to these consequences as the "irrationality of rationality" (p. 12). In the case of McDonaldization, irrationalities may result in inefficiency, incalculability, unpredictability, and lack of control, which may have serious effects on penal policies and practices.

Inefficiency

One of the inefficiencies of fast-food sites is that although they are meant to be "fast," often long lines of people have to wait to be served (Ritzer, 1993). In the criminal justice system, three-strikes laws contribute to the clogging up of courts and the overcrowding of confinement facilities. The measure also seems to have had a major impact on the number of cases that go to trial. In California, before the new law came into effect in March 1994, about 90 percent to 94 percent of all criminal cases were settled through plea bargaining. But in the summer of that year, Santa Clara County projected a 160 percent increase in the number of criminal trials (Cushman, 1996). In an assessment of the preliminary impacts of the three-strikes implementation for the first eight months, the California Legislative Analyst's Office (1995b) found a 144 percent increase in jury trials in Los Angeles County. In San Diego County, it is expected that there will be a 300 percent increase in jury trials. The decline in plea bargaining is the result of the mandatory aspect of the three-strikes law. Many offenders feel that they cannot gain much from a negotiated settlement under the new law and that it is preferable to exercise their constitutional right to jury trials without increasing their risks of substantially more severe sentences. The increase in the number of trials not only has affected the three-strikes cases but also has caused delays in nonstrike criminal and civil cases. For example, the Los Angeles district attorney transferred a large number of attorneys who previously were handling white-collar cases to work on three-strikes offenses.

The growing backlog in the courts also has had an impact on county jails because more suspects are detained for longer periods of time prior to their trials (McCarthy, 1995). Although some early studies indicate that the expected effects are evolving at a slower pace than as projected (Cushman, 1996), there is a strong potential for major "gridlocks" in jails. The California Legislative Analyst's Office (1995b) elaborated on this situation:

> Because offenders charged under the "three-strikes" law face significant prison sentences, most counties set bail for second-strike offenders at twice the usual amount and refuse bail for third-strike offenders. These bail charges, coupled with more offenders taking their cases to trial, result in more offenders being incarcerated in county jails. (p. 5)

Another efficiency issue is concerned with the type of offenders handled by the three-strikes law. This law was enacted to curb violent crime, or at least "serious" crime, through the incapacitation of "dangerous" and violent criminals. However, early findings in California indicate that most offenders prosecuted and convicted under this measure have been brought into the system for nonviolent offenses (California Legislative Analyst's Office, 1995b). Furthermore, this measure inevitably will increase the numbers of elderly inmates in prisons because of the long terms mandated in this legislation.[8] In 1994, inmates age 50 years or older represented about 4 percent of the California prison population, but it was estimated that by 2005 they will constitute around 12 percent of the inmates (National Council on Crime and Delinquency, 1994). Studies of crime patterns indicate that violent predatory crime tends to decline sharply with age (Shichor and Kobrin, 1978); thus, a rapidly growing segment of the prison population will be confined in spite of the facts that its members pose little danger to society and that keeping them in prison is unlikely to reduce the volume of crime (Benekos and Merlo, 1995). This is an ineffective use of limited criminal justice resources.

Also, the cost of implementation of the three-strikes law is related to effectiveness in that incarceration is an expensive correctional option.

Although the three-strikes law is presented as a rational measure to curb serious crime and to punish serious habitual offenders, it may be a very expensive or even wasteful policy (O'Connell, 1995), a suggestion that certainly merits a careful cost-benefit analysis. Ritzer (1993:123) cited the columnist Richard Cohen, who observed that rational systems are not less expensive than other systems; indeed, they may cost more. According to all indications, the three-strikes law will increase considerably the cost of criminal justice operations because (a) more people will be detained in jails, (b) the increase in the number of trials will necessitate the building of more courts and the hiring of more judges and other court personnel, (c) the number of long-term prisoners will grow and so more prisons will have to be built, (d) the growing number of elderly prisoners will need additional (and more expensive) health care than prisons usually provide (Merianos, Marquart, Damphouse, and Herbert, 1997), and (e) welfare agencies will have to support a larger number of dependents of incarcerated felons for longer periods of time than ever before.[9]

It is a major concern that rapidly increasing correctional expenditures will have detrimental effects on other public services. For example, Greenwood et al. (1994) projected that, in California, "to support the implementation of the law, total spending for higher education and other services would have to fall by more than 40 percent over the next 8 years" (p. 34).

Incalculability

The outcomes of three-strikes cases, which were supposedly easily calculable, often are not so. Concerning mandatory laws, Blumstein, Cohen, Martin, and Tonry (1983) observed that they are "vulnerable to circumvention because they are inflexible and require imposition of penalties that judges and prosecutors may believe to be inappropriate in individual cases" (p. 179). The situation is similar in jurisdictions that use sentencing guidelines that "do not assure the elimination or even the reduction of sentencing disparity" (Kramer and Ulmer, 1996:81).

This observation seems to be valid regarding three-strikes laws as well. One reason is that they are not being applied uniformly by prosecutors in the different jurisdictions. Cushman (1996) and Feeley and Kamin (1996) documented differences among California counties in the extent of use of this measure. Also, there have been many instances in which the incalculability of punishment has been demonstrated in jurisdictions where the three-strikes law was widely applied. For example, because of overcrowding of jails by detainees who were reluctant to plea bargain, many minor offenders have been released early from jail, and a large number of misdemeanants have not even been prosecuted. Thus, the calculability of punishment for minor offenders has been neglected and even sacrificed for that of three-strikes offenders. In other instances, some arrests that could have been qualified as three-strikes cases have been processed as parole violations rather than new offenses and, thus, were not considered as felonies (Spiegel, 1994). In other cases, prosecutors and judges have ignored some previous felonies or redefined them as non-strike offenses (Colvin and Rohrlich, 1994). The recent California Supreme Court ruling, mentioned earlier, that gives judges the discretion to overlook a defendant's prior convictions (Dolan and Perry, 1996) is a reinforcement of the authority of the courts to determine the punishment of convicted offenders and to curb somewhat the gains of the prosecutors' influence on sentencing.

As noted, the quantity of punishment delivered (i.e., the length of incarceration) has been touted as a major virtue of three-strikes measures, whereas its effects on other aspects of social life and culture have not been considered to be important. For example, little concern has been paid to the concept of justice that requires a balance between the seriousness of the crime and the severity of punishment. In 1994, a California offender was sentenced to prison for 25 years to life for grabbing a slice of pepperoni pizza from a youngster (this sentence was reduced in January 1997, and he will be released by 1999). Another offender received 30 years to life for stealing a video recorder and a coin collection. Still another three-striker got 25 years to life for stealing a package of meat worth $5.62, apparently to feed his family (Slater, 1995). More recently, a heroin addict with a record of previous theft-related offenses was sentenced to 25 years to life for stealing two pair of jeans worth $80 from a store (Abrahamson and Maharaj, 1996). These and similar cases pose serious questions concerning the proportionality of punishment even though the offenders had prior felony convictions. One Los Angeles County Superior Court judge declared in this regard, "I refuse to dispense injustice" (Colvin and Rohrlich, 1994:40). Similarly, another aspect of justice, equal treatment, is being neglected because three-strikes measures focus almost exclusively on street crimes that usually are committed by poor offenders. Meanwhile, crimes of the middle and upper classes either are not affected or will be handled even more leniently than before because the criminal justice system that is overoccupied by predatory street crimes will have diminishing resources to deal with them. Geis's (1996) comments in this regard are well taken: "The failure to extend the 'three strikes and you're out' policy to white-collar offenders provides persuasive evidence of the class bias that fuels this viciously punitive policy" (p. 244). Thus, the implementation of this measure will increase perceptions, which already are pervasive among many, that the criminal justice system is biased, discriminatory, and unjust.

Another factor that adds to the incalculability of this measure is that it is not applied uniformly. Data pertaining to the first six months of implementation compiled by the Los Angeles Public Defender's Office indicate that minorities with criminal histories comparable to those of White offenders were being charged under the three-strikes law at 17 times the rate of Whites (Donziger, 1996).

Although many citizens see the long sentences meted out under the three-strikes law as indicators of "high-quality" justice, there are others who will raise questions concerning justice, just desert, and injustice in American society. Some will consider this measure as an expression of the "triumph of vengeance over retribution" (Haas, 1994:127) when vengeance becomes institutionalized as a public policy (Shichor and Sechrest, 1996).

Unpredictability

Several of the issues concerning predictability resemble those that emerged in relation to efficiency and calculability. For various reasons, the outcomes of three-strikes cases are not as clearly predictable as they were intended to be, based on this law's mandatory and determinate nature. For example, in some instances victims refuse to testify when the convictions would carry sentences of long-term incarceration under the three-strikes law ("California Judge Refuses," 1994). In other cases, juries may fail to convict for the same reason. Forst (1983) cited studies of mandatory sentencing laws that found that

> they tend to induce dismissals, acquittals, and other outcomes that make the laws ineffective, so that the longer average sentences for those convicted are approximately offset by increases in the number of persons not convicted and sentenced. Thus, sentence disparity actually increases under mandatory sentencing. (p. 179)

As noted previously, because of jail overcrowding caused by the growing numbers of detainees waiting for trials, many sheriff departments release minor offenders early to ease the situation. Sometimes this is done because of court orders that limit facility crowding. According to court sources, in Los Angeles County, misdemeanor offenders sentenced to one year in jail are serving on the average only 19 days (Lindner, 1995). Thus, the implementation of the three-strikes law, instead of increasing the predictability of punishment, may have an opposite impact in non-strike cases. Moreover, as has been seen, the outcome of a case under this law may be entirely different from what was foreseen because juries may refuse to convict, authorities may refuse to press a felony charge, or the courts may not count previous felonies. Also, by decreasing considerably the number of plea bargains and by increasing the number of jury trials, a larger number of outcomes may become unpredictable. Although plea bargaining should not be considered as the best method of dispensing justice, it does provide a certain level of predictability, being an almost permanent fixture of the criminal justice process. Thus, it seems that in many instances, including three-strike laws, instead of increasing the predictability of punishment as they were meant to do, determinate and mandatory sentences may contribute to unpredictability.

Similarly, by placing the emphasis on the predictability of "aggregate control and system management rather than individual success and failure" (Feeley and Simon, 1992:455), three-strikes laws cannot predict, and are not interested in predicting, the effects of the punishment on individual convicts, and they may waste a great deal of money, time, and effort on false positives by keeping those who would not cause further harm to society incarcerated for long periods of time. Farrington (1987) pointed out, concerning prediction of criminal behavior, that "it is inevitably difficult to predict a rare phenomenon such as [the] high rate of offending, and it seems both unjust and inefficient to apply penal measures to persons who neither deserve nor need them" (p. 91). Three-strikes legislation was based on the assumption that the high rate of criminal behavior of "dangerous" offenders already has been proven; however, many times it is dependent on how the offenders' criminal records are being used by the prosecution and the courts. Although the predictability of the outcome of three-strikes measures is focused only on the punishment factor, the predictability of other outcomes that are influenced by the punishment does not seem to constitute a genuine concern for those who advocate such measures.

Finally, because the application of three-strikes laws may vary from one jurisdiction to another, the extent and accuracy of predictability also may vary among jurisdictions, as was the case concerning the calculability of punishment.

In short, like the case with many other public policies, the implementation of three-strikes laws is likely to lead to many unintended consequences that may defeat some of the very same purposes that the laws were supposed to fulfill.

Lack of Control

Rational systems often can spin out of the control of those who devise and use them (Ritzer, 1993). Sentencing based on an almost automatic decision-making system drastically reduces the court's authority to consider particular circumstances of offenses and individual differences among offenders. However, there are experts who maintain that to render a high quality of justice, a certain degree of judicial discretion is essential. The dilemma of sentencing under a mandatory system of punishment was noted by Tonry (1996):

> The quality of justice is impoverished when sentencing laws or guidelines, in the interest of treating like cases alike, make it difficult or impossible for judges to treat different cases differently. The quality of justice and public respect for legal institutions likewise are diminished when judges, forced to choose between their oaths to do justice and to enforce the law, participate in disingenuous circumvention of mandatory minimum sentence laws and rigid guidelines in order to do justice. (pp. 165–66)

There also is the issue of "hidden discretion"; that is, whereas the court's decision-making power in the imposition of punishment is severely curtailed, the discretion of law enforcement, and especially that of the prosecution, increases greatly. The charges brought against a suspect will be determined by these agencies. The major discretionary decision in many instances will be whether a case should be filed as a misdemeanor or a felony, which bears directly on the application of three-strikes laws. The changes in the locus of discretion in the criminal justice process mean that decision making will become less visible than before because courts are an open forum, and their decisions, even in plea bargaining cases, can be scrutinized and monitored much more easily than the ones made by law enforcement and the prosecution behind closed doors. Consequently, the ability of the judicial system to control the imposition and administration of the law will be affected. In many instances, the lack of control will stem not from the latitude in sentencing but rather from the growing discretionary powers given to agencies in the pretrial stages of the criminal justice process. Because of the reduced visibility of decision making in the determination of charges, in many cases sentencing disparities among jurisdictions may become even greater in spite of the promise of increased control over such differences under three-strikes laws.

Another related aspect of control, namely ensuring that the most "dangerous" offenders who are the most harmful to society will be the ones incapacitated for long periods of time, also is not fulfilled. Many three-strikes cases involve property offenders and drug abusers rather than vicious, violent criminals.

In sum, the promise of a high level of control over punishment, which was one of the major aims of mandatory and determinate sentencing including three-strikes laws (the other was the increase in the severity of punishment), can spin out of control and result in unintended and unforeseen consequences.

Conclusion

The three-strikes laws that have spread recently in the United States are a reaction to a moral panic that has swept the country since the late 1970s. On the public policy level, these measures can be viewed as being related to the new penology trend. They are based on the concern for managing aggregates of "dangerous" people rather than being concerned with rendering justice, protecting the community, or attempting to rehabilitate individual offenders. The emphasis is on rational criminal justice operations that apply management methods based on statistical estimates of patterns of crimes and future inmate populations, risk indicators of future criminal behavior, operations research, and system analysis.

Three-strikes laws also are in line with the modern sociocultural ethos of McDonaldization (Ritzer, 1993), a model built on the principles of rationality embodying an attitude that "it is possible to calculate and purposively manipulate the environment" (Chirot, 1994:63). However, the quest for extreme rationality can lead to irrationalities in the practical workings of this model (Weber, 1968; Ritzer, 1993). Often, the application of three-strikes laws results in inefficiency of the criminal justice process, punishments are not always clearly calculable, predictability of outcomes may be negatively affected by rational procedures, and the system may lose control over the nature of punishment. In short, as is the case with many other public policies, three-strikes laws could lead to a host of unintended consequences that may defeat the purposes for which they were intended. Probably, the greatest irrationality of the penal policy represented by three-strikes laws is their tremendous economic cost. Various studies have indicated that three-strikes laws will cost such sums of public money that they can hardly be characterized as rational on the basis of any cost-benefit calculation. In fact, these laws may seriously endanger the quality, or even the existence, of some important and essential social programs such as support for higher education, welfare, environmental protection, or cultural programs and may have a negative impact on the quality of life for millions of people (see Greenwood et al., 1994). In sum, it seems that, as Ritzer (1993) claimed, modern contemporary society is locked into the "iron cage of rationality," which is characterized by policies made on a rational basis that lead to irrational consequences. This is demonstrated in current penal policies given that punishment "relies on meanings and symbols and representations that construe its own actions and weave them into the belief systems, sensibilities, and cultural narratives of the social actors and audiences involved" (Garland, 1991:192–93).

Some advocates of these measures, especially politicians such as California's attorney general (who is a potential Republican candidate for governor in 1998), attribute the major part of the decline in the crime rates in 1994 to the application of the state's three-strikes law (Ingram, 1995). However, others maintain that mandatory sentences have not made the streets safer (e.g., O'Connell, 1995) and that although Americans are proud of their personal freedoms and their constitutional rights, many of them do not feel free to walk the streets of their own neighborhoods.

The general results of three-strikes laws remain to be analyzed. Future studies will have to evaluate a wide range of policy-related issues in addition to the crime rates. They also will have to gauge public perceptions regarding crime including the fear of crime, the readiness to continue costly incapacitation policies, and the willingness to deal with societal problems related to crime and social control. As Mauer (1994) pointed out, the "overriding problem with this legislation is that it is diverting our attention from a serious discussion of how the nation could go about addressing the crime problem in a comprehensive way" (p. 12). Finally, there should be some concern with theoretical and ethical issues such as justice and injustice, the proportionality of punishment, the amplification of crime in the media, the symbolic meanings of three-strikes laws, the racial aspects of the application of these measures, and the degree of punitiveness that a free society can tolerate.

Endnotes

[1] In a review of three-strikes laws nationwide, Turner, Sundt, Applegate, and Cullen (1995) found that 37 jurisdictions had proposed three-strikes legislation by 1995; out of these 37 jurisdictions, 15 actually enacted such laws, which are not exactly the same in all the jurisdictions.

[2] Citizens in nineteenth-century England distinguished between the "deserving" and the "undeserving" poor. The undeserving urban poor were seen as paupers or the "criminal class." The Poor Laws of 1834 were enacted to regulate the growing population of the urban poor in large industrial cities (Tobias, 1972). Also in America during the colonial period, there was a negative public attitude toward certain types of poor people, especially "vagrants." For example, the Poor Law of North Carolina in 1754 was titled "An Act for the Restraint of Vagrants and for Making Provisions for the Poor." A 1699 Massachusetts law was titled "An Act for Suppressing and Punishing Rogues, Vagabonds, Common Beggars . . . and Also for Setting the Poor to Work." Workhouses were established in several colonies with their primary function being to prevent vagrants from endangering the peace of the towns. Later, in the nineteenth century, there also was public sentiment against the "paupers" who were held responsible for their own situations and who were seen by many people as potential criminals (Rothman, 1971). Wilson (1987) and most other social scientists relate the development of "underclass" or "dangerous classes" to the social arrangements of modern industrialized societies and do not imply that members of these classes are responsible for their own predicaments.

[3] There is a contrast between "substantive rationalization" of the law, which "means the intrusion of economic, sociological, and ethical criteria upon formal-rational reasoning and decision making" (Savelsberg, 1992:1346–47), and "technocratization," which is "the movement toward exclusive use of causal reasoning by scientific-technical experts to make and administer state policy" (Stryker, 1989:342). Both the new penology and McDonaldization are based on technocratization.

[4] Cost estimates of three-strikes implementation indicate that in California, correctional expenses by 2002 will double their share in the general budget from 9 percent to 18 percent (Greenwood et al., 1994). The California Legislative Analyst's Office (1995:7) forecasted that the costs for the California Department of Corrections in 1999–2000 would be about $5 billion (in 1994–95 dollars), an increase of nearly 60 percent in five years. These projections come on top of the increase in correctional expenses that has occurred during the "imprisonment binge" of the 1980s. During that period, "Absolute spending on corrections has increased 217 percent, far outstripping any other segment of the criminal justice system. . . . During the past decade, state spending in corrections was the fastest-growing category of all state spending categories" (Irwin and Austin, 1994:13).

[5] Three-strikes measures do not focus on the celerity and certainty of punishment. Although they try to make sure that convicted offenders will receive harsher sentences, they do not focus on the apprehension rate. Regarding the celerity of punishment, indications are that this law may slow down rather than accelerate the criminal justice process.

[6] The tendency to use quantity as a measure of quality is a characteristic of American culture that has a global influence and is seen by many as the model of modern society (see Kuisel, 1993).

[7] An example of this type of control is the maximum-security prison in Pelican Bay, California, that was opened in the late 1980s and was designed to hold the most dangerous prisoners in the state. The prison is subject to several lawsuits claiming that its confinement conditions violate the Eighth Amendment prohibition against "cruel and unusual punishment."

[8] The definitions of "elderly offenders" or "elderly prisoners" are not standard. Several studies dealing with elderly offenders have followed Shichor and Kobrin's (1978) defini-

tion of age 55 years or older, whereas others have used 65 years of age as an indicator of "older." There are some correctional statistics that group "older" prisoners into a category of "age 40 years or older."

[9] The California Legislative Analyst's Office (1995b) calculated that to maintain the current 182 percent occupancy rate in California prisons, the state will have to build 15 prisons at a cost of about $4.5 billion by 1999. Greenwood et al. (1994) estimated that the implementation of the three-strikes law in the same state will cost between $4.5 billion and $6.5 billion per year. Mandatory sentences for "habitual offenders" cost extraordinarily large sums of money in other states as well.

References

Abrahamson, A., & Maharaj, D. (1996, June 21). O.C. judges hail change in their role. *Los Angeles Times*, pp. A1, A22.

Alschuler, A. W. (1990, May). The failure of sentencing commissions. Paper presented at the Conference of Growth and Its Influence on Correctional Policy: Perspectives on the Report of the Blue Ribbon Commission, University of California, Berkeley.

Benekos, P. J., & Merlo, A. V. (1995). Three strikes and you're out! The political sentencing game. *Federal Probation, 59*(1), 3–9.

Blumstein, A. (1993). Making rationality relevant: The American society of criminology 1992 presidential address. *Criminology, 31*, 1–16.

Blumstein, A., Cohen, J., Martin, S. E., & Tonry, M. H. (1983). *Research on sentencing.* Washington, DC: National Academy Press.

Bonger, W. ([1916] 1969). *Criminality and economic conditions.* Bloomington: Indiana University Press.

Bottoms, A. E. (1980). An introduction to "the coming crisis." In A. E. Bottoms & R. H. Preston (Eds.), *The coming penal crisis* (pp. 1–24). Edinburgh, UK: Scottish Academic Press.

California judge refuses to apply a tough new sentencing law. (1994, September 20). *The New York Times*, pp. A9.

California Legislative Analyst's Office. (1995a). *Status: Accommodating prison population growth.* Sacramento: California Legislative Analyst's Office.

California Legislative Analyst's Office. (1995b). *Status: The three strikes and you're out law – A preliminary assessment.* Sacramento: California Legislative Analyst's Office.

Chirot, D. (1994). *How societies change.* Thousand Oaks, CA: Pine Forge.

Cohen, S. (1973). *Folk devils and moral panics.* St. Albans, UK: Paladin.

Cohen, S. (1985). *Visions of social control.* Cambridge, UK: Polity.

Colvin, R. L., & Rohrlich, T. (1994, October 23). Courts toss curves at "3 strikes." *Los Angeles Times*, pp. A1, A40–43.

Cushman, R. C. (1996). Effect on a local criminal justice system. In D. Shichor & D. K. Sechrest (Eds.), *Three strikes and you're out: Vengeance as public policy* (pp. 90–113). Thousand Oaks, CA: Sage.

Dixon, J. (1995). The organizational context of criminal sentencing. *American Journal of Sociology, 5*, 1157–1198.

Dolan, M., & Perry, T. (1996, June 21). Justices deal blow to "3 strikes." *Los Angeles Times*, pp. A1, A21.

Donziger, S. R. (1996). *The real war on crime: The report of the national criminal justice commission.* New York: Harper & Row.

Farrington, D. P. (1987). Predicting individual crime rates. In D. M. Gottfredson & M. Tonry (Eds.), *Prediction and classification: Criminal justice decision making* (pp. 53–101). Chicago: University of Chicago Press.

Fattah, E. A. (1986). *From crime policy to victim policy: Reorienting the justice system.* London: Macmillan.

Feeley, M. M., & Karnin, S. (1996). The effects of "three strikes and you're out" on the courts: Looking back to see the future. In D. Shichor & D. K. Sechrest (Eds.), *Three strikes and you're out: Vengeance as public policy* (pp. 135–154). Thousand Oaks, CA: Sage.

Feeley, M. M., & Simon, J. (1992). The new penology: Notes on the emerging strategy of corrections and its implications. *Criminology, 30,* 449–474.

Forst, B. (1983). Prosecution and sentencing. In J. Q. Wilson (Ed.), *Crime and public policy* (pp. 165–182). San Francisco: ICS Press.

Foucault, M. (1977). *Discipline and punish: The birth of the prison.* New York: Random House.

Garland, D. (1990). *Punishment in modern society.* Chicago: University of Chicago Press.

Garland, D. (1991). Punishment and culture: The symbolic dimension of criminal justice. In A. Sarat & S. S. Sibley (Eds.), *Studies in law, politics, and society* (Vol. 11, pp. 191–222). Greenwich, CT: JAI.

Geis, G. (1996). A base on balls for white-collar criminals. In D. Shichor & D. K. Sechrest (Eds.), *Three strikes and you're out: Vengeance as public policy* (pp. 244–264). Thousand Oaks, CA: Sage.

Goode, E., & Ben-Yehuda, N. (1994). *Moral panics: The social construction of deviance.* Cambridge, UK: Blackwell.

Goodstein, L., & Hepburn, J. (1985). *Determinate sentencing and imprisonment: A failure of reform.* Cincinnati, OH: Anderson.

Gottfredson, D. M. (1987). Prediction and classification in criminal justice decision making. In D. M. Gottfredson & M. Tonry (Eds.), *Prediction and classification: Criminal justice decision making* (pp. 1–20). Chicago: University of Chicago Press.

Gottfredson, M. R., & Hirschi, T. (1987). *Positive criminology.* Newbury Park, CA: Sage.

Gottfredson, M. R., & Hirschi, T. (1990). *A general theory of crime.* Stanford, CA: Stanford University Press.

Greenwood, P. W., et al. (1994). *Three strikes and you're out: Estimated benefits and costs of California's new mandatory sentencing law.* Santa Monica, CA: RAND.

Haas, K. C. (1994). The triumph of vengeance over retribution: The United States Supreme Court and the death penalty. *Crime, Law and Social Change, 21,* 127–154.

Hagan, J. (1995). Rethinking crime theory and policy: The new sociology of crime and disrepute. In H. D. Barlow (Ed.), *Crime and public policy: Putting theory to work* (pp. 29–42). Boulder, CO: Westview.

Henry, S., & Milovanovic, D. (1996). *Constitutive criminology: Beyond postmodernism.* Thousand Oaks, CA: Sage.

Ingram, C. (1995, May 13). Overall state crime rate drops 7.2 percent, Lundgren says. *Los Angeles Times,* p. A16.

Irwin, J., & Austin, J. (1994). *It is about time: America's imprisonment binge.* Belmont, CA: Wadsworth.

Kramer, J. H., & Ulmer, J. T. (1996). Sentencing disparity and departures from guidelines. *Justice Quarterly, 13,* 81–105.

Kuisel, R. (1993). *Seducing the French: The dilemma of Americanization.* Berkeley: University of California Press.

Lewis, N. A. (1994, August 27). President foresees safer U.S.: Others see crime bill as symbolic. *The New York Times,* p. 6.

Lindner, C. L. (1995, May 7). Commit a misdemeanor — Don't worry about jail. *Los Angeles Times,* p. M1.

Martinson, R. M. (1974). What works? Questions and answers about prison reform. *The Public Interest, 35,* 22–54.

Mauer, M. (1994, March 1). Three strikes and you're out. Testimony before the House Judiciary Committee, Subcommittee on Crime and Criminal Justice, Washington, DC.

McCarthy, N. (1995, March 1). A year later, "3 strikes" clogs jails, slows trials. *California Bar Journal,* 6–7.

Merianos, D. E., Marquart, J. W., Damphouse, K., & Herbert, J. L. (1997). From the outside in: Using public health data to make inferences about older inmates. *Crime & Delinquency, 43,* 298–313.

Morris, N., & Tonry, M. (1990). *Between prison and probation: Intermediate punishment in a rational sentencing system.* New York: Oxford University Press.

National Council on Crime and Delinquency. (1994). *The aging of California's prison population: An assessment of the three strikes legislation.* San Francisco: NCCD.

O'Connell, J. R., Jr. (1995, Winter). Throwing away the key (and state money). *Spectrum,* 28–31.

Ritzer, G. (1993). *The McDonaldization of society.* Newbury Park, CA: Pine Forge.

Rothman, D. J. (1971). *The discovery of the asylum: Social order and disorder in the new republic.* Boston: Little, Brown.

Saint-Germain, M. A., & Calamia, R. A. (1996). Three strikes and you're in: A streams and windows model incremental policy change. *Journal of Criminal Justice, 24,* 57–70.

Sanders, C. R., & Lyon, E. (1995). Repetitive retribution: Media images and the cultural construction of criminal justice. In J. Ferrell & C. R. Sanders (Eds.), *Cultural criminology* (pp. 25–44). Boston: Northeastern University Press.

Savelsberg, J. J. (1992). Law that does not fit society: Sentencing guidelines as a neoclassical reaction to the dilemmas of substantivized law. *American Journal of Sociology, 97,* 1346–1381.

Shichor, D. (1987). Penal policies: Some recent trends. *Legal Studies Forum, 11,* 55–78.

Shichor, D., & Kobrin, S. (1978). Criminal behavior among the elderly: A survey of the arrest statistics. *The Gerontologist, 18,* 213–218.

Shichor, D., & Sechrest, D. K. (1996). Three strikes as public policy: Future implications. In D. Shichor & D. K. Sechrest (Eds.), *Three strikes and you're out: Vengeance as public policy* (pp. 265–277). Thousand Oaks, CA: Sage.

Simon, J. (1988). The ideological effects of actuarial practices. *Law and Society Review, 22,* 771–800.

Simon, J. (1993). From confinement to waste management: The postmodernization of social control. *Focus on Law, 8*(2), 4, 6–7.

Simon, J., & Feeley, M. M. (1994, November). True crime: The new penology and public discourse on crime. Paper presented at the annual meeting of the American Society of Criminology, Miami, FL.

Slater, E. (1995, March 3). Pizza thief gets 25 years to life term. *Los Angeles Times,* p. B14.

Spiegel, C. (1994, October 24). 3 strikes has escape loophole. *Los Angeles Times*, pp. A3, A14–15.

Stryker, R. (1989). Limits on technocratization of the law: The elimination of the national labor relations board's division of economic research. *American Sociological Review, 54*, 341–358.

Surette, R. (1996). News from nowhere, policy will follow: Media and the social construction of "three strikes and you're out." In D. Shichor & D. K. Sechrest (Eds.), *Three strikes and you're out: Vengeance as public policy* (pp. 177–202). Thousand Oaks, CA: Sage.

Sutton, J. R. (1987). Doing time. *American Sociological Review, 52*, 612–630.

Tobias, J. J. (1972). *Crime and industrial society in the nineteenth century*. London: Penguin.

Tonry, M. (1996). *Sentencing matters*. New York: Oxford University Press.

Turner, M. G., Sundt, J. L., Applegate, B. K., & Cullen, F. T. (1995). "Three strikes and you're out" legislation: A national assessment. *Federal Probation, 59*(3), 16–35.

Van den Haag, E. (1975). *Punishing criminals: Concerning a very old and painful question*. New York: Basic Books.

Visher, C. A. (1987). Incapacitation and crime control: Does a "lock 'em up" strategy reduce crime? *Justice Quarterly, 4*, 513–543.

Weber, M. (1968). *Economy and society*. Totowa, NJ: Bedminster.

Wilson, W. J. (1987). *The truly disadvantaged: The inner city, the underclass, and public policy*. Chicago: University of Chicago Press.

Zeigler, F. A., & Del Carmen, R. V. (1996). Constitutional issues arising from "three strikes and you're out" legislation. In D. Shichor & D. K. Sechrest (Eds.), *Three strikes and you're out: Vengeance as public policy* (pp. 3–23). Thousand Oaks, CA: Sage.

Zimring, F. E., & Hawkins, G. (1991). *The scale of imprisonment*. Chicago: University of Chicago Press.

Chapter 28

Jails and Judicial Review
Special Problems for Local Facilities

N. E. Schafer

County jails are unique institutions bound by their own histories to a local perspective and limited by local control and local budgets to traditional methods of operation. They are short-term facilities that house both pretrial and sentenced prisoners and thus differ from state and federal prisons in both function and orientation. When in the 1970s federal courts began to intervene in jail and prison management, many jail administrators reacted with anger and hostility to what they viewed as the court's interference in a purely local matter. Although in applying constitutional standards the courts recognized differences in the functions of jails and prisons. Most correctional case law arose from prison cases and many of these were applied equally to jails. Remedy formulations in jail suits should have differed from those arranged in prison suits because most defendant jails were not only unwilling but *unable* to respond to judicial review.

The jail's inability to deal with judicial intervention is the subject of this paper. Differences in jail and prison lawsuits are noted, and jails and prisons are contrasted for their preparation for, and response to, court review. A case study of one jail's response to a class action suit filed in federal court serves to underscore the inability of jails to deal in a timely fashion with court orders.

From D. B. Kalinich and J. Klofas, "Sneaking Inmates Down the Alley: Problems and Prospects," in *Jail Management*, 1986. Courtesy of Charles C. Thomas, Publisher, Springfield, Illinois.

The federal courts had traditionally been loath to intervene in the internal operation of jails and prisons. They had preferred to rely on the professional expertise of correctional administrators and entertained few suits from jail and prison inmates until the mid-1960s. However, following passage of the 1964 Civil Rights Act the courts increasingly responded to suits from all classes of prisoners for relief of the conditions of their confinement. The majority of these suits relied on Section 1983 of the Civil Rights Act:

> Every person who, under color of any statute, ordinance, regulation, custom, or usage of any State or Territory, subjects or causes to be subjected, any citizenry of the United States or other persons within the jurisdiction thereof to the deprivation of any rights, privileges or immunities secured by the Constitution of laws, shall be liable to the party injured at an action at law, suit in equity, or other proper proceeding for redress. (42 U.S.C. 1983, 1964)

This law had a role in changing the "hands off" policy of the federal courts whose reluctance to interfere in jail and prison management was overcome by their unwillingness to allow deprivations of federal rights.

The courts seem to have been especially solicitous of the status of pretrial detainees because of the presumption of innocence. Indeed, Eighth Amendment standards were sometimes more strictly applied for pretrial detainees than for convicted prisoners and the equal protection clause of the Fourteenth Amendment was invoked to compare their rights with the rights of those admitted to bail (e.g., Inmates of Milwaukee County Jail v. Peterson, 353 F. Supp. 1157, 1160, E.D. WIS, 1973). These higher standards changed in 1979 when the Supreme Court established that the prohibition of punishment for the legally innocent should be balanced against necessary jail security (Bell v. Wolfish, 441 U.S. 520, 995C 1979). Presumption of innocence does, however, require that the equal protection clause of the Fourteenth Amendment be strictly applied to detainees in relation to those convicted of crimes. Pretrial prisoners must not be confined under conditions worse than those of convicted prisoners (Rhem v. Malcolm, 371 F. Supp. 594 [S.D.N.Y., 1974]; Hamilton v. Love, 328 F. Supp. 1182 [E.D. ARK, 1971] and others). The special attention given to the presumption of innocence reveals that judges recognized differences in function between jails and prisons but, in ordering relief, the courts did not seem to recognize the limitations implied by other differences.

Jails are defined as local institutions (U.S. Dept. of Justice et al., 1978) while prisons are defined as state or federal facilities housing prisoners with sentences of more than one year. Most state prisons are part of a larger state corrections system and, of course, the Federal Bureau of Prisons constitutes a federal prison system. Prison officials have access to a larger network of information and assistance as well as to a larger tax base than do jails that are county funded and often operate in isolation from similar institutions.

Prisons have long been defined as correctional institutions and the officials who operate them have professional affiliations with correctional associations. Jails have only recently been included under the corrections label. History and tradition have placed pretrial facilities outside the corrections category. The National Advisory Commission on Criminal Justice Standards and Goals found it necessary to justify the inclusion of jails in their volume *Corrections* (1973:98) and suggested that the "stepchild" status of jails reflected an abdication of responsibility for pretrial detainees.

The chief administrator of the county jail is usually a locally elected official, the county sheriff, who has, among other duties, a centuries old responsibility to assure the appearance at trial of persons who could not post bond. Except for this custodial function the sheriff's is primarily a law enforcement department and, unlike prison administrators, the sheriff and his deputies are more likely to be professionally affiliated with the police than with corrections.

The difference in professional orientation is an important one. Professional affiliations permitted prison personnel to participate in a dialogue on judicial review at national conferences and in professional publications. The American Correctional Association (ACA) frequently reviewed court suits in its member journal between 1969 and 1980, and the topic of judicial review was regularly on the program at the annual conference. The ACA developed a proactive response to litigation that served to defuse some of the charges and to persuade judges to rely again on their professional expertise in prison management. The movement for accreditation of correctional facilities and agencies accelerated while court suits proliferated. A Self-Evaluation and Accreditation Project was conducted by ACA between 1968 and 1970 and in 1974 a Commission on Accreditation for Corrections was funded by LEAA to develop and apply operational standards for correctional agencies. Accreditation standards were published in 1977 (ACA, 1977). Judges welcomed this trend and some prison suits were settled pending accreditation by the national association (Jones, 1982). In contrast, jail administrators remained outside the corrections network until fairly late in the decade and many remained unaware of judicial review in other parts of the country. Their isolation locked them into reactive responses as defendant institutions.

Articles in scholarly journals assessing responses to judicial review appeared in the late 1960s. Kimball and Newman (1968) addressed only suits filed against state and federal prison authorities and identified three postures taken by defendant agencies. The "defensive response" was tied to the prison officials' belief in their own expertise and in their legislatively delegated authority. This response was based upon the impropriety of any judicial review of the activities of corrections professionals. A second reaction, "apathy/acquiescence," was a passive response that denied any role for corrections in the review outcome and was, in effect, a denial of professionalism. The third and most desirable response was "prevention" or "rational persuasion," an active response that involved persuading the court that review was unnecessary by improving procedures, encouraging professionalization of staff, etc.

Rubin (1969) suggested a reaction beyond defensive that he called "provocative." This reaction was based on illegality or actual defiance of the law. He cited as an example Jordan v. Fitzharris (257 F. Supp. 674 [1966]) in which the court required a prison to maintain certain conditions of "elemental decency" in its strip cells. The prison administration fought for its right to impose whatever treatment it deemed best under whatever conditions. Rubin's characterization of the "defensive response" fits that described by Kimball and Newman though he also appears to assimilate within it the "apathy/acquiescence" posture they discussed. In a later article he calls this a "sit-tight" response (1974). Rubin's third "positive" response is characterized by anticipating court requirements and/or providing more than the minimum. Such a response includes "rational persuasion," i.e., convincing federal judges that their professionalism makes review unnecessary.

The courts had never fully abandoned their reliance on the professional expertise of defendant administrators. They maintained that judges were qualified only to assess the constitutionality of prison conditions not to manage the institution. Usually they left the means of correcting conditions to the defendant facility. Such language as "make a prompt and reasonable start toward eliminating the unconstitutionalities . . ." (Holt v. Sarver, 309 F. Supp. 362 [E. D. ARK, 1970]) implies continued reliance on the experience and expertise of prison or jail officials.

Isolated from networks of information and expertise and bound by local tradition and history, jails were unable to respond professionally to such language and were locked for a much longer period of time into defensive, or even hostile, postures when suits were filed against them. Judge Young, in Jones v. Wittenburg (330 F. Supp. 707, W.D. Ohio 1971) noted some of the problems he found more common in local than in state compliance: local appropriations, archaic laws and customs, and the actions and attitudes of responsible public officials. Two years after this opinion the court found no changes in the jail and faulted the sheriff for deliberate delay based on a desire for revenge against the court. (Jones v. Wittenburg, 357 F. Supp. 696, N.D. Ohio, 1973.)

Four case studies of implementation of court orders by Harris and Spiller (1977) illustrate some of the problems of responding in isolation. The only prison case reviewed was Holt v. Sarver, in which an entire state prison system was found to be operating unconstitutionally. The quality of Arkansas prison personnel and the nature of administrative appointments suggest that there was little, if any, tie to professional networks and the conditions revealed in the court suits and reported by Murton (1976) describe a system so bound by its antiquated traditions and so thoroughly directed inward that it could only be impacted by the very drastic measures required by the court.

The three remaining cases involved jails. Like most jails they were locally funded, locally operated, locally staffed. All were old and all were designed for short-term confinement and strict custody. Crowding, poor conditions, and unconstitutional processes and procedures were cited in all three suits. In only one case was assistance sought from outside. One year after the Baltimore City Jail (Collins v. Schoonfield, 344 F. Supp. 257 [1972]) suit was filed, the mayor of the city requested an inspection of the jail by the Federal Bureau of Prisons.[1] Problems with compliance noted by Harris included lack of funds, inadequate staff, and inadequate facilities (1977:386).

The other jails studied were Louisiana Parish jails. In Holland v. Donelon the initial complaint was filed in 1971 and court orders were handed down in 1972, 1973, and 1974. When Harris conducted the study in 1975 the jail was still not in full compliance. Reasons cited included budget, physical limitations, and "lack of clarity as to who was responsible and for what . . ." (1977:165).

In Hamilton v. Schiro, Spiller noted that "divided administrative responsibility" (between city and sheriff) was a special problem in compliance (1977:296) and also noted animosity between sheriff and city government. At the time the fieldwork was completed this jail, too, was still not in compliance.

In each of these cases anger and disbelief were the initial responses to the filing of the suits and to the courts' willingness to hear the plaintiffs. There was also an attempt to place blame upon Legal Aid lawyers, "radicals," and on co-defendants.

While responses to the court's review are part of these implementation studies, the emphasis in the studies is on assessing compliance rather than on assessing responses. In the following case study the focus is on the reaction of public officials to judicial intervention, and note is made of the court's contribution to the delay and confusion that marked compliance.

Marion County Jail Suit

The Marion County Jail serves as the detention facility for the county, the city of Indianapolis, and the cities of Beech Grove, Lawrence, Southport, and Speedway—a total population of approximately 800,000. The four-story jail, completed in 1965, had an official capacity of 776. It was built with security and control as the primary concerns and was, according to one observer, obsolete before it opened.

Just a few years after the jail opened it was the subject of a lawsuit that was not fully settled until a new jail addition wing was completed. Figure 1 lists sequentially the events related to the suit and the resulting actions of the defendants. Some of these will be discussed in detail. Briefly, the events and charges are as follows: In September 1972, a suit was filed

Date	Court Action	Compliance Activity
Sept. 1972	Suit filed	
Nov. 1972	Amended complaint	
March 1973	Order to proceed as class action suit	
1974–75		New jail rules formulated for submission to court resulting in consent decree and partial judgment
June 1975	*Consent Decree and Partial Judgment* contact visiting out of cell block recreation overcrowding	
March 1976	*Court Order*	
April 1976		Steering Committee appointed to select consultants
June 1977		Consultants' report submitted
Jan. 1978	Mayor's memorandum re. compliance	
Feb. 1978	Sheriff's memorandum re. compliance	
Aug. 1978	Plaintiff's interrogatories to Sheriff	
Sept. 1978	Sheriff's response to interrogatories	
April 1979		Consolidation of Jail & City-County lockup
Autumn 1979		Jail sends letters to facilities around the country seeking assistance and advice
Dec. 1979	—Motion for order to show cause —Motion to appoint special master —Motion to restrain further incarceration	
Jan. 1980		Ad Hoc Jail Committee recruited
Feb. 1980		New classification system in operation
May 1980	Stipulation and order programs ordered Commission appointed Commissioners appointed	GIPC begins to monitor compliance
July 1980		Contact visits begin
Aug. 1980		Indoor recreation area opened Outdoor exercise begins TVs installed Cubicles for attorney/client conferences
April 1981		City-County Special Resolution to commence expansion of jail
March 1982	Stipulation and order 1979 motions held in abeyance until July 1982	
June 1982		Architect's drawings
July 1982	Report of Commission filed	
Dec. 1982		Jail addition construction contracts signed
April 1983	Construction begins	

Figure 1   Sequence of events (partial)

by the Legal Services Organization (LSO) on behalf of pretrial detainees at the Marion County jail. Named as defendants in the suit were the Sheriff of the County, the jail commander, the Commissioner of the State of Indiana Department of Corrections, the Mayor of Indianapolis, and specific members of the Board of County Commissioners. The complaint, brought under Section 1983 of the Civil Rights Act (42 U.S.C. 1983), alleged violations of the pretrial detainees' rights under the First, Fourth, Fifth, Sixth, Eighth, Ninth, Thirteenth, and Fourteenth Amendments to the United States Constitution. At issue were overcrowding, physical and sanitary conditions, failure to classify prisoners for housing assignments, inadequate medical and dental care, lack of recreation, of contact visits, and of access to telephone and mail services.

Because of crowding, detainees were sometimes required to sleep on the floor in the shower rooms. Although mattresses were provided, mattress covers often were not. Jail issue clothing consisted of dresses for females and trousers for males. The prisoners wore the underwear they had on when admitted. Although they could purchase more underwear, as well as towels and pillows, or receive them from a visitor, indigent prisoners often had to do without. No provision was made to launder clothing or towels. Though these could be washed in the cellblock basins, it was against regulations to hang them up to dry.

All detainees could purchase postage and writing materials. They were allowed to mail only one letter per day containing no more than one piece of paper. Jail officials read all correspondence to and from family and friends. Telephone calls were not permitted except by special arrangement.

There was no recreation program or exercise area. Playing cards could be purchased and there was a meager library. Detainees could exercise only in the open area of the cellblock. No televisions or radios were available.

There was no regular dental program, no provision for medical examinations, no law library. Visits were "closed." The detainee visited from inside the cellblock looking through a small Plexiglas window and talking through a metal grating. Only two visitors were allowed per week. Children were never permitted.

In 1975 a consent decree and partial judgment corrected many of the physical and sanitary problems. New jail rules were formulated and submitted to the court. These covered the sanitizing of mattresses, issuance of jail clothing and provisions for laundering these, improvements in medical and dental care, counseling services, and more liberal correspondence rules. However, many of these were "paper" changes only.

In 1976 a court order required attention to all areas left unresolved by the consent decree. The judge ordered that clothing be issued and laundered weekly; that a bed above floor level be provided for each detainee along with sheets, pillow, blanket, and mattress cover. He ordered that telephone calls be permitted "in reasonable number and for a reasonable length of time without censorship," and that correspondence opportunities be greatly expended.

Contact visiting was ordered with the visitation schedule to be equal to that provided by the state for the convicted. Reasonable facilities for both indoor and outdoor recreation were also ordered. The court recognized that many deficiencies resulted from lack of funds but ordered that appropriations be made in order to correct them.

Defendants' official response was the appointment of a Steering Committee, with representatives of the Mayor, the county commissioners, and the Sheriff as members, to select consultants who would propose solutions. The contract to the consultants was let by the Department of Metropolitan Development, an arm of city government attached to the Mayor's office.

The Consultants' Report was submitted fourteen months later in June of 1977. In January and February, 1978 the Mayor's office and the Sheriff's office submitted memoranda based on the report to the court advocating certain of the compliance options which particularly addressed the problem of overcrowding. These memoranda were followed by the plaintiffs' memorandum in opposition to some of the proposed solutions.

In August 1978, interrogatories to the Sheriff were propounded by attorneys for the plaintiffs and were answered in the required thirty days by the Sheriff. There were 87 questions and it was clear from the responses that no major concerted effort had been made to implement the judgment of the court. Neither the 1977 nor the 1978 Sheriff's budgets had allocated funds for compliance, nor had the sheriff requested special funds. Whatever improvements had been made had come from the jail's normal operating budget. The 1979 budget request included $12 million for an addition to the jail but it was denied by the County Commissioners.

In 1979, seven years after the suit was initiated, the jail commander sent letters to jail officials throughout the country seeking advice and assistance in achieving compliance. During this year also, the Sheriff's Department assumed command of the city lockup. All prisoners were than booked at the lockup and transient prisoners (held for up to three days) were not transferred to the jail. This had the immediate effect of reducing the population. But on December 28 lawyers for the plaintiffs filed three motions: an order to show cause why defendants should not be held in contempt of court and assessed fines and damages of over $300,000; a motion to appoint a Special Master to oversee compliance with the order issued three years earlier; and a motion to restrain further incarceration of detainees at the Marion County Jail.

These motions produced immediate action. By January 14, 1980, an Ad Hoc Jail Committee had been appointed which included criminal court judges, City-County Councilmen, representatives of the Mayor's office, the Sheriff's office, the Prosecutor's office, the Auditor's office, and the Greater Indianapolis Progress Committee (GIPC), a privately funded citizens group advisory to the Mayor.

In the Court's Stipulation and Order of May 1980, GIPC was appointed jail commission and two commissioners were named. The Court held in abeyance the show cause order and the motion to restrain incarceration but ordered further progress toward compliance within six months and recreation, televisions, and radios and private attorney-client conference booths by July 1, 1980. Threatened with a contempt of court citation, the defendants began to engage seriously in compliance attempts. A new classification system went into effect in March 1980; in July, both contact visits and outdoor exercise were begun; by August, private attorney-client cubicles were in use; and by the end of the summer there was a television set for each cell block.

The Ad Hoc Jail Committee met regularly throughout the year and ordered an update of the 1977 consultants' study that was submitted in December. In December the City-County Council passed a resolution to undertake a survey of jail renovations and additions. The federal court judge cooperated in this progress by accepting improvements and postponing action on the 1979 motions.

In April 1981, expansion of the jail and a necessary bond issue were approved by the City-County Council. Architects' drawings were approved in June of 1982, construction bids were accepted in the fall, and contracts signed in December. Construction began in April 1983. This new addition would bring the jail into full compliance in all areas requiring additional space and structural change.

By March 1983, compromises had been made on the larger issues: outdoor recreation was available once per week rather than daily; holding cages had been converted for contact visitation by setting up folding chairs on each side of the bars; cubicles were made available for attorney-client conferences; telephones had been installed in each cell block with 16–24 hours of access per day (collect calls only); and a law library was in operation. Compliance was lax in other areas: mattresses were not hygienically treated on a regular basis; clean clothing was not regularly issued; the promised counselors were interns from a nearby university's School of Social Work; and often there were not quite enough blankets, pillows, or towels for every inmate.

The Response: Problems and Issues

Resentment is a natural response to what was perceived as unnecessary interference in a local matter. While state and federal prison officials had already begun to discuss the "threat" of judicial intervention (Kimball and Newman, 1968), officials of local jails were not engaged in the late 1960s and early 1970s in dialogues with one another. Each jail decision was a surprise to the defendants in it and sheriffs in other states and counties remained unaware of the growing willingness of the federal courts to entertain suits from jail inmates.

Their ignorance of this trend was compounded by local laws and local traditions. Jails are, in the main, locally funded and operated facilities. Pretrial detention is their *raison d'être* and the statutory responsibility of the sheriff to assure the appearance at trial of those who do not post surety leads to an emphasis on custody and security. Since detention is usually a matter of days or weeks rather than years the conditions of such short-term confinement had been typically overlooked and traditional means of maintaining secure custody were perpetuated. The uniqueness of each jail in terms of local customs and local context results in a local perspective that courts should not intervene in what are perceived of as purely local matters and often results in anger and resentment among defendants in a jail lawsuit.

Indiana is a conservative, even insular, state that has traditionally viewed federal intervention in local matters with suspicion and resentment. The state, as well as various local governments, had avoided the use of federal funds for a variety of programs out of a fear that accepting federal funds would invite federal control. In this political climate the federally funded Legal Services Organization (LSO) filed a class action suit against the Marion County Jail inviting the intervention of the Federal Court. The defendants named in the suit were unaware that the suit was being considered and were thus taken by surprise when it was filed. To add insult to injury their first knowledge of the suit came from stories in the local news media. The press was apparently notified by representatives of LSO. This "leak" raised the level of anger and resentment among the defendants. The sheriff, in an immediate though irrelevant gesture of defiance, called the U. S. Marshal's office to insist on the removal of all federal and military prisoners and terminated all agreements to detain them in the future.

The initial response was in line with the one Rubin (1969) characterized as "provocative" rather than "defensive" but the "sit tight" response soon followed. In many ways the defendants treated the suit as if it had no real meaning and did not require any serious response. It was eight years before serious attempts were made to correct the problems identified in the suit filed in 1972.

One factor in the delay was an especially serious problem in jail administration known as "discontinuity of management" which is a result of the political nature of the Sheriffs office (Pappas, 1970). In Indiana the Sheriff, by law, cannot serve more than two terms. In the case of the Marion County Jail this fact, coupled with some unexpected events, led to considerable "discontinuity of management." In the twelve years between the filing of the suit and the achievement of full compliance there had been four Marion County Sheriffs.

Sheriff Eads was named in the initial suit in 1972. While his initial negative reaction to the suit suggests that he would not have become a willing participant in the formulation of remedies, it is also true that he was in the final two years of his second term and could not run again. He may have decided to let his successor assume the responsibility of compliance. In any event, no action other than his angry refusal to house federal prisoners was taken during the remainder of his term.

Sheriff Broderick, elected in November 1974, had formulated by June 1975 a new set of jail rules based on the facts of the case. These were submitted to the Court and resulted, in 1975, in a consent decree and partial judgment in which the court noted that with these rules some issues were fully resolved, some were partially resolved, and some were still awaiting resolution. This Sheriff was clearly concerned about the suit and anxious to settle the issue. Since he had ahead of him a possible seven years of responsibility for the administration of the jail, it was in his best interest to seek solutions early in his tenure and move on to other concerns. It should be noted, however, that no means of implementing many of the new rules were sought. This sheriff was involved in the Jail Task Force, formed in response to the 1976 court order. Less than a year later he was killed in a traffic accident and his political party appointed a replacement, Gilman.

Under Gilman, the Sheriff's department showed little interest in achieving compliance and the problem of management discontinuity increased. He replaced the Jail Commander who had served under both Eads and Broderick with a Sergeant who had been on road patrol. Both the Sheriff and the new major needed time to learn jail operations and to study the problems associated with the court order. There was, in effect, a two-year lull in the jail's efforts at compliance.

In 1978 the appointed Sheriff was defeated in an election and a fourth Sheriff became a defendant in the case. Sheriff Wells recalled the previous jail commander and began seriously to consider compliance alternatives. One of his early actions (1979) was to hire a number of new deputies and stipulate that they would serve five years' jail duty. Prior to this the jail deputies had been new hires on six months' probation who were promoted to road duty after completing the probationary period. The move to create a staff of career jail deputies was a step toward professionalization of jail personnel.

In the autumn 1979 he sought advice and assistance from sheriffs throughout the nation who had been involved in court actions. Defendants had only recently become aware that jail suits were common and that theirs was not a singular event arising out of political differences with the federal judge. By 1979, however, eight years had passed since the suit was filed, more than four years since the 1975 consent decree, and more than three since the court order. Counsel for the plaintiffs had become understandably impatient.

Three motions filed in December 1979 led to immediate action; one was an order to show cause why the defendants should not be held in contempt of court. Although the Sheriff has statutory responsibility for the jail the plaintiffs must take care to name as defendants all those who might reasonably be involved in relief since the court cannot enforce a decree against those who are not named (Buckholz et al., 1978). The Sheriff, the jail commander, the Mayor of Indianapolis, the County Auditor, and others were, therefore, threatened with a contempt of court citation. Another of the motions was to enjoin further incarceration of pretrial detainees at the Marion County Jail. This would have created extraordinary political problems for the county. These two motions were held in abeyance, but the third was approved — the appointment of a Special Master to oversee compliance. In addition LSO (counsel for plaintiffs) were to be included in plans and negotiations. While the new Sheriff, facing a possible eight years of responsibility for the jail, might have continued his efforts to comply, these motions certainly had an impact on the speed of the responses.

It should be noted that none of the four defendant sheriffs requested additional funds for compliance, except for Sheriff Wells' request for funds to enclose an outside recreation area. (The City-County Council denied this request.) All compliance activities had been funded through the Sheriff's normal operating budget or from special jail funds.

Still at issue in December 1979 were outdoor recreation, contact visiting, a classification system, a basic law library, private attorney-client cubicles, and access to telephones, radios, and television. The county officials in charge of appropriations were not in sympathy with these requirements, nor, they were sure, were their constituents. Funds were appropriated for enclosing a small outdoor exercise area and ultimately (1981) the City-County Council did approve, "with reluctance, but with a sense of reality," (Proposal 103, 1981) construction of an addition to the jail. The other issues were negotiated and went into effect in one form or another in the eight months after the three motions were filed.

The new classification system went into effect in February 1980. No budget appropriations were necessary. Contact visiting was begun in July. The jail purchased used folding chairs which could be set up on either side of the bars of a holding cage in which prisoners had lined up to await sick call, counseling appointments, etc. Kisses and handshakes could be made through the bars while standing, but once seated a clear plastic barricade prevented continued contact. Visits were considerably less frequent than had been promised in the 1975 consent decree.

The same source for the folding chairs also provided materials for the construction of booths for private attorney-client conferences. The materials had been left behind after the closing of a local elementary school, were then used in the building by a neighborhood organization, and were at last given to the Marion County Jail. Jail carpentry staff constructed the cubicles. Books to complete the law library, equipment for the recreation area, and televisions (one for each cell block) were purchased from the jail's commissary fund.[2]

The telephone company installed special telephones on the cellblocks that could be used only for collect calls. This is one area that exceeded the "reasonable access" requirement of the court order. The prisoners have unlimited access to the telephones 14–18 hours per day.

Negotiations led to compromise on many of the other issues, particularly the scheduling of visits and recreation. It was understood that full compliance could not be achieved until the new jail addition was completed, and good faith attempts at partial compliance were accepted by attorneys for the plaintiffs.

Discussion

Remedy formulation in judicial orders vis-à-vis prisons and jails includes: remedial abstention, court imposition, court selection, master-supervised formulation and negotiation (Buckholz et al., 1978). The first of these is the most common and reflects the judge's willingness to rely on the defendant institution to formulate remedies to correct the problems established in the suit. In effect the Court retains jurisdiction and orders responsible officials to submit plans that address the facts of the suit.

In the Marion County suit remedial abstention was the first of three methods of remedy formulation attempted by the Court. The only response by jail officials was a new set of jail rules based specifically on the facts of the case that they submitted to the court in 1975. No plan for implementation of the rules was included. Personnel involved in the submission state that the intent was to mollify the court and convince the judge to terminate the case. The process of putting the new rules into practice was never considered. Though the submission of new rules resulted in a consent decree and partial judgment, the court retained jurisdiction. By 1979, so little had been done by way of implementation that the Court turned to two other judicial prerogatives: a special master was appointed and negotiations between defendants' and plaintiffs' counsel were ordered. These methods of remedy formulation began to produce results. Probably one or the other should have been tried much earlier in the process.

While defendants in all jail or prison lawsuits may be unwilling to cooperate in remedy formulation, defendants in jail suits may not only be unwilling, but also *unable*. Lawsuits arise, after all, out of conditions in the defendant jail, and defendant officials' expertise in jail management is usually based on experience in that jail alone. Participation in the formulation of remedies requires the defendant sheriff to criticize his own prior performance and to do so in isolation since he has seldom had an opportunity to compare his facility with others. Prison officials on the other hand have traditionally had access to a network of information and expertise which has enabled them to respond rapidly and rationally to court orders and to participate knowledgeably in remedy formulation.

In jail suits the Court should consider, very soon after the plaintiff's need for relief has been established, appointment of a special master to assist jail officials in remedy formulation. In the suit studied here there was confusion about what was expected. For example, the court ordered contact visiting at least equal in quality and frequency to that provided for convicted felons in a nearby state prison. Jail personnel were unfamiliar with these visiting facilities and some were unaware that contact visitation was not a euphemism for conjugal visitation. The search for advice from other defendant jails that was undertaken in 1979 illustrated the sheriffs' uncertainty about how to deal with judicial review. It also reflected the new realization that this suit was not a local quarrel with the federal court, but part of a national trend.

In the case of Marion County the initial resentment and outright antagonism engendered by the suit made negotiation an unacceptable early method of remedy formulation. However, a special master could have been ordered to negotiate remedies between counsel for the plaintiffs and defendant officials. Early appointment of such a master might have kept the attention of jail personnel focused on the suit even during the transition between changing administrations.

The master finally appointed in 1980 was a person of such prestige in the community that he might have been able to influence the local governing body to appropriate funds for at least partial compliance. No requests for compliance funds were included in the sheriffs' budgets until 1979. Earlier budget requests, even though denied, might ultimately have underscored the need for compliance and resulted in earlier acquiescence by the Council. This is, of course, speculation. Since the City-County Council officially inserted the word "reluctantly" into its approval of new jail construction in 1981, they were clearly resistant to the idea of allocating funds for improvement of the jail. It is possible that they would have been moved to action only by the threat of contempt of court citations and of an imposed moratorium on acceptance of prisoners at the jail.

Judicial intervention on behalf of pretrial prisoners has helped to focus national attention on county jails. The result has been a growing professionalism among jail administrators and increasing interest, among local sheriffs, in quality jail management. The National Sheriffs Association published a jail administration manual in 1974. The American Correctional Association and the National Institute of Corrections offer assistance and training to local facilities and more and more jails have taken advantage of these opportunities.

The jail studied here remained outside this opportunity network for many years after the suit was filed. Some jails continue to operate in isolation, and if they fall under judicial review will be unable to formulate remedies. Courts should consider defendant jails' involvement in professional networks before deciding on a method of remedy formulation.

In Marion County defendants were plagued with all the handicaps to compliance which isolation breeds and were, in large measure, unable to find ways to comply with the orders of the court. For some of the defendants the compliance process was a learning experience. They moved through several responses: defiance and anger, "sit-tight," and, at the last, active involvement. According to one of the originally named defendants the hardest part about responding to the court order was changing attitudes, "including my own." Pleased with the new professionalism among jail personnel and anticipating completion of the new jail extension, he acknowledged that the court order "may have been the best thing that ever happened to us."

Endnotes

[1] Baltimore's proximity to the nation's capital was an advantage in knowing that other agencies might play a role. It is unclear from the study if this was a request for assistance or for confirmation that the jail was fine and the court in error.

[2] All of the money each prisoner has when arrested is placed in an account from which he may draw to purchase commissary items (candies, cookies, cigarettes, items of personal hygiene, etc.). Visitors may deposit additional money in the prisoner's account. Profits from the sale of these items are spent on jail improvements. This was a fairly new source of funds since, until 1977, commissary profits had gone to the Sheriff and were considered one of the perquisites of the office.

References

Buckholz, R. E., Jr., et al. (1978). The remedial process in institutional reform legislation. *Columbia Law Review, 78*, 784–929.

Civil Rights Act of 1964, Public Law No. 88–352, 78 STAT. 241 (July 2, 1964).

Harris, M. K., & Spiller, D. P. (1977). *After decision: Implementation of judicial decrees in correctional settings.* Washington, DC: U.S. Government Printing Office.

Jones, B. (1982, November). Impact of courts on correctional management. Paper presented at the regional conference of ASPA. Louisville, KY.

Kimball, E. L., & Newman, D. J. (1968). Judicial intervention in correctional decisions: Threat and Response. *Crime and Delinquency, 14*, 1–14.

Murton, T. O. (1976). *The dilemma of prison reform.* New York: Holt, Rinehart and Winston.

National Advisory Commission on Criminal Justice Standards and Goals. (1973). *Corrections.* Washington, DC: U.S. Government Printing Office.

President's Commission on Law Enforcement and Administration of Justice. (1967). Task force reports. *Police, courts, corrections.* Washington, DC: U.S. Government Printing Office.

Rubin, S. (1969). The administrative response to court decision. *Crime and Delinquency, 15*, 377–386.

Rubin, S. (1974). The impact of court decisions on the correctional process. *Crime and Delinquency, 20*, 129–134.

U.S. Department of Justice, Bureau of Statistics. (1978). *Census of jails.* Washington, DC: U.S. Government Printing Office.

Cases Cited

Bell v. Wolfish — 441 U.S. 520, 995C 1979.

Collins v. Schoonfield — 344 F. Supp. 257 (D.M.D. 1972).

Hamilton v. Love — 328 F. Supp. 1182 (E.D. ARK, 1971).

Hamilton v. Schiro — 338 F. Supp. 1016 (E.D. LA, 1970).

Holland v. Donelon — Civil Action No. 71-1442 Sec. C (E.D., LA, 1973).

Holt v. Sarver — 309 F. Supp. 362 (E. D. ARK, 1970); Aff'd 442 F. 2d 304 (8th Cir. 1971).

Inmates of Milwaukee County Jail v. Peterson — 353 F. Supp. 1157, 1160 (E.D. WIS, 1973).

Jones v. Wittenberg — 330 F. Supp. 707 (W.D. OHIO, 1971).

Jordan v. Fitzharris — 257 F. Supp. 674 (N.D. CAL, 1966).

Rhem v. Malcolm — 371 F. Supp. 594 (S.D. NY, 1974).

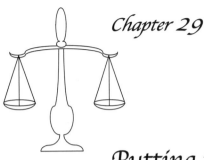

Chapter 29

Putting the "What Works" Research into Practice
An Organizational Perspective

Jennifer L. Ferguson

Over the past decade, significant advances have been made in correctional research. This research has resulted in an increased sense of optimism that correctional assessment and treatment can be effective. "What works" has emerged as a popular theme to describe effective correctional services. Some attempt has been made to describe how organizations can take this research and implement it into daily practice (Bonta, 1997). However, the focus has been on what should be done and the steps that need to be taken without giving attention to how to implement these steps or the challenges that might be experienced while doing so. The lack of attention to the practical implementation of what works is problematic for organizations that wish to engage in effective correctional services. This article aims to address this issue by describing how one probation department implemented research-based practice as part of the daily routine of the organization.

What Works

In the 1970s, the phrase "nothing works" took hold with the publication of Martinson's (1974) article titled "What Works? Questions and

Jennifer L. Ferguson, *Criminal Justice and Behavior*, Vol. 29 No. 4, copyright © 2002 by Sage Publications. Reprinted by permission of Sage Publications.

Answers About Prison Reform." This phrase was used to describe the apparent lack of effectiveness of correctional rehabilitation and helped steer correctional practice in a more punitive direction, with an increased reliance on sanctions as a means of crime control. Since that time, the research has been reviewed again and new research has been conducted, resulting in a recognition that criminal sanctions alone have a minimal effect on recidivism (Andrews et al., 1990). This research has also found that treatment can be effective and can reduce recidivism. The key ideas of correctional research have changed and the focus is now on what works.

What has emerged as key principles of effective correctional intervention are the principles of risk, need, and responsivity (Andrews and Bonta, 1994; Andrews, Bonta, and Hoge, 1990). These principles help define the appropriate targets for treatment and how treatment should be delivered. They also help link assessment to treatment and highlight the importance of assessment to the delivery of effective treatment programs (Gendreau, 1996).

The risk principle states that treatment services should be matched to the risk level of the offender (Andrews and Bonta, 1994; Andrews, Bonta, and Hoge, 1990). Individuals who are high risk should receive the most intensive services, whereas those who are low risk should receive minimal intervention and services. This principle is supported by research that has found that low-risk individuals who have received intensive services have had no change or increases in their level of recidivism, whereas high-risk individuals who receive intensive services show reductions in levels of recidivism (Andrews, Bonta, and Hoge, 1990).

The need principle focuses on the factors that should be targeted through intervention and states that appropriate targets for correctional intervention are criminogenic needs. Criminogenic needs are dynamic risk factors that can be changed through treatment and where change is known to reduce recidivism (Andrews and Bonta, 1994).

The responsivity principle suggests that characteristics of the offender, such as personality and learning style, influence how he or she responds to different types of treatment. As a result, for treatment to be more effective, the style and mode of services should be matched to the individual. For example, clients who are anxious may do better in a supportive, nonconfrontational treatment environment.

Assessment is a key component to effectively implementing the risk, need, and responsivity principles. Because advances have been made in learning what is needed for effective correctional intervention, advances have also been made in the type of assessment that should be conducted to help with the delivery of effective treatment programs. Bonta (1996) has identified different generations of assessment to highlight the advances that have been made. The first generation of correctional assessments conducted was primarily based on the professional judgment, intuition, and gut-level feelings of the individual conducting the assessment. The information collected and the way that information was interpreted could vary from person to person.

The second generation of assessment moved toward a more standardized assessment. Specific criteria were identified to be included in each assessment conducted. However, the focus was primarily on static risk factors, which are factors that contribute to an individual's risk to reoffend but cannot be changed. For example, an individual's age at first juvenile adjudication is a factor that is often measured through risk assessment tools. However, no intervention can be conducted that will change the age the first juvenile adjudication occurred. During this generation of assessment, the information provided by the risk assessment was used primarily to determine appropriate levels of supervision.

The second generation of assessment also gave some attention to assessing an individual's needs to identify potential targets for treatment. These assessments were conducted independently of the risk assessment, and risk and needs were viewed as separate concepts.

Building on the second generation of assessment, a third generation of risk and needs assessment has been identified. In the third generation of assessment, risk and needs are viewed as related concepts that should be included in a single assessment tool. Needs are recognized as dynamic risk factors that contribute to an individual's overall risk to reoffend. When both static and dynamic risk factors are included within a single assessment tool, the assessment is strengthened and can help direct offenders to the type of services they should receive and also to the appropriate level of services.

Recent research also has identified key predictors of recidivism. Both static (historical) and dynamic (changeable) factors have been found to be significant predictors of recidivism, although some factors are stronger predictors than others. The strongest predictors have been identified as adult criminal history, antisocial personality, criminal attitudes, and companions (Andrews and Bonta, 1994; Gendreau, Little, and Goggin, 1996). The research has also found that composite risk scores, which combine information from several predictor domains (as is usually done in a combined risk and needs assessment), are the strongest predictors of recidivism (Gendreau et al., 1996).

Along with the advances in assessment, the correctional research highlights characteristics of effective treatment programs. This research has found that when certain characteristics are present, reductions in recidivism can range from 25 to 60 percent (Gendreau, 1996). Effective treatment programs are those that adhere to the principles of risk, need, and responsivity; provide cognitive behavioral programming; enforce program rules in a firm but fair manner; provide more positive reinforcers than punishers; use therapists that respond in sensitive and constructive ways; and use therapists who have appropriate training and supervision.

The shift in research findings away from "nothing works" to a focus on "what works" means that correctional practice also must shift from a get-tough law-and-order focus, relying strictly on sanctions, to a more balanced approach that includes both sanctions and treatment. There is some evidence that organizations that are in the business of correctional practice are willing to make this shift. For example, in its position paper on probation, the American Probation and Parole Association (APPA, 1987) stated that "probation . . . views itself as an instrument for both control and treatment appropriate to some, but not all, offenders" (p. 1). However, although the knowledge base of what contributes to effective correctional services has grown and organizations appear committed to implementing what works, there has been little practical guidance on how organizations can take this research and implement it in daily practice. The title of Bonta's (1997) recent article, "Offender Rehabilitation: From Research to Practice," suggests that this type of guidance exists. In that article, Bonta identified three steps that should be followed to put research findings on assessment and treatment into practice. First, there needs to be an organizational commitment to the value of rehabilitation. This commitment must include the dedication of time and resources. Second, valid instruments need to be used to accurately assess offender risk and needs. The final step is to use cognitive-behavioral approaches to improve the effectiveness of treatment. Although these are necessary steps, little guidance is provided about how to achieve them. There is no discussion of the practical challenges that might be experienced while trying to implement any of the steps. These shortcomings pose problems for organizations that wish to implement research findings and engage in effective correctional services.

The Maricopa County Adult Probation Department (MCAPD)

The MCAPD is an organization that is trying to take the current findings of correctional research and implement them in the daily practice of the organization. The current strategies being used to accomplish this include conducting a combined risk and needs assessment and providing programs that attempt to adhere to the principles of effective correctional intervention.

A primary responsibility of the MCAPD is to provide supervision to individuals sentenced to probation through the Superior Court of Arizona, in Maricopa County. At any given time, active supervision is provided to approximately 23,000 individuals on standard probation and 1,800 individuals on intensive probation supervision. The department also provides presentence recommendations for all individuals coming through the Superior Court of Arizona, in Maricopa County. Approximately 15,000 presentence investigations are conducted each year.

In addition to the supervision and presentence investigation services provided by the department, efforts are made to provide a number of programs that meet the needs of the offenders. These programs may be provided internally by the department, or other agencies may be used to provide these services.

A key component that shapes how the MCAPD operates is the use of a combined risk and needs assessment tool. The remainder of this article focuses on how the department implemented this tool as part of everyday practice of the organization and includes a discussion of how it was developed and implemented, the challenges faced, and the lessons learned.

Implementing a Risk and Needs Assessment Tool

Organizational Commitment to Research-Based Practice

As a first step toward implementing a risk and needs assessment tool and similar to the first step that Bonta (1997) identified for putting research into practice, the MCAPD made a commitment to implementing research-based practice and to using the findings of research to guide the strategies used by the organization. The importance of organizational commitment has been cited as important to obtaining quality work (Crosby, 1984; General Accounting Office, 1993; Hunt, 1993). If something is important to management, it will be viewed as important to staff.

The MCAPD made the commitment to conducting research-based practice by incorporating it in the strategic plan of the department, which outlines the priorities of the organization. The commitment to research-based practice first appeared in the strategic plan developed in 1996. This commitment could be seen in statements such as "All department programs will be based on empirically validated research" and "The department will use (a risk/needs assessment tool) and individual screening tools to assess client needs."

The organizational commitment to research and to implementing research-based practice was maintained and strengthened when the strategic plan was revisited at the end of 1999. One of the strategies identified for accomplishing the mission of the department was "working in partnership with the community to provide research-based prevention and intervention services." Although providing prevention and intervention services was part of the 1996 strategic plan, the words "research-based" were added, demonstrating the commitment to putting research into practice.

New goals were also developed that highlighted the commitment to research. One goal was "to utilize proven and effective methodology to assess and change behavior of offenders through effective case management." A goal specific to research was also added that stated that the department wanted "to increase our use of internal research-based information to make quality decisions."

Selecting an Assessment Tool

The commitment to implementing research-based practice also included conducting the type of assessment that was supported by the research literature. The MCAPD wanted to conduct meaningful assessments of the individuals coming through the department that would allow assessment information to guide decisions about its level of supervision an individual should receive and also to guide program planning. However, in 1996, when the department reviewed the current assessment practices, it recognized that there were some problems with the assessments that were being conducted.

First, different instruments were being used to assess risk and to assess needs. The risk assessment and the needs assessment were modeled after the Wisconsin risk and needs assessment tools (Baird, 1981). Although the instruments were standardized and allowed the same information to be gathered on each individual, risk and needs were treated as separate entities. An individual's risk level was not being used to inform decisions about the level of treatment services that should be received.

Second, the risk assessment conducted focused primarily on static factors. Whereas conducting both the risk and the needs assessment allowed static and dynamic factors to be assessed, the dynamic risk factors were not considered when determining the individual's overall risk level, and they did not inform the level of services needed.

Finally, concerns existed about the quality with which the assessments were being conducted. The risk and needs assessments were often conducted as an afterthought and completed quickly at the last minute. They were viewed as something that had to be done, and the information contained in the assessment was not necessarily viewed as useful to staff. Staff generally did not use the assessment information that was available to make decisions.

As a result of the review of existing assessment practices, the MCAPD recognized a need to change the assessment tool that was being used. In particular, an assessment tool was desired that would provide a broad, overall assessment of the risk and needs of the offender. The assessment tool should contain both static and dynamic risk factors that focus on the key predictors of criminal behavior. Also, the assessment tool should allow the information to be used to determine the overall risk the individual posed to reoffend, the appropriate targets for services or intervention, and the appropriate level of services. The department also wanted to select an assessment tool and develop an assessment process that would make risk-needs assessment more meaningful and valuable to staff.

The MCAPD considered two options when selecting an assessment tool that would meet its needs. One was to use an existing validated risk and needs assessment tool, and the other was to create a new tool that incorporated the existing research. The advantages and disadvantages of each approach were considered before making a decision.

Assessment tools do exist that would meet the needs of the MCAPD. One of the most commonly used assessment tool is the Level of Service Inventory-Revised (LSI-R) (Andrews and Bonta, 1995). There are a number of advantages to using an existing assessment tool. An existing tool is likely to have many resources already in place, such as the forms, training curriculum, a pool of trainers, and software. It is also likely that an existing tool has already been validated, increasing the amount of confidence that people have in the instrument. For example, a significant body of research literature exists that discusses the reliability and validity of the LSI-R (Andrews, Kiessling, Mickus, and Robinson, 1986; Loza and Simourd, 1994) and that discusses its use with different offender populations (Bonta and Motiuk, 1987; D. J. Simourd and Malcolm, 1998). One of the disadvantages is the cost of purchasing the tool, which may be an ongoing expense.

Developing a new assessment tool also has advantages and disadvantages. When developing a new tool, staff can be involved in the process, which may help increase staff willingness to use the information provided by the assessment. There may also be fewer ongoing costs. However, developing a new tool has the disadvantage of not being validated, and more work is required to develop the instrument, the training curriculum, and to train trainers.

The Offender Screening Tool (OST)

The MCAPD made the decision to develop its own tool, called the OST. One reason for the decision was the cost required to use an existing tool given the large number of assessments the department conducts each year, along with the department's desire to engage in reassessment. Another key factor was a concern about resistance of staff to a change in the way assessment was being conducted. Because there was a desire to conduct assessment that was meaningful to staff, the decision was made to involve staff in the development of the OST.

At the same time that a decision was made to develop the OST, the decision was also made to reengineer the presentence division. The reengineering decision was made because the presentence process had become complex and labor intensive. There were also a number of areas where work was being duplicated. The redesigned process would eliminate the duplication of effort and also introduce the OST as the risk and needs assessment tool of the department.

The current version of the OST was developed and implemented in 1998. The OST is administered at the presentence level, and information used to score the OST is gathered as part of a larger presentence interview. The presentence interview is automated, so interviewers enter the information directly into the computer. At the end of the interview, the OST is automatically scored.

The content of the OST incorporates the existing research on assessment. The OST gathers information in 10 categories that are supported by the research as predictors of an offender's criminal behavior. The 10 categories are (a) physical health/medical, (b) vocational/ financial, (c) education, (d) family and social relationships, (e) residence and neighborhood, (f) alcohol, (g) drug abuse, (h) mental health, (i) attitude, and (j) criminal behavior. The items on the OST include both static and dynamic criminogenic risk factors.

The OST also focuses on those factors that are the strongest predictors of recidivism. Although all the factors included in the OST are predictors of recidivism, those categories that are stronger predictors are weighted more and contribute more to the offender's composite risk score. For example, where an individual lives and who an individual lives with can influence criminal behavior. This is measured through the residence and neighborhood category of the OST. However, residence and neighborhood is not as strong a predictor as attitudes that may be supportive of criminal behavior. As a result, the residence and neighborhood section of the OST contains two items, whereas the attitude section contains seven items and makes a greater contribution to the overall risk score.

Once scored, the OST provides information about an offender's risk and needs. All the items on the OST are used to create a composite risk score. Cutoff scores have been statistically determined based on Maricopa County's offender population to identify risk levels of low, medium, and high. Need scores also exist for each category. A rational cutoff has been created to highlight those areas where an individual may need treatment or intervention. The risk score, in combination with the information provided in each category, can also help identify the level of services needed. Preliminary validation research (Grobe, Simourd, Lessard, and Ferguson, 2000) has been conducted on the OST, which suggests the tool has considerable promise as an appropriate risk and needs assessment instrument.

The risk and need information generated by the OST is used by staff throughout the MCAPD. The OST is implemented as part of the presentence investigation and can be used, along with other information, to inform the recommendations of presentence officers. It is also intended for probation officers in the field to inform their case management and supervision plans.

Training on the OST

Once the OST was developed, a key to successful implementation was to provide staff with enough information and training to allow them to incorporate the assessment and its results into their daily work. Multiple trainings were developed. The presentence division was trained on both the administration of the OST and how to interpret the results. The rest of the department, from support staff to probation officers to upper management, was trained on how to interpret the OST and how to use it to develop case management and supervision plans. What was important in developing each training was to tailor the training as much as possible to the needs of the group being trained.

The most significant training component was the training provided to the entire department on how to interpret the OST and use it for case plans. To help this training go more smoothly, the MCAPD developed a written training curriculum to ensure the essential information was consistently provided to staff. The key information the department hoped to convey through the training included (a) a discussion of the history of assessment and the advances that have been made; (b) specific information about the OST, including how it was developed and the categories that were assessed; (c) a discussion of OST scores and the information they provide; and (d) a discussion of how to interpret the OST and use the information to guide decisions. Sample cases were included, so training participants could practice interpreting the scores.

At the end of the training, a training assessment was conducted. The assessment was designed to gather information in two areas. One was to test participants' knowledge of the information provided during the training. In general, it was important to know if the participants understood the concepts that were presented. Some of the issues tested through the MCAPD's assessment included the following questions; (a) Is the difference between static and dynamic risk factors understood? (b) Is the importance of assessing multiple risk factors understood? (c) Do participants understand how to interpret the composite risk score? (d) Do participants understand how to identify areas in need of treatment or intervention? (e) Do participants understand how risk level influences the level of services an individual should receive?

The second type of information that was gathered was participants' perceptions of the OST. For example, do participants believe they could explain the purpose of the OST to others? Questions were also asked about whether probation staff believe the OST will help them in their jobs. Finally, the training assessment asked staff to identify any concerns they had about the OST or about using the information the OST provides to guide decisions.

The training assessment conducted by the MCAPD provided administrative staff with confidence that the trainers did a good job of conveying the essential information of the training. However, the assessment also highlighted which concepts were most difficult for people to understand. One of the most difficult concepts was the idea that someone who poses a low risk to reoffend may not need to receive intensive services, even if they do have a need that should be addressed. Receiving this information helped the trainers identify some different ways to present this information so it could be more easily understood.

The training assessment also highlighted the concerns that staff had about using the OST to do their jobs. Some of the common concerns were potentially receiving inaccurate information through client self-report and the loss of professional judgment. Receiving this information helped highlight some of the potential obstacles that may interfere with staff using the information provided by the OST to guide their decisions. With this information, the department could work to identify strategies to help address these concerns.

Another component of the implementation of the OST and the reengineered presentence process was the creation of the Quality Assurance Council (QAC). The QAC was created to help demonstrate the commitment to quality, which has been identified as a key to success (Crosby, 1984; General Accounting Office, 1993; Hunt, 1993). The purpose of the QAC was to help identify where errors could occur in the presentence process and to identify ways to minimize or eliminate those errors. The MCAPD wanted to be sure that quality information was gathered through the presentence interview and used to make informed decisions. It also wanted to be sure there was a mechanism in place to address questions and concerns about the OST and about the presentence process. The QAC addressed issues such as the need for ongoing training, workload concerns, and the need for technical support. It was in the meetings of the QAC that many of the challenges faced during the implementation of the OST were discussed.

Challenges

The MCAPD has been successful in developing and implementing the OST as the risk and needs assessment being conducted by the department. As a result, the MCAPD has achieved its goal of incorporating research-based assessment in the daily practice of the organization. However, the implementation of the OST did not occur without significant challenges, some of which are still ongoing. Some of the challenges experienced by the MCAPD, as well as the strategies used to address them, are described in this section.

Perceived Loss of Discretion

Research on assessment acknowledges that structured assessments are better predictors of criminal behavior than clinical judgment (Glaser, 1987; Meehl, 1954). As a result, assessments are better when they are structured and objective, ensuring that all clients are assessed using the same criteria. This shift to a more structured assessment resulted in concerns of probation staff that they no longer had any discretion when making presentence recommendations or when developing case management plans. The following quotes describe the essence of their concerns: "It (the

OST) will be too standardized so that individual judgment will be lost." Another person expressed a concern "that the professional judgment aspect will slowly fade out." This perceived loss of discretion poses a significant challenge when implementing research-based assessment because it can contribute to a resistance to change.

While implementing the OST, it was important for the MCAPD to acknowledge this concern of staff. As one staff member commented, "Officers need to be reassured the OST does not replace professional judgment, it complements it." Trainers tried to respond to this concern. They drew on the work of Andrews and Bonta (1994) when presenting this message. Andrews and Bonta highlighted that in addition to the principles of risk, need, and responsivity, professional judgment plays a role in effective assessment. Trainers presented the message that the information provided by the OST, along with their professional judgment, was a powerful tool. Trainers also acknowledged that the information provided by the OST was not the only information that needed to be considered when making a decision. For example, when making a presentence recommendation, the officer also needs to consider the seriousness of the offense and the concerns of the victims so that there is a balance between the needs of the victim, the offender, and the community. These messages helped staff feel they were still a valued part of the assessment process and that their experience was still valued. It also helped to reassure them that the department would still support them if they used their professional judgment.

Obtaining Quality Information

Another area that posed a challenge was obtaining quality information. Quality assessment information is essential if the assessment tool is going to be used to inform decisions. Two challenges were experienced related to quality information. One was a concern of probation staff about the quality of the information contained in the OST The second challenge was making sure that probation staff gathered quality information.

Probation staff members were concerned that the information provided by the OST would not be meaningful because it was gathered through self-report. They were concerned that the offender may not be honest and that information provided by the offender may not be accurate or give a true picture of the client. Trainers acknowledged that sometimes offenders are not honest or provide misleading information. They also emphasized that although information is initially gathered from the offender through an interview, the offender should not be the only source of information used to gather information for the OST. Information should still be verified through official records. Trainers stated that when there were inconsistencies between the information provided by the client and the information obtained from other sources, the information should be changed to reflect the official records.

Staff also expressed a concern that the OST does not address all factors. As an example of this concern, one person commented that "human behavior is more complex than a questionnaire." Related to this, staff was concerned that the OST would not provide enough information for specialized caseloads, such as sex offenders. To address this concern, several key messages were presented. One was to emphasize that the OST was designed to be a general risk and needs assessment tool that could be administered to a broad offender population. The assessment tool would become too long and cumbersome if all potential risk factors were included. However, the OST did consider multiple risk factors and incorporated those that were considered some of the strongest predictors of criminal behavior.

Another message was that there was value in having a general assessment conducted on each offender. There are common risk factors across offender groups that contribute to the risk to reoffend (D. J. Simourd and Malcolm, 1998; L. Simourd and Andrews, 1994). A general assessment tool can help identify areas in need of treatment or intervention that may not be recognized if the only assessment conducted was related to the offending behavior. At the same time, there is value to specialized assessment, and a general assessment can identify areas where there might be a need for further assessment. For example, when there is an elevated score in the drug category of the OST, a more detailed substance abuse assessment is conducted. Additional assessments are also conducted when there is an elevated score in the attitude category of the OST.

Although staff members were concerned about the quality of the information provided by the offender, the MCAPD also wanted to ensure that quality data were collected and maintained by probation staff. Having quality data was viewed as important not only for the case-by-case decisions but also for research that would be done to validate the OST. One issue was making sure staff members were conducting quality interviews. A number of strategies were used to address this. Prior to conducting any interviews, the presentence screeners were provided training that included a component on interviewing skills. The training addressed issues such as how to listen effectively, how to treat the offender with respect, and how to ask probing questions to obtain more detailed information. Once a number of interviews were conducted, focus groups were held with interviewers to obtain feedback. The key questions for the focus groups were whether there were any questions that the offenders had difficulty understanding and whether there were any questions where the interviewers were uncertain about the question's intent. Clarifying item intent was important to ensure that everyone was interpreting and answering the questions the same way. The feedback provided during the focus group was used to develop refresher training.

Another step taken to verify consistency across interviewers was to have an independent observer attend a number of interviews and record responses to the questions. The similarity between the interviewer's

OST scores and the observer's OST scores were then compared. The close relationship that was found between the two scores gave the department confidence that when properly trained, the OST could be administered consistently.

Mechanisms were also built into the automated system to help ensure quality. One feature was to make each question that contributed to the OST score a required question. If the question was not asked and answered, a drop-down menu box would appear on the computer screen informing the interviewer that he or she had missed a question. The interviewer was prevented from continuing until the question had been answered. This was important because the OST was designed as a structured assessment, and it helped ensure that each person was assessed using the same questions.

It was also important to ensure that all staff members were using the same version of the automated system because enhancements or corrections were occasionally made. To do this, whenever a change had been made, staff members were prompted to update their version of the program. They could not access the system until it had been updated.

Maintaining Appropriate Levels of Resources and Support

The changes that were made to the presentence process, which included the implementation of the OST, were significant. The process was reengineered in part to help use existing resources more effectively and efficiently. At the same time, it was important that the number of resources and support that were dedicated to the effort were sufficient to ensure its successful implementation. The resources and support included organizational commitment, staff, time, training, equipment (e.g., computers, software, printers), and technical support. The OST was initially implemented as a pilot project in the presentence division. The intent of the pilot project was to help manage the change and to help identify the resources that would be needed. Once the department was comfortable with the new presentence process and the implementation of the OST on a small scale, it was implemented departmentwide.

One of the biggest challenges was anticipating and maintaining resource levels once the project was implemented. It was difficult to anticipate the ongoing resource needs. The Quality Assurance Council played a key role in identifying those needs because it provided a forum to raise concerns and identify problems so resources could be directed to the issue.

Managing Workload

It has been noted that the OST was implemented as one part of a reengineered presentence process. One of the reasons for undertaking the reengineering project was to minimize the duplication of effort that previously existed. One description of the presentence process called it a "a complex process that is difficult to describe and labor intensive." The example that was often used to highlight the duplication of effort that occurred was that an individual name had to be entered into the system 20 different times. Although an exaggeration, it highlighted the problem. As a result, there was a concern with managing workload. This was also a concern of staff who were trained in the OST. They expressed concerns about the amount of time it would take to complete and that it would add more paperwork.

It was difficult to address concerns about workload. Trainers tried to emphasize that this was a new and different way to look at risk and needs rather than something additional that needed to be done. However, trainers also had to acknowledge that it might require more time. What trainers tried to emphasize was how the OST could benefit staff and help them do their job. Based on responses to a training assessment item, it appears that trainers were effective in conveying this message. Staff members were asked to state in their own words why the department was using the OST. One of the top responses was to help officers do their job. Other responses also identified ways the OST could help, such as by identifying levels of treatment supervision, prioritizing treatment needs, and developing case management plans. They also stated it could help supervise clients better and help officers make better decisions.

Resistance to Change

By definition, reengineering involves making radical changes in the way work is done. As a result, significant changes were taking place that staff needed to adjust to. Comments made during the training acknowledge staff concern about the changes being made. One comment was "It will be a major shift in the way we do business and that will be difficult for officers to adjust to the change." Staff also raised a concern about continual change and suggested that by the time they adjusted to this change, it would be changed again. One staff person said, "I'll get used to it and be told there is a new tool to use."

As with the other concerns raised by staff, it was important to acknowledge this concern. It was more difficult to respond to it because change can be necessary to remain a vital organization. What was emphasized was the need for this change and how it would add value to the work that staff members do.

Lessons Learned

With all the challenges experienced, an important question to ask is whether the investment of time and resources was worth the effort. To answer that question, it is important to go back and review what the MCAPD hoped to accomplish by reengineering the presentence process and implementing the OST. The MCAPD hoped to develop a process that would allow it to use resources wisely while responding to growth in the number of cases coming through the presentence division. The MCAPD also wanted to conduct a more systematic assessment that would be meaningful to probation staff.

Some noticeable changes have occurred that suggest the investment made was worth the effort. The workload of the presentence division has continued to grow, but the increase in workload has been managed with the existing resource levels. Information is also being gathered more systematically at the presentence level, and assessment is a routine part of the staff's job. The information gathered also appears to be meaningful and is allowing more time to be devoted to the high-risk and high-needs cases.

Because of the positive results, the MCAPD will continue its efforts to implement research into practice. At the same time, the MCAPD hopes to remember some key lessons learned from this experience. First, it is important to have the commitment of the organization, especially the top levels of management, for implementation to be successful. The support of management will help address other challenges experienced along the way, such as the need for sufficient resources, how to manage the changes that are taking place with the organization, and providing a consistent message to staff about the need for the change.

Second, once a commitment has been made, sufficient resources need to be committed to the effort. Resource needs should be anticipated beyond the initial implementation and should include the resources needed to sustain the project or program.

Third, it is important to invest in good-quality training. Devoting resources to training, such as developing a written training curriculum and developing a pool of quality trainers, will help sustain the project.

Fourth, as something new is implemented, be sure to acknowledge the concerns of staff as they adjust to the change. This includes providing them with opportunities to voice their concerns and planning for ways to respond to those concerns.

Finally, be prepared to face challenges and anticipate what those challenges may be. It will not be easy to implement the findings of research into practice and organizations need to be prepared for that. The experience of the MCAPD in implementing risk and needs assessment helps highlight the practical steps needed to implement the findings of research in the daily practice of an organization. While specifically applied to the implementation of risk and needs assessment, they can also be applied to the implementation of other research findings, such as appropriate treatment programs. MCAPD's experience helps fill a gap that has existed in the literature by addressing how to implement research findings. The lessons learned can help organizations committed to implementing effective correctional service and research-based practice achieve that goal.

References

American Probation and Parole Association. (1987). *Probation*. Retrieved July 26, 2001, from the American Probation and Parole Association Web site: http://www.appa-net.org.

Andrews, D. A., & Bonta, J. (1994). *The psychology of criminal conduct*. Cincinnati, OH: Anderson.

Andrews, D. A., & Bonta, J. (1995). *The level of service inventory – revised*. Toronto, Canada: Multi-Health Systems.

Andrews, D. A., Bonta, J., & Hoge, R. D. (1990). Classification for effective rehabilitation: Rediscovering psychology. *Criminal Justice and Behavior, 17*, 19–52.

Andrews, D. A., Kiessling, J. J., Mickus, S., & Robinson, D. (1986). The construct validity of interview-based risk assessment in corrections. *Canadian Journal of Behavioral Science, 17*, 19–52.

Andrews, D. A., Zinger, I., Hoge, R. D., Bonta, J., Gendreau, P., & Cullen, F. T. (1990). Does correctional treatment work? A clinically relevant and psychologically informed meta-analysis. *Criminology, 28*, 369–404.

Baird, C. (1981). Probation and parole classification: The Wisconsin model. *Corrections Today, 43*, 36–41.

Bonta, J. (1996). Risk-needs: Assessment and treatment. In A. T. Harland (Ed.), *Choosing correctional options that work: Defining the demand and evaluating the supply* (pp. 18–32). Thousand Oaks, CA: Sage.

Bonta, J. (1997). Offender rehabilitation: From research to practice. Retrieved October 21, 1998, from the Solicitor General Canada Web site: http://www.sgc.gc.ca/epub/corr/e199701/e199701.htm.

Bonta, J., & Motiuk, L. L. (1987). The diversion of incarcerated offenders to correctional halfway houses. *Journal of Research in Crime and Delinquency, 24*, 302–323.

Crosby, P. B. (1984). *Quality without tears: The art of hassle free management*. New York: McGraw-Hill.

Gendreau, P. (1996). Offender rehabilitation: What we know and what needs to be done. *Criminal Justice and Behavior, 23*, 144–161.

Gendreau, P., Little, T., & Goggin, C. (1996). A meta-analysis of the predictors of adult offender recidivism: What works! *Criminology, 34*, 575–607.

General Accounting Office. (1993). *An audit quality control system: Essential elements*. Washington, DC: Author.

Glaser, D. (1987). Classification for risk. In D. M. Gottfredson & M. H. Tonry (Eds.), *Prediction and classification: Criminal justice decision making*. Chicago: University of Chicago Press.

Grobe, B., Simourd, D. J., Lessard, S., & Ferguson, J. (2000, July). *The offender screening tool: One department's answer to risk assessment*. Paper presentation at the annual convention of the American Probation and Parole Association, Phoenix, AZ.

Hunt, V. D. (1993). *Quality management for government: A guide to federal, state and local implementation*. Milwaukee, WI: ASQC Quality Press.

Loza, W., & Simourd, D. J. (1994). Psychometric evaluation of the Level of Supervision Inventory (LSI) among male Canadian federal offenders. *Criminal Justice and Behavior, 21*, 468–480.

Martinson, R. (1974). What works? Questions and answers about prison reform. *The Public Interest, 35*, 22–54.

Meehl, P. E. (1954). *Clinical versus statistical prediction: A theoretical analysis and a review of the literature.* Minneapolis: University of Minnesota Press.

Simourd, D. J., & Malcolm, P. B. (1998). Reliability and validity of the Level of Service Inventory-Revised among federally incarcerated sex offenders. *Journal of Interpersonal Violence, 13,* 261–274.

Simourd, L., & Andrews, D. A. (1994). Correlates of delinquency: A look at gender differences. *Forum on Correctional Research, 6,* 26–31.

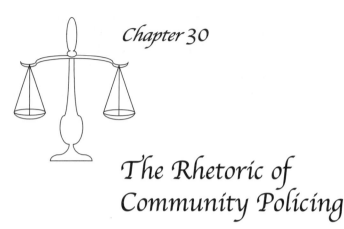

Chapter 30

The Rhetoric of Community Policing

Carl B. Klockars

The police are a mechanism for the distribution of non-negotiably coercive force employed in accord with an intuitive grasp of situational
exigencies. The proposed definition of the role of the police entails a
difficult moral problem. How can we arrive at a favorable or even accepting judgment about an activity which is, in its very conception, opposed to the ethos of the polity that authorizes it? Is it not well nigh
inevitable that this mandate be concealed in circumlocution?

Egon Bittner (1970)

In *The Functions of Police in Modern Society*, Egon Bittner (1970) posed
the problem of the relationship between police and the people they police
in an extremely general but remarkably provocative form. Bittner
advanced the argument that for nearly two centuries the core culture goal
of Western society has been the establishment of peace, both international
and domestic, as a condition to everyday life. Our failures to achieve
peace between nations are no secret, but each one of these failures, be it
either of two world wars, Korea, or Viet Nam, seems to have strengthened both our cultural commitments to the virtue of peace, as well as our
resolve that such destructive failures to secure it should not occur again.
While diplomacy, treaties, trade, and aid are pursued as alternatives to

Carl B. Klockars, "The Rhetoric of Community Policing," *Community Policing: Rhetoric or Reality*, edited by Jack R. Greene and Stephen D. Mastrofski. Copyright © 1988 by Praeger Publishers. Reproduced with permission of Greenwood Publishing Group, Inc., Westport, CT.

forceful conflict on the international level, bureaucracy, democracy, education, and a host of social services are promoted as the proper, noncoercive terms of the relationship between the state and citizens domestically. In both domestic and international relations, it is not merely that peace has become a nearly universal cultural goal, but that it is believed to be a goal that can *only* be successfully secured through the development and application of peaceful means to its achievement.

In ways wholly consistent with this aspiration to achieve peace through peaceful means as a condition of everyday domestic life, Western societies have sought to circumscribe to the greatest degree possible the legitimacy of the use of force by its citizens. Save for occasions of self-defense from criminal attack and intrafamily discipline of children by their parents, Western states have all but eliminated the rights of its citizens to use coercive force. The historical trade-off for this elimination of citizen rights to employ coercive force is, of course, the allocation of an exclusive right to it to police. After repeated failures of attempts to do so otherwise, a major component in the move toward the elimination of violence as a condition of everyday domestic life in every modern Western society has been to seek to extend a virtual monopoly on the legitimate right to use coercive force to police.

While no one whom it would be safe to have home to dinner argues that modern society could be without police, this situation places police in a most uneasy relationship with both the society and the state that authorize it. In their aspiration to eliminate violence as an acceptable means of conducting human affairs, both are forced to accept the creation of a core institution whose special competence and defining characteristic is its monopoly on a general right to use coercive force. Understood in this light, the police are not only fundamentally and irreconcilably offensive in their means to the core cultural aspiration of modern society, but an ever present reminder that all of these noble institutions, which should make it possible for citizens to live in nonviolent relations with one another and with the state, often come up very short.

It is this truth that Bittner argues must be "concealed in circumlocution." That is, in order to reconcile itself with an institution whose means are irreconcilably offensive to it, society must wrap that institution in signs, symbols, and images that effectively conceal, mystify, and legitimate police actions. In *Functions*, Bittner attends to three of these circumlocutions, the legalization, the militarization, and the professionalization of police in considerable detail.

The thesis of this chapter is that the modern movement toward what is currently called "community policing" is best understood as the latest in a fairly long tradition of circumlocutions whose purpose is to conceal, mystify, and legitimate police distribution of nonnegotiably coercive force. However, before we look directly at the cluster of circumlocutions that constitute the community policing movement, it will be helpful to follow some of Bittner's leads in analysis of legalization, militarization, and professionalization.

Legalization

> As late as 1900 when Chicago's police department numbered 3,225 men, there was no organized training. New policemen heard a brief speech from a high-ranking officer, received a hickory stick, a whistle, and a key to the call box, and were sent out to work with an experienced officer. Not only were policemen untrained in law, but they operated within a criminal justice system that generally placed little emphasis on legal procedure. Most of those arrested by police were tried before local justices who rarely had legal training. Those arrested seldom had attorneys so that no legal defense was made. Thus, there were few mechanisms for introducing legal norms into street experience and crime control activities of police. (Haller, 1976:303)

Although the quote above from Mark Haller's "Historical Roots of Police Behavior, Chicago, 1890–1925" describes Chicago police at the turn of the century, the situation was not very different in any major U.S. city at that time. At the turn of the century, the newly formed U.S. police were under no illusions that they were a "law enforcement" agency nor that their mandate or principal activity was to enforce law. While there is no question but that they understood that they were engaged in law enforcement in some formal sense, "the law" for U.S. police in their early years was but one of many tools they might be called upon to use in their work. By no means was it as crucial to that work as their whistle, call box key, or hickory stick.

Things are, of course, very different today, and Haller's observations on big city policing at the turn of the century provide an ideal vantage point from which to lay a perspective on those changes. Although, in fact, contemporary police may not mobilize the law with any greater frequency than their turn-of-the-century predecessors, modern police view themselves, at least publicly, as "law enforcement agencies" and are widely understood to be fairly closely governed in their work by the courts through the procedural and evidentiary requirements of the criminal law. Historically, this process of the progressive legalization of the enterprise of policing is widely appreciated to have begun at the federal level in 1914 with the *Weeks* decision, a decision whose exclusionary rule principles were extended to all jurisdictions in 1961 by *Mapp*. Since *Mapp*, literally dozens of fourth, fifth, eighth, and fourteenth amendment decisions have promoted this view of the intimate and binding relationship between the police, the courts, and the law.

In light of these and other developments in laws that bear upon police behavior, it is probably fair to say that no other police anywhere in the world are as thoroughly "legalized" as the U.S. police. How then can we, following Bittner, speak of their "legalization" as a "circumlocution?" To do so requires the appreciation of three major points, one of which is analytical and the other two of which are empirical. The analytical point is offered by Bittner (1970:25): "Our courts have no control over police work, never claimed to have such control, and it is exceedingly unlikely that they will claim such powers in the foreseeable future, all things being equal." Bittner's point hinges on the meaning of "control." He argues that the relationship between the courts, the law, and police is rather like that between independent consumers and suppliers of services. What the courts offer to police is the opportunity, if they wish to take advantage of it, to seek the state's capacity to punish. In effect, the courts say to the police that if they wish to make use of that capacity, they must demonstrate to the courts that they have followed certain procedures in order to do so. Thus it is Bittner's point that only on those occasions that the police wish to employ the state's capacity to punish do the two institutions have any relationship of any kind. Despite the enormous growth in police law in the past quarter century, the courts have no more "control" over the police than local supermarkets have over the diets of those who shop there.

Even that analogy, however, may give more substance to the relationship between the police and the courts than is actually warranted in fact. Empirically, it is probably the case that the cost and kind of products supermarkets offer do influence the diets of the people who shop there. It is likewise the case with police that it is almost inevitable that they will seek to secure the state's capacities to punish in certain instances. For example, in cases of reported homicides, police behave on the assumption that the case may well end up in court. On these occasions, procedural requirements certainly influence how police behave (and what they choose to report to the courts on their behavior).

Empirically, however, we know two major things about the terms of this relationship between the police, the law, and the courts. The first is that the felony arrest rate for patrol officers is very, very low even in areas in which felony offense rates are very high. For example, a recent study by Walsh (1986) found that 40 percent of the 156 patrol officers assigned to a very high crime area in New York City did not make a single felony arrest during the entire year under study, and that 68.6 percent of these officers made no more than three felony arrests.

The second empirical fact we know about police behavior has to do with the frequency with which police choose not to arrest when they have every legal right and all the evidence necessary to do so, or, alternatively, choose to make arrests when they have no legal grounds to do so whatsoever. For example, in his well-known study of 299 cases of dispute settlements by police, Black (1980:183) found that in 52 cases in which there was ample evidence that a violent felony had occurred, police made arrests in only 27 percent of those cases. In cases of violent misdemeanor offenses, the arrest rate dropped to 17 percent. Black also found that in 78 cases in which police had no grounds for legal action of any kind, they nevertheless made arrests in 17 percent of those cases as well. Similar results are reported in many other studies. Collectively, they constitute the major empirical discovery of police research of the past two decades: the discovery of selective enforcement and the enormous influence on police discretion of such things as suspect demeanor, complainant preferences, and a host of other factors that have nothing to do with "the law."

Militarization

While legalization is probably the most powerful circumlocution currently mystifying the institution and functions of police in modern society, the militarization of police runs a close and complicating second. Begun as a reform movement in the history of U.S. police, an effort to establish discipline within police ranks and to extricate police from the stink of municipal machine politics, militarization drew upon a powerful and abiding analogy (Fogelson, 1977, especially chapter 2, "The Military Analogy": 40–67). The analogy held that police were, in effect, a domestic army engaged in a "war" on crime.

The analogy drew upon three compelling themes. First, by associating police with the heroes and victories of the military rather than the back rooms of city politics, the military analogy sought to confer some honor and respect on the occupation of policing. Second, the idea of a war on crime struck a note of emergency that gave the movement to militarize the U.S. police a moral urgency and a rhetorical tone that was difficult to resist. To fail to support the police in their war on crime, to stand in their way, or to be stingy with the resources they would need to fight it was siding with the enemy and metaphorically tantamount to treason. Third and finally, the military analogy sought to establish a relationship between local politicians and police chiefs that was analogous to the relationship between elected executives at the national level and the general of the U.S. military. The politicians would, of course, retain the right to decide whether or not a given war ought to be fought, but the conduct of the battles and the day-to-day discipline and management of the troops was to be left to the control of the generals. At bottom then, the military analogy was a way of talking about police that sought to wrest from the hands of local politicians and place into the hands of police chiefs the administrative tools—hiring, firing, promotion, demotion, assignment, and discipline—that those chiefs needed to manage the organizations they headed.

To a degree that no turn-of-the-century police chief could have imagined, the military analogy proved a smashing success. The popularity of police and the size of police budgets have grown enormously. While no one would argue that the police are free of political control or influences (and no thoughtful person in a democratic society can argue that they should be), the political "autonomy" of police makes them a major, independent political force in many U.S. cities. The real problem in policing today is more often to find ways of putting politics into policing than it is to find ways of taking it out.

While extricating police from the shabby sides of urban politics and establishing discipline within the ranks were no small achievements in the history of U.S. police, the military metaphor that made those achievements possible brought with it some mighty long-term costs. Administratively, it left U.S. police with a quasi-military administrative structure that is wholly inappropriate as a device for managing the highly discretionary activity of police work. Almost wholly punitive in its approach to controlling employee behavior, it stifles innovation, imagination, experimentation, and creativity. It is no accident that the CYA (cover-your-ass) syndrome is endemic in U.S. police agencies, supported as it is by the absolute organizational truth that the department administration is preoccupied with punishment.

Equally important as a long-term cost of the militarization of the U.S. police is the dramatization of the police role in fighting crime that the military metaphor required. The fact is that the "war on crime" is a war police not only cannot win, but cannot in any real sense fight. They cannot win it because it is simply not within their power to change those things — such as unemployment, the age distribution of the population, moral education, freedom, civil liberties, ambitions, and the social and economic opportunities to realize them — that influence the amount of crime in any society. Moreover, any kind of real war on crime is something no democratic society would be prepared to let its police fight. We would simply be unwilling to tolerate the kind of abuses to the civil liberties of innocent citizens — to us — that fighting any kind of a real war on crime would inevitably involve.

These absolute limitations on the police capacity to influence crime notwithstanding, the expectation that police should be able to do so remain and are routinely reinforced by police themselves. Police take credit for drops and blames for rises in the crime rate. So strong is the crimefighting image of the U.S. police, that for the past 50 years virtually every purchase of equipment, every request for additional personnel, and every change in operating procedure has had to be promoted or defended in terms of its role in fighting crime.

The impassioned, crime-fighting rhetoric of militarization is often juxtaposed to the supposedly restraining metaphor of legalization. For example, we find that motif magnified in images suggesting that the courts are "handcuffing" the police. However, in two important ways, both of which mystify police activity and shield it from scrutiny, the rhetorics of militarization and legalization are profoundly complementary. First, both focus exclusively on crime. While the military analogy holds that fighting crime is the *raison d'être* of police, the circumlocution of legalization holds that police are controlled by the courts because they must show compliance with certain procedures on occasions when they petition the courts to punish.

Second, both legalization and militarization tend to discourage police accountability to political authorities. Legalization does so by sponsoring the impression that the courts oversee and control police practice. Insofar as the police function can be understood as simply "law enforcement" and the consequences of law enforcement governed by the judgments of the courts, there is apparently very little room or need for legitimate political accountability of police. The metaphor of militarization makes essentially the same point, only more strongly. It holds that in the war against crime, political involvement is suspect. Only someone interested in aiding the enemy would have reason to interfere with police.

Professionalization

Like militarization and legalization, the circumlocution that police administrators were to call "professionalization" also sought to distance police from the influence of the political process. And, like militarization, it did so by drawing upon an analogy. The professional analogy held that, like doctors, lawyers, engineers, and other professionals, police possessed a body of special skills and knowledge that were necessary both to do and to understand their work. Hence it would be no more appropriate for a politician to instruct a police officer on how to do his or her work than it would be for a politician to instruct a doctor on how to remove an appendix, or an engineer on how to build a bridge. It followed from this analogy that to do the work of professional policing, police administrators would require not only the highly sophisticated technological tools of professional policing, but also officers of intelligence and education to employ them. Only in a police agency equipped and staffed in this way, and working in an environment free from political interference, could truly professional policing flourish.

Although the professional analogy was effective in getting improved personnel and technical resources for police, in encouraging police research, and in increasing the political autonomy of police, the analogy was not without its difficulties. Even on its own metaphorical terms, it was defective. While it is true that no politician should have a hand on a surgeon's scalpel during an appendectomy or calculate weight displacement factors for an engineer's bridge, political involvement in medicine, engineering, and numerous other professions is thoroughgoing and, by most accounts, needs to be. While politicians do not dictate the depth of a surgeon's cut, they do influence where hospitals are built, what kinds of health insurance programs may be offered in a state, how and in what form health care will be provided for indigent patients, and to what extent the government will support specialized clinics, medical certification, education, and specialization. On a still broader political scale, state agencies review petitions for experimental surgical procedures and supervise in minute detail the development of all new medications. On balance and despite the intended political thrust of the professional analogy, it is probably fair to say that the state plays a much larger and more systematically influential role in the practice of medicine than it does in influencing the practice of policing.

The professional analogy also concealed a second major circumlocution. The fact is that the "professional" police officer, as conceived by the professional police model, was understood to be a very special kind of professional, a kind of professional that taxes the very meaning of the idea. The distinctive characteristic of the work of professionals is the range of discretion accorded them in the performance of their work. By contrast, the police view of professionalism was exactly the opposite. It emphasized centralized control and policy, tight command structure, extensive departmental regulation, strict discipline, and careful oversight. While the professional model wanted intelligent and educated police officers and the technological appearance of modern professionals, it did not want police officers who were granted broad, professional discretion. It wanted obedient bureaucrats.

Of course, it never really got them. The reason it did not is that the shape and variety of tasks and situations police encountered in their day-to-day work were too complex to be covered by the crude provisions of general bureaucratic regulations. Understanding this, the professional model focused its regulatory apparatus not on what police do with citizens, but on the behavior of police within the department bureaucracy. If one looks at the manuals that most modern police departments publish, some of which are hundreds and even thousands of pages long, one finds that virtually all the rules within them govern how the officer is supposed to behave within the department. With the exception, perhaps, of a policy on when to use deadly force, they are silent on the question of how they should treat the people they police.

It is against this backdrop of the three major circumlocutions in the history of the U.S. police that the emerging circumlocution of community policing must be considered. Although the mystiques of legalization, militarization, and professionalization have been largely demystified in the scholarly literature, they remain a part of the popular consciousness and continue to influence police conceptions of themselves. While they are assuredly myths about policework, they are not myths that can be dismissed. They have hardened into beliefs that govern police management and officer self-conceptions. They are driven deeply into the organizational structure and administrative apparatus of police agencies. Community policing thus must face the twin problems of dealing with the long-term consequences of those circumstances, and of replacing those circumlocutions with others powerful and compelling enough to permit a societal reconciliation with an "activity which is, in its very conception, opposed to the ethos of the polity that authorizes it" (Bittner, 1970).

The Circumlocutions of Community Policing

There are many notions of what community policing is, what it means, and what it can mean (Kelling, 1985; Wilson and Kelling, 1982; Sykes, 1986; Klockars, 1985). Perhaps the most comprehensive attempt to identify the critical elements of the movement is to be found in Jerome Skolnick and David Bayley's *The New Blue Line* (1986). The chief virtue of that book from our perspective is that it is uniformly cheerful about the movement and wholly without critical reservations as to its capacities and limits. Conceding that a more measured advocacy of community policing might provoke a less-revealing analysis of the rhetoric of community policing, we will, nevertheless, focus on what Skolnick and Bayley identify as the four elements of community policing that make it the "wave of the future" (p. 212): (1) police-community reciprocity, (2) areal decentralization of command, (3) reorientation of patrol, and (4) civilianization.

Police-Community Reciprocity

The first and most distinctive element of the community policing movement is what Skolnick and Bayley term "police-community reciprocity." The term as Skolnick and Bayley employ it embodies practical, attitudinal, and organizational dimensions. Practically, it implies that "the police must involve the community . . . in the police mission." Attitudinally, police-community reciprocity "means that police must genuinely feel, and genuinely communicate a feeling, that the public they serve has something to contribute to the enterprise of policing" (p. 211). Organizationally, police-community reciprocity implies that "the police and the public are co-producers of crime prevention. If the old professional leaned toward, perhaps exemplified, a 'legalistic' style of policing . . . the new professionalism implies that the police serve, learn from, and are accountable to the community" (p. 212).

Two central circumlocutions mark this vision of the relationship between police and the people they police. They are: (1) the mystification of the concept of community, and (2) the mixed metaphors of reduced crime. Although the two circumlocutions are heavily intertwined, let us begin by considering each of them separately.

The Mystification of the Concept of Community. Sociologically, the concept of community implies a group of people with a common history, common beliefs and understandings, a sense of themselves as "us" and outsiders as "them," and often, but not always, a shared territory. Relationships of community are different from relationships of society. Community relationships are based upon status not contract, manners not morals, norms not laws, understandings not regulations. Nothing, in fact, is more different from community than those relationships that character- ize most of modern urban life. The idea of police, an institution of state and societal relations, is itself foreign to relations of community. The modern police are, in a sense, a sign that community norms and controls are unable to manage relations within or between communities, or that communities themselves have become offensive to society. The bottom line of these observations is that genuine communities are probably very rare in modern cities, and, where they do exist, have little interest in culti- vating relationships of any kind with police. University communities, for example, have often behaved in this way, developed their own security forces and judicial systems, and used them to shield students (and fac- ulty) from the scrutiny of police.

The fact that genuine communities do not exist or are very rare and are largely self-policing entities in modern society raises the question of just why it is that the community policing movement has chosen to police in their name. An hypothesis suggests itself. It is that nonexistent and unin- terested communities make perfect partners for police in what Skolnick and Bayley have termed the "co-production of crime prevention." What makes them perfect partners is that while they lend their moral and politi- cal authority as communities to what police do in their name, they have no interest in and do not object to anything that might be done.

The flaw in this thesis is that it asks police to behave like good soci- ologists and use their concepts carefully. Of course, police do not behave in this way and it is probably unfair to ask them to do so. If we admit this flaw and excuse police for using the concept of "community" in far too casual a sense, we are obliged to ask what "police-community reciproc- ity" implies if it is not policing "communities." One answer is "neighbor- hoods," "districts'" and "precincts," each of which can often be spoken of as having legitimately identifiable characters and characteristics that police rightly and routinely take into account when working there.

There are, however, two major difficulties with substituting real entities like neighborhoods, districts, or interest groups for the concept of community. The first is that doing so misrepresents what working police officers in those places do. Those officers who actually work in those areas see themselves policing people and incidents, perhaps even "cor- ners," "houses," "parks," "streets," or even a "beat." But the concept of a patrol officer policing an entire neighborhood, district, or precinct extends the notion of a police officer's sense of territorial responsibility beyond any reasonable limits.

The only persons in police departments who can be said to police entities as large as entire neighborhoods, districts, or precincts are police administrators. It is police administrators who can be pressured by repre- sentatives of groups or associations from those areas. In policing such areas, police captains, inspectors, and police chiefs have rather limited resources and a rather limited range of real things they can do for or offer to such groups. By and large, police administrators at captain rank or above, the only persons in police agencies who can be said to police areas of the size of communities, police those areas with words. Thus the idea of police-community reciprocity becomes a rhetorical device for high-command-rank police officers to speak to organizations or groups in areas that are at once, geographically, too large to be policed and, politically, too large to be ignored.

The second major difficulty with substituting a concept like neighborhood for the too casual police use of community is that such a term tends to belie the character of the entities with which police leaders interact. In speaking to traditional neighborhood groups, police community relations officers have always had their "community-is-the-eyes-and-ears-of-the-police" speeches. But what is distinctive about the community policing movement is that it places the burden of bringing those groups into being and giving them an institutional or organizational reality on police. The typical strategy involves creating some form or organization that can act as a public forum for information exchange. In Santa Ana, California, the model community policing agency in Skolnick and Bayley's study, the department's organizational efforts are described as follows:

> Each of the four community areas has 150–250 block captains who may be responsible for thirty or forty neighbors. . . . Block captains are actively involved as liaisons, communicating with the Police Department. The result is quite extraordinary. The Police Department has not only responded to the community; it has, in effect, created a community—citywide—where formerly none existed. Neighbors who were strangers now know each other. A sociologist who wants to consider the "positive functions" of the fear of crime need only look at the Santa Ana team policing experience. Consider that up to 10,000 residents annually participate in a "Menudo cook-off and dance" organized by participants in community-oriented policing programs. This sort of community support is obviously important for social adhesion. It is equally significant for the Police Department. Community support is not simply an abstraction. It is also a grass-roots political base, assuring the department a generous portion of the city budget (of which in 1983 it received 30.7 percent) (pp. 28–29).

The city-wide community the Santa Ana police have created is, of course, not in any meaningful sense of the word a community at all. Nor is it a neighborhood, precinct, district, or any other form of indigenous, area-based entity. It is, rather, a grass-roots political action organization, brought into being, given focus, and sustained by the Santa Ana police.

As such, it is a very new form of political organization and one that our review of the history of circumlocutions in U.S. policing has prepared us to understand. Historically, each of those circumlocutions has served to increase the autonomy and independence of police, making them not only less receptive to demands from indigenous neighborhood action and interest groups, but also less tractable to control by elected political leaders. Progressively, these movements eventually left a void in municipal government. For while they increased the autonomy of police, they robbed them of both their popular and political support.

From the police point of view, the type of organization Skolnick and Bayley describe in Santa Ana as a model for community-oriented policing fills the void perfectly. It does so because it creates a political base for police that is not only independent of other municipal political organizations—indeed it deems itself "apolitical" in the case of the Santa Ana organization—but is totally dependent upon, organized by, and controlled by police themselves.

The Mixed Metaphors of Reduced Crime. Despite the fact that for the past 50 years the police have been promoting themselves as crime fighters, devoting enormous resources to the effort, taking credit for drops in the crime rate and criticism for rises in it, the best evidence to date is that no matter what they do they can make only marginal differences in it. The reason is that all of the major factors influencing how much crime there is or is not are factors over which police have no control whatsoever. Police can do nothing about the age, sex, racial, or ethnic distribution of the population. They cannot control economic conditions; poverty, inequality; occupational opportunity; moral, religious, family, or secular education; or dramatic social, cultural, or political change. These are the "big ticket" items in determining the amount and distribution of crime. Compared to them what police do or do not do matters very little.

While all of this is true for police, it is equally true of the kind of political entities the community policing movement calls communities. This reality is not lost on Skolnick and Bayley. Unlike some authors in the community policing movement (Kelling, 1985; Wilson and Kelling, 1982; and Sykes, 1986) and some community action groups, Skolnick and Bayley have chosen poses with respect to the prospect of controlling crime that leave the community policing movement some important outs and may even have diversified sufficiently to withstand the depression that is inevitable when it is realized that they have failed once again.

The Skolnick and Bayley construction of the relationship of community-oriented policing to crime control appears to consist of three images. The first is the image of the police and the people working side by side as coproducers of crime prevention. Describing community-oriented policing as the "new professionalism," Skolnick and Bayley (pp. 212–213) write: "The new professionalism implies that the police serve, learn from, and are accountable to the community. Behind the new professionalism is a governing notion: that the police and the public are co-producers of crime prevention." If ordinary citizens are actually to become crime prevention co-producers, reciprocity is a necessity. Communities cannot be mobilized for crime prevention from the top down. Members of the community have to become motivated to work with and alongside professional law enforcement agents.

Prevention.   Historically, the most significant semantic shift in the relationship between police and crime is the shift from promises to reduce it to promises to prevent it. The difference is important because, practically speaking, failures of crime reduction are measurable while failures of crime prevention are not. It is possible, though difficult, to test promises of crime reduction by determining whether there is more or less crime today than last year or the year before. By contrast, the success of crime prevention can only be evaluated against a prediction of what would have happened had the crime prevention effort not been made. Given that such predictions are presently impossible and that prevention efforts of any kind are able to produce at least some anecdotal evidence of occasional successes, the promise of successful prevention is virtually irrefutable. Skolnick and Bayley (p. 48) write of Santa Ana:

> Measures of police department effectiveness continue to baffle those inside departments as well as those who try to write about them. One measure is the crime rate. Santa Ana Police Department statistics show crime rising less than had been projected between 1970 and 1982. It is possible, however, that the overall rise in reported crime rates is attributable to citizen willingness to report having been victimized. Another [sic.!] indicator of Santa Ana success is the willingness of banks to provide loans to residents where they would not have been so willing a decade earlier.

Skolnick and Bayley do not report how the 12-year predicted rise in crime rates was arrived at, what the actual rise in crime rates was, nor how they arrived at measures of the "not so" willingness of banks to provide loans a decade ago, or of their alleged willingness to do so today.

Coproduction.   Even though prevention efforts will invariably be judged successful, a second rhetorical line of defense should prevention somehow be found to be slightly less successful than was hoped is provided by the contention that it is the product of the police and community coproduction. As this coproduction cannot be imposed from the top down, shortcomings in preventive efforts will be attributable to a lack of genuine community support. Although police may then step up their community organizing efforts, the blame for shortcomings will fall on the community.

The Virtue of Crime.   Skolnick and Bayley lay atop the notions of prevention and coproduction a third theme to guard against the possibility that community-oriented policing might be judged a failure against some crime control standard. Even though controlling crime is the manifest justification for coproductive prevention efforts, Skolnick and Bayley suggest a line of argument that, if taken seriously, leads to the conclusion that even if such efforts failed completely, coproductive prevention efforts would in and of themselves be sufficient evidence of community-oriented policing's success (1986:214):

> We have spoken freely about "neighborhoods" and "communities." In actuality, these forms of social organization—implying face-to-face interaction and a sense of communal identity—may be weak . . . [T]he police may find they have to activate neighborhood and community associations. In our often anomic urban society, the transcendent identity of many city dwellers is that of crime victim. Their neighbors may be the very people they fear. In such circumstances, police departments can facilitate, even create, a sense of community where one did not previously exist or was faintly imprinted. . . .
>
> Could it be that crime, like war and other disasters, might turn out to be America's best antidote to anomie in the United States?

It is with this third theme that Skolnick and Bayley's circumlocution of the idea of community-oriented policing comes full circle. Community-oriented policing is brought into being with the expectation that it will reduce crime. Political action groups are organized by police under that assumption. The assumption itself is converted into an untestable and irrefutable promise of prevention, coupled with an escape clause under which failure to achieve prevention becomes the fault of the "community." Finally, in the face of their failure to reduce crime, the organizations police created for the manifest purpose of reducing it become ends in themselves—success as antidotes to the problems of urban anomie. Indeed, such success would appear to be much like the success of war and other disasters.

Areal Decentralization of Command

After police-community reciprocity, understood as we have outlined it above, the second theme Skolnick and Bayley identify as crucial to community-oriented policing is "areal decentralization of command." It refers to the creation of ministations, substations, storefront stations, and the multiplication of precincts, each of which is given considerable autonomy in deciding how to police the area in which it is located. "The purpose behind all of them," explain Skolnick and Bayley (p. 214), "is to create the possibility of more intensive police-community interaction and heightened identification by police officers with particular areas."

As a symbolic gesture of police focus on a particular area, the ministation concept has considerable surface appeal. But as Skolnick and Bayley themselves admit, such decentralization does not automatically lead to the kind of community-oriented policing they advocate. They merely create conditions under which police assigned to these substations might engage in that type of behavior if they were motivated to do so. For example, Detroit had over 100 ministations before 1980, which were considered a joke by local residents, an administrative nightmare by police administrators, and a rubber-gun assignment by police officers.

The Skolnick and Bayley position on ministations, which is that unless they are genuinely committed to and motivated to do neighborhood organization, they will not promote community-oriented policing, conceals an administrative paradox. The paradox is that the more latitude and autonomy one gives to ministations to decide what is best for their local area, the less capacity one has to insure that those decisions are made in the genuine interest of that local area. Under such conditions, one simply has to trust that ministation crews embrace the community-oriented policing philosophy to a degree that will prevent them from perverting their autonomy for their own ends.

Perhaps the greatest danger in a police administrative structure in which command is radically decentralized to hundreds of ministations is corruption. Skolnick and Bayley (p. 215) are well aware of this problem and in acknowledgment of it they write:

> [T]here is a significant potential problem with the delegation of command to relatively small areas. Where a department has an unfortunate history of corruption, decentralization could prove to be a disaster, creating the exact conditions that facilitate further corruption. Where corruption prevails, however, it is unlikely that one would find much genuine interest in the sort of community crime prevention philosophy we have described here.

Their words are not, to say the least, very assuring. Their argument is that only a department with an "unfortunate history" of corruption would be subject to the danger of corruption in their ministations. The fact is that such decentralization of command invites new corruption to develop as surely as it invites old corruption to spread. Their further argument that departments in which corruption prevails would not have much "genuine" interest in developing an operating philosophy that creates the "exact conditions that facilitate further corruption" is even less comforting.

Reorientation of Patrol

The third rhetorical pillar in Skolnick and Bayley's construction of the idea of community policing is what they term the "reorientation of patrol." Practically speaking, the term means two things: increased use of foot patrol, and a reduction in police response to telephone calls for emergency service.

Skolnick and Bayley offer four claims in favor of foot patrol, all of which they report are supported by their observations and other studies. According to Skolnick and Bayley, foot patrol: (1) prevents crime, (2) makes possible "order maintenance" in ways motor patrol does not, (3) generates neighborhood goodwill, and (4) raises officer morale.

While it is not possible to refute Skolnick and Bayley's observational claims for these meritorious effects of foot patrol—except perhaps to say that they were made by observers who were categorically convinced of its virtues before they began their observations—at least some of those observations run directly counter to systematic, empirical evaluations of the effects of foot patrol. It is generally conceded that foot patrol can have some effect in reducing citizen fear of crime and in affecting positively citizen evaluations of the delivery of police service. It is also accepted that in certain very high-density urban areas foot patrol officers can engage in certain types of order maintenance policing that motor patrol officers cannot easily do. However, there is no evidence whatsoever that foot patrol can reduce or prevent crime (Police Foundation, 1981).

Moreover, it is of utmost importance to add to these observations on the effects of foot patrol that all of them are the product not of foot patrol alone, but of foot patrols added to areas already patrolled at normal levels by motor patrol. This fact is especially bothersome in light of the second theme in Skolnick and Bayley's idea of "reorientation of patrol." In *The New Blue Line* (pp. 216–217), they write:

> Police departments are also trying in various ways, though they don't like to admit it, to unplug the 911 emergency dispatch system selectively for patrol officers. By doing so, they free themselves for community development and crime prevention activities of their own devising. In many cities, the 911 system with its promise of emergency response has become a tyrannical burden. . . . The pressure of 911 calls has become so great that few officers are available for proactive community development. Moreover, patrol personnel can exhaust themselves speeding from one call to another, using up the time needed for understanding the human situations into which they are injected.
>
> . . . So, cautiously, [community-oriented police departments] are experimenting with measures that have the effect of reducing 911 pressure. Some departments are directing officers to park patrol cars periodically and patrol on foot; . . . others encourage patrol officers to take themselves "out of service" and simply stop and talk to people; and still others help them to prepare individualized plans for meeting local crime problems, even if it means not responding to calls or going under cover.

We are obliged to point out that not one of the measures Skolnick and Bayley identified above has, as they claim, "the effect of reducing 911 pressure." The pressure remains constant. Only the level of police response to it changes when patrol officers take themselves out of service or otherwise make themselves unavailable to respond.

Civilianization

The fourth and final rhetorical dimension Skolnick and Bayley fashion into the circumlocution of community policing is "civilianization"— the employment of nonsworn employees to do jobs that were formerly done by police officers. "Where civilianization does not prevail—and it does not in most police departments—it is difficult to offer much more than lip service to crime prevention" (p. 219).

Of all the arguments in *The New Blue Line,* the argument linking civilianization to community policing may be the most puzzling. There is, of course, a simple, powerful, and straightforward argument in favor of civilianization. It is that it can be significantly cheaper to have civilian employees do certain types of tasks than to have full-fledged, sworn officers do them. This argument is well accepted in police agencies in the United States, virtually all of which are concerned with finding ways to save money. In fact, it is probably difficult to find a U.S. police department that has not already civilianized at least a portion of its traffic control, motor pool, maintenance, clerical, and communication functions. At present, about 20 percent of the employees of the typical U.S. police agency are civilians. Moreover, it is quite likely that as the costs of police officers' salaries and benefits increase, police agencies will continue to civilianize certain routine tasks and duties that are unlikely to require the use of coercive force.

It is obvious that this economic argument in favor of civilianization is totally salient on the question of community-oriented policing. Its only premise is that police agencies have some interest in saving money and its only promise is that through civilianization they may do so. However, while Skolnick and Bayley accept this economic argument, they find that civilianization leads almost directly to the creation of successful community organization and crime prevention programs. "[O]ur investigations have persuaded us," say Skolnick and Bayley, "that the more a department is civilianized, the greater the likelihood that it will successfully introduce and carry out programs and policies directed toward crime prevention" (p. 219).

Skolnick and Bayley attempt to link the economic argument for civilianization to successful community crime prevention via two different but parallel arguments. The first argument holds that once some portion of their present duties are civilianized, police officers can be made available for crime prevention and community liaison activities. The second argument holds that by civilianizing the community liaison or crime prevention activities in a police officer's role, the officer can be freed to attend to genuine emergency situations.

Both arguments rest upon four highly questionable assumptions. The first assumption is that civilianization will be achieved by adding civilian employees to an agency's payroll rather than replacing sworn employees with civilians. No one is freed for any new forms of work if a department merely replaces retired police officer clerks, evidence technicians, or dispatchers with less costly civilian employees.

The second assumption is that new civilian employees performing tasks formerly assigned to police officers are not hired in lieu of needed additional police officers. If, for example, an agency concludes that it needs ten new police officers in its patrol division but obtains them by hiring ten civilian employees who, in turn, free ten officers already employed for patrol duty, no one, neither sworn officer nor civilian, is freed for any new form of work.

The third assumption linking the economic argument for civilianization with the conclusion that it leads to community-oriented policing is the belief that any additional funds or personnel resources, police or civilian, gained by civilianization will be devoted to crime prevention and community organization. Needless to say, such additional funds and resources must compete with every other need for funds and resources in a modern police agency and there is no reason to believe that crime prevention will gain or merit first priority.

Fourth and finally, Skolnick and Bayley link civilianization with community-oriented policing with the assumption that civilian employees will be more sensitive, receptive, and responsive to community needs and values than sworn police officers. "If civilians are drawn from within the inner-city communities that are being policed, they are likely to possess special linguistic skills and cultural understandings . . . [which can] further contribute to strengthening mobilization efforts to prevent crime" (p. 219). This assumption pales quickly when one begins to examine its credibility in numerous other municipal government agencies. Consider it in light of urban education, transportation, social welfare, public housing, and sanitation, none of which are much appreciated for their sensitivity, receptivity, or responsiveness to the communities they serve, even though all of them are 100 percent civilianized.

Whither the Circumlocution of Community Policing?

This chapter attempts to point out the errors, in fact, logic, and judgment, that mark the modern movement that goes by the name of community policing. Whatever the merit of the arguments and observations advanced here, they will undoubtedly strike some readers as misdirected and perhaps even mean spirited. Its difficulties, exaggerations, misrepresentations, and shortcomings notwithstanding, some will find it offensive to be critical of a movement that aspires to diminish urban anomie, to prevent crime by enlisting local support for police, and to make police agencies more sensitive to the cultural complexities of the areas they police. This reaction is to be anticipated and its appearance is central to the core argument of the chapter.

The only reason to maintain police in modern society is to make available a group of persons with a virtually unrestricted right to use violent and, when necessary, lethal means to bring certain types of situations under control. That fact is as fundamentally offensive to core values of modern society as it is unchangeable. To reconcile itself to its police, modern society must wrap it in concealments and circumlocutions that sponsor the appearance that the police are either something other than what they are or are principally engaged in doing something else. Historically, the three major reform movements in the history of the U.S. police, their militarization, legalization, and professionalization, were circumlocutions of this type and all sought to accomplish just such concealments. To the extent that these circumlocutions worked, they worked by wrapping police in aspirations and values that are extremely powerful and unquestionably good.

The movement called community policing is precisely this type of concealment and circumlocution. It wraps police in the powerful and unquestionably good images of community, cooperation, and crime prevention. Because it is this type of circumlocution, one cannot take issue with its extremely powerful and unquestionably good aspirations. Who could be against community, cooperation, and crime prevention? To do so would not only be misdirected and mean spirited, it would be perverse.

This chapter is not against any of these aspirations. What it does oppose is the creation of immodest and romantic aspirations that cannot, in fact, be realized in anything but ersatz terms. Police can no more create communities or solve the problems of urban anomie than they can be legalized into agents of the courts or depoliticized into pure professionals. There is no more reason to expect that they can prevent crime than to expect that they can fight or win a war against it.

Be that as it may, the circumlocution of community policing, like the circumlocutions of militarization, legalization, and professionalization before, enjoys a peculiar form of rhetorical immunity that it is likely to sustain in the face of even the most damaging criticism. At the International Conference on Community Policing at which an early draft of this chapter was first presented, Chris Murphy of the Office of Canadian Solicitor General captured the sense of this immunity elegantly by observing that criticizing community policing was "like criticizing the tune selection of the singing dog." It is not that the police dog is singing well that is so remarkable, but that he is in fact singing.

What this chapter attempts to show is that it is not at all remarkable that we should find the new song of community policing being sung by or about police. We have heard the songs of militarization, legalization, and professionalization in the past and we will no doubt continue to hear the tunes of community policing in the future. An echo of the songs that preceded it, this tune also is about some very good things we might gladly wish, but which, sadly, cannot be.

References

Bittner, E. (1970). *The functions of police in modern society.* Washington, DC: National Institute of Mental Health.

Black, D. (1980). *Manners and customs of police.* New York: Academic Press.

Fogelson, R. M. (1977). *Big-city police.* Cambridge, MA: Harvard University Press.

Haller, M. H. (1976). Historical roots of police behavior: Chicago, 1890–1925. *Law and Society Review, 10*(2), 303–323.

Kelling, G. L. (1985). Order maintenance, the quality of urban life, and police: A line of argument. In W. A. Geller (Ed.), *Police leadership in America: Crisis and opportunity* (pp. 296–308). New York: Praeger.

Klockars, C. B. (1985). Order maintenance, the quality of urban life, and police: A different line of argument. In W. A. Geller (Ed.), *Police leadership in America: Crisis and opportunity* (pp. 309–321). New York: Praeger.

Mapp v. Ohio. 1961 81 Sup. Ct. 1684.

Skolnick, J. H., & Bayley, D. H. (1986). *The new blue line: Police innovation in six American cities.* New York: The Free Press.

Sykes, G. (1986, December). Street justice: A moral defense of order maintenance. *Justice Quarterly, 3*(4), 297–512.

Walsh, W. F. (1986). Patrol officer arrest rates: A study of the social organization of police work. *Justice Quarterly, 2*(3), 271–290.

Wilson, J. Q., & Kelling, G. L. (1982, March). The police and neighborhood safety: Broken windows. *Atlantic Monthly, 127,* 29–38.

Chapter 31

Research Utilization in Complex Organizations
A Case Study in Corrections

Rick Lovell

Nearly 50 years have passed since Robert S. Lynd (1939) posed the question to social scientists: "Knowledge for what?" During the past two decades in particular there has been increasing interest in the potential of social science research information, or information developed through the use of social science methods, to "routinely guide policy and practice in people-changing organizations" (Glaser, 1973:2). As in other areas of public policy, importance has been attached to the possibility of empirical information serving as a significant input, if not as the predominant basis, for policy development and decision making in corrections and in other criminal justice agencies (Glaser, 1973; Gottfredson and Gottfredson, 1980).

The literature on research utilization (RU) is growing. Most of the available literature points to the "general failure" of research information to "affect decision making in a significant way" (Patton, 1978:2). The perceived lack of effect of empirical information on decision making in public agencies has led to much discussion and to some research. In criminal justice, particularly in corrections, there is scant research on the use of empirical information and too little consideration of the potential role of research information as an input in decision making and policy formulation.

Rick Lovell, "Research Utilization in Complex Organizations: A Case Study in Corrections," *Justice Quarterly* Vol. 5 No. 2, 1988, pp. 257–280. Reprinted by permission of the Academy of Criminal Justice Sciences.

It has long been assumed that research information is underutilized in correctional decision making and policy development. Yet, as noted, there is little empirical evidence about the level or scope of utilization in corrections: what information is used, by whom, for what purposes, and with what result. This article reports and discusses an exploratory study on the use of research information by upper-level administrators and staff members in a state department of corrections. The purposes of the study were 1) to examine the use of social science research information in policy development and decision making and 2) to develop an understanding of factors which influence or shape use in the department. The aims of the following discussion are 1) to stimulate consideration of the predominant expectations about research use in corrections and 2) to encourage dialogue on possible directions for further inquiry and on the development of an adequate integrative model of the research utilization process in corrections.

Defining Utilization

Asking questions about research utilization proves to be difficult. Many of our images of RU are conditioned, if not determined, by rigorous and demanding notions rooted in the analytic paradigm of decision making in complex organizations. Many common images are associated with normative expectations derived from viewing social science research information as "conclusive," "useful," and "authoritative."

The most rigorous conceptualization of RU is defined operationally in terms of documentable or observable changes in programs or policies, based directly on the information supplied by empirical studies (Patrick, 1979). Such a conception generally is described by the terms *instrumental use* or *impact*. The predominant expectation about instrumental use is that research information would enter into an analytic, rational decision-making process and that the findings and/or conclusions would be incorporated directly into the outcome. In short, the empirical information would affect the outcome significantly.

Scholars, researchers, and practitioners have recognized the shortcomings of simply assuming that research information will achieve instrumental use regularly. Such expectations and their resultant definitions, according to Weiss and Bucuvalas (1980:10), "identify what program directors in the applied research offices of [The National Science Foundation] used to call 'nuggets,' those occasional gems of direct application that they mined and cherished for their value in proving the utility of their research programs to a hostile Congress." Weiss also states, "It probably takes an extraordinary concatenation of circumstances for research to influence policy *directly*" (1979:428).

An awareness that empirical findings seldom achieve instrumental use has led to broader conceptualizations. Many scholars now find it acceptable to define utilization in terms of consideration. From this perspective, research information is seen as a tool for enlightenment "in sorting out assumptions, clarifying logic, or arriving at a better understanding of the range of activities and constraints involved in a particular decision [or set of decisions]" (Rich, in Grosskin, 1981:9). In other words, research information is used to guide and clarify the decision-making process. Such application generally is termed *conceptual use*.

Now it is also recognized generally that utilization may include symbolic functions; that research information may be put to *persuasive use*. In other words, empirical information may be used to "substantiate a previously held position, marshal support, or cast doubt on propositions at odds with those of the user, among other such possibilities" (Knorr quoted in Weiss, 1977:152).

Broader operational definitions of utilization corresponding to the latter conceptualizations (conceptual use and symbolic use) must emphasize research information as a competing rather than a dominating input among other sources of information. Furthermore, the corresponding view of the utilization process may need to replace the rational, analytic image, and admit to a dynamic process in which individuals with diverse interests and unequal influence affect actively the process of utilization.

Perspectives on Research Utilization

Even among those who employ broad definitions of use there remains an overall impression and a rather pervasive belief that research information is underutilized in decision making in public agencies. Several perspectives have been employed by those seeking to account for the modest levels of use observed in most studies.

Relying on a belief that differences in the culture of science and the culture of government (following Snow, 1962) lead to less effective utilization, some scholars have focused on the processes of knowledge production and transfer to locate the major variables that account for use or nonuse of research information (see Caplan, 1979; Weiss and Bucuvalas, 1980:17–23). "Proponents [of this approach] assume that bridges need to be constructed to link the worlds of policymakers and researchers and analysts" (Rich, 1981:12). The reasons offered for the alleged lack of effect of research information have been summarized in long lists which include such items as poor methodological quality of the research, lack of relevance of research information to decision making, and inadequate, ineffective, and untimely communication of results (Grosskin, 1981:1).

Scholars also have employed varying perspectives (often presented as mutually exclusive) to explore barriers to utilization associated with individual characteristics and/or orientations of decision makers, political constraints, and the linkage system for transmitting results. It is reasonable to expect that barriers to utilization can arise in any or all of these areas (for excellent discussions see Glaser, Abelson, and Garrison, 1983 and Weiss and Bucuvalas, 1980). No adequate theoretical framework exists yet, however, to integrate the various perspectives.

A few students of utilization have focused on the nature of organizational decision making and on the processes through which use of research information may occur in complex, bureaucratic organizations. Lindblom and Cohen (1979) attempt to come to an understanding of use/ nonuse by conceptualizing the potential role of such information in the problem-solving process of complex organizations. They remind us that decision makers

> always have a choice between trying to find "solutions" by arranging to have a given problem frontally attacked by persons who will think it through to a solution, or by managing to set in motion interaction, that will, with the help of analysis adapted to the interaction, eventuate in a solution or a preferred outcome (25).

Further, Lindblom and Cohen provide a critical insight in suggesting that research information must compete with a "mountain of ordinary knowledge which it cannot replace but only reshape here and there" (32). Their insights are crucial in directing our attention to the interactive nature of the decision-making process and in sensitizing us to the descriptive inaccuracy of the images associated with the rational, analytic paradigm of decision making. As emphasized in the quote above, Lindblom and Cohen point out the need to consider the potentially active focus of decision makers regarding information requirements. They also suggest the need to pay attention to patterns of information search and to the bureaucratic decision making norms of tailoring the search for information to problems at hand and of addressing problems sequentially, as these arise and become important enough to require resolution.

Robert Rich (1981) focuses on *bureaucratization* to locate a set of variables associated with internal agency control and with bureaucratic interests as important factors in utilization. According to Rich, one can assume that the characteristics of knowledge—its quality or perhaps its conclusiveness—establish a necessary but not a sufficient condition in accounting for its application or utilization (159). He concludes that research information is less likely to be used because of its quality or its appropriateness to the substantive policy or problem area than because of its value in enhancing bureaucratic interests (158–64).

Scholars disagree on what the important determinants of utilization may be. No completely adequate theoretical framework exists from which to investigate it. As noted, much of the discussion of utilization has been impressionistic, and empirical work to date has been exploratory.

Framework for This Study

Corrections policy presents a challenge to the study of utilization. Decision makers in corrections operate in complex, bureaucratic environments, in a rather visible and competitive policy arena. They occupy the unenviable position of needing to be "successful" (perhaps in terms of loyalties to the organization, perhaps in other ways); at the same time, these administrators are the focal points for scrutiny and review by a number of outside sources, including legislative bodies, state executives, the judiciary, reform groups, and other significant parties. Decisions and policies in this context emerge from compromise, confusion, and conflict among many actors, engaged in some version of what Allison (1971) would term "bureaucratic politics." Because powerful external elites may be important in shaping use within correctional agencies, attention to the overall decision-making and policy-making context is required.

The array of findings and thought on utilization suggests a variety of possibilities for organizing a study of this subject. The most promising perspectives are suggested in work by Lindblom and Cohen (1979) and by Rich (1981); their conceptualizations and findings urge consideration of the context in which utilization is expected to occur. The complexity of the issues to be addressed, the possibility that relevant variables will be influenced by or will stem directly from the decision-making context, and the lack of available evidence or use in corrections argue for an exploratory, qualitative approach. This study proceeded with a framework of basic concepts derived from a review of the RU literature and the literature on complex organizations and decision making. The empirical intent of the study was 1) to ascertain patterns of use (with particular attention to availability of research information as well as types and scope of use) and 2) to determine whether factors associated with the bureaucratization of the decision-making process would prove important in understanding use in the department under study here.

Methods

This study examined the use of social science research information at the upper levels of management in a state department of corrections. The author used a qualitative design to provide depth and variety within a limited context and to allow for examination of foci that emerged as the author moved toward grounded theory.

The study interviewed a sample of 27 top-level administrators, major division managers, and research/information-producing personnel in the central headquarters of the organization. The respondents were responsible for or contributed directly to systemwide planning and decision making for the department. The working universe consisted of all persons in the groups defined above.

The author employed a semistructured interview schedule. The procedure was flexible; it permitted respondents to develop their thoughts and allowed the interviewer to pursue leads that emerged. The tape-recorded interviews averaged 90 minutes in length.

In addition to the interview data, a variety of other sources provided evidence on utilization and on the processes and context in which use might occur. These sources included agency records, project memoranda and documents, and illustrative material such as study reports, journals, and other information provided by respondents. This material was used in examining the flow of research information within the department, to document use where possible, and to provide information on organization structure and relevant formal policies within the department.

Setting

The chief executive officer of a state department of corrections (DOC) granted access for the study; this is a medium-sized DOC located in a southern state. The organization is headed by a chief executive appointed by and primarily accountable to the governor of the state. Upper-level management positions are unclassified and appointed.

The department has a complex mission to perform and is highly differentiated structurally. The operating environment and the projected operating environment at the time of the study were turbulent. Leaders of the department faced stiff competition for resources in a state struggling to reconcile large budget deficits with expectations of an uncertain economic future. The operating environment was one of fiscal retrenchment stemming from economic crises.

In addition, the department was experiencing a major problem with over-crowding, it had come under increasing scrutiny from an array of outside observers including the judiciary, the state legislature, the governor's office, the news media, and special interest groups. The external pressures compounded the usual difficulties found in the internal environment of a large, complex public organization.

Gaining access for this study required that a research understanding be reached. The agreement involved a promise that the author would control the data developed in this study and would assure confidentiality regarding the data and the respondents. To comply with the request, the author has generalized descriptions of the organization and the respondents. He has made an effort to avoid using names, titles, and other designations which may reveal identities.

Analysis of the Data

The interviews provided the bulk of the data concerning use in the department. Collateral evidence in the form of agency documents, project memoranda, and other material provided verification of some responses, data on use, and data concerning the dissemination networks and structural features of the department.

The data were submitted to a qualitative analysis. The coding of interview responses corresponded to categories established on the basis of subjective analysis of the content of responses, together with basic questions established and a general conceptual framework rooted in the utilization literature.

The following basic questions were addressed:

Category	Questions
1. type of information	Is research information available? If so, what information is available?
2. type of use	If research information is used, how is it used? What types of use occur? Is use immediate or does it occur in a diffuse way?
3. user's identity	Who uses research information? Individuals? Groups? Who is more likely to use research information?
4. scope of use	Is research information systematically used? Is it put to greater/equal/less use than other types of information? Are there certain individuals/groups/areas where research information is more likely to be used? To be ignored?

A portion of the data collection was devoted to investigating the information dissemination process in the department and to obtaining data on the possible bureaucratization of the utilization process. To suggest possible categories for analysis the author drew on the work done by Rich (1981) in his assessment of use of Continuous National Survey information in federal policy making. In addition, the author left leeway to explore emerging foci and to allow for creation of categories based on content analysis of the data.

Discussion of Findings

The following discussion is organized 1) to address the basic questions concerning use in the department and 2) to present findings of primary interest in coming to understand utilization in the department; such findings may be important in considering the RU process in general.

Availability of Research Information

Members of the department had access to research information in a number of forms and from a variety of sources. A substantial amount of research-based information was physically present and at least ostensibly was available for use. In many instances this information had not been acquired for specific purposes; in most instances no discernible attempt had been made to categorize or evaluate it in terms of potential identifiable use by members of the department. In other words, a great deal of research-produced knowledge was merely present and might possibly be put to some use ad hoc and rather haphazardly. Most of this "information" could be said more appropriately to consist of pieces of knowledge which happened to be present in the department.

Externally Produced Information

Much of the research-based information in the department could be characterized as "routinely encountered material." Various individuals in the department received such information rather regularly. Research-based information was received routinely from a variety of sources:

1. professional journals and publications (e.g., *ACA Journal* and *Federal Probation*); psychological journals; juvenile justice publications; professional business journals.

2. material disseminated from national clearing houses and from federal agencies such as NIC and NCJRS.

3. material disseminated by other agencies, such as studies on risk prediction or on riot situations in other states.

The department, as an organization, was on no dissemination lists; only individuals were included on such lists. There was no central coordination of information resources and no centralized process for acquiring, assessing, or disseminating such resources. In fact, the department had no formal policies regarding the dissemination or potential use of this type of information. It was left to the discretion of individual department members to decide whether to acquire certain research-based information or any information, and whether (as well as to whom) to pass along information.

One administrator reflected the organization's short-term focus and summarized management's views on routinely encountered material:

> A lot of this material is looked on as a frivolous encumbrance. No, we do not centrally acquire this material on a day-to-day basis and distribute it. There is actually little forethought about this. [We] do not acknowledge the utility of acquiring this kind of information in doing business. There is a large body of knowledge out there, but a lot is not valuable. There is little utility in it in addressing day-to-day problems.

A member of the in-house research staff assessed this issue as follows:

> Information [of this type] comes in at different points. It may be sent on to so and so, but this is [done] purely on personal initiative. Information sent on to an individual is done on the basis of who you think might be interested. If information comes in to [the chief executive's] office it might be disseminated. A lot of information comes in. We do crisis-oriented search.

Regarding routinely encountered empirical knowledge, the department could be said to have a *distributed-information problem*. No formal policies governed the acquisition, assessment, dissemination, or use of such information; consequently, much potentially useful information simply was shelved and disregarded. The author found no formal decision rules which would encourage use of research information.

In-House Research: Internally Produced Empirical Information

Members of the department visualized "research" with a great deal of variability. The participants in this study evidenced widely differing conceptions of research and notions of the processes and outcomes associated with research. The term "research" might be applied to activities ranging from tightly designed and rather rigorously conducted empirical investigations to compiling basic data (as in daily census totals and counts on bed space); decision makers were expected to evaluate this material heuristically and to put it to some use. Most respondents, with the notable exception of the in-house research personnel, tended to refer to any "special" or specific data collection activity as research. In this study the interviewer had to be specific about the meaning of the term "research information"; perhaps the same would be true in other studies.

Tangible evidence showed that members of the department conduct empirical studies using social science research methods. Most of the studies would fall loosely into the category of program evaluation. The department's structure included a program evaluation section which had been in existence for two years at the time of the study. This section had completed three major studies, each involving survey techniques combined with collection of collateral evidence and qualitative analysis, as well as some descriptive quantitative analysis. A separate statistics section also developed a limited amount of empirical information, primarily descriptive analyses intended for use by top-level administrators.

The mental health division of the department also engaged in empirical research. The division administrator, a clinical psychologist with a Ph.D., provided evidence of several projects completed or under way. This administrator also provided evidence of recent publication in a professional journal and furnished a copy of an article submitted for publication.

Again, research-based information was present. There were no formal policies regarding the dissemination or potential use of the information produced in-house. None of the work reviewed included a utilization scheme or plan. The author noted evidence, however, of an informal but quite explicit policy regarding the products of the program evaluation section. Respondents, including administrators and research personnel, stated that information developed by this section would be disseminated on a "need-to-know" basis. "Need to know" would be determined situationally by the chief executive officer.

Knowledge Possessed by Individuals

The study could not ascertain how much scientific knowledge was possessed by individual respondents. The respondents' credentials were impressive; many possessed considerable experience in corrections as well as substantial educational attainment. As one top-level administrator observed, "Many of these people are experts in their own minds." The primary base of information in the department existed in the form of the knowledge and expertise possessed by the individual members of the department.

Use of Research Information

The primary evidence of use in the department was drawn from responses of the participants in the study. Very little evidence of use was present in agency documents, project memoranda, or other material.

It is impossible to make absolute statements about levels of use of research information, but relative to the use of other forms of information, the use of this information for decision making or policy formulation was minimal. Even so, some research information was used in what must be termed circumscribed ways, and the diversity of types of use was somewhat surprising.

Instrumental Use

Interviews and review of documents covering a two-year period revealed only three instances of instrumental use. Even these instances, although documentable, arguably could be placed in the category of symbolic use. In one instance where documentation revealed instrumental utilization of study findings, a researcher explained:

> We were assigned to do this study. But you have to understand that the decision had already been made. The outcome was obvious. We knew what we were going to find, and that is why we were asked to do what we did. We didn't have time for adequate study, but it didn't matter anyway.

An administrator noted further:

> Recommendations, findings, from [that study] were made use of in making the change. They [the legislature] already knew what they wanted, so the study didn't decide that. It helped to justify the changes.

The other two instances of instrumental use were surrounded by circumstances that also could have led to categorization as symbolic use. The data collection in the present research was centered on the upper levels of management in the department; that focus could be significant in considering the small amount of instrumental use and the circumstances surrounding the instances noted.

Conceptual Use

Most of the evidence for use of research information in this study was provided by respondents who discussed instances of conceptual use. The accounts of conceptual use often were cloudy or nonspecific in the sense that respondents were attempting to describe instances in which they considered research information in coming to understand the issues confronting them. Research/information-producing personnel more often were able to point out specific instances of conceptual use by referring to studies completed or under way which involved a preliminary review of literature or collection of research information as a foundation for a study or project. Administrators' responses were less specific; their responses conveyed the idea that even conceptual use was minimal, although several indicated a *belief* that conceptual use occurred.

The following statements represent the range of responses among administrators:

> Administrator: For the most part, I think there is strong consideration of research results. I can name areas where we look at research of a general nature. The process of using this information is more informal. We rely heavily on other kinds of information-practical information.

> Administrator: Sometimes there are so many recommendations. They tell you too much. You get tired. Research can become word-of-mouth. Something gets translated, becomes part of what someone believes, gets used in this way.

> Administrator: I can't point to anything right now.

Specifically mentioned instances of conceptual use included consideration of research information concerning work on a hostage policy, reviews of crowding and risk prediction studies, design work for a pilot study using the M-C inkblot test to detect inmates faking psychoses, review of recent findings on the Rorschach method, design work on education evaluations, and review of studies on riots and riot situations to identify possible policy needs. In addition, research information produced in house was put to conceptual use. One administrator noted:

> Like this one study program evaluation did. If nothing else, it enlightened me. I used it to critique some of the things we were doing. I also looked at information from other states. I put these things together, and if it's reasonable, we might try some tests.

Symbolic Use

Most administrators reported that their primary use of research information involved supporting budget requests, justifying grant or funding requests, or strengthening policy recommendations already formulated. One administrator noted:

> We use research mostly in our budget requests; to get funding — as a justification.

Another administrator summarized the statements made by most respondents:

> We'll recommend what we *feel*—but that won't be without as much backup as we can get.

Yet another administrator commented on the products of the program evaluation section:

> Program evaluation is used as a management tool—to get budget increases.

Type of Use in Perspective

This study focused on diversity in types of use, not on quantity. In view of all the data, however, it is possible to form a rather clear picture of use. It is apparent that symbolic or persuasive use of research information was the primary mode of use among administrators in the department. Among research/information-producing personnel, however, conceptual use was the primary application; conceptual use was described by all respondents. Instrumental use was minimal.

Scope of Use

Systematic use of research information was found to be limited in the department. Yet a pattern emerged which was supported both in the responses of study participants and to some degree in agency documents and memoranda.

The respondents agreed that the operational (program) level in the department contained the areas where the greatest amount of use had probably taken place, and certainly where the greatest levels of use had probably taken place, and certainly where the greatest levels of use could be expected. Small program sections, such as those involved with mental health, classification, and certain treatment interventions, were seen as the areas where research information could find consistent application.

One administrator provided a summary of most respondents' perceptions:

> Research is going to be useful in program areas—almost any treatment program. From my level [division manager] on up, almost everything is geared for planning for budget. If we had more time, maybe it would be different. Here we live from day to day, and here there are value choices.

Another administrator addressed the scope of use in the following way:

> It depends on the issue. At the operational level, the decision is going to be based about 60 percent on experience. The other 40 percent depends on reviewing policies and regulations. We *need* a body of knowledge—a statistical base to draw on. If we had that we might use

it. Managers are not acclimated to research. I don't know that many researchers who are top-line managers. Empirical data is *boring* to legitimate power brokers.

During the study and in analyzing the data it became rather obvious
that persons in certain subunit sections at the operational level were most
likely to be seen as the users of research information. Also it was clear
that use could vary among individuals and groups within hierarchical
levels. Respondents perceived the use of research information as more
appropriate in certain subsections with limited "scientific" missions. In
addition, it was clear that use—both type of use and the degree of reliance on research information—would vary between hierarchical levels.
At the division-manager level and particularly at the top management
level, the likelihood of instrumental or strictly conceptual use was diminished greatly, whereas the use of research information for symbolic or
persuasive purposes was somewhat more likely, when it was considered
necessary. Stated in another way, an inverse relationship exists between
hierarchical level and research utilization. In the agency studied, the
higher an individual ascends in the hierarchy, the less that individual
uses research information. At the upper levels, research information
might prove useful only for symbolic or persuasive purposes.

Moreover, the use of research information was a matter of individual determination in the department. Most respondents were rather pes-
simistic about the likelihood that research information would affect
policy or decision in a significant way. Further, evidence of any concerted
effort to use research information in a systematic way (formal policies,
decision rules or structure, systematic procedures) was totally absent.

Research Information versus
Other Forms of Information

Relative to reliance on other forms of information, research information was used only minimally, except for certain circumscribed purposes.
As noted earlier, Lindblom and Cohen (1979:32) hypothesize that
research information must compete with a "mountain of ordinary knowledge which it cannot replace but only reshape here and there." Consideration of the data in regard to this notion sheds light on the role accorded
to research information in the department.

With little variation, the respondents described the preference for
practical policy without research. The separation of research data from policy data or data for decision making was pervasive; with few exceptions
(notably among the researchers) the respondents did not recognize a direct
relationship between research information and the development of policy.
The issue of reliance on research information compared to other forms of
information is illuminated by the following representative comments:

> Administrator: The need for policy takes priority over the need to review research. The kinds of information decision makers look to are not necessarily what you would call research. Definitely the need for policy takes priority over the need for evaluation.

> Researcher: I don't think we use research. I may be biased. We use historical data. We use aggregate data: looking at today, last week, last year—strictly numbers. I think these numbers have a stronghold on the formulation of policy and on making decisions in general.

> Administrator: Research, even reviewing research, is a luxury—whatever the source. Needs and resource-oriented constraints and the personal time factor make it so.

> Administrator: Decisions are political. To have the greatest impact for research information, you have to learn the secret; learn how to market it in a political environment—to influence decision makers to change their behaviors.

> Administrator: Expertise is used more than any other source of information for policy and decisions.

> Administrator: Whatever information supports the budget, we use that and go that way.

Finally,

> Administrator: We use the resources at hand: experience, expertise, and the legislature.

The study participants made it quite clear that information drawn from experience and expertise dominated decision making and policy development in the department. Even though one might argue that individuals may have knowledge of specific research findings and conclusions, and might put these to conceptual use in a diffuse way, the respondents generally distinguished individual knowledge and expertise from research information. The role accorded to individual knowledge and expertise, together with other forms of "ordinary" information (e.g., "strictly numbers"), was patently greater than that accorded to research information except where the use of research information received validation for limited purposes.

Factors Which Emerge as Important in Understanding Use/Nonuse in the Department

The department studied here is a complex, bureaucratic organization in which more than 5,000 persons are employed. The department has a differentiated structure and is characterized by the generally accepted features of a bureaucratic organization.

Every participant in the study characterized the management climate in the department as "crisis-oriented." All the participants characterized the department's external environment as uncertain; perceptions of a turbulent environment were pervasive. It appeared to the author that the respondents viewed "crisis" as a general, understandable rationale for an overall management approach based on incrementalism. Administrators interviewed gave little indication that rational analysis would be important for decision making unless the appearance of rationality would assist in persuading a particular audience.

Concern with established routine and with safe, incremental adaptation was evident in the responses of top administrators in the department. "Success" for the department was linked to preservation of staff and budget in the face of what the participants perceived to be an uncertain future. Understanding research utilization (or the lack of it) in the department requires the realization that the potential role of research information is limited by the orientation of the decision system (incrementalism as opposed to rational, analytic process) and by the corresponding logic and processes which facilitate decision making and policy formulation.

The department is structured along functional lines; problem solving is partitioned across and among subelements, as well as being ordered hierarchically. Members of the department were left relatively free to create what may be described best as "information spaces," based on the selective perception of information considered (on whatever basis) to be relevant to task accomplishment and/or to the resolution of immediate or anticipated problems.

One must suggest that the partitioning of problems, coupled with the absence of any formal forethought concerning information resources, was important in understanding the patterns of use noted previously. Members of the department viewed research information as relevant for certain limited purposes. In other words, the types of problems to be addressed and the perceptions of the nature of problems (technical as opposed to involving questions of value) contributed at least in a basic way to perceptions of the appropriateness of research information as an input; thus they must be seen as contributing to the pattern of circumscribed use.

The hierarchical ordering of problems also must be considered. At upper management levels, where intra-organizational interests, external interests, and questions of value were emphasized by respondents as more important, it is apparent that the potential role for research information diminished significantly and changed from perceptions of potential instrumental and conceptual use to a role with more practical importance for symbolic or persuasive purposes.

This study developed data on the patterns of search for information in problem solving. Overall, problem solving in the department could be described best as "problemistic" (Cyert and March, 1963). In other words, it appeared that the general tendency was to address immediate problems sequentially and to tailor the search for information to perceptions of what would be necessary to resolve the problem or problems at hand.

All respondents except research/information-producing personnel evidenced a strong inclination to rely on the expertise and experience of department staff members as the primary source of information for problem solving. As identified, the sources of information for problem solving fell into six categories, ranked as follows: 1) staff (experience/expertise); 2) standards and laws; 3) other systems' activities (direct observation of practices); 4) in-house research information; 5) research information from external sources; 6) review by consultants.

The crisis orientation of management appeared to reinforce perceptions of the need to address immediate problems sequentially. Respondents perceived that resource and time constraints related to crisis would preclude most attempts to use research information as a basis for decision. Review of research information or in-house production of empirical information was viewed in general as a "luxury" or, as one administrator put it, "a waste of time better applied to other pursuits." Conducting in-house research was perceived in general as a way to supplement problem-specific interactions aimed at resolving immediate problems, primarily to gain leverage for budget requests or for other symbolic purposes.

Bureaucratic Interests

It could not be said that as a group, the administrators had discounted research information completely as a possible input. They did show a preference for receiving information which already had been digested and evaluated by persons trusted to apply expertise and experience in determining its relevance and importance. Consider the following comments:

> Administrator: I always staff the problem. I expect the staff to use whatever resources are available — whether that means journals, the library, civil service regulations, other states, get in touch with universities — whatever. After that they give me a summary. I write a decision and distribute it for consideration. That usually generates a response. Then I act on it.

> Administrator: I prefer statistics to back up a decision. My people give me a capsule version and their recommendations. I look at what is necessary. You have to have a feel for the politics of it. I seldom look at an entire study.

Rich (1981) draws attention to the "selective utilization" of research information within complex organizations. His work emphasizes the need to examine the upward dissemination of research information as a process in which "trusted aides" are relied on to select safe and bureaucratically useful information. In the department under study, some evidence indicated that upper-level administrators relied on trusted staff to send them appropriate information. One researcher stated quite directly:

> Reliability is the key. It depends on the subject matter, but if you find the "right ear" [to transmit information], then you get this halo effect.

In pursuing the issue of "selective utilization," the author asked all respondents whether research information that comes directly to a decision maker through a trusted staff aide would be of great importance, of some importance, or of no importance in understanding utilization in the department. Twenty of the 27 respondents had an opinion on this issue; 12 stated that they would judge the issue to be of great importance and eight considered it to be of some importance, reflecting a strong perception of the possible importance of selectivity in transmitting information in the department. Future studies may attend to this issue quite fruitfully. It is intriguing and important to consider the possibility that the use of research information is influenced by implicit, informal information policies concerning what administrators may want to see. It may be an important possibility that certain information is used or ignored because it is transmitted by "trusted staff," as opposed to others, especially when (as this study finds) upper-level administrators use research information more for symbolic than for other purposes.

The issue of bureaucratic interest and research use/nonuse was more pronounced in another vein. It is natural that upper-level decision makers place faith in reliable subordinates; delegation of authority demands such an attitude. In addition, however, upper-level administrators discussed the potential nonuse of research information (any information) in connection with risk avoidance and perceptions of uncertainty. Candid comments from two administrators were ominous in their possible effect on RU:

> Administrator: Our biggest problem is, do we even want to develop certain information? If we are not prepared to handle it—deal with the results—do we even want to develop it? If we can't handle what they want to tell us, I don't even want to generate it right now. Because if you do there is a tremendous push from the outside, from the legislature, from do-gooders, from the media, saying, "You mean you were aware of this all the time and didn't do anything about it?"

> We'll back-burner things. That's a terrible thing to admit, but it's true. We have limited resources. If a federal judge says, "You will do this," then we'll do that. We've got state laws and regulations to respond to. Then we can get to other things.

> Administrator: All you have to do is have one disgruntled employee. The information becomes a matter of public record. If I don't like you or you don't like me, all you have to do is call this reporter and say, "Hey, go check on this." This has happened. Frankly, I don't want some of our employees to have the information they request . . . People do not know some of the information that does exist, and we can't make it available to them.

The respondents associated issues of bureaucratic interest particularly with the possible use of products of the in-house evaluation section. One top administrator characterized evaluation information as a "management tool." Respondents expressed concern that research information produced by the in-house evaluation section might be used to promote bureaucratic interests and therefore would become suspect.

A researcher commented on perceived conflict regarding evaluation information:

> You have to consider that there are adversary relationships within the department.

An administrator noted:

> There is some defensiveness about evaluation research. It loses credibility when you have the feeling that it is promoted to do somebody in. The research in this department has not been formative. Many administrators are concerned with boundary maintenance. Hidden agendas discourage the circulation of some information.

Another administrator stated:

> People react to evaluation with some apprehension. It's like sending out eyes and ears. Their reaction may be antagonistic. Any utilization may be antagonistic utilization.

The attitudes expressed above indicate a belief among some respondents that certain research information (particularly that produced in house) could have an adverse effect. As the comments show, this effect could be associated 1) with uncertainty as to the possible use of research information by powerful external elites, especially the legislature and the judiciary, and/or 2) with the conflict resulting from internal bureaucratic antagonisms.

All the study respondents appeared to understand decision making and policy development as part of a larger political process. It was apparent during the study that bureaucratic politics and bureaucratic interest, both internal and involving external relationships, were important in influencing perceptions of research and the use of research information. The comments above, other responses, and the general attitude about crisis support an inference that uncertainty, risk avoidance, and bureaucratic interest could constitute a critical overlay in understanding use/nonuse. Future studies might address the possibility that uncertainty over the ability of external elites to request or commission research and to use research information in a challenging manner could result in implicit or explicit information policies affecting use. In addition, future inquiry should take into account the possibility that internal bureaucratic struggles may lead to similar potential effects on the role for research and on use. The existence of implicit or explicit informal information policies could be very important in understanding the RU process.

The Findings in Perspective

This study was undertaken to contribute to the development of a body of data and to increase our basic understanding of the role and the potential of research information in order to help identify possibilities for conceptual development. Generalizing from limited data can be risky; the critic of information presented in this paper could ask whether the empirical base — a southern DOC facing a state of crisis — is atypical. One must suggest that the limitations of coverage do not invalidate the utility of the findings. The core features of this DOC — its bureaucratic arrangements — are similar to most if not all state DOCs. The most important question is whether the crisis overlay contributes to a characterization of this DOC as idiosyncratic.

Considering nationwide trends, one must think not. As Jurik and Musheno (1986:457) observe, "The 1980's mark a new era of crises for correctional systems in the United States." They point out appropriately that "the instability of corrections today revolves around a reconsideration of system goals with a renewed emphasis on deterrence and incapacitation, and on an exploding population of inmates unaccompanied by adequate fiscal support for correctional bureaucracies" (457). This statement describes aptly the situation in the DOC studied here.

Nonetheless, it is important to realize that "crisis" and crisis perceptions are relative. Perhaps one should compare these findings to expectations about use in state DOCs that are not characterized by perceptions of crisis. Yet demarcating possible differences places one in the realm of speculation; ultimately, comparing these findings in a series of further studies is the only sure way to know how valid they may be. (The author hopes that this research will encourage further efforts.) Such consideration may help clarify the limits and the value of this research.

As explained earlier, the existing literature on RU points out the strong expectation that research information will not have a direct influence on policy-making or decision-making outcomes. The findings in this study are in accord with such an expectation. Even in the "noncrisis" situation, if the RU literature is to be believed, instances of instrumental use will be minimal.

What differences, then, can one expect? One might find a more generally positive attitude toward use. The participants in this study indicate that research information assumes a very low priority as an input to policy making and decision making ("It is a luxury to review research"; "There is actually very little forethought"). What one could expect is that a state DOC with adequate resources and a more research-oriented leadership might invest both energy and dollars in coordinating inputs of information, including research information. In such a situation one might find more commitment to in-house and external studies and more forethought about the potential use of the resulting information, as well as more attention to the acquisition, assessment, dissemination, and use of the type of information characterized in this study as routinely encountered material. In general, one might expect a great deal more attention to conceptual use and possible instrumental use, primarily because one would conceive of a situation where time and resource constraints were not presented as a rationale for a lack of attention. Even so, one hardly could conceive of a reality approaching normative expectations for a research-oriented, rationalistic decision system.

Even when resources are plentiful enough to allow an agency to be characterized as "fat," they do not necessarily ensure a great deal of instrumental research use. Questions of policy — in fact, most decisions at the upper levels of management — involve the resolution of questions of value or preference. The participants in this study recognize their environment as political; accordingly one must consider the ways of doing business in complex, bureaucratic organizations that operate within complex, bureaucratic systems. In view of the research on corrections organizations and systems which addresses these issues (e.g., Conley, 1981; Jacobs, 1983; McEleney, 1985), it appears that this DOC is not unusual.

Conclusion

The findings and the insights obtained in this study point to the need for further research examining utilization in corrections and other criminal justice agencies. Baseline data must be established and effort must be devoted to understanding the potential role of research information in corrections agencies. The state of knowledge concerning RU in criminal justice requires additional explanation and conceptual development before we attempt quantitative cross-sectional studies of determinants and outcomes (Ellickson, 1981:54).

This study yields several points that are worth consideration. First, it cannot be assumed simply that patterns of research use will be consistent throughout an organization. This statement seems obvious, but much of the literature on RU fails to emphasize this issue. Use may vary within and between hierarchical levels.

The literature on RU attends to the possibility that use may be affected by the substantive issue, but it does not direct sufficient attention to the possibilities of variability in uses within the organization. In the department under study here, levels and types of use appeared to be associated with the hierarchical ordering and the partitioning of problems. Utilization appeared to be associated with perceptions of the appropriateness of research information to fulfill limited purposes.

In addition, the parceling out and the incremental, sequential ordering of problems contributed to the creation of information spaces and to variation in attention to information resources. These are important foci in constructing a useful conceptual framework for inquiry; they point to the need to turn to the rich literature on organizations and decision making in order to develop sets of propositions to be addressed in studying utilization.

Second, this study supports the contention that bureaucratic interests constitute a key overlay in developing an understanding of use. Again the literature on organizations and decision making may provide the basis for propositions about the relationship of uncertainty, risk avoidance, and associated concepts to the use/nonuse of research information. This study supports Rich's (1981) contention that "bureaucratization," as expressed in terms of informal policies and selective use, is crucial in understanding use. Evidence in this study points to the possibility that intentional control of information and intended control of the decision process deserve attention in further research. These points are important in developing an adequate model of the RU process; they indicate a major direction for incorporating related variables, such as individual interest, and for developing hypotheses.

Finally, the study suggests that those who develop prescriptions about systematic use of research information must attend to the structure and the dynamic nature of the decision system and to the overlay of bureaucratic interests. The patterns of circumscribed use noted in the study seem to be regularized. Perhaps conceptual development must proceed to identify characteristic modes of organizational learning and related processes in criminal justice agencies. This direction may be promising in attempts to clarify basic assumptions and expectations about use and in locating sets of variables from an integrative perspective.

References

Allison, G. T. (1971). *Essence of decision*. Boston: Little, Brown.

Caplan, N. S. (1979). The two-community theory and knowledge utilization. *American Behavioral Scientist, 22*, 459–470.

Conley, J. (1981, Winter). Beyond legislative acts: Penal reform, public policy, and symbolic justice. *The Public Historian, 3*, 26–39.

Cyert, R. M., & March, J. G. (1963). *A behavioral theory of the firm*. Englewood Cliffs, NJ: Prentice-Hall.

Ellickson, P. (1981). *Knowledge utilization in local criminal justice agencies: A conceptual framework*. Santa Monica: Rand.

Glaser, D. (1973). *Routinizing evaluation: Getting feedback on the effectiveness of crime and delinquency programs*. Rockville, MD: NIMH.

Glaser, E. M., Abelson, H. H., & Garrison, K. N. (1983). *Putting knowledge to use: Facilitating the diffusion of knowledge and the implementation of planned change*. San Francisco: Jossey-Bass.

Gottfredson, M., & Gottfredson, D. (1980). *Decision making in criminal justice: Toward the rational exercise of discretion*. Cambridge, MA: Bellinger.

Grosskin, R. (1981). Toward the integration of evaluation in criminal justice policy: Constructing alternative interpretational models of the evaluation utilization process. Unpublished paper.

Jacobs, J. (1983). *New perspectives on prison and imprisonment*. Ithaca, NY: Cornell University Press.

Jurik, N. C., & Musheno, M. C. (1986). The internal crisis of corrections: Professionalization and the work environment. *Justice Quarterly, 4,* 457–480.

Lindblom, C., & Cohen, D. (1979). *Usable knowledge.* New Haven, CT: Yale University Press.

Lynd, R. S. (1939). *Knowledge for what?* Princeton, NJ: Princeton University Press.

McEleney, B. L. (1985). *Correctional reform in New York: The Rockefeller years and beyond.* Lanham, MD: University Press of America.

Patrick, M. S. (1979). Utilizing program evaluation products: A rational choice approach. Paper presented at the annual meeting of the Midwest Political Science Association, Chicago.

Patton, M. (1978). *Utilization-focused evaluation.* Beverly Hills, CA: Sage.

Rich, R. (1981). *Social science information and public policy making.* San Francisco: Jossey-Bass.

Snow, C. P. (1962). *Science and government.* New York: New American Library.

Snow, C. P. (1979, September/October). The many meanings of research utilization. *Public Administration Review,* 426–431.

Weiss, C. (1977). *Using social science research in public policymaking.* Lexington, MA: Heath.

Weiss, C., & Bucuvalas, M. (1980). *Social science research and decision-making.* New York: Columbia University Press.